Sources in American History

A BOOK OF READINGS

Sources in American History

A BOOK OF READINGS

HBJ **Harcourt Brace Jovanovich, Publishers**
Orlando   San Diego   Chicago   Dallas

Note: Some of the material in this work previously appeared in RISE OF THE AMERICAN NATION, Volume 1, and RISE OF THE AMERICAN NATION, Volume 2, by Lewis Paul Todd and Merle Curti, copyright © 1982 by Harcourt Brace Jovanovich, Inc.

Printed in the United States of America   ISBN 0-15-375956-9

ACKNOWLEDGMENTS

For permission to reprint copyrighted material, grateful acknowledgment is made to the following sources:

American Enterprise Institute for Public Policy Research: Adapted from "The American Revolution As a Successful Revolution" (Retitled: "The Success of the Revolution") by Irving Kristol in *America's Continuing Revolution: An Act of Conservation.* Copyright 1973, 1974, 1975 by the American Enterprise Institute for Public Policy Research.

Arbor House Publishing Company, Inc.: Adapted from "Ricky's Story" (Retitled: "Four Minority Voices") in *Growing Up Puerto Rican* by Paulette Cooper. Copyright © 1972 by Paulette Cooper. Published by Arbor House Publishing Company. All rights reserved.

Asian Cine Vision: Adapted from "The Security Blanket of Racial Anonymity" (Retitled: "Four Minority Voices") by Clarence Chen in *Bridge: An Asian American Perspective.* Copyright © by Asian Cine Vision, Inc.

Atheneum Publishers, Inc.: Adapted from *Breach of Faith* (Titled: "The Meaning of Watergate") by Theodore H. White. Copyright © 1975 by Theodore H. White. Adapted from *Equal Time: The Private Broadcast and the Public Interest* (Titled: "A Critical Look at Television") by Newton M. Minow, edited by Lawrence Laurent. Copyright © 1964 by Newton M. Minow.

The Julian Bach Agency, Inc.: Adapted from "The Shaping of the Presidency 1984" by Theodore H. White in *Time* Magazine, November 19, 1984. Copyright © 1984 by Theodore H. White.

Basic Books, Inc., Publishers: From *The Zero-Sum Society* (Titled: "A Troubled Economy") by Lester C. Thurow. © 1980 by Basic Books, Inc., Publishers.

Robert Bendiner: Adapted from pp. 178–300 in "WPA, Willing Patron of the Arts" (Retitled: "WPA and the Arts") in *Just Around the Corner* by Robert Bendiner. Copyright © 1967 by Robert Bendiner.

Laura Benet: "Fifth Avenue and Grand Street" (Titled: "Women Unite to Support the War") by Mary Carolyn Davies.

Continued on page 455.

CONTENTS

UNIT ONE   Building the Colonies

v

UNIT TWO   Winning Independence

CHAPTER 6 **The Struggle for Independence**
(1775–1783)

CHAPTER 7 **Forming a Confederation**
(1775–1787)

CHAPTER 8 Creating a Federal Union
(1787–1789)

UNIT THREE   Building the Nation

CHAPTER 9 A Strong Start for the Nation
(1789–1801)

UNIT FOUR The Rise of Sectionalism

UNIT FIVE   The Nation Torn Apart

UNIT SIX Rebuilding the Nation

UNIT SEVEN   The Rise of Industrialism

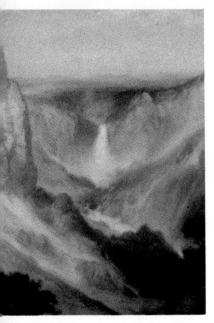

UNIT EIGHT The Arrival of Reform

UNIT NINE Becoming a World Power

UNIT TEN   The Golden Twenties and the New Deal

UNIT ELEVEN   Isolation Through World War II

UNIT TWELVE   Reshaping the Postwar World

UNIT THIRTEEN   Into a New Era

Sources in American History

A BOOK OF READINGS

TO THE STUDENTS: Reading Historical Sources

This book of readings contains primary and secondary sources. Such sources are invaluable in the interpretation of American history. A primary source, as you know, is one that originated in the period under study. A primary source may be a letter, a diary, a journal, a newspaper article such as an editorial, a birth notice, death notice, and a stockmarket quotation. It may be a public record such as a birth certificate, a death certificate, a deed to property, a legal opinion, minutes of a meeting, or a law. It may also be a painting, a drawing, a photograph, a song, or even an object, or artifact, manufactured during the period under study.

Secondary sources are writings about a period by someone who lived at another time or by someone who reported what another person had seen without the reporter being an eyewitness.

Each reading has an introduction to give you some background about the reading, the author of the reading, or the time period in which the reading originated. A list of questions follows the introduction to give a focus, or direction, to your study of the reading. The questions that follow each reading help you make use of the information the reading provides. In addition, illustrations accompany each reading, many of which are themselves primary sources.

Remember, as you read, to think critically. Look for clues that help you understand each author's point of view. Relate the information in the reading to the content of your textbook. You are not expected to agree with the viewpoints expressed in every reading. By thinking critically about a reading, you can determine the points with which you agree and those with which you disagree.

Building the Colonies

CHAPTER 1 Exploring the Americas
(Beginnings to 1624)

1 The Aztec Marketplace

Present-day knowledge of the Aztec civilization is incomplete because the Spanish conquerors of Mexico destroyed many of the buildings and temples, books, and works of art that these civilizations had produced. Much of what is known about the Aztecs comes from letters and diaries written by the Spanish conquerors. One such account comes from Bernal Díaz who was with Cortés in Mexico during the conquest of the Aztecs.

In the following excerpt, Bernal Díaz described his first visit to the marketplace in Tenochtitlán, the

An Aztec marketplace

Aztec capital. This visit took place when the Spaniards were still on friendly terms with the Aztecs, so Díaz was able to move about freely and record what he saw in great detail.

READING FOCUS
1. What features of the marketplace impressed Díaz the most?
2. How was the marketplace divided?

The moment we arrived in this huge market we were shocked at the great numbers of people, the amount of merchandise that it contained, and at the good order that was maintained.

We first visited those areas of the market set aside for the sale of gold, silver, jewels, of cloths woven with feathers, of other manufactured goods, and of slaves. To keep these slaves from running away, they were fastened with halters about their neck, though some were allowed to walk freely. Next to these came the dealers in cotton, twisted thread, and cacao.

In another area of the market there were the skins of tigers, lions, jackals, otters, red deer, wild cats, and of other animals, some of which were tanned. Another place sold beans, sage, herbs, and vegetables. A particular market area was set aside for the merchants in fowls, turkeys, ducks, rabbits, hares, deer, and dogs. Also, there were sellers of fruit, pastry, and tripe.

Not far away were all types of pottery, from large clay pots to small pitchers. Then came the dealers in honey and honey-cakes, and other sweetmeats. Next to these, the timber merchants and furniture dealers displayed tables, benches, cradles, and all sorts of wooden tools, all separately arranged. In this marketplace there were also courts of justice, to which three

Adapted from The Memoirs of the Conquistator Bernal Diaz de Castillo . . . , *translated by J. I. Lockhart, 1844.*

judges were appointed, who inspected the goods for sale.

I had almost forgotten to mention the salt, and those who made the flint knives; also the fish, and a type of bread made of a kind of mud or slime gathered from the surface of Lake Texoco and eaten in that form tastes like our cheese.

The bustle and noise caused by this large crowd of people was so great that it could be heard more than four miles away. Some of our men, who had traveled through Italy, said that they never had seen a marketplace that covered so large an area, which was so well regulated, and so crowded with people as this one at Mexico.

READING REVIEW

1. Name three areas of the marketplace that Díaz visited.
2. Why were there "courts of justice" in the marketplace?
3. What three characteristics of the marketplace did Díaz find most impressive?
4. List two items sold at this market that are unfamiliar to you. Use the dictionary and define each.

2 A Clash of Cultures

The people who first settled the American continents over the centuries developed their own special ways of living. When the European explorers and settlers arrived in the Americas, they brought with them their own outlooks and ways of living. These often clashed sharply with those of the original settlers, whom the Europeans called Indians.

Conflicts between the Indians and the newcomers continued for hundreds of years and led to much bitterness and bloodshed. This reading is taken from a speech that Corn Tassel, a Cherokee leader, made to representatives of the United States government in 1785. In it, Corn Tassel argued that whites had no claim to Indian lands.

READING FOCUS

1. On what grounds did Corn Tassel reject the whites' claim to Cherokee land?
2. Why did Corn Tassel believe that the whites and the Indians could become more alike?

It is a little surprising that when we entered into treaties with our brothers, the whites, their whole cry is *more land!* Indeed, it once seemed to be a matter of formality with them to demand what they knew we dare not refuse. But on the principles of fairness, and in the name of free will and equality, I must reject your demand [in this proposed treaty].

Suppose I were to ask one of you under what kind of authority, by what law, or on what pretense he makes this huge demand of nearly all the lands we hold between your settlements and our towns.

Would he tell me that it is by right of conquest? No! If he did, I should reply that *we* had last marched over his territory. Nay, some of

From Peter Nabakov, ed., Native American Testimony.

Colonists and Indians clash over conflicting land claims.

our young warriors (whom we have not yet had an opportunity to recall or notify of the general treaty) are still in the woods, and continue to keep his people in fear.

If merely marching through a country is sufficient reason to lay claim to it, we shall insist upon your giving up your settlements and moving one hundred miles back towards the east, whither some of our warriors advanced against you in the course of last year's campaign.

Let us examine the facts of your present eruption into our country. What did you do? You marched into our territories with a superior force. Your numbers far exceeded us, and we fled to the stronghold of our extensive woods, there to secure our women and children.

Thus, you marched into our towns; they were left to your mercy. You killed a few scattered and defenseless individuals, spread fire and desolation wherever you pleased, and returned again to your own settlements.

Were we to inquire by what law or authority you set up a claim, therefore, I answer, none! Your laws do not apply in our country, nor ever did. You talk of the law of nature and the law of nations, and they are both against you.

Indeed, much has been spoken about the lack of what you term civilization among the Indians. Many proposals have been made to us to adopt your laws, your religion, your manners and your customs. But, we confess that we do not yet see the rightness, or practicality of such a step. We should be better pleased with beholding the good effect of these doctrines in your own practices than with hearing you talk about them, or reading your papers to us upon such subjects.

You say: Why do not the Indians till the ground and live as we do? May we not, with equal justice, ask, Why do the white people not hunt and live as we do? You pretend to think it no injustice to warn us not to kill our deer and other game from the mere love of waste. But it is very criminal in our young men if they kill a cow or a hog for food when they happen to be in your lands. We wish, however, to be at peace with you, and to do as we would be done by. We do not quarrel with you for killing an occasional buffalo, bear or deer on our lands when you need one to eat. But you go much farther. Your people hunt to gain a livelihood by it; they kill our game. Our young men resent the injury, and it is followed by bloodshed and war.

The great God of Nature has placed us in different situations. It is true that he has endowed you with many superior advantages. But he has not created us to be your slaves. *We are a separate people!* He has given each their lands, under distinct considerations and circumstances. He has stocked yours with cows, ours with buffalo; yours with hog, ours with bear; yours with sheep, ours with deer. He has, indeed, given you an advantage in this, that your cattle are tame and domestic while ours are wild and demand not only a larger space for range, but art to hunt and kill them. They are, nevertheless, as much our property as other animals are yours, and ought not to be taken away without our consent, or for something equivalent.

READING REVIEW

1. Name two reasons that the American colonists gave as their right to claim Indian land.
2. How did Corn Tassel respond to each claim of the white man?
3. (a) How did Corn Tassel feel about the whites and the Indians becoming more alike? (b) How did he justify his position?

3 The Riches of the Orient

Marco Polo had gone to China with his father and uncle to establish and gain control of the Chinese trade for Venice, one of the richest of the Italian city-states. Kublai Khan, the emperor of China, made Marco one of his advisers. During his years in the service of the Khan, Marco traveled through many parts of Asia. Eventually he returned to Italy and wrote *The Book of Sir Marco Polo*.

At first Marco's stories were mocked and regarded as lies. After several years, however, explorers anxious to find a new trade route to China began to read Marco's fascinating descriptions of the Orient. One of the explorers was Christopher Columbus.

The following passage is an excerpt from Marco's writings. It describes one of his journeys in the service of the Khan.

READING FOCUS

1. What features of Oriental civilization impressed Marco Polo?
2. What was the most important manufactured product of the Orient?

After going thirty miles in a westerly direction, through a country filled with fine buildings, among vineyards and many cultivated and fertile fields, we arrived at a handsome and considerable city, named Gouza. The townspeople lived by commerce and manual arts. They manufactured the finest kind of cloth.

From the city of Gouza we journeyed ten days through Cathay to the kingdom of Ta-in-fu, in the course of which we passed many fine cities, in which manufactures and commerce flourished. We saw many vineyards and much cultivated land. From here grapes were carried to Cathay, where the vine does not grow. Here we found an abundance of mulberry-trees, the leaves of which allow the inhabitants [worms] to produce large quantities of silk. We noticed a degree of civilization which existed among all the people of this country, because of their frequent contacts with the towns, which are not far from each other. To these towns the merchants continually traveled carrying their goods from one city to another.

At the end of ten days journey from the city of Gouza we arrived at the kingdom of Ta-in-fu, whose chief city, the capital of the province, bears the same name. Ta-in-fu is very large and beautiful. A great deal of trade is carried on in this city. A variety of articles are manufactured, including weapons which are used by the grand Khan's armies. There were many vineyards from which large quantities of grapes were gathered. Although this is the only district within the borders of Ta-in-fu that has vineyards, there is still a large enough supply for the entire province. Other fruits also grow here in plenty, as does the mulberry-tree, together with the worms that yield the silk.

Upon leaving Ta-in-fu, we traveled for seven days through a fine country in which there were many cities, where commerce and manufactures prevailed. We reached a large city named Pi-an-fu, which is very famous. Like Ta-in-fu, this city contains numerous merchants and artisans. Silk is produced here also in great quantity.

READING REVIEW

1. Name two features of the Oriental civilization that Marco Polo found impressive.

From the Travels of Marco Polo: The Venetian, *edited by William Marsden, 1948.*

From **The Book of Sir Marco Polo**

2. According to the author, why was there "a degree of civilization" among the people of the Orient?
3. **(a)** What was the most important manufactured product? **(b)** Why was the mulberry-tree important?
4. Based on this reading, why do you think merchants and explorers were eager to find new routes to the Orient?

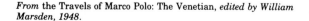

4 Columbus in the New World

Columbus was not the first European to reach America. But it was his voyage that made the people of Europe aware of North America and South America. Because Europeans had not known about these continents before, they now called them the New World.

On his first voyage, in 1492, Columbus kept a journal, which has since been lost. Luckily a Spanish priest copied out parts of it before it disappeared. He retold most of the account in the third person. This is why Columbus is referred to as "the Admiral" and the crews of his ships as "they." (Note, however, that the last two paragraphs are in Columbus' own words.)

READING FOCUS

1. What evidence proved that Columbus had found a New World?
2. How did Columbus describe the Indians he met?

Wednesday, 10th of October

The course was west-southwest, and they sailed at the rate of 10 miles an hour, occasionally 12 miles, and sometimes 7 [18, 22, and 13 kilometers]. Finally the crew could endure no longer. They complained of the length of the voyage. But the Admiral cheered them up in the best way he could, giving them hope that they might profit from the voyage. He added that no matter how they might complain he had to reach the Indies, and that he would go on until he found that land, with the help of our Lord.

Thursday, 11th of October

The course was west-southwest, and the sea was rougher than it had been during the whole voyage. They saw sandpipers and a green reed near the ship. The crew on the ship *Pinta* saw a cane and a stick. And they took out of the water another small stick, which appeared to have been shaped by a tool of some sort, as well as another bit of cane, a land plant, and a small board. The crew of the *Niña* also saw signs of land, such as a small branch covered with berries. Everyone on the ship breathed fresh hope and rejoiced at these signs.

Adapted from Clements R. Markham, The Journal of Christopher Columbus (During His First Voyage, 1492-1493), *1893.*

After sunset the Admiral returned to his original west course, and they went along at the rate of 12 miles [22 kilometers] an hour. By two hours after midnight they had gone 90 miles [166 kilometers]. Since the *Pinta* sailed faster than the Admiral's ship, it found the land first and made the signals ordered by the Admiral.

The land was first seen by a sailor named Rodrigo de Triana. But at ten o'clock the Admiral, standing high up in the ship's stern, saw a light, though it was so dim that he could not be sure it was land. He called Pedro Gutierrez and said that there seemed to be a light and he should look at it. He did so, and he too saw it. The Admiral told the same thing to Rodrigo Sanchez of Segovia, whom the king and queen had sent with the fleet as inspector, but he could see nothing.

After the Admiral had spoken, he saw the light once or twice again and it was like a flickering candle. A few of the crew were sure that it was a sign of land, but the Admiral wanted to be certain that land was near. He asked the crew to keep a careful lookout and to watch well for land. To the first person who cried out that he saw land the Admiral promised to give a silk jacket, besides the other rewards promised by the king and queen. At two hours after midnight the land was sighted.

The vessels stayed in place, waiting for daylight. On Friday they arrived at a small island of the Lucayos Indians, called Guanahani in

The Niña, Pinta, and Santa Maria sail for the New World.

the Indians' language. Presently they saw naked people. The Admiral went on shore in an armed boat, with Martin Alonso Pinzón and his brother Vicente Yañez, captain of the *Niña*. The Admiral took the royal flag, and the captains carried two banners bearing the initials of King Ferdinand and Queen Isabella.

Having landed, they saw many green trees, much water, and fruits of various kinds. The Admiral called to the two captains, to the others who leaped on shore, and to Rodrigo Sanchez of Segovia. He said that they should bear witness that he, in the presence of all, now claimed possession of the island for the king and for the queen.

* * * *

This island is rather large and very flat, with bright green trees, much water, a very large lake in the center, and without any mountains. The whole land is so green that it is a pleasure to look on it. The people are very friendly. They long to possess our things, but not having anything to give in return they take what they can get, and presently swim away.

Still, they give away all they have in return for whatever may be given to them, even broken bits of crockery and glass. I saw one of them trade 16 skeins of cotton for three small Portuguese coins, the skeins weighing as much as 25 pounds [11 kilograms] of cotton thread. I shall keep it and allow no one to take it, preserving it all for your Highnesses, for it may be obtained in great quantities. I think it is grown on this island, though my short stay did not allow me to find out for sure. Here also is found the gold that the people wear fastened in their noses. But in order not to lose time, I intend to depart from here and see if I can discover the island of Cipango [Japan].

READING REVIEW

1. Cite two items of evidence that support Columbus' claim that he had found the New World.
2. What was Columbus' impression of the Indians he met?
3. How did the Indians react to the landing party?
4. What evidence is there that Columbus failed to realize he had discovered a land previously unknown to Europeans?

5 A First Claim for France

Like other nations of Europe, France was jealous of the wealth that Spain got from her colonies in the New World. France hoped to gain wealth by finding a "Northwest Passage," a route through North America that would allow them to continue sailing west to China. Eventually, the French realized there was no Northwest Passage. The search for it, however, resulted in claims to large areas of North America for France. Jacques Cartier was one of these explorers.

The following excerpt is from the memoirs of Jacques Cartier. In the spring of 1534, Cartier left France with two ships bound for the New World to search for the Northwest Passage. He did not, of course, find the "Northwest Passage," but he did explore the Gulf of St. Laurence, observe the Indians, and claim the land for his king, Francis I.

READING FOCUS

1. What was Cartier's impression of the Indians he met?
2. How did the Indians react to Cartier and his men?

Evil weather caused us to stay in this harbor and stream until the 25th day of July, 1534. During the time we saw a great number of Indians, who had come into the stream to fish for mackerel.

There were men, women, and children as well. There were more than two hundred persons in about forty boats. They came freely with their boats close alongside our ships. We gave them knives, combs, and other articles of little worth, for which they made many signs of joy, raising their hands to the sky while singing and dancing in their boats. These people are the poorest folks that there may be in the world, for altogether they have not the value of five sous [a French coin], their boats and their fishing nets excepted. They wear old skins of beasts which they throw over them scarf-wise. They have their heads shorn close all about, except a clump on the top of the head, which they leave long like a horse's tail, which they tie upon their heads with strips of leather. They have no other lodging but under their said boats, which they turn over before lying down

Adapted from James Phinney Baxter, A Memoir of Jacques Cartier, 1906.

This detailed drawing from an old map shows Jacques Cartier founding Quebec in 1534.

on the ground. Under these they eat their food almost raw after being a little warmed on coals, and likewise their fish.

We went with our boats to the place where they were on the shore of the stream, and landed freely among them. All the men began to sing and dance in two or three bands, making great signs of joy at our coming. But they had caused all the young women to flee into the woods, save two or three who remained, to whom we gave each a comb, and to each a little tin bell. And seeing what the captain had given to those who had remained the Indian men made those women return who had fled into the woods.

We found a great quantity of mackerel that they had caught near the shore. The nets which they have for fishing, are of hemp, a plant that grows where they ordinarily abide; for they only come to the sea in the season of fishing. Likewise there grows a large millet like peas, the same as in Brazil, which they eat in place of bread, of which they name in their language *Kagaige.* [*Kagaige* was Maize, or Indian corn.] If one shows them anything they may not have and know nothing about, they shake their heads and say, "Nouda." They have showed us by signs how things grow, and how they prepare them for eating. They never eat a thing wherein there may be a taste of salt. They are to a marvelous degree thieves of all that they can steal.

The 24th day of July, 1534 we made a cross, thirty feet in height. On the cross-bar we put a shield embossed with three fleurs-de-lis, [symbols of the King of France] and above was an inscription graven in wood in large letters, "Long Live The King of France". And this cross was planted on the point of the harbor.

READING REVIEW

1. Give three reasons why Cartier called the Indians the poorest people in the world.
2. Did the Indians seem afraid of the French explorers? Cite evidence from Cartier's memoirs to support your answer.
3. Do you think the Indians understood what Cartier was doing when he claimed the land for the King of France? Explain.

6 Coronado's Search for Gold

Thousands of Spaniards followed Columbus to the Americas seeking their fortunes. Among them was Francisco Vasquez de Coronado, a colonial governor in Mexico. In 1540 Coronado set out in search of the Seven Cities of Cibola, cities believed to be filled with gold and great riches. His search for gold led him farther into the interior of what is now the United States than any European before him.

The following selection is from a report that Coronado wrote to King Charles I of Spain after he returned to Mexico.

READING FOCUS

1. What were Spain's ambitions in the New World?
2. Why was Coronado's expedition useful to Spain?

After nine days' march I reached some plains. They were so vast that I did not find their end anywhere that I went, although I traveled over them for more than 900 miles [1,448 kilometers]. And I found so many cows [buffalos], of the kind that I wrote Your Majesty about, that it was impossible to count them. There was not a day that I lost sight of them as I traveled through these plains.

After traveling for 17 days, I came to a settlement of Indians who are called Querechos. They do not plant crops. They travel around with these cows, and they eat the raw flesh and drink the blood of the cows they kill. They tan the skins of the cows, with which all the people of this country dress themselves. They have small field tents made of the cow's hides, tanned and greased and very well made. They

---

Adapted from George Parker Winship, editor and translator, The Journey of Coronado, 1540-1542, *1922.*

live in these tents while they travel with their herds of cows. They have dogs which they use to help move their tents and poles and belongings. These people are the best looking that I have seen in America. They could not give me any information about the country where the guides were taking me. I traveled for five days following the guides until I reached some new plains. This land had no landmarks of any kind. There was not a stone, not a bit of hilly ground, not a tree, not a shrub—nothing to help guide our travels. However, there was much very fine pasture land, with good grass.

It seemed to me best to continue with only 30 horsemen. I wanted to explore the country, so that I could give Your Majesty a true account of what was to be found in it. I sent all the rest of the force I had with me to Mexico. And with only the 30 horsemen as my escorts, I traveled 42 days. We lived all this while solely on the meat of the bulls and cows we killed. This was at the cost of several of our horses which the cows killed, because, as I wrote Your Majesty, they are very brave and fierce animals. We went many days without water. We cooked the food using cow dung as fuel because there is not any kind of wood in all these plains, away from the gullies and rivers, which are very few.

It was the Lord's pleasure that, after having journeyed across these deserts for 77 days, I arrived at the province they call Quivira, to which the guides were leading me. They had described to me houses of stone, many stories high. But instead we found houses made of straw, not stone, and the people in them were as barbarous as all those I have seen and passed before this. They do not have cloaks, nor cotton to make them from. Instead they use the skins of the cattle they kill, which they tan; and they eat raw meat of these animals like the Querechos. They are enemies of one another, but all of them are the same sort of people. The people at Quivira do, however, build better houses and plant corn. Since the guides who brought me are natives of this province, the people received me here peaceably. They told me when I set out for this region that I would not be able to see it all in two months. And, in fact, I saw and learned about only 25 or so villages of straw houses in this province and in all the rest of the country. The people of Quivira swore to obey Your Majesty and placed themselves under your rule.

The province of Quivira is 2,850 miles [4,586 kilometers] from Mexico. The country

Coronado's party searching for gold

itself is the best I have ever seen for raising all the products of Spain. The soil is very fertile and black and very well watered by springs and rivers. I found prunes like those of Spain and nuts and very good sweet grapes and mulberries. I have treated the natives of this province, and all the others I found wherever I went, as well as was possible, as Your Majesty had commanded. They have received no harm in any way from me or from those who went in my company.

I remained in this province of Quivira for 25 days, in order to see and explore the country. I also wanted to find out whether there was anything beyond this province which could be of service to Your Majesty, because the guides who brought me had told me of other provinces beyond this. And what I am sure of is that there is not any gold nor any other metal in all that country. The other places of which they had told me are nothing but little villages. In many of these villages they do not plant anything and do not have any houses except those made of skins and sticks, and the people move from place to place with their herds of cows. After having heard the account of what was beyond, which I have given above, I returned here, to Mexico. I wanted to provide for the force I had sent back here and to give Your Majesty an account of what this country is like.

READING REVIEW

1. **(a)** What did Spaniards hope to accomplish in the New World? **(b)** Were they successful?
2. **(a)** What was Coronado's first impression of Quivira? **(b)** Did it match his expectations?
3. Why did Coronado conclude that there is "not any gold nor any other metal in all that country"?
4. List two ways Spain benefited as a result of Coronado's expedition.

9

7 Civilizing the Indians

It has often been said that the Spanish had three main motives for colonizing the New World: gold, glory, and God. The Spaniards craved the gold and other riches of the New World. They hoped also to glorify their country through their conquests in the New World. Finally, the Spaniards felt duty bound to convert the Indians of the New World to the Roman Catholic religion.

These three motives were often interrelated. Some of the things the Spaniards did to convert the Indians also helped to gain more riches and glory for Spain, as this reading illustrates. The reading is from a royal order concerning Indian policy that the King of Spain issued on May 26, 1570. The order was addressed to Spanish officials in a province of Mexico.

READING FOCUS

1. Why did the King want the Indians gathered into towns?
2. How did the Indians react to the Spaniards' attempts at "civilizing" them?

Juan de la Peña has reported to me saying that because the Indians of this province are not gathered into towns where they may be governed and controlled much harm is done. Many difficulties arise in their conversion because they are not taught to live under the control and ordered system leading to their salvation and welfare. For scattered as they are over the mountains and deserts, the missionaries are unable to visit them. Moreover, the Indians resist the changes to their way of life. They assault, rob, and kill both Spaniards and peaceful Indians on the highways. De la Peña asked me to order that the Indians of that province who are wandering about in the mountains should be gathered together and made to live in established towns where they might be controlled. The plan suggested has been discussed by the members of our Council of the Indies, who considered how the Indians would benefit from it. I have therefore approved it, and do now command you to issue orders and instructions for gathering the Indians of that province who are wandering in the mountains into towns. Here they may live in a civilized manner and be governed, may better communicate with each other, have order and system in their living, and be more easily taught the Catholic religion. They may also escape the dangers which result from living in the mountains and deserts. Whatever you may do in this matter above your ordinary obligation we shall accept as service to us, and you will report to us how this order is complied with and carried out.

READING REVIEW

1. List two reasons why the King wanted the Indians gathered into towns.
2. What two things did the Spaniards hope to accomplish once they had the Indians gathered into towns?
3. Based on this reading, what was the King's attitude toward the culture of the Indians?

Adapted from Charles W. Hackett, ed., Historical Documents Relating to New Mexico, Nueva Vizcaya, and Approaches Thereto, to 1773, *Vol. I.*

8 Why England Should Colonize the New World

Many Englishmen such as Sir Francis Drake, Humphrey Gilbert, and Walter Raleigh dreamed of the adventure and wealth that would be theirs if England could successfully challenge Spain's hold on the New World.

A friend of Gilbert and Raleigh, Richard Hakluyt, urged England to establish permanent colonies in the New World. In a series of writings in the late 1500's, Hakluyt argued that England would solve many of her economic and social problems by establishing colonies in the New World.

In this reading Hakluyt outlined some of the reasons why the English government should support exploration and colonization.

READING FOCUS

1. Why should the English government support colonization in the New World?
2. How would the colonization of the New World benefit England?

This painting by an artist in the 1800's shows the arrival of the first Catholic settlers in Maryland. A group of Indians join the settlers in a celebration of thanksgiving.

A short collection of certain reasons to convince her Majesty [Queen Elizabeth of England] and the state to pay for western voyages and the establishment of colonies in the New World.

The passage there and home is neither too long nor too short, but easy, and to be made twice in the year.

The passage is not near the trade of any kings nor near any of their countries or territories, and is a safe passage.

It can be made at all times of the year.

This enterprise may keep the Spanish King from taking over all of America.

We shall be planting there the glory of the gospel, and offer a safe and a sure place to receive people from all parts of the world that are forced to run away for the truth of God's word.

Many men of intelligence and of different talents who are defeated by the loss of money, by the sea, or by some foolish act of youth, that are not able to live in England, may they be raised again, and do their country good service.

Many soldiers and servants, in the end of their services may there be settled to the common profit and quiet of this kingdom.

The wandering beggars of England, that grow up idly, and hurtful and burdensome to this kingdom, may there be settled and better brought up.

READING REVIEW

1. List four reasons why England should colonize the New World.
2. Which of Hakluyt's reasons do you think especially appealed to the upper-class in England? Explain.
3. Why was Hakluyt concerned with the ease and safety of possible English trade routes to the New World?
4. What three groups of people did Hakluyt feel would prosper in the New World? Why?

Adapted from Richard Hakluyt, "A Discourse on Western Planting," Documentary History of the State of Maine, *1877.*

Captain John Smith

June, 1607
The 22nd, Captain Newport returned to England. We said many prayers to our Almighty God for his good passage and safe return.

June the 25th
An Indian came to us from the chief, the great Powhatan, with the word of peace. He said that Powhatan greatly desired our friendship, and that chiefs Pasyaheigh and Tapahanagh wanted to be our friends. Powhatan said that we would be able to sow and reap our crops in peace or else he would make war upon our enemies. This message turned out to be true, for these chiefs have ever since remained in peace and continued to trade with us. We rewarded the messenger with many small gifts, which were great wonders to him.

This Powhatan lives 10 miles [16 kilometers] from us along the Pamunkey River, which lies north of us.

9 The First Summer at Jamestown

In the spring of 1607 the first permanent English colony was established at Jamestown in Virginia. When the ship that had brought the settlers returned to England, the newcomers faced the wilderness alone. Their first summer in Jamestown was a terrible time, as Edward Maria Wingfield, the colony's first president, reported in the journal that he kept. (He refers to himself as "the President.")

In the fall Wingfield was accused of favoring some settlers over others and was removed from office. Although he probably had governed as fairly as anyone could have under extremely difficult circumstances, Wingfield nevertheless was tried, convicted, and sent back to England to prison.

READING FOCUS

1. What were some of the problems that the first settlers at Jamestown faced?
2. How did the colony's president try to deal with these problems?

Adapted from Edward Maria Wingfield, A Discourse of Virginia, *edited by Charles Deane, 1860.*

July the 3rd
Seven or eight Indians presented the President with a deer from Pamunkey, a chief who desires our friendship. They asked about our ship, which the President said had gone to Croatoan. They greatly fear our ships. Therefore, the President did not want them to think that our ship was far away. Then their chief sent a hatchet to him. They were very pleased by the small gifts we gave them in return. Shortly after this a deer was sent to the President from the Great Powhatan. He and his messengers were pleased by the gifts we gave them. The President paid good prices to the Indians for beavers and other game, which he always divided equally among members of the colony.

About this time several of our men fell sick. About 40 died before September. Among them was the worthy and religious gentleman, Captain Bartholomew Gosnold. He had been responsible for a great part of the success and fortune of our government and colony.

Sickness had now left us only six ablebodied men in our town. God's mercy did now watch over us. The President carefully hid our weakness from the Indians, never allowing them to come into our town in all this time.

September the 6th

Pasyaheigh sent us a boy who had run away from us. This was the first sign that he was at peace with us.

Now the colony's supply of oil, vinegar, wine, and brandy was all used up except for two gallons [7.6 liters] of each. The wine was reserved for church services and the rest for emergencies. The President had explained this only to Captain Gosnold. After Mr. Gosnold died, the President told the rest of the council about the amount that remained. Lord, how they then longed to drink up the little that was left. For they had now emptied all of their own bottles, and all the others that they could find.

READING REVIEW

1. What message did Powhatan bring to the settlers at Jamestown?
2. Why was the giving of gifts important in keeping peaceful relations?
3. What effects did sickness have on the settlement at Jamestown?
4. How did the settlers know that Pasyaheigh was at peace with them?

10 Massachusetts, a Land of Plenty

The early days at Plymouth were full of hardships, but the tough-spirited settlers made the colony survive. In 1621 Edward Winslow, one of the Pilgrim settlers, wrote the first account of the settlement's beginnings, including the first Thanksgiving. Winslow also had other firsts to his credit. His marriage, to a widow of one of the colonists, was the first among the European settlers in Massachusetts. And he made the Massachusetts colonists' first treaty with the Indians.

In the following selection Winslow was writing to the people in England who might have been interested in coming to Plymouth.

READING FOCUS

1. How did Winslow describe the colonists' relations with the Indians?
2. According the Winslow, what natural resources were found in abundance in Massachusetts?

The Pilgrims and Indians celebrate the first American Thanksgiving in 1621.

Edward Winslow

In the short time that we few settlers have been here, we have built seven houses and four buildings for the colony's use, and have made preparation for several others. Last spring we planted some 20 acres [8 hectares] of Indian corn, and sowed some 6 acres [2 hectares] of barley and peas. Using the Indians' method, we fertilized the soil with herrings, which we have in great abundance. Our corn did well, and our barley fairly well. But our peas were not worth gathering probably because they were planted too late. They came up very well and blossomed; but then the sun parched the blossoms.

After our harvest was gathered, our governor sent four people out hunting, so that we might have a special celebration together after all our hard work. Those four killed almost enough fowl in a single day to last the settlers almost a week. During this time we also held shooting contests. Many of the Indians came to visit us, including their greatest king, Massasoit, who brought about 90 of his followers. We entertained and feasted them for three days. The Indians went out and killed five deer, which they presented to our governor. Although food is not always as plentiful as it was

at this time, yet by the goodness of God we are so far from want that we often wish you were here to share our plenty.

We have found the Indians very faithful in their pact of peace with us, very kind, and ready to please us. We often go to them, and they come to visit us. Some of us have traveled 50 miles [80 kilometers] inland with them. We walk as peaceably and safely in the woods as on the roads in England. We entertain the Indians in our houses, and they give their deer meat to us. They are a people without any religion or knowledge of any God. Yet they are very trustworthy, quick to learn, intelligent and just.

The climate here is like that in England. If there is any difference at all, it is somewhat hotter here in summer. Some think it colder in winter, but I do not think so from my experience. The air is very clear, not foggy, as has been reported. I cannot remember a more agreeable year than the one we have enjoyed here. Once we have cattle, horses, and sheep, I see no reason why people may not live as happily here as in any part of the world. As for fish and fowl, we have both in great abundance. Fresh cod fish is plentiful in the summer. Our bay is full of lobsters, as well as a variety of other fish, all summer. In September we can catch a barrel of eels in a night, with little labor, and can dig them out of their beds all winter. We have mussels in nearby waters. We have no oysters near, but we can have them brought by the Indians wherever we want. In the spring the land produces very good salad herbs. There are also grapes, both white and red, which are very sweet and strong, plus strawberries, gooseberries, raspberries, and so on. There are plums of three sorts—white, black, and red. There is also an abundance of roses—white, red, and pink—all very sweet smelling, indeed.

The land needs only industrious people to work. It would make you unhappy—as it does me—to see so much land, located near good rivers, without settlers, while your part of the world is overcrowded with people.

READING REVIEW

1. List two ways in which the Indians helped the colonists.
2. According to Winslow, were the climatic conditions good for farming?
3. Name the two most important natural resources found in Massachusetts. Why were these important for the survival of the settlers?

Adapted from Edward Winslow, Relation or Journall, etc. *(1622) in Alexander Young,* Chronicles of the Pilgrim Fathers, *1841.*

11 In Praise of Philadelphia

William Penn, a devout Quaker, founded the colony of Pennsylvania in 1682. He wanted to establish a colony that offered religious and political freedom to all those who settled there.

Pennsylvania attracted many settlers and became one of the most successful of the thirteen colonies. It owed much of this success to the driving energy of its founder, William Penn. His zeal is evident in this description of Philadelphia and its surroundings.

William Penn landing in Pennsylvania, 1682

READING FOCUS
1. What statements in this section indicated Penn's pride in the progress of his colony?
2. What did he say about the colony's location?

Philadelphia has long been the dream of those people who are concerned with this colony. At last it has been planned and designed, to the great happiness of the settlers. The location chosen is a neck of land between two navigable rivers, the Delaware and the Schuylkill. The land itself is one mile [1.6 kilometers] or two wide from river to river. The Delaware is a glorious river. But the Schulykill will probably be more important in settling the colony because it is navigable 100 miles [161 kilometers] above the falls and along its course northeast toward the Susquehannah River.

I say little about the town itself, because you will be shown a plan by my agent. On it those who are purchasers will find their names and their properties. But this I will say, for the goodness of God, that of all the many places I have seen in the world, I do not remember one better located. It seems to me to have been meant for a town—whether we look at the rivers, or the coves, docks, and springs, or the land, or even the air, which the people here say is very good.

The town has grown within less than a year to about 80 houses and cottages, where merchants and artisans are hard at work. The farmers' lands are nearby. Some of them planted winter corn last season. Most have had a very good summer crop, and they are now preparing for their winter wheat crop. They reaped their barley this year in May and their wheat in the following month. There is still time to grow another crop of various other things before the winter season.

Every day we hope for ships that will bring people, for—blessed be God!—there is both room and resources for them here. The stories of our difficulties are either the needless fears of our friends or the scarecrows of our enemies. The greatest hardship we have suffered has been eating dried, salted meat. But with fowl in winter and fish in summer, together with some poultry, lamb, mutton, veal, and plenty of venison most of the year, things are not too bad.

I bless God I am fully satisfied with the country. I am as contented here as I have been wherever God by his will has made it my place and service to reside. At present I am very busy, and it is difficult work. But the way things are going will make my work easier. It is some people's duty to plow, some to sow, some to water, and some to reap. So it is our wisdom as well as our duty to yield to the mind of God, and cheerfully as well as carefully to follow his guidance.

READING REVIEW
1. Where was Philadelphia first located?
2. Why was its location a good one?
3. What evidence was there of the colony's eventual success?
4. What did Penn have to say about the difficulties of settlement?

Adapted from "William Penn, 1683," in Samuel M. Janney, The Life of William Penn, *1852.*

15

12 A British Governor's Warning of French Danger

During most of the colonial period, the British and the French were bitter rivals over their New World possessions. In the colonies themselves there were frequent clashes between British and French settlers over land. Yet people in the colonies often felt that officials in the homeland did not clearly understand the tense situation in America.

Alexander Spotswood, deputy governor of Virginia, was one of those in America who was concerned about Great Britain's future in the region. In 1718 he wrote this letter to the Board of Trade, the British agency responsible for shaping royal policy in and toward America.

READING FOCUS

1. What were the chief dangers from the French, as Spotswood saw them?
2. What suggestions did Spotswood make on how to prevent dangers caused by the French?

For a long time I have tried to learn about the French traders living to the west of us, and the advantages they gain from their line of communications along the Great Lakes. I shall here

The French trade with an Indian tribe.

take the liberty of sharing my thoughts with Your Lordships. I shall describe the dangers to which His Majesty's settlements may be exposed and suggest how these dangers may best be prevented. I have often regretted that after so many years we have made no attempts to discover the sources of our rivers. Also, we have not tried to establish relations with the Indians to the west of us, even though we know of the progress the French have made in surrounding us with settlements.

The French have already built so many forts that the British settlements almost seem surrounded by French trade with the numerous Indian tribes on both sides of the lakes. The French may, in time, take over the whole fur trade. But even if they do not they can, whenever they please, send bands of Indians to the outskirts of our settlements and greatly threaten His Majesty's subjects there. If the French should increase their settlements along these lakes, in order to join their lands in Canada to their new colony of Louisiana, they might take over any English settlements they please.

Nature, it is true, has formed a defense for us with that long chain of mountains which runs from the west of South Carolina as far north as New York and which is passable only in a few places. But even this natural defense may become a danger to us, if we do not take over before the French do. Now, while both nations are at peace, is the time to prevent all such dangers caused by the growing power of the French which threaten His Majesty's holdings. While the French are still unable to seize all that vast area west of our lands, we should attempt to make some settlements along the Great Lakes. At the same time we should also take over the passes of the mountains in order to safeguard communications with such settlements.

As Lake Erie lies almost in the center of the French lines of communication it seems the best place for founding a settlement. With it, we could share with the French in the commerce and friendship of those Indians living along the Great Lakes. We could also cut off or disturb the communication between Canada and Louisiana if a war should break out. Once such a settlement was made, I can't see how the French could dispute our right of possession.

Adapted from R. A. Brock, ed., The Official Letters of Alexander Spotswood.

The law of nations recognizes the right of the first nation that settles an area. And if the French should try to make us leave by using force, we are closer to our settlements and aid than they are to theirs.

READING REVIEW

1. **(a)** What type of defense has nature provided for the colonists? **(b)** Why would this defense be helpful to them?
2. How could this natural defense become a danger to the colonists?
3. According to the author, what was the best place for founding a settlement? List two advantages this location would have.

13 A French Settler's Warning of British Danger

As the years passed, the rivalry between Great Britain and France over their colonial possessions steadily grew. And the rivalry between the British colonists and the French settlers in America also grew. Each side continued to establish forts and settlements to protect itself, and each side saw the other's settlements as threats to its own existence.

This report from a French settler in Canada was sent to the homeland in 1750.

READING FOCUS

1. What were the writer's main objections to actions already taken by the British?
2. What were his fears about the future?

The St. Lawrence River and the lakes which supply the waters of that great river stretch across the interior of Canada. Its navigation and trade can be halted more easily than people may think. One of the best ways to avoid this misfortune is further to strengthen not only Quebec and Montreal, but also Fort St. Frederic [Crown Point]. It is essential to establish at that fort a large, well-fortified French village

Adapted from Documents Relative to the Colonial History of the State of New York, *Vol. X. edited by E. B. O'Callaghan, 1858.*

in time of peace and to attract an Indian village in time of war. This effort will cost little if we settle some farmers on Lake Champlain at the same time and form some villages there.

Fort Frontenac [now Kingston, Ontario] is at the outlet of Lake Ontario, on which the English have established a post or fort called Oswego. This is clearly illegal, and is a serious threat to Canada. This Oswego post is located on a lake that has long been claimed by France. And it has been built by the English during a period of peace. The Governor of Canada has protested but taken no further action. Although it ought to have been pulled down in the beginning by using force, the post is still there.

This post, which has been regarded as of little importance, can, in fact, destroy Canada, and it has already caused the greatest harm. It is at Fort Oswego that the French often carry on an illegal trade, which sends to England profits that Canada should send to France. It is there that the English hand out rum to the Indians, even though the King of France has forbidden this trade. It is there that the English try to win over all the Indian nations. They not only try to corrupt them with gifts but also urge them to kill the French traders throughout the vast forests of New France.

As long as the English occupy Fort Oswego, we must distrust even those Indians who are most loyal to the French. We will have to keep twice as many troops in Canada as the colony needs or can afford in times of peace. Forts will have to be built in a great number of places, and many expensive military units will have to be sent out almost every year to keep the Indians under control. Shipping on the lakes will always be exposed to danger. Agriculture will make very slow progress, and will be limited to the heart of the colony. In short, we will face a situation that has all the difficulties of war and none of its advantages. Everything possible, then, must be done to destroy this dangerous post.

We must also have free and dependable communication from Canada to the Mississippi. This chain, once broken, would leave an opening where the English would doubtless move in. The Ohio River, also called the Beautiful River, is of the greatest importance here. It rises near the country at present partly occupied by the Iroquois, runs southward, joins the Wabash, and as part of that river, flows into the Mississippi.

Fort St. Frederic, Crown Point

The English have no posts, or forts, out there. Nor did they go to that area to trade, except secretly, until the last war [King George's War]. Then the revolt of some Indian nations there against the French encouraged the English to enter the area.

Since the peace, the English have been asked to leave. If they do not do so, there is no doubt that the Governor of Canada will force them to. Otherwise, we would soon face the same kind of problem as we do at Fort Oswego. In fact, it would be even more disastrous, for a military post on the Ohio River would provide more opportunities to endanger Canada. The English would then have more ways of breaking the communication line between Canada and Louisiana. For the Ohio River offers almost the only route to move troops from Canada to the Mississippi River, and thus protect that still weak colony against the Indians of Carolina (whom the English stir up against the French). Only with such a fort would the English be able to attack, with a sizable force and hope of success, the Illinois outposts and those others which we will establish along the Mississippi River.

The establishment of French posts on the Ohio River is considered, then, one of our most urgent needs.

READING REVIEW

1. Why was it important to establish a French village at Fort St. Frederic?
2. According to the author, why was the English fort at Oswego illegal?

3. Name three ways in which Ft. Oswego could have caused harm to Canada.
4. Why did the author feel it was important to have "free and dependable communication from Canada to the Mississippi"?

14 How Half a Continent Changed Hands

The conflicting claims of Great Britain and France were finally settled—in North America, at least—in the French and Indian War. With the victory of the British, "half the continent had changed hands at the scratch of a pen," as the famous historian Francis Parkman put it. In this selection, Parkman described the French surrender and analyzed the special nature of the war.

READING FOCUS

1. What was Parkman's attitude toward the British colonists? toward the French?
2. What advantages and disadvantages did each side possess?

On September 8, 1760, the French governor signed the surrender agreement by which Canada and all its dependencies passed to the British Crown. French military officers and government officials, with French troops and sailors, were to be sent back to France in British ships. Freedom of religion was assured to the people of the colony. All those who might wish to leave for France were allowed to do so. The Canadians were to keep all their property, including Negro and Indian slaves.

Half the continent had changed hands at the scratch of a pen. Governor Bernard of Massachusetts proclaimed a day of thanksgiving for the great event. The Boston newspapers told how the occasion was celebrated with a parade of young soldiers and other volunteers, a grand dinner in Faneuil Hall, music, bonfires, fireworks, and the firing of cannons. Above all, there were sermons in every church, for the heart of early New England always spoke through its ministers.

On the American continent the war was ended. The British colonists rested for a while, as they drifted unaware toward a deadlier

---

Adapted from Francis Parkman, Montcalm and Wolfe, *1885.*

struggle. They had learned hard and useful lessons. Jealousies and disputes among the colonies, the quarrels of their governors and assemblies, the lack of any general military organization, and the absence, in most of them, of military habits had left them unprepared to carry on offensive war. Nor did the British troops sent to support them show good discipline or efficient command in the beginning. When the fighting broke out, the army of Great Britain was so small that it could hardly be called an army at all. A new one had to be created. Besides their own lack of ability, the English generals had the disadvantage of inexperienced troops and officers. Against them was an enemy who, though weak in numbers, was strong in its military organization. The French had skillful leaders, experienced soldiers, and a population that not only was brave but also was used to war.

The nature of the country itself also made the war last longer. Canada was fortified with its vast defenses of the wilderness forests, marshes, and mountains. Its only "highways" were streams filled with fallen trees that led to dangerous waterfalls and rapids. Thus the problem of moving troops loaded down with supplies and artillery could hardly have been a more difficult one. The question was not so much how to fight the enemy as how to reach him. If there had been a few usable roads in this vast wilderness, the war would have been shortened and the fighting very different.

For these and other reasons, the fact that the English had a larger army was not necessarily an advantage. French writers did perhaps overemphasize the size of the English army. Even so, it was a very large military force if judged by the number of men involved. However, only a part of this large army could be used in offensive military action. The rest was needed for duty in forts and blockhouses and to guard the long frontier from Nova Scotia to South Carolina. And their enemies were foxy, silent and secret; they chose their own time and place to attack, and struck suddenly at every unguarded spot. Thus thousands of English troops had to be scattered at countless points of defense in order to guard against a few hundred savage attackers. At least half the troops of the English colonies, and many of the British regulars, were used for defense in this way.

In actual encounters, the French often were able to outnumber the British, because it was

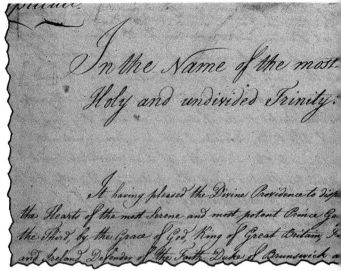

Treaty of Paris, 1760

fairly easy for them to concentrate their forces at a given place. Of the ten important sieges or battles of the war, five (besides the great ambush in which the Indians defeated Braddock) were victories for France. In four of them—Oswego, Fort William Henry, Montmorenci, and Ste. Foy—the French greatly outnumbered the British.

In this very colorful and dramatic American war, nothing is more notable than the skill with which the French and Canadian leaders used their advantages. Their unconquerable spirit and courage helped them, despite little aid from France, to overcome tremendous difficulties. Their defense of Canada deserves praise and admiration.

READING REVIEW

1. List five terms of the Treaty of Paris which ended the war.
2. According to Parkman, what lessons had the colonists learned that would be beneficial to them in the future?
3. How did the "nature of the country" make the war last longer?
4. How might the war's outcome have differed if there had been a network of roads through the wilderness?

CHAPTER 3 American Cultural Beginnings
(1607–1763)

15 Adapting to a New Environment

The European settlers in North America faced new and unfamiliar surroundings. At first they tried to do things as they had done them in their homeland. But often their old ways simply did not work. In order to survive, they had to adjust to their new surroundings. This selection described some of the ways in which the settlers adapted.

READING FOCUS

1. What did the author mean by the "backwoods system"?
2. What items did the Americans adapt to fit their new environment?
3. How did the American environment influence the development of a distinctive American culture?

Savannah, Georgia 1732

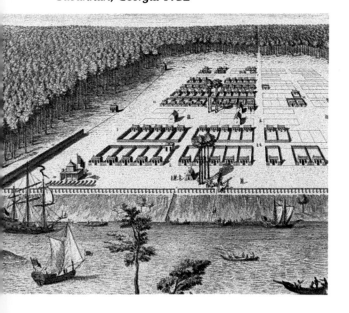

The Europeans who moved to North America in the 1600's faced many hardships. They traveled westward against ocean and wind currents across the Atlantic, the stormiest ocean in the world. The voyage was long, rough, and dangerous. They suffered weeks of seasickness and epidemics of smallpox and scurvy. But the voyage was only the first big obstacle that the settlers had to overcome.

In America the weather was different from the fairly mild, stable climate of Western Europe. Summers were drier and winters were cooler than in Western Europe. There were stormy rains, heat waves, raw winds, hurricanes, blizzards, droughts, lightning storms, and sudden, violent weather changes. The need for shelter from bad weather was an everpressing problem. Food was an even more serious one. Many European seeds and plant cuttings died in the new environment. Starvation, disease, and injury threatened the settlers.

Travel by land was blocked by thick forests in which the newcomers easily became lost. All work—even the settlers' lives—was threatened by the Indians, who fought so well with new tactics and weapons that they confused men who had learned military strategy from famous European generals. Aid and supplies from Europe were all-important. Yet the stormy, gray Atlantic Ocean greatly limited communication, completely isolating colonists for months at a time.

At first it appeared that the French, English, Swedes, Dutch, Spaniards, Germans, and Scots would keep their own cultures and establish communities just like those in their mother countries. Thus the Puritan settlements were religious communities based on English middle-class values. In the French and Swedish settlements, priests and military governors ruled with the same unlimited power that they used to control the villages in their mother countries. From New York to South Carolina, wealthy people brought over a social structure based on Europe's feudal society. They expected indentured servants and slaves to accept this kind of society. European ways of doing things were followed in the coastal settlements.

But when disaster struck at Jamestown, at Plymouth, at the Spanish forts on the Gulf of

Adapted from The Great Forest *by Richard G. Lillard, 1947.*

Mexico and the French missions in Canada, people had to change or die. Their most urgent needs forced them (through slow and costly learning) to imitate the Indians, to keep the most useful parts of their own culture, and to try new and different ways of doing things. Thus, in America, many things about European civilization had to be changed, although the major things did not change immediately.

The result was the backwoods system—a pattern of life and labor based on cutting down forests and using "new ground." It included new crops and farming methods, certain changes in basic tools and weapons, new methods of transportation, a type of house that was new to most Europeans, the new woodcraft of hunter, scout, and settler, and gradual changes in social institutions.

Since Dutch settlers came from a country where there were few trees, they built "colonial Dutch" farmhouses like those in the Netherlands. During the 1600's English settlers (who like the Dutch were used to a scarcity of lumber) used only thin boards of wood to build frame houses. The New Englanders went to great trouble to saw tree trunks lengthwise into frame timbers and split the trunks into boards. They built houses that were made of closely jointed and fitted sills, posts, rafters, and beams. In some towns the second story of the house was overhung, as if they were trying to fit the house in a narrow London street.

But the wooden frame house was too expensive and too difficult to build for the many poor settlers who were untrained in carpentry and who lacked tools. They had to build a shelter quickly while performing the other tasks of daily living. Moreover, the frame dwelling did not meet the needs of the Southern Colonies, where oak boards often warped, creating drafts and fire hazards. Thus the frame house was not to be the shelter used by people in the westward movement. Instead, the log cabin was to provide their shelter. From 1638 on, the Swedes, Finns, and the southern Germans, who came from heavily forested lands, brought over their traditional styles—blockhouses, or log cabins, built of whole trees split through the middle or notched on the ends and placed on top of one another to form a square. After 1700, Scotch-Irish immigrants in Pennsylvania copied these houses and spread them along the frontier. The log cabin—simple, cheap, easy to build and repair, warm and dry, durable, offering protection from bullets—became the proper house for the forest.

The ax that the colonists brought from Europe was of Roman design, influenced perhaps by still older German and Irish war axes. It had a long, straight handle and a shaped blade about eight inches [20 centimeters] long. Altogether it weighed only about three pounds [1.36 kilograms]. It had no pounding edge opposite the blade. And it was hard to balance and could not make deep cuts. This ax did not meet the demands of settlers or wood cutters. So local blacksmiths designed and forged the exact instrument they needed for clearing the forests.

These men forged sharp axheads, putting together steel strips to act as the cutting edge. They experimented until they had axes that balanced well and cut deeply. In short, they invented what the English called the "American ax."

The settler holding an ax in his hand cut down a tree without stopping for breath. He struck his blows with vigorous and rapid strokes, with an accurate, on-target aim. He produced a chip with every blow. Once the tree was down, the settler stood on the trunk and swung his ax in a bold, graceful curve from above his head clear down to the notch beneath his feet. In a rapid rhythm the ax gleamed in the air, buried itself in the log, and gleamed in the air again. It quivered, changed its direction, flashed down and drove into the log, while out flew chips, two inches thick and a foot square. He left the sides of the notch as clean as if it had been cut by a chisel.

Early colonial hunters had only short muskets. These firearms were large and had smooth gun barrels. They were slow to load and fire, required large amounts of powder and bullets, and were very inaccurate. They killed deer and turkeys, and human foes, but they were not as accurate as bows and arrows, and they were noisier. English muskets were so heavy and clumsy, and had such a short range, that they hit their target largely by chance.

There was no accurate weapon in America until the Germans and Swiss, fleeing religious persecution, brought their Jaeger guns to Pennsylvania. These guns, too, were short, heavy, and inaccurate. But they had a grooved gun barrel. The grooves spun the bullet at right angles to the line of shot, giving it distance and power.

To meet the demands of backwoods hunters, the German blacksmiths rapidly changed the design of these traditional rifles. They pro-

A log cabin in the wilderness

duced a gun for people living far from supplies in a wilderness where sharpshooting was necessary. The barrel became longer—up to four or five feet [1.2-1.5 meters]—the inside diameter of the barrel was made smaller, the aiming devices and trigger guards were improved. The new weapon, called the Pennsylvania or Kentucky rifle, did not require constant cleaning, and it was accurate time after time, unlike any previous gun in history.

After the French and Indian War and the American Revolution, the backwoods system began to spread rapidly from the narrow strip of settlements along the Atlantic coast into the interior valleys. When the United States was half a century old and had reached the Missouri River, it was a nation unified by common experiences. Most Americans had cleared land, built cabins, and lived on corn and pork and game. They had drunk sassafras tea as a spring tonic, fought Indian style, and built roads. They had shared a group effort that helped mold the American character and personality and helped to shape people's feelings that they were members of a great nation.

READING REVIEW

1. What was the "backwoods system"?
2. How did the American environment change each of the following: the "colonial Dutch" house, the Roman ax, and the short musket?
3. Which was the most important in settling the American frontier—the log cabin, the American ax, or the Kentucky rifle? Why?
4. According to the author, by the end of the French and Indian War the colonists were a people unified by common experiences. Name two of these experiences and explain why you feel they had a unifying effect.

16 On the Need for Settlers

Benjamin Franklin traveled about the colonies a good deal. Like many other observers, Franklin was impressed by the rapid growth in population. By the 1750's, when Franklin wrote this article, as many as 1.5 million people were living in the colonies. This number was expected to double by 1775. But impressive as this population growth was, it did not meet the demand for workers. Some people thought that slavery was the answer to the shortage of workers. Franklin disagreed with this view.

READING FOCUS

1. Why did Franklin think the population of the colonies would double every 20 years?
2. Why did he think labor would never be cheap in the colonies?

Land is in good supply in America. It is so cheap that a laborer can, in a short time, save enough money to purchase a piece of new land large enough to support a family. Thus people are not afraid to marry. For, even if they look far enough ahead to consider how their children are to be provided for when grown up, they see that more land probably will be available at prices equally cheap, everything considered. Therefore marriages in America are more common and generally occur earlier than in Europe. According to my arithmetic, based on the high birth rate caused by these early marriages, the population should at least double every 20 years.

But in spite of this increase, the territory of North America is so vast that it will require many ages to settle it fully. And until it is fully settled, labor will never be cheap here. No newcomers continue long as laborers for others, but instead get farms of their own. No laborers continue long as journeymen to a trade, but instead move to new settlements and set up for themselves. Hence labor is no cheaper now in Pennsylvania than it was 30 years ago, though many many thousands of laboring people have been brought over here.

It is an incorrect opinion that, by using the labor of slaves, America may possibly compete with Britain in the cheapness of its manufac-

Adapted from Jared Sparks, ed., The Works of Benjamin Franklin, *1856.*

tures. The labor of slaves can never be as cheap as the labor of workers in Britain. Slaves are expensive. Figure the purchase price of a slave, the insurance or risk on his life, the cost of his clothing and food and the expenses of his sicknesses and loss of work. There is also loss caused by the slave's neglect of his work. (Such neglect is natural when a person does not benefit by his own efforts and hard work.) Add the cost of a driver to keep him at work and the cost of his stealing from time to time. Then compare all this expense with the wages paid by a manufacturer of iron or wool in England. You will see that labor is much cheaper there than that of Negro slaves here can ever be.

Why then do Americans purchase slaves? Because slaves may be kept as long as a person pleases or has need of their labor. By contrast, hired workers may decide to leave their masters (often in the midst of a job) and work for themselves.

READING REVIEW

1. Why did Franklin say that people would never be afraid to marry?
2. Why did Franklin think that labor would never be cheap in the colonies?
3. What was Franklin's attitude toward slavery?

17 The Life of Indentured Servants

The need for workers in the colonies led to the practice of hiring indentured servants. People who came to the colonies as indentured servants signed contracts in which they agreed to work in America for a period of two to seven years in return for their passage to the colonies.

Indentured servants came from many different backgrounds. In this selection, a historian gives some of the reasons why some got used to the new conditions and the hard work while many others did not.

READING FOCUS

1. What were the chief difficulties faced by indentured servants in terms of climate? in terms of their work?
2. What single factor, according to Smith, was most important in making a servant's life one of "bondage" (slavery)?

Benjamin Franklin

Of all the things which caused misery to white indentured servants [in the Southern Colonies], the most important was not the temper of their masters nor the unfairness of officials. It was simply the climate of the new country. Men and women of low status were used to obeying masters in England, and often to suffering great cruelties from them. But they were not used to the heat and glaring sun of tropical countries, nor even to the milder temperatures of Virginia. The English, masters as well as servants, had to learn about such climates. Their knowledge was gained at the price of the lives and happiness of many thousands from both classes. In early days the death rate from fevers and epidemic diseases was very high indeed.

Eventually the settlers learned that people should be brought over toward the beginning of the winter season. Though this became the rule for ships from the Netherlands, it does not appear that British and Irish newcomers were treated this way. They were treated better, however, as conditions in the colonies became more stable, and as masters provided against the worst effects of the climate.

The servants' hours of labor had to be adjusted because of the climate. One observer declared that the servants in Virginia had five hours of rest in the heat of the day, but this statement seems hard to believe. Three hours'

From Colonists in Bondage: White Servitude and Convict Labor in America, 1607-1776, *by Abbot Emerson Smith.*

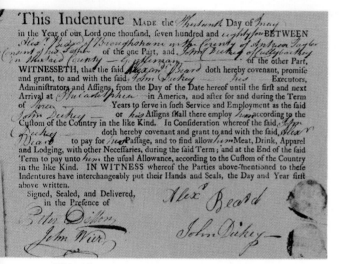

This contract dated May 13, 1784 shows the standardized form that indentured servants from England signed.

daily rest was the average in Maryland. Servants also were free from labor on Saturday afternoons and Sundays in all the colonies; in Maryland, for example, masters were taken into court for working their servants on the Sabbath.

Indentured servants generally lived in huts or cabins, which they built themselves. Apparently they never lived with the Negroes, although the two groups worked side by side in the fields. Food in the early years consisted largely of a mush called "lob-lolly," made from ground Indian corn. In Barbados servants drank a liquid brewed from potatoes called "mobbie" or a mixture of spring water, orange juice, and sugar. English servants complained if they did not eat meat three or four times a week. From New Jersey one observer wrote in 1684 that servants had "beef, pork, bacon, pudding, milk, butter and good beer and cider for drink," a diet of which no one could complain.

One kind of plantation labor which servants had to perform was certainly more difficult and exhausting than the work which was generally done by workers in England. This was the preparing of new land for planting. Trees had to be cut down, trimmed, and dragged away. Brush had to be cleared away. The soil had to be turned for the first time, often without the help of good plows and sometimes even without animals to pull the plows. Even if such clearing was delayed, it had to be done eventually on nearly all land. And immigrants groaned under this burden, which was new to them.

It is clear that all servants usually were required to work in the fields. This was what they were primarily needed for, at least until the Negroes came. Even artisans were used in this way unless their written indenture contract freed them from such a duty. Servants who arranged their contracts before leaving England were often careful to include a statement in it providing that they should work only at their own trades or crafts. In 1741 a court in Pennsylvania ordered a master to let his servant labor as a weaver "according to the meaning of his Indenture," and not to use him for field labor under penalty of having the servant set free. Such cases are frequent in the records, but it appears that the servant had to have a clear statement in his indenture contract in order to free him from toil "in the ground."

These facts provide a basis for understanding the true difficulties of the servant population. People at that time, observing the shorter hours of labor and other advantages enjoyed by servants, compared them with agricultural workers in Europe and thought that they were well off. People who wrote such things generally were interested in giving a favorable report. They overlooked the important fact that many servants were not used to agricultural labor, and therefore found it extremely difficult. The English or German farmers found their work no great hardship in the New World. But it was very different for the tailor, or shoemaker, or weaver who was forced into the tobacco fields. Perhaps it was worst of all for the idle rascals, the thieves, pickpockets, and beggars who were sent to the colonies. They suffered great hardships, and few people wasted sympathy on them.

The basic human problem in colonization was simply one of conditions. White indentured servants did not come from the groups in society that are best able to face changes in their ways of living. People who had been idle now had to work. People whose occupations had not involved hard physical labor found themselves plowing the soil. They had to go without fresh meat. They had to eat Indian corn instead of wheat and rye. They had to wear cotton or linen instead of wool, and sleep in hammocks instead of beds. Probably for the most part they had to drink water. It was these things that made life very difficult for so many servants. Hours of labor might be shorter in the colonies than in

England, and rewards for hard work might be greater. But the servant who was not able to adjust to colonial conditions and do physical labor could be described, without much exaggeration, as in bondage [slavery] worse than that of the Jews in Egypt.

READING REVIEW

1. Why was the climate the most difficult factor for indentured servants to overcome?
2. According to Smith, why did they change the working hours?
3. (a) What was the most difficult labor the servants had to perform? (b) Why was it so hard?

18 A Slave's Middle Passage

In the days when travelers had to cross the oceans in sailing ships, the voyage to America was difficult and dangerous for everyone. But it was most terrible of all for Africans who were captured and sold into slavery.

What was this experience like? The following account was written by Olaudah Equiano, a young African who was taken from his home in Nigeria in the late 1750's and sold into slavery. He was brought to the island of Barbados in the West Indies, and after several years as a slave he was able to buy his freedom. In this selection, Equiano told of the horrors of the voyage to America—what it was like living for weeks, in chains, in the dark hold of a slave ship.

READING FOCUS

1. What did this account tell you about the Middle Passage and the treatment of slaves?
2. Why do you think slavers did not take better care of their "valuable property"?

I loved my family, I loved my village, and I especially loved my mother because I was the youngest son—and her favorite. She made great efforts to develop my mind. She trained me from my earliest years to be skilled in agriculture and war. She rewarded me whenever I did well on the lessons she gave me. I was very happy. But my happiness ended suddenly when I was eleven years old. The end came like this:

Adapted from Olaudah Equiano, The Interesting Narrative of the Life of Olaudah Equiano, or Gustavus Vassa, The African, *Vol. I, 1791.*

One day when all of our people had gone off to their work as usual, and only my dear sister and I were left to guard the house, two men and a woman leaped over our wall and seized us both. Without giving us time to cry out or to resist, they gagged our mouths, tied our hands, and took us away to the nearest woods. They continued to carry us as far as they could until it was dark and we reached a small house, where they stopped to eat and spent the night.

Our only comfort was being with each other all that night and sharing our tears with each other. The next day my sister was separated from me, and the grief it caused me was almost unbearable. I cried and grieved continually, and I ate nothing but what they forced into my mouth.

Finally, after many days of travel during which I had often changed masters, I was sold to a chieftain in a very pleasant country. Although this place was many days' journey from my own land, the people there spoke our language. This first master of mine was an iron smith and I was given the job of working the bellows. Although they treated me well, I missed my mother and my family so much that I made plans to run away.

I hid in the woods all day, planning to start for home after dark. But home was now so far away, I did not know how to reach it. As darkness came I became more and more afraid. At last my fear made me leave my hiding place and return to my master.

Soon after this, I was sold to another chief. I found myself traveling from kingdom to kingdom, changing masters several more times, going farther from my own land and my mother and family. Still, the nations I passed through were like our own in manners, customs, and language. From the time I left my own nation until I arrived at the seacoast, I always found somebody who understood me.

The first thing I saw when I arrived at the coast was the sea, and a slave ship, which was anchored there, waiting for its cargo. The sight filled me with astonishment, then with a feeling of terror which I am still not able to describe.

When I was carried onto the ship, I was immediately handled and tossed up in the air by some of the crew to see if I were strong and healthy. I was now certain that I had gotten into a world of evil spirits, and that they were going to kill me. The color of their skin, which was so different from ours; their long hair; and

African slaves form a human chain as they are led to coastal markets.

the language they spoke, which was very different from any I had ever heard, all strengthened this belief. Indeed, I was so terrified that if I were the ruler of ten thousand empires I would gladly have given them all up just to change places with the lowliest slave in my own country. When I looked around the ship and saw the large group of black people of all kinds who were chained together, their faces expressing great unhappiness, and sorrow, I no longer doubted that something terrible was going to happen to me. Overpowered by terror and anguish, I fell on the deck and then fainted.

I now knew I had lost all chance of returning to my own country, or even of getting back to the shore. I even wished to be back in my recent slavery, rather than in my present situation. My mind was filled with horrors of every kind, made even worse by my ignorance of what was going to happen to me.

I was not permitted to grieve for very long, however. I was soon placed below the decks. The experience there was one of the worst in my life. The terrible smells and the crying made me so sick that I was not able to eat. I now wished for that final friend, Death, to take me.

Soon two white crew members offered me something to eat. When I refused to eat, one of them held me fast by the hands and tied my feet, while the other beat me severely. I had never experienced anything of this kind before. If I could have gotten over the netting, I would have jumped over the side. But I could not. Besides, the crew watched us very carefully, especially those of us who were not chained to the decks—to prevent us from jumping overboard into the water. I have seen some poor African prisoners very severely cut for attempting to jump overboard, and others whipped for hours for not eating.

When the ship had loaded all its cargo, we were all put below deck. The number of people was so great that each person barely had room to move. The stale air and the heat almost choked us. Everyone was dripping with sweat, so that the air became unfit to breathe, from a variety of foul smells. These conditions caused sickness among the slaves, and many died—in this way becoming victims to the short-sighted greed of their purchasers.

This wretched situation was made even worse by the rubbing of the chains against the slaves' skin, which became unbearable, and by the filth of the tubs, into which the children often fell and were almost drowned. The screams of the women, and the moans of the dying, made this a scene of horror almost beyond belief.

At last we came within sight of the island of Barbados [in the West Indies]. The white crew members gave a loud shout and showed their excitement and joy. We did not know what to think of this.

Many merchants and planters now came on board the ship, though it was evening. They put us in separate groups, and examined us carefully. They pointed to the land, showing us that we were to go there. We thought this meant that we should be eaten by these ugly men! There was so much dread and trembling among us that at last the crew brought some old slaves from the island to talk to us and calm us. They told us we would not be eaten; we had been brought here to work and we would soon go ashore, where we could see many people from our own country. Their words succeeded in calming our fears.

As we had been told, as soon as we landed Africans of all languages came to us. We were taken immediately to the merchant's yard. There we were all crowded together, like so many sheep, without regard to sex or age.

We were not many days in the merchant's custody before we were sold according to their usual manner: On a given signal, such as the beat of a drum, the buyers rush into the yard where the slaves are kept, and choose the group they like best. The noise and clamor of this action, and the eagerness on the faces of the buyers, only greatly increases the fear of the terrified Africans.

In this manner, without a thought about it, family members and friends are separated—most of them never to see each other again.

READING REVIEW

1. Who kidnapped Equiano and his sister, a European or an African? Cite two pieces of evidence that support your answer.
2. What conditions did the slave endure during the Middle Passage?
3. Why did some slaves feel that death would be preferable to the treatment they received?
4. List two reasons why the slavers did not take better care of the slaves.

19 A Traveler's Connecticut Report

In 1704 Sarah Kemble Knight, a hardy Bostonian, set out on horseback for New York City to settle some business matters. Travel in those days was difficult, but her enthusiasm and zest for new experiences helped her overcome the problems that travelers faced.

During her five-month trip from Boston to New York and home again, Sarah Knight kept a journal. It gives a vivid picture of colonial life, enlivened by her witty comments about the people she met. In this selection, she gives her impressions of the people of Connecticut.

READING FOCUS

1. What comparisons did Sarah Knight make with the people of Massachusetts?
2. How do the people recreate in Connecticut?

About two o'clock in the afternoon we arrived at New Haven, where I was treated with all possible respect and politeness. Here I dismiss-ed my guide, paying him for his services, and took some time to rest after the long and difficult journey. I studied the manners and customs of the place, and also took care of some business matters.

In this colony of Connecticut, the people are governed by the same or similar laws as we are in Boston. They also have much the same kind of church organization. Many of them are good, sociable people, and I hope religious too, but they are a little too independent in their principles. I have been told that in the past they showed rigorous zeal in punishing those who broke the law, including even young people guilty of a harmless kiss or innocent merriment. Whipping was a frequent punishment, and judges were severe in their sentences.

Their recreations in this part of the country are mostly on church Lecture Days and military Training Days. On Lecture Days there is riding from town to town. On Training Days the young men enjoy themselves by shooting at a target. The one who hits nearest the bull's-eye is presented with yards of red ribbon. This is tied to his hatband, with the two ends streaming down his back. The youth is then led away in triumph, with great applause, like a winner at the Greek Olympic games.

People generally dress very simply throughout the colony. In each area, however, they have a special style. Thus you can tell where people come from—especially the women—no matter where you meet them.

Their chief holiday is St. Election Day, which is observed every year as provided in their colonial charter. They then choose their governor—a blessing for which they can never be thankful enough, as they could have had the bad luck to lose it.

READING REVIEW

1. Where was Sarah Knight from?
2. What criticism did she make about their independence? What do you think she meant by this remark?
3. Cite evidence from the excerpt that shows she admired democracy.

Adapted from The Journal of Madam Knight, *1920.*

20 A Letter from South Carolina

Eliza Lucas was born in the West Indies, where her father, a British officer, was stationed. She moved to South Carolina as a teen-ager. In the 1740's on the plantation where the Lucas family lived, she experimented with growing indigo, a plant which produced a blue dye. Helped by professionals whom she hired, she became the first planter in the American colonies to grow indigo as a successful commercial crop. A few years later she married Charles Pinckney. Two of their sons were prominent in the American Revolution.

In this letter to her brother, written in 1742, Eliza Lucas describes the colony of South Carolina and the people who lived there.

READING FOCUS

1. What favorable characteristics of North Carolina did Lucas list?
2. What unfavorable characteristics did she mention in the letter?

Now, dear brother, I will obey your command and give you a short description of the part of the world in which I now live. South Carolina is a vast region near the sea. Most of the settled part of it is flat. The soil near Charleston is sandy, but farther away one finds clay and swamp lands. South Carolina is filled with fine navigable rivers and great forests of fine timber. The soil in general is very fertile. There are few European or American fruits or grains that cannot be grown here. The country is full of wild fowl, deer, and fish. Beef, veal, and mutton are much better here than in the West Indies, though not as good as meat in England. The fruit is extremely good and plentiful. The oranges are superior to any I ever tasted in the West Indies or to those from Spain or Portugal.

The people in general are hospitable and honest. The better sort of people are polite and gentle. The poorer sort are the laziest people in the world. Otherwise they would never be poor and wretched in a land as rich as this.

Adapted from Eliza Lucas, Journal and Letters, *edited by Mrs. H. P. Holbrook, 1850.*

The winters here are fine and pleasant. But the four months in the summer are extremely disagreeable and hot. There is much thunder and lightning, and great swarms of mosquitoes and sand flies are all around.

Charleston, the main city, is a neat, handsome place. The people who live here are polite and have a gentle manner. The streets and houses are attractively built. Both ladies and gentlemen dress fashionably. On the whole you will find as many agreeable people of both sexes here as in any other city of this size. St. Philip's Church is very elegant and much visited. There are several other places of public worship in town, and most people are of a religious turn of mind.

I began this letter in haste, and have been writing without a plan. I should have told you before I wrote about summer that we have had a most charming spring in this region, especially for those who travel through the countryside. The scent of new myrtle and yellow jasmine flowers, so abundant in the woods, is delightful.

READING REVIEW

1. What did Lucas say about South Carolina in general? About Charleston in particular?
2. How do the seasons in South Carolina differ from each other?

21 An English Visitor in New York City

By the mid-1700's many Europeans were visiting the American colonies. Andrew Burnaby, a minister of the Church of England, spent several months touring North America during 1759-60. For the most part, he liked what he saw in the colonies. But he also reported that there were weaknesses that were impossible to overcome—among them slavery—and that they would prevent the region from ever being a strong nation.

In this selection Burnaby gave his impressions of the city of New York. The Kissing Bridge he wrote about spanned a creek in what is now the Bowery in southern Manhattan, the most familiar part of New York City.

New York City in 1757 is shown as an important commercial center and thriving port.

READING FOCUS

1. Why did Burnaby say that the province of New York is "flourishing"?
2. What was Burnaby's impression of the people of New York?

At Staten Island I boarded a ship for New York. It was a pleasant trip across the bay, with delightful views of rivers, islands, fields, hills, woods, New York City, vessels sailing to and fro, and the many porpoises playing on the surface of the water. The evening was so peaceful that the sky was not disturbed by a single cloud. I arrived about sunset.

This city is located at the tip of a small island, lying open to the bay on one side, and enclosed on the other side by the North [Hudson] and East rivers. It has between 2,000 and 3,000 houses and 16,000 or 17,000 inhabitants. It is well laid out and has several truly fine houses. The streets are paved and very clean, although in general they are narrow.

Arts and sciences have made no greater progress here than in the other colonies. But a library supported by members' payments has recently opened, and everyone seems eager to promote learning. Thus it may be hoped that the arts and sciences will now make faster progress than they have done before this time. King's College [now Columbia University] is

Adapted from Burnaby's Travels Through North America, *with Introduction and Notes by Rufus Rockwell Wilson, 1904.*

established upon the same plan as the college in the Jerseys [now Princeton University], except that this New York college follows the teachings of the Church of England. At present it is far from flourishing, or as good as might be wished. Its budget is small, and there are few professors. Nevertheless, a graduation ceremony was held this summer, and seven gentlemen were awarded degrees. About 25 students are now attending King's College.

The character of the people of New York is very much like that of Pennsylvania. More than half of them are Dutch, and almost all are traders. Therefore they are industrious and save their money. Since the people of New York are of so many different nationalities, different languages, and different religions, it is almost impossible to describe them. New York women are beautiful and pleasant, though more reserved than women in Philadelphia.

Their amusements are much the same as in Pennsylvania. There are balls and sleigh rides in the winter. In the summer they go out in boats and fish, or take trips to the country. There are several houses pleasantly located along the East River, near New York, where it is common to have turtle feasts. These happen once or twice a week. Thirty or forty gentlemen and ladies meet and dine together, drink tea in the afternoon, and fish and amuse themselves till evening. Then they return home in carriages, a gentleman and a lady riding in each one. On the way there is a bridge, about 3 miles [5 kilometers] distant from New York, which they always pass over on their return, called the Kissing Bridge. There it is considered polite for the gentleman to salute the lady who has put herself under his protection.

At present this province is flourishing. It has an extensive trade with many parts of the world, particularly the West Indies, and has grown rich from this commerce.

Before I left New York, I took a ride out to Long Island, the richest spot in all America in the view of New Yorkers. There many New Yorkers have their villas, or country houses. The area is truly beautiful, and some parts of it are remarkably fertile, though not equal to the Jerseys in my opinion.

READING REVIEW

1. Name two reasons Burnaby gave for the lack of progress of the arts and sciences in the colonies.
2. How did Burnaby describe the character of the people of New York?
3. What did the New Yorkers do for amusement?
4. According to Burnaby, the province of New York was "flourishing". What evidence did he give to support this conclusion?

22 A Colonial College

Nine colleges in the United States today were started during colonial days. One of these was Princeton University. In the fall of 1770, when Philip Fithian started college there, Princeton was called the College of New Jersey and was less than 25 years old. Like other colonial colleges, its main purpose was to prepare young men to become ministers.

As this letter to his father showed, Fithian, then 22, was favorably impressed by the school's atmosphere and strict rules. One wonders whether other students at that time—such as James Madison and Aaron Burr—liked the strict rules as much as Fithian did.

READING FOCUS

1. What aspects of college life did Fithian talk about in his letter?
2. How did Fithian feel about the strict rules?

Very Dear Father,

As you know, I began to study three weeks later than the rest of the class. But even though

Nassau Hall (left) is the oldest building now standing on the Princeton University campus.

I am very busy as a result, I think it my duty to tell you about my admission to this seminary of learning. It is another grand step toward my goal of becoming a minister. I shall also describe as many of the customs as I can, given my short acquaintance with the college and students.

I was admitted into the junior class on the 22nd day of November, after passing an examination given by the president, the tutors, and some graduates. This was about three weeks after the college term began.

The rules of conduct for scholars and students here are, in my opinion, very well suited to restrain wicked students, to assist studious students, and to encourage virtuous ones.

Every student must rise in the morning by 5:30 A.M. at the latest. The bell rings at 5 A.M., after which everyone has a half hour to dress. Then the bell rings again, and prayers begin. In case anyone did not hear the bell, the servant who rings goes to every door and knocks until he wakens the boys. Thus they have no excuse for being late.

There are record keepers in each class, usually appointed by the president or in his absence by one of the tutors. They take down the names of those who are absent from the morning or evening prayers. Once every week they present their record to the president or to one of the tutors, who calls in those named and demands to hear their excuse. If their excuses are not acceptable, they are fined or privately rebuked. If the same person is frequently found guilty without good reason, he receives a public reproach in the hall for refusing to obey authority.

After morning prayers, we can, now that it's winter, study for an hour by candlelight every morning.

We eat breakfast at 8 o'clock. From 8 to 9 o'clock, we have free time to play games or to exercise.

At 9 A.M. the bell rings for classroom instruction. After classes end, we study until 1 o'clock, when the bell rings for lunch. We all dine in the same room, at three tables. We have breakfast and supper in the same way.

After lunch we are at liberty to do as we please until 3 P.M. From 3 until 5 P.M. we study until the bell rings for evening prayers.

Adapted from John Rogers Williams, ed., Philip Vickers Fithian Journal and Letters, 1767-1774.

We eat at 7 P.M. At 9 o'clock the bell rings for study. A tutor goes through the college to see that every student is in his own room. If he finds anyone absent, or that more students are in a room than belong there, he notes this down and the following day calls these students in and asks them to explain.

After 9 P.M. anyone may go to bed; however, if you go before that hour, it is considered a sign of laziness.

No student is allowed to be absent on Sunday from public worship for any reason except sickness. We have two sermons every Sunday. One is given at 11 o'clock in the morning in the church. The other is given at 3 o'clock in the afternoon in the college hall. I am very pleased indeed with Dr. Witherspoon [John Witherspoon, president of the college from 1768 to 1794]. I find his sermons almost without equal.

We rise on Sunday mornings and have prayers as usual.

There is a group that meets every Sunday evening at 6 P.M. for religious worship. This is a voluntary group made up of those who go to the college and want to attend.

There are now more than a hundred students in the college. I am, through divine goodness, very well. And I am more willing than I was at first to get up so early in the morning.

From your dutiful son.

READING REVIEW

1. To whom was Fithian writing? How might this have influenced what he wrote about?
2. What was Fithian's purpose in writing this letter?
3. What was Fithian's opinion concerning the "rules of conduct for scholars and students"?
4. How do these rules compare with those at your school?

23 What an American Is

Over the years, the questions "What is an American?" and "How are Americans different from other peoples of the world?" has been asked many times by many different people. One of the first persons who attempted to answer these questions about America and Americans was J. Hector St. John de Crèvecoeur. Crèvecoeur was a French

Americans today represent a variety of cultural backgrounds.

immigrant who became a successful farmer in the colony of New York. Between 1769 and 1776 he wrote *Letters from an American Farmer*. In these letters Crèvecoeur gave his impressions of many aspects of life in the colonies. An excerpt from one of his letters, "What is an American?," appears below. As you read the excerpt remember that it was written from the point of view of a person living in the late 1700's.

READING FOCUS

1. What features make Americans different from other peoples of the world?
2. What did Crèvecoeur think about the future of Americans?

What, then, is the American, this new man? He is neither an European nor the descendant of an European; hence that strange mixture of blood, which you will find in no other country. I could point out to you a family whose grandfather was an Englishman, whose wife was Dutch, whose son married a French woman, and whose present four sons have now four wives of different nations. *He* is an American, who, leaving behind him all his ancient prejudices and manners, receives new ones from the new way of life he has embraced, the new gov-

ernment he obeys, and the new rank he holds. Here individuals of all nations are melted into a new race of men, whose labors and descendants will one day cause great changes in the world.

The Americans were once scattered all over Europe; here they are united into one of the finest systems of population which has ever appeared, and which will hereafter become distinct by the power of the different climates they inhabit. The American should love this country much better than where either he or his forefathers were born. In America the rewards of his industry follow with equal steps the progress of his labor; his labor is founded on the basis of nature, that is, his own self-interest. Wives and children, who before in vain demanded of him a morsel of bread, now, fat and frolicsome, gladly help their father to clear those fields where plentiful crops are to arise to feed and to clothe them all, without any part being claimed, either by a despotic prince, a rich religious leader, or a mighty lord. Here religion demands but little of him: a small voluntary salary to the minister and gratitude to God; can he refuse these?

The American is a new man, who acts upon new principles; he must therefore entertain new ideas and form new opinions. From involuntary idleness, servile dependence, poverty, and useless labor he has passed to work of a very different nature, rewarded by a good life. This is an American.

Adapted from Hector St. John de Crèvecoeur, "What is an American?" in Letters from an American Farmer and Sketches of Eighteenth-Century America, *1963.*

32

READING REVIEW

1. What did Crèvecoeur mean when he said that in America there is "that strange mixture of blood, which you will find in no other country"?
2. Did Crèvecoeur imply that there was political and religious freedom in America? Give evidence from the reading to support your answer.
3. According to Crèvecoeur, what did an American have to do in order to be rewarded with a good life?

24 Travels in the Wilderness

Well before the American Revolution, colonists had begun pushing beyond the settled territories into the Allegheny Mountains and beyond. One of the best known of these pioneering colonists was Daniel Boone. In 1769, with a small group of adventurers, he explored what he called the paradise of Kentucky. Boone's story—as told to writer John Filson in later years—was no doubt changed somewhat for publication. For example, the language was certainly not that of a simple backwoods hunter. But the descriptions of Boone's experiences were probably fairly accurate.

READING FOCUS

1. Why did Boone explore Kentucky?
2. Was his expedition successful?

It was on the 1st day of May in the year 1769 that I left my family and peaceful home on the Yadkin River, in North Carolina. I left to wander through the wilderness of America, searching for the country of Kentucky. I went with John Stewart and four other companions.

After a long and tiring journey through a mountainous wilderness, we found ourselves at the Red River. From the top of a hill we saw the beautiful plain of Kentucky. At this place we camped, made a shelter, and began to hunt and to explore the country. Everywhere we found an abundance of wild animals of all sorts. There are more buffalo here than there are cattle in most settlements. They are fearless, because they are ignorant of the violence of

Adapted from "Daniel Boone's Own Story" from The American Reader *by Paul M. Angle. Published by Rand McNally & Company.*

human beings. Sometimes we saw hundreds together, and the numbers around the salt springs were amazing. This forest was the home of animals of every kind known in America, and we hunted them with great success until the 22nd of December.

That day John Stewart and I took what seemed to be a pleasant stroll, which fortune determined would end quite differently. We had passed through a vast forest. Late in the day, near the Kentucky River, a number of Indians suddenly appeared and took us prisoners. The time of our misfortunes had arrived. The Indians robbed us, and kept us prisoners for seven days. During this time we showed no uneasiness or desire to escape, which made them less suspicious of us. But one night when they were asleep, we escaped, leaving them to enjoy their sleep. We fled back to our old camp, but found that everything there had been stolen, and that our group had separated and returned home. About this time, my brother, with another adventurer, accidentally found our camp. Despite our group's misfortunes, we were very happy at our good luck in finding each other in the wilderness.

Soon after this, John Stewart, my companion and former fellow prisoner, was killed by the Indians. And the man who had arrived with my brother returned home. We were then in a dangerous situation. We now faced danger and death every day from the Indians and wild animals. There was not a white settler in the country except us.

We hunted every day, and prepared a small shelter to protect us from the winter storms. We remained there undisturbed during the winter. On the 1st of May, 1770, my brother returned home to the settlement to get more horses and ammunition. This left me alone, without bread, salt, or sugar, without company of my fellow-creatures, or even a horse or dog. I confess I never before had had greater need of courage.

One day I walked through the countryside and the variety and beauties of nature I saw drove away all my gloomy thoughts. Toward evening the gentle wind died down and all was calm and peaceful. Not a breeze shook a leaf. I had reached the top of a lofty mountain. Looking round with delight, I saw the wide plains and the beautiful land below. From the other side, I looked down at the famous Ohio River, which flowed in silent dignity, marking the western boundary of Kentucky. In a few days I explored a considerable part of the area, and each day I was just as pleased as on the first. I even returned to my old camp, which had not been disturbed in my absence.

Thus I spent the time until the 27th day of July 1770, when my brother met me at our old camp, as we had planned. Shortly afterward, we left, thinking it might not be safe to stay there longer. We traveled to the Cumberland River, giving names to the different rivers and exploring that part of the country until March 1771. Soon afterward, I returned home to my family. I was determined, even at the risk of my life and fortune, to bring them with me as soon as possible to live in Kentucky, which I now considered to be a second paradise.

Daniel Boone

READING REVIEW

1. What was Boone's impression of Kentucky?
2. How did he describe it?
3. Why did the Indians attack Boone and later kill Stewart?
4. **(a)** If you had read this account in 1771, would you have wanted to move to the new territory? **(b)** List the advantages and disadvantages you would have had to consider before making such a decision.

25 A Seneca Chief's Speech

To Daniel Boone, and to many other white Americans, Indians were dangerous nuisances who had to be dealt with or gotten rid of, if possible. Another group of settlers, the missionaries, wanted to convert the tribes to Christianity. Neither group of settlers realized that the Indians had highly advanced cultures and profound beliefs of their own on life, the natural environment, and religion. These beliefs were so different from those of the white settlers that the Indians and the settlers seldom understood one another.

In 1805 a group of Iroquois chiefs met with a Boston missionary for a discussion of religion and other matters. One of the observers wrote down what was said, including this remarkable speech by Red Jacket, a chief of the Seneca tribe.

READING FOCUS

1. How did Red Jacket describe the relationship between the whites and the Indians?
2. Why did the Indians refuse to accept the white man's religion?

Brother, listen to what we say.

There was a time when only our ancestors lived in this great land. Their lands extended from the rising to the setting sun. The Great Spirit had made it for the use of Indians. He had created the buffalo, the deer, and other animals for food. He had made the bear and the beaver. Their skins served us for clothing. He had scattered these animals over the country, and taught us how to catch them. He had caused the earth to produce corn for bread. All this he had done for his red children, because

Adapted from a pamphlet entitled Indian Speeches; Delivered by Farmer's Brother and Red Jacket, Two Seneca Chiefs, *1809.*

he loved them. If we had some disputes about our hunting ground, they were generally settled without the shedding of much blood. But an evil day came upon us. Your ancestors crossed the great water, and landed on this land. Their numbers were small. They found us to be friends and not enemies. They told us they had fled from their own country for fear of wicked men, and had come here to enjoy their religion. They asked for a small piece of land. We took pity on them, and granted their request, and they settled down among us. We gave them corn and meat. They gave us poison [strong liquor] in return.

The white people had now found our country. News of it was carried back, and more came among us. Yet we did not fear them. We took them to be friends. They called us brothers. We believed them, and gave them more land. After a time their numbers had greatly increased. They wanted more land. They wanted our country. Our eyes were opened, and our minds became uneasy. Wars took place. Indians were hired to fight against Indians, and many of our people were killed. They also brought strong liquor among us. It was strong and powerful, and has slain thousands.

Brother, our lands were once large and yours were small. You have now become a great people, and we have scarcely a place left to spread our blankets. You have got our country, but you are not satisfied. You want to force your religion upon us.

You say that you are sent to teach us how to worship the Great Spirit. You say that if we do not accept the religion which you white people teach, we shall be unhappy hereafter. You say that you are right and that we are lost. How do we know this to be true? We understand that your religion is written in a book. If it was intended for us as well as you, why has not the Great Spirit given this book to us? And why did he not give our ancestors knowledge of that book, with the means of understanding it? We only know that you tell us about it. How shall we know when to believe, being so often tricked by white people?

Brother, you say there is only one way to worship and serve the Great Spirit. If there is only one religion, why do you white people disagree so much about it? Why are you not all agreed, as you all read the same book?

Brother, we do not understand these things. We are told that your religion was given to your ancestors, and has been handed

Red Jacket worked his entire life to preserve the ancient customs of his people.

down from parent to child. We also have a religion, which was given to our ancestors, and has been handed down to us their children. We worship in that way. It teaches us to be thankful for all the favors we receive, to love each other, and to be united. We never quarrel about religion.

Brother, the Great Spirit has made us all, but he has made a great difference between his white and red children. He has given us different skin colors and different customs. To you he has given learning and science. He has not opened our eyes to such things. Since he has made so great a difference between us in other things, why may we not conclude that he has given us a different religion according to our understanding? The Great Spirit does what is right. He knows what is best for his children. We are satisfied.

Brother, we do not wish to destroy your religion, or take it from you. We only want to enjoy our own. We are told that you have been preaching to the white people in this place. These people are our neighbors. We know them well. We will wait a little while, and see what effect your preaching has upon them. If we find it does them good, makes them honest and less ready to cheat Indians, we will then consider again what you have said.

Brother, you have now heard our answer to your talk, and this is all we have to say at present. Since we are going to part, we will come and take you by the hand. We hope the Great Spirit will protect you on your journey, and return you safe to your friends.

READING REVIEW

1. According to Red Jacket, how did the Indians greet white people?
2. What were the main points Red Jacket made against accepting Christianity?
3. How would you describe Red Jacket's speech?

CHAPTER
4 Democracy in Colonial America
(1607–1763)

---

26 The Body of Liberties

Civil rights were among the most important ideas that the English colonists brought to the New World. One of these rights was the right to elect representatives to pass laws.

The legislature of Massachusetts Bay Colony was known as the General Court of Massachusetts. In 1641 the General Court adopted a code of laws known as the Body of Liberties. The specific laws in the Body of Liberties reflected the basic rights of the English and had a great impact on laws made by other legislatures in colonial New England.

The following excerpt contains some of the laws in the Body of Liberties.

READING FOCUS

1. What important civil rights were included in the Body of Liberties?
2. When may a person loose their civil rights?

1. No man's life shall be taken away. No man's honor or good name shall be stained. No man's person shall be arrested, restrained, banished, dismembered, nor any ways punished. No man shall be deprived of his wife or children. No man's goods or estate shall be taken away from him, nor in any way damaged, unless it be by authority of some express law of the country warranting the same.

2. Every person within this colony, whether inhabitant or foreigner, shall enjoy the same justice and law.

*   *   *   *

7. No man shall be made to go out of the limits of this plantation except to defend it.

8. No man's cattle or goods shall be taken for any public use or service, unless it be by legal order of the General Court. A reasonable price based on the ordinary rates of the country will be paid for any goods taken for public use or service. And if his cattle or goods shall perish or suffer damage in such service, the owner shall be paid for his loss.

*   *   *   *

45. No man shall be forced by torture to confess any crime against himself nor any other unless it be in some case involving the death penalty, where he is first fully convicted by clear and sufficient evidence to be guilty.

46. For bodily punishments we do not allow any that are inhumane, barbarous or cruel.

47. No man shall be put to death without the testimony of two or three witnesses.

READING REVIEW

1. Name three important civil rights listed in the Body of Liberties.
2. Under what circumstances could a man's cattle or goods be taken from him?
3. Under what circumstances could a person be put to death?

Adapted from The Colonial Laws of Massachusetts, *edited by William H. Whitmore, 1889.*

27 A Quaker Defense of Conscience

One of the ironies of early American history is that the Puritans, who were themselves denied religious freedom in England, denied it to others in Massachusetts. Among those they opposed were the Quakers, who believed that an individual's conscience was more important than any church or doctrine. The Puritan rulers of Massachusetts feared this idea and saw it as a threat to their religion.

As a result, in 1658 Massachusetts passed a law banning Quakers from the colony on pain of death. When Mary Dyer, a Quaker, visited friends there a year later, she was imprisoned and sentenced to death. The following selection is from her speech to the court that sentenced her. Although she was freed at the last minute, Mary Dyer returned to Massachusetts in 1660, was sentenced again, and this time was hanged.

A Quaker meeting

READING FOCUS

1. To what did Mary Dyer refer when she spoke of the "seed"?
2. What warning did she issue to the Puritans?

I am blamed by many for being the cause of my own death. If they mean by my coming to Boston, I am justified by the Lord, by whose will I come. You have made a law to take away the lives of innocent servants of God, whom you call "cursed Quakers" if they come among you. I say that God has blessed them and sent them to you. Be not fighters against God, but accept my advice. You should end all such laws, so that the truth and the servants of the Lord may move freely among you. You would then be kept from shedding innocent blood, which I know many among you would not do if you could help it.

Out of the love for your souls, I must persuade you. I have no selfish goals, as the Lord knows. If my life were now spared, it would not help if I still had to see the sufferings of my people – my dear fellow Quakers who share the seed of true faith with which my life is bound up.

Adapted from Mary Dyer, by Edward Burrough—A Declaration of the Sad and Great Persecution and Martyrdom of the People of God, called Quakers, in New-England, for the Worshipping of God, 1660.

Were such laws found among people who say they believe in Christ? And have you Puritans no other weapons except such laws to fight against "spiritual wickedness," as you call it? I pity you if you do not!

It is not my own life I seek – only the life of the seed of true faith, which I know the Lord has blessed. The devil seeks to destroy its life, as he had in all ages. Oh, do not follow him, I beg you, for the seed's sake. It is dear in the sight of God.

Know this also. If you enforce your law by hatred, and take the life of only one of us, the Lord will destroy both your law and you. If you do not hear and obey the Lord or his servants, he will send more of his servants among you. You may try to prevent those you call "cursed Quakers" from coming among you. But God has planted a seed here among you, for which we have suffered all this while and still suffer. The Lord of the harvest will send forth more servants to gather this seed into his fold of true believers.

In love and in the spirit of meekness I again beg you, for I have no hatred toward any of you. But you should know that God will not be defied. What you sow, that shall you reap.

READING REVIEW

1. What did Mary Dyer seek?
2. What warning did she issue to the Puritans?

28 An Early Condemnation of Slavery

Slavery existed in all the colonies by the mid-1600's. Most American settlers probably gave little thought to slavery and simply accepted the practice.

But in 1688 a group of Quakers at their monthly meeting in Germantown, Pennsylvania, voted in favor of this statement, or resolution, against slavery. The resolution is unusual because at this time almost no one thought of protesting the use of Africans as slave laborers. The resolution was sent to the annual Quaker meetings, but was voted down there.

READING FOCUS

1. What arguments did the Quakers make against slavery?
2. Do they regard black people as their equals?

These are the reasons why we are against the buying and selling of human beings: How fearful and worried do many Europeans feel at sea when they see a strange ship. They are afraid that it might be a Turkish ship and that they will be taken and sold as slaves in Turkey. Now, is slavery here any better than in Turkey? Rather it is worse when practiced by those people who say they are Christians. We believe that most Negroes are brought here against their will, and that many of them are stolen.

Now, because they are black, we cannot agree that people are freer to own them as

Slaves packing tobacco on a colonial plantation

slaves than to own white slaves. There is a saying that we should do unto others as we would have others do unto us, no matter what their social class, their background, or color. And those who steal or rob other human beings, and those who buy or purchase them, are they not all alike?

Here we have freedom of religious belief, which is right and reasonable. Here we should also have personal freedom, except for evildoers, which is another case. Thus we protest against bringing people here, and robbing and selling them against their will. In Europe many people are oppressed for religion's sake. Here they are oppressed because of their black color.

This gives us a poor reputation in all the countries of Europe, when they learn that the Quakers here treat people as they treat the cattle there. And for that reason some people have decided not to come here.

We ask, what worse thing could happen to us than if people should rob or steal us away and sell us as slaves to strange countries, separating husbands, wives, and children? We who believe that it is not lawful to steal must also avoid purchasing things that are stolen. Rather we should help stop this robbing and stealing, if possible. And the people who have been stolen ought to be taken from the robbers and set free as in Europe. Then Pennsylvania would have a good reputation, just as now it has a bad one.

If these slaves (who are said to be so wicked and stubborn) should join together to fight for their freedom, and treat their masters and mistresses as they were treated, will these masters and mistresses decide to use weapons and make war against these poor slaves? Or, have these poor Negroes not as much right to fight for their freedom as you have to keep them as slaves?

READING REVIEW

1. What did the Quakers say about the relationship of Christianity to slavery?
2. What did the Quakers say about the relationship of skin color to slavery?
3. What did the Quakers say about slavery and rights?

Adapted from George H. Moore, ed., Notes on the History of Slavery in Massachusetts, *1866.*

29 In Zenger's Defense

The trial of John Peter Zenger, in 1735, helped to establish the principle of freedom of the press in the American colonies. Zenger was accused of publishing newspaper articles which criticized the British colonial governor of New York. His lawyer, Andrew Hamilton, admitted immediately that Zenger was guilty of publishing the articles in question. He tried to base his case on the fact that the material published was true. However, the law was plainly against Zenger. At that time the publishing of even a true statement could be considered illegal.

The jurors had no legal choice but to vote guilty. If they did not, they could be fined and imprisoned. But the trial was being widely followed in the colonies, and feeling ran high. When the jury cleared Zenger, the judge did not dare reject the verdict and punish the jurors. This account of some of the speeches by Andrew Hamilton and a government attorney at the trial was published by Zenger himself a few years later.

READING FOCUS

1. What were the main points in Mr. Hamilton's argument?
2. What were the main points in the government attorney's arguments?

MR. HAMILTON: I represent Mr. Zenger, the defendant, in this case. I do not deny that these articles were published. I think it is the right of every freeborn citizen to take such action when the thing published can be proven to be truthful. Therefore I will save the Government Attorney the trouble of examining his witnesses on this point. I confess that Mr. Zenger both printed and published the two newspapers described in the charge against him. And I hope that in doing so he has committed no crime.

GOVERNMENT ATTORNEY: The case before the court is whether Mr. Zenger is guilty of publishing damaging statements—or libeling—his excellency, the governor of New York, and indeed the whole administration of the government. Mr. Hamilton has confessed that he printed and published these statements. Nothing is plainer than that the words are scandalous and tend to cause great unrest among the

---

Adapted from A Brief Narrative of the Case and Tryal of John Peter Zenger, Printer of the New-York Weekly Journal, *1738.*

people of this province. If such newspaper articles are not libelous, I think it may be said there is no such thing as a libel.

MR. HAMILTON: I cannot agree with the Government Attorney. For though I freely admit that there are such things as libels, I must insist that what my client is charged with doing is not a libel. I noticed just now that the Government Attorney did not include the word "false" in defining "libel."

GOVERNMENT ATTORNEY: I believe that I did not leave out the word "false." In any case it already has been said that something may be a libel even if the statements published are true.

MR. HAMILTON: In this I still must disagree with the Government Attorney. Mr. Zenger is charged with printing and publishing a certain false, evil, and scandalous libel that could cause discontent with the government. This word "false" must have some meaning, or else why is it there?

MR. CHIEF JUSTICE: You cannot argue, Mr. Hamilton, the point of whether a libel is true or false. A libel cannot be justified even if it is true.

MR. HAMILTON: I thank your Honor. Then, gentlemen of the jury, I must now appeal to you. And let it not seem strange that I do so. You have been chosen from the neighborhood where the action is said to have taken place because you are supposed to have the best knowledge of the action that is being considered at this trial. And if you decided that Mr. Zenger is guilty, you must take it upon yourselves to say that the papers which we admit he printed and published are false, scandalous, and could cause a rebellion.

But I have no fear of this happening. You are citizens of New York. You are really what the law supposes you to be, honest and lawful people. In your justice lies our safety. We are denied the right to present evidence to prove the truth of what we have published. I believe that not allowing such evidence to be presented itself becomes very strong evidence supporting our case. I hope it will have that meaning for you.

I hope to be pardoned, your Honor, for my zeal on this occasion. It is a wise old saying that when your neighbor's house is on fire, you ought to take care of your own. Blessed to God, I live in a government where liberty is well understood and freely enjoyed. Yet experience has shown us all—I'm sure it has me—that a

A colonial American print shop

bad example in one government soon becomes a precedent in another. And therefore I think that while we owe obedience to those who govern we ought at the same time to guard against such power wherever we fear it may harm us or our fellow subjects.

Those who injure and oppress the people they govern cause them to cry out and complain. And then those same officials make these complaints the reason for new oppressions and arrests. I wish I could say there were no examples of this kind. But I must conclude my case. The question before the court and you, gentlemen of the jury, is not a matter of private concern. It is not the cause of a poor printer, nor of New York alone, which you are now trying. No! Its results may affect every free person who lives under British government on the mainland of America. And it is the best cause. It is the cause of liberty.

And I am sure that your honest conduct this day will entitle you to the love and respect of your fellow citizens. Everyone who prefers freedom to a life of slavery will bless and honor you for having halted tyranny and this attempt to misuse the power of government. By an impartial and honest verdict, you can lay a noble foundation for securing for ourselves, our neighbors, and future generations that to which nature and the laws of our country have

given us a right—the liberty to uncover and to oppose the misuse of power by government by speaking and writing the truth.

READING REVIEW

1. What was the charge brought against John Peter Zenger?
2. What distinction was made about the meaning of libel by Mr. Hamilton? by the Chief Justice?
3. Why, then, did the jury acquit Mr. Zenger?

30 A Colonial Election in Philadelphia

In the 1760's Philadelphia was the largest and busiest city in the colonies. The city's inhabitants took their politics seriously, as the following account by Joseph Reed indicates.

Joseph Reed was a lawyer, revolutionary leader, and soldier. He served as George Washington's military secretary and was elected to the First Continental Congress. In this account, he told of an election in Philadelphia. By today's standards, the election procedures would be considered strange and irregular.

READING FOCUS

1. What were the two political parties?
2. Who were members of each party?

I don't remember that I have told you anything about our recent election, which was really a hard-fought one. It was managed with more honesty and good manners than you might have expected from the strong-minded supporters on each side. The Dutch Calvinists and the Presbyterians all assisted the new party. Members of the Church of England were divided and so were the Dutch Lutherans. The Czech Moravians and most of the Quakers were the chief supporters of the old party.

The voting place, or poll, was opened at about 9 o'clock in the morning, on October 1st. The steps there were so crowded until 11 and 12 o'clock in the evening that at no time was a person able to vote in less than a quarter of an

Adapted from William B. Reed, ed., Life and Correspondence of Joseph Reed, *Vol. I, 1847.*

hour after he got to the steps. Voters could go no faster than the whole line moved. About 3 o'clock in the morning, those who favored the new party proposed that the poll be closed. But (O! fatal mistake for them!) supporters of the old party kept it open. They had a group of aged and lame people who could not come to vote while the place was so crowded. This group now was brought out in chairs and stretchers all during the night, between 3 and 6 o'clock—a total of about 200 voters.

As both sides took care to have watchers at the polls all night, the alarm was given to the new party people. Horsemen and footmen were immediately sent off to Germantown and elsewhere. By 9 or 10 o'clock the next morning, new party voters began to pour in. Thus 700 or 800 more votes were obtained in this way after the first proposal to close the poll was made. About 500 of these votes were for the new party. The officials did not close the poll until 3 o'clock that afternoon. Then it took them until 1 o'clock the next day to count the votes. The candidates of the new party won, but the vote was extremely close.

READING REVIEW

1. Who belonged to the old party? the new party?
2. How long were the polls opened?
3. How did this differ from the way an election is held today?

31 English No More

Stephen Vincent Benét, an American poet, planned a long poem about the movement of peoples westward across the American continent. This poem was to be contained in several books. Although he never finished this project, he did publish one book of the poem in 1943. This volume told of the lives of a newcomer who settled in Virginia and of a family who made their new home in Massachusetts. Benét's aim was to make these people come to life. Part of the poem follows.

READING FOCUS

1. With what resolve did Englishmen come to America?
2. How did this resolve change?

And we look back, and see how the thing was done
And, looking back, think, "So, of course, it must be."
And are wrong by a million miles, and never see
The daily living and dying, under the sun.

For they did not know what would happen. No one knew.
No one knew, though the men of England planned,
Planned with cunning of brain and strength of hand,
And their plans were deer-tracks, fading out in the dew.

They planned for gold and iron, for silk and wood,
For towns and settled farming and steady things,
And an Indian pipe puffed out its blue smoke-rings,
And, where they had made their plans, the tobacco stood.

And those who came were resolved to be Englishmen,
Gone to world's end, but English every one,
And they are the white corn-kernels, parched in the sun,
And they knew it not, but they'd not be English again.

They would try, they would swear they were, they would drink the toast,
They would loyally petition and humbly pray
And over them was another sort of day
And in their veins was another, a different ghost.
For the country is where the life is, not elsewhere.
The country is where the heart and the blood are given.
They could swear to be English by every oath under heaven.
It did not alter the country by a hair.

From Western Star *by Stephen Vincent Benét, 1943.*

READING REVIEW

1. What was the colonists' resolve?
2. What happened to this resolve?

UNIT TWO READINGS
Winning Independence

5 Moving Toward Independence
(1763–1775)

the American colonists and the British began a struggle that eventually led to war and independence for the colonies.

READING FOCUS
1. Why were the colonists growing less fond of their native country?
2. Why was the presence of the French in North America considered the best way of keeping the colonies under British authority?

32 Independence Predicted

Peter Kalm, a Swedish scientist, spent three years in America, from 1748 to 1751, studying plant and animal life. After he returned home he wrote a book about the colonies. Along with detailed scientific information, he included his observations about the land and the people.

Kalm's book contained one of the earliest suggestions that the colonists were beginning to think about independence. Three years after Kalm left the colonies, the British and French began their final struggle for control of North America. By 1763 the French had been defeated. But soon afterward

It is a great advantage to the king of England that his North American colonies are near a country, such as Canada, that is governed by the French. Some people suspect that the king was never sincere in his attempts to drive the French from his territory, although he could have done it without much difficulty.

The English colonies have increased so rapidly in population and in riches that they almost rival England itself. Therefore, in order to maintain the power and trade of England (as well as for other reasons), the colonists are forbidden to establish new crafts and trades that might hurt British commerce. They are not allowed to hunt for gold or silver, unless they send what they find to England immediately. They are forbidden to trade with places that are not under British control. Nor are foreign traders allowed to send ships to the colonies. These and other severe laws cause the inhabitants of the English colonies to grow less fond of their mother country. This loss of fond feelings is made worse by the fact that many foreigners, including Germans, Dutch, and French, have

One view of British policies

Adapted from Peter Kalm, Travels into North America, *Vol. I, 1770.*

settled here in the colonies, and they have no strong ties to England.

I have been told by English settlers—not only those born in America, but also those from Europe—that the English colonies in North America will be able to form their own nation, entirely independent of England, in 30 to 50 years. But today this whole area along the eastern coast is unprotected, and the interior of the colonies is often attacked by the French. So in times of war these dangerous neighbors are enough to prevent the colonies from breaking their ties with their mother country. Thus the English government has good reason to regard the presence of the French in North America as the best means of keeping the colonies obedient to British authority.

READING REVIEW

1. List three things the colonists were forbidden to do in an effort to maintain the power and trade of England.
2. To what extent do you think the French threat from Canada kept Americans under British control?

33 The Colonists' Rights and British Policy

James Otis, a Massachusetts lawyer, was one of the most eloquent Patriots to speak out against British rule of the colonies. In this pamphlet, written in 1764, he summarized the colonists' rights and argued that these rights have grown out of the British constitution. (Unlike the American Constitution, the British constitution is not a single written document. Instead, it is made up of a series of laws, proclamations, and customs that have accumulated over centuries.)

Otis accused the British government of violating these long-honored rights of British citizens. In this selection he attacked the government for imposing taxes on the colonies to support the British army stationed in America and hinted at the dangers brought on by such a policy.

READING FOCUS

1. What reasons did Otis give for writing his pamphlet?
2. Why did he object to having a British army stationed in the colonies?

I have waited for years to hear some friend of the colonies pleading in public for them. I have waited in vain. One privilege after another is taken away. Where we shall end up only God knows. I trust he will protect and provide for us, even if we are driven and persecuted—as many of our ancestors were driven to these once inhospitable shores of America. It is unfortunate that those people in America who are best qualified to support the rights of the colonists have reasons that prevent them from doing so. Thus there are many people who are infinitely better able than I to serve this cause. But they are prevented from doing it because of fear, laziness, or the pressures of business. There has been a very long and, I think, shameful silence. It seems almost too late to assert our undeniable rights as human beings and as citizens. What will future generations think of us? The trade of the whole continent is taxed by Parliament. Stamps and other internal duties and taxes are discussed. But there is not one petition to the king and Parliament urging the ending of these injustices.

It is unjust that a heavy burden should be laid on the trade of the colonies to maintain an army of soldiers, customhouse officers, and fleets of guardships. All the wealth both from trade and the colonies themselves was not enough to support these groups during the last war. How can anyone suppose that all of a sudden the trade of the colonies alone can bear such a heavy burden? The recent territory gained in America, as glorious and as profitable as it has been to Great Britain, to the colonies is only a safeguard against the attacks of the French and Indians. Our trade on the whole has not benefited by them one bit. All the time the French islands were controlled by us, all the fine sugar and other products were shipped to England. None were allowed to be brought to the colonies.

If an army must be kept in America and paid for by the colonies, this might not seem quite so harsh if Parliament determined the sum to be raised, then divided it and allowed each colony to assess what it owed, and raise it as best it could. But to have the whole sum levied and collected without our consent is extraordinary. The way these provinces are treated is certainly likely to be the harshest case in recorded history. Was ever such a

Adapted from James Otis, "The Rights of the British Colonies Asserted and Proved," Boston, 1765, in Pamphlets of the American Revolution 1750-1776, *edited by Bernard Bailyn.*

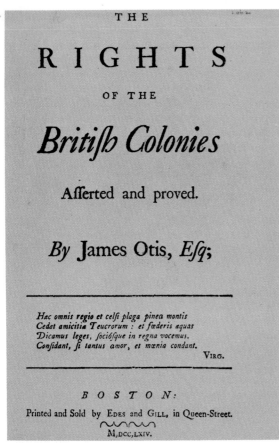

The title page of James Otis' pamphlet.

demand for money forced even on a conquered nation?

To say the Parliament has absolute and arbitrary power does not make sense. Parliament cannot make two and two equal five. Parliament can declare that something is being done for the good of the whole, but this declaration by Parliament does not make it true. There must be a higher power—that is, God. Should any act of Parliament be against any of his natural laws, which are eternally true, such an act would be contrary to eternal truth and justice. Therefore, it would be void. It is this great principle that causes Parliaments to repeal such unjust acts as soon as they find that they have been mistaken when they declared them to be for the public good when in fact they were not.

We see here the grandeur of the British constitution! We see here the wisdom of our ancestors! The legislative and the executive branches are always a check and balance on each other. If the executive makes a mistake, it is corrected by the legislative in Parliament. If the legislative makes a mistake, it is corrected by the executive in the king's courts of law. Here the king, as represented by his judges, appears as supreme agent of the commonwealth. This is government! This is a constitution! To preserve it from foreign and domestic foes has cost oceans of blood and treasure in every age. The blood and the treasure have on the whole been well spent. British America has given its blood and treasure to this cause from the beginning of its settlement. We have contributed all we could raise and more, for, despite payments, we are still deep in debt. The province of Massachusetts, I believe, has contributed more men and money in war since the year 1620—when the first few families landed at Plymouth—in relation to its size and ability than has all of Great Britain. The same, I believe, is true of many of the other colonies, though Massachusetts has undoubtedly carried the heaviest burden.

We all regard ourselves as happy under Great Britain's rule. We love, esteem, and revere our mother country, and honor our king. If the colonies were offered a choice between independence and subjection to Great Britain upon any terms other than absolute slavery, I am convinced they would accept subjection. The British government in all future generations may be sure that the American colonies will never try to leave Britain's rule unless driven to it as the last desperate action against oppression. It will be an oppression that will make the wisest persons mad and the weakest strong.

The colonies are and always have been "entirely subject to the crown" in the legal sense of the term. Few examples can be given where colonies have forsaken or disobeyed a wise mother country. But history is full of examples where armies guarding over provinces have seized those lands for their general and given him a crown at the expense of his master. Are all ambitious generals dead? Will no more appear in the future? The danger of a standing army in faraway places is much greater in the colonies than at home. Rome discovered the truth of this in the actions of its ambitious generals, but it discovered this too late. And eighteen hundred years have passed since Rome's ruin.

A continuation of the same liberties enjoyed by the colonists since the [English] Revolution, and the same moderate government they have known since then, will bind them in a lasting and willing subjection, obedience, and love to Great Britain. Both Britain and its colonies will prosper and flourish. The British monarchy will then remain in sound health even if the proud tyrants of Europe unite to deliver the human race or resign their crowns. Human nature must and will be rescued from the general slavery that so long has ruled over humankind. Great Britain has done much toward achieving this goal. What a glory will it be if it can complete this noble goal throughout the world!

What will be the unavoidable result of all this taxation if another war occurs and it is necessary to recruit as many colonists in America as in the last war? Would it be possible for the colonies, after being burdened in their trade, perhaps after it is ruined, to raise an army? Will they have enough will left to make this effort? If someone says that other American duties must then be levied, it would be impossible for us to pay them. Also, there is the danger of a large standing army so far away from home. A good provincial militia, aided by the mother country when required, never was and never will be dangerous. But the experience of past times will show that an army of 20 or 30 thousand veterans is very apt to proclaim dictators like Caesar. Caesar, the assassin of his country, gained his false glory by stealing the affections of his army away from the government.

I hope these hints regarding the fate of Rome will not be misunderstood. They are delivered in pure affection to my king and country, and are not a reflection on any individual. The best army and the best people may be led into temptation. All I know is that it is easier to prevent evil than to escape from it once it is here.

READING REVIEW

1. According to Otis, what was the "higher power" and how did it affect any actions taken by the British Parliament?
2. What did Otis think was the "grandeur" of the British constitution?
3. According to Otis, what would it take to bind the colonists to Great Britain?
4. (a) What did Otis say would be the unavoidable result of taxation? (b) Do you agree with this statement? Why or why not?

34 A Colonial Defense of British Taxation

A Rhode Island lawyer named Martin Howard published several pamphlets signed "A Gentleman of Halifax." In one pamphlet, written in 1765 and addressed to "a friend in Rhode Island," he dared to defend British taxation and to question American attitudes toward it. At the time expressing such opinions was a dangerous thing to do. An angry mob destroyed his house in Newport, Rhode Island, and eventually Howard was forced to flee to England.

READING FOCUS

1. What distinction does Howard make about rights?
2. What is his idea about representation in regard to taxation?
3. Why does he think the colonists are ungrateful?

Depend upon it, my friend, that a people like the English, who risked everything in the recent war for the defense and safety of America, will not want to be told what to do by those they have always considered dependent upon them.

The charters of the New England colonies define and limit the rights and privileges of each colony. I cannot understand how it happens that the colonies now claim other or greater rights than are expressly granted to them in these charters. When we speak about the rights of freeborn English citizens, we sometimes confuse those rights which are personal with those rights which are political. However, there is a distinction between them, which always ought to be kept in mind.

Our personal rights of life, liberty, and property are guaranteed to us by the law of England. These form the birthright of every citizen, whether born in Great Britain, on the ocean, or in the colonies. The political rights of the colonies are more limited. The nature, quality, and scope of these political rights depend completely upon the charters which first established them.

Adapted from Martin Howard, A Letter from a Gentleman at Halifax, . . . The Rights of Colonies Examined, *1765.*

Customs House, Boston

I am aware that this reasoning will be argued against by quoting the saying "No English subject can be taxed without his consent, or the consent of his representatives."

It is the opinion of the members of the House of Commons that they are the representatives of all British subjects, wherever they may live. From their point of view, the saying about taxation is fully respected, and its benefit applies to the colonies. And indeed, the saying must be viewed in this way, for in a strict sense taxation with consent always was and always will be impractical. Let me ask what is the value or amount of each citizen's representation in the kingdom of Scotland? Scotland has nearly 2 million people, and yet not more than 3,000 have the right to vote in the election of members of Parliament.

Now, consider the merchant class of Britain. Though it is very large it has no share in this same representation. A poor land owner earning 40 shillings a year can vote for a member of Parliament. By contrast, a merchant who is worth 100,000 pounds sterling has no vote if his wealth consists only of merchandise. But does anyone suppose that the interest of the merchant is not as much the object of Parliament's attention?

Parliament may levy internal taxes as well as regulate trade. There is no important difference in the rights involved. A stamp duty is the most reasonable and fairest tax that can be devised. I do not want to see it established among us, but I fear that it is now too late to prevent this blow.

Many people have complained about the increased power of the court of admiralty. I shall state my ideas on this matter to you freely.

It is well known that smuggling had become a common practice in some of the colonies. Acts of Parliament had been ignored by those who were supposed to carry them out. Corruption had become commonplace. Courts of Admiralty, with authority within small areas, came under the influence of powerful merchants.

If, my friend, customs duties are to be paid to the government, if smuggling is to be stopped,—if these goals cannot be achieved in the usual way, what can the government do but use a remedy as serious as the disease? I admit that the method of prosecution of the newly established court of admiralty is harsh. But we have brought this harshness upon ourselves. When every reasonable effort to stop the dreadful practice of smuggling has been tried in vain, the government is justified in passing laws against it.

Believe me, my friend, it causes me great pain to see that the colonies are so ungrateful to the mother country, whose army and money have just rescued them from being ruled by a French government. I have been told that some colonists have gone so far as to say that, the way things are, they would even prefer a French government to an English one. Heaven knows I have little ill will for anyone. Yet for a moment how I wish that those unworthy subjects of Britain could feel the iron rod of a

Spanish inquisitor or a French tax agent. This would indeed be a punishment suited to their ungrateful feelings.

READING REVIEW

1. What did Howard say is the difference between political and personal rights?
2. How did Howard defend the colonists' lack of representation in Parliament?
3. How did Howard feel about the establishment of the increased power of the Courts of Admiralty?

35 A Plea for Moderation

By March of 1775 Great Britain and the colonies seemed to be heading toward a crisis. Edmund Burke, like William Pitt, was a well-known member of Parliament who felt that the American colonies were being treated too harshly. Burke, a noted speaker, on March 22, 1775, delivered a famous speech in Parliament urging improved relations between Great Britain and the colonies. Burke felt that conciliation, not force, was the best policy. In his speech he proposed 13 resolutions to achieve such a policy, but they were voted down in Parliament by a vote of 270 to 78. In the following part of the speech (the entire speech lasted several hours), Burke warns the British government against forcing the colonies into obedience.

READING FOCUS

1. What did Burke say about the use of force?
2. What common principles of English liberty did Burke discuss?

People say America is a noble object well worth fighting for. Certainly it is, if fighting a people is the best way of winning them over. But I confess I favor wise government much more than the use of force. I consider force to be a very poor way of keeping a people who are as numerous, as active, and as proud as the Americans tied to us in a profitable and subordinate relationship.

First, let me say that the results of using force may not be lasting ones. Force may stop people's actions for a moment, but it does not

Adapted from Edmund Burke's Speech in Conciliation with America, *edited by Albert S. Cook, 1896.*

end the need of using it again. And no nation can be governed if it must continually be conquered.

My next objection concerns the uncertainty of using force. That is, if the use of force does not succeed, you have no other action left to take. If attempts at peace fail, you can then use force. But if force is used and fails, no further hope of re-establishing peace is left. Power and authority are sometimes achieved by kindness. But they can never be achieved after violence and force have failed to gain them.

Another objection to force is that you damage the thing you are fighting for by your very efforts to preserve it. The thing you fought for is not the thing that you gain. It has been ruined in the struggle. Nothing less will content me than a whole America. I do not want to use up its strength along with our own, because on both sides it is the British strength that I use up. I do not want to be attacked by a foreign enemy at the end of such a conflict, or even less in the middle of it. Let me add that I do not want to break the American spirit, because it is that very spirit which has made America important to us.

These are the reasons I do not favor the use of force, which some people seem to do so strongly. But there is another thing which influences my opinion about the kind of policy we should follow toward America. I am talking here about Americans.

The love of freedom is the outstanding feature in the Americans' character. This fierce spirit of liberty is probably stronger in the English colonies than in any other people on earth—and for many good and powerful reasons.

First, the people of the colonies are descendants of English men and women. England is a nation which, I hope, still respects freedom, as it once deeply honored it, indeed. The colonists emigrated from England when this feature of the English character was strongest. They took this point of view with them when they parted from our soil. They are therefore not only devoted to liberty itself but to liberty based on English ideas and on English principles.

It happened, you know, that from the earliest times the great struggles for freedom in this country have chiefly concerned the question of taxing. The ablest writers and most expressive speakers have devoted themselves to this matter of taxes. They took great effort to teach as a basic principle that in all monarchies the people must keep the power of granting their own money, or no shadow of liberty could remain alive.

The colonies draw these ideas and principles from you. Their love of liberty, like yours, is attached to this specific point of taxing. Liberty might be safe, or might be endangered, in twenty other ways without their being much pleased or alarmed. On the matter of taxation they felt its pulse. And depending on what beat they felt, they thought themselves sick or well. I do not say whether they were right or wrong in applying your general arguments to their own case. The fact is that they did apply your general arguments in this way. And your manner of governing them—whether through lenience or laziness, through wisdom or mistake—confirmed their belief that they, as well as you, had an interest in these common principles.

READING REVIEW

1. What objections did Burke have to using force on the American colonies?
2. What did Burke say is the outstanding feature of American character?
3. Why did Burke think the Parliament should respect this feature?
4. Why do you think the majority of Parliament's members voted down Burke's resolutions?

36 A Call to Battle

The idea of conciliation did not appeal to Patrick Henry, who believed that war was coming and welcomed it. In a fiery speech before the Virginia legislature in March of 1775 he condemned those Americans who still hoped to settle peacefully the problems between Great Britain and the colonies and to avoid warfare. Henry felt that the time for peaceful policies was clearly past. Instead he urged Virginia and the other colonies to arm their militia, not caring that such actions might be considered acts of treason.

Actually, Henry's exact words were not recorded. However, many delegates were so moved by his speech that they remembered nearly every word and later reconstructed it from memory.

READING FOCUS

1. According to Henry, what was the purpose of Great Britain's display of military strength in the colonies?
2. Why did Henry feel that war was inevitable?

No one thinks more highly than I do of the patriotism, as well as abilities, of the worthy gentlemen who have just spoken to the legislature. But different people often view the same subjects in different ways. Therefore, I hope that it will not be thought disrespectful to those gentlemen, if I speak my mind freely and without reserve, even though my opinions are the opposite of theirs.

This is no time to be bound by custom. The question before this legislature is one of great importance to this country. For my own part I consider it as nothing less than a question of freedom or slavery.

It is natural for people to cling to the illusions of hope. We are likely to shut our eyes against a painful truth. But is this the course to be followed by a wise people engaged in a great and difficult struggle for liberty? For my part, whatever pain of spirit it may cost, I am willing to know the whole truth, to know the worst and to prepare to meet it.

I have but one lamp by which my feet are guided. That is the lamp of experience. I know of no way of judging the future but by the past. And judging by the past, I wish to know what there has been in the conduct of the British government for the last ten years to justify those hopes with which gentlemen have tried to comfort themselves and the legislature.

Is it that crafty smile with which our petition has recently been received? [Patrick Henry is referring to a petition sent to King George III by the First Continental Congress in hopes of settling the colonies' grievances.] Trust it not. It will prove a trap to your feet. Ask yourselves how this gracious reception of our petition fits with the warlike preparations which cover our waters and darken our land. Are fleets and armies necessary to a plan of love and renewed understanding? Have we shown ourselves so unwilling to reach an agreement that force must be called in to win back our love? Let us not deceive ourselves. These are the instruments of war and conquest, the last arguments to which kings resort.

Adapted from Sketches of the Life and Character of Patrick Henry, *3d ed., edited by William Wirt, 1818.*

I ask what this military display means if its purpose is not to force us into submission? Can gentlemen give any other possible motives for it? Has Great Britain any enemy in this part of the world to call for all this massing of navies and armies? No, it has none. They are meant for us. They can be meant for no one else. They are sent over to bind and rivet upon us those chains which the British government has been forging for so long.

And what do we have to oppose them? Shall we try argument? We have been trying that for the last ten years. Have we anything new to offer on the subject of our complaints? Nothing. We have held the subject up to every light, but it has been all in vain. Shall we resort to pleas and humble appeals? What expressions shall we find which have not already been exhausted? Let us not, I beg you, deceive ourselves longer. We have done everything that could be done to turn aside the storm which is now coming on. We have petitioned; we have pleaded; we have humbled ourselves before the tyrannical hands of the English government and Parliament.

Our petitions have been slighted; our protests have produced additional violence and insult; our appeals have been ignored. And we have been turned away, with contempt, from the foot of the throne. After these things, we may indulge in vain in the fond hope of peace and understanding. There is no longer any room for hope.

If we wish to be free—if we mean to preserve those privileges for which we have been fighting so long—if we do not mean to abandon the noble struggle in which we have so long been engaged—we must fight! I repeat it, we must fight! An appeal to weapons and to God is all that is left us!

They tell us that we are weak, unable to deal with so powerful an enemy. But when shall we be stronger? Will it be next week, or next year? Will it be when we are totally disarmed, and when a British guard shall be stationed in every house? Shall we gain strength by inaction? Shall we acquire the means of effective resistance by lying on our backs and hugging the illusion of hope until our enemies have bound us hand and foot?

We are not weak if we make proper use of the means which the God of nature has granted us. Three million people, armed in the holy cause of liberty, and in such a country as ours, cannot be conquered by any force which our

Patrick Henry

enemy can send against us. Besides, we shall not fight our battles alone. There is a just God who rules over the fates of nations. He will raise friends to fight our battles for us.

The battle is not won by the strong alone. It is won by the alert, the active, the brave. Besides, we have no choice. Even if we were cowardly enough to desire it, it is now too late to back down from the conflict. There is no retreat but in submission and slavery! Our chains are forged! Their clanking may be heard on the plains of Boston! The war is inevitable— and let it come! I repeat it, let it come!

It is in vain to drag the matter out. Gentlemen may cry peace, peace. But there is no peace. The war is actually begun! The next gale that sweeps from the north will bring to our ears the clash of resounding arms! Our brethren are already in the field! Why stand we here idle! What is it that gentlemen wish? What would they have? Is life so dear, or peace so sweet, as to be purchased at the price of chains and slavery? Forbid it, Almighty God! I know not what course others may take; but as for me, give me liberty, or give me death!

READING REVIEW

1. How did Great Britain react to the colonists' petitions, protests, and appeals?
2. Why did Henry say that it was too late to back down from the conflict?

Angry colonists in Boston provoke British troops into fighting.

37 A British View of the Boston Massacre

In 1770 the incident occurred that came to be known as the Boston Massacre. The reading below gave a British version of the Boston Massacre. It was part of a report from General Thomas Gage, the commander-in-chief of the British Army in North America, to one of his superiors in England.

READING FOCUS

1. According to General Gage, why did the people of Boston plan a general uprising against the British troops?
2. Why did the British troops fire at the citizens?

In my letter to Your Lordship I mentioned a misunderstanding between the citizens and soldiers in this town, soon after which a message was sent from Boston that it was unsafe for officers or soldiers to appear in the streets after dark. The people there had quarreled with the troops. They lay in wait for them in the streets to knock them down. A particular quarrel happened with a few soldiers of the 29th Regiment; the cause was given by some citizens of Boston though it may be imagined in the course of it that there were faults on both sides. This quarrel, it is supposed, excited the people to plan a general rising . . . on March 5.

Colonists began by attacking a few soldiers in a lane next to a barrack of the 29th Regi-

Adapted from Selection 45 in The Correspondence of General Thomas Gage with the Secretaries of State 1763-1775, *Vol. I.*

ment. The officers of the regiment found some of their men greatly hurt and carried all the soldiers to their barracks. The mob followed, menacing and brandishing their clubs over the officers' heads, to the barrack door. The officers tried to pacify the citizens and begged them to retire. Part of the mob broke into a meeting-house and rang the fire bell, which appears to have been a signal because many people immediately assembled in the streets. Many were armed, some with muskets, but most with clubs, bludgeons, and suchlike weapons.

Many people came out of their houses supposing a fire in the town. Several officers on the same supposition were going to their posts. On meeting with mobs the officers were insulted and attacked. Those who could not escape, were knocked down and treated with great inhumanity. Different mobs paraded through the streets. As they passed several barracks, they taunted the soldiers to come out.

One mob went to the main guard station where every provocation was given, without effect, for the guard remained quiet. From thence the mob proceeded to a sentinel posted upon the customhouse, at a small distance from the guard station, and attacked him. He defended himself as well as he could, calling out for help. Some people ran to the guard station to give information of his danger. Captain Preston of the 29th Regiment was Captain of the Day. Hearing the fire alarm he went to the main guard station. Thinking the sentinel was in danger of being murdered, he detached a sergeant and twelve men to relieve the guard. And soon after he followed to prevent any rash act on the part of the troops. This party as well as the sentinel were immediately attacked by

Bostonians. Some threw bricks, stones, pieces of ice and snowballs at the soldiers. Others advanced up to their bayonets, and brandishing their bludgeons and clubs, called out to them to fire if they dared.

Captain Preston stood between the soldiers and the mob, using every method to persuade the mob to retire peaceably. Some amongst the mob asked him if he intended to order the men to fire. He replied by no means, and observed he stood between the troops and them.

All he could say had no effect, and one of the soldiers, receiving a violent blow, instantly fired. Captain Preston turned round to see who fired, and received a blow upon his arm, which was aimed at his head. And the mob, at first seeing no one shot, and imagining the soldiers had only fired powder to frighten them, grew more bold and attacked with greater violence, continually striking at the soldiers and pelting them and calling out to them to fire.

The soldiers thought their lives were in danger. Hearing the word fire all round them, three or four of them fired one after another, and again three more in the same hurry and confusion. Four or five persons were unfortunately killed, and more wounded. Captain Preston and the party were soon afterward delivered into the hands of the magistrates, who committed them to prison [to await trial].

Some have sworn that Captain Preston gave orders to fire. Others who were near, that the soldiers fired without orders because of the provocation they received. None can deny the attack made upon the troops, but differ in the degree of violence in the attack.

I hope and believe that I have given Your Lordship in general a true account of this unhappy affair. I am sorry to say that neither Captain Preston nor the soldiers can have a fair and impartial trial for their lives. The utmost ill will and hatred has been shown already, in attempts to bring on the trials whilst the people are heated by resentment and the thirst of revenge.

READING REVIEW

1. What earlier quarrel led the colonists to plan a general uprising?
2. What alarm did the colonists use to signal the beginning of the uprising?
3. Who commanded the British troops that were involved in the Boston Massacre?
4. Does General Gage think that the soldiers can get a fair trial? Why or why not?

The Struggle for Independence
(1775–1783)

38 Lexington and Concord: Views from Both Sides

Early on the morning of April 19, 1775, the first shots of the Revolutionary War rang out. Within a few hours, both the Americans and the British wrote accounts of what had happened at Lexington and also at the nearby town of Concord. The American account appeared in the *Salem Gazette*, and it may be considered the story most colonists read. Across the Atlantic, the British people read the *London Gazette's* account of the events. Both these accounts are included here.

READING FOCUS

1. On what important points did the two accounts disagree? On what points did they agree?
2. Which account seems more believable? Why?

The American Account

Last Wednesday, the 19th of April, the troops of His Britannic Majesty began hostilities against the people with a cruelty no less brutal than that received by our ancestors from the worst savages of the wilderness. We have tried to collect the details of this interesting event as well as we can under the present confused state of affairs.

On Tuesday evening a detachment of the [British] army moved silently and with speed on their way to Concord. The people soon became alarmed and began to assemble in several towns before daylight in order to watch the movement of the troops. At Lexington a company of militia, about 100 strong, gathered near the meeting house. The troops arrived within sight of the militia, just before sunrise.

Adapted from American Archives, *Fourth Series, Vol. II, edited by Peter Force, 1839.*

The British redcoats encounter armed colonists as they march into Lexington.

Approaching within a few feet of them, the commanding officer spoke to the men of the militia roughly as follows: "Disperse, you rebels—throw down your arms and disperse!" At this the British troops cheered. Immediately one or two officers fired their pistols, and then instantly four or five of the soldiers fired their guns. Then all of the troops seemed to fire their weapons. Eight of our men were killed, and nine were wounded.

A few minutes after this action the enemy renewed their march toward Concord. When they arrived there, they destroyed several carriages, carriage wheels, and about 20 barrels of flour. There, about 150 Americans were moving toward a bridge which the enemy held. The British fired and killed two of our men, who then returned the fire and forced the enemy to retreat to Lexington. There the British troops met Lord Percy, who brought large reinforcements and two cannons.

In Lexington the enemy set fire to Deacon Joseph Loring's house and barn, Mrs. Millikin's house and shop, and Mr. Joshua Bond's house and shop, which were all destroyed. They also set fire to several other houses, but our people put out the flames. They robbed almost every house they passed by, breaking in and carrying off clothing and other valuable articles. It appeared to be their intention to burn and destroy everything along their way. Only our vigorous pursuit prevented them from doing so.

The bodies of our fallen comrades were treated with an almost incredible savage barbarity. The British soldiers were not content to shoot down unarmed, aged, and helpless people. They disregarded the cries of the wounded, killing them without mercy and mangling their bodies in the most shocking manner.

We have the pleasure to report that, despite the greatest provocation from the enemy, not one instance of cruelty that we have heard of was committed by our victorious militia. Following the merciful teachings of the Christian religion, they "breathed higher sentiments of humanity."

The British Account

Lieutenant Nunn brought letters from General Gage, Lord Percy, and Lieutenant Colonel Smith containing the following details of what happened on the 19th of April.

Lieutenant Colonel Smith found, after he had advanced some miles on his march, that the country people had been alerted by the firing of guns and ringing of bells. He sent six companies of light infantry in order to protect two bridges on different roads beyond Concord.

When they arrived at Lexington they found an armed group of the country people on a village green close to the road. When the king's troops marched up to them to ask why they were assembled there, they ran off in great confusion. Then several guns opened fire upon the king's troops from behind a stone wall, and also from the meeting house and other houses. One man was wounded and Major Pitcairn's horse was shot in two places. Because of this attack by the rebels, the troops returned the fire and killed several of them.

After this, the detachment marched on to Concord without anything further happening. There the troops carried out their original orders. They knocked the iron supports off three cannons, burned some new gun carriages and a great number of carriage wheels, and threw a considerable amount of flour, gunpowder, musket balls, and other articles into the river. Large numbers of the rebels assembled in many places. A large group of them attacked the light infantry posted at one of the bridges. In this action several men were killed and wounded.

Our troops were very much harassed as they returned from Concord. Several men were killed or wounded by the rebels firing from behind walls, ditches, trees, and other hiding places. A brigade under the command of Lord Percy joined them at Lexington with two cannons, so they dispersed the rebels for a while. But as soon as the troops again started their march, the rebels began to fire upon them from behind stone walls and houses. They kept up this scattered firing during the whole 15-mile [24-kilometer] march, and thus several of our soldiers were killed and wounded. Such was the cruelty and barbarity of the rebels that they scalped and cut off the ears of some of the wounded men they captured.

General Gage says that our troops behaved with their usual bravery.

READING REVIEW
1. List two items on which each report agreed.
2. List two items on which each report disagreed. Why do you think the two accounts differ so much?
3. Was either report an eyewitness account? What was each author's source of information?
4. Which account do you believe? Cite two pieces of information given in these reports to support your opinion.

39 Why One Man Fought

More than 60 years after the battle of Concord, a historian interviewed Levi Preston, who had fought on the American side. In this interview, Preston was asked why he fought at Concord. His answer may help you to understand the colonists' feelings just before the Revolution.

READING FOCUS
1. Why did Preston take part in the fighting?
2. Why did the historian think the fighting had taken place?

I began: "Captain Preston, why did you go to the Concord fight, the 19th of April, 1775?"

The old man, bowed down by the weight of years, raised himself upright and turning to me said: "Why did I go?"

"Yes," I replied. "My histories tell me that you men of the Revolution took up arms against 'intolerable oppressions.' What were they?"

"Oppressions? I didn't feel them."

"What, were you not oppressed by the Stamp Act?"

"I never saw one of those stamps, and always understood that Governor Bernard [of Massachusetts] put them all in Castle William [Boston]. I am certain I never paid a penny for one of them."

"Well, then, what about the tea tax?"

"Tea tax! I never drank a drop of the stuff; the boys threw it all overboard."

"Then I suppose you had been reading Harrington or Sidney and Locke about the eternal principles of liberty?" [These men were English political thinkers whose writings deeply influenced Americans in the Revolutionary years.]

"Never heard of 'em. We read only the Bible, the Catechism, Watts' Psalms and Hymns, and the Almanac."

"Well, then, what was the matter? And what did you mean in going to the fight?"

"Young man, what we meant in going for those Redcoats was this. We always had governed ourselves, and we always meant to. They didn't mean we should."

Adapted from Mellen Chamberlain, John Adams, the Statesman of the American Revolution, *1898.*

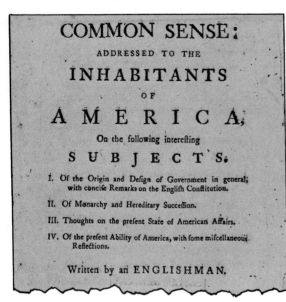

The first page of Thomas Paine's famous pamphlet

READING REVIEW

1. Why do you think Preston saw the reason for fighting differently than the historians do years later?
2. Do you think Preston's simplification of the issues was unusual? Why or why not?

40 An Influential Demand for Independence

Thomas Paine arrived in the colonies from England on November 30, 1774, with a letter of introduction to Benjamin Franklin. In January 1776, he published his 50-page pamphlet *Common Sense*. Within a few months, nearly half a million copies had been sold in the colonies. To Americans who were still uncertain over the question of independence, Paine spoke firmly and clearly: " 'Tis time to part." Paine's pamphlet convinced many Americans that independence from Great Britain was the only course of action possible. And within six months, the Continental Congress had taken steps to separate the colonies from Great Britain and had formed a committee to draft a declaration of independence.

READING FOCUS

1. What were Paine's arguments for independence?
2. Why did Paine say that America is only of minor importance in the system of British politics?

In the following pages I offer nothing more than simple facts, plain arguments, and common sense. I request only that the reader rid himself of prejudice and allow his reason and his feelings to determine things for themselves. I ask that the reader liberally enlarge his point of view by looking beyond the present.

Volumes have been written on the subject of the struggle between England and America. People of all ranks have entered into the controversy, out of different motives and with various goals. But the period of debate now is closed. Arms as the last resort must decide the contest.

The sun never shone on a cause of greater worth. 'Tis not the affair of a city, a country, a province, or a kingdom, but of a continent—of at least one eighth of the habitable globe. 'Tis not the concern of a day, a year, or an age. Future generations are involved in the contest, and will be affected to the end of time by what is happening now. Now is the seedtime of continental union, faith, and honor.

By going from argument to arms, a new era of politics is opening—a new method of thinking has arisen. All plans, proposals, etc., prior to the 19th of April—that is, before the beginning of hostilities—are like the almanacs of last year, which, though useful then, are useless now.

I have heard it said by some that since America has flourished under its former connection with Great Britain, this same connection is necessary for its future happiness. Nothing can be more false than this kind of argument. We may as well say that because a child has thrived upon milk, it will never need to have meat. America would have flourished as much, and probably more, if no European power had taken notice of it. The commerce by which it has enriched itself consists of the necessities of life. America will always have a market as long as eating is a custom in Europe.

But England has protected us, say some. That it has defended the continent (at our expense as well as its own) is admitted. It would have defended Turkey for the same reason—that is, for the sake of trade and domination.

We have taken pride in the protection of Great Britain without considering that its motive was its own interest, not attachment to

Adapted from The Writings of Thomas Paine, *Vol. I, edited by Moncure D. Conway, 1894.*

us. It did not protect us from our enemies on our account, but from its enemies on its own account.

But Britain is the parent country, say some. Then the more shame on it for its conduct. Even brutes do not devour their young, nor savages make war upon their families. But this happens not to be true, or only partly so. Europe, not England, is the parent country of America. This new world has been the asylum for the persecuted lovers of civil and religious liberty from every part of Europe. They have fled here, not from the tender embraces of the mother, but from the cruelty of the monster. And as for England, the same tyranny which drove the first emigrants from home pursues their descendants here.

I challenge the most ardent supporter of reconciliation with England to show a single advantage that this continent can reap by being connected with Great Britain. I repeat the challenge; not a single advantage is obtained.

But the injuries and disadvantages which we bear because of that connection are without number. Our duty to all peoples as well as to ourselves, requires us to renounce the alliance. Any submission to, or dependence on, Great Britain tends to involve this continent in European wars and quarrels. It sets us against nations that would otherwise seek our friendship and against whom we have neither anger nor complaint. Europe is too closely crowded with kingdoms to be long at peace. Whenever a war breaks out between England and any foreign power, the trade of America is ruined because of its connection with Britain.

Everything that is right or reasonable pleads for separation. The blood of the slain, the weeping voice of nature cries, 'Tis time to part. Even the distance at which the Almighty has placed England and America is a strong and natural proof that the authority of the one over the other was never the plan of heaven.

America is only of minor importance in the system of British politics. England consults the good of this country no further than this suits its own purpose. Its own interest leads it to suppress the growth of ours in every case which does not promote its advantage.

I have never met anyone, either in England or America, who has not felt that a separation between the countries would take place sooner or later.

These proceedings toward independence from Great Britain may at first seem strange and difficult. But like all other steps which we have already passed, it will in a little time become familiar and agreeable. Until independence is declared, the continent will feel like a person who continues putting off some unpleasant business from day to day, yet knows it must be done. The person hates to set about it, wishes it were over, and is continually haunted by the thought of the need to do it.

READING REVIEW

1. List two reasons Paine gave for supporting independence.
2. Why did Paine feel that America would have flourished even if no European power had taken notice of it?
3. According to Paine, why was America only of minor importance in the overall structure of the British Empire?

---

41   A Loyalist's Reply to *Common Sense*

Many colonists agreed with Thomas Paine when he wrote in *Common Sense* that it was time for America to break away from Great Britain. There were, however, many colonists who bitterly disagreed with him. They hoped that the colonies and Britain could settle their difficulties peacefully, and that America would continue to be part of the mighty British Empire.

In an effort to limit the influence of *Common Sense,* several Loyalists wrote their own pamphlets attacking Paine's ideas. The excerpt below came from the pen of an Anglican clergyman from New York City named Charles Inglis. His essay appeared several weeks before the Declaration of Independence was signed.

READING FOCUS

1. Why did Inglis think the colonies should have peacefully settled their difficulties with Britain and remained a part of the British Empire?
2. What evils did Inglis think would result from a declaration of independence?

Thomas Paine

By a settling of differences with Britain an end would be put to the present terrible war, by which so many lives have been lost, and so many more must be lost, if it continues. This alone is an advantage devoutly to be wished for. Paine says—"The blood of the slain, the weeping voice of nature cries. 'Tis time to part." I think they cry just the reverse. The blood of the slain, the weeping voice of nature cries—it is time to be reconciled. It is high time that those who are connected by the ties of religion, kinship, and country, should resume their former friendship and be united in the bond of mutual affection.

By a connection with Great Britain, our trade would still have the protection of the greatest naval power in the world. The protection of our trade, while connected with Britain, will not cost us a *fiftieth* part of what it must cost, were we ourselves to raise a naval force sufficient for this purpose. The manufactures of Great Britain confessedly surpass any in the world—particularly those in every kind of metal, which we want most. And no country can supply linens and woollens of equal quality cheaper.

When a Reconciliation is made, a few years of peace will restore everything. Emigrants will flow in as usual from the different parts of Europe. Population will advance with the same rapid progress as formerly, and our lands will rise in value.

Adapted from Charles Inglis, "The True Interest of America Impartially Stated, 1776".

These advantages are not imaginary but real. They are such as we have already experienced; and such as we may derive from a connection with Great Britain for ages to come.

Let us now, if you please, take a view of the other side of the question. Suppose we were to revolt from Great Britain, declare ourselves Independent, and set up a Republic of our own—what would be the consequence?—I stand aghast at the prospect—my blood runs chill when I think of the calamities, the complicated evils that must follow, and may be clearly foreseen—it is impossible for any man to foresee them all.

What a horrid situation would thousands be reduced to who have taken the oath of allegiance to the King [colonists who served as officials under the British government]. They must renounce that allegiance, or abandon all their property in America! By a Declaration of Independency, every avenue to a compromise with Great Britain would be closed. The sword only could then decide the quarrel. And the sword would not be sheathed till one had conquered the other.

Devastation and ruin must mark the progress of this war along the sea coast of America. Hitherto, Britain has not exerted her power. Her number of troops and ships of war here at present, is very little more than she judged necessary in time of peace. The troops amount to no more than 12,000 men. The ships to no more than 40, including frigates. Both Great Britain and the colonies, hoped for and expected compromise. Neither of them has lost sight of that desirable object.

The seas have been open to our ships. Although some skirmishes have unfortunately happened, yet a ray of hope still cheered both sides that, peace was not distant. But as soon as we declare for independency, every prospect of this kind must vanish. Ruthless war, with all its aggravated horrors, will ravage our once happy land—our seacoasts and ports will be ruined, and our ships taken. Torrents of blood will be spilled, and thousands reduced to beggary and wretchedness.

But supposing once more that we were able to cut off every regiment that Britain can spare or hire, and to destroy every ship she can send. Suppose we could beat off any other European power that would presume to invade this continent. Yet, a republican form of government would neither suit the spirit of the people, nor the size of America.

1. List the advantages of making peace and remaining part of the British Empire that were noted by Inglis.
2. What did Inglis predict would result from a declaration of independence?
3. What did Inglis think about a republican form of government?
4. To which of the following do you think Inglis' essay might have had the most appeal: a colonial merchant, a farmer on the frontier, or a colonist who served as a tax collector? Explain your answer.

42 Ordeal at Valley Forge

When Washington's army set up its winter headquarters at Valley Forge in Pennsylvania, no one realized what extreme hardships these troops would face in the next few months. During that long winter, the army suffered from inadequate supplies of food and clothing, from lack of shelter against the freezing cold and snow, and from sickness and disease. This ordeal weakened and discouraged Washington's army. In this reading, Albigence Waldo, a doctor from Connecticut, records his impressions of the terrible winter at Valley Forge.

READING FOCUS

1. How did Waldo describe the conditions at Valley Forge?
2. What did Waldo think about General Washington's leadership?

Dec. 14th, 1777

English prisoners and deserters are continually coming in. The soldiers, who have been surprisingly healthy up to this time, now begin to be sick from the endless hardships they have suffered in this campaign. Yet they still show a courage and contentment that is unusual in such young troops.

I am sick, unhappy, and bad tempered. Poor food—bad lodging—cold weather—fatigue—nasty clothes—bad cooking—I am sick to my stomach half the time. I can't endure it. Why are we sent here to starve and freeze? What happiness did I leave at home—a charming

Adapted from the Diary of Doctor Albigence Waldo, 1777-1778, from The Historical Magazine, *May-June 1861.*

wife, pretty children, a good bed, good food, all of them agreeable and pleasant things, indeed. Here all is confusion, hunger, and filth.

See the poor soldier there—with what cheerfulness he meets his enemies and encounters every hardship. If his feet are bare, he struggles through mud and cold with a song on his lips praising the war and Washington. If his food is bad, he eats it anyway and blesses God for a good stomach. But here comes another soldier. His bare feet can be seen through his worn-out shoes. His legs are nearly bare, with only the tattered remains of his only pair of stockings. His shirt hangs in strings, his hair is tangled, his face is thin. He cries with an air of wretchedness and despair: "I am sick—my feet lame—my legs sore—my body covered with this tormenting itch. I am fast growing weaker, and shall soon be dead!"

Dec. 21st

Preparations are made for huts. Food is scarce. A general cry went up through the camp this evening among the soldiers: "No meat! No meat!" The distant valleys echoed back this sad sound.

Dec. 25th, Christmas

We are still in tents when we ought to be in huts. The poor sick soldiers suffer greatly in their tents during this cold weather.

Dec. 26th

The city [Philadelphia] is at present nearly clear of the enemy. Why doesn't his Excellency [Washington] rush in and retake the city, in which he will doubtless find much to rob? Because he knows better than to leave his post and be caught like a fool, trapped in the city. He has always acted wisely. His action when examined closely cannot really be criticized. If only his officers were as skillful as he is, we would have the best group of officers God ever made.

Jan. 1st, 1778

I am alive. I am well. Hut building goes on briskly, and our camp begins to look like a spacious city.

Jan. 4th

I was called to ease the pain of a soldier thought to be dying. He died before I reached the hut. He was an Indian—an excellent soldier and a loyal, good-natured fellow.

The bitter winter of 1777 at Valley Forge, Pennsylvania

READING REVIEW

1. What hardships did the soldiers have to endure?
2. According to Waldo, why did General Washington not march into Philadelphia?
3. What was his opinion of General Washington?
4. Did Waldo seem to you to be an objective observer? Why or why not?

43 The Need for Black Soldiers

From the beginning, black Americans fought alongside other Patriots in the Revolutionary War. In fact, one of the heroes at the Battle of Breed's Hill in 1775 was Peter Salem, a black man. At first, official army policy was against the enlistment of black soldiers. But General Washington soon changed his mind, especially when many slaves joined the British army after it had promised them their freedom once the war ended.

The state of South Carolina, however, refused to allow black men to fight. In this letter Alexander Hamilton writes to General Washington about a project—which was unsuccessful—to recruit some Negro battalions in South Carolina.

READING FOCUS

1. What was Lauren's project?
2. Why did Hamilton recommend it?
3. What prediction did Hamilton make?

Headquarters, March 14th, 1779

Dear Sir,

Colonel Laurens, who will have the honor of delivering this letter to you, is on his way to South Carolina to carry out a project which I think is a very good one and which deserves

Adapted from a letter by Alexander Hamilton to John Jay, 1779, from The Life of John Jay: with Selections from his Correspondence.

every kind of support. This project is to raise two, three, or four battalions of Negroes, with the assistance of the government of South Carolina, by contributions from slaveowners in proportion to the number of slaves they own. If you want to discuss the subject with him, he will give you details of his plan. He wishes to have it recommended by Congress to the state. As encouragement Congress would give these battalions the same pay as continental soldiers.

It appears to me that the way things now are going in the South a plan of this kind is the most reasonable that can be adopted. It promises to have very important advantages. Indeed, I hardly see how a large enough military force can be collected in that region without it. The enemy's operations there are growing much more dangerous. I have not the least doubt that the Negroes will make very excellent soldiers with proper leadership. I will venture to say that they cannot be put into better hands than those of Colonel Laurens. He has the zeal, intelligence, energy, and every other qualification necessary to succeed in such an undertaking.

I often hear people object to the scheme of enlisting Negroes by saying they are not intelligent enough to make good soldiers. This is far from being a valid objection, in my opinion. I think their lack of education (for their natural faculties are probably as good as ours), plus that habit of depending on others that they acquire from a life of slavery, will make them better soldiers than our white troops. Let their officers exercise good judgment. The closer soldiers are to being like machines, perhaps the better.

I predict that this project will face much opposition because of prejudice and self-interest. The contempt we have been taught to feel for black people makes us imagine many things that are based neither on reason nor experience. Those who are unwilling to part with such valuable property will give a thousand arguments to show how unworkable this scheme is which requires such a sacrifice. But it should be remembered that if we do not use Negroes in this way, the enemy probably will.

An essential part of the plan is to give the Negroes their freedom when they are given their muskets. This will secure their loyalty and increase their courage. I believe it will also have a good influence upon those who remain slaves, by opening a door to their emancipation. This last point, I confess, strongly moves me to hope for the success of the project. For both the principles of humanity and good policy lead me to take an interest in favor of this unfortunate class of people.

With the truest respect and esteem,
I am, sir, your most obedient servant,
Alexander Hamilton

READING REVIEW

1. Why did Hamilton encourage the enlistment of black troops?
2. Why did Hamilton think blacks would make good soldiers?
3. What prediction did Hamilton make?
4. Cite evidence from the readings to support Hamilton's belief in equality of the races.

44 Rough Fighting in the South

Like most colonial women, Mercy Otis Warren did not receive a formal education. But, like some women who showed intellectual promise, she attended the tutoring sessions of her brothers. (One of her brothers was James Otis.)

During the Revolutionary War, Mercy Warren, an ardent Patriot, wrote plays attacking the British. She also wrote a history of the conflict, which she published in 1805.

This excerpt from Mercy Warren's history describes the fighting in the Carolinas in 1781. It focuses on the battle at Guilford Court House between the British army led by Lord Cornwallis and the American army led by General Nathanael Greene. It also describes some of the fighting that took place afterward.

READING FOCUS

1. What did Mercy Otis Warren think of General Greene's actions? Of Lord Cornwallis' actions?
2. What evidence is there to suggest this account was objective?

On the fifteenth of March the two armies met at Guilford, and seemed at first to fight with equal strength. But as usual, the inexperienced Carolina militia were made fearful by the courage and discipline of the British veterans.

Adapted from Mercy Warren, History of the Rise, Progress and Termination of the American Revolution. *Vol. II, 1805.*

Almost all the Carolinians threw down their weapons and fled, many without firing even once. This of course was a blow to the American army, yet this army fought with great bravery for an hour and a half. By then its lines were completely broken, and it had to retreat hastily. Both armies suffered the loss of many gallant officers and soldiers.

Lord Cornwallis held the field, and claimed a complete victory. Later events showed, however, that the advantage was on the American side.

After the action at Guilford and the departure of the American troops, Lord Cornwallis found it difficult to get supplies for his army. He left the field of action and marched toward eastern North Carolina. He and his army met many difficulties on the way, but they continued their march with great bravery. They cheerfully withstood the severest hardship. However, as they had frequently done before, they marked their path with the slaughter of innocent people all the way from Charleston to Yorktown. It was later estimated that fourteen hundred women became widows in one district of South Carolina alone during this year's campaign.

After the defeat at Guilford, General Greene, the commander of the Americans, was far from discouraged. He retreated with a steady step, and set up his camp only 10 or 15 miles [16 or 24 kilometers] from the scene of the recent action. He had every reason to expect a second encounter with the British army.

When Lord Cornwallis withdrew from Guilford, it seemed less the result of a systematic plan and more like the retreat of a conquered army. This, as well as other circumstances, caused General Greene, after he had gathered together most of his scattered troops, to follow Cornwallis rather than to retreat. The people of the area (unusual as it may seem) now tended to flock to the camp of the defeated, rather than to the conquering general. Large numbers of people came to join, and General Greene soon was well enough prepared to pursue the enemy.

Details of all the minor actions that took place in this period in the Carolinas might tire

A regiment of British soldiers

more than inform the reader. It is enough to note that the Americans, under various leaders and some excellent commanders, were continually attacking the chain of British posts in the Carolinas.

Unfortunately, the actions of many Americans were influenced either by feelings of hatred or by feelings of resentment for personal injuries. Many took advantage of the public confusion to take their own private revenge. A number of others seemed to fight under the banners of liberty with no aims other than looting, assassination, and robbery. After they had practiced such violence for a time, they frequently deserted to the British camp, where they acted in this same way against the Americans.

READING REVIEW

1. How did the inexperience of the Carolina militia contribute to their defeat.
2. What difficulties did Cornwallis' army meet on the way to eastern North Carolina?
3. According to Warren, what influenced the actions of some Americans?

45 The Success of the Revolution

The American Revolution brought independence to the thirteen American colonies. But it also was successful in other ways. In this reading, a modern scholar, Irving Kristol, summarizes some of the important results of the Revolution.

READING FOCUS

1. Why could the American Revolution be called a successful revolution?
2. What were the advantages of the Revolution?

In what sense can the American Revolution be called a successful revolution? To begin at the beginning: The American Revolution was successful in that those who led it were able, in later years, to look back peacefully at what they had done and to say that it was good. This was a revolution that, unlike all later revolu-

Adapted from "The American Revolution As a Successful Revolution" by Irving Kristol in America's Continuing Revolution: An Act of Conservation.

tions, did not destroy its creators. The people who made the revolution were the people who went on to create the new political system. They then held the highest elected positions in this system, and they all died in bed.

Indeed, in one important respect the American Revolution was so successful that it was almost self-defeating. It turned the attention of thoughtful people away from politics, which now seemed utterly settled. Political theory lost its vigor. Even the political thought of the Founders was not seriously studied. The American political tradition became an undebated tradition. It worked so well we did not bother to ask why it worked. (And we are therefore surprised during those moments when it suddenly seems not to be working so well after all).

The American Revolution was also successful in another important respect. It was a mild and relatively bloodless revolution. A war was fought, to be sure, and soldiers died in that war. But the rules of civilized warfare, as then established, were for the most part quite carefully observed by both sides. There was little of the butchery that we have come to accept as a natural part of revolutionary warfare. More important, there was practically none of the off-battlefield savagery that we now believe always happens in revolutions. There were no revolutionary courts dealing out "revolutionary justice." There was no reign of terror. There were no bloodthirsty proclamations by the Continental Congress. Tories had their property taken away, to be sure, and many were rudely forced to go into exile. But so far as I have been able to learn, not a single Tory was executed for holding counter-revolutionary opinions. Nor, in the years after the Revolution, were Tories persecuted to any significant degree (at least by today's standards) or their children discriminated against at all. As de Tocqueville [the great French writer and political thinker] later remarked, with only a little exaggeration, the Revolution "made no alliance with the violent passions of anarchy. Its course was marked, on the contrary, by a love of order and law."

READING REVIEW

1. What did Kristol mean when he called the American Revolution a revolution that did not destroy its creators?
2. Why did he say that the American Revolution was so successful that it was self-defeating?

CHAPTER 7 Forming a Confederation (1775–1787)

46 The Abolition of Slavery in Massachusetts

Some Americans realized that slavery was a denial of the principles of freedom they had fought to uphold during the Revolution. One of the accomplishments of the Confederation period was the abolition, or ending, of slavery in several northern states. Slavery was ended in Connecticut and Rhode Island in 1784, in New York in 1785, and in New Jersey in 1786. In Massachusetts, the state supreme court declared slavery to be illegal in a 1783 ruling in the case of *Quack Walker v. Nathaniel Jennison*. A part of the court's opinion in this case appears here.

READING FOCUS

1. In the court's opinion how did slavery arise?
2. Why did the court abolish slavery?

As to the doctrine of slavery and the right of Christians to hold Africans in permanent servitude and to sell and to treat them as we do our horses and cattle: It is true that this has been allowed by this province's laws. But nowhere is slavery expressly enacted or established. It has been a custom—a custom which began in some of the European nations for the benefit of trade and wealth. But whatever ideas once prevailed in this matter, or were imposed on us by the example of others, a different idea now has grown up among the people of America. This idea is more favorable to the natural rights of human beings and to that natural, inborn desire of liberty which Heaven (without regard

Adapted from Commonwealth History of Massachusetts, *Vol. IV,* edited by A. B. Hart, 1874.

to color, complexion, or physical features) has inspired among all the human race.

Upon this ground our [state] Constitution, by which the people of this commonwealth have solemnly bound themselves, begins by declaring that all people are born free and equal. It states that every subject is entitled to liberty, and that, like life and property, it should be guarded by the laws. In short it is totally opposed to the idea of being born a slave. This being the case, I think the idea of slavery goes against our own conduct and our Constitution. There can be no such thing as permanent servitude of a reasonable creature, unless the individual gives up his liberty because of criminal conduct.

READING REVIEW

1. Why did Massachusetts allow slavery before 1783?
2. What did the state Constitution declare regarding all people?
3. What did the court say is the only reason to allow permanent servitude?

47 A Foreigner's View of the Confederation

Johann David Schoepf was a German doctor who served with Hessian troops fighting on the British side during the Revolution. After the war, he remained in America and traveled around the new nation for several months. Here, he describes the Congress during the Confederation period and its frequent changes in meeting places during those years—its moves from Annapolis to Trenton and then to New York City.

READING FOCUS

1. How did the press treat the Confederation Congress?
2. What criticisms did the writer state about the Congress?
3. Who did the writer blame for the weaknesses of Congress?

The newspapers of Philadelphia find a good deal of amusement in the frequent changes of residence by Congress, especially its yearly

A contemporary political cartoonist satirizes President Reagan.

move from Jersey to Maryland and back again.

Under the protection of an almost complete freedom of press, which properly used can be one of the solidest supports of the Constitution, every day the bitterest mockeries of the Congress appear, and nobody is made to take the blame. The people, who mistake rudeness for liberty, would defend the author as well as the publisher against every attack.

I need to give only an example or two to show how rudely this notable assembly is treated. Congress decided to erect a statue on horseback to the defender of the nation, General Washington. The work was to be done by the best artist of France, and the statue was to be set up at the meeting place of Congress. This resolution was followed shortly afterward by another, designating two "federal-towns," on the Delaware and the Potomac rivers, in which the Congress was to meet alternately. Someone

then wrote in the *Freeman's Journal* that when Congress migrated from one town to the other, the mounted statue should go along. The writer added that this horse, like the Trojan horse, probably should be hollow-bellied in order to house the members of Congress on this journey.

Then a newspaper proposed the building of a floating town for Congress, known to be poor and greatly in debt. Congress and its members' luggage could be sent down the Delaware River from Trenton, along the coast into the Chesapeake Bay, and up the Potomac River to Georgetown comfortably and at a great savings of money. It was announced further that at the earliest possible opportunity an unmeasurably large pendulum would be swinging in America. Why? The Americans had observed the uncertain way that the machinery of government worked in European nations. Therefore, they invented an automatic mechanism—a great pendulum—for keeping their affairs going on an orderly course. The pendulum will hang from the planet Mars, and be composed of certain materials of great specific gravity known as the American Congress. This pendulum will swing across a space of 180 miles [290 kilome-

Adapted from Johann David Schoepf, Travels in the Confederation. 1783–1784, *translated by Alfred J. Morrison.*

63

ters] between Annapolis and Trenton. But even the best mathematician will be unable to calculate its true line of movement, since it will follow neither a straight line, nor a curved one, but will go its own crooked way!

These and many other similar anecdotes should show plainly enough that this notable assembly receives no special reverence or great honor in America. It appears from other circumstances, too, that Congress has neither the weight nor solidity it needs. Therefore its activities are very restricted and it faces all kinds of problems.

It was natural that a people so enthusiastic for liberty should grant their Congress only a shadow of dignity and watch its proceedings carefully. Insofar as its activities may be compared with those of similar groups in other nations, Congress is responsible for the wellbeing and the safety of the people. But in actual practice, there are a thousand difficulties in the way. The United States authorized Congress to borrow money and to do so by pledging the honor of the nation. But there is no authority granted Congress to pay these debts. Each state has its own independent government which is concerned with its special welfare and security. Each state has its own laws, police, and system of justice, free and regulated according to its own wishes. The state governments have the right to resist all laws and proposals of Congress which do not please them. (And if they did not have this right, they would do so nonetheless.)

The power given by the people to the government of each state, and given by these governments to Congress, is subject to constant change, because the members of these assemblies are always being replaced by others. Thus the private citizen is continually taking up the business of a national leader, and after a time returns to being a private citizen and gives his place to another. The purpose of this arrangement is to guard against the misuse of the highest power, which an unchanging group of leaders might allow themselves to drift into. Every member of a provincial assembly, as well as of Congress, will be careful about approving an ordinance which as a private person he might hesitate to obey. He will be slow to impose heavy taxes, which must be a burden to himself as well. And he will hesitate to make poor use of public money, because similar action by those who are elected after him would be disagreeable to him.

But also, useful institutions come into being more slowly if it appears that special interests might suffer. Thus there will be a hampering of the best and wisest plans of Congress. Congress can give no decisive orders; it can only make proposals and recommendations. But even to carry these out, it must rely chiefly on influence and dishonest ways.

The Congress is very well aware of its increasing weakness. It does not fail to inform the people of the necessity of increasing its powers and widening its scope of action.

READING REVIEW

1. What did the writer say about freedom of the press?
2. What did the story about the statue say about the Congress?
3. What action of Congress were the newspapers criticizing most?
4. Summarize the writer's statements about the role of the states in the Confederation.

48 The Problems of the Confederation

John Adams served as the first American minister, or ambassador, to Great Britain from 1785 to 1788. It was a difficult period in which to represent the United States abroad. A vivid picture of some of the problems facing Americans in these years is found in the letters of Abigail Adams, the wife of John Adams. Her correspondence is notable for its wide range of interests and its clear writing style. The selections that follow are from letters to her son John Quincy, her sister, and her niece Lucy. The letters show Abigail Adams' concern with important events—both domestic and foreign—taking place in her day.

READING FOCUS

1. From what country did Abigail Adams write her letters?
2. What message did she give to her son?
3. What two events did she write about?

To John Quincy Adams

Grosvenor Square, London
6 September, 1785

Our countrymen have injured themselves by coming here in great numbers since the peace, and running up bills they cannot pay. They have so loaded themselves with debts that they cannot get free. Merchants who have given them credit are now suffering, and that naturally creates illwill and harsh words. His Majesty and the government show every personal respect and civility which we have any right to expect.

It is astonishing that the English grab at every straw that floats. The people delude themselves that we are weary of our independence and wish to return under their government again. Their attitude toward us arises more from this idea than from any generous plans that would honor them as able leaders and a great nation. They propose to carry out their plans by prohibitive acts and high import taxes. They say they can injure us much more than we can them, and they seem determined to try.

Those who look beyond the present moment foresee the consequences. The English will never leave us alone until they drive us into the power and greatness that will finally shake this kingdom. We first must struggle very hard and encounter many difficulties. But we can be a great and a powerful nation if we try. Industry and thrift, wisdom and virtue, must make us so.

I think America is taking steps toward a reform, and I know it is capable of whatever it undertakes. I hope you will never lose sight of its interests. Make its welfare your study. Spend those hours which others devote to cards and folly in investigating the great principles by which nations have risen to glory and eminence. For your country will one day call for your services, either in the government or in the army. Qualify yourself to do honor to it.

To Mrs. Cranch

London,
21 May, 1786

There is no office more undesirable than that of Minister of the United States. Under the

Abigail Adams

present embarrassing conditions, there is no reputation to be acquired and there is much to lose. Negotiations with other nations may be and have been carried out. But with England there is not the least chance of a treaty until the states are united in their measures and give Congress full powers to regulate commerce. A minister here can be of very little service until that event takes place.

It is true that he may be given other powers. One, more important than negotiating with this country, is making peace with the Barbary States. But the demand for the poor sailors who are in captivity is a thousand dollars per man, and there are 21 of them. The sum voted by Congress is so inadequate that we can only look forward to the outbreak of war. Unless Congress tries to borrow the sum demanded and negotiates immediately, the pirates' demands will increase in proportion to the number of captures they make. These are dull subjects for one lady to write about to another. But our country is so much interested in these affairs, that you must excuse me for troubling you with them.

To Miss Lucy Cranch

London,
20 July, 1786

The riots and dissensions in our state of Massachusetts [because of Shays' Rebellion] have been of very serious concern to me. No one

Adapted from Letters of Mrs. Adams, 1840.

can suppose that our situation here is better because of it. I hope it will lead the wise and sensible part of the community in our state, as well as in the whole Union, to reflect seriously upon their situation. Since we have wise laws, let us execute them with vigor, justice, and punctuality. Mr. Adams has been employed in strengthening and supporting our governments. He has spared no pains to collect examples for them, and to show them the dangerous results of unbalanced power. We have the means of being the first and the happiest people upon the globe.

To Mrs. Cranch

London,

25 February, 1787

When I came to that part of your letter where you say that you hoped to see only peace in the future, after overcoming the horrors of one war, the idea was too powerful for me, and my tears involuntarily flowed. The thoughts which naturally occurred to me were: Why have we been battling against the tyranny of Britain if we are to become the victims of lawless bandits? Is it an unimportant matter to destroy a government? Will my countrymen justify the belief of tyrants that human beings are not made for freedom? I will, however, still hope that the majority of our fellow-citizens are too wise, virtuous, and enlightened to permit these outrages to triumph. The spirit shown by the volunteers does honor to our state. Quicker action by the government would have prevented the evil from spreading so far as it has done.

We shall wait with impatience to learn the result of General Lincoln's expedition. Much depends upon his success. The government seems afraid to use the power it has. It recommends and begs when it ought to *command*. This makes me fear that the evil lies deeper than Shays.

From letters received here both from Boston and New York, it is to be feared that some wealthy and educated citizens are considering visionary schemes and ambitious projects. But before so important a structure as an established government is altered or changed, its foundation should be carefully examined and the materials of which it is made should be fully investigated.

READING REVIEW

1. What complaint did Adams voice regarding the job of minister of the United States?
2. What did she think about the negotiations with the Barbary pirates?
3. What did Adams think about Shays' Rebellion?
4. Cite evidence from the letters to show that Adams was concerned about the weaknesses of the Confederation government.

49 A French Report on the Annapolis Convention

Louis Guillaume Otto served as French consul, or representative, in New York City during the Confederation period. In 1786 he wrote a detailed report about the Annapolis Convention for his superior, Count Vergennes, the French ambassador to the United States. In his report Otto discussed the Annapolis Convention and also his analysis of the background of this meeting.

READING FOCUS

1. In what ways did the author compare "gentlemen" to European nobility?
2. What was the reason for calling the Annapolis Convention?

Although there are no nobles in America, there is a class of "gentlemen." Because of their wealth, talents, education, families, or the offices they hold, they desire power that the people refuse to grant them. Almost all of them dread the efforts of the people to strip them of their possessions. Moreover, they are creditors and therefore interested in strengthening the government and its laws.

The majority of these people are merchants. It is in their interest to establish the credit of the United States in Europe on a solid foundation by the payment of debts, and to grant Congress enough power to force the people to pay taxes to repay these debts. Proposing a new organization of the federal government would

Adapted from George Bancroft, History of the Formation of the Constitution of the United States, *Vol. II, 1882.*

The Maryland statehouse, site of the Annapolis Convention

have alarmed the people. But difficulties threatening American commerce have given them an excuse for introducing new ideas.

The reformers declared that the flag of the United States was everywhere exposed to insults and annoyance. Farmers, no longer able to export their produce freely, would soon suffer extreme hardship. Therefore, the nation must respond. But strong measures could be taken only with the consent of the thirteen states. Since Congress lacked the necessary powers, it was essential to form a general assembly instructed to present the plan to Congress for its approval.

The people were generally discontented with the obstacles in the way of commerce. They hardly suspected the secret motives of their opponents. Adopting this measure, they appointed commissioners who were to meet at Annapolis in the beginning of September.

The authors of this proposal did not hope, nor even desire, to see this assembly of commissioners succeed. The proposal was intended only to deal with a question much more important than that of commerce. The matter was handled so well that at the end of September no more than five states were represented at Annapolis. The commissioners from the northern states stayed in New York several days in order to arrive late.

The commissioners who met waited nearly three weeks. Then they disbanded, with the excuse that not enough states were represented to deal with the issues. To justify their actions, they sent a report to the different legislatures and to Congress. In it, the commissioners discussed the present crisis of public affairs and the necessity of uniting the interests of all the states. They closed by proposing that a new assembly of commissioners meet next May. It is to consider not only a general plan of commerce, but the means of making the federal government more effective.

You will notice, my lord, that the commissioners were unwilling to consider the problems of commerce, which are of great interest to the people, without at the same time considering fundamental changes in the powers of Congress.

READING REVIEW

1. How did the "gentlemen" merchants use the idea of strengthening commerce as a means of gaining unity?
2. What criticisms did the writer level against the people who called the Annapolis Convention?
3. Why do you think the writer seemed so critical in his report?

50 The Bill of Rights of the Northwest Ordinance

In 1787 Congress passed one of its most important measures, the Northwest Ordinance. The Northwest Ordinance outlined the procedures by which new states would be created from the Northwest Territory (see text page 175). It also included a Bill of Rights for the citizens of the Territory. This was the first national bill of rights, and it was patterned after the bills of rights that had been included in many of the new state constitutions.

READING FOCUS

1. What basic freedoms were guaranteed to citizens of the Northwest Territory?
2. Why were schools considered important?
3. What did the Bill of Rights say about slavery and Indians?

It is hereby ordained and declared by the authority of the Continental Congress, that the following articles shall be considered as Articles of agreement between the Original States and the people and States in the Northwest Territory and forever remain unalterable, unless by common consent.

Article the First. No person who behaves in a peaceable and orderly manner shall ever be molested on account of his way of worship or religious beliefs in the said territory.

Article the Second. The inhabitants of the said territory shall always be entitled to the benefits of the writ of habeas corpus [a court order guaranteeing a prisoner a hearing before a judge], and of the trial by Jury; of a proportionate representation of the people in the legislature, and of judicial proceedings according to the course of the common law. All persons shall be bailable, unless for capital offences [crimes punishable by death], where the proof shall be evident or the presumption great. All fines shall be moderate and no cruel or unusual punishments shall be inflicted. No man shall be deprived of his liberty or property, but by the judgment of his peers or the law of the land. Should public necessities make it vital for the common preservation to take any persons property, or to demand his particular services, full compensation shall be made for the same. And in the just preservation of rights and property it is understood and declared that no law ought ever to be made, or have force in the said territory, that shall in any manner whatever, interfere with or affect private contracts or engagements, bona fide, and without fraud previously formed.

Article the Third. Religion, morality, and knowledge being necessary to good government and the happiness of mankind, Schools and the means of education shall forever be encouraged. The utmost good faith shall always be observed towards the Indians; their lands and property shall never be taken from them without their consent. In their property, rights, and liberty, they shall never be invaded or disturbed, unless in just and lawful wars authorized by Congress; but laws founded in justice and humanity shall from time to time be made, for preventing wrongs being done to them, and for preserving peace and friendship with them.

*   *   *   *   *

A facsimile of the Northwest Ordinance

Adapted from Journals of the Continental Congress, 1774-1789, *edited by Worthington C. Ford.*

Article the Sixth. There shall be neither Slavery nor involuntary Servitude in the said territory otherwise than in the punishment of crimes, whereof the party shall have been duly convicted, Provided, always, That any person escaping into the same, from whom labor or service is lawfully claimed in any one of the original States, such fugitive may be lawfully reclaimed and conveyed to the person claiming his or her labor or service as aforesaid.

READING REVIEW

1. What freedom was guaranteed in Article I?
2. List the rights granted to citizens in Article II.
3. Why were the building of schools and education encouraged by the Bill of Rights?
4. What was required in order to take over Indian lands in the Northwest Territory?
5. While Congress prohibited slavery in the Northwest Territory, it did not prohibit slavery in the Old Southwest Territory. Why do you think this was so? Use the map on page 173 of the text to help explain your answer.

Freedom to disagree

51 Reaction to Shays' Rebellion

Some Americans were so disturbed by Shays' Rebellion that they even began to view the American Revolution as a mistake. They argued that America enjoyed peace and prosperity as part of the British Empire, and that independence brought about mob rule (such as Shays' Rebellion), hurt trade, and led to several other ills.

This view was summarized in the following excerpt from a speech given in 1786 by a student at Brown University in Rhode Island.

READING FOCUS

1. Why did the student like the British form of government?
2. What problems did he say were brought about by independence from Great Britain?
3. Why did the states refuse to give Congress the power it needs to run the country?

It is agreed by all good Politicians that no form of government was ever better calculated to preserve the rights of mankind and make the subjects happy than that of Great Britain.

It joins the two extremes of Monarchy and Democracy and forms that Glorious balance of Power which checks Usurpation [unlawful seizure of power] and Tyranny in the throne and equally checks the Power in the hands of the people.

It appears evident from the nature of governments that Republics can flourish or answer the end of Society only in Countries of Small size.

We have heard much said in favor of the Glorious Liberty we have obtained by independence. But let us stop a moment and count the Cost. Before the American Revolution England stood in the same Relationship to us as a Parent does to his child. She was honorable amoung the nations. Like the Lionness in the forest her voice protected her young wherever it went.

Her Arm she extended over these Colonies. When our enemies invaded us She sent her veteran troops Commanded by some of the greatest Generals Europe ever boasted. They United with Americas Sons to Drive our enemies from our borders. With their blood they bought us

Adapted from "Oratorical Afterthoughts on American Independence," New England Quarterly, *VIII (September, 1935), edited by Robert E. Moody.*

the victory! These were the most flourishing most happy days America ever saw.

But in that fatal hour in which the Sword of the American Revolution was drawn, this pleasing Scene was changed. Worry and distress sat on every face. Fifty thousand souls fell victims to this Cruel war. Our Towns and lands were laid waste.

Our Fathers, Brothers, and Children in thousands fell around us. Our Breavest youth in the gay morn of Life were cut off by untimely Death. Where ere we turned our Eyes we saw the breathless corpse. Mourning and sorrow Continually sounded in our Ears. To these we must now add the flood of Luxury and vice introduced by this unnatural war. The vices have Corrupted our former honest simple manners and will soon fix us down in abject Slavery and ripen us for heaven's severest Judgment. Add to these an immense debt foreign and domestic.

Here then is a Sacrifice of Life, Virtue, and property. To gain what? An imaginary Liberty! Are we more free than we used to be? We enjoyed under Great Britain all the Liberty Consistent with good government. What has since been added is but immoral behavior.

Thus we are without money, Trade, and permanent Alliances. Our repeated Attempts to supply the Defficiency of money by a paper Currency have destroyed our national Faith at home and abroad.

The large size of each State together with their Different manners and Customs fills them with Jealousies and animosities towards each other and prevent their giving to Congress that Power which is absolutely necessary in all governments. Our public officials are more numerous now than ever they were under the British Administration.

READING REVIEW

1. What two extremes were checked by the British form of government?
2. Why did he say a republic was not a good form of government for the United States?
3. How did Britain treat the colonies before the Revolution?
4. What problems did the student say America faced?
5. Did this student favor the creation of a stronger national government? Give evidence from the speech to support your answer.

52 On the Need for a New Constitution

Concern over the political situation in the 1780's was shown in many of the letters written during these years by leading Americans. This letter from John Jay to George Washington revealed the serious problems faced by the leaders of the new nation. Jay wrote that changes in the Confederation government were needed. However, he felt that the convention called to deal with the problem had not received its power from the people but only from the state legislatures. He therefore questioned the authority of the convention to make any basic changes either in the government or in its powers.

READING FOCUS

1. What changes did Jay suggest be made in the Nation's government?
2. According to Jay, where did the true source of authority come from?

Our situation requires not only careful thought and wisdom but action. What is to be done is a common question but not an easy one to answer.

Would giving more power to Congress make it more effective? I am very inclined to think that it would not. Among other reasons, there will always be members who will find it easy enough to use their power for personal gain. Those who may be able and willing to promote useful measures for the nation will often be hindered by the ignorance, prejudices, fears, or selfish views of others.

The business of using the power of government will be handled poorly if it depends on so many wills, wills moved by so many different and contradictory motives. The great power of government cannot be effective without an adequate system of justice. I think, therefore, that any change should divide the power of government into its proper departments. Let Congress legislate—let others execute—let others judge.

Shall we have a king? Not in my opinion while other ways of governing remain untried. Might we not have a governor-general with

Adapted from Correspondence and Public Papers of John Jay, *Vol III, edited by Henry P. Johnson, 1891.*

limited powers and a limited term of office? Might not Congress be divided into an upper and lower house—the former appointed for life, the latter newly appointed each year? Let the governor-general (to preserve the balance), with the advice of a judicial council, have a veto on Congress's acts. Our government should in some degree be suited to our manners and circumstances, which, you know, are not strictly democratic.

What powers should be granted to such a government is a question which deserves much thought. I think the more thought the better. The states should keep only enough power to handle local matters. All their highest officers, civil and military, should be commissioned and removable by the national government. These are only some sketchy ideas, of course, since detailed ideas would exceed the limits of a letter.

A convention is being planned, and I am glad to find your name among those who are going to be members. To me the policy of such a convention appears questionable. Its authority is to be derived from acts of the state legislatures. But are the state legislatures authorized, either by themselves or others, to alter constitutions? I think not. Perhaps it is intended that this convention shall not enact but only recommend. If so, there is a danger that its recommendations will cause endless discussion, perhaps jealousies and party quarrels.

Would it not be better for Congress to declare plainly and in strong terms that the present federal government is inadequate? Its members should keep from pointing out particular defects or asking for more power. But they could recommend that the people of the states appoint state conventions with the sole power of appointing deputies to a general convention. This convention, in turn, would meet to consider the Articles of Confederation and make such alterations, amendments, and additions to them as would appear necessary and proper.

No changes in the government should, I think, be made—nor could they actually be made—unless they come from the only source of true authority—the People.

1. List the changes Jay felt were necessary for the American government to be successful.
2. Why did Jay question the state legislatures' authority to call a convention?

CHAPTER 8 Creating a Federal Union
(1787-1789)

53 Why Slavery Remained

Slavery was one of the most difficult issues discussed at the Constitutional Convention. Its continued existence in some parts of the nation struck many Americans as a violation of basic American principles. The three-fifths compromise had settled the problem of representation, but those who were against slavery refused to accept a clause stating that the importation of slaves could not be prohibited or taxed.

The reading that follows is taken from James Madison's record of the debates of the convention. In it Madison has recorded the arguments regarding the clause of the Constitution that allowed slavery to continue.

READING FOCUS
1. How many people's arguments are presented in Mr. Madison's record?
2. What is the principle argument stated by each person?
3. Which men were opposed to the slave trade?

Mr. Martin [Maryland] proposed to change Article VII, Section 4 to allow a prohibition or tax on the importation of slaves. First, as five slaves are to be counted as three free persons in the apportionment of representatives, such a clause would encourage the slave trade. Second, slaves weakened one part of the Union, which the other parts were bound to protect; the privilege of importing them was therefore unreasonable. Third, it was inconsistent with the principles of the Revolution and dishonorable to the American character to have such a feature in the Constitution.

Adapted from Max Farrand, ed., The Records of the Federal Convention of 1787.

Signing the United States Constitution

Mr. Rutledge [South Carolina] did not see how the importation of slaves could be encouraged by this section. He was not fearful of slave revolts, and would readily exempt the other states from [the obligation to protect the southern states against revolts]. Religion and humanity had nothing to do with this question. Self-interest alone is the governing principle of nations. The true question at present is whether the southern states shall or shall not be members of the Union. If the nothern states consider their real interests, they will not oppose the increase of slaves, which will also increase the quantities of goods which these states will be able to trade.

Mr. Ellsworth [Connecticut] was for leaving the clause as it stands. Let every state import what it wishes. The morality and wisdom of slavery are considerations for the states themselves to decide. What enriches a part enriches the whole, and the states are the best judges of their own interests. The old confederation had not meddled with this point, and he did not see any greater necessity now for the new government to do so.

Mr. Pinckney [South Carolina] can never accept the plan if it prohibits the slave trade. In every proposed increase of the powers of Congress, that state has expressly and carefully made certain that meddling with the importation of Negroes was outside this power. If the states are all left at liberty to act as they wish on this matter, South Carolina may perhaps, by degrees, do what is wishes [prohibit the importation of slaves], as Virginia and Maryland have already done.

Mr. Sherman [Connecticut] was for leaving the clause as it stands. He disapproved of the slave trade. Yet as the states now had the right to import slaves, as the public good did not require that this right be taken from them, and as it was advisable to have as few objections as possible to the proposed plan of government, he thought it best to leave the matter as we find it. He observed that the abolition of slavery seemed to be going on in the United States and that the good sense of the various states would probably, by degrees, complete it.

Colonel Mason [Virginia]. This infernal slave trade originated in the greed of British merchants. The British government constantly prevented the attempts of Virginia to put a stop to it. The present question concerns not the importing states alone but the whole Union. Maryland and Virginia, he said, had already expressly prohibited the importation of slaves. North Carolina had done the same in practice. All this would be useless, however, if South Carolina and Georgia were free to import slaves. The western people are already demanding slaves for their new lands, and will fill that country with slaves if they can get them from South Carolina and Georgia.

Slavery discourages arts and manufactures. The poor despise the idea of labor when labor is performed by slaves. It prevents the immigration of white settlers, who really enrich and strengthen a country. Slaves produce the most harmful effect on manners. Every master of slaves is born a petty tyrant. They bring down the judgment of Heaven on a country. As nations cannot be rewarded or punished in the next world, they must be in this. By an inevitable chain of causes and effects, Providence punishes national sins by national calamities. He lamented that some of our eastern brethren's lust of gain caused them to take part in this evil slave trade. He held it essential, from every point of view, that the national government should have power to prevent an increase of slavery.

Mr. Ellsworth [Connecticut]. As he had never owned a slave, he could not judge the effects of slavery on people's character. He said, however, that if slavery was to be considered in a moral light, we ought to go further and free those already in the country. Inasmuch as slaves multiply so fast in Virginia and Maryland that it is cheaper to raise than import them, while in the rice swamp regions imports of slaves are necessary, if we go no further than is proposed, we shall be unjust toward South Carolina and Georgia. Let us not interfere. As population increases, poor laborers will become so plentiful they will make slaves useless. Slavery, in time, will not be a speck in our country.

General Pinckney [South Carolina] declared it to be his firm opinion that if he and all his colleagues were to sign the Constitution, and use their personal influence, it would still not cause the people they represented to agree to this action. South Carolina and Georgia cannot do without slaves. As to Virginia, it will gain by stopping the importation. Its slaves will rise in value, and it already has more than it wants. It would be unfair to require South Carolina and Georgia to join on such unequal terms.

He contended that the importation of slaves would be in the interest of the whole Union. The more slaves, the more products for commerce; the more consumption also; and the more of this, the more revenue for the national treasury. He admitted it was reasonable that a duty should be paid on slaves as on other imports, but he would consider a rejection of the clause as an exclusion of South Carolina from the Union.

READING REVIEW

1. Which men were opposed to slavery in general?
2. Which men were opposed only to the continuation of the slave trade?
3. Review your textbook to state the compromise that turned out to be the final solution to the issues debated here.
4. Cite evidence from Madison's record to prove that a compromise was needed.

54 Slavery and the Constitution: A Historian's View

Some of the decisions made at the Constitutional Convention may seem questionable, if judged on the basis of today's ideas and standards. The decisions made by the Framers of the Constitution regarding slavery may seem especially questionable. Did these leaders, many of whom saw slavery as wrong and inhuman, try to abolish it? Did they even try to end its most terrible features? The answer, of course, is no. They simply did not deal with the question of slavery. In this selection, Clin-ton Rossiter, a modern historian, explained in this why the Constitutional Convention did not try to solve the problem of slavery.

READING FOCUS

1. What limited the conduct of the Framers of the Constitution in the matter of slavery?
2. What was the principal concern of the Framers of the Constitution?
3. How did the Constitution achieve their goal?

The most fateful decision *not* made at the Convention—or so it appears to people today and must have appeared to people of the 1860's—was to do something imaginative about Negro slavery. It had long been recognized in at least half the states as a terrible injustice to the slaves themselves, a mockery of the principles of 1776, and a menace to free government. Slavery was a problem for many leading framers. This is clear in the remarks of Madison, Luther Martin, Mason, King, Gerry, and Gouverneur Morris. There is something unconvincing in the prediction of framers Ellsworth and Sherman that slavery would someday be no more than "a speck in our country." The framers, like almost all people of their time, may have had trouble thinking of slaves as persons. But they were, with few exceptions, painfully aware of slavery as an institution.

What the Convention did about slavery is beyond dispute. At four points in the Constitution the framers confirmed its existence in guarded language—the "three-fifths clause" in Article I, section 2; the "1808 clause" in Article I, section 9; the provision for surrender to one state by another of an escaped "person held to service or labor" in Article IV, section 2; and the extra protection given in the "1808 clause" in Article V. What they did not do is also beyond dispute. They did not outlaw slavery, nor in any way seek to soften its effects. Also, they did not give Congress the power to outlaw slavery in the states. They did not arrange either to help or hinder free Negroes in their attempt to win the status and rights of citizenship.

What the framers could have done is, of course, a more hotly disputed question. Many Americans have insisted that the Convention of 1787 missed a splendid opportunity to settle the issue once and for all. Most such persons have wished that the framers would have pro-

Thirteenth Amendment, the United States Constitution

vided for the freeing of all slaves, either immediately or by stages, and also perhaps for including them in the American community. A few people have wished that the framers could have guaranteed to each state the exclusive right to deal with slavery in its own time and way. This might have included the right to strengthen it as well as to abolish it.

All such persons, in my opinion, have failed to "think themselves back into the twilight" of 1787 and to understand the limits under which the framers were operating in this manner. These limits permitted them as builders of a nation to do nothing positive and only a few things negative about slavery, their potentially most explosive social problem. On one hand, a blow at slavery in the Constitution itself would have invited certain rejection by the southern states. Even the acknowledgment of a power to suppress the slave trade at a future date was a gamble with opinion in South Carolina. On the other hand, any additional display of tolerance toward slavery—indeed the very mention of the word "slaves" or "slavery" or "slave trade" in the Constitution—would have invited rejection by the North. Even the concession that a slave might be considered as three-fifths of a person (for the political purposes of the white South) was a gamble with both the conscience and self-interest of Massachusetts or Pennsylvania.

Here, as in the attempt to work out a com-

promise on representation acceptable to both Delaware and Virginia, the framers were searching for the workable middle road. Here, as in every decision, their principal concern was to give the nation a new government, one that could win support in all parts of the Union. Their strongest fear was that certain important states would reject their proposal, and at least three of these states had economies built squarely on slavery. And so they believed John Rutledge when he said that the question of what to do about slavery was really a question of "whether the Southern states shall or shall not be parties to the Union." And they believed General Pinckney when he warned that the elimination of the 20-year period of delay before outlawing the slave trade would mean "an exclusion of South Carolina from the Union."

The decisions and non-decisions of 1787 about slavery and the slave trade were, to be brief, decisions for the Union. Those who criticize the framers for not acting boldly in this matter see them as people they never were or could have been—bold supporters of a social revolution. Rather they were cautious builders of a nation. Both the angry people of the North and the troubled ones of the South were limited by a whole set of circumstances—inertia, tradition, sectionalism, poor timing, lack of imagination, the preference for "essential principles only," and above all their great desire for a nation—from striking for the freedom of a misunderstood and, for that matter, feared group of people. This was, they were certain, their last chance to forge a political unity out of the thirteen states that stretched from Canada to Florida. They were not disposed to lose it by gambling that the Southern states would now see a light where they had never seen one before.

The United States of America has repeatedly paid a high price for its precious Union over the years since 1776. It laid out a huge sum of moral and political currency for the charter upon which the Union was to rise. Yet the sum, surely, was not too huge. For we must recognize, despite our misgivings, that any determined step against slavery in the Constitution would have been an act of pure political insanity. Simply to make it possible for the new government to move against the slave trade in 20 years (and to tax it in the meantime) was as decisive a victory for human decency as people who loved the Union and hated slavery could have won at Philadelphia.

Adapted from "Why Slavery Remained: An Historian Looks Back"
in 1787: The Grand Convention by Clinton Rossiter.

1. List the three areas in which the convention did nothing in regard to slavery.
2. **(a)** How would Southern states have reacted to the outlawing of slavery? **(b)** How would the Northern states have reacted to any additional display of tolerance toward slavery?
3. In order to receive support from both geographic areas, what actions did the Framers of the Constitution take?

55 Article 15, *The Federalist*

The strength of the Anti-Federalists in New York was enough to cause Alexander Hamilton, James Madison, and John Jay to write a series of 85 articles, or essays, urging ratification of the Constitution. These essays appeared as letters in a New York newspaper and were later published in a book titled *The Federalist*. They were thought to be a strong factor in achieving ratification of the Constitution. In this selection, taken from Article 15, Hamilton denounces the shortcomings of the government under the Confederation.

READING FOCUS

1. What weaknesses of the Confederation government did Hamilton attack?
2. What was Hamilton's solution for the problems of the nation?

It can indeed be justly said that we have reached about the last state of national humiliation. There is scarcely anything that can wound the pride or degrade the character of an independent nation that we have not experienced.

Are there treaties for which we are responsible? These are constantly and shamelessly violated.

Do we owe debts to foreigners and to our own citizens, debts begun at a time of great peril in order to preserve our political existence? These remain unpaid, without provision for paying them.

Have we valuable territories and important posts in the possession of a foreign power which it ought to have surrendered long ago? These

Adapted from The Federalist, *edited by H. C. Lodge, 1895.*

THE FEDERALIST:

ADDRESSED TO THE

PEOPLE OF THE STATE OF NEW-YORK.

NUMBER I.

Introduction.

AFTER an unequivocal experience of the inefficacy of the subsisting federal government, you

Opening passage of The Federalist.

are still being kept, against both our interests and our rights. Are we in a condition to resent or to turn back this aggression? We have neither troops, nor money, nor government. Are we even in a condition to protest with dignity?

Are we entitled by nature and treaty to free navigation on the Mississippi River? Spain excludes us from it.

Is commerce of importance to national wealth? Our trade is at its lowest ebb.

Is respectability in the eyes of foreign powers a safeguard against foreign aggression? The unwise policies of our government even forbid them to deal with us. Our ambassadors abroad are merely playacting.

Is private credit the friend and supporter of industry? That most useful kind of credit, which relates to borrowing and lending, is kept within the narrowest limits. This results more from a feeling of insecurity than from the scarcity of money.

In short, what sort of national disorder, poverty, and insignificance is not part of the dark catalog of our public misfortune?

This is the sad situation to which we have been brought by those same groups which would now discourage us from adopting the proposed Constitution.

1. What was Hamilton's purpose in writing this essay?
2. List the weaknesses of the Confederation government.
3. What did Hamilton feel we should do to correct this situation?

56 One Massachusetts Delegate on the Constitution

Jonathan Smith was a delegate to the Massachusetts ratification convention in 1788. Because of what he had seen and experienced during Shays' Rebellion, he felt that the government under the Confederation was too weak. In this speech, he described the results of the Confederation government's weaknesses, and explained why he supported ratification of the Constitution.

READING FOCUS

1. Why did Smith favor the Constitution?
2. Why did he think that it must be ratified without delay?

I am a plain man, and earn my living by farming. I am not used to speaking in public, but I want to say a few words to my fellow farmers in this house. I have lived in a part of the country where I have learned the worth of good government by the lack of it. There was a black cloud of rebellion that rose in the east last winter and spread over the west. The cloud burst upon us and produced a dreadful result. It brought on a state of anarchy, and that led to tyranny. People that used to live peaceably, and were good neighbors, took up weapons against the government.

I am going to show you, my brother farmers, what were the results of anarchy, so you may see the reasons why I wish for good government. People, I say, took up arms. If you went to speak to them, you had the musket of death presented to your chest. They would rob you of your property, threaten to burn your houses, and force you to be on your guard night and

Adapted from Debates on the Adoption of the Constitution, *Vol. II, edited by Jonathan Elliot, 1861.*

day. Warnings spread from town to town. Families were broken up. Then we would hear of an action, and the poor prisoners were stood in the front to be killed by their own friends. Our distress was so great that we should have been glad to grab at anything that looked like a government, even though our savior was a monarch.

Now when I saw this Constitution, I found it was a cure for these disorders. It was just such a thing as we wanted. I got a copy of it, and read it over and over. I did not go to any lawyer to ask his opinion. I formed my own opinion, and was pleased with this Constitution. My honorable old daddy there (pointing to Mr. Singletary) won't think that I expect to be a member of Congress and swallow up the liberties of the people. I never had any post, nor do I want one. But I don't think the worse of the Constitution because lawyers, and educated people, and wealthy people are fond of it. I don't suspect that they want to get into Congress and misuse their power. I am not of such a jealous nature.

Some say, don't be in a hurry; take time to consider. I say, take things in time; gather fruit when it is ripe. There is a time to sow and a time to reap. We sowed our seed when we sent men to the federal Convention. Now is the harvest, now is the time to reap the fruit of our labor. If we won't do it now, I am afraid we never shall have another opportunity.

READING REVIEW

1. What were the results of anarchy after Shays' Rebellion?
2. Why did Smith, a Massachusetts farmer, feel the need to speak out in favor of the Constitution's ratification?

57 Another Massachusetts Delegate on the Constitution

The proposed Constitution caused uneasiness among many of the small farmers, artisans, and townspeople who distrusted any change in government. At the Massachusetts ratification convention, held early in 1788, one such delegate, Amos Singletary, voiced his opinion.

1. What, in Singletary's view, was the reason the
Revolutionary War was fought?
2. What was Singletary's greatest objection to
government?

We fought against Great Britain—some said
for a three-penny duty on tea—but it was not
that. It was because they claimed a right to tax
us and control us in all cases as they pleased.
And does this Constitution not do the same
thing? Does it not take away all we have—all
our property? Does it not levy all taxes, duties,
tariffs, and excises? And what more have we to
give?

They tell us Congress won't place taxes
upon us, but will collect all the money it wants
by tariffs. I say there has always been difficulty
with tariffs. They won't be able to raise enough
money that way, and then they will tax the
land and take all we have got.

These lawyers and men of learning and
wealthy men who talk so finely and cover over
difficult matters so smoothly to make us poor
uneducated people swallow the pill—they
expect to get into Congress themselves. They
expect to be the managers of the Constitution
and to get all the power and all the money into
their own hands. And then they will swallow
up all us common people just as the whale swallowed up Jonah. This is what I am afraid of.

Adapted from Debates on the Adoption of the Federal Constitution,
Vol. II, edited by Jonathan Elliot, 1861.

READING REVIEW

1. What objection did Singletary have to men of
learning and men of wealth?
2. Do you think Singletary's judgment about the
delegates was a fair one? Explain.
3. According to Singletary, why did we fight the
Revolutionary War?

58 A New Yorker's Reservations

The two groups favoring and opposing ratification
of the new Constitution soon became known as the
Federalists and the Anti-Federalists. The Anti-Federalists were especially strong in New York, and
many of them argued in favor of their viewpoint in
letters to newspapers.

The following letter appeared in a New York
newspaper on November 8, 1787, not long after the
Constitutional Convention had ended.

READING FOCUS

1. What were the two arguments seemingly in the
Constitution's favor?
2. How did the writer feel about the strength of each
of the arguments?
3. What would the writer have urged instead of
ratification?

A facsimile of the Preamble to the United States Constitution

Po·lar·oid [pō′lə·roid′] *n.* **1** A transparent plastic material that polarizes light and reduces glare: a trademark. **2** A camera that develops the picture it shoots, producing a finished print in seconds. Also called **Polaroid Land Camera** and **Polaroid camera**: a trademark.

pol·der [pōl′dər] *n.* A low area of land that has been protected by dikes and emptied of water, as in the Netherlands.

pole¹ [pōl] *n., v.* **poled, pol·ing** **1** *n.* A long, thin, wooden or metal rod, usually rounded. **2** *v.* To push along with a pole, as a boat.

pole² [pōl] *n.* **1** Either end of the axis of a sphere. **2** Either end of the earth's axis; the North Pole or the South Pole. **3** A point of maximum strengh in a magnetic or electric field.

Pole [pōl] *n.* A person born in or a citizen of Poland.

pole·cat [pōl′kat′] *n.* **1** A European animal related to a weasel, known for its foul odor when annoyed or frightened. **2** *U.S.* A skunk.

po·lem·ic [pə·lem′ik] **1** *adj.* Of or having to do with dispute or argument. **2** *n.* An argument, especially about political or religious beliefs.

pole·star [pōl′stär′] *n.* **1** The North Star; Polaris. **2** Something that guides or governs.

How does the definition of polemic apply to Reading 58?

I have read with attention several publications which have recently appeared in favor of the new Constitution. As far as I am able to understand, the most serious arguments (if they can be so termed) in its favor may be summed up in the two following:

First: The men who formed it were wise and experienced. They were a highly distinguished group of patriots who had the happiness of their country at heart. They spent four months carefully considering the matter. Therefore, it must be a perfect system.

Second: If the system is not adopted, this country will be without any government. As a result, it will experience a state of anarchy and bloodshed. In the end a government will be imposed upon us that is not the result of reason and reflection, but the result of force.

With respect to the first argument, it is easy to see that it prevents all investigation of the merits of the proposed Constitution. It leads to an adoption of the plan without inquiring whether it is good or bad. For if we are to judge the perfection of this system by the characters and abilities of men who formed it, we may as well accept it without any inquiry at all. Using such reasoning, a number of persons in this

as well as other states have decided to agree to it without even reading it or knowing its contents.

In answer to the second argument, I deny that we are in immediate danger of anarchy and bloodshed. Nothing but the passions of wicked and ambitious men can cause us the least danger on this score. Those who are anxious to push something through will always tell us that the present is the critical moment: Now is the time, the crisis is arrived, and the present minute must be seized. Tyrants have always used this plea, but nothing in our present circumstances can justify it.

The country is in a state of complete peace, and we are not threatened by invasion from any region. The governments of the states are in full control to exercise their powers. The lives, the liberty, and property of individuals are protected.

It is true that we need to regulate trade and provide for the payment of interest on the public debt. But no immediate difficulties will arise from this fact. There is time for calm discussion and carefully thought-out decisions. Individuals are just recovering from their losses during the last year. Industry and careful use of resources are driving idleness from the community. Individuals are reducing their personal debts.

There is no reason, therefore, why we should rashly adopt a system which is imperfect. We should confidently consider and propose amendments and alterations. I know it is said that we cannot change our systems of government for the worse. But if we are wise, we shall take care that we change for the better. It will be labor lost, if we are in no better circumstances after all our efforts than we were before.

If any violent disorders arise, they will be the fault of those clever and ambitious men who are determined to force this government down the throats of the people before they have time to examine it carefully.

Adapted from the Journal and Weekly Register, *New York, November 8, 1787.*

READING REVIEW

1. What two arguments in favor of ratifying the Constitution does the writer advance?
2. How did he answer each argument?
3. Which argument, in your estimation, did the writer refute more convincingly? Explain your reasoning.

59 A Letter on Federalism

The Framers of the Constitution determined that the United States should be organized under the principle of federalism. Under the federal system the central government divided and shared powers with the state governments. The decisions regarding which powers were to belong to the central government and which were to belong to the states were made with much argument and debate at the Constitutional Convention. Even after the Constitution was adopted and the government was established, there was great difference of opinion about how much power the central government should really have.

The reading below is from a letter written by Thomas Jefferson in 1800, more than a decade after the Constitution went into effect. In it Jefferson gave some of his ideas about the roles of the central and state governments.

READING FOCUS

1. Why did Jefferson oppose having the United States governed only by a central government?
2. Why did he feel a large central government would be corrupt?
3. What should be the main job of the central government?

Our country is too large to have all its affairs directed by a single government. Public servants, at such a distance and away from the watchful eye of the people who elected them would be unable to administer and overlook all the details necessary for the good government of the citizens; and such a far distance from the people who elected them will tempt the public officials to be corrupt, to steal and to waste public money. And I do truly believe that if the central government took over all the powers of the state governments, thus eliminating states, that the central government would be the most corrupt government on earth. What opportunities there would be for thefts, bribery, plundering, and the placing of friends in government jobs if the central government took over all the powers of the state governments! The true theory of our Constitution is surely the wisest and best; that the states are independent as to

Thomas Jefferson, staunch advocate of federalism

everything within themselves, and united under the central government as to everything regarding foreign nations. Let the central government take care of foreign affairs only, and let the United States keep out of entangling alliances with other nations. Let us trade with foreign nations, but let the merchants manage matters of trade—they can do it best if left free by the central government to manage it themselves. This will allow the central government to be a very simple and inexpensive one—a few plain duties to be performed by a few public servants.

READING REVIEW

1. What were two reasons why Jefferson felt the United States was too large to be governed by only the central government?
2. What would happen to the size of the central government if it took over the powers of the states?
3. Why would taking over the powers of the states tend to make the central government corrupt?
4. What did Jefferson say should be the responsibility of state governments? Of the central government?
5. Did Jefferson favor the idea of federalism? Cite evidence from the reading to support your answer.

Adapted from Thomas Jefferson Randolph, Memoirs, Correspondence, and Private Papers of Thomas Jefferson, 1829.

Building the Nation

60 Washington's Inauguration

George Washington's inauguration as first President took place Thursday, April 30, 1789, in New York City, the temporary capital of the nation. This reading is from a report written by a representative of the government of the Netherlands to the head of the Netherlands foreign office. The report described Washington's arrival in New York City and his inauguration. The writer frequently referred to Washington as "his Excellency."

George Washington takes the oath of office.

READING FOCUS

1. How did the citizens feel about Washington?
2. What was the writer's opinion of the first President of the United States?

President George Washington made his entry into New York on Thursday, April 23d. On the previous day a barge left this city. The barge was built expressly by the citizens of New York, and was rowed by thirteen pilots, all dressed in white. His Excellency was also accompanied by some well-equipped sloops and by a multitude of small craft with citizens of New Jersey and New York on board, and a Spanish royal packet-boat, anchored at the entrance of the harbor. At sight of the barge, on board of which was the President, the Spanish packet-boat fired a signal-shot, whereupon that vessel saluted his Excellency by firing thirteen guns. The salute was repeated by the Battery, and again thirteen guns were fired by the fort when the President landed.

His Excellency was received by Governor George Clinton, the mayor of the city and other officers, and, after a procession had formed, consisting of some companies of uniformed citizens and the merchants and other citizens of the city, the President walked with his escort, and Governor Clinton at his side, to the house prepared by Congress for his use. Shortly afterward his Excellency was called for in a coach by Governor Clinton, without any ceremony. At Governor Clinton's residence he took a midday meal, though a magnificent dinner had been prepared for his Excellency at his own residence. Both these personages were on that day dressed very plainly in civilian clothes, without any display.

Adapted from Clarence Winthrop Bowen, ed., The History of the Centennial Celebration of the Inauguration of George Washington as First President of the United States, *1892.*

The rush of the people to see their beloved General Washington was amazing, and their delight and joy were truly universal and cordial. At night the whole city was illuminated. No accident occurred, and everything passed off very well and quietly.

On Thursday, April 30th, General Washington was inaugurated President of the United States. New York was represented by the same companies of citizens under arms as on his arrival. After the President, in accordance with the new Constitution, had publicly taken the oath of office, in presence of an innumerable crowd of people, his Excellency was led into the Senate-chamber and there delivered an address. By this address this admirable man made himself all the more beloved. His Excellency was dressed in plain brown clothes, which had been presented to him by the mill at Hartford, Connecticut. At night there was a display of fire-works at the State-House.

The next day the President received congratulations. The President adopts no other title than simply President of the United States. He receives visits twice a week, Tuesdays and Fridays, from two to three o'clock, and not at other times. It is further stated that his Excellency returns no visits. Nor will he accept invitations to attend banquets or other entertainments. The reason is that his Excellency, as head of the Executive Department of the new Government, has his time fully occupied.

This gentleman alone, by his courteous and friendly demeanor and still more so by his frugal and simple mode of living, is able to unite the parties in America and to make the new Government effective and regular in execution, if such be possible.

READING REVIEW

1. What evidence in the reading allows you to infer that Washington was warmly received?
2. According to the writer, what personal qualitites made Washington a good choice for the first President?

61 On American Manufacturing

Tench Coxe was appointed assistant Secretary of the Treasury in May 1790. His ideas on the growth of industry in the United States coincided with Alexander Hamilton's. The following is an excerpt from a speech Coxe gave in 1787, a few years before Hamilton developed his five-part financial program for the economic growth of the United States.

READING FOCUS

1. What reasons did Coxe advance for the importance of developing manufacturing after the Revolution?
2. Why did some people oppose the growth of manufacturing?
3. What role did Coxe expect immigrants from Europe to play in the growth of American manufacturing?

Providence has bestowed upon the United States of America means of happiness as great and numerous as are enjoyed by any country in the world. A soil fruitful and varied—a healthful climate—mighty rivers and seas abounding with fish are the great advantages for which we are indebted to a beneficent Creator.

Agriculture, manufacturing, and commerce, naturally arising from these sources, offer to our industrious citizens certain subsistence and innumerable opportunities of acquiring wealth.

The situation of America before the Revolution was very unfavorable to manufacturing. Some manufacturing was carried on with great advantage. But in our colonial situation our progress was very slow, and indeed, the necessity of attention to manufactures was not so urgent as it has become since we won independence. We need to employ those whom the decline of shipping has deprived of their usual occupations. We also need the certainty of supplies in the time of war.

Factories which can be run by watermills, windmills, fire, and horses are not burdened with any heavy expense of boarding, lodging, clothing, and paying workmen. And they supply the force of hands to a great extent without taking our people from agriculture. By wind and water machines we can make pig and bar iron, nail rods, tire, sheet-iron, sheet-copper, sheet brass, anchors, meal of all kinds, gunpowder, writing, printing and hanging paper, snuff, linseed oil, boards, plank, and scantling;

Adapted from A View of the United States of America, _1794._

and they assist us in finishing scythes, sickles, and woolen cloths. Strange as it may appear, they also card, spin, and even weave, it is said, by water in the European factories. Bleaching and tanning must not be omitted, while we are speaking of the usefulness of water.

The lovers of mankind, supported by experienced physicians and the opinions of enlightened politicians, have objected to manufactures as unfavorable to the health of the people. I give this humane and important consideration its full weight. Indeed, it furnishes an equal argument against several other occupations by which we obtain our comforts and promote our agriculture. The painting business, for instance, reclaiming marshes, clearing swamps, the culture of rice and indigo, and some other employment are even more fatal to those who are engaged in them.

Emigration from Europe will also assist us in developing manufacturing. The blessings of civil and religious liberty in America and the oppressions of most foreign governments, the lack of employment at home and the expectations of profit here, curiosity, domestic unhappiness, civil wars, and various other circumstances will bring many manufacturers to this asylum [refuge] for mankind. Ours will be their industry, and, what is of still more consequence, ours will be their skill.

READING REVIEW

1. List the three areas of work in which Americans could make a living and acquire wealth.
2. List two reasons why Coxe said the development of manufacturing was important.
3. (a) Why did some people oppose the encouragement of manufacturing? (b) How did Coxe respond to them?
4. Explain the reasons why Coxe felt immigrants would help American manufacturing develop.

62 An Attack on Jay's Treaty

When President Washington sent John Jay to Britain, it was hoped that Jay would be able to work out a treaty that would peacefully settle the disagreements between the United States and Britain. When the terms of Jay's Treaty were made known, they aroused a storm of protest. Many of the attacks against the treaty came from the followers of Jefferson. These opponents felt that Jay had gained nothing and had actually betrayed America's ally, France. The following excerpt is from an essay written by Robert Livingston in 1795.

READING FOCUS

1. Why did Livingston think that Jay should have been able to get better terms from the British?
2. What previous treaty with the United States had Britain already violated by not evacuating the western posts?
3. Why was June 1796, too late a date for the British to evacuate the western posts?

Britain, on the day of the signature of the treaty, was involved in a war with the French in Europe. In the whole course of this war, Britain had experienced continued defeats and disgraces. Its treasures were wasted upon allies that either deserted Britain or were too feeble to give it aid. Britain's debt had grown to the enormous sum of three hundred millions. Its Navy could only be manned by the most destructive burdens upon its commerce. Its manufactures were declining. Its fleets were unable to protect British trade, which had suffered unexampled losses. And while Britain was sinking under its burdens, France was making stronger its government and growing so rapidly in strength, reputation, and vigor, as to threaten Britain's existence as a nation.

The United States was, on the other hand, in the highest prosperity. Its numbers had doubled since the United States had successfully measured swords with Britain. The United States possessed men, arms, military stores, and an ally France, who was alone too powerful for her enemies. Sweden and Denmark, who had received insults from Britain, were ready to make a common cause with France. As the navies of Britain and France were nearly balanced, the weight of America, had she been forced into the war, would have turned the scale and completed the ruin of British commerce.

And, indeed, so fully satisfied were the Americans, of every party, of the superiority of our situation, that a favorable conclusion to Mr. Jay's negotiation was not in doubt.

Adapted from Examination of the Treaty of Amity, Commerce and Navigation, Between the United States and Great Britain, *by Cato [Robert Livingston's pen name], 1795.*

Colonists, angered at terms of the treaty he negotiated, hang John Jay in effigy.

Following the War for Independence, the British nation, in direct violation of the Treaty of Paris, refused to surrender the western posts. The British extended the limits of their control. They possessed the Indian trade, and stimulated the Indians to ravage our frontiers. British officers even accompanied them in their attacks.

It was necessary for the honor of the United States to demand a delivery of the posts—reparation for the loss of trade—a compensation for the expense of the war the British had excited with the Indians—a public punishment of the British subjects who had personally appeared in arms against us. A final demand was the removal from office of Lord Dorchester, who had, in his address to the Indians, encouraged them to violate the treaty of peace. Mr. Jay was thought the properest person to make this demand. Let us see how far he has justified that sentiment, in fulfilling his duty with respect to evacuation of western posts.

By the 2nd Article of the Jay treaty, the British promised to evacuate the western posts by the 1st of June, 1796. By the Treaty of Paris, in 1782, they had promised to evacuate with all convenient speed. All that the Jay Treaty does with respect to the western posts is less than we were entitled to by the Treaty of Paris. Surely we might expect better security than a mere promise from a nation which has already shown, in their violation of the past, the little reliance that can be placed on their future engagements. But are we not at this moment at war with Indians? Is not this war attended with much expense to the nation, and much private distress? Is not the blood of our citizens daily shed? These evils must continue as long as the posts are in the hands of the British. . . .

If it is said that these terms were the best that could be obtained by Mr. Jay, I boldly deny the assertion.

READING REVIEW

1. What were conditions like in the United States when Jay was sent to negotiate with the British?
2. What country was America's powerful ally in 1795?
3. What treaty had the British violated by not evacuating the western posts following the War for Independence?
4. List the four demands that Livingston felt Jay should have made of the British.
5. According to some historians, the United States either had to approve Jay's Treaty or go to war with Britain. If you were a Senator, would you have voted for or against the Treaty? Explain your answer.

63 The First American Political Parties

Washington and many other government leaders did not want to see the development of political parties, calling them factions. Moreover, the Constitution made no provision for political parties. Yet within just a few years they developed. These political parties reflected the different attitudes Americans held about the nation and how it should be governed.

In this selection, William Winterbotham, an English minister, wrote about the two political parties in 1795. Note that Winterbotham used the term *republicans* to describe most Americans, not to indicate a specific political party. He meant that most Americans favored a government in which ultimate power rested with the people, not with a monarch or any other ruler.

READING FOCUS

1. What were the characteristics of the two political parties?
2. How did British actions aid the Anti-Federalist party?

One cartoonist's view of Jefferson's "Anti-Federalist Club"

With respect to the state of politics in America, they have among them a few people who secretly favor a monarch. There are also some English people settled in the large towns, whom the Americans regard as unreasonably prejudiced against their government.

The rest of the Americans were republicans, but of two different political parties. One party favors an extension rather than a limitation of the powers of the legislative and executive government. It leans more to British than to French politics. Its members want to strengthen the banking, manufacturing, and commercial systems. In this party are almost all the executive officials of government, with the President at their head. The party also includes most members of the state senates and most rich merchants in the large towns. This party is called "Federalist," for two reasons. Its members were the chief planners and supporters of the present federal government and the Constitution of 1787. The second reason is that very skillful series of letters in favor of that Constitution by Mr. Hamilton, known as *The Federalist*. [*The Federalist* letters actually were written by Hamilton, Madison, and Jay.]

The other party is called "Anti-Federalist." This is not because its members are against a federal government. The name simply shows their distinction from the other party. The Anti-Federalists, at the time when the present American Constitution was being drafted, opposed the extensive powers given to government. They wanted the people to have more control over those to whom they delegated authority. This party objects to the salaries given to the officers of government as too large. The Anti-Federalists also dislike the pomp and reserve shown by some officials, including President Washington. His manners and way of living—cold, reserved, and ceremonious, it is said—have tended in some degree to work against the effect of his great abilities and services.

The Anti-Federalists, favoring the French, feel that the English display an insulting arrogance and superiority. This anger toward Great Britain has been greatly increased by the part it is supposed to have taken in encouraging Indian warfare and the hostilities of the

Adapted from William Winterbotham, An Historical, Geographical, Commercial and Philosophical View of the American United States, *Vol. III, 1795.*

Algerians; in seizing the ships and obstructing the commerce of American merchants; and in refusing or neglecting to give up posts upon the Great Lakes. The conduct of the British has certainly given strength to the Anti-Federalist party. It now includes the majority of the people and most members of the state houses of representatives.

It will be easy to guess from this account that the Federalists are the *ins,* and the Anti-Federalists the *outs* of the American government. This is true for the most part, but not entirely.

READING REVIEW

1. According to Winterbotham, what did the term *republican* mean? How does this meaning differ from the meaning of the word today?
2. How did the Federalist party get its name? The Anti-Federalist party?
3. List four characteristics of each political party.
4. Name three ways in which the conduct of the British gave strength to the Anti-Federalists.
5. Do you think Winterbotham's description of the two political parties was objective? Why or why not?

64 In Defense of the Alien and Sedition Acts

The Alien and Sedition Acts were passed at a time when many Americans were fearful of France and its growing power. According to the Federalists, the purpose of these laws was to protect the United States from foreign danger. However, the Democratic-Republicans (the Anti-Federalists), were outraged by these laws. They regarded them as an effort to destroy the Democratic-Republican Party. And they felt these laws were a clear violation of the Constitution. In this selection from 1798, Secretary of State Timothy Pickering defended the laws and argued against criticism of them.

READING FOCUS

1. How did Pickering justify the Alien Act? The Sedition Act?
2. What was Pickering's main concern?

The Alien Law has been bitterly criticized as a direct attack upon our liberties. In fact, it

Adapted from Life of Timothy Pickering, *Vol. III, edited by Charles W. Upham, 1873.*

affects only foreigners who are plotting against us, and has nothing to do with American citizens. It gives authority to the President to order out of the country all aliens he judges dangerous to the peace and safety of the United States, or whom he suspects of treason or secret plots against the government.

All we need to ask is whether, without such a power, any government ever did, or ever can, long protect itself. The objects of this act are strangers, persons who have not been naturalized. They have no interests in common with us. Some are even hostile to this country, while it gives them safety and protection. It is absurd to say that, in providing by law for their removal, the Constitution is violated. For only the ignorant do not know that the Constitution was established for the protection and security of American citizens, not for scheming foreigners.

The Sedition Act has likewise been wrongly criticized as an attack upon freedom of speech and of the press. On the contrary, it allows punishment only for disturbers of order "who write, print, utter, or publish any false, scandalous and malicious writings against the government of the United States, or either house of the Congress of the United States, or the President, with intent to slander or bring them into contempt or disrepute, or to excite against them the hatred of the good people of the United States; or to stir up sedition, or to aid the hostile designs of any foreign nation."

What honest person can justly be alarmed at such a law? Who can wish that unlimited permission be given to publish dangerous lies! People who complain about laws for punishing slander and lies as limiting freedom of speech and of the press might as well complain about laws for punishing assault and murder as limits upon the freedom of people's actions.

Because we have the right to speak and publish our opinions, it does not necessarily follow that we may use it to utter lies about our neighbor or our government. After all, freedom of action does not give us the right to knock down the first person we meet and excuse ourselves from punishment by pleading that we are free persons. We may indeed use our tongues [speak], employ our pens [write], and carry our muskets [guns] whenever we please. But at the same time we must be accountable and punishable for making such "improper use of either as to hurt others in their characters, their persons, or their property."

1. What two powers did the Alien Act give the President of the United States?
2. Who did the Alien Act affect?
3. What was the intent of the Sedition Act?
4. What was Pickering's reason for supporting the Sedition Act?
5. Do you find his arguments in favor of these laws convincing? Why or why not?

65 Federal Supremacy

Today we expect the national government to represent all Americans. We also know that when state laws conflict with the Constitution they may be declared null and void by the Supreme Court. But these ideas were not always a part of the American system of government. They were shaped and defined in the nation's early years by leaders such as Chief Justice John Marshall. In this Supreme Court opinion, written in 1821, Marshall emphasized the supremacy of "the general government"—that is, the federal government.

READING FOCUS

1. What does the United States Constitution say about the sovereignty of the national, or "general," government?
2. What happens to the laws of a state when they conflict with the laws or the Constitution of the national government?
3. What limits are put on the states?

The American States, as well as the American people, have believed that a close and firm union is essential to their liberty and to their happiness. They have been taught by experience that this union cannot exist without a government for the entire nation. They have been taught by the same experience that this government would be useless, that it would disappoint all their hopes, unless it had the sovereignty [supreme power] that belongs to independent nations. Under the influence of this opinion, and taught by experience, the American people, in their state conventions, adopted the present Constitution.

Adapted from Cohens v. Virginia, _6 Wheaton 264 (1821)._

If there were any doubt about this, it should be removed by the declaration that "this Constitution, and the laws of the United States which shall be made in pursuance thereof, . . . shall be the supreme law of the land; . . . anything in the constitution or laws of any state to the contrary notwithstanding."

This is the authoritative language of the American people and of the American states. It clearly marks the distinction between the government of the Union and those of the states. The general government, though limited as to its powers, is supreme with respect to those powers. This principle is a part of the Constitution. Some may deny its necessity, but none can deny its authority.

To this supreme government ample powers are given. The people of the United States have declared that they are given "in order to form a more perfect Union, establish justice, insure domestic tranquillity, provide for the common defense, promote the general welfare, and secure the blessings of liberty" to themselves and their posterity. With the ample powers given to this supreme government for these purposes are connected many specific limitations on the sovereignty of the states.

The powers of the Union on the subjects of war, peace, and commerce, and on many others, are in themselves limitations of the sovereignty of the states. In addition to these, the sovereignty of the states is given up in many instances where it benefits the people. In such cases, no other power may be conferred on Congress than a power to maintain the principles established in the Constitution.

A constitution is framed for ages to come. It is designed to be as nearly immortal as human institutions can be. Its course cannot always be calm. It is exposed to storms and tempests. Its framers would not have been wise leaders if they had not provided it with the means to preserve itself against the dangers it would surely encounter. No government ought to be so weak as to lack ways of carrying out its own laws in the face of dangers.

That the United States forms a single nation has not yet been denied. In war we are one people. In making peace we are one people. In all commercial regulations we are one and the same people. In many other respects the American people are one, and the government, which alone can control and manage their interests in all these respects, is the government of the Union. It is their government, and in these respects they have no other.

America has chosen to be, in many respects and for many purposes, a nation. For all these purposes its government is complete and qualified. The people have declared that it is supreme in the exercise of all the powers given it. It can, in carrying out its given powers, legitimately control all individuals or governments within the American territory. The constitution and laws of a state, when they conflict with the Constitution and laws of the United States, are absolutely void. These states are parts of the United States. They are members of one great empire.

READING REVIEW

1. According to Marshall, who gave the national government its supremacy?
2. How were these "ample powers" given to it?
3. What limits does the Constitution put on the states?
4. Why should a nation be strong enough to carry out its own laws in the face of dangers?

66 A Dissenting Voice

The Federalists no longer controlled the national government after Jefferson was elected President. But John Marshall, a Federalist, was appointed Chief Justice of the United States by outgoing President John Adams in 1801. Marshall served as Chief Justice for 34 years, and during his long term in office Justice Marshall made the Supreme Court a powerful branch of the nation's government.

Marshall's views on the need for a strong central government were not shared by Jefferson and the Republicans. When Marshall died in 1835, the New York *Evening Post* printed this article on his death.

READING FOCUS

1. What view of Marshall the man was expressed?
2. What view of Marshall the Chief Justice was expressed?

The Philadelphia papers of yesterday bring us news of the death of Chief Justice John Marshall, of Virginia, in his eightieth year. He kept

Chief Justice John Marshall

his abilities to the last, and a few days before his death is said to have written an inscription for his own tomb.

Judge Marshall was a man of very considerable talents and great character. His political principles, unfortunately, were of the ultrafederal or aristocratic kind. He was one of those who, like Hamilton, distrusted the virtue and intelligence of the people. He was in favor of a strong general government at the expense of the rights of the states and of the people. His judicial decisions on all questions involving political principles have been all on the side of implied powers and a loose construction of the Constitution. Such also has been the tendency of all his writings.

That he was sincere in these views we do not doubt, nor do we doubt that he truly loved his country. But no one can deny that he has been, all his life long, a stumbling block in the way of democratic principles. Therefore, his position at the head of an important court has always been to us a violation of the very first principles of democracy and most unfortunate. That he has at long last been removed from that position is reason for satisfaction. At the same time we express regret at the death of a good and worthy man.

READING REVIEW

1. What statements indicate the article appeared in a newspaper that followed Republican rather than Federalist thinking?
2. With which statement, if any, do you most strongly disagree?

Adapted from the New York Evening Post, *July 8, 1835.*

CHAPTER 10 The Nation's Growth
(1801-1817)

67 How the Louisiana Purchase Changed America

In 1803 Jefferson solved the problem of frontier trade on the Mississippi River by making a "noble bargain"—the purchase of the Louisiana Territory from France. Not until the Lewis and Clark expedition returned, however, did most Americans have even a vague idea of what they had gained.

John Bakeless, author and editor, considered the significance of this purchase and the expedition that explored the vast new territory.

READING FOCUS
1. According to Bakeless, why was the Louisiana Purchase the "making of the modern United States"?
2. How did the Louisiana Purchase promote feelings of national unity in the United States?
3. Why did so few white explorers travel in this territory?

The Louisiana Purchase has been called "the greatest real estate bargain in history." That judgment is probably correct. At any rate, it would be hard to think of a better bargain, though the United States has always done pretty well in its real estate deals. Manhattan Island wasn't a bad buy. Neither was Alaska nor the Gadsden Purchase.

But the Louisiana Purchase was much more than a smart bargain in real estate. It was really the making of the modern United States. Or, if that is putting it too strongly, it was one of half a dozen events without which there would never have been anything like the present United States.

Adapted from "History's Greatest Real Estate Bargain" by John Bakeless in The American Story, edited by Earl Schenck Miers.

The Louisiana Purchase made it possible for the United States eventually to become a two-ocean world power. It gave us control of some of the most fertile land and some of the richest mines in the world. It gave us control of the Mississippi River, which, in the days before transportation by air and rail, was a vital transportation route. Thus the Louisiana Purchase united our country as nothing else could have done. The West—in those days that meant Kentucky and the country around it—decided to stick with the United States.

Before the Purchase there had been continual trouble. Farm products could be sold only by sending them down the Mississippi, but the Spaniards controlled New Orleans. Western Pennsylvania even rose in armed rebellion—the Whisky Rebellion—which had to be put down. There was always the chance that the westerners might leave the United States entirely and throw in their lot with Spain. Even Daniel Boone had been forced to leave the country he had opened up and settle in Missouri, then part of what was called "Louisiana." Boone was even, for a time, an official of the Spanish government in Missouri.

But when the Louisiana Purchase made the Mississippi, as well as the vast stretch of country reaching to the Rockies, firmly American, the United States could turn its back on the Atlantic world and forget Europe's quarrels for at least a century. We could now develop our own immense resources and internal trade without being held back by tariffs between the states or frontier jealousies. We could provide for a growing population.

The strange thing is that in 1803 nobody quite knew what the United States had bought. North America had already been crossed overland, but not through this territory. Clearly, Mr. Jefferson thought, the thing to do was to send an expedition up the Missouri River to its source. Nobody knew where the source was, but it simply had to be somewhere in the Rocky Mountains. Then, if the expedition crossed the Rocky Mountains alive, it could go beyond the Purchase territory, down the Columbia River to the Pacific coast—that is, if it could find the Columbia. Adventurous Mountain Men knew where the river's mouth was. A few of them had gone some distance up its length. Beyond that—no one knew.

The things that Lewis and Clark discovered in the Louisiana Purchase were stranger and more valuable than anything imagined. They

American negotiators sign the Louisiana Purchase treaty in Paris, April 30, 1803.

found a wonderful stretch of fertile land, the enormous plains, the towering Rockies, buffalo herds, grizzly bears, trees towering 200 feet [61 meters] in the air, unknown rivers, and strange plants.

The Lewis and Clark expedition told America for the first time what it had acquired by its great Purchase. After it came trappers, traders, soldiers, settlers, farmers, and ranchers who laid the foundations for the America of today.

READING REVIEW

1. Name two sources of trouble the West had encountered before the Purchase.
2. How did the Purchase allow the United States to "forget Europe's quarrels"?
3. Did the majority of Americans realize the significance of the Louisiana Purchase in 1803? Why or why not?
4. What were some of the things Lewis and Clark discovered on their expedition?

68 Exploring the Louisiana Purchase

The Lewis and Clark Expedition left its winter camp near present-day Bismarck, North Dakota, in the spring of 1805. The explorers continued up the Missouri River enroute to the Pacific Ocean. On May 14, the expedition had two experiences that left the men badly shaken. Meriwether Lewis recounted these two incidents. Notice that Lewis did not spell all the words as they are spelled today.

READING FOCUS

1. What were the two experiences that left the explorers badly shaken?
2. Why were the contents of the canoe important to the success of the Expedition?

Tuesday, May 14th, 1805

Some fog on the river this morning, which is a very rare occurrence. The country much as it was yesterday with this difference—that the bottoms are somewhat wider. Passed some high black bluffs. Saw immence herds of buffaloe today, also elk, deer, wolves, and antelopes. Passed three large creeks—one on the right, and two others on the left side, neither of which had any runing water.

Capt. Clark walked on shore and killed a very fine buffaloe cow. I felt an inclination to eat some veal and walked on shore and killed a

From "A Day With Lewis and Clark" from The American Reader *by Paul M. Angle.*

very fine buffaloe calf and a large woolf. The Woolf was much the whitest I had seen, it was quite as white as wool of the common sheep. One of the party wounded a brown bear very badly, but being alone did not think proper to pursue him.

In the evening the men in two of the rear canoes discovered a large brown bear lying in the open grounds about 300 paces from the river. Six of them went out to attack him, all good hunters. They took the advantage of a small rise of ground which concealed them and got within 40 paces of him. Two of them reserved their fires as had been previously planned. The four others fired nearly at the same time and put each his bullet through him. Two of the balls passed through the bulk of both lobes of his lungs.

In an instant this monster ran at them with open mouth. The two who had reserved their fires discharged their pieces at him as he came towards them. Boath of them struck him, one only slightly and the other fortunately broke his shoulder. This however only retarded the bear's motion for a moment.

The men unable to reload their guns took to flight, the bear pursued and had very nearly overtaken them before they reached the river. Two of the party betook themselves to a canoe, and the others seperated and concealed themselves among the willows. Reloading their pieces, each discharged his piece at him as they had an opportunity. They struck him several times again but the guns served only to direct the bear to them.

In this manner he pursued two of them seperately so close that they were obliged to throw themselves into the river altho' the bank was nearly twenty feet perpendicular. So enraged was this animil that he plunged into the river only a few feet behind the second man he had forced to take refuge in the water. Finally one of those who still remained on shore shot him through the head and killed him. They then took him on shore and butchered him. They found eight balls had passed through him in different directions. The bear being old, the flesh was indifferent not tasty. They therefore only took the skin and fleece, the latter made us several gallons of oil.

It was after the sun had set before these come up with us, where we had halted by an occurrence, which I have now to describe. Altho' the occurrence happily passed without ruinous injury, I cannot recollect it but with the utmost fear and horror. This is the upsetting and narrow escape of the white perogue [canoe].

It happened unfortunately for us this evening that Charbono was at the helm of this perogue, instead of Drewyer, who had previousely steered her. Charbono cannot swim and is perhaps the most timid waterman in the world. Perhaps it was equally unluckey that Capt. C. [Clark], and myself were both on shore at that moment, a circumstance which rarely happened; and tho' we were on the shore opposite to the perogue, were too far distant to be heard or to do more than remain spectators of its fate.

In this perogue were embarked our papers, instruments, books, medicine, a great part of our merchandize and in short almost every article indispensibly necessary to further the views, or insure the success of the enterprize in which we are now launched to the distance of 2200 miles. Surfice it to say, that the perogue was under sail when a sudon squal [sudden gust] of wind struck her obiquely [at an angle], and turned her considerably.

The steersman alarmed, instead of puting her before the wind, lufted her up into it. The wind was so violent that it drew the brace of the squarsail out of the hand of the man who was attending it, and instantly upset the perogue and would have turned her completely topsaturva [upside down], had it not have been for the resistance made by the oarning [awning] against the water.

In this situation Capt. C. and myself both fired our guns to attract the attention if possible of the crew and ordered the halyards [ropes used to raise or lower sails] to be cut and the sail hawled in, but they did not hear us. Such was the crewman's confusion and consternation [fear] at this moment, they they suffered the perogue to lye on her side for half a minute before they took the sail in. The perogue then wrighted but had filled within an inch of the gunwals [upper edge of the ship's side]. Charbono still crying to his god for mercy, had not yet recollected the rudder. Nor could the repeated orders of the bowsman, Cruzat, bring him to his recollection. Cruzat finally threatened to shoot him instantly if he did not take hold of the rudder and do his duty.

The waves by this time were runing very high, but the fortitude, resolution, and good conduct of Cruzat saved her. He ordered two of the men to throw out water with some kettles

In this Charles Russell painting Captain Lewis watches as Sacagawea (Charbono's wife) is reunited with her Shoshone relatives.

that fortunately were convenient, while himself and two others rowed her ashore, where she arrived scarcely above the water. We now took every article out of her and lay them to drane as well as we could for the evening, baled out the canoe and secured her. There were two other men beside Charbono on board who could not swim, and who of course must also have perished had the perogue gone to the bottom.

READING REVIEW

1. Summarize the attack on the large brown bear.
2. Describe the capsizing and righting of the perogue, or canoe.
3. What man was responsible for saving the perogue?
4. Why would the loss of the perogue, and especially its cargo, have been a disaster for the Lewis and Clark Expedition?

69 Opposition to the Embargo

Josiah Quincy was a Federalist who represented Massachusetts in Congress during the embargo crisis of 1807-09. He was a strong and vocal opponent of the embargo. Quincy felt that the embargo was doing great economic damage to the United States as a whole, and especially to the shipping interests of his native New England. He also believed that if the embargo was not repealed, the people would soon openly rebel and resist the law.

In the following speech before Congress, Quincy gave some of his views on the embargo.

READING FOCUS

1. What were the two important characteristics of the embargo as stated by Quincy?
2. How did the embargo affect different groups of citizens?

The entire nation is suffering under a most serious oppression, the embargo. All the business of the nation is in disorder. All the hopes of the people are frustrated. All the nation's industry is at a standstill. Its many products hastening to the market are stopped in their course. With every passing hour the desire of the citizens to resist the embargo increases.

The embargo, which holds in its crippling grip all the hopes of this nation, has two important characteristics: it hurts all Americans, and nothing like it has ever been tried before. Every interest in the nation is affected by the

"Ograbme" is embargo spelled backwards.

embargo. The merchant, the farmer, the planter, the craftsman, the laboring poor—all are sinking under its weight. The embargo especially hurts the poor. From those who have much, it takes something. But from those who have little, it takes all. What hope is left to the hard-working poor when they lose their jobs because of the embargo?

The embargo affects the hopes and interests of all the people. But it is also remarkable because it has never been tried before. In fact it never before entered into the human imagination! There is nothing like it in all of history or in the tales of fiction. All the habits of our mighty nation are at once frustrated. All property of our people sinks in value. Five million Americans are trapped by this embargo. They can neither travel nor trade outside our once free country.

I ask whether the embargo, which affects so many Americans and which is so new, and which interferes with the desires and interests of the whole nation, ought to be left in effect. Who can predict when the British and French will honor American trading rights and bring an end to the embargo? And who can guarantee that the patience of the citizens will not soon give out and lead them to resist the embargo?

Adapted from Josiah Quincy, "How Jefferson's Embargo Paralyzed Trade," in America: Great Crises in Our History Told by Its Makers, *Vol. V, 1925.*

READING REVIEW

1. **(a)** How did the embargo affect business and industry in the United States? **(b)** How did it affect poor people?
2. What two characteristics of the embargo did Quincy point out?
3. Quincy was most interested in protecting the merchants. Why do you think he mentioned the other groups in his speech?

70 A War Hawk's Demands

Henry Clay, one of the great speakers in American history, represented Kentucky in the United States Senate and House of Representatives several times between 1806 and 1852. As a young senator in 1810, Clay was one of the leading War Hawks who called for war with Great Britain.

The following is an excerpt from the speech Clay delivered in the Senate on Washington's birthday, February 22, 1810. It clearly represented the attitude of the War Hawks.

READING FOCUS

1. Why did Clay choose to go to war with Great Britain instead of France?
2. Why did some Americans oppose war with Britain?
3. Why did Clay want the United States to gain control of Canada?

No man in the nation wants peace more than I. But I prefer the troubled ocean of war, with all its disasters and desolation, to the calm decaying pool of dishonorable peace. If we can settle our differences with one of the enemies—Britain or France—I should prefer that one to be Britain. But if with neither, and we are forced into a selection of our enemy, then I choose war with Britain. I believe her first in aggression and her injuries and insults to us were extremely cruel in character.

Britain stands out in her outrage on us, by her violation of the sacred personal rights of American freemen, in the arbitrary and lawless imprisonment of our seamen.

From Annals of Congress, *11th Congress, 1st Session, (1809-1810).*

But we [Congress] are asked for the means of supporting the war, and those who oppose it triumphantly appeal to the empty vaults of the Treasury. We have, I am credibly informed, in the city and vicinity of New Orleans alone, public property sufficient to pay off the debt noted in the Treasury report. And are we to regard as nothing the patriotic offers so often made by the States, to spend their last cent, and risk their last drop of blood, in the preservation of our neutral privileges?

It is said, however, that it is hopeless to go to war with Great Britain. If we go to war, we are to estimate not only the benefit to be gained for ourselves, but the injury to be done the enemy. The conquest of Canada is in your power. I trust I shall not be thought to be bold when I state that I truly believe that the militia of Kentucky are alone competent to place Montreal and Upper Canada at your feet. Is it nothing to the pride of the King, to have the last of the immense North American possessions held by him in the beginning of his reign taken from him? Is it nothing to us to put out the torch that lights up Indian warfare? Is it nothing to gain the entire fur trade connected with Canada?

War with Great Britain will deprive her of those supplies of raw materials and provisions which she now obtains from the United States.

A certain portion of military enthusiasm or spirit is necessary for the protection of the country. The withered arm and wrinkled brow of the illustrious founders of our freedom [Soldiers of the War for Independence] are sad signs that they will shortly be removed from us. Their deeds of glory and renown will then be felt only through history books. We shall want the presence and living example of a new race of heroes to supply their places, and to encourage us to preserve what they achieved.

If we surrender without a struggle to maintain our rights, we forefeit the respect of the world and (what is worse) of ourselves.

READING REVIEW

1. Why did Clay favor war against Britain?
2. Why did some Americans oppose war with Britain?
3. (a) List three reasons why Clay wanted the United States to gain control of Canada. (b) Did Clay think it would be difficult to conquer Canada? (c) Cite evidence from the reading to support your answer.

Senator Henry Clay

4. Do you think Clay was more interested in defending the neutral rights of American ships and sailors or with gaining control of Canada? Explain your answer.

71 A Request for a Declaration of War

After many years of tension over Indian uprisings incited by the British, over western land hunger, and over resentment of British impressment policies, the United States finally declared war on Great Britain in 1812. President Madison sent a war message to Congress on June 1. Days of heated debate between the War Hawks, on the one hand, and their opponents, on the other hand. After a close vote, Congress declared war against Great Britain on June 18. The Senate vote was 19 to 13 for war; in the House of Representatives the vote was 79 to 49.

READING FOCUS

1. What reasons did Madison give for declaring war against Great Britain?
2. What was the intent of Great Britain's actions?

President James Madison

British ships have continually violated the American flag on the great highway of nations, and have seized and carried off persons sailing under its protection. Britain has done this, not as a wartime right, founded on the law of nations, against an enemy, but in exercising its power over British subjects. British authority is thus extended to neutral ships.

If the seizure of British subjects could be regarded as a wartime right, the laws of war—which forbid an article of captured property to be awarded without a regular investigation before a court—would demand the fairest trial where the sacred rights of persons were at issue. In place of such a trial, these rights are subject to the will of every petty commander.

Thousands of American citizens under the safeguard of public law and of their national flag have been torn from the country and from everything dear to them. They have been dragged on board warships of a foreign nation. They may be exiled to distant and deadly lands. They may have to risk their lives in the battles of their oppressors, and even fight against their own people.

Against these injustices the United States has objected in vain. It has formally assured the British government of its readiness to enter into arrangements that could not be rejected if the recovery of British subjects were the real

and the sole object. But this message was received by Britain and not replied to.

British ships have also violated the rights and the peace of our coasts. They harass our trade. They spill American blood within the waters under our territorial control. The principles and rules enforced by Britain against armed ships disturbing its trade are well known. When called on, nevertheless, by the United States to punish the greater offenses committed by its own ships, the British government has instead given the commanders of these ships additional marks of honor and confidence.

It has become certain that Great Britain intends to destroy the trade of the United States. This has resulted not because the United States interfered with the wartime rights of Great Britain, not because it supplied the wants of Britain's enemies, but because the United States is in the way of the monopoly which Britain wants for its own trade and navigation.

In reviewing the conduct of Great Britain toward the United States, our attention is necessarily drawn to the warfare just started by the Indians on one of our extensive frontiers. In this warfare, both women and children are killed and the Indians use brutal fighting methods. It is difficult to account for the activity among tribes in constant communication with British traders and garrisons without connecting their hostility with that influence.

We see, in essence, on the side of Great Britain a state of war against the United States, and on the side of the United States a state of peace toward Great Britain.

Whether the United States shall continue not to do anything about these accumulating wrongs or use force in defense of its national rights is a solemn question which the Constitution wisely leaves to the legislative branch of the government. In recommending it to their early consideration, I am sure that the decision will be worthy of the enlightened and patriotic councils of a virtuous and powerful nation.

READING REVIEW

1. According to the President, what two things have the British done to violate American rights?
2. Why, according to the President, would American sailors benefit if war were declared?
3. If you had been in Congress at this time, how would you have voted? Cite passages from Madison's speech to support your decision.

Adapted from James D. Richardson (comp.), Messages and Papers of the Presidents, *Vol. I, 1896.*

72 Bostonians' Objections to War

The close vote in Congress on President Madison's war message reflected Federalist New England's disapproval of the War of 1812. As the conflict continued, this disapproval and opposition to the war increased. By 1814 feelings in New England against the war were so strong that a convention met in Hartford, Connecticut, to consider secession. This Boston newspaper editorial, written in 1813, clearly showed the growing opposition in New England to the war.

READING FOCUS

1. Why did New Englanders object to the war?
2. Whom did they blame for it?

The feeling is growing by the hour that we are in a condition no better in relation to the South than that of a conquered people. We have been forced, without the least necessity, to give up our habits, occupations, means of happiness, and means of support. We are plunged into a war without feeling that there has been sufficient cause for it. We are obliged to fight the battles of a conspiracy which, while pretending to defend republican equality, aims at trampling into the dust the weight, influence, and power of trade.

We, whose ships were the training ground of sailors, are insulted with the pretense of a devotion to sailors' rights by those whose region knows nothing of navigation beyond the size of a ferryboat or an Indian canoe. We have no interest in fighting this sort of war, at this time and under these circumstances, at the command of Virginia.

The consequences must be either that the southern states must drag the northern states farther into the war or we must drag them out of it, or the union of our nation will break apart. We must no longer listen to those foolish outcries against a separation of the states. It is an event we do not desire. But the states are separated in fact when one section continues in actions fatal to the interests and opposed to the opinions of another section because of a geographical majority.

Adapted from Columbian Sentinel *(Boston), Jan. 13, 1813.*

READING REVIEW

1. Give two reasons why the New Englanders objected to war.
2. According to the author, what were the two alternatives from which the nation had to choose at this time?
3. Why did the author not consider a "separation of the states" as an alternative?
4. What did the editorial indicate about national feeling—or the lack of it—at this time?

73 A Kentuckian at the Battle of New Orleans

The most important battle of the War of 1812, the Battle of New Orleans, was fought after the war was over. Because of slow communications, news of the peace treaty did not reach New Orleans in time to stop the battle. This battle made Andrew Jackson a national hero, and Americans gained a victory that made them proud.

To the people of Kentucky, the battle had special importance. A group of soldiers from that state had fought to take back Detroit from the British late in 1812. When they were defeated in January 1813, near the Raisin River, many of those who surrendered were killed by Great Britain's Indian allies.

READING FOCUS

1. Why was this battle so important to the soldiers from Kentucky?
2. From this account, what seems to you to be the major differences between war then and war today?

Colonel Smiley, from Bardstown, was the first one who gave us orders to fire. Then, I reckon, there was a pretty considerable noise. Then the heavy iron cannon, toward the river, and some thousands of small arms, joined in and made the ground shake under our feet. As soon as the firing began, Captain Patterson came running along. He jumped upon the defensive wall and stopping a moment to look through the darkness, he shouted, "Shoot low, boys! shoot low! rake them! They're comin' on their all fours!"

Adapted from William Matthews and Dixon Wecter, Our Soldiers Speak, 1775-1918.

Jackson's men defeat the British at the battle of New Orleans.

The official report said the action lasted two hours and five minutes, but it did not seem half that length of time to me. It was so dark that little could be seen, until just about the time the battle ended. The morning had dawned to be sure, but the smoke was so thick that everything seemed to be covered up in it. Our troops did not seem to fear any danger, but loaded and fired as fast as they could, talking, swearing, and joking all the time. All ranks and sections were soon broken up. After the first shot, everyone loaded and fired away on his own. Henry Spillman did not load and fire quite so often as some of the rest, but every time he did fire he would go up to the defensive wall, look over until he could see something to shoot at, and then take aim and fire. Lieutenant Ashby was very busy and it was evident that the River Raisin was on his mind all the time. He kept running about. Every now and then he would call out, with an oath, "We'll pay you now for the River Raisin! We'll give you something to remember the River Raisin!" When the British had come up to the opposite side of the defensive wall, having no gun, he picked up an empty barrel and threw it at them. Then finding an iron bar, he jumped upon the wall and threw that at them.

It was near the end of the firing. About the time that I saw three or four men carrying away the body of one of the Tennessee men, a white flag was raised on the opposite side of the defense wall and the firing stopped.

The white flag was raised about ten or twelve feet [3 or 4 meters] from where I stood, close to the defensive wall and a little to the right. As soon as it was seen, we stopped firing. Just then the wind picked up a little and blew the smoke off, so that we could see the field. It then appeared that the flag had been raised by a British officer. I was told he was a major. He stepped over the defensive wall and came into our lines.

A good many others came in just about the same time. Among them I noticed a very neatly dressed young man, standing on the edge of the defensive wall, offering his hand, as if asking for some one to help him. He looked to be about nineteen or twenty years old. He held his rifle in one hand, while he was offering the other. I took hold of his rifle and set it down, and then giving him my hand, he jumped down quite lightly. As soon as he got down, I noticed a red spot of blood on his clean white underjacket. I asked him if he was wounded. He said that he was, and he feared pretty badly. Captain Farmer came up, and said to him, "Let me help you, my man!" The captain and myself then helped him to take off his things. He begged us not to take his canteen, which contained his water. We told him we did not wish to take anything but what was in his way. Just then one of the Tennesseans, who had run down to the river for water as soon as the firing stopped, came along with some in a tin coffeepot. The wounded man looked at him and asked if he would please give him a drop. "O! Yes," said the Tennessean, "I will treat you to anything I've got." The young man took the coffeepot and swallowed two or three mouthfuls. He then handed back the pot, and in an instant, we saw him falling backward. We eased him down against the side of a tent, when he gave two or three gasps and was dead. He had been shot through the chest.

When the smoke had cleared away and we could obtain a clear view of the field, it looked, at first glance, like a sea of blood. It was not blood itself which gave this appearance but the red coats in which the British soldiers were dressed. Straight out before our position the field was completely covered with bodies. In some places they were lying in piles, one on top of the other.

When we first got a clear view of the field in our front, individuals could be seen in every possible position. Some lying quite dead, others mortally wounded, pitching and tumbling about in the agonies of death. Some had their heads shot off, some their legs, some their arms. Some were laughing, some crying, some groaning, and some screaming. There was every variety of sight and sound. Among those that were on the ground, however, there were some that were neither dead nor wounded. A great many had thrown themselves down behind piles of dead soldiers for protection. As the firing stopped, these men were every now and then jumping up and either running off or coming in and giving themselves up.

READING REVIEW

1. What feelings did the soldier who wrote this account seem to have about the enemy?
2. How would you describe Ashby's actions?
3. List two differences between war then and war today.

CHAPTER
11 Gaining Prosperity and Respect
(1817–1825)

74 A Keelboat Journey

As Americans' feelings of pride in their new nation grew in the early 1800's, the United States was enjoying increasing prosperity. One sign of the nation's strong economic development was improved methods of transportation. During these years water transportation was especially important. In this selection, Timothy Flint, a missionary and writer, described a journey he took in a keelboat—a shallow riverboat that was used to carry products and goods on inland rivers in the United States. His trip, from Cincinnati, Ohio, to St. Charles, Missouri, took place in 1816.

READING FOCUS

1. What were some of the dangers of keelboat travel?
2. What kind of traveler was the writer?

Our keelboat was between 80 and 90 feet [24 and 27 meters] in length, had a small but comfortable cabin, and carried 17 tons [15 metric tons]. It was an extremely hot afternoon when we left. The river was almost to the top of its banks, and the current was very rapid. We

Adapted from Timothy Flint, Recollections of the Last Ten Years, *1826.*

A family travels to a new home by keelboat.

looked out over a deep, green forest with a richness of plants and trees and a grandeur of size and height, that characterize the forest in this part of Ohio.

We started this trip under favorable signs. We experienced in a couple of hours what has so often been said of all earthly enjoyments—how near to each other are the limits of happiness and trouble. Banks of thunderclouds were on the horizon when we left Cincinnati. They gathered over us, and a violent thunderstorm followed. We had no time to reach the shore before it burst upon us, accompanied by strong gusts of wind. The gale was too violent for us to think of landing on a rugged, rockbound shore. We protected the open part of the boat as well as we could, and began scooping out the water which the boat took in from the waves. We had women passengers on board, whose screams added to the uproar outside. I faced the storm up on the deck, ready to help the "patron," or skipper, to steer the boat. The thunder was continuous, and the air was ablaze with flashes of lightning.

The storm continued to rage for more than an hour. Such storms are always dangerous and sometimes fatal to a small keelboat so heavily loaded down. The patron, who had done this work for many years and who had been, as he said, "boatwrecked" half a dozen times, kept perfectly cool. But his face showed great anxiety. We made it through the storm, however, with no other inconvenience than getting soaked with rain and hearing the frequent claims of our passengers that they would never risk the danger of such a storm again.

Then the sky brightened. As happens to those who depend upon nature for the tone of their minds, our thoughts began to brighten. Our strength and courage to continue our journey were renewed. We landed in the evening near General Harrison's mansion and were well received by him.

READING REVIEW
1. How did Flint describe a keelboat?
2. How did this boat aid in the settlement and beginning of trade in the West?
3. Why were thunderstorms such as the one described by Flint especially dangerous to a keelboat?

The Ohio River port of Cincinnati, 1800

75 A Race Between Two Steamboats

The great age of steamboats on American rivers lasted from the 1820's to the 1860's. And no one has described this colorful period better than Mark Twain, who worked on steamboats as a young man.

Twain, whose real name was Samuel Clemens, took his pen name from the language of steamboat crews. On every steamboat, crew members called "leadsmen" tested the depth of water by using a line marked into segments by pieces of lead. One of these measurements, called "twain," meant 2 fathoms, or 12 feet (3.6 meters). Thus "mark twain," or "by the mark twain," meant that the line showed that the river water was 2 fathoms deep.

In this selection, Mark Twain described a race between two steamboats—the *Boreas* and the *Amaranth.*

READING FOCUS

1. Why was this race between steamboats taking place?
2. What was the outcome of the race?

At night the *Boreas* moved ahead on the river, hardly ever passing a light to indicate a human presence. Mile after mile, the *Boreas* passed thick forest that had never been disturbed by human beings.

An hour after supper the moon came up. Presently the pilot [a person who knew the river well and helped the captain navigate] said:

"By George, yonder comes the *Amaranth!*"

He bent over a speaking tube and said:

"Who's on watch down there?"

A hollow voice rumbled up through the tube in answer:

"I am. Second engineer."

"Good! You want to get busy now, Harry. The *Amaranth's* just turned the point."

The pilot took hold of a rope, jerked it twice and a big bell rang. The pilot shouted down to the sailor on deck:

"Wake up the old man. Tell him the *Amaranth's* coming. And go and call Jim. Tell *him.*"

Adapted from Mark Twain and Charles Dudley Warner, The Gilded Age, *1874.*

"Aye, aye, sir!"

The old man was the captain—he is always called so on steamboats. Jim was the other pilot. Within two minutes both of these men were flying up the pilothouse stairway three steps at a jump.

The three men in the pilothouse began to talk in short, sharp sentences, low and earnestly. As fast as one of them put down the spyglass another took it up. Each time the decision was:

"It's a-gaining!"

The captain spoke through the tube:

"What steam are you carrying?"

"A hundred and forty-two, sir! But it's getting hotter and hotter all the time."

The boat was straining and groaning and shaking like a monster in pain. Both pilots were at work now, one on each side of the wheel, with their coats and vests off, their collars wide open, and the perspiration running down their faces. They were holding the boat so close to the shore that the willow trees swept the rails. The captain put down the spyglass.

"Lord, how the *Amaranth* creeps up on us! I do hate to be beat!"

"Jim," said George, looking straight ahead, "how'll it do to try Murderer's Chute?"

"Well, it's—it's taking chances. We can just barely get through if we hit it exactly right. But it's worth trying. The *Amaranth* don't dare tackle it!"

In another instant the *Boreas* plunged into a crooked creek known as Murderer's Chute, and the *Amaranth's* approaching lights were shut out in a moment. Not a whisper was uttered now, but the three men stared ahead into the shadows and two of them spun the wheel back and forth with anxious watchfulness while the steamer tore along. The chute seemed to come to an end every 50 yards [46 meters], but always opened out in time. Now the end of it was at hand. George tapped the big bell three times. Two leadsmen sprang to their posts, and in a moment their cries were heard.

"By the mark twain!"

"Quar-ter-her-*er-less* twain!"

"Eight *and* a half!"

"Eight feet!"

"Seven-and-a-half!"

A jingling of little bells and the wheels stopped turning. The whistling of the steam was something frightful now. It almost drowned out all other noises.

The boat hesitated—seemed to hold its breath, as did the captain and pilots—and then it began to fall away to the right.

"Now then! Turn the wheel!"

The wheel flew to the left very fast. The swing of the boat lessened and it steadied.

Bang! The boat hit bottom! George shouted through the tube:

"Turn up the steam!"

Pow-wow-chow! The escape pipes belched snowy pillars of steam, the boat ground and surged and trembled.

And away it went, flying up the shore with the whole Mississippi stretching ahead.

No *Amaranth* in sight!

"Ha-ha, boys, we took a couple of tricks that time!" said the captain.

And just at that moment a red glare appeared in the opening of the chute and the *Amaranth* came springing after them!

"Well, I swear!"

The *Amaranth* was within 300 yards [274 meters] of the *Boreas* and still gaining. The old man spoke through the tube:

"What steam is it carrying now?"

"A hundred and sixty-five, sir!"

"How's your wood?"

"Pine all out—cypress half gone—eating up cottonwood like pie!"

"Break into that rosin on the main deck. Pile it in. The boat can pay for it!"

Soon the boat was shaking and screaming more madly than ever. But the *Amaranth's* bow was almost next to the *Boreas's* stern.

"How's your steam now, Harry?"

"Hundred and eighty-two, sir!"

"Break up the casks of bacon in the forward hold! Pile it in! Pour on that turpentine. Drench every stick of wood with it!"

The boat was a moving earthquake by this time.

"How is your steam now"?

"A hundred and ninety-six and still aswell-ing! Carrying every pound it can stand!"

The *Amaranth* drew steadily up till the boats were wheel to wheel. Then they closed up with a heavy jolt and locked together tight and fast in the middle of the big river under the moonlight! A roar and a hurrah went up from the crowded decks of both steamers. All hands rushed to the rails to look and shout and wave their arms. Officers flew here and there cursing and storming, trying to drive the people below deck. Both captains were leaning over their railings, shaking their fists, swearing and threatening. Black columns of smoke rolled up. Two pistol shots rang out, and both captains dodged unhurt. The packed masses of passengers were tossed back and forth while the shrieks of women and children were heard above the terrible noise.

And then there was a booming roar, a thundering crash, and the *Amaranth* dropped loose and drifted helplessly away!

Instantly the fire doors of the *Boreas* were thrown open and men began dashing buckets of water into the furnaces, for it would have been death and destruction to stop the engines with such a head of steam on.

As soon as possible the *Boreas* dropped down to the floating wreck of the *Amaranth* and took off the dead, the wounded, and the unhurt—at least all that could be got at. The whole forward half of the boat was a shapeless ruin. The great chimneys lay crossed on top of it, and underneath were a dozen victims imprisoned alive and screaming for help. While men with axes worked to free these poor fellows, the *Boreas's* boats went about picking up people from the river.

When the boys came down into the main lounge of the *Boreas,* they saw a pitiful sight and heard a world of pitiful sounds. Eleven poor people lay dead and 40 more lay moaning or pleading or screaming.

But these things must not be dwelled upon.

Steamboat racing was a popular sport on the Mississippi River.

The *Boreas* landed its dreadful cargo at the next large town—a cargo amounting by this time to 39 wounded persons and 22 dead bodies. And with these it delivered a list of 96 missing persons that had drowned or otherwise died at the scene of the disaster.

A jury of inquest was held. After due deliberation and inquiry they returned the inevitable American verdict which has been so familiar to our ears all the days of our lives—"Nobody to blame."

READING REVIEW

1. What caused the explosion on the *Amaranth*?
2. Do you agree or disagree with the inquest verdict? Explain your reasoning.

76 Pioneering in Illinois

Between 1791 and 1819, as settlers moved south and west, traveling by river and by road, nine new states joined the Union. By this time, life in the states along the Atlantic coast had become comfortable for most Americans. But conditions were very different for those who went into distant, unsettled areas. In Illinois, for example, life was harsh and demanding as late as the 1830's.

The story in this selection is told by Rebecca Burlend, who left England with her family in 1831. The Burlends bought farmland near Quincy, Illinois. After years of hard work, the family farm prospered enough for Rebecca to travel back to England to visit relatives. This account, written by Rebecca and her son Edward, was published in 1848.

READING FOCUS

1. What kind of help did the Burlends receive from their neighbors?
2. What hardships did they face?

Toward the end of June our three acres [1.2 hectares] of wheat began to look ripe, and we had to consider how we were going to cut and

---

Adapted from Rebecca and Edward Burlend, A True Picture of Emigration, *edited by Milo Milton Quaife.*

gather it. We had no sickles, nor were any to be had for less than a dollar each. We therefore, myself and my husband, decided to go to our friend Mr. B. He lent us two sickles, for which we were thankful although they were poor ones. As we were returning home, my husband had the misfortune to stumble over a log. Having a sickle in his hand, he fell on the edge of it with his knee, and cut himself severely. We were then a mile from home, and the wound bled heavily. I bound it up with a handkerchief, and after a little faintness he was able to go on.

The next day, on examining the cut, we found it to be more serious than we had imagined. The symptoms were bad. Instead of being warm and irritated, it was cold and numb. Although we applied lotions, it kept growing worse and worse. The following day it began to swell very much, and to be exceedingly painful. The pain took away my husband's appetite for food, and symptoms of inflammation and fever came on rapidly. After several days, he began to perspire, and his leg had feeling again. A change for the better had taken place. Slowly the bad symptoms disappeared.

I felt myself the happiest woman on earth, although my situation was still difficult. Our wheat was ripe, indeed almost ready to shake. If it was not cut soon, it would be lost. We had no money to hire workers, and my husband could not go out. I was therefore forced to begin myself. I took my eldest child, who was nine, into the field to help me, and left the next in age to take care of his father and baby brother. I worked as hard as my strength would allow. The weather was intolerably hot, so that I was almost melted. In little more than a week, however, we had it all harvested. But the wheat was still not stored away. Left in the burning sun, it was in danger of being dried out. It was absolutely necessary to gather it together right away. Having neither horses nor wagon, we faced another difficulty. The work, however, could not be postponed.

With a little trouble I got two strong rods, and placed a number of sheaves near one end. I then had my young son take hold of the lighter end, and in this manner we gathered the whole of the three acres [1.2 hectares]. My husband had by this time recovered enough to be able to move about with the help of a crutch. He came to the door to show me how to place the sheaves in forming the stack.

The reader may think I am trying to magnify my own labors when I describe how I cut,

Pioneering on the western frontier was a very difficult and often lonely existence.

carried home, and stacked our whole crop of wheat with no other assistance than that of my little boy. But my statements are facts. What is more, I did the work in addition to caring for my young family and sick husband during the hottest part of the year.

Having thrashed and winnowed our wheat, our next consideration was how to sell it. The produce of the three acres [1.2 hectares] might be about 80 bushels [2,819 liters], one fourth of which was not well threshed and was therefore unsalable. My husband took a sample of wheat to Mr. Varley, the storekeeper. He offered us half a dollar per bushel [35 liters], in money, or a few cents more in barter. We borrowed a wagon and a yoke of oxen of one of our neighbors, and carried to the store 50 bushels [1,762 liters].

The first thing we did was to pay our flour account. We next bought two pairs of shoes for myself and my husband. We had intended to buy a little more clothing, but finding the prices so high, we had to give up that intention. For a yard [.9 meter] of common printed calico cloth, they asked half a dollar or a bushel [35 liters] of wheat, and proportionate prices for other goods. We gave 10 bushels [352 liters] of wheat for the shoes.

Our next purchase was a plow, bought in hopes that we should at some time have cattle to draw it, as we were tired of the hoeing system. We also bought two tin milk bowls; these and the plow cost about 20 bushels [705 liters]. We also obtained a few pounds of coffee, and a little flour. The coffee cost us a dollar for four pounds [1.8 kilos]. Thus we laid out the greater part of our first crop of wheat. We had reserved only about 20 bushels [705 liters] for seed. On balancing our account with Mr. Varley, we found we still had about five dollars, which we received in paper money, since coins are very scarce in Illinois.

READING REVIEW

1. **(a)** What problems did Mrs. Burlend face when she tried to harvest the wheat? **(b)** How did she overcome them?
2. Using the reading, draw up three general statements about frontier life that could be supported by evidence in the reading.

77 Westward on the National Road

America's rivers provided an extensive inland water transportation system. But they could not meet all of the nation's transportation needs. A road was needed that would go through the Appalachian Mountains and reach the sparsely settled areas of the West. The National Road, begun in 1811, provided this new and improved land route to the West. Charles Fenno Hoffman, a poet, described what the National Road was like by the year 1833. The "emigrants" he wrote about are the pioneers moving westward that he saw on the road.

Roads helped to open the frontier.

READING FOCUS

1. How did Hoffman describe the road?
2. What was his attitude toward the people he saw on the National Road?

About 30 miles [48 kilometers] from Wheeling, Virginia, we first entered the National Road. It appears to have been originally constructed of large round stones, thrown without much arrangement on the surface of the soil after the road was first leveled. These are now being plowed up, and a thin layer of broken stones is in many places spread over the renewed surface. It yields like a snowdrift to the heavy wheels which cross it.

Even the very best parts of the road that I saw are not to be compared with a Long Island turnpike. Two thirds of the road was worse than any paved road I ever traveled. The ruts are worn so broad and deep by heavy travel that an army of pygmies might march into the depths of the countryside under the cover they would provide.

There is one feature, however, in this national road which is truly fine—I mean the massive stone bridges which form a part of it. When the road crosses a winding creek, they may occur a dozen times within twice as many miles. These bridges are monuments of taste and power that will speak well for the country when the brick towns they bind together have crumbled in the dust.

Adapted from Charles Fenno Hoffman, A Winter in the West, Vol. I, 1835.

Though most westerners generally travel on horseback, one does meet numbers of people on foot on the western side of the Alleghenies. They generally have a knapsack, or light leather bag, hung across their backs, and are often well dressed in a blue coat, gray trousers, and round hat. They travel about 40 miles [64 kilometers] a day.

Those on horseback usually wear an overcoat, fur cap, and green cloth leggings. In addition to a pair of well-filled saddlebags, they very often have strapped to their saddle a convenience you would not expect to find in the wardrobe of a backwoodsman—an umbrella.

But by far the greatest portion of travelers one meets with, not to mention the ordinary stagecoach passengers, consists of teamsters and the emigrants. The teamsters generally use six horses to pull their enormous wagons— stout, heavy-looking beasts. They go about 20 miles [32 kilometers] a day. The lead horses are often ornamented with a number of bells hanging from a square raised framework over their collars. This was originally used to warn others of their approach.

As for the emigrants, it would astonish you to see how they get along. A covered one-horse wagon generally contains all of the goods owned by the family, often consisting of a dozen members. The tools are so high along this western turnpike and horses are so cheap in the region he is going to that the emigrant rarely provides more than one miserable nag to transport his whole family to the Far West. The strength of the poor animal is, of course, half the time unequal to the demand upon it. Therefore, unless it is raining very hard, you will rarely see anyone in the wagon, except perhaps some child who is sick or a mother nursing a young infant. The man of the family walks by the horse, cheering and encouraging him on his way. The woman of the family either walks along with her husband or, leading some weary little child by the hand far behind, tries to keep the rest of her children from dropping behind.

The hardships of such a trip must be a good preparation for the hard life which the new settlers are about to begin. Their horses, of course, frequently give out on the road. And in such large families sickness frequently overtakes some of the members.

READING REVIEW

1. List two things that Hoffman found wrong with the National Road.
2. According to Hoffman, what were the two groups that made up the largest number of travelers?
3. List two good things that Hoffman had to say either about the road itself or the travelers on it.

78 A Plea for an American Language

By 1800 it had become clear that, although Americans spoke English, they spoke and wrote it in their own way. No one encouraged an American style of English more than Noah Webster.

Webster began by writing spellers, grammars, and readers for schoolchildren that stressed American scenes and subjects. He later published a dictionary that helped to standardize American language usage. For instance, it was Webster who chose to use the spelling "or" instead of "our" in words such as "color" and "honor." Webster managed to substitute "jail" for the English "gaol," but he had less success in persuading people to write "wurd" for "word" and "iz" for "is."

Adapted from Noah Webster, An Essay on the Necessity, Advantages and Practicability of Reforming the Mode of Spelling, and of Rendering the Orthography Correspondent to the Pronunciation, *1789.*

READING FOCUS

1. Why did Webster propose the establishment of an American language?
2. Why did he think 1789 was a good time for a change?

Changes in spelling, however small, would encourage the publication of books in our own country. It would make it, in some measure, necessary that all books be printed in America. The English would never copy our spelling rules for their own use. Consequently the same printing of books would not be suitable for both countries.

Besides this, a national language is a bond of national union. Every means should be used to make the people of this country nationalistic, to inspire them with the pride of national character. They may boast of independence and the freedom of their government, yet their opinions are not sufficiently independent. An astonishing respect for the arts and literature of England and a blind imitation of its manners are still common among Americans. Thus a continuing respect for another country turns the attention of Americans from their own interests and prevents their respecting themselves.

I am aware that is is much easier to propose improvements than it is to introduce them. But American is in a most favorable situation for great reforms, and the present time is extremely favorable. The minds of people in this country have been awakened. Unexpected problems have caused them to invent new ways of doing things. The application of new methods has demanded every possible use of wisdom and talents. Attention is roused, the mind expanded, and the intellectual abilities stimulated. Here people are prepared to receive improvements which would be rejected by nations whose habits have not been shaken by similar events.

Let us then use the present moment to establish a national language as well as a national government. As an independent people, our reputation abroad demands that in all things we should be federal, be national. If we do not respect ourselves, other nations will not respect us. In short, every American should realize that to neglect the means of commanding respect abroad is treason against the character and dignity of a brave and independent people.

READING REVIEW
1. According to Webster, what would changes in spelling encourage?
2. In Webster's view, why would a national language encourage a bond of union?
3. Why did Webster think 1789 was a good time to make a change?

A Mandan Village

79 A Description of the Indians West of the Appalachians

During the late 1700's and early 1800's, Americans moved into the lands beyond the Appalachian Mountains in search of farmland. Some of the early explorers into the lands west of the Appalachians left written accounts of the Indians they encountered. Jonathan Carver of Connecticut was one of these explorers. During the 1760's, he explored the region that is today the north central part of the United States. The following account from Carver's journal described the Indians he met.

READING FOCUS

1. What were some characteristics of the Indians' civilization?
2. What types of homes did the Indians build?
3. According to Carver, what was the greatest fault of the Indians' character?

The Indians, in general, are slender and rather tall. Their skin is of a reddish or copper color. Their eyes are large and black, and their hair is of the same hue, but very rarely is it curled. They have good teeth, and their breath is as sweet as the air they draw in. Their cheekbones are raised, but more so in the women than the men. The women are not quite so tall as the European women. However, you frequently meet with good faces and agreeable persons among them.

The men of every nation differ in their dress very little from each other, except those who trade with the Europeans. These exchange their furs for blankets, shirts, and other appar-

Adapted from J. Carver, Travels Through The Interior Parts of North-America, *1778.*

el, which they wear as much for ornament as necessity. Those who wear shirts never make them tight either at the wrist or collar; this would be uncomfortable and confining to them. They paint their faces red and black, which they regard as greatly ornamental. They also paint themselves when they go to war.

The women wear a covering of some kind from the neck to the knees. Those who trade with the Europeans wear a linen garment the same as that used by the men. Some women dress like their ancestors and make a kind of shirt with leather, which covers the body but not the arms.

The Indians, in general, pay greater attention to their dress and to the ornaments with which they decorate themselves, than to the accommodations of their huts or tents. They construct their tents in the following simple, and speedy manner.

Being provided with poles of a proper length, they fasten two of them across, near their ends, with bands made of bark. Having done this, they raise them up, and extend the bottom of each as wide as they purpose to make the area of the tent. They then erect others of an equal height, and fix them so as to support the two principal ones. They lay skins of the elk or deer, sewed together, in quantity sufficient to cover the poles, and by lapping over to form the door. A great number of skins are sometimes required for this purpose, as some of their tents are very spacious.

The huts also, which some erect when they

travel, for very few tribes have fixed homes or regular towns or villages, are equally simple and almost as quickly constructed.

They fix small flexible poles in the ground, and bending them till they meet at the top and form a semi-circle, then lash them together. These they cover with mats made of woven swamp grass, or with birch bark, which they carry with them in their canoes for this purpose.

These cabins have neither chimnies nor windows. There is only a small hole left in the middle of the roof, through which the smoke is discharged, but when this is stopped up when it rains or snows violently, the smoke proves exceedingly troublesome.

They lie on skins, generally those of the bear, which are placed in rows on the ground. If the floor is not large enough to contain enough beds for the whole family, a frame is erected about four or five feet from the ground, in which the children sleep.

Every nation pays a great respect to old age. The advice of a father will seldom meet with any extraordinary attention from the young Indians. But they will tremble before a grandfather, and submit to his commands with the utmost speed. The word of the older members of their community are regarded by the young as the words of prophets. If they take during their hunting parties any game that is thought by them especially delicious, it is immediately presented to the oldest of their relatives.

They never cause themselves to be overburdened with care, but live in a state of perfect peace and contentment. Being naturally lazy, if just enough food can be gotten with little trouble, and near at hand, they will not go far, or take any extra pains for it, though by so doing they might acquire greater plenty, and of a better kind.

Having much leisure time they give in to this laziness to which they are so prone, by eating, drinking, or sleeping, and rambling about in their towns or camps. But when necessity obliges them to take the field, either to oppose an enemy, or to find themselves food, they are alert and tireless.

The spirit of gambling is not confined to Europe. The Indians also feel the bewitching impulse, and often lose their weapons, their clothing, and every thing they possess.

The greatest fault in their character is that disposition which causes them to treat their enemies with cruelty. But if they are barbarous to those with whom they are at war, they are friendly, hospitable, and humane in peace. It may with truth be said of them that they are the worst enemies, and the best friends, of any people in the whole world.

READING REVIEW

1. List three characteristics of Indian civilization. Explain why you feel each was important.
2. Describe the two types of dwellings built by the Indians.
3. What did Carver consider the greatest fault of the Indians' character?
4. Why did Carver say that the Indians were the worst enemies and the best friends of any people in the whole world?

80 On American Railroad Travel

Once Americans realized the advantages of the railroad over other means of transportation, rail lines began to be built all over the country. Despite the conditions on early passenger cars, Americans appreciated the speed of rail travel compared to travel by foot, horse, wagon, or canal.

In 1842, Charles Dickens, the great English author, was on a tour of America. The following account gave Dickens' impressions of a railroad trip from Boston to Lowell, Massachusetts.

READING FOCUS

1. How were passenger cars differentiated?
2. What was Dickens' opinion of American railroads?

There are no first and second class carriages as with us [the English]; but there is a gentlemen's car and a ladies' car. The main distinction between which is that in the first, everybody smokes; and in the second, nobody does. As a black man never travels with a white one, there is also a negro car. There is a great deal of jolting, a great deal of noise, a great deal of wall, not much window, a locomotive engine, a shriek, and a bell.

Adapted from Charles Dickens, American Notes, _1842._

Typical rail travel in the 1840's

The cars are shabby, and hold fifty people. The seats, instead of stretching from end to end, are placed crosswise. Each seat holds two persons. There is a long row of seats on each side of the car, a narrow passage up the middle, and a door at both ends. In the center of the carriage there is usually a stove, fed with coal, which is for the most part red-hot. It is very stuffy.

In the ladies' car, there are a great many gentlemen who have ladies with them. There are also a great many ladies who have nobody with them. Any lady may travel alone, from one end of the United States to the other, and be certain of the most courteous and considerate treatment everywhere. The conductor wears no uniform. He walks up and down the car, and in and out of it, as his fancy dictates; leans against the door with his hands in his pockets and stares at you, if you chance to be a stranger; or enters into conversation with the passengers about him. A great many newspapers are pulled out, and a few of them are read. Everybody talks to you, or to anybody else who hits his fancy.

If a lady takes a fancy to any male passenger's seat, the gentleman who accompanies her gives him notice of the fact, and he [the male passenger] immediately surrenders it with great politeness.

Except when a branch road joins the main one, there is seldom more than one track of rails. The character of the scenery is always the same. Mile after mile of stunted trees. Now you emerge for a few brief minutes on an open country, glittering with some bright lake or pool. You catch hasty glimpses of a distant town, with its clean white houses when whir-r-r-r! almost before you have seen them, comes the same dark screen: the stunted trees—all so like the last that you seem to have been transported back again by magic.

The train calls at stations in the woods, where the wild impossibility of anybody having the smallest reason to get out, is only to be equalled by the apparently desperate hopelessness of there being anybody to get in.

READING REVIEW

1. List and describe three types of passenger cars.
2. How were lady travelers treated? Explain.
3. What opinion did Dickens have of traveling on American railroads? Cite evidence from the reading to support your answer.

81 An Attack on American Ignorance

In their struggle to get ahead, Americans tended to neglect "book learning." Many people in frontier communities could not read or write, and there were few schools where they could learn these skills. Many people felt this was an unfortunate situation, especially in a democracy.

Among those who disapproved of this situation was Anne Royall, a writer who had been brought up on the Pennsylvania frontier. She was taught to read and write by her father. After writing the book of essays, from which this selection is taken, she became a newspaper publisher in Washington. She was known for her effective writing style and her fearless attacks on government officials.

READING FOCUS

1. According to the writer, what does education do for people?
2. According to the writer, what was the source of most evils?

A lady asked me one day, "What state is Virginia in?" Another asked, "Is Canada in Kentucky?" Another supposed that "Joe Graphy [geography] was very hard to learn." Such is the cause of all our mistakes in religion, morals, and politics. When we are educated we can cast off prejudice and superstition. Education improves our judgments and restrains our passions. In short, it enables us to discover what is best for our welfare.

I was reading a newspaper today in which there was something about Ireland. A genteel, well-dressed looking man was standing by, and he asked me if Ireland was in South America! He lives here and is worth not less than twenty thousand dollars. He is a candidate for the office of sheriff in this county, which is the second wealthiest in the state. There are eight or nine other candidates in the election, but the misfortune is that the voters, or a majority of them, and the other candidates are equally ignorant!

Now, what sort of government are we to

Adapted from Anne Newport Royall, Letters From Alabama, 1817–1822.

expect when responsibility and power is held by such people as these? This will be the downfall of our country some day! This ignorance is not limited to any one part of the Union; it is everywhere. I happened to be in court once in a county in Virginia. The court was just beginning, and the judge ordered the sheriff to command silence until he "read the charge to the grand jury." The sheriff replied that he would thank him (the judge) to do it himself, as he was "a new hand at the business." This was the high sheriff of the county!

A person who is said to know anything of geography, philosophy, or astronomy is so disliked by the great mass of the people one would think he was a friend of the devil. They are jealous of rich and famous people. Why, then, don't they seek to have their minds enlightened? That is their only security against the oppression and inroads of the wealthy.

In a country like this, where the freedom of elections makes it possible for every man to hold office, how can he carry out duties of his office with honor to himself, or benefit to his country, if he is ignorant of the principles of his government? How can he tell if the government is run correctly by others, when he has no way of finding out?

Is not something wrong with our system of education? If there is, where does the defect lie? I have seen many evils, much sorrow, much oppression and much wickedness of all descriptions and degrees. I have traced these evils to their source, and find their origin in ignorance. If I were to speak from experience upon this subject, I would say in the first place that humans are reasonable beings. Reason is improved by observation and study. As we see, hear, and understand from the cradle to the grave, we are constantly learning. Our education, therefore, begins at birth and ends at death. But first impressions are the most permanent, because a person's mind then is empty and is prepared to take in more than it is ever able to do thereafter. How necessary it is then to teach young children the importance of justice and humanity! How necessary to enforce them, both by ideas and example, so they will influence them all their lives afterwards. But when parents are ignorant themselves, deplorable indeed must be the condition of their children. This is the misfortune, and here I fear it is long to remain. Most parents are not only ignorant but are highly prejudiced against learning.

READING REVIEW

1. What were two main reasons according to Royall, why Americans needed to be educated?
2. Which of the two reasons do you think is more important?
3. Which statements in this reading might still apply today? Explain your reasoning.

82 A Defense of American Manners

Americans had their share of critics, foreign as well as native-born. However, Timothy Dwight, a minister who was president of Yale from 1795 to 1817, was a firm defender of the American people. Every fall he traveled around New England. Then, when he returned home, he wrote about his travels. Like many writers of the time, he wrote his letters to an imaginary correspondent. In this selection, Dwight is writing to an imaginary English friend.

Americans travel west over the National Road.

READING FOCUS

1. How did Dwight characterize the visiting English that he met?
2. How did English visitors generally treat Americans?
3. How did Dwight characterize Americans?

Of the numerous English people who have visited these states, I have seen many. Their manners have, with few exceptions, been less civil, more distant, and more self-satisfied than those of my own countrymen.

A principal reason why your countrymen complain of discourteous conduct in America is that they bring about this treatment. When an English traveler enters an inn, he treats the innkeeper as if he were his servant or even his slave. Whether this behavior is proper I shall not now stop to ask. It is not customary; and for this reason, at least, it is unwelcome. As every New England man feels entirely independent, it is not strange that he should not stand for what he considers undeserved abuse. A little politeness would have encouraged every effort by the innkeeper to please the traveler.

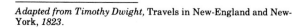

Adapted from Timothy Dwight, Travels in New-England and New-York, *1823.*

Many people complain that we Americans are inquisitive, or nosy. We are but very rarely, I suspect, so much as to justify the complaints. I have traveled in New England and New York during the last sixteen years. I do not remember that I have been once asked by an innkeeper, during the whole of this time, who I was, where I came from, where I was going, or what was my business. Nor do I remember having been shown a single example of rudeness.

Our government, our laws, our religion, our manners, the state of arts and manufacturers, our literature, our science, our climate, even our plant life, are poorly understood by every foreigner who passes through the United States.

You will object to these observations. You will say that our government is the same as yours, except for some slight differences. You will say that our religion is the same in all its varieties, that our manners are the same, and that our whole society is the same as that of Great Britain. But there are more differences in the two countries than an Englishman can possibly realize.

The people of New England are not inferior, and in some cases are superior, to those of

A colonial schoolhouse

England. In the older settlements they are more religious, and have better morals. We have fewer corruptions, we have more of the simplicity and innocence of youth. We are behind you in learning, in science, and in many of the mechanical and manufacturing arts. Still we have fewer prejudices, both because we are a less important part of the human family, and because we have had less time to form them. Great, powerful, and splendid nations never do justice to those that are inferior. At the same time, we are more friendly, more social, and more ready to please. We are also more orderly, quiet, and peaceful. We are governed with less difficulty, and by milder measures.

Our common people are far better educated than yours, both in the school and in the church. The reason for this is that they all go to school, and almost all go to church. All of them can read, write, and keep accounts. Almost all of them are able to read. To end the subject, there is a vein of practical good sense, the most valuable of all intellectual possessions, running through the people of New England. This may be considered as their most characteristic feature.

READING REVIEW

1. According to Dwight, why do visiting English people often receive discourteous treatment?
2. According to Dwight, what are the main differences between English visitors and the people of New England?
3. Why might an intelligent American reader have objected to this article?

83 The People of the Western Frontier

The number of settlers moving into the lands west of the Appalachian Mountains increased rapidly during the late 1700's and early 1800's. These "westerners" had to adapt to their new surroundings. As they did so, they developed customs and manners that were much different from those of the Americans back East.

The following was written by an Englishman, Elias P. Fordham. It gives his impressions of the westerners he encountered on a trip through the Ohio River Valley in 1818.

READING FOCUS

1. What were the four classes of westerners Fordham observed?
2. Did the westerners believe in and practice equality toward one another?
3. Which class did Fordham seem to most admire?

The people who live on these frontiers may be divided into four classes:

1st. class.—The hunters, a daring, hardy, race of men, who live in miserable cabins, which they strengthen in times of War with the Indians, whom they hate but much resemble in dress and manners. They [the hunters] are unpolished, but hospitable, kind to Strangers, honest and trustworthy. They raise a little

Adapted from Elias P. Fordham, Personal Narrative of Travels in Virginia, Maryland, Pennsylvania, Ohio, Indiana, Kentucky; and a Residence in the Illinois Territory: 1817-1818.

Indian corn, pumpkins, hogs, and sometimes have a Cow or two, and two or three horses belonging to each family: But their rifle is their principal means of support. They are the best marksmen in the world, and such is their skill that they will shoot an apple off the head of a companion. Some few use the bow and arrow. I have spent seven or eight weeks with these men, have had opportunities of testing them, and believe they would sooner give me the last shirt off their backs, than rob me of a charge of powder. Their wars with the Indians have made them bitter. This class cannot be called first Settlers, for they move every year or two.

2d. class.—First settlers—a mixed set of hunters and farmers. They possess more property and comforts than the first class [the hunters]; yet they are a half barbarous race. They follow open land, selling out when the Country begins to be well settled, and their cattle cannot be entirely kept in the woods.

3d. class.—is composed of ambitious men from Kentucky and the Atlantic States. This class consists of Young Doctors, Lawyers, Storekeepers, farmers, mechanics and craftsmen, who found towns, trade, and speculate in land. There is in this class every level of *intellectual* and *moral* character; but the general tone of Social manners is yet too much relaxed. There is too much reliance upon personal ability, and the laws have not yet acquired enough force to prevent violence.

4th. class.—old settlers, rich, independent, farmers, wealthy merchants, possessing a good deal of information, a knowledge of the world, and an adventurous spirit. Such are the Ohio men, Western Pennsylvanians, Kentuckians, and Tennessee men. The young men have a military taste, and most of them have served in the late war. They were great duellists, but now the laws against duelling are more strictly enforced; they carry dirks [daggers], and sometimes decide a dispute on the spot. Irritable and lazy in youth, yet they are generally steady and active in Manhood. They begin, and carry on any business or speculation that promises great profit, and suffer the greatest losses with a firmness that resembles indifference.

The Backwoods men, as they are called somewhat contemptuously by the Inhabitants of the Atlantic States, are admirably adapted by Nature and education for the scenes they live and act in. The outstanding feature of their character is power. The young value them-

Pioneers on the western frontier

selves on their courage, the old on their shrewdness. The worst villains have something grand about them. They expect no mercy and they show no fear; "every man's hand is against them, and their hand is against every man's."

As social Comforts are less under the protection of the laws here, than in old countries, friendship and good neighbourhood are more valued. A man of good character is a treasure; not that there is a small number of such men, but because the bad are as terribly bad, as their opposites are especially good. This is not the land of Hypocrisy. It would not here have its reward.

I wish I could give you a correct idea of the perfect equality that exists among these republicans. A Judge leaves the Court house, shakes hands with his fellow citizens and retires to his loghouse. The next day you will find him holding his own plough. The Lawyer has the title of Captain, and serves in his Military capacity under his neighbour, who is a farmer and a Colonel. The shop keeper sells a yard of tape, and sends shiploads of produce to New Orleans; he travels 2000 miles a year; he is a good hunter, and has been a soldier; he dresses and talks as well as a London Merchant, and probably has a more extensive range of ideas; at least he has

111

fewer prejudices. One prejudice, however, nothing will cause him to give up—he thinks the Americans in general, and particularly those of his own state, are the best soldiers in the world.

I have not seen a feeble man, in mind or body, belonging to these Western Countries. The most ignorant, compared with men of the same standing in England, are well informed. Their manners are coarse; but they have amongst themselves a code of politeness, which they generally observe. Drinking whiskey is the greatest problem and cause of disorder, amongst them. When intoxicated by it, they sometimes fight most furiously.

READING REVIEW

1. List the four classes of people that lived on the frontier and describe two characteristics of each.
2. Did the westerners believe in equality? Cite evidence from the reading to support your answer.
3. Describe the character of the typical westerner. What personal qualities did westerners especially value?
4. Which class do you think the writer admired the most? Explain your answer.

84 "Our Andy's Inauguration"

Large crowds gathered in Washington, D.C., to see Andrew Jackson sworn in as President. But these crowds were different from those that had witnessed other inaugurations. Many who came to celebrate Jackson's inauguration were "common people"—farmers, laborers, pioneers, backwoodsmen. They felt that Jackson was one of them. They had come to Washington to celebrate the inauguration of "our Andy."

Many of the old-line politicians and Washington society people took a dim view of some of the events surrounding Jackson's inauguration. One such person was Mrs. Samuel Harrison Smith, who wrote down her impressions of the inauguration and the White House reception that followed.

READING FOCUS

1. Describe the crowd's behavior at Jackson's inauguration.
2. According to Mrs. Smith, what did Jackson's bow to the people symbolize?
3. What was Mrs. Smith's opinion of the "common people"?

The inauguration was an imposing and majestic event, and one of inspiration. Thousands and thousands of people, without distinction of rank, gathered round the Capitol, silent, orderly, and peaceful, with their eyes fixed on the front of that building, waiting the appearance of the President.

The door from the rotunda opens; preceded by the marshals, surrounded by the judges of the Supreme Court, the old man [Jackson] with his gray locks, advances, bows to the people who greet him with a shout that rends the air. The cannons from Alexandria and Fort Warburton proclaim the oath he has taken, and all the hills echo the sound.

It was grand—it was magnificent! An almost breathless silence followed, and the crowd was still, listening to catch the sound of his voice, though it was so low as to be heard only by those nearest to him. After reading his speech the oath was administered to him by Chief Justice Marshall. Then Marshall presented the Bible. The President took it from his hands, pressed his lips to it, laid it reverently down, then bowed again to the people—yes, to the people in all their majesty.

President-elect Andrew Jackson on the way to his inauguration

---

Adapted from Mrs. Samuel Harrison Smith, The First Forty Years of Washington Society, Portrayed by Family Letters of Mrs. Samuel Harrison Smith, *edited by Gaillard Hunt, 1908.*

The day was delightful, the scene animating. We walked around town and at every turn met some new acquaintance and stopped to talk and shake hands. We continued strolling here until near three, then returned home unable to stand, and threw ourselves on the sofa. Some one came and informed us the crowd before the White House was so far lessened that they thought we might enter.

This time we were able to enter. But what a scene did we witness! The *majesty of the people* had disappeared, and a rabble, a mob, of boys, Negroes, women, and children, were scrambling, fighting, and romping. What a pity, what a pity! No arrangements had been made, no police officers placed on duty, and the whole house had been flooded by the rabble mob.

We came too late. The President, after having been *literally* nearly pressed to death and almost suffocated and torn to pieces by the people in their eagerness to shake hands with Old Hickory, had retreated through the back way and had escaped to his lodgings.

Cut glass and china to the amount of several thousand dollars had been broken in the struggle to get the refreshments. Punch and other articles had been carried out in tubs and buckets, but had it been in barrels it would not have been sufficient; for it is said that twenty thousand people were there, though I think the number exaggerated. Ladies fainted, men were seen with bloody noses, and such a scene of confusion took place as is impossible to describe.

Those who got in the White House could not get out by the door again but had to scramble out of windows. At one time the President, who had retreated until he was pressed against the wall, could only be protected by a number of gentlemen forming round him and making a kind of barrier of their own bodies. The pressure was so great that Colonel Bomford, who was one, said that he was afraid they should have been pushed down or on the President. It was then the windows were thrown open and the torrent found an outlet, which otherwise might have proved deadly.

This crowd had not been anticipated and therefore not provided for. Ladies and gentlemen only had been expected at this reception, not the people en masse. But it was the people's day, and the people's President, and the people would rule. God grant that one day or other the people do not put down all rule and rulers. I fear, as they have been found in all ages and countries where the people get the power in their hands, that of all cruel rulers, they are the most ferocious, cruel, and oppressive.

The noisy and disorderly rabble in the President's house brought to my mind descriptions I had read of the mobs in Tuileries and at Versailles during the French Revolution. I expect to hear the carpets and furniture are ruined; the streets were muddy, and these guests all went there on foot.

READING REVIEW

1. Describe the mood of the crowd when Jackson was sworn into office.
2. (a) To whom did Jackson bow after taking the oath of office and kissing the Bible? (b) What did Mrs. Smith seem to think this bow symbolized?
3. Compare the behavior of the crowds at the inauguration and at the White House reception.
4. What was Mrs. Smith's opinion of the common people? Explain your answer.

85 Officeholders in Government

Andrew Jackson firmly believed in the ability of average people to govern themselves. To put this belief into practice, he made many changes in government officeholders when he became President. He extended the so-called "spoils system," that is, the practice of appointing party supporters to serve in various government jobs. Jackson stated some of his beliefs about government in his first annual message to Congress, part of which follows.

READING FOCUS

1. How did Jackson think that government efficiency could be improved?
2. What views did Jackson express about officeholders?

There are few people who can for any great length of time hold office and power without being more or less influenced by feelings unfa-

Adapted from James D. Richardson (comp.), Messages and Papers of the Presidents, *Vol. II, 1896.*

Jackson often rewarded loyal supporters.

Offices were not established to support particular people at the public expense. No wrong is done by removing a person from office, since neither appointment to nor continuance in office, is a matter of right. It is the people, and they alone, who have a right to complain when a bad official is substituted for a good one.

The person who is removed from office has the same means of earning a living as are enjoyed by the millions who never held office. The proposed limitation on appointments of officeholders would destroy the idea of property now so generally connected with public office. Although individual distress may sometimes result, the change would, by promoting rotation in officeholders, be healthy for the system.

READING REVIEW

1. What did Jackson mean when he said, "Public office is considered as a kind of property"?
2. According to Jackson, what harm could come about if a person continued in office for a long time?

vorable to faithfully carrying out their public duties. Their integrity may prevent them from actual wrongdoing, but they are apt to become indifferent to the public interest and to tolerate conduct that would not be accepted by an inexperienced person. Public office is considered as a kind of property. And government is thought of more as a means of promoting individual interests than as an instrument created solely for the service of the people. Corruption and distortion of values turn government away from its proper ends and make it a way to support the few at the expense of the many.

The duties of all public officials are so plain and simple that people of intelligence may readily qualify themselves to perform them. I believe that more is lost by people continuing in office for a long time than is generally gained by their experience. I ask you, therefore, whether government efficiency would not be increased by a general extension of the law limiting appointments of officeholders to four years.

In a country where offices are created solely for the benefit of the people, no one person has any more right to hold office than another.

86 A Great Chief's Farewell

In the 1830's the nation was making remarkable progress in manufacturing, in transportation, and in settling western lands, as well as in strengthening democracy. However, while most free Americans shared in the nation's progress, the Indians did not. Instead, they were being pushed from their lands by white settlers. American and Indian cultures were in conflict and this conflict often resulted in warfare.

In the Black Hawk War of 1832, American soldiers wiped out most of the Sac tribe after it had surrendered. The following is part of a farewell speech given by Black Hawk, the chief of the tribe, after he was forced to surrender.

READING FOCUS

1. What is Black Hawk's attitude in the face of defeat?
2. What does Black Hawk think of whites?

You have taken me prisoner with all my warriors. I am much grieved, for I expected, if I did not defeat you, to hold out much longer, and give you more trouble before I surrendered. I fought hard. But your guns were well aimed. The bullets flew like birds in the air, and whizzed by our ears like the wind through the trees in the winter. My warriors fell all around me; it began to look very bad. I saw my evil day at hand. The sun rose dim on us in the morning, and that night it sunk in a dark cloud, and looked like a ball of fire. That was the last sun that shone on Black Hawk. He is now a prisoner of the white men. They will do with him as they wish. But he can stand torture, and is not afraid of death. He is no coward. Black Hawk is an Indian.

He has done nothing for which an Indian ought to be ashamed. He has fought for his countrymen, the squaws and papooses, against white men, who came, year after year, to cheat them and take away their lands. You know the cause of our making war. It is known to all white men. They ought to be ashamed of it. The white men hate the Indians, and drive them from their homes. But the Indians are not dishonest. The white men speak evil of the Indian and look at him spitefully. But the Indian does not tell lies. Indians do not steal.

An Indian who is as bad as the white men could not live in our nation. He would be put to death and eaten up by wolves. The white men are bad teachers. They carry false looks and deal in false actions. They smile in the face of the poor Indians to cheat them. They shake them by the hand to gain their trust and make them drunk.

Black Hawk is a true Indian, and refuses to cry. He feels sympathy for his wife, his children, and his friends. But he does not care for himself. He cares for his nation and the Indians. They will suffer. He regrets their fate. The white men do not scalp the head but they do worse—they poison the heart. Black Hawk's countrymen will not be scalped, but they will, in a few years, become like the whites so that you can't trust them.

Farewell, my nation! Black Hawk tried to save you, and avenge your wrongs. He drank the blood of some of the whites. He has been taken prisoner, and his plans are stopped. He can do no more. He is near his end. His sun is setting, and he will rise no more. Farewell to Black Hawk.

Adapted from Samuel G. Drake, Biography and History of the Indians of North America, *1841.*

READING REVIEW

1. What, according to Black Hawk, should the white people be ashamed of?
2. Why did Black Hawk surrender?
3. How does Black Hawk show his pride as an Indian?

87 In Praise of the Union

In 1830 Congress held a long, bitter debate on states' rights. This debate was brought about by the South's growing opposition to high tariffs on imported goods. The most memorable debates were those between Robert Hayne of South Carolina and Daniel Webster of Massachusetts. They have become known as the Webster-Hayne debates. Webster's best known speech of these debates was a moving tribute to the ideal of national unity. Americans of the 1830's were used to listening to long speeches. This one, lasting several hours, took Webster two days (January 26 and 27) to complete. Only parts of the speech are given here.

READING FOCUS

1. What is Webster's position on states' rights?
2. What does Webster say would be the result of giving in to the tariff's opponents?

What is the origin of this government, and the source of power? Whose agent is it? Has it been created by the state legislatures or by the people? It is the people's Constitution, the people's government, made for the people, and by the people, and answerable to the people. The people of the United States have declared that this Constitution shall be the supreme law. We must either agree or dispute their authority. The states are, unquestionably, sovereign, so far as their sovereignty is not affected by this supreme law. But the state legislatures, as political bodies, however sovereign, are yet not sovereign over the people.

The people created this government. They gave it a Constitution. In that Constitution

---

Adapted from Congressional Debates, *Vol. VI, 21st Cong., 1st session, 1830.*

they have listed the powers they have given to this government. They have made it a limited government. They have defined its authority. They have limited it to certain powers. All others, they declare, are reserved to the states or to the people. But they have not stopped here. If they had, they would have accomplished only half their work. No definition can be made so clear as to avoid all possibility of doubt. Who then shall interpret the people's will, where it seems to be in doubt? With whom do they leave this right of deciding on the powers of the government? They have left it with the government itself, in its appropriate branches.

The people have wisely provided, in the Constitution itself, a proper, suitable way to settle questions of constitutional law. There are, in the Constitution, grants of powers to Congress and restrictions on these powers. There are also prohibitions on the states. Some authority must therefore have the ultimate power to interpret these grants, restrictions, and prohibitions. The Constitution itself established that authority. How has it accomplished this great and essential end? By declaring that "the Constitution, and the laws of the United States made in pursuance thereof, shall be the supreme law of the land, anything in the constitution or laws of any state to the contrary notwithstanding."

This was the first great step. By this, the supremacy of the Constitution and laws of the United States is declared. The people so will it. No state law is to be valid which comes in conflict with the Constitution or any law of the United States. But who shall decide if a state law interferes with the Constitution or a federal law? This the Constitution itself decides also, by declaring "that the judicial power shall extend to all cases arising under the Constitution and laws of the United States." These two provisions cover the whole ground. They are, in truth, the keystone of the arch. With these, it is a constitution. Without them, it is a confederacy.

If the people, in these respects, had done otherwise, their Constitution could neither have been preserved, nor would it have been worth preserving. And if its clear provisions shall now be disregarded, it will become as feeble and helpless a being as its enemies could possibly desire.

In my career up to now, I have always kept in view the prosperity and honor of the whole country, and the preservation of our federal Union. It is to the Union we owe our safety at home and our dignity abroad. It is to the Union that we are chiefly indebted for whatever makes us most proud of our country. Every year it has lasted has brought fresh proofs of its usefullness and its blessings. Although our territory has stretched out wider and wider, and our population spread farther and farther, they have not outrun its protection or its benefits. It has been to us all a fountain of national, social, and personal happiness.

I have not allowed myself to look beyond the Union, to see what might lie hidden there. I have not coolly weighed the chances of preserving liberty, when the bonds that unite us might be broken apart. I have not let myself think of the horrible effects that would result from the breakup of our Union. While the Union lasts, we have high, exciting, gratifying prospects spread out before us, for us and our children. Beyond that, I seek not to look. God grant that, in my day at least, I shall not have to look beyond it.

When my eyes shall be turned to look for the last time on the sun in heaven, may I not see it shining on the broken and dishonored fragments of a once glorious Union—on states in conflict and belligerent; on a land filled with civil feuds, or drenched, it may be, in brothers' blood! Let my eyes' last feeble and lingering glance, rather, see the gorgeous flag of the republic, now known and honored throughout the earth, still flying high, not a stripe erased, nor a single star obscured. Let its motto not be Liberty first and Union afterward. Let its motto—spread all over in characters of living light, blazing on all its ample folds, as they float over the sea and over land, and in every wind under the whole heavens—be that other sentiment, dear to every true American heart—Liberty *and* Union, now and forever, one and inseparable!

READING REVIEW

1. According to Webster, who gave the government its authority?
2. How did the people provide a suitable way to settle questions of constitutional law?
3. What is Webster's attitude toward the Union?
4. What response might you have made to the last sentence of the reading?

88 Proclamation to the People of South Carolina

On December 10, 1832, President Andrew Jackson issued a "Proclamation to the People of South Carolina." This was the President's answer to South Carolina's Ordinance of Nullification. The fact that Jackson was a southern cotton planter led some of the supporters of nullification to hope that he would support the Ordinance. In his Proclamation, however, Jackson made it clear that he strongly opposed nullification and would use force, if necessary, to carry out the laws of the United States.

READING FOCUS

1. Why did Jackson oppose the nullification?
2. What was his opinion of the right of a state to leave the Union?
3. What was the intent of the Proclamation which Jackson issued?

Andrew Jackson as President

The Ordinance of Nullification is not based on the right to resist acts which are unconstitutional and oppressive, but rather on the strange position that any one state may declare an act of Congress void and prohibit the act from being carried out. If this Ordinance had been put into effect when our nation was young, the Union would have been dissolved in its infancy.

I consider that the power of one state to annul a law of the United States is not consistent with the survival of the Union. Nullification is forbidden by the Constitution; it violates the spirit of the Constitution; it is not consistent with the principles on which the Constitution was founded; and it is destructive of the great object for which the Constitution was written.

Furthermore, to say that any state may secede, or leave the Union, is to say that the United States are not a nation. The supporters of nullification and secession say that the Union was formed by a contract among the states. They go on to say that if the parties to that contract feel that they have been injured, then they may break the contract and leave the Union. But a contract is an agreement, a binding obligation. So it is exactly because the Constitution is a contract that they cannot leave the Union!

This, then, is the position in which we stand. A small majority of the citizens of South Carolina have elected delegates to a state convention. That convention has proclaimed that all the revenue laws of the United States must be repealed or that South Carolina will leave the Union. The governor of South Carolina has recommended the raising of a state army to carry out a secession from the Union. No act of violent opposition to the laws of the United States has yet been committed, but such an act is feared to occur soon.

It is the intent of this proclamation (1) to declare that the duty imposed on me by the Constitution to faithfully carry out the laws of the United States shall be performed to the full extent of the powers given to me, and (2) to warn the citizens of South Carolina of the danger they will face if they obey the illegal and disorganizing Ordinance of Nullification.

Consider the following questions. If your state leaders were successful in separating

Adapted from Messages and Papers of the Presidents, *Vol. II, edited by J.D. Richardson, 1898.*

South Carolina from the Union, what would be your situation? Are all the people of your state united? Don't you fear civil war with all of its consequences?

The laws of the United States must be carried out. Those leaders in your state who told you that you might peaceably prevent the laws from being carried out deceived you. They know that force alone can prevent the laws from being put into effect. Their real object is disunion. But disunion by armed force is *treason*. Are you really ready to suffer the punishment for treason? On South Carolina will fall all of the evils of any conflict you force upon the government of your country.

I rely with confidence on your undivided support in my determination to carry out the laws, to preserve the Union by all constitutional means, and to prevent by moderate and firm measures the necessity of the rise of force.

Fellow-citizens, the momentous case is before you. On your undivided support of your government depends the decision of the great question it involves—whether your sacred Union will be preserved and the blessings the Union guarantees us as one people shall continue.

READING REVIEW

1. List three reasons why Jackson opposed the Ordinance of Nullification.
2. What were Jackson's two main purposes in issuing his Proclamation?
3. According to Jackson, what was the real reason that the leaders of South Carolina supported nullification?
4. Why do you think that Jackson specifically addressed his Proclamation to the "People" of South Carolina rather than to the government of the state?

89 Advice on Politics

"Davy" Crockett was a rough-and-tumble frontiersman. He fought under Andrew Jackson in the War of 1812, served three terms in the House of Representatives, and died a hero at the Alamo.

Crockett's folksy speaking style and warm humor made him popular in his home state of Tennessee as well as in Washington, D.C. In this reading, Crockett gives advice on how to succeed as a politician.

READING FOCUS

1. What was Crockett's eight-step plan for success?
2. What do you think Crockett really meant by his advice?

Attend all public meetings and get some friend to make a motion that you become presiding officer. If you fail in this attempt, make a push to be appointed secretary. The records of the meeting of course will be published, and your name is introduced to the public. If you fail in both undertakings, get two or three acquaintances over a bottle of whiskey to pass some resolutions, no matter on what subject. Publish them, even if you pay the printer. It will break the ice, which is the main point in these matters.

Intrigue until you are elected an officer of the militia. This is the second step toward promotion, and can be accomplished with ease. I know of one election where nobody showed up. The innkeeper, at whose house it was to be held, elected himself colonel of his regiment.

If your ambition or circumstances force you to serve your country and earn three dollars a day by becoming a member of the legislature, you must first publicly swear that the constitution of the state is a restraint upon free and liberal legislation. It is, therefore, of as little use in the present enlightened age as an old almanac of the year in which the document was written. There is a point to this. By making the constitution a dead document, your rash proceedings will be thought of as resulting from a bold mind. Otherwise people might think they arose from sheer mule-like ignorance.

When the day of elections approaches, visit the voters. Treat them generously and drink freely in order to rise in their estimation, though you fall in your own. True, you may be called a drunken dog by some of the upper class, but the real roughnecks will think you are a jovial fellow. Their votes are certain, and frequently count double.

Adapted from David Crockett, Exploits and Adventures in Texas, *1836.*

Do all you can do to win the favor of the women. That's easily done. You have only to kiss and slobber over their children, wipe their noses, and pat them on the head. This cannot fail to please their mothers.

Promise all that is asked and more if you can think of anything. Offer to build a bridge or a church, to divide a county, create a bunch of new offices, build a turnpike, or anything they like. Promises cost nothing. Therefore, deny nobody who has a vote or sufficient influence to obtain one.

Get up on all occasions and sometimes on no occasion at all, and make long-winded speeches. Talk of your devotion to your country, your modesty, or any such fanciful subject. Speak against taxes of all kinds, officeholders, and bad harvest weather. Wind up your speech with a flourish about the heroes who fought and bled for our liberties in the times that tried men's souls.

If any charity is being carried on, be at the head of it, provided it is to be advertised publicly. If not, it isn't worth your while. None but a fool would keep his light under a bushel on such an occasion.

These few directions, if properly attended to, will take care of things. And when once elected—why, never mind the dirty children, the promises, the bridges, the churches, and the taxes. For it is absolutely necessary to forget all these before you can become a true politician and patriot.

READING REVIEW
1. Why do you think Crockett was joking when he stated these ideas?
2. (a) What was Crockett really saying? (b) How would you translate his remarks into "good" advice for success as a politician?
3. Are any of Crockett's techniques in use today? Explain.

---

90 An Accusation of Hypocrisy

Frances Trollope came to the United States in 1827 in hopes of earning money for her family. She opened a shop in Cincinnati but it failed, and she returned to England in 1831. She took back to

Davy Crockett

England a book she had written while in America. When it was published it angered Americans and continued to do so for many years. Here, during a visit to Washington she writes about Americans' hypocrisy—"the contradictions between their principles and practice."

READING FOCUS
1. How did Trollope characterize American–Indian relations?
2. What upset Trollope the most about Americans?

The Bureau of Indian Affairs contains a room of great interest. The walls are completely covered with original portraits of all the chiefs who, from time to time, have come to negotiate with their great father, as they call the President. The faces in the portraits are full of expression, but the expression in most of them is extremely similar. Rather, I should say that they have but two sorts of expression. The one is that of very noble and warlike daring, the other of a gentle simplicity. These portraits were touching, perhaps because at the moment we were looking at them they were suffering

---

Adapted from Mrs. Trollope, Domestic Manners of the Americans, *1832.*

from a base, cruel and oppressive action by their *great father*.

We were at Washington when a law forcing several tribes of Indians from their forest homes was passed by Congress and signed by the President. If the American character may be judged by their conduct in this matter, they are lacking honor and integrity. It is among themselves, and from themselves, that I have heard the statements which show them treacherous and false almost beyond belief in their relations with the unhappy Indians.

Had I, during my residence in the United States, seen any single feature in their national character that could justify their never-ending boast of generosity and love of freedom, I might have respected them, however much my taste was offended by their peculiar manners and customs. But it is impossible for any person not to be very upset by the contradictions between their principles and practice. They attack the governments of Europe, because as they say, they favor the powerful and oppress the weak. You may hear this said in Congress, roared out in taverns, discussed in every living room, poked fun at upon the stage, even discussed in the churches. Listen to it, and then look at them at home. You will see them with one hand lifting the cap of liberty, and with the other whipping their slaves. You will see them one hour lecturing their mob on the rights of man, and the next driving from their homes the Indians, whom they have bound themselves to protect by the most solemn treaties.

READING REVIEW

1. According to Trollope, what characterized American dealings with the Indians?
2. What contradiction in the national character did Trollope find most upsetting?
3. What examples were given to support the statement on contradictory actions and beliefs?

91 In Praise of American Democracy

In 1831 Alexis de Tocqueville traveled from France to the United States to study prisons in America. He saw much more, however, during his travels. The book he wrote, *Democracy in America,* was full of insights about American society. De Tocqueville was especially interested in how the American government worked and its relation to the people of the nation.

READING FOCUS

1. According to de Tocqueville, what makes America great?
2. What are the two kinds of rights he talks about?

No man can be great without goodness, nor any nation great without respect for rights. One might almost say that without it there can be no society, for what good is a combination of rational and intelligent beings held together by force alone?

I kept asking myself how, in our day, this idea may be taught to people. I find one way only—namely, to give them all the peaceful use of certain rights. One can see how this works among children. When a baby first begins to move among things, instinct leads him to make use of anything his hands can grasp. He has no idea of other people's property, not even that it exists. But as he is taught the value of things and discovers that he too may be robbed, he becomes more careful. In the end, he respects for others that which he wishes to be respected for himself.

Just as for a child with his toys, so is it later for a man with all his belongings. Why is it that in America, the land of democracy, no one makes that outcry against property in general that is often heard in Europe? Is there any need to explain? It is because there are no propertyless people in America. Everyone, having some possession to defend, recognizes the right to property in principle.

It is the same in the world of politics. The Americans have formed a high idea of political rights because they have some political rights. They do not attack those of others, because they do not want their own to be violated. Whereas the same person in Europe would be prejudiced against all authority, even the highest, the American obeys the lowest officials without complaint.

Adapted from Democracy in America *by Alexis de Tocqueville, edited by J. P. Mayer and Max Lerner.*

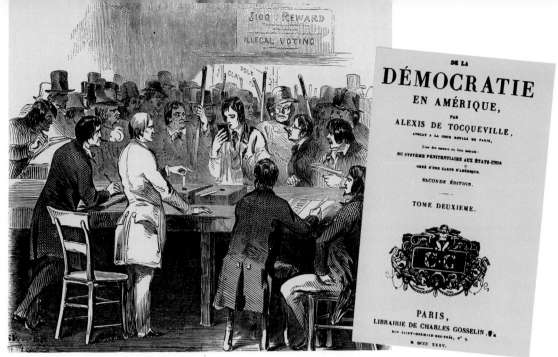

The spectacle of Americans voting in general elections inspired Alexis de Tocqueville to write Democracy in America.

Democratic government makes the idea of political rights spread to all citizens, just as the division of property puts the general idea of property rights within reach of all. That, in my view, is one of its greatest advantages.

I am not saying that it is an easy matter to teach all people to make use of political rights; I only say that when that can happen, the results are important.

And I would add that if ever there was a century in which such an attempt should be made, that century is ours.

Do you not see that religions are growing weak and that the idea of the sanctity of rights is vanishing? Do you not see that customs are changing and that the moral idea of rights is going with them?

Do you not notice how on all sides beliefs are given way to arguments, and feelings to planned behavior? If amid this collapse you do not succeed in linking the idea of rights to personal interest, what other means will be left to you to govern the world, if not fear?

In America the people were given political rights at a time when it was difficult for them to misuse them because the citizens were few and their ways of life simple. As they have grown more powerful, the Americans have not greatly increased the powers of democracy. Rather they have extended their democracy by increasing the number of people who have political rights.

There can be no doubt that the moment when political rights are granted to a people who have till then not had them is a time of crisis. A crisis which is often necessary but always dangerous.

A child may kill when he does not understand the value of life. He carries off other people's property before he knows that his own may be taken from him. At the moment when political rights are granted to a person, he is in much the same position with respect to those rights as is a child faced by unknown things.

This truth can be tested even in America. Those states in which the citizens have longest enjoyed their rights are those in which they still best know how to use them.

It cannot be repeated too often. Nothing is more wonderful than the art of being free, but nothing is harder to learn how to use than freedom.

READING REVIEW

1. Why is respect for rights important to a nation, in de Tocqueville's estimation?
2. Why have Americans, according to de Tocqueville, formed a high idea of political rights?
3. Why did so little misuse of political rights take place in America?
4. Explain why de Tocqueville thinks the price of liberty is high?

121

UNIT FOUR READINGS

The Rise of Sectionalism

CHAPTER **13** **Building New Northern Industries**
(1820's–1860's)

American ships loaded with trade goods sailed all the world's major trade routes. Seaports such as Boston, New York, and New Orleans served as home ports for the merchant fleet. In each port city hundreds of young boys roamed the docks, gazed at the ships, and dreamed of a life at sea.

Charles Low was one of those boys. Charles' dream came true in 1842, when, at age fourteen, he made his first voyage as a crew member of the *Horatio.*

92 **A Young Sailor's First Voyage**

In the years between 1800 and 1860, the United States merchant fleet grew at an amazing pace.

READING FOCUS
1. How did Charles get his job on the ship?
2. What aspects of life at sea did Charles enjoy?

The Flying Cloud *and other clipper ships sailed the major trade routes of the world.*

In May, 1842, my brother William married Miss Bedell of Brooklyn, and it was understood that in the fall they were to go to China. So about the middle of October they engaged passage on the *Horatio*. What was better than that, my brother Abbot secured a cabin for me as boy on board the same ship. After he had secured it, he wanted to know how I was going to make a living, as boys had no wages. I immediately replied, "As soon as the voyage is over, I will ship again." On departure, my father gave me fifty dollars, a sailor's outfit, and my freedom; that is, I was not to depend upon him any further, but make my own way in the world.

The fifth day of November, 1842, was the day set for sailing and I could hardly wait. At ten o'clock a.m. the tug came alongside, and my brothers and sisters and some six or eight of the Bedell girls, sisters of my brother William's wife, went down to Sandy Hook to see us off. The day was pleasant, and we had a good start.

After leaving the pilot [person who guides ships in and out of harbors] and guests, we were kept hard at work stowing the anchors and getting sail on the ship. It being a fair wind we did not stop work till all the studding-sails were set and we were nearly out of sight of land. After the decks were cleared up all hands were called aft [rear part of the ship] and the watches chosen.

The watches were chosen by the first and second mates. One chooses a man, and then the other chooses, till the crew are equally divided. The captain then addresses the men, telling them he expects them to be quick at a call and to do their duty at all times, and that if they do, they will be well fed and have a pleasant voyage, but if they do not, they will have a rough time of it. At six p.m. the captain's watch went below, ready to come back on deck at eight p.m. and stay on deck till midnight. The rule on board ship is for the captain to take the ship out, and the mate to bring her home; that is, the captain's watch, which is looked out for by the second mate, has the first eight hours on deck from eight to twelve p.m. and from four to eight a.m. And, coming home, the mate's watch has the same time the first night out.

The sailmaker and carpenter and we four boys had bunks in the between-decks, just for-

---

Adapted from Some Recollections *by Captain Charles P. Low, 1847-1873.*

ward of the cabin. The men all slept forward in the forecastle [a cabin at the front of the ship]. The ship not being full of cargo, there was plenty of room. The sailmaker and carpenter both worked down in the between-decks. Our cargo consisted of two or three hundred tons of lead, lumber, and cotton goods, which filled up the lower hold. Water, ship stores, and spare sails were all that were in between-decks.

The first two days out we had fine weather, but the ship rolled enough to make all the boys seasick. I escaped, however, not feeling the least uncomfortable, but enjoying it all.

The living I stood very well, for I had a hugh appetite. Mondays we had salt beef and bread for breakfast, dinner, and supper, with a mixture at breakfast called coffee. Tuesday we had salt pork for breakfast, bean soup and salt pork for dinner, and a quart of vinegar was allowed us on bean day. Wednesday we has scouse [meat stewed with vegetables and ship's biscuit]. Thursday we had scouse for breakfast and flour pudding, or duff, for dinner. Friday the same as Tuesday, bean soup. Saturday and Sunday, codfish and potatoes or rice. Such was the bill of fare through the voyage. I got used to it and enjoyed all my meals.

As the weeks flew by I became more in love with my sea life, and I got along well with officers and men. I was perfectly fearless. I could hold my weight with one hand, and I was as much at home on the royal yard [part of the ship's rigging] as on deck.

READING REVIEW

1. How did Charles get a job as a boy on the ship *Horatio*?
2. Do you think Charles Low enjoyed his first voyage at sea? Cite evidence from the reading to support your answer.
3. What did Charles plan to do when his voyage on the *Horatio* was over?

---

93 Industry in the United States

When the Industrial Revolution began, Great Britain jealously guarded the secrets of designing and building industrial machines. However, the British found it impossible to protect their industrial secrets forever. American manufacturers, with the help of British immigrants, began to develop industry in the United States. Most of the early factories were located in New England. The following

READING FOCUS

1. What natural resources encouraged the growth of industry in New England?
2. What affect did increases in population and acquisition of new territory have on industry?
3. How was industry affected by improvements in transportation?

The Northern or New England States are endowed by nature with a mountainous and barren soil, which poorly rewards the labor of the farmer. However, its wooded slopes, and tumbling streams, which fall into spacious harbors, showed the first settlers the direction in which their industry was to be employed. Shipbuilding and navigation at once became the leading industry, bringing with it wealth.

The harsh rule of the mother country forbade a manufacturing development, and that branch of industry never got a footing in the colonies. Independence from Britain opened up manufacturing, and also provided a large market for the sale of manufactures to the agricultural laborers of the more fertile fields of the Middle and Southern States.

The genius of Northern industry was quick in applying the profits earned in commerce to

Adapted from Thomas P. Kettell, Southern Wealth and Northern Profits, *1860.*

the development of manufacturing. With every increase in population, and every extension of national territory, the New England States gained a larger market for their wares, while the foreign competing supply has been restricted by high duties on imports.

The mountain rivers of New England have become motors, by which annually improving machinery has been driven. These machines require only the attendance of females, but a few years since a non-producing class, to turn out immense quantities of textile fabrics. In the hands of the male population, other branches of industry have multiplied, in a manner which shows the stimulant of an ever-increasing demand.

At about the time that New England became free to manufacture, the discoveries in navigation brought about that change in commerce by which Charleston, S.C., was no longer regarded as the nearest port to Europe, and New York assumed its proper position, as the leading seaport. The commerce of the Middle States rapidly increased, and with that increase a larger demand for the manufactures of New England was created.

When population spread west of the Allegheny Mountains, and the annexation of Louisiana opened the Mississippi River to a market for western produce, a new demand for New England manufactures was felt. This was further enhanced by the opening of the Erie Canal. In later years, the vast foreign immigration, pouring over new lands opened up by railroads, has given a further stimulus to the demand for New England manufactured goods.

Textile factories flourished throughout New England.

READING REVIEW

1. What natural resources caused shipbuilding and navigation to become important occupations in New England?
2. (a) How was manufacturing in New England affected by increases in population? (b) By the addition of new territory to the United States?
3. How did the opening of the Erie Canal affect manufacturing in New England?
4. Why was a demand for manufactured goods necessary for the development of industry in New England?

94 Discontent in Lowell

The textile mills of Lowell, Massachusetts, were well known in the United States in the 1830's and 1840's. The women and young girls who worked in the mills were called "Lowell girls." They lived in well-supervised boarding houses near the mill and spent their spare time at school or in church. When Davy Crockett visited the Lowell Mills in the 1830's, he described the women he saw leaving work as "well dressed, lively, and genteel."

However, according to this account by Harriet Hanson Robinson, conditions at Lowell were not quite as pleasant as this. Harriet was only ten when she started to work in the mills. She was eleven at the time of the famous Lowell strike in 1836, which she described in this selection.

READING FOCUS

1. Why did the workers decide to strike?
2. Why did the strike fail?

One of the first strikes of cotton-factory workers that ever took place in this country was in Lowell, in October 1836. When it was announced that the workers' wages were to be cut, there was great anger. The workers decided to strike.

Cutting the wages was not the only grievance, nor the only cause of this strike. Up till now the corporation had paid 25 cents a week toward the board of each worker. Now it intended to have the girls pay the sum. This, in addition to the cut in wages, would make a difference of at least one dollar each week.

Adapted from Harriet Hanson Robinson, Loom and Spindle: Life Among the Early Mill Girls, *1898.*

A "Lowell Girl" operates a loom in a textile mill.

It was estimated that as many as 1,500 girls went on strike and walked as a group through the streets. They had neither flags nor music; instead, they sang songs, a favorite one being:

Oh! Isn't it a pity, such a pretty girl as I—
Should be sent to the factory to pine away and die?
    Oh! I cannot be a slave,
    I will not be a slave,
    For I'm so fond of liberty
    That I cannot be a slave.

My own memory of this strike (or "turn out," as it was called) is very vivid. I worked in a lower room, where I had heard the proposed strike discussed. I had been an eager listener to what was said against this attempt at "oppression" on the part of the corporation. Naturally I took sides with the strikers. When the day came on which the girls were to strike, those in the upper rooms started first. So many of them left that our mill was at once shut down. But the girls in my room stood about, uncertain what to do. They asked each other, "Would you?" or "Shall we strike?" Not one of them had the courage to lead off. I began to think they

125

would not go out after all their talk. Growing impatient, I started on ahead, saying, with childish bravado, "I don't care what you do, *I* am going to turn out, whether anyone else does or not?" So I marched out, and was followed by the others.

As I looked back at the long line that followed me, I was more proud than I have ever been since at any success I may have achieved, and more proud than I shall ever be again until my own beloved state gives to its women citizens the right to vote.

The agent of the corporation where I then worked took revenge on those thought to be the strike leaders. My mother was evicted from her boarding house. The agent said, "Mrs. Hanson, you could not prevent the older girls from turning out. But your daughter is a child, and *her* you could control."

So far as results were concerned, this strike did no good. The dissatisfaction of the workers burned itself out. Though the authorities did not give in to their demands, most of them returned to their work, and the corporation went on cutting the wages.

READING REVIEW

1. Name two grievances the girls at Lowell had against the factory.
2. What did the workers hope to accomplish by striking?
3. (a) How did the agent treat Harriet's mother after the strike? (b) What caused his actions? (c) What happened to Harriet's mother?

95 A German Newcomer on Immigration

Many immigrants to the United States came from the German states. Gustave Koerner was one of the many thousands of German immigrants who arrived in America in the 1830's. He was a lawyer who had taken part in an unsuccessful attempt to set up a more liberal government in the German states. When the effort failed, Koerner had to flee from Frankfort in order to avoid arrest.

After he arrived in the United States, he settled in St. Louis because he had read a very favorable account about Missouri by a German writer, Gottfried Duden. However, since he was opposed to slavery, he soon decided to leave Missouri and move to Illinois. In later years, Koerner served as a judge, was elected lieutenant governor of Illinois, and was appointed United States minister to Spain.

READING FOCUS

1. What advice did Koerner give his family about immigrating to America?
2. Why were large emigration societies formed?
3. Why did the Giessen Society fail?

During the fall I received many letters from home and from my friends. Those from my family were full of love and tenderness. All of them more or less spoke of a hope of reunion in America. My brother Charles had serious thoughts of coming over, if he could get rid of his business, and of bringing our mother and sisters. My family were all troubled by the political reaction which had set in. They feared for Charles, whose liberal views were well known, and who was suspected of having some knowledge of our uprising at Frankfort.

I did not encourage their idea of coming to America. For Charles there was no chance of opening up a bookseller's business, either in the East or in the West. I had carefully looked into this, having written to friends in Philadelphia. Many years ago attempts were made in St. Louis by Germans to open bookstores, but they all failed. There was not even an English bookstore in St. Louis at this time. It was not until 20 years after our arrival that there was one there that could be called respectable.

Mother's health was good for her age. But my sister Augusta, who had been sickly from youth, suffered from stomach trouble, so that the climate might have been very harmful to her. And my sister Pauline had weak lungs.

There was great enthusiasm in Germany at that time for migrating to America. A great many families in and around Frankfort, whom my family knew, were preparing to leave for America, or speaking seriously about it. No wonder my family spoke of coming too. And not only individuals and families decided to come over. Large emigration societies were formed in hopes of founding German settlements in some western state or territory. Some people thought that it might even be possible to form a German state.

One of these societies became rather famous. It was the Giessen Society, which was headed by some very important men. Among

Adapted from Gustave Koerner, Memoirs, 1809-1896, *Vol. I, edited by Thomas J. McCormack.*

them was Frederick Muench, a Protestant minister, known in later times as "Far West." He was a man of great character, very well informed, with an iron will and very strong. A German patriot, he had lost hope in his country and had longed to become a citizen of the United States. Though violently opposed to slavery, he—along with others—was misguided by Gottfried Duden's book and made the great mistake of settling in Missouri. When the slavery question became a burning one, he had a difficult time with those who favored secession. The German men in Missouri who favored the Union were in constant danger of their lives. "Far West" acted most ably and stood his ground. His young son later died on the battlefield for the Union.

Paul Follenius was another member of this society. He also was a very noble person. Like Muench, he had given up all hopes of a political rebirth for Germany. He was an important lawyer, and when he came to this country, he had to give up a large and profitable law practice. The idea of forming a new state for German immigrants, not a mere colony, won his warm support.

The Giessen Society was the best organized colonization group that ever left Germany. Its constitution and bylaws were admirable. Its leaders were men of importance and integrity. Yet, like all similar societies, it eventually failed, bringing financial loss and shame to most of its members.

I have never favored such schemes, for many reasons. A bigoted group may follow a religious leader. They look upon him as a sort of prophet and are kept together by religious bonds. But the more intelligent the members of an immigration society are, the less authority can be exercised over them even by the best leaders. Without rule by one authority, settlements in new countries or in countries already fully organized cannot be successfully established. If my family had come over at all, I would have advised it to come entirely by itself or with a few other families or traveling companions.

READING REVIEW

1. Why did Koerner advise his family against coming to the United States?
2. Cite evidence to support the statement that Koerner was opposed to slavery.
3. Why did Koerner not favor the Giessen Society?

96 The Hard Lot of the Irish

During the mid-1840's, a disease destroyed most of the potato crop in Ireland. The results were disastrous, for the Irish people depended largely on potatoes for their food. By 1850 nearly one million people had died of starvation and another million had left Ireland to seek new lives in the United States. The Irish faced many difficulties in their new land. An especially serious problem facing Irish newcomers was the rise of nativism—a movement by native-born Americans to discriminate against those who came to the United States from foreign lands.

This selection was written in a humorous and sarcastic manner. The author was not criticizing the Irish. Instead he was poking fun at the nativist viewpoint about the Irish.

READING FOCUS

1. How did the "famine Irish" differ from immigrants of earlier times?
2. How did the nativists compare blacks and the famine Irish?

It is no secret that the Irish were not especially welcomed when they entered the United States. One can understand this reaction. Most earlier immigrants had been, if not wealthy, at least reasonably skilled workers or artisans. They were the most ambitious and vigorous of the Europeans seeking to make new lives for

A "nativist" view of the new immigrants

themselves in a richer country. But the famine Irish were poor, uneducated, and confused. They fled not to a better life but from almost certain death. They were dirty, undernourished, disease-ridden, and incapable of anything but the most unskilled labor. That they arrived in great numbers and filled up whole sections of cities almost overnight did not go unnoticed by native Americans. They saw that when the Irish moved in, the neighborhood went to pieces. They did not take care of property, and foolishly allowed great overcrowding in their houses. Nor did they understand how important it was to keep clean, especially when there was almost no provision made for sewage disposal. They failed to understand the importance of health and seemed satisfied to live in crowded, dark basements.

If the Irish were to be accepted into American society they must be sober, industrious, and ambitious, like the Protestant immigrants who had come before them. There, of course, was the heart of the problem. Not only were they poor, sick, dirty, and uneducated. They were also Catholic.

The Irish Catholics, with their unmarried clergy, had an equally strange tendency not to want to send their children to public schools, where every effort would be made to turn them into good Americans—this meant, of course, good Protestant Americans. From the nativist point of view, it was no wonder that churches were burned and that Catholics were occasionally murdered in riots.

The nativists were fond of comparing the Irish with the blacks. If they were northern Protestant abolitionists, they were especially fond of such a pastime. The comparison was always favorable to the blacks. The freed blacks "knew their place" and the Irish did not. The blacks were properly grateful for what the abolitionists had done for them, and the Irish seemed not at all grateful for their second-class citizenship. On the contrary, hardly had they been permitted to become citizens when they promptly joined with others of their kind in political organizations which threatened native American control of the cities. The Irish, then, were not only bigoted Catholics, they also were organizers of political "machines" that were a direct challenge to the established powers. The Know-Nothings and other nativist organizations gained much of their support from their strong appeals to anti-Catholic sentiment.

Practically every charge that has been made against the American blacks was also made against the Irish. They had no ambition. They did not keep up their homes. They drank too much. They were not responsible. They had no morals. It was not safe to walk through their neighborhoods at night. They voted the way crooked politicians told them to vote. They were not willing to pull themselves up by their own efforts. They were not capable of education. They could not think for themselves. They would always remain social problems for the rest of the country.

It was extremely difficult for us to understand what life in the early immigrant ghettos must have been like. There are practically no Americans today who live in anything even resembling the immigrant sections in Boston and New York. The psychological degradation of the Irish was certainly no worse than that to which blacks have been subjected. But it must also be said that from 1850 to 1950 there were no dissenting voices raised on the subject of the American Irish. No one suggested that Irish might be beautiful. No one argued that their treatment was both unjust and bigoted.

The Irish crawled out of the mud huts and wooden hovels in which they lived, and left behind the day labor and domestic service by which they made a living. They managed to do this not because American society offered special opportunities (as the native Americans would like to believe), nor because of a superior merit which enabled them to overcome obstacles (as the Irish would like to believe). The Irish "made it" because the American economy was growing at a fantastic rate, and the Irish were a large group of workers with knowledge of English. The growing economy and the almost unlimited number of jobs allowed the American Irish to move first into the respectable working class, then into the lower middle class, and more recently into the upper middle class. An occasional well-to-do Irish family like the Kennedys shows that even the Irish can become aristocrats.

From canal workers and railroad builders they became police officers, streetcar conductors, schoolteachers, and clerks. From the coal

"The Hard Lot of the Irish" from That Most Distressful Nation: The Taming of the American Irish *by Andrew M. Greeley.*

mines, stockyards, and steel mills they moved into offices, classrooms, and political headquarters. Then some began to go to law school, medical school, and dental school. Their heroes were political leaders, entertainers, singers, comedians, and athletes.

These changes took generations. The rate of social improvement increased as the economy grew and slowed down as the economy went down. The Irish were probably on the verge of making it when the Great Depression came. It took the prosperity of World War II and the postwar economic boom, plus the G.I. Bill, to enable the Irish to make it into the upper middle class. In other words, the worst of the immigrant experience was over about a hundred years after the famine. When John Kennedy was elected President, 110 years after the famine, the immigrant period of American history came to an end.

READING REVIEW

1. What similarities did the nativists find between the Irish and the blacks?
2. What difference did they find between the two groups?

Alexis de Tocqueville

CHAPTER 14 Creating a Southern Economy
(1820's–1860's)

97 Northern and Southern Society Compared

Alexis de Tocqueville came to the United States from France in 1831. He traveled throughout the country studying the American people and their institutions, their economy, and their ways of living. In 1832 de Tocqueville arrived in New Orleans. On this trip he was interested in finding out about some of the differences between the North and South. He was especially interested in observing slavery and gave his views about its effects upon Americans and their nation. He also wrote about the rapid expansion of the United States.

READING FOCUS

1. What was de Tocqueville's viewpoint about how slavery affected the areas where it existed?
2. How did it affect the people who lived in slave areas?

Scarcely a hundred years after the settling of the colonies, the planters were struck by the extraordinary fact that the states that had few slaves increased in population, in wealth, and in prosperity more rapidly than those states that had many slaves. This result seemed difficult to explain, especially since all the settlers, who were Europeans, had the same habits, the same civilization, and the same laws.

The difference was vividly shown when settlements reached the banks of the Ohio River. Rolling lands with rich soil extend along both shores of the Ohio. On either bank of the river the air is equally wholesome and the climate equally mild. Each bank forms the frontier of a large state. The state upon the left bank is called Kentucky. The one upon the right bank

Adapted from Democracy in America, *Vol. I, by Alexis de Tocqueville, translated by Henry Reeve, revised by Francis Bowen, and edited by Phillips Bradley.*

Differing ways of life along the Ohio River: Kentucky (foreground) and Cincinnati, Ohio, across the river

is called Ohio. These two states differ only in one way. Kentucky has admitted slavery, while Ohio has prohibited it. Thus the traveler who floats down the Ohio River may be said to sail between liberty and servitude. A brief inspection will convince anyone which of the two states is more favorable to humanity.

Upon the left bank (Kentucky) the population is small. From time to time one sees a group of slaves in the poorly farmed fields. Forest lands are everywhere. Society seems to be asleep; the people seem to be idle. Nature alone offers a scene of activity and life.

From the right bank (Ohio), on the contrary, a busy hum is heard, proclaiming the presence of activity. The fields are full of abundant harvests. The elegance of the houses indicates the taste and activity of the workers. People seem to be enjoying that wealth and satisfaction which is the reward of work.

The influence of slavery extends still further. It affects people's character. Upon both banks of the Ohio the character of the people is enterprising and energetic. But this vigor is used very differently in the two states. The white inhabitants of Ohio, forced to live by their own efforts, regard prosperity as the chief aim of their existence. Since the land they occupy presents inexhaustible resources for their activity, their greed is extraordinary. They desire wealth, and boldly seize every opportunity that fortune opens to them.

The Kentuckians scorn not only labor but all the undertakings that labor promotes. As they live in idleness, their tastes are those of idle people. Money has lost some of its value in their eyes. They want wealth much less than pleasure and excitement. The energy which their neighbors devote to becoming wealthy is used by them for field sports and military exercises. Thus slavery prevents the whites not only from becoming wealthy, but even from desiring to become so.

In Europe it is generally believed that slavery has made the interests of one part of the Union opposite to those of the other. I have not found this to be the case. Slavery has not created interests in the South opposite to those of the North. But it has changed the character and the habits of the people of the South.

The citizens of the southern states become domestic dictators from infancy. The first idea they acquire in life is that they are born to command. The first habit they learn is that of ruling. Their education tends, then, to give them the character of a proud and hasty people—angry, violent, impatient toward obstacles but easily discouraged if they cannot succeed at the first attempt.

Americans of the North see no slaves around them in their childhood. They are not even taken care of by free servants, for they are usually obliged to provide for their own wants. As soon as they enter the world, they see the need to do things for themselves. They soon learn to know exactly the limits of their power. They never expect to use force against those who oppose them. They know that the surest means of obtaining the support of other people is to win their favor.

If two people are united in society by the same interests and, to a certain extent, the same opinions but with different characters and a different style of living, these people will probably not agree. The same is true of two societies within a nation.

It is difficult to imagine a strong union between a nation that is rich and strong and one that is poor and weak. Union is even more difficult to maintain when one side is losing strength and the other is gaining it. The rapid increase in population and wealth in certain northern states threatens the independence of the southern states. The weak generally mistrust the justice and the reason of the strong. The states that increase less rapidly than the others look upon those others with envy and suspicion. This is the cause of the deep-seated uneasiness and unrest one sees in the southern states. These states are a striking contrast to the confidence and prosperity common to other parts of the Union.

If the changes I have described were gradual ones, the danger would be less. But the progress of American society is rapid. Thus the prosperity of the United States is the source of its most serious dangers. It tends to create in some of the states that overpowering excitement which accompanies a rapid increase of fortune. Meanwhile it awakens in other states those feelings of envy, mistrust, and regret which usually accompany the loss of wealth. The Americans look at their extraordinary progress with joy, but they would be wiser to consider it with sorrow and alarm. The people of the United States must inevitably become one of the greatest nations in the world. Their offspring will cover almost the whole of North America. What urges them to take possession of it so soon? Riches, power, and fame cannot fail to be theirs at some future time. But they rush in search of this large fortune as if only a moment remained for them to make it their own.

READING REVIEW

1. According to de Tocqueville, how did people in Ohio and Kentucky differ?
2. Why did he say that Northerners were better off without slaves?
3. Why did de Tocqueville think that rapidly growing prosperity was dangerous for the United States?

Harvesting the cotton crop

98 Life on a Georgia Plantation

Fanny Kemble, who was born in England, became an actress who was well known to playgoers in both England and the United States. After a successful career on the stage she married an American, Pierce Butler, in 1834. Her husband and his brother owned several plantations in Georgia. This selection told about an incident that occurred during the year she spent in Georgia.

READING FOCUS

1. What system was set up on the plantation to establish discipline among the slaves?
2. How did Fanny's views on slavery differ with those of her husband?

On my return from the river I had a long and painful talk with Mr. Butler on the subject of the whipping of Teresa [a slave worn out from childbearing and field work, who asked the author to try to get her work load reduced]. Those discussions are terrible. They throw me into great distress for the slaves, whose position is completely hopeless; for myself, whose efforts on their behalf sometimes seem to me worse than useless; and for Mr. Butler, whose part in this horrible system fills me by turns with anger and pity. But, after all, what can he

Adapted from Journal of a Residence on a Georgian Plantation in 1838-1839 *by Frances Anne Kemble, edited by John A. Scott.*

Actress Fanny Kemble

do? How can he help it all? Moreover, born and raised in America, how should he care or wish to help it? And of course he does not, and I am in despair that he does not.

He said that there had been neither hardship nor injustice in the case of Teresa's whipping. Moreover, he added, she had not been whipped for complaining to me, but simply because her work was not done on time. Of course this lateness was the result of her having come to appeal to me instead of working. Since she knew perfectly well the punishment she would receive, my husband believed that there was neither hardship nor injustice in the case. The whole thing was a regularly established law, which all the slaves knew perfectly well. This case was no exception. My being here could not, of course, be allowed to overthrow the whole system of discipline established to secure the labor and obedience of slaves. If the slaves chose to challenge that fact, they and I must accept the consequences.

At the end of the day, the driver of the gang to which Teresa belongs reported that her work was not done. The overseer ordered him to give her the usual number of lashes. The driver obeyed this order, without of course, knowing how Teresa had spent her time instead of hoeing. But the overseer knew well enough, for Teresa told me that she had told him she would appeal to me about her weakness and suffering and inability to do the work.

When I was thus silenced on the particular case under discussion, I turned in my distress to abstract questions, which I never can stop from doing. When Mr. Butler defended the justice of Teresa's punishment, I attacked the obvious injustice of unpaid forced labor, the brutal inhumanity of allowing a man to whip a woman who was the mother of ten children. I declared that all of her work went to keep in luxury two idle young men, the owners of the plantation. I said I thought female labor such as that of these slaves, and the punishment they suffer, must be hateful to any manly or humane man. Mr. Butler said he thought it *was* disagreeable, and then left me to my thoughts.

*   *   *   *

I must tell you that I have been delighted, surprised, and puzzled by the sudden request of our young waiter, Aleck, that I teach him to read. He is a very intelligent lad of about 16, and he asked it in a way that was very touching. I told him I would think about it. I mean to do it. I will do it. And yet, it is breaking the laws of the government under which I am living. Unrighteous laws are made to be broken— *perhaps*—but then, you see, I am a woman, and Mr. Butler stands between me and the penalty. If I were a man, I would do so. Doubtless I should be shot some fine day from behind a tree by some good neighbor, who would do the community a service by quietly getting rid of a troublemaker. But teaching slaves to read is a finable offense, and, since I am a married woman, my fines must be paid by my legal owner. The first offense of the sort is heavily fined, and the second more heavily fined. For the third, one is sent to prison. What a pity it is I can't begin with Aleck's third lesson, because going to prison would fall upon me. I certainly intend to teach Aleck to read. I certainly won't tell Mr. Butler anything about it. I'll leave him to find it out. This is the way things are done by slaves and servants and children and all oppressed, ignorant, uneducated, and unprincipled people.

I begin to see one very great advantage in this slavery: you are the absolute ruler on your own plantation. No slave's testimony counts against you, and no white testimony exists but what you choose to admit. Some owners injure their slaves, some brand them, some pull out their teeth, some shoot them a little here and there (all details gathered from ads for runaway slaves in southern papers). They do all this on their plantations, where nobody comes to see.

I'll teach Aleck to read, for nobody is here to see, at least nobody whose seeing I mind. And I'll teach every other person that wants to learn. I haven't much more than a week to remain in this place. In that last week perhaps I may teach the boy enough to go on alone when I am gone.

READING REVIEW

1. Why was Teresa whipped?
2. **(a)** What objections did Fanny offer to the whipping? **(b)** How did Mr. Butler respond to these objections?
3. What was the penalty for teaching a slave to read?
4. Despite the punishment, why did Mrs. Kemble want to teach the slave to read?

99 In Defense of Slavery

From its beginning in America, there were many people who defended the system of slavery. Most of its early defenders, however, saw slavery as a "necessary evil." But after the 1830's, many defenders of slavery began to argue that the system was not only necessary but a positive good. Part of this changed attitude was caused by slave revolts, like that of Nat Turner, as well as by the growth of antislavery feeling. B. F. Stringfellow, a proslavery leader from Missouri, was typical of those who maintained that slavery was good both for black Americans and white Americans.

READING FOCUS

1. Why did Stringfellow say that "slavery is no evil" to black Americans?
2. What advantages did Stringfellow say came to whites because of slavery?

Negro slavery, as it exists in the United States, is neither a moral nor a political evil. On the contrary, it is a blessing to the Negro and to the white race.

Slavery is no evil to the Negro. If we look at the condition of Negroes in Africa, the land of their birth, we find the most pitiable victims of cruel masters. The most unfortunate slave in America, when contrasted with a prince of a tribe in the deserts of Africa, is as a person contrasted with a beast! The mightiest of the Negroes, in their native land, not only sacrifice their human victims to gods of stone, but are so horrible in their filth and nakedness that abolitionists would fly from them. It is certain that the only Negroes that have been rescued from the lowest stage of barbarity are those who have been made slaves to the whites.

But I go further and say that whenever Negroes have been the slaves of whites, their condition has been better, not only than that of their race in the deserts of Africa, but better than when freed from the control of whites.

Negro slavery is no evil to the white race either. Negro slavery produces effects which are not shown in the census, and which cannot be set down in figures, of far more importance than the acquisition of wealth or mere increase of population. These are its tendency to raise the character of the white race and to give to

Adapted from B. F. Stringfellow, Negro Slavery, No Evil, *1854.*

A slave auction in Richmond

that race a more noble moral tone. Slavery gives to the white race a higher, holier, more stern and unyielding love of liberty. It makes the white race a race of rulers, fit members of a free government.

Not only does the institution of slavery raise the character of the master. But where, as in our country, the slave is of a different race, marked and set apart by color, slavery raises the character not only of the master, the actual owner of slaves, but of all who wear the color of the free person. With us, color, not money, marks the class. Black is the badge of slavery, white the color of the free. And the white person, however poor, whatever the occupation, feels like a ruler.

Where Negro slavery exists, money is not necessary to make a person free. Whites take their rank by color. It is their sign of nobility. Through it, they are entitled to all the privileges of their class.

Things are not like this in the North. There money distinguishes the classes—marks the masters, separates them from the servants. There color gives no privilege. The white man and the white woman driven to "service" are excluded from the presence of their masters, and dare not claim to be their equals. Where money means honor, poverty is looked upon as a disgrace.

Let the foreign laborers continue to come daily, lowering wages. Let the prisons and poorhouses of Europe be emptied on us. Let labor thus be destroyed by its own strength, capital be thus still further taken over by the few. What then shall save the Republic from ruin?

The North can depend upon the South, as upon the strong arm of a brother, so long as Negro slavery exists. The South will furnish materials for its workshops, a market for its manufacturers, wealth for its capitalists, wages for the laborers. In the South no struggle between labor and capital can take place. Where slavery exists, capital and labor are one, for labor is capital. There the capitalists, instead of exhausting their laborers, must strengthen, protect, and preserve them. The interest of the laborer and the capitalist, slave and master, are the same; they cannot conflict. The prosperity of the master is the happiness of the slave. The master prospers as the slaves are healthy, vigorous, and happy.

Let abolitionists succeed, let slavery be abolished, let the Negroes be turned loose. The whites, driven from their homes, will seek a refuge among the crowded population of the North. If the whites are victorious in the conflict, the Negroes will fly to their northern friends. The northern laborer would find a ruinous competitor; the northern capitalist, a fearful addition to the strength of his enemy. In either event the fall of the South would bring ruin on the North.

1. According to Stringfellow, why are blacks better off under slavery than freedom?
2. How does he say the slave system benefits whites?
3. What danger does Stringfellow believe the end of slavery would bring to northerners?

100 At a Slave Auction

Many white people wrote about slavery. But what did the slaves think and feel about slavery? Since slaves were forbidden to learn to read or write, they left few written records. Most of those that do exist are stories of men and women who escaped to the North. Often their stories were heavily edited or written entirely by abolitionists.

Solomon Northup was a free black man who wrote an account of his years as a slave. Northup had been kidnapped in Washington, D.C., and sold into slavery. After working for many years on a Louisiana cotton plantation, he finally was freed in 1853. Historians regard Northup's writing as one of the more accurate accounts of slavery.

READING FOCUS

1. How were the slaves at the auction treated?
2. What happened to make the slave seller threaten Eliza with a whipping?

Mr. Theophilus Freeman, keeper of the slave pen in New Orleans, was out among his slaves early in the morning. He gave an occasional kick to the older men and women, and many a sharp crack of the whip about the ears of the younger slaves. It was not long before they were all wide awake. Mr. Theophilus Freeman moved about in a very industrious manner, getting his property ready for the salesroom, intending to do a rousing business that day.

First we were required to wash thoroughly, and if we had beards, to shave. We each were then given a new suit, cheap but clean. The men got a hat, coat, shirt, pants, and shoes. The women had dresses of calico, and handkerchiefs

Adapted from Solomon Northup, Twelve Years a Slave, *1853.*

to bind about their heads. We were then led into a large room in the front part of the building in order to be properly trained before the buyers came. The men were arranged on one side of the room, the women on the other. The tallest was placed at the front of the row, then the next tallest, and so on in the order of height. Freeman instructed us to remember our places and urged us to appear smart and lively—sometimes threatening, sometimes holding out various rewards. During the day he rehearsed us in the art of "looking smart" and of moving to our places. After being fed in the afternoon, we were again paraded and made to dance. Bob, a colored boy who belonged to Freeman, played on the violin.

Next day many customers arrived to examine Freeman's "new lot." He was very talkative, spending much time explaining our good points and qualities. He would make us hold up our heads and walk briskly back and forth. Customers would feel our hands and arms and bodies, turn us about, ask us what we could do, and make us open our mouths and show our teeth. It was just the way a jockey examines a horse. Sometimes a man or woman was taken back to the small house in the yard, stripped, and inspected more closely. Scars on a slave's back were considered evidence that the slave was rebellious or restless, and this hurt sales.

One old gentleman, who said he wanted a coach driver, appeared to take a liking to me. From his talk with Freeman, I learned he lived in the city. I very much wanted him to buy me, because I thought it would not be difficult to make my escape from New Orleans on some northern ship. Freeman asked him to pay fifteen hundred dollars for me. The old gentleman insisted it was too much, as times were very hard. Freeman replied that I was sound and healthy, strong and intelligent. The old gentleman argued that there was nothing extraordinary about me. Finally, to my regret, he left, saying he would call again.

During the day, however, a number of sales were made. David and Caroline were both bought by a Natchez planter. They left us, grinning broadly. They were happy because they had not been separated. Lethe was sold to a planter of Baton Rouge, her eyes flashing with anger as she was led away. The same man also purchased Randall. The little fellow was made to jump and run across the floor, and perform many other acts to show his activity and condition. All the time the trade was going on his mother Eliza was crying aloud and wringing her hands. She begged the man not to buy him unless he also bought her and her daughter Emily. She promised, in that case, to be the most faithful slave that ever lived. The man answered that he could not afford it, and then Eliza burst into sobs. Freeman turned round to her savagely, with his whip in his uplifted hand, ordering her to stop her noise or he would whip her. He would not have such whining, he said. Unless she stopped that minute, he would take her to the yard and give her a hundred lashes. Yes, he would take the nonsense out of her pretty quick.

Eliza cringed and tried to wipe away her tears, but it was all in vain. She wanted to be with her children, she said, for the little time she had to live. All the frowns and threats of Freeman could not silence her. She kept on begging that he not separate the three of them. Over and over again she told how she loved her boy. She repeated how very faithful and obedient she would be, how hard she would work day and night, to the last moment of her life, if only he would buy them all together. But it was of no use. The man could not afford it. The bargain was agreed upon, and Randall had to go alone. Then Eliza ran to him and embraced him. She kissed him again and again, and told him to remember her. All the while her tears fell like rain on the boy's face.

Freeman ordered her to go to her place and behave herself. He swore he wouldn't allow such action any longer. He would soon give her something to cry about, if she was not mighty careful, and that she could depend upon.

The planter from Baton Rouge, with his new purchases, was ready to depart.

"Don't cry, mama. I will be a good boy. Don't cry," Randall yelled, looking back as they passed out of the door.

What has become of the boy, God knows. It was a sad scene indeed. I would have cried myself if I had dared.

READING REVIEW

1. Why were the slaves cleaned up and told to look smart for the auction?
2. Why did Northup want to be bought by the man from New Orleans?
3. Explain the reactions of David and Caroline and Eliza and Randall.

101 How Slaves Survived

The treatment of slaves varied. But no matter how kind owners might be, they had complete control over the blacks they owned. They were free to split up slave families and to punish blacks in almost any way they chose.

According to a modern black historian, Nathan Huggins, slaves developed their own way of looking at life. This ethical framework, or system of values, gave them the courage they needed to withstand the dehumanizing circumstances in which they were forced to live.

READING FOCUS

1. According to Huggins, why did relatively few slaves try to escape?
2. Why did most slaves not rebel?

By the mid-nineteenth century, the only way out of slavery was escape. Yet to escape from the Deep South was almost impossible. The distances were long, the countryside hostile. Most fugitives in the Deep South escaped only for short distances from their places and for short periods of time.

It was much less difficult to make it to freedom from the Upper South. But, after 1850, the refugee was in constant danger. Kidnappers, anxious for rewards, would seize blacks on the streets of northern cities and bring them to trial as fugitives to be returned to slavery. If refugees could make it to Canada, they would be safer, but even there they could not be sure.

The decision to escape filled slaves with anxiety and doubt. The fear and concern over the difficulties, the likely consequences of failure, were part of it, to be sure. But there was more. To leave meant to abandon parents, friends, or children. Outside the plantation, on the long road north, was a dark emptiness, a loneliness that few slaves would want to endure.

Most slaves would not become refugees, nor would they lead revolts. They had a stake in order. They would try to hold the family and the group together. To find room in which to

Adapted from Nathan I. Huggins, Black Odyssey, *1977.*

live as human beings and to find ways to improve life became primary goals for the greatest number of slaves. Threats to order, even from rebellious blacks, were threats to the marginal existence that slaves had carved out for themselves and would strive to protect.

Some people called slaves fatalists because they seemed resigned to their condition. But their fatalism has to be qualified. They accepted, through their faith, their own worthiness as children of God. They had no doubt that they, in their essence, were as capable of freedom as anyone. Indeed, they assumed freedom to be their right. Their Bible was filled with examples of deliverance. In time, the circumstances would change and they would assume their rightful place. Thus slavery was their condition, not their destiny.

Whites of the time and some historians have taken this attitude as a suggestion that slaves were content with their lot. Far from it. They tried to find a bit of happiness within brutalizing circumstances. There is a heroism in this, but we must consider their ethical framework to appreciate it.

Slaves understood and accepted, as few of their masters could, that pain was as much a part of life as pleasure. From infancy, the slave's experience was so filled with pain, the anticipation of pain, the witnessing of pain in others, that there could be no surprise or shock when the lash stung against one's back or when one's heart was crushed in the sorrow of separation. White Americans had always thought of the pursuit of happiness as a right. The weight of pain was not their heritage. Rather, it was something that could be minimized or avoided.

In learning to accept pain and injury as natural to the human condition, the slave came to see a truth: that true damage to the soul was not in injury inflicted by others but in inflicting injury *on* others. The ideal person was one who had become detached enough to protect his or her emotions from the accidents of life.

The central ethical demand for the slave was duty, to accept one's duty and to be honest in it. Most slaves saw themselves obliged by their condition to labor for their owner on his place. This was no comment on the rightness or justice of slavery. It was merely to say that given their predicament, there was an honorable way of surviving it, and it was their duty to find that way and live it.

Music helped slaves survive.

READING REVIEW

1. Why was it difficult for slaves to escape?
2. What arguments did the writer present to prove that slaves were not fatalists?
3. List three opinions that Huggins offered to convince readers that slaves were survivors.

102 A Black's Stand Against Colonization

One of the most outstanding black abolitionist leaders was Frederick Douglass. An escaped slave, he became a powerful and effective speaker and writer in the antislavery movement. Douglass told of the horrors of slavery from his own experience and never failed to move his audiences by telling of the inhumanity and cruelty of slavery.

In addition to speaking at antislavery meetings, Douglass also published an abolitionist newspaper, the *North Star,* and aided escaped slaves. In this selection, Douglass argues against the colonization of black Americans in Liberia.

READING FOCUS

1. For whom was Douglass speaking?
2. What was Douglass' main objection to sending free blacks to Liberia?

We are of the opinion that the *free* colored people generally mean to live in America, and not in Africa. To set aside a large sum of money for our removal would merely be a waste of the

Colonization society membership certificate, 1842

public money. We do not mean to go to Liberia. Our minds are made up to live here if we can, or die here if we must. Every attempt to remove us will be, as it ought to be, labor lost. Here we are and here we shall remain. While our brothers and sisters are in bondage on these shores, it is idle to think of persuading many free colored people to leave this for a foreign land.

For two hundred and twenty-eight years the colored people have worked in the soil of America, under a burning sun and a driver's whip. They have plowed, planted, and reaped so that whites might live in ease, their hands unhardened by labor, their brows unwet by the sweat of work. Now that the moral sense of humanity is beginning to revolt at this system of cruel wrong and is demanding its overthrow, the mean and cowardly oppressor is planning to expel the colored people entirely from the country. Shame upon the guilty wretches that dare propose or consider such a plan. We live here—have lived here—have a right to live here—and mean to live here in the future.

Adapted from Frederick Douglass, speech published in The North Star, *January 26, 1849.*

READING REVIEW

1. List two pieces of evidence that Douglass cited in opposition to colonization.
2. What "loaded" words did Douglass use to convince people of the rightness of his stand?

CHAPTER 15 Expanding the Nation's Boundaries
(1820's–1860's)

---

103 Santa Fe in 1831

Josiah Gregg was born in Missouri in 1806. He was "weakly" (as people then described someone with poor health), probably suffering from tuberculosis. After training as a doctor, he joined a wagon caravan and traveled westward to Santa Fe. The climate in Santa Fe attracted him because it was supposed to help those in poor health. In the selection that follows Gregg describes the town of Santa Fe and the trading that took place there. On this trip, Gregg was part of an advance scouting party that arrived in Santa Fe a few days ahead of the wagon caravan.

Gregg settled in Santa Fe and became a merchant there. During the Gold Rush of 1849 he traveled to California, where he later died of exposure and starvation while exploring the region around Humboldt Bay.

READING FOCUS

1. How did Gregg describe Santa Fe?
2. Why was the arrival of the caravan significant for the people of Santa Fe?

A few miles before reaching the city, the road again runs onto an open plain. Climbing a hill, we saw a valley to the northwest with occasional groups of trees in green corn and wheatfields. Here and there a square blocklike struc-

Adapted from The Commerce of the Prairies *by Josiah Gregg.*

Santa Fe, New Mexico, as an early trading center.

ture rose up. A little farther ahead of us to the north more structures appeared. "Oh, we are coming to the outskirts!" I said, seeing the cornfields and what I thought were ovens for baking bricks located in every direction. When a friend heard these remarks, he said: "It is true those are heaps of unbaked bricks. Nevertheless, they are also houses—this *is* the city of Santa Fe."

Five or six days after our arrival the caravan finally arrived, and wagon after wagon poured down the last hill about a mile from the city. To judge from the loud shouts of the men and the excitement of the mule drivers, the sight must have been as exciting to them as it had been to me. It was truly a scene for an artist to draw. Even the animals seemed to share in the mood of their riders, who grew more and more merry and noisy as they rode toward the city.

The caravan's arrival produced a great deal of movement and excitement among the natives. Shouts of "Los Americanos!"—"Los carros!"—"Ahi viene la caravana!" ["The Americans!"—"The wagons!"—"The caravan is coming!"] were heard in every direction. Crowds of women and children came to see the newcomers, while gangs of thieves hung about, as usual, to see what they could steal.

The wagoners also were excited on this occasion. Told of the ordeal they had to face, they had spent the previous morning freshening up. Now they were prepared, with clean faces, combed hair, and their best Sunday suits, to meet the fair, sparkling dark eyes of the young women who were sure to stare at them as they passed.

Our wagons were soon unloaded in the cus-

toms house. We now had a few days' leisure—and time for the rest and enjoyment which a journey of ten weeks had made so necessary. The wagoners and many of the traders went to the many parties that are given after the arrival of a caravan. But most of the merchants were anxiously and actively engaged in their business affairs. They were trying to see who would be first to get their goods out of the customs house and have a chance at the hard cash of the many country dealers who come to the capital each year on these occasions.

Since only a few of the traders are able to write Spanish, they are forced to hire interpreters. They pay these people to make the arrangements and to act as interpreters during the customs inspection.

The inspection takes place but is rarely carried on strictly according to the rules. Sympathy for the merchants and a desire to encourage trade causes the customs inspector to open only a few packages.

The *derechos de arancel* [tariffs] of Mexico are extremely high, averaging about 100 percent. But there are very few places in Mexico where these rigid rules are strictly carried out. An arrangement—a compromise—is expected in which the inspectors are sure to provide something for themselves. At some places, it has been said that the tariff duties are divided into three equal parts: one for the officers, a second for the merchants, the third for the government.

The arrival of a caravan at Santa Fe changes the place at once. Instead of stillness in the streets, one now sees everywhere the movements, noise, and activity of a lively market town. Since the Mexicans very rarely speak

English, the negotiations are mostly in Spanish. Taking a tour of the stores, I found they usually contained goods much like those in the stores of the West.

READING REVIEW

1. How did Gregg react to Santa Fe? How did he react to its people?
2. Why were the merchants of Sante Fe excited about the arrival of the caravan?
3. Give two reasons why the custom inspection rules were not strictly enforced.
4. Why did the traders "compromise" with the inspectors?
5. What was Gregg's attitude toward "compromise" between traders and Mexican government officials regarding tariffs?

104 Two Messages from the Alamo

On February 23, 1836, a large Mexican army under the command of Santa Anna laid siege to the Alamo. Inside the Alamo was a force of fewer than 200 Texans. They were under the command of William Barret Travis, a twenty-seven-year-old lawyer, who had been appointed a Lieutenant Colonel in the Texas army. The outnumbered Texans held off Santa Anna's army for several days. But, finally, on March 6, 1836, the Mexican army broke through the Texans' defenses. The defenders of the Alamo were wiped out to the last fighting man.

The following reading includes two messages from Travis. The first was sent the day after the siege began, the second three days before the Alamo fell.

READING FOCUS

1. How did Travis respond to the Mexican demand to surrender?
2. Why did Travis not want the Mexican army to reach the Texas settlements?

TO THE PEOPLE IN TEXAS, AND ALL AMERICANS IN THE WORLD: COMMANDANCY OF THE ALAMO, BEJAR, Feb. 24, 1836.

FELLOW-CITIZENS AND COMPATRIOTS [countrymen]:

I am besieged by a thousand or more of the Mexicans, under Santa Anna. I have sustained a continual bombardment and cannonade for twenty-four hours, and have not lost a man. The enemy have demanded a surrender, otherwise the garrison is to be put to the sword, if the

Outnumbered by Santa Anna's troops, Texans bravely defend the Alamo.

fort is taken. I have answered the summons with a cannon-shot, and our flag still waves proudly from the walls. *I shall never surrender or retreat:* then I call on you, in the name of Liberty, of Patriotism, and of every thing dear to the American character, to come to our aid with all despatch. The enemy are receiving reinforcements daily, and will no doubt increase to three or four thousand in four or five days. Though this call may be neglected, I am determined to sustain myself as long as possible, and die like a soldier, who never forgets what is due to his own honor and that of his country. *Victory or Death!*

W. BARRET TRAVIS,
Lieutenant Colonel, Commanding.

P.S. The Lord is on our side. When the enemy appeared in sight, we had not three bushels of corn. We have since found, in deserted houses, eighty or ninety bushels, and got into the walls twenty or thirty head of beeves.

T.

TO THE PRESIDENT OF THE CONVENTION: COMMANDANCY OF THE ALAMO, BEJAR, March 3, 1836.

SIR:

From the 25th to the present date, the enemy have kept up a bombardment from two howitzers [short cannons] and a heavy cannonade from two long nine-pounders, mounted on a battery on the opposite side of the river, at the distance of four hundred yards from our walls. During this period, the enemy have been busily employed in encircling us with intrenched encampments on all sides. Notwithstanding all this, a company of thirty-two men from Gonzales, made their way into us on the morning of the March 1, at three o'clock, and Col. J. B. Bonham (a courier from Gonzales) got in this morning at eleven o'clock, without molestation. I have so fortified this place, that the walls are generally proof against cannon-balls; and I still continue to intrench on the inside, and strengthen the walls by throwing up the dirt. At least two hundred shells have fallen inside of our works without having injured a single man; indeed, we have been so fortunate as not

to lose a man from any cause, and we have killed many of the enemy. The spirits of my men are still high, although they have had much to depress them. We have contended for ten days against an enemy whose numbers are estimated at from fifteen hundred to six thousand men, with Gen. Ramirez Sezma and Col. Bartres, the aid-de-camp of Santa Anna, at their head. A report was circulated that Santa Anna himself was with the enemy, but I think it was false. A reinforcement of about one thousand men is now entering Bejar from the west, and I think it more than probable that Santa Anna is now in town, from the rejoicing we hear.

I look to the Texas settlements for aid; unless it arrives soon, I shall have to fight the enemy on his own terms. I will, however, do the best I can under the circumstances, and I feel confident that the determined heroism and desperate courage, shown by my men, will not fail them in the last struggle.

The power of Santa Anna is to be met here or in the colonies; we had better meet them here, than to suffer a war of desolation to rage in our settlements. A blood-red banner waves from the church of Bejar, and in the Mexican camp above us, in token that the war is one of revenge against rebels. They have declared us as such, and demanded that we should surrender sensibly, or that this garrison should be put to the sword. Their threats have had no influence on me or my men, but to make all fight with desperation, and that high-souled courage which characterizes the patriot, who is willing to die in defence of his country's liberty and his own honor.

The bearer of this message will give your government of the rebellion, a statement more in detail, should he escape through the enemy's lines. *God and Texas!—Victory or Death!!*

Your obedient ser't [servant],
W. BARRET TRAVIS
Lieut. Col. Comm. [Lieutenant Colonel, Commanding]

READING REVIEW

1. **(a)** What did the Mexicans threaten if Travis and the other defenders of the Alamo did not surrender? **(b)** How did Travis respond to this?
2. **(a)** How many Mexicans did Travis estimate opposed the Texans at the Alamo? **(b)** Why would it have been difficult for Travis to make an accurate count of his enemy?

Adapted from Henry Stuart Foote, Texas and the Texans, *1841.*

3. Why did Travis prefer to fight the Mexicans at the Alamo rather than in the Texas settlements?
4. Do you think that Travis made the correct decision when he refused to surrender? Explain your answer.

105 Manifest Destiny: An American View

Many Americans in the 1840's favored the spread of American power and influence. One of the most enthusiastic of these nationalists was John L. O'Sullivan. His magazine, *United States Magazine and Democratic Review*, expressed the ideas of those who favored the territorial expansion of the United States. The article that follows appeared in O'Sullivan's magazine in 1845 and was probably written by him. The famous phrase "manifest destiny"—which came to mean America's vital need and right to expand its territory—may have been used for the first time in this article and was a catchy phrase probably thought up by O'Sullivan.

New Yorkers celebrate news of victory over Mexico.

1. What were O'Sullivan's arguments in favor of annexing territory from Mexico?
2. Describe O'Sullivan's attitude toward Mexico?

It is time now for opposition to the annexation of Texas to end. It is time for the common duty of patriotism to the country to take over. If this duty is not recognized, it is at least time for common sense to give in to what is inevitable.

Texas is now ours. Already before these words are written, Texas's convention has surely ratified our invitation to join the Union. Its star and its stripe may already be said to have taken their place in the nation's glorious flag. The sweep of our eagle's wing already includes its fair and fertile land.

Texas is no longer to us a mere geographical place—a certain combination of coast, plain, mountain, valley, forest, and stream. It is no longer to us a mere country on the map. It is included within the cherished and sacred designation of Our Country. Patriotism, which is at once a sentiment and virtue, already begins to thrill for it within the national heart.

If we needed a reason for taking Texas into the Union, it surely is to be found in the manner in which other nations have interfered in the matter. Their object is to oppose our policy and hold back our power, to limit our greatness, and to check the fulfillment of our manifest destiny to spread over the continent. This we have seen done by England, our old rival and enemy, and by France, strangely allied with England against us.

It is wholly untrue and unjust to say that the annexation has been unlawful and unrighteous. It is wrong to say that it was a form of military conquest, of territorial enlargement at the cost of justice. This view of the question is wholly false.

The independence of Texas was complete and absolute. It was an independence not only in fact but of right. If Americans settled in Texas, they did not do so because of our government but at the invitation of Mexico itself, which offered guarantees of state independence and the maintenance of a federal system. When

Adapted from John L. O'Sullivan, "Annexation," Democratic Review, *July-August, 1845.*

Mexico violated these guarantees, the strongest measures were fully justified.

Texas was released, rightfully and absolutely released, from all allegiance to Mexico by the acts and fault of Mexico itself, and by Mexico alone. There never was a clearer case. And it was under such circumstances as left independence the only course. What then can be more absurd than these outcries by Mexico against annexation as a violation of its rights?

California will probably be the next area to break away from Mexico. Reckless and troubled by unrest, Mexico never can hold any real governmental authority over such a country. Its weakness and distance from California must make their relation one of almost independence, unless tyranny takes over, and in the case of California this is now impossible. Americans are already beginning to settle there. A population will soon occupy the region which Mexico cannot dream of dominating. These people will necessarily become independent. All this without the action of our government, without the responsibility of our people, is a natural course of events.

And these people will have a right to independence—to self-government, to possession of homes conquered from the wilderness by their own labors and dangers, sufferings, and sacrifices. They will have a better and a truer right there than Mexico, a thousand miles away.

READING REVIEW

1. Give two reasons why the United States should annex Mexican territory.
2. Do you think they are valid arguments? Why or why not?

106 Manifest Destiny: A Mexican-American View

In the 1840's, many Americans believed it was their destiny to take over all of the American continent. However, the Mexicans had a very different view of America's "manifest destiny."

In recent years, Americans of Mexican ancestry have begun to recognize and reclaim their Mexican heritage and traditions. Many, like the authors of the following selection, have proudly called themselves "Chicanos," a shortened form of "Mexicanos," meaning Mexicans. They presented a different view of manifest destiny.

READING FOCUS

1. What were the authors' views of "manifest destiny"?
2. What were the authors' purpose in writing this article?

People from the East had already begun to arrive in Téjas—part of Mexico—in the 1700's. [The authors used "Téjas," an Indian term meaning "allies," instead of "Texas"; it is pronounced TAY·hass.] There were no great mountain ranges to separate Téjas from Anglo-America [the United States], and there were rivers as well as coastline to encourage travel. These first people fought their way in—killing and ruining the area around San Antonio. Most of them came from the slave states, and they brought a racist attitude with them. They treated the Mexicans living in Téjas the same way they treated black people, and they showed no respect for the laws of Mexico. When Mexico abolished slavery in 1826, the filibusterers just ignored the new law and kept on bringing in slaves.

President Jackson and his friends wanted to do more than force their way into Téjas, especially since the law against slavery made it hard to establish big plantations. So they drew up a plan. The United States would try to buy Téjas from Mexico. But in case that didn't work, Anglo settlers [white settlers from the United States] would be brought into Téjas until there were enough of them there to declare a "revolution" against Mexico. The Mexicans would be kicked out, and then the United States would annex Téjas.

The conspiracy was in full operation by 1829. Jackson's good friend, Sam Houston, went to New York and Washington looking for people to take part in the conquest of Téjas. Houston sent agents all over the country to find "settlers" for Téjas. Another person who played an important part in the whole plan was Moses Austin and later his son, Stephen.

Moses Austin asked the Mexican government for a large grant of land in Téjas, where he would establish a settlement of 300 Anglo-American families. All the families would be Roman Catholics and of good character, he said, and they would swear allegiance to the

Adapted from Viva la Raza.

Mexican government. Mexico agreed to grant this land to Moses Austin. Later his son, Stephen, got more contracts to settle Téjas. By 1833 he had issued land titles to 2,000 Anglo families. Austin and also Sam Houston even became Mexican citizens to convince Mexico of their honest intentions.

In 1836 it was clear that Mexico would not sell Téjas. But there were enough Anglos there for the other plan to be put into effect. So the Anglos decided that they would declare their "independence" from Mexico. Having received the land from Mexico on certain conditions, they simply broke the agreement and called it a "revolution." To make the so-called revolution look more legal, Houston and his friends set up a so-called government. They wrote a constitution. Everybody knew it was just a trick.

The United States whipped up a tremendous national enthusiasm for helping "Texas" win its "independence." In New York, Boston, Philadelphia, and many other cities, rallies and benefits were held to raise funds for the "Texans" against what were called "the Mexican tyrants." Money poured in. Sam Houston was named commander of the army and Téjas was named Texas.

The president of Mexico quickly sent in troops to put down the phony revolution, and they won several victories. The most famous of these was retaking the Alamo fort in San Antonio. "Remember the Alamo" is the famous cry that has come down to us from that battle. We are told that the Mexicans massacred hundreds of helpless Anglos who had taken refuge in the Alamo. "Remember the Alamo" has always meant: remember the massacre and get revenge on Mexico. But what really happened at the Alamo?

When Mexico's troops began winning in Texas, many Anglos became frightened and went to the Alamo fort for safety. A small number of Mexicano women and children also went there. Houston ordered that the fort be abandoned because it couldn't be defended and he couldn't promise any help. But Jim Bowie, the man in command at the fort, didn't want to give up. With Bowie were William Travis and Davy Crockett.

The Mexican attack on the Alamo began on February 23, 1836. Soon after, General Santa Anna sent word to the people inside that if they would just put down their weapons and swear never to use them again to fight Mexico, their lives and property would be respected. This offer was answered with cannon fire. The Mexican troops continued to shell the fort and then stormed it on March 6.

They took the fort, but paid heavily for the victory. Mexico lost many more men at the Alamo than the Anglos. Bowie, Travis, and Crockett all died fighting, as did the other men. It was not a massacre, it was a battle. The women and children were all removed safely from the Alamo and given money and blankets. The two slaves who had been inside were freed by the Mexicanos.

That is the true story of the Alamo. Yet "Re-

Mexican soldiers open fire on Americans at the Alamo.

member the Alamo" has come down to us as a cry of anger and bitterness from the Anglos. It is we Chicanos who should really feel bitter, because we see the hypocrisy and falseness of "Remember the Alamo." That cry is taught to encourage hatred toward Mexico, Mexicans, and ourselves. For us, the Alamo was a victory in the struggle by Mexico to defend itself against invasion and aggression. For us, the Alamo was the birth of the gringo [an uncomplimentary way of referring to so-called Anglo-Americans]—when the gringo first showed us *his* true colors.

The Alamo was the last of Mexico's victories. Soon afterward, General Santa Anna was defeated and captured in a surprise attack, and he signed a treaty recognizing the "independence" of Texas in return for his freedom. The Mexican government did not confirm that treaty, so the war went on. The gringos in Texas even sent a band of 270 men to invade Nuevo Mexico [New Mexico]. They were defeated, but that was the beginning of a new move—to take over still more of Mexico's territory.

The truth was that the United States had decided it would expand all the way to the West Coast. It wanted to obtain ports on the Pacific Ocean and build up its commerce. A name was invented for this plan: "manifest destiny." War on Mexico was just a matter of "destiny," of "God's will," officials of the United States government said. It was the God-given destiny of the United States to expand all the way to the Pacific. The magic words "manifest destiny" were repeated over and over again. They were used to justify the takeover of anything and everything.

READING REVIEW

1. According to the authors, why did the United States want to annex Mexican territory?
2. Do you agree or disagree with this view of manifest destiny?
3. How does this account of the Battle of the Alamo compare with the one on text page 390?
4. Were the authors' views one-sided or impartial? Explain.

107 A Rendezvous on the Green River

The Mountain Men were trappers and explorers who roamed the western territories in search of fur-

bearing animals. As the fur trade grew, trappers and the fur-trading companies developed the "rendezvous system." Each year, at a prearranged time and place, trappers and Indians would meet with merchants and representatives of the fur-trading companies. At this rendezvous, or meeting, the trappers and Indians would trade the furs they had caught during the year for money and supplies. The rendezvous also gave the trappers a chance to renew old friendships, exchange news, and generally take a break from the dangers and hardships of trapping in the wild.

The following reading described a rendezvous in 1839, on the Green River in the southwestern part of present-day Wyoming. The description was written by a German immigrant who attended the rendezvous as an employee of the Fur Company of St. Louis.

READING FOCUS

1. Why was the rendezvous important to the trappers and explorers?
2. How were the trappers and Indians similar?
3. Why did the writer think that the days of the trapper would soon come to an end?

We reached the camping place. What first struck our eye was several long rows of Indian tents, extending along the Green River for at least a mile. Indians and whites were mingled here in varied groups. Of the Indians present, there were chiefly Snakes, Flatheads, and Nez Perces, all peaceful tribes, living beyond the Rocky Mountains. Of the whites present, there were agents of the different trading companies and a large number of trappers. They came to buy and to sell, to renew old contracts and to make new ones, to make arrangements for future meetings, to meet old friends, to tell of adventures they had been through, and to spend for once a jolly day.

These trappers are such a peculiar set of people that it is necessary to say a little about them. They roam throughout the mountains in small groups. No rock is too steep for them; no stream too swift. They are in constant danger from hostile Indians, whose delight it is to ambush, plunder, and scalp them. But this daily danger seems to exercise a magic attraction over most of them.

In manners and customs, the trappers have borrowed much from the Indians. Many of

Adapted from F.A. Wislizenus, A Journey to the Rocky Mountains in the Year 1839.

145

them, too, have taken Indian women as wives. The trappers' dress is generally of leather. The hair of the head is usually allowed to grow long. In place of money, they use beaver skins, which they trade at the forts to satisfy all their needs. A pound of beaver skins is usually paid for with four dollars worth of goods; but the goods themselves are sold at enormous prices, so-called mountain prices.

At the yearly rendezvous the trappers seek to make up for the sufferings and privations of a year spent in the wilderness. With their beaver skins, they can obtain all the luxuries of the mountains, and live for a few days like lords. Coffee and chocolate is cooked; the pipe is kept aglow day and night; the spirits circulate; and whatever is not spent in such ways the squaws coax out of them, or else it is squandered at cards. Formerly single trappers on such occasions have often wasted a thousand dollars.

But the days of their glory seem to be past, for constant hunting has very much reduced the number of beavers. This decrease in the beaver catch was noticeable at this year's rendezvous in the quieter behavior of the trappers. There was little drinking of spirits, and almost no gambling. Another decade perhaps and the original trapper will have disappeared from the mountains.

The Indians who had come to the meeting were no less interesting than the trappers.

Mountain men at a yearly rendezvous

There must have been a thousand of them. Their tents are made of buffalo hides, tanned on both sides and sewed together, stretched in cone shape over a dozen poles, that are leaned against each other, their tops crossing.

I visited many tents, partly out of curiosity and partly to barter for trinkets. An army of Indian dogs very much resembling the wolf, usually beset the entrance. From some tents comes the sound of music. An Indian musician beats a sort of kettle drum with all his might, and the chorus accompanies him with strange monotone sounds. A similar heart-rending song drew me to a troop of squaws that were engrossed in the game of "the hand," so popular with the Indians. Some small object, a bit of wood, for instance, is passed from hand to hand among the players seated in a circle; and it is someone's part to guess in whose hands the object is.

Other groups of whites and Indians were engaged in barter. The Indians had for trade chiefly tanned skins, moccasins, thongs of buffalo leather or braided buffalo hair, and fresh or dried buffalo meat. They have no beaver skins. The articles that attracted them most in exchange were powder and lead, knives, tobacco, cinnabar, gaily colored kerchiefs, pocket mirrors and all sorts of ornaments. Before an Indian begins to trade he demands sight of everything that may be offered by the other party to the trade. If there is something there that attracts him, he, too, will produce his wares, but discovers very quickly how much or how little they are coveted. If he himself does not want to sell some particular thing, he refuses, though ten times the value be offered him.

The rendezvous usually lasts a week. Then the different parties move off to their destinations and the plain that today echoed with Indian music, that was thronged with people of both races, with horses and dogs, returns to its old quiet, interrupted only now and then by the muffled roar of the buffalo and howl of the wolf.

READING REVIEW

1. Give five reasons why fur trappers attended the yearly rendezvous.
2. List three customs the trappers borrowed from the Indians.
3. Why did the writer think that the days of the trapper would soon be ended?

In the gold rush, many people abandoned their homes, hoping to strike it rich.

108 California in the Gold Rush Days

What was life like in California after gold was discovered there in 1848? Most Americans were eager to learn all they could about the land of the Gold Rush. As a result, in 1849 the New York *Tribune* sent Bayard Taylor, an eager young reporter, to California to find out. He visited miners who were digging for gold, talked to everyone he could, and sent back vivid reports about California to his newspaper. In this selection Taylor described what mining for gold was like along the Mokelumne River, not far from Stockton, California.

READING FOCUS

1. What was mining for gold like?
2. What was life like in California after the Gold Rush of 1848?

The first group of miners we saw had just finished digging a new channel for the waters of the Mokelumne River. Now they were beginning to mine the old riverbed. There were ten of them, and their only tools were shovels, a rude cradle for sifting the top layers of dirt, and flat wooden bowls for washing out the sands. One of them took a bowl which was full of sand, and in five minutes showed us a dozen grains of bright gold. In the morning the men had mined about three pounds [1.3 kilograms] of gold. We watched them at their work till the evening, by which time they had produced three pounds more, making an average of seven ounces [198 grams] of gold for each man. The gold was of the purest quality and the most beautiful color.

When I first saw the men there in the hot sun carrying heavy stones, standing nearly waist deep in water, and digging with their hands in the gravel and clay, there seemed to me little sense in digging for gold. But when the shining particles of gold were poured out from a tin basin, I admit I was tempted to grab

Adapted from Bayard Taylor, Eldorado, *1949.*

147

the heaviest crowbar and the biggest shovel and to start looking for gold myself.

We found many persons at work in the higher part of the valley, searching for veins and pockets of gold in the holes which had already produced their first gold finds. Some of them were well repaid for their steady work. Others had been working for days without finding anything.

There are thousands of similar valleys among the mountains, nearly all of which undoubtedly contain gold. Those who are familiar with geology [the study of rock formations of the earth] usually find new spots for digging. A great many who are disappointed in their high hopes, disheartened by the hard work, cry out in great bitterness against the stories of gold which first attracted them to the country. I met hundreds of such persons, many of whom have returned home disgusted forever with California. They compared the diggings to a lottery, in which people grew rich only by accident or luck. There is no such thing as accident in Nature. The better people understand Nature, the more sure a clue they have to its

A lone prospector pans for gold.

buried treasures. There is more gold in California than ever was imagined. Ages will not exhaust the supply

The first result of the rush of emigrants from all parts of the world into California—a country almost unknown—was to nearly end all law. The countries which were nearest the golden coast sent forth thousands of adventurers, who speedily outnumbered the American population. Another factor that threatened serious consequences was the large numbers of worthless and wicked people from our own country who came to the Pacific coast. From the beginning, a lack of government or law might have been expected. Instead of this, there was a desire to maintain order and protect the rights of all throughout the mining districts. In the absence of all law or available protection, the people met and adopted rules for their mutual security—rules adapted to their situation, where they had neither guards nor prisons. Small thefts were punished by banishment from the diggings. For those of large amount or for more serious crimes, there was the single alternative of hanging.

In all the large digging districts, which had been worked for some time, there were established rules, which were faithfully obeyed. Mayors were elected. They decided on all disputes of right or complaints of trespass, and had power to summon juries for criminal trials. When a new mine was discovered, the first thing done was to elect officers and extend the area of order.

The rights of the diggers were also definitely marked and strictly obeyed. Among the hundreds of miners I saw on the Mokelumne River and among the valleys, I did not see a single dispute nor hear a word of complaint. A man might dig a hole and so long as he left a shovel, pick, or crowbar to show that he still intended working it, he was safe from trespass. His tools might remain there for months without being disturbed. I have seen many such places, miles away from any camp or tent, which the digger had left, in perfect confidence that he should find everything all right on his return.

Abundance of gold does not always lead to a grasping and greedy spirit. The principles of hospitality were as faithfully followed in the crude tents of the diggers as they would be by thrifty farmers of the North and West. In no part of the world have I ever seen help more freely given to the needy, or more ready cooperation. Personally, I can safely say that I never met with such kindness from people who were strangers.

I do not believe, however, that the majority of California's native population is happy at the change which has come over the region. On the contrary, there is much jealousy and bitter feeling among some of the people. The large numbers of emigrants from the Atlantic states outnumbered the native population three times over within a single year, and consequently placed them forever in a hopeless minority. They witnessed the swift loss of their own political importance, and the introduction of a new language, new customs, and new laws. It is not strange that many of them should be opposed to us at heart, even while growing wealthy and prosperous under the changes brought by the hard work of our citizens. Nevertheless, we have many warm friends among them. Our authorities have acted toward them with fairness and kindness. By following a similar course, the future government of the state will soon remove the differences of race and condition, and all the people will then be equally Californian and American citizens.

READING REVIEW

1. Was Taylor correct in his estimate of California's gold resources?
2. Why did some people compare their mining experience to a lottery?
3. What feature of life among the miners pleased Taylor? Why?
4. Name two results of the rush of immigrants to California.
5. How do you think newspaper readers in the eastern United States reacted to Taylor's reports?

CHAPTER
16 Working for Reform
(1820's–1860's)

109 On the Roles of Women

Many Americans were critical of conditions in society in the mid-1800's. They felt that important changes had to be made in the nation. Many of those who felt this way were from New England and were abolitionists. One of them, Lydia Maria Child, started a successful children's magazine when she was only 24. However, her outspoken antislavery views turned many people against her, and the magazine went bankrupt. Afterward, she spent much time writing and working for the abolitionist cause. In this selection, Lydia Maria Child gave her views on the role of women.

READING FOCUS

1. What roles did the author consider proper for women?
2. What did Child say about "the ownership principle"?

You ask what my opinions about "Women's Rights" are. I confess a strong dislike for the subject as it has been generally treated. On no other subject has there been so much false sentiment, shallow philosophy, and sputtering wit. Still, if the style of its supporters has often been offensive and unreasonable, surely that of its opponents has been more so. College boys have amused themselves writing dreams in which they saw women in hotels with their feet up and chairs tilted back, or growling and bickering at each other in legislative halls, or fighting at the election polls with eyes blackened by fistfights. But it never seems to have occurred to these writers that the proceedings which appear so silly and improper in *women* are also ridiculous and disgraceful in *men*. *Men* should learn not to put their feet up above their heads and tilt their chairs backward, nor to growl and snap in the halls of legislation, nor to give each other black eyes at the election polls.

It seems that men are willing to give women the exclusive benefit of gospel-teaching. "*Women* should be gentle," say those who favor women's subordination. But when Christ said, "Blessed are the meek," did he preach to women only? "*Girls* should be modest," is the language of common teaching. Would it not be an improvement for men also to be pure in manners, conversation, and life? Books written for young married people give plenty of advice

Adapted from *Lydia Maria Child,* Letters from New York, *1852.*

149

American abolitionist and writer, Lydia Maria Child

to the *wife*. She should control her temper and never complain or be angry when her husband comes home irritable and unreasonable from his conflicts with the world. Would it not be as appropriate if the husband were advised to control *his* temper and stop *his* complaints in consideration of his wife's ill health, tiring cares, and thousand chores? In short, whatever can be called the loveliest, best, and most graceful in woman would likewise be good and graceful in man.

You will perhaps remind me of courage. If you use the word in its highest meaning, I answer that woman, above others, has abundant need of it. The true woman wears it with a quiet grace. If you mean mere animal courage, *that* is not mentioned in the Sermon on the Mount as among those qualities which enable us to inherit the earth or become the children of God.

That the present position of women in society is the result of physical force is obvious enough. If any woman doubts it, she should consider why she is afraid to go out in the evening without the protection of a man. What makes up the danger of aggression? Superior physical strength, uncontrolled by moral sentiments.

There are few books which I can read through without feeling insulted as a woman. But this insult is almost always expressed in words meant as praise. Just imagine, for a moment, what impression it would make on men if women authors should write about *their* "rosy lips," and "melting eyes" and "voluptuous forms," as they write about *us*! I readily admit that most women do not feel this kind of flat-

tery to be an insult. For, in the first place, they do not realize the ownership principle it expresses. Moreover, they have become used to thinking of themselves as household conveniences or painted toys. Hence they consider it feminine and pretty to give up all use of the abilities that would make them co-workers with men in the advancement of society.

The nearer society approaches to divine order, the less separation there will be in characters, duties, and pursuits of men and women. Women will not become less gentle and graceful. But men will become more so. Women will not neglect the care and education of their children. But men will find themselves becoming better persons by sharing those duties with them. They will receive, in return, cooperation and sympathy in handling various other duties now thought unsuitable for women. The more women become rational companions, partners in business and in thought, as well as in affection and amusement, the more highly men will appreciate *home*—that blessed word which opens to the human heart the most perfect glimpse of heaven.

The conviction that woman's present position in society is a false one, and therefore has disastrous effects on the happiness and improvement of man, is becoming clearer to everyone. As man approaches the truest life, he will realize more and more that there is no separation or conflict in their mutual duties. They will be one. But it will be as affection and thought are one—the treble and bass of the same harmonious tune.

READING REVIEW

1. Do you think this letter was written to a man or woman?
2. What did the writer say about the "mutual duties" of men and women?

110 The Seneca Falls Declaration

The first women's rights convention was held at Seneca Falls, New York, in 1848. There, on July 19, the delegates to the convention adopted the following "Declaration of Sentiments and Resolutions." It was based on the Declaration of Independence and much of it was written by Elizabeth Cady Stanton. When she read the Declaration to her husband, he threatened to leave town during the convention—which he did. The declaration was signed at the convention by 68 women and 32 men.

READING FOCUS

1. How did the format of the Seneca Falls Declaration compare with that of the Declaration of Independence?
2. What facts did the Declaration list to "prove" the "tyranny" of man over woman?

1. Declaration of Sentiments

When, in the course of human events, it becomes necessary for one part of the family of man to assume a position different from that which they have held up to now, but one to which the laws of nature and of God entitle them, respect for the opinions of mankind requires that they should declare the causes that lead them to such a course.

We hold these truths to be self-evident: that all men and women are created equal; that they are endowed by their Creator with certain unalienable rights; that among these are life, liberty, and the pursuit of happiness; that to secure these rights governments are instituted, deriving their just powers from the consent of the governed. Whenever any form of government becomes destructive of these ends, it is the right of those who suffer from it to refuse allegiance to it, and to insist upon the institution of a new government, laying its foundation on such principles, and organizing its powers in such form, as to them shall seem most likely to effect their safety and happiness. Caution, indeed, will dictate that governments long established should not be changed for light and passing causes: and accordingly all experience shows that mankind are more given to suffer while evils are sufferable, than to right themselves by doing away with the forms which they are used to. But when a long train of abuses and usurpations, following unchangingly the same object, shows a plan to bring them under absolute control and tyranny, it is their duty to throw off such government, and to provide new safeguards for their future security. Such has

been the patient suffering of women under this government, and such is now the necessity which forces them to demand the equal position to which they are entitled.

The history of mankind is a history of repeated injuries and usurpations on the part of man toward woman, having as its direct object the establishment of an absolute tyranny over her. To prove this, let facts be given to a candid world.

He has never permitted her to exercise her unalienable right to vote.

He has forced her to submit to laws which she had no voice in forming.

He has withheld from her rights which are given to the most ignorant and degraded men—both natives and foreigners.

Having withheld from her this first right of a citizen, the vote, thereby leaving her without representation in the legislatures, he has oppressed her on all sides.

He has made her, if married, in the eye of the law, civilly dead.

He has taken from her all right to property, even to the wages she earns.

He has made her, morally, an irresponsible being, as she can commit many crimes without punishment, provided they be done in the presence of her husband. In the marriage ceremony, she is compelled to promise obedience to her husband, he becoming, to all intents and purposes, her master—the law giving him power to take away her liberty, and to punish her.

He has so written the laws of divorce as to what shall be the proper causes, and in case of separation, to whom the guardianship of the children shall be given, as to wholly ignore the happiness of women—the law, in all cases, going upon a false supposition of the supremacy of man, and giving all power into his hands.

After taking away all her rights as a married woman, if single, and the owner of property, he has taxed her to support a government which recognizes her only when her property can be made profitable to it.

He has kept for himself nearly all the profitable jobs, and from those she is permitted to follow, she receives but a small payment. He closes to her all the avenues to wealth and distinction which he considers most honorable to himself. As a teacher of theology, medicine, or law, she is not known.

He has denied her the opportunity of obtaining a thorough education, all colleges being closed to her.

From The History of Woman Suffrage, Vol. I, edited by E. C. Stanton, S.B. Anthony, and M. J. Gage, 1881.

151

He allows her in church only a subordinate position, claiming the authority of God for her exclusion from the ministry, and, with some exceptions, from any public participation in the affairs of the church.

He has created a false public sentiment by setting forth a different code of morals for men and women by which moral delinquencies which exclude women from society, are not only tolerated, but deemed of little account in man.

He has taken over the right of God himself, claiming it as his right to assign for her a sphere of action, when that belongs to her conscience and to her God.

He has tried in every way that he could to destroy her confidence in her own powers, to lessen her self-respect, and to make her willing to lead a dependent and hopeless life.

Now, in view of not allowing one half the people of this country to vote, of their social and religious degradation—in view of the unjust laws above mentioned and because women do feel themselves harmed, oppressed, and wrongfully deprived of their most sacred rights, we insist that they have immediate admission to all the rights and privileges which belong to them as citizens of the United States.

In entering upon the great work before us, we anticipate mistaken ideas, misrepresentation, and ridicule; but we shall make every effort within our power to secure our object. We shall employ agents, circulate pamphlets, petition the state and national legislatures, and work to enlist the help of the churches and the press in our behalf. We hope this convention will be followed by a series of conventions in every part of the country.

2. Resolutions

WHEREAS, The great order of nature is admitted to be that "man shall pursue his own true and substantial happiness," Blackstone [a famous British scholar of the law] remarks, that this law of Nature being equal with mankind, and dictated by God himself, is of course superior in obligation to any other. It is binding everywhere, in all countries and at all times; no human laws are of any validity if contrary to this, and such of them as are valid, obtain all their force, and all their validity, and all their authority, from this original; therefore,

Resolved, That all laws which prevent woman from occupying such a position in society as her conscience shall dictate, or which place her in a position inferior to that of men, are contrary to the great order of nature, and therefore of no force or authority.

Resolved, That woman is man's equal—was intended to be so by the Creator, and the highest good of the race demands that she should be recognized as such.

Resolved, That the women of this country ought to be instructed in regard to the laws under which they live, that they may no longer announce their degradation by declaring them-

An artist's view of the Seneca Falls Convention

selves satisfied with their present position, nor their ignorance, by declaring that they have all the rights they want.

Resolved, That inasmuch as man, while claiming for himself intellectual superiority, does accord to woman moral superiority, it is his duty to encourage her to speak and teach, as she has an opportunity, in all religious assemblies.

Resolved, That the same amount of virtue, delicacy, and refinement of behavior that is required of woman in society, should also be required of man, and the same violations should be treated with equal harshness in both man and woman.

Resolved, That the objection of indelicacy and impropriety, which is so often brought against a woman when she speaks to a public audience, comes with a very ill grace from those who encourage, by their attendance, her appearance on the stage, in the concert hall, or in performances at the circus.

Resolved, That woman has too long rested satisfied in the limits which corrupt customs and a perverted application of the Bible have marked out for her, and that it is time she should move in the greater area which her Creator has assigned her.

Resolved, That it is the duty of the women of this country to secure to themselves their sacred right to vote.

Resolved, That the equality of human rights results necessarily from humans having the same capabilities and responsibilities.

Resolved, That the speedy success of our cause depends upon the zealous and untiring efforts of both men and women, for the overthrow of the monopoly of the churches, and for the securing for women an equal participation with men in the various trades, professions, and commerce.

Resolved, therefore, that, being provided by the Creator with the same capabilities, and the same realization of responsibility for their exercise, it is demonstrably the right and duty of woman, equally with man, to promote every righteous cause by every righteous means; and especially in regard to the great subjects of morals and religion, it is self-evidently her right to participate with her brother in teaching them, both in private and in public, by writing and by speaking, by any efforts proper to be used, and in any assemblies proper to be held; and this being a self-evident truth growing out of the divinely given principles of human nature, any custom or authority against it, whether modern or ancient, is to be regarded as a self-evident falsehood, that is at war with mankind.

READING REVIEW

1. Which of the restrictions on women listed in the Declaration do you feel were the most discriminatory? Why?
2. By today's standards some of the language in the Declaration could be called "sexist". Can you pick out these so called "sexist" usages?
3. Which document do you find more relevant for today—the Declaration of Independence or the Seneca Falls Declaration?

111 In Defense of Women's Rights

Sojourner Truth was born a slave in New York State and was freed when New York ended slavery in 1827. After she was freed, she changed her name to Sojourner Truth—she had been called Isabella by her master—and she began to travel around the country and to speak against slavery at revival meetings. Although she was more interested in ending slavery than in women's rights, Sojourner Truth also had strong feelings on this subject.

The following reading describes a speech Sojourner Truth made at a woman's rights convention in 1851. The presiding officer, Frances Dana Gage, said of Sojourner Truth's speech: "She had taken us up in her strong arms and carried us safely over the bog of difficulty, turning the whole tide in our favor."

READING FOCUS

1. What three claims were made against the equality of women with men?
2. How did Sojourner Truth respond to each of these claims?

At Akron, Ohio, a woman's rights convention was held at the end of May. Heavy rains poured down on opening day, but a large, generally unsympathetic crowd filled the Universalist

Sojourner Truth

church. The galleries were filled with boys looking forward to seeing women embarrassed. Members of the unpopular women's rights movement shuddered at the appearance of a tall black woman in a soaked gray dress, her white turban covered by a sunbonnet. Resentment rustled alongside Sojourner Truth, as she walked up the aisle and sat on the pulpit steps.

She heard people muttering: "An abolition affair. . . . Woman's rights and Negroes—we told you so! . . ."

A big, strong-faced woman in the chair asked for order and got it. The business of the convention went on, with Sojourner huddled against the side wall of the pulpit, elbows on her knees, chin in her palms. Above her, she heard voices appealing to the president: "Don't let her speak, Mrs. Gage! It will ruin us! Every paper in the land will have our cause mixed up with abolition and Negroes—"

"We'll see when the time comes," said the strong-faced woman.

The evening session came and went, and the next morning found Sojourner back in her place. Methodist, Baptist, Episcopal, Presbyterian, and Universalist ministers came to hear and discuss the resolutions offered. Sojourner listened, hardly lifting her head. One of the ministers told women to be careful not to trade their birthright of consideration for equality.

Adapted from Hertha Pauli, Her Name was Sojourner Truth, *1962.*

What man, he asked, would help a political or business rival into a carriage, or lift her over a ditch? Another claimed superior rights for man on the ground of superior intellect. A third claimed superior privileges for men because of the manhood of Christ. "If God had desired the equality of women," he said, "he would have given some token of his will through the birth, life, and death of the Saviour."

The men in the church sneered, and rude noises rang down from the galleries, where the boys were having fun.

Sojourner got up slowly.

"Don't let her speak!" gasped half a dozen as she walked to the front, laid down her worn bonnet, and turned her eyes on the president. Hissing greeted the announcement that Sojourner Truth would now speak. But when Mrs. Gage [the presiding officer] asked for silence, the noise stopped. Everyone stared at the six-foot figure in the pulpit.

"Well, chillun [children], where there's so much racket there must be something out of kilter [wrong]. I think 'twixt [between] the Negroes of the South and the women of the North all a-talking about rights, the white men will be in a fix pretty soon."

The deep voice could be heard by everyone in the church and by those outside the open doors and windows.

"But what's all this here talking about? That man over there says that women need to be helped into carriages, and lifted over ditches, and to have the best place everywhere. Nobody ever helps me into carriages, or over mud puddles, or gives me any best place—and aren't I a woman?"

"Look at me! Look at my arm!" She bared her right arm to the shoulder, showing powerful muscles. "I've plowed and planted and gathered crops into barns—and aren't I a woman? I could work as much as a man, and eat as much, when I could get it, and bear the whip as well. And aren't I a woman? They talk about this thing in the head—what's this they call it?"

"Intellect," whispered someone nearby.

"That's it, honey. What's that got to do with women's rights or Negroes' rights? If my cup won't hold but a pint and yours holds a quart, wouldn't you be mean not to let me have my little half-measure full?"

Amid cheers and loud laughter, her finger pointed at one of the ministers.

"That little man in black there, he says women can't have as much rights as men 'cause

Christ warn't [wasn't] a woman. Where did your Christ come from?"

She paused. No one answered. She repeated her question.

"Where did your Christ come from?" The voice rang out. "From God and a woman! Man had nothing to do with it!"

The cheers grew deafening.

READING REVIEW

1. Why did it take courage for Sojourner Truth to attend the convention?
2. Why were members of the convention afraid to let Sojourner Truth speak?
3. Why were Sojourner Truth's responses to the critics of equality effective?

112 A Pacifist Declares War

Henry David Thoreau felt strongly about opposing the brutal effects of industrialization and powerful, impersonal government. The only way to express opposition, he felt, was for each individual to take responsible action according to his or her conscience. If laws were wrong, then citizens should oppose them through passive resistance—an idea that became known as civil disobedience. Thoreau himself believed that the Mexican War was an immoral act of aggression designed to spread slavery, and he decided to take strong personal action to oppose it.

READING FOCUS

1. What three alternatives did Thoreau offer for dealing with unjust laws?
2. Why did Thoreau refuse to pay the poll tax?

Government is at best simply a means to an end. Most governments are usually, and all governments are sometimes, inefficient. The objections which have been brought against a permanent army may also be brought against

Adapted from Henry David Thoreau, "Resistance to Civil Government," in Henry David Thoreau: Representative Selections, with Introduction, Bibliography, and Notes, *1934.*

any permanent government. A permanent army is only an arm of the permanent government. The government itself, which is only the means the people have chosen to carry out their will, can be misused before the people can act through it. Consider the present Mexican War, the work of a few individuals using the government as their tool. At the outset, the people would not have agreed to it.

This American government—what is it but a tradition, though a recent one. This government never by itself accomplished anything except through the speed with which it got out of the way. *It* does not keep the country free. *It* does not settle the West. *It* does not educate.

Must the citizen even for a moment or in the least degree turn over his or her conscience to the legislator? Why has everyone a conscience then? I think that we should be human beings first and subjects afterward. It is not desirable to develop a respect for the law so much as for the right. The only obligation which I have a right to assume is to do at any time what I think right.

Law never made people a bit more just. And, by means of their respect for it, people are every day made the agents of injustice. A common and natural result of an undue respect for law is that you may see a file of soldiers—colonel, captain, corporal, privates, and all—marching in order over hill and dale to the wars against their wills. They act against their common sense and consciences, which makes it very difficult marching indeed.

How should a person behave toward this American government today? I answer that no one can be associated with it without disgrace. I cannot for an instant recognize that political organization as *my* government which is the *slave's* government also.

In other words, when a sixth of the population of a nation are slaves, and a whole country [Mexico] is unjustly overrun and conquered by a foreign army and subjected to military law, I think that it is not too soon for honest people to rebel. What makes this duty the more urgent is the fact that the country so overrun is not our own, and ours is the invading army.

There are thousands who are opposed to slavery and to the war, and yet do nothing to put an end to them. They sit with their hands in their pockets and say that they do not know what to do, and do nothing. They hesitate, and they regret, and sometimes they petition, but they do nothing in earnest and with effect.

They will wait for others to fix the evil so that they no longer have to regret it.

Unjust laws exist. Shall we be content to obey them? Or shall we try to change them and obey them until we have succeeded in changing them? Or shall we disobey them at once? Most people under such a government as this think that they ought to wait until they have persuaded the majority to change the unjust laws. They think that if they resist, the remedy would be no worse than the evil. But it is the fault of the government itself that the remedy is worse than the evil. Why does the government not anticipate and provide for reform? Why does it not cherish its wise minority? Why does it try and resist before it is hurt? Why does it not encourage its citizens to be on the alert to point out its faults?

If a thousand people were not to pay their tax bills this year, that would not be as violent and bloody a measure as it would be to pay them and enable the state to commit violence and shed innocent blood. This is, in fact, the definition of a peaceable revolution, if such is possible. If the tax collector or any other public officer asks me, as one has done, "But what shall I do?" my answer is, "If you really wish to do anything, give up your office." When citizens refuse allegiance and public officers give up their offices, then the revolution is accomplished.

When I speak with the freest of my neighbors, I see that whatever they may say about their regard for public tranquillity, the long and short of the matter is that they cannot do without the protection of the existing government. They dread the consequences to their property and families of disobedience. For my own part I should not like to think that I depend on the protection of the state. But if I deny the authority of the state when it presents its tax bill, it will soon take all my property, and harass me and my children without end. This is hard. This makes it impossible for a person to live honestly and at the same time comfortably.

I have paid no poll tax for six years. I was put into a jail once for this for one night. As I stood considering the walls of solid stone, the door of wood and iron, and the iron grating, I

Thoreau's Walden *and the pond that inspired the book*

WALDEN.

BY HENRY D THOREAU,
AUTHOR OF "A WEEK ON THE CONCORD AND MERRIMACK RIVERS."

I do not propose to write an ode to dejection, but to brag as lustily as chanticleer in the morning, standing on his roost, if only to wake my neighbors up. — Page 92.

BOSTON:
JAMES R. OSGOOD AND COMPANY,
LATE TICKNOR & FIELDS, AND FIELDS, OSGOOD, & CO.
1875.

could not help being struck with the foolishness of that government. It treated me as if I were just flesh and blood and bones to be locked up. I was amazed that it should have thought that this was the best use it could put me to and had never thought of making use of my services in some way.

I saw that if there was a wall of stone between me and the townspeople, there was a still more difficult one to climb or break through before they could get to be as free as I was. I did not for a moment feel shut in. The walls seemed a great waste of stone and mortar. I felt as if I alone of all my neighbors had paid my tax. They plainly did not know how to treat me, but behaved crudely. They thought that my chief desire was to stand on the other side of that stone wall. I had to smile to see how they locked the door on my thoughts, which followed them out again without difficulty. And it was only my thoughts that were dangerous.

As the authorities could not reach me, they had decided to punish my body. I saw that the state was half-witted, and that it did not know its friends from enemies. I lost all my remaining respect for it and pitied it.

Thus the state never confronts a person's sense, intellectual or moral, but only the body. It is not armed with superior wit or honesty but with superior physical strength. I was not born to be forced.

I have never refused to pay the highway tax, because I am as eager to be a good neighbor as I am to be a bad citizen. As for supporting schools, I am doing my part to educate my fellow citizens now. It is for no particular item in the tax bill that I refuse to pay it. I simply wish to refuse allegiance to the state, to withdraw and stand away from it. I do not care to follow the course of my dollar, if I could, till it buys a man or a rifle to shoot one with—the dollar is innocent—but I am concerned to follow the effects of my allegiance. In fact, I quietly declare war against the state in my own way.

READING REVIEW

1. According to Thoreau, what is government at its best?
2. (a) What did Thoreau consider as his only obligation? (b) How did this obligation cause Thoreau problems?
3. What was the "war" that Thoreau declared?
4. What effect did Thoreau's jail experience have on him?

113 A Scene from *Uncle Tom's Cabin*

When President Lincoln met Harriet Beecher Stowe during the Civil War, he is reported to have said, "So you're the little woman who started this great war." His words did, of course, exaggerate the truth. However, few novels have ever had such great influence. It turned many people in the North against slavery, and deeply angered many Southerners. In 1852, the year it was published, *Uncle Tom's Cabin* sold 300,000 copies in the United States. The same year, an English edition of the book sold 1.5 million copies.

The main character in the book is Uncle Tom, a slave who is beaten to death by his owner. But it was not Uncle Tom's story alone that so aroused readers. Rather it was the vivid picture the author painted of the horrors of slavery. The following reading is taken from this famous novel.

READING FOCUS

1. According to Stowe's account what was the relationship of a slave to his or her master?
2. On whom did Stowe place the blame for the brutality of slave masters?

Mr. Simon Legree, Tom's master, had bought eight slaves in New Orleans. He had walked them handcuffed in couples of two, down to a steamer which was ready for a trip up the Red River.

After settling them on board, with the boat underway, he came around, to look them over. He stopped next to Tom, who had been dressed for sale in his best suit, with a well-starched shirt and shining boots. Legree spoke as follows:

"Stand up."

Tom stood up.

"Take off that collar!" As Tom, hindered by his chains, tried to do it, Legree helped him by pulling it—with no gentle hand—from his neck, and putting it in his pocket.

Legree now turned to Tom's trunk, which he had been looking through. Taking from it a pair of old pants and a worn-out coat, he said, freeing Tom's hands from the handcuffs, and pointing to a space among the boxes,

"You go there, and put these on."

Tom obeyed, and in a few moments returned.

Adapted from Harriet Beecher Stowe, Uncle Tom's Cabin.

"Take off your boots," said Mr. Legree.

Tom did so.

"There," said Legree, throwing him a pair of coarse, stout shoes common among the slaves, "put these on."

In Tom's hurried change of clothes, he had not forgotten to move his cherished Bible to his pocket. It was well he did so. For Mr. Legree, having put back Tom's handcuffs, proceeded to go through the pockets of the suit. He drew out a silk handkerchief, and put it into his own pocket. Several little things, which Tom had treasured, he looked upon with a scornful grunt, and tossed them over his shoulder into the river.

Tom's Methodist hymn-book, which in his hurry Tom had forgotten, he now held up and turned over.

"Humph! Religious, to be sure. So, what's yer name—you belong to the church, eh?"

"Yes, Mas'r," [Master] said Tom, firmly.

"Well, I'll soon have that out of you. I'll have none of yer bawling, praying, singing niggers on my place; so remember. Now, mind yourself," he said, with a stamp and a fierce glance of his gray eye, directed at Tom. "I'm your church now! You understand—you've got to be as I say."

An 1853 children's edition of Uncle Tom's Cabin

Something within the silent black man answered NO! He seemed to hear the words,— "Fear not! for I have redeemed thee. I have called thee by my name. Thou art MINE!"

But Simon Legree heard no voice. That voice is one he never shall hear. He only glared for a moment on the downcast face of Tom, and walked off. He took Tom's trunk, which contained a very neat and abundant wardrobe, and it was soon surrounded by deckhands. With much laughing at Negroes who tried to be gentlemen, the articles were very readily sold and the empty trunk finally put up at auction. It was a good joke, they all thought, especially to see how Tom looked as his things were going this way and that.

After it was over, Simon walked up again to his property.

"Now, Tom, I've taken care of your extra baggage, you see. Take mighty good care of them clothes. It'll be long enough before you get more. I go in for making niggers careful. One suit has to last one year, on my place."

Simon next walked up to the place where Emmeline was sitting, chained to another woman.

"Well, my dear," he said, touching her under the chin, "keep up your spirits."

The look of horror, fright, and hatred with which the girl regarded him did not escape his eye. He frowned fiercely.

"None of your looks, gal! You's got to keep a pleasant face when I speak to ye,—d'ye hear? And, you," he said, giving a shove to the mulatto woman to whom Emmeline was chained, "don't you look like that! You's got to look chipper, I tell ye!"

"I say, all of ye," he said, stepping back a bit, "look at me—look at me—look me right in the eye—*straight,* now!" said he, stamping his foot at every pause.

"Now," said he, doubling his large, heavy fist, "d'ye see this fist? Lift it!" he said, bringing it down on Tom's hand. "Look at these bones! Well, I tell ye this fist has got as hard as iron knocking down niggers. I never see the nigger yet I couldn't bring down with one crack," said he, bringing his fist down so near to Tom's face that he winked and drew back. "I don't keep none of yer cussed overseers. I does my own overseeing. And I tell you things is seen to. You's every one of ye got to toe the mark, I tell ye; quick—straight—the moment I speak. That's the way to last. Ye won't find no soft spot in me, nowhere. So, now, mind yerselves. For I don't show mercy!"

Simon turned away and marched up the bar of the boat for a drink.

"That's the way I begin with my niggers," he said to a gentlemanly man who had stood near him during his speech. "It's my system to begin strong—just let 'em know what to expect."

"Indeed!" said the stranger, looking upon him with the curiosity of a scientist studying an unusual specimen.

"Yes, indeed. I'm none o' yer gentlemen planters, with lily fingers, to be cheated by some old cuss of an overseer! Just feel my knuckles, now; look at my fist. Tell ye, sir, the flesh on it has gotten just like a stone, practicing on niggers—feel it."

The stranger applied his fingers to the hand in question, and simply said,

"'Tis hard enough. And, I suppose," he added, "practice has made your heart just like it."

"Why, yes, I may say so," said Simon, with a hearty laugh. "I reckon there's as little soft in me as in anyone going. Tell you, nobody out-smarts me!"

"You have a fine lot there."

"Real fine," said Simon. "There's that Tom, they told me he was something uncommon. I paid a little high for him, intending him to be a driver and managing chap. If I get rid of the ideas he learned by being treated the way a nigger never ought to be, he'll do fine! The yellow woman I got took on. I rather think she's sickly, but I shall put her through for what she's worth. She may last a year or two. I don't go for saving niggers. Use up and buy more, it's my way—makes you less trouble, and I'm quite sure it's cheaper in the end," said Simon.

"And how long do they generally last?" asked the stranger.

"Well, I dunno. Depends on their make-up. Stout fellers last six or seven years. Trashy ones gets worked up in two or three. When I first begun, I used to have considerable trouble fussing with them and trying to make them hold out—doctoring them when they's sick, and giving them clothes and blankets and what not, trying to keep them decent and comfortable. Twasn't no use. I lost money on them, and 'twas heaps of trouble. Now, you see, I just put them straight through, sick or well. When one nigger's dead, I buy another. I find it comes cheaper and easier, every way."

The stranger turned away, and seated himself beside a gentleman who had been listening

Harriet Beecher Stowe

to the talk uneasily.

"You must not take that fellow to be an average Southern planter," said he.

"I should hope not," said the young gentleman with emphasis.

"He is a mean, low, brutal fellow!" said the other.

"And yet your laws allow him to hold any number of human beings subject to his absolute will, without even a shadow of protection. And, low as he is, you cannot say that there are not many such."

"Well," said the other, "there are also many considerate and humane planters."

"Granted," said the young man. "But, in my opinion, it is you considerate, humane planters that are responsible for all the brutality and outrage caused by these wretches. If it were not for your influence, the whole system could not last an hour. If there were no planters except ones like him," said he, pointing with his finger to Legree, "the whole thing would go down like a millstone. It is your respectability and humanity that allows and protects his brutality."

READING REVIEW

1. How did Legree make Tom feel inferior?
2. What did Stowe mean when she said that it was some planters "respectability and humanity" that allowed and protected other's brutality?
3. Why do you think this book aroused such strong feelings among readers in the 1850's?

114 "The Village Blacksmith"

Henry Wadsworth Longfellow was born in Portland, Maine, on February 27, 1807. During his career he was more widely read and better paid than any other American poet. Today Longfellow's poetry is often criticized for being simple and sentimental. However, these were two of the qualities that made him popular with Americans of his day. His poetry generally had a moral that was easy to understand, and it expressed the ideals and feelings of many Americans of the mid-1800's.

Below is one of Longfellow's most popular poems, "The Village Blacksmith." It appeared in 1841 in Longfellow's second book of poetry, *Ballads and Other Poems.* "The Village Blacksmith" is one of his sentimental classics.

READING FOCUS

1. How did Longfellow describe the village blacksmith?
2. What personal qualities of the blacksmith would the people of Longfellow's day have admired?

From Henry Wadsworth Longfellow, "The Village Blacksmith," *in* The Annals of America, *Vol. 4, 1797-1820.*

American poet Henry Wadsworth Longfellow, 1850

Under a spreading chestnut tree
  The village smithy stands;
The smith, a mighty man is he,
  With large and sinewy hands;
And the muscles of his brawny arms
  Are strong as iron bands.

His hair is crisp, and black, and long,
  His face is like the tan;
His brow is wet with honest sweat,
  He earns whate'er he can,
And looks the whole world in the face,
  For he owes not any man.

Week in, week out, from morn till night,
  You can hear his bellows blow;
You can hear him swing his heavy sledge
  With measured beat and slow,
Like a sexton ringing the village bell,
  When the evening sun is low.

And children coming home from school
  Look in at the open door;
They love to see the flaming forge,
  And hear the bellows roar,
And catch the burning sparks that fly
  Like chaff from a threshing floor.

He goes on Sunday to the church,
  And sits among his boys;
He hears the parson pray and preach,
  He hears his daughter's voice
Singing in the village choir,
  And it makes his heart rejoice.

It sounds to him like her mother's voice,
  Singing in Paradise!
He needs must think of her once more,
  How in the grave she lies;
And with his hard, rough hand he wipes
  A tear out of his eyes.

Toiling—rejoicing—sorrowing,
  Onward through life he goes;
Each morning sees some task begun,
  Each evening sees its close;
Something attempted, something done,
  Has earned a night's repose.

Thanks, thanks to thee, my worthy friend,
  For the lesson thou hast taught!
Thus at the flaming forge of life
  Our fortunes must be wrought;
Thus on its sounding anvil shaped
  Each burning deed and thought!

READING REVIEW

1. Describe the physical characteristics of the village blacksmith.
2. List three personal qualities of the village blacksmith.
3. Do you think Americans in Longfellow's time would have admired and respected the village blacksmith? Explain your answer.

115 On Reform and Reformers

In the 1840's industry was developing rapidly and the nation was expanding its borders. Americans also found that they faced many new problems. Reform movements developed in an effort to solve these problems.

During this period of reform in the 1840's, the most influential thinker and writer was Ralph Waldo Emerson. Although he admired many of the reform movements, he did not admire some of the reformers. In this 1842 lecture, Emerson gave his views on reform and the reformers.

READING FOCUS

1. Why did Emerson say that the different reform movements are all parts of one movement?
2. According to Emerson, why were reform movements important?

The present age will be known for its many projects for the reform of domestic, civil, literary, and religious institutions. The leaders of the movements against war, Negro slavery, intemperance, government based on force, and so on are proper successors of Luther, Knox, and Penn [religious leaders]. They have the same virtues and vices, the same noble motives, and the same bigotry.

These movements are important. They not only check the abuses about which they are concerned, but educate the conscience and mind of the people. How can a question such as the slave trade be discussed for 40 years with-

out throwing great light on moral principles? The fury with which slave traders defend their bloody decks and auction platforms alarms all people, and drives all those who are neutral to take sides. Political questions involving the banks, the tariff, the limits of executive power, the treatment of the Indians, and boundary wars all present moral questions.

The different reform movements are really all parts of one movement. Each cherishes some part of the general idea. All must be seen in order to do justice to any one. The conscience of the age shows itself in this effort to improve our life by putting it in harmony with our idea of the beautiful and the just.

These reforms are our contemporaries. They are ourselves, our own light and sight and conscience. They are our simplest statements in these matters, the plain right and wrong. They are to be honored.

So much for the reforms. But we cannot say as much for the reformers. Beautiful is the motive and the theory. The practice is less beautiful. The reforms have their origin in an ideal justice, but they do not keep the purity of an idea. Quickly organized in some inadequate form, they present no better image than the evil tradition they attack. They mix the fire of moral sentiment with personal and party fervor, wit exaggerations, and the blindness that prefers some favorite solution to justice and truth. Those who are most in favor of what are called the greatest benefits to humanity are narrow, self-pleasing, conceited people.

I think the work of the reformer is no worse than other work. But when I have seen it close up, I do not like it better. It is done in the same way. It is done profanely, not piously. It is done by management, by tactics and clamor. It is a buzz in the ear.

This then is our criticism on the reforming movement: In its origin it is divine, but in its management and details it is timid and profane.

Adapted from Ralph Waldo Emerson, "Lectures on the Times." The Dial, July 1842.

READING REVIEW

1. According to Emerson, what benefits did reform movements bring to the people?
2. What criticisms did Emerson level against reforms and reformers?

The Nation Torn Apart

CHAPTER 17 Crisis and Compromise
(1845–1861)

116 On The Missouri Compromise

The debate surrounding the passage of the Missouri Compromise of 1820 was deeply disturbing to most Americans. John Quincy Adams, the son of former President John Adams, was the Secretary of State in President Monroe's Cabinet when the Missouri Compromise went into effect. Even though he considered slavery to be a terrible evil, he advised President Monroe to sign the Compromise into law.

The following selection, from the diary of John Quincy Adams, gave some of his opinions about Southerners, slavery, and the Missouri Compromise.

READING FOCUS

1. According to Adams, what was one of the "great evils of slavery"?
2. What was Adams' position regarding the Missouri Compromise?

The discussion of whether or not Missouri should be admitted to the Union as a slave state has shown the two-sided nature of the white Southerners. They admit that slavery is an evil. They refuse to accept any blame for the

Adapted from Memoirs of John Quincy Adams, Comprising Portions of his Diary from 1795 to 1848, *edited by Charles Francis Adams, Vol. V, 1875.*

introduction of slavery to North America. Instead they blame Great Britain for the introduction of slavery on this continent. But when questioned about the continued existence of slavery in the South, they show their feelings of pride and the love of being masters over other human beings. The Southerners think they are more generous and noblehearted than the plain freemen who labor for a living. They look down upon the simplicity of a Yankee's manners, because a Yankee doesn't act like a bully and cannot treat Negroes like dogs.

One of the great evils of slavery is that it establishes a false basis for judging good and bad. For what can be more false and heartless than judging people based on the color of their skin? This false basis for judging good and bad confuses human reason. It allows Southerners to hold many false beliefs. They believe that slavery is approved of by the Christian religion. They believe that slaves are happy and content to be slaves. They believe that there are ties of mutual affection between slaves and their masters. They believe that the master becomes more refined and dignified as he degrades his slaves. At the same time these Southerners curse the slave trade, curse Britain for having introduced slavery to America, burn Negroes convicted of crimes at the stake to serve as examples to other slaves, and cry out in fear at the very mention of human rights applied to men of color.

I have favored this Missouri Compromise because I believed it to be the best that could be done under the Constitution. I also favored it because I was unwilling to endanger the future of the United States. But perhaps it would have been a wiser as well as a bolder course to have opposed the extension of slavery into Missouri. Perhaps I should have argued for a convention of the states to revise and amend the Constitution to prohibit slavery in all the states. This would have caused a division of the country and produced a new Union of thirteen or fourteen

States, unpolluted with slavery. If the Union must be dissolved, slavery is precisely the question upon which it ought to break. For the present, however, the Missouri Compromise has laid the question of slavery to sleep.

READING REVIEW

1. Name four false beliefs that slavery led Southerners to hold.
2. (a) List two reasons why Adams supported the Missouri Compromise? (b) Why did Adams later think that perhaps he should have opposed the Missouri Compromise?
3. Do you think Adams felt that the slavery issue was forever settled by the Missouri Compromise? Explain your answer.

Representative Robert Toombs

117 Why Slavery Must Be Allowed in the New Territories

The Wilmot Proviso once again forced Americans to face the issue of slavery. The question of whether or not slavery should be allowed in the territories won from Mexico caused bitter debate in Congress. When California asked to be admitted to the Union as a free state, Southerners angrily protested.

The following is an excerpt from a speech made by Representative Robert Toombs of Georgia. He made this speech in Congress in December 1849. This was a little more than a month before Henry Clay made the proposals that later became the Compromise of 1850. Toombs' speech showed the bitterness caused by the issue of slavery.

READING FOCUS

1. Why did Toombs think slavery should be allowed in the California and New Mexico territories?
2. What did he threaten if slavery were outlawed in the territory won from Mexico?
3. Did he expect that the North would treat the South fairly?

I have as much attachment to the Union of these States, under the Constitution of our fathers, as any freeman ought to have. I am ready to sacrifice for it whatever a just and honorable man ought to sacrifice—I will do no more.

I do not, then, hesitate to swear before this house and the country, and in the presence of the living God, that if by your laws you seek to drive us from the territories of California and New Mexico, purchased by the common blood and treasure of the whole people, and to abolish slavery in this District of Columbia, thereby attempting to fix a national shame upon half the States of this Confederacy, *I am for disunion.* I will devote all I am and all I have on earth to secession.

From 1787 to this hour, the people of the South have asked nothing but justice—nothing but the maintenance of the principles and the spirit which controlled our fathers in the formation of the Constitution. Unless we are unworthy of our ancestors, we will never accept less as a condition of union.

The territories are the common property of the people of the United States, purchased by their common blood and treasure. Congress is responsible for governing the territories and it is our duty, while they are territories, to remove all obstacles to their free enjoyment by all sections and people of the Union, the slaveholder and the nonslaveholder. You have given the strongest indications that you will not perform this trust—that you will take for yourselves all of this territory.

Adapted from Congressional Globe, *29th Congress, 1st Session.*

READING REVIEW

1. Give two reasons why Toombs thought Southerners had the right to expand slavery into the territories of California and New Mexico.
2. What did Toombs threaten if slavery were outlawed in the territories of California, New Mexico, and in the District of Columbia?
3. Did Toombs think that the South would be treated fairly? Cite evidence from the reading to support your answer.

118 A Southerner's Solution

Many Americans thought the problem of slavery had been settled by the Missouri Compromise of 1820. But between 1820 and 1850 the issue of slavery continued to trouble the nation.

The slavery issue came up again when California applied for admission to the Union in 1849. For a time, it looked as if the Union was in danger of breaking apart. Henry Clay offered several proposals that became the basis for the Compromise of 1850. The debate over Clay's proposals lasted for more than six months and became known as the Great Debate. In this selection, John C. Calhoun gave his opinion of Clay's compromise bill. It was Calhoun's last speech and was read by a colleague in the Senate on March 4, 1850.

READING FOCUS

1. According to Calhoun, what is it that has put the Union in danger?
2. How did Calhoun propose to save the Union?

I have, Senators, believed from the first that agitation over slavery would end in disunion, if not prevented by some effective measure. I have often tried to get the two great parties to adopt some measure to prevent so great a disaster, but without success. The agitation has been allowed to continue with almost no attempt to stop it. We have reached a period when we can no longer cover up or deny the fact that the Union is in danger. You have thus had forced upon you the greatest and the most important question that can ever come under your consideration: How can the Union be preserved?

Adapted from Congressional Globe, 31st Congress, 1st Session, March 4, 1850.

The first question I propose to raise in order to solve this problem is: What is it that has put the Union in danger?

One of the causes is the long-continued agitation of the slave question on the part of the North and the many aggressive actions it has directed toward the South during this time.

There is another reason that may be regarded as the great and basic cause. This is the fact that the balance between the two sections in the government, as it stood when the Constitution was ratified and the government began, has been destroyed.

Since independence, the United States has acquired 2,373,046 square miles [6,146,189 square kilometers] of territory. If the North should succeed in taking over most of the newly acquired territories, it will possess about three fourths of the whole, leaving to the South only about one fourth.

As the North has absolute control over the government, it is clear that on all questions between it and the South where there is a conflict of interests, the interests of the South will be sacrificed to the North. The South has no means by which it can resist the actions of the federal government.

I return to the question with which I began: How can the Union be saved? There is only one way. That is by a full and final settlement based on the principle of justice, of all the disputes between the two sections. The South asks for justice, simple justice. Less it ought not to accept. It has no compromise to offer but the Constitution, and no concession or surrender to make. It has already surrendered so much that it has little left to surrender.

Such a settlement would remove all the causes of dissatisfaction. It would satisfy the South that it could remain honorably and safely in the Union. It would bring back the harmony and good feelings between the sections that existed before the Missouri question. Nothing else can finally and forever settle the questions at issue, end agitation, and save the Union.

But can this be done? Yes, easily. Not by the weaker party, for it can of itself do nothing—not even protect itself—but by the stronger.

The North has only to will it to bring it about. It can do justice by granting to the South an equal right in the acquired territory. It can do its duty by seeing that laws regarding fugitive slaves are faithfully carried out. It can stop agitating on the slave question. And it can provide for an amendment to the Constitution which will return to the South the power it had to protect itself before the balance between the sections was destroyed by the action of this government.

California will become the test question. If you admit it under all the circumstances that oppose admission, you force us to conclude that you plan to exclude us from all the acquired territories.

READING REVIEW

1. What did Calhoun think had put the Union in danger?
2. How did Calhoun think the danger could be overcome?
3. Why did Calhoun say that the South was the "weaker" party?

Senator William Seward

119 Appeal to "a Higher Law"

To solve the problem raised when California asked to join the Union as a nonslave state, Henry Clay proposed a compromise that led to a long and heated debate in Congress.

Many members of Congress did not want to compromise on the slavery issue. Calhoun wanted a solution favorable to the South. Senator William H. Seward of New York also refused to compromise and wanted a solution favorable to the North. He believed that it was wrong to make any concessions on slavery, which he regarded as evil. The following selection is from a speech Seward made in the Senate on March 11, 1850.

READING FOCUS

1. Why did Seward object to compromise?
2. What did Seward mean by a "higher law than the Constitution"?

It is insisted that the admission of California be accompanied by a compromise on the questions which have arisen out of slavery!

I am opposed to any such compromise in any and all the forms in which it has been proposed. While admitting the patriotism of all those

---

Adapted from Congressional Globe, *Appendix, 31st Congress, 1st Session, March 11, 1850.*

with whom I differ, I think all legislative compromises, which are not absolutely necessary, are wrong and essentially vicious.

What am I to receive in this compromise? Freedom in California. Good. It is a noble benefit and one worth a sacrifice. But what am I to give in return? A recognition of the claim to continue slavery in the District of Columbia; and tolerance of stricter laws concerning the arrest of persons suspected of being slaves who are found in the free states. What I give in return then is some part of liberty, some part of human rights, in one region for liberty in another region.

It is now declared by the honorable Senator from South Carolina, Mr. Calhoun, that nothing will satisfy the slave states but a compromise that will convince them that they can remain in the Union with their honor and their safety.

These terms amount to this: That the free states with majorities of population and majorities in both houses of Congress, shall give to the slave states with a minority in both an unequal advantage. That is, that we shall change the Constitution in order to change the government from a national democracy operating by a constitutional majority into a federal alliance in which the minority has a veto over the majority. This would be to return to the original Articles of Confederation.

There is another aspect which deserves consideration. It assumes that slavery, if not

165

the only institution in a slave state, is at least a ruling institution, and that it is recognized by the Constitution. But slavery is only one of many institutions there. Freedom is an institution there too. Slavery is only a temporary, accidental, and partial one. Freedom, on the contrary, is a permanent, essential, and universal one, in harmony with the Constitution of the United States.

There is yet another aspect to be examined. It concerns the national territory. It is true that this territory is ours. It is true that it was acquired by bravery and with the wealth of the nation. But we hold no arbitrary power over it. We hold no arbitrary authority over anything, whether we acquired it lawfully or seized it by force. The Constitution devotes the territory to union, to justice, to defense, to welfare, and to liberty.

But there is a higher law than the Constitution which regulates our authority over the territory and devotes it to the same noble purposes. The territory is a part, no small part, of the common heritage of humankind. It was given to humans by the Creator of the universe. We are his stewards and must carry out our trust so as to secure the highest possible degree of happiness.

And now a simple, bold, and awful question presents itself to us. We are founding institutions, social and political, for countless millions. We know by experience the actions that are wise and just, and are free to choose them, and reject the wrong and unjust. Shall we establish human slavery or permit it to be established?

Our ancestors would not have hesitated an hour. They found slavery existing here and left it only because they could not remove it. No free state would now establish it. Nor would any slave state have established slavery if it had had the alternative we now have. Indeed, our revolutionary forebears had exactly the same question before them in establishing a law under which the states of Ohio, Indiana, Michigan, Illinois, and Wisconsin have since come into the Union. They excluded slavery from those states forever.

The fearful issue is whether the Union shall continue with slavery and under steady, peaceful action of moral, social and political causes, have slavery removed by gradual, voluntary effort and with compensation. Or will the Union be broken apart and civil wars follow, bringing on violent but complete and immediate emancipation? We have now arrived at that time in our nation when that crisis can be foreseen, when we must foresee it. It is directly before us. Its shadow is upon us. It darkens the legislative halls, the churches, and the home.

READING REVIEW

1. What did Seward think about all "legislative compromises"?
2. Why did Seward think that the Constitution's recognition of slavery should be disregarded?
3. What did Seward think were the consequences of accepting the compromise of 1850?

---

120 Violence in "Bloody" Kansas

The Kansas-Nebraska Act allowed the people in the Kansas-Nebraska Territory to decide whether slavery should exist there. One northern senator said that this law, passed in 1854, "puts freedom and slavery face to face and asks them to grapple." And soon afterward, the settlers in that territory did grapple, or fight, over the issue of slavery in Kansas.

Thomas H. Gladstone, an English traveler in the United States, reached Kansas just as the fighting broke out there. Later he wrote a book in which he described what happened in the town of Lawrence. The fighting in and around Lawrence became known as the Wakarusa War of 1855.

READING FOCUS

1. Who was attacking the people in Kansas?
2. What happened in the sack of Lawrence?

In the fall of 1854, a few families of New England settlers built the first log huts in Lawrence. During the year 1855 its population increased rapidly, chiefly through the arrival of emigrants from the northern states. Buildings of brick and stone went up. The growing prosperity of the "Yankee town" began to make those who favored slavery jealous.

The proslavery forces viewed Lawrence as the stronghold of the Free State Party. Consequently, Lawrence was made the point of

---

Adapted from Thomas H. Gladstone, The Englishman in Kansas, *F.L. Olmstead, ed., 1857.*

attack during what was called the Wakarusa War in the winter of 1855. Before the end of this, the people who lived in Lawrence realized that they needed some means of defense, and began to fortify their town by building defensive walls. The inhabitants were also given guns and formed into companies with commanders. They had their daily drill, they kept guard day and night upon the forts; at night they sent out a horse patrol to watch the outer posts and to warn of approaching danger.

The peace that followed the Wakarusa campaign in December 1855 brought only a short halt to the struggle. Although fighting had stopped, the people did not stop carrying weapons. When the time was right, they used them with deadly effect. The settlers from Missouri did not hide the fact that they were organizing another invasion, which would "wipe out Lawrence" and win Kansas for slavery, even if they had to "wade up to their knees in blood to obtain it." The southern states were being appealed to for men and money to wipe out every northern settler.

Finally the day approached when Lawrence was to fall. On the night before May 21, anyone taking a look at the countryside would have seen at Franklin, 4 miles [6 kilometers] southeast of Lawrence, Colonel Buford's [a proslavery agitator from the South] companies, brought from the United States. This formed the lower division of the invading army. West of Lawrence, 12 miles [19 kilometers] away, was another military camp.

On May 21, Jones [a proslavery agitator from the South] rode into Lawrence at the head of 20 or more men, mounted and armed. He placed himself in front of the Eldridge House Hotel, demanding that General Pomeroy [a leader of the free-state forces] surrender all his arms. He gave him five minutes for his decision. Then they would bombard the town. General Pomeroy gave up their cannons and some small weapons. Jones then demanded that the furniture be removed from the hotel. He said that the district court for Douglas County had ruled that the hotel and the two newspaper offices were public nuisances. Therefore, they were to be removed, and he, as sheriff, was to carry out the orders.

The newspaper offices were the first objects of attack. First the office of the *Free State* was destroyed, then that of the *Herald of Freedom*. The presses were broken down to pieces and the type carried away to the river.

The papers and books were treated the same way, until the soldiers became tired of carrying them to the river. Then they piled them in the street, and burned, tore, or otherwise destroyed them.

From the printing offices the attackers went to the hotel. By evening, all that remained of the Eldridge House Hotel was a part of one wall. The rest was a shapeless heap of ruins.

The sack of Lawrence occupied the rest of the afternoon. Sheriff Jones, after looking at the flames rising from the hotel and saying that it was "the happiest day of his life," dismissed his troops, and they immediately began their lawless destruction.

Fortunately, no lives were lost. The people of Lawrence deprived their invaders of a fight by not resisting them.

Among all the scenes of violence I witnessed, the groups responsible were always on the proslavery side. The free-state people appeared to me to be intimidated, not merely because of the determination and boldness of their opponents, but more because the government approved of their acts.

The free-state people were driven to take extreme action. Some of them organized guerrilla groups to try to recover stolen horses and other property. Other acts of revenge also occurred. In several cases the opposing groups met, and violence resulted. For some time after the attack upon Lawrence, some fighting con-

Freesoilers protect Topeka.

tinued. Bitter memories filled people's minds and led to daily acts of hostility—and frequently to bloodshed.

READING REVIEW

1. Did Gladstone favor the North or the South? Give two pieces of evidence to support your conclusion.
2. Why do you think the newspaper offices were attacked first by the proslavery forces?
3. What effect might this account have had on Northern readers? on Southern readers? on English readers?

121 The Raid on Harpers Ferry

John Brown's raid on Harpers Ferry in 1859 was one of the most significant events in the long series of events that led to the Civil War. Brown hoped to seize guns stored there and start a slave rebellion. The raid was unsuccessful. However, it once more aroused the deep feelings in the North and the South on the slavery issue and moved the nation closer to disunion.

After John Brown was captured, on October 18, he was taken to a room in the armory at Harpers Ferry. There he was questioned about the reasons for his action by a group of politicians and newspaper reporters. One of the reporters who were present wrote this account of the interview for the *New York Herald,* and it appeared in that paper five days after the raid.

READING FOCUS

1. What was the purpose of Brown's raid?
2. How did Brown justify his actions?

When I arrived in the armory, Brown was answering questions put to him by Senator Mason; Colonel Faulkner, a member of Congress; Mr. Vallandigham, a member of Congress from Ohio; and several other distinguished gentlemen. The following is a report of the conversation:

MR. MASON: Can you tell us who provided the money for your expedition?

Adapted from New York Herald, *October 21, 1859.*

MR. BROWN: I provided most of it myself. I cannot involve the others.

MR. VALLANDIGHAM: Mr. Brown, who sent you here?

MR. BROWN: No person sent me here. It was my own idea and that of my Maker, or that of the devil, whichever you please to blame.

MR. VALLANDIGHAM: Did you organize the expedition yourself?

MR. BROWN: I did.

MR. MASON: What was your object in coming here?

MR. BROWN: We came to free the slaves, and only that.

A YOUNG MAN (in the uniform of a volunteer company): How many men in all did you have?

MR. BROWN: I came to Virginia with 18 men, besides myself.

VOLUNTEER: What in the world did you suppose you could do here in Virginia with so few men?

MR. BROWN: Young man, I don't wish to discuss that question here.

VOLUNTEER: You could not do anything.

MR. BROWN: Well, perhaps your ideas and mine on military subjects would differ.

MR. MASON: How do you justify your acts?

MR. BROWN: I think, my friend, you are guilty of a great wrong against God and humanity. It would be perfectly right for anyone to interfere with you in order to free those you willfully and wickedly hold in slavery. I do not say this insultingly. I think I did right and that others will do right who interfere with you at any time and at all times.

A BYSTANDER: Do you consider this a religious movement?

MR. BROWN: It is, in my opinion, the greatest service a person can give to God.

BYSTANDER: Do you consider yourself an instrument in the hands of Providence?

MR. BROWN: I do.

MR. VALLANDIGHAM: Did you expect a general uprising of the slaves in case you succeeded?

MR. BROWN: No, sir, nor did I wish it. I expected to gather them up from time to time and set them free.

REPORTER: I do not wish to bother you, but if you have anything further you would like to say, I will report it.

MR. BROWN: I have nothing to say, only that I claim to be here carrying out an action that I believe perfectly justifiable—not to act the part of an agitator or ruffian, but to aid those suffering great wrong.

REPORTER: Brown, suppose you had every Negro in the United States, what would you do with them?

MR. BROWN: Set them free.

A BYSTANDER: To set them free woud cost the life of every person in this community.

MR. BROWN: I do not think so.

BYSTANDER: I know it. I think you are fanatical.

MR. BROWN: And I think you are fanatical. "Whom the gods would destroy they first make mad," and you are mad.

READING REVIEW

1. From what you have read, do you think John Brown was telling the truth about the purpose of his raid? Explain.
2. Why do you think he claimed to be "an instrument in the hands of Providence"?
3. Why did Brown say that the bystander was fanatical?

John Brown's last moments

---

122   A Southerner's Opinion of Brown's Raid

The southern reaction to John Brown's raid against Harpers Ferry was one of great anger and distrust. Many southerners were greatly upset and outraged by John Brown's daring action. They believed that this event was proof that northerners planned to use force in order to end slavery. Despite the heated reactions that the raid caused in many Americans, however, there were some Americans who viewed the raid as merely an isolated incident. The following selection expresses such a viewpoint. The selection is taken from a letter written by James A. Seddon, who was a Virginia lawyer, to Senator Robert Hunter of Virginia.

READING FOCUS

1. According to the writer, how should the raid on Harpers Ferry been treated?
2. Whom did the writer blame for the mismanagement of public opinion?

I left Virginia, although I did not want to go, just as the Harpers Ferry raid took place. I knew it was a crisis of great importance to our state and country and of deep interest to your political future. I must say that in my opinion events that followed and the course of public conduct and opinion, especially in Virginia, have been mismanaged and misdirected. I think that the unsound judgment, vanity, and selfish policy of Governor Wise were mainly responsible for this.

The Harpers Ferry affair ought to have been treated either as the insane folly of a few mistaken cranks branded fanatics or—more accurately—as the crime of a group of reckless ruffians, ready for any scheme of murder. They should have been tried and executed as criminals in the fastest possible manner. They should not have had the chance to pose as political criminals or as representatives and champions of northern sentiment.

Our honorable governor could not resist making speeches about Brown's group. By insisting that they were the leaders of an organized conspiracy in the North, he encouraged sympathy and praise from many people and respected journals of public opinion in the North.

Adapted from American Historical Association, Annual Report, *1916, Vol. II, "Correspondence of Robert M. T. Hunter, 1826–1876," Charles H. Ambler, ed. Washington, 1918.*

In Virginia and throughout the South, every possible effort has been made to turn these lawbreakers into political criminals. Southern opinion identifies them with the North itself, or at least the Republican Party, causing the greatest indignation against that whole section and its people. In short, with his policy of swaggering and bullying, the governor has used this whole affair for his own advantage in order to aid his vain hopes for the Presidency and to strengthen the fragment of a southern party he heads. As a result, he has called up a devil neither he nor perhaps anyone else can control. By appealing to the pride and hatred of both sections, he has brought on a real crisis dangerous to both.

READING REVIEW

1. Why was the raid on Harpers Ferry an event of great importance to the South?
2. Why was the event seemingly blown out of proportion to its effects?
3. On the basis of this reading, do you agree or disagree that often it is not the event itself, but the reaction of people to the event that is important? Explain your thinking.

123 John Brown, a Hundred Years Later

John Brown became a martyr to many of those Americans who opposed slavery. Just months after his death, soldiers marched off to war singing what one observer called "a queer, rude song" about how his soul was marching on. John Brown has remained a fascinating and controversial figure ever since.

In this selection, Lerone Bennett, a modern black writer, praises John Brown as a man willing to take action to achieve what he believed was right. Bennett contrasts white liberals of his own period to John Brown, and concludes that they lacked his spirit and determination. He strongly criticizes them for spending so much time talking of problems of the 1960's and failing to take decisive actions. John Brown, Bennett points out, talked little; he felt the oppression of the slaves—and he acted.

READING FOCUS

1. According to the writer, why did John Brown suffer so much?
2. Why did Shields Green "go with the old man"?

It is to John Brown that we must go if we want to understand the limitations and possibilities of our situation. He was of no color, John Brown, of no race or age. He was pure passion. He was basic force like the wind, rain, and fire. "A volcano beneath a mountain of snow," someone called him.

A great gaunt man with a noble head, the look of a hawk and the intensity of a saint, John Brown lived and breathed justice. As a New England businessman, he sacrificed business and profits, using his warehouse as a station on the Underground Railroad. In the 1850's he became a fulltime friend of freedom, fighting small wars in Kansas and leading a group of Negro slaves out of Missouri. Always, everywhere, John Brown was preaching the importance of the act. "Slavery is evil," he said, "kill it."

"But we must study the problem . . ."
Slavery is evil—kill it!
"We will hold a conference . . ."
Slavery is evil—kill it!
"But our allies . . ."
Slavery is evil—kill it!

John Brown was scornful of conferences and study groups and graphs. "Talk, talk, talk," he said. Women were suffering, children were dying—and grown men were talking. Slavery was not a word; it was a fact, a chain, a whip, an event. It seemed obvious to John Brown that facts could be opposed only by facts, a life by a life.

There was in John Brown a complete identification with the oppressed. It was his child that a slaveowner was selling; his sister who was being whipped in the field; his wife who was being assaulted in the barn. It was not happening to Negroes; it was happening to him. It was said that he could not bear to hear the word "slave" spoken. John Brown was a Negro, and it was in this aspect that he suffered.

More than Frederick Douglass, more than any other Negro leader, John Brown suffered with the slave. "His zeal in the cause of freedom," Frederick Douglass said, "was far superior to mine. Mine was as the candle's light; his was as the burning sun. I could speak for the slave; John Brown could fight for the slave. I could live for the slave; John Brown could die for the slave."

In the end, John Brown chose a superhu-

Adapted from "Tea and Sympathy: Liberals and Other White Hopes."

man act. The act he chose—the tools, the means, the instruments—does not concern us here. His act, as it happened, was violent. But it could have been as gentle as rain in the spring.

John Brown chose to attack the arsenal at Harpers Ferry, in the hope of creating a situation in which slaves all over the South would flock to him. He begged his old friend, Frederick Douglass, to come with him, but Douglass insisted that the time was not right. The old white man and the young Negro argued from eight one night to three the next morning. While they argued, a tough, cynical fugitive slave named Shields Green watched and listened. After the argument, Douglass rose and asked Shields Green if he were ready to go. Green thought for a moment and then said: "I believe I'll go with the old man." Shields Green was in the mountains and could have escaped when federal troops closed in on John Brown. A man suggested running away, but Shields Green said: "I believe I'll go down with the old man." And he did—all the way to his death by hanging.

Why did Green sacrifice his life?

Not because he was committed to John Brown's way but because he was committed to John Brown. In a horribly bloody and horribly real way, a prayer had been answered. He had at long last found a man, neither black nor white, who was willing to go all the way.

Who?

"I believe I'll go with the old man."

Who?

"A man for all seasons," a pillar of fire by night and a cloud by day.

Who?

A John Brown. It may be that America can no longer produce such men. If so, all is lost. Cursed is the nation, cursed is the people, that can no longer breed its own radicals when it needs them.

There was an America once that was big enough for a Brown.

What happened to that America?

Who killed it?

We killed it, all of us, Negroes and whites, with our petty lies and our frantic flights from truth and risk and danger. We killed it, all of us, liberals and activists with the rest. It is my faith that buried somewhere deep beneath the detergents and lies is the dead body of the America that made Thomas Jefferson a lawbreaker and John Brown a martyr.

Segregation is evil—kill it!

"We will hold a conference . . ."

Segregation is evil—kill it!

"But our allies . . ."

Segregation is evil—kill it!

For the Jew in Germany, the African in Salisbury, the Negro in New York:

Who?

A man beyond good and evil, beyond black and white.

Who?

"A man for all seasons," a pillar of fire by night and a cloud by day.

Who?

"I believe I'll go down with the old man."

READING REVIEW

1. What did Bennett mean when he said that "John Brown was a Negro"?
2. Why, according to Bennett, does a nation need to produce radicals?
3. What did Bennett admire most about John Brown?

A cartoonist stresses the need for interracial cooperation in the civil rights movement.

Hesse in The St. Louis Globe-Democrat

"It takes two to lay the cornerstone."

124 A Southerner on Secession

To many Southerners, secession was an exciting adventure. They felt that their states, which had long been oppressed, were at long last standing firm and united in order to defend their rights. For example, when South Carolina seceded, the people of Charleston celebrated the event. Shops and businesses closed, church bells rang, people ran excitedly into the streets, houses were lit up, and military bands played.

This selection, written by Susan Bradford, who lived on a large plantation in Leon County, Florida, captured this sense of excitement on the eve of the war. She was just 15 years old when she went with her father to the state's secession convention.

READING FOCUS

1. What events of the convention impressed Susan Bradford the most?
2. Do you think she was for or against secession?

January 1, 1861

As we sat around the long table today the talk turned to the convention, so soon to meet in Tallahassee. Father said he considered this the most important year in the history of the South. He is for secession, and he does not think that war will necessarily follow. Brother Junius is a strong Union man, and he thinks we will certainly have war. If the South secedes, the North will fight to keep us. If we do not secede, all property rights will be taken from us and we will be forced to fight to hold our own. He says he is for the fight, but he wants to fight in the Union, not out of it. Father thinks it is more honorable to take an open and decided stand and let all the world know what we are doing. Mother says she wants the Negroes freed, but she wants the United States government to make laws which will free them gradually. All agree on one point—if the Negroes are freed, our lands will be worthless.

January 6, 1861

Father told me to get ready to go with him to town next morning. He said he was going to show me what a convention was like. I was so

Adapted from Heroines of Dixie, *edited by Katherine M. Jones.*

happy at the thought of going that my heart sank when Mother said: "Surely, Dr. Bradford, you are not going to take the child away from school?" but Father said, "Yes, I am going to take her with me in the morning. This is history in the making. She will learn more than she can get out of books, and what she hears in this way she will never forget." I am so glad. I am so excited I cannot hold my pencil steady.

January 7, 1861

The convention was assembling in the hall of representatives when we entered the Capitol, and soon everybody was in place. A small man, very erect and slender, was being introduced as Mr. Leonidas Spratt of South Carolina. Mr. Spratt said he felt some hesitation in appearing before this convention. But the heart of South Carolina was filled with love and sympathy for Florida, who now was standing where Carolina had so lately stood. Then he read aloud a communication from his state, repeating the grievances which had led it to break the ties which bound it to the Union. You never heard such cheers and shouts, and it lasted so long.

When the speaking was over and a few resolutions had been passed, the convention adjourned and we came home. We left a noisy crowd behind us.

January 8, 1861

We are at home again after a day filled to overflowing with excitement and interest. I had never seen a convention until Father brought me here and it is strange to me. I wish I could tell all I heard today but the language the members used is not familiar to me and some of the things they talk about are just as new. Then, too, I am just a little girl.

A message was read on the floor of the convention, from Governor Brown of Georgia. As near as I can remember, it was this way: "Georgia will certainly secede. Has Florida occupied the fort?"

Mr. Sanderson was very interesting. He repeated the rights which the states kept when they delegated other rights to the central government in the Constitution. He made it so perfectly clear that every state had the right to withdraw from the Union, if its rights and liberty were threatened. He said a committee had carefully examined the question and could find no reason why Florida should not exercise its right to withdraw from an agreement that now threatened it with such disaster.

January 9, 1861

There has been a hot time in the convention today. The nearer they get to a final decision, the hotter it gets. Colonel Ward made a most eloquent speech to the convention. He told them that he was a Union man but it was in this way: in his opinion the South had done more to establish that Union than any other section. It was a southerner who wrote the Declaration of Independence. It was a southerner who led the American army. It was southerners who framed the Constitution. A southerner wrote our National Anthem. He thought we should hold on to that which we had done so much to bring about. He was willing to fight, if fight we must, but he wanted to fight in the Union and under that flag which was doubly ours. The heartiest applause greeted him as he sat down. It was plain to see that his audience was tremendously moved. But the next speaker tore his fine argument apart. So it went on all day.

Our old friend Mr. Burgess says: "If Mrs. Harriet Beecher Stowe had died before she wrote *Uncle Tom's Cabin,* this would never have happened." He says, "She has started a fire which all the waters of the earth cannot put out." Isn't it strange how much harm lies can do?

January 10, 1861

It is night and I am very tired, but there is much to tell. The Ordinance of Secession was voted on today, 62 for and 7 against. It was resolved that at one o'clock on the next day, January 11th, the Ordinance of Secession should be signed. The convention then adjourned until the afternoon session.

Mississippi seceded last night and it seems we will have plenty of company. The Union men in the hall looked very sad. They have worked hard for their side, but they had only a few followers.

January 11, 1861

Capitol Square was so crowded you could see nothing but heads. As the old town clock struck one, the members of the Convention walked out. In a few moments they were grouped about the table on which someone had put the Ordinance of Secession. Colonel Ward held his pen up and said, in the saddest of tones, "When I die I want it inscribed upon my tomb-

A Southern newspaper proclaims secession.

stone that I was the last man to give up the ship." Then he wrote slowly across the sheet before him, "George T. Ward."

The stillness could almost be felt. One by one they came forward.

When at length the names were all written, cheer after cheer filled the air. It was deafening. Our world seemed to have gone wild.

General Call is an old man now, and he is a strong Union man. Chancing to look toward him, I saw that the tears were streaming down his face. Everybody cannot be pleased and we are fairly launched on these new waters. May the voyage be a prosperous one.

READING REVIEW

1. Why did Susan's father take her to the secession convention?
2. How did Susan react to Colonel Ward's speech and General Call's show of emotion once Florida had signed the Ordinance of Secession?
3. Was Susan for or against secession? Give two pieces of evidence that support your conclusion.

18 A Nation Divided
(1861–1865)

125 The First Modern War

No one in the North or the South was prepared for the death and destruction caused by the Civil War. Its devastation was greater than that of any previous conflict the nation had ever fought. And it was a different kind of war.

No people had ever before fought a war like the Civil War. For the first time, a modern industrialized nation was fighting a war using its new technology, machinery, and organization. This meant that instead of older, inaccurate weapons that killed relatively few people, guns that were deadly accurate could be used to kill many. It also meant that the war was no longer fought only between armies, since fighting now was brought directly to the people—to their cities, towns, and homes. In this selection historian Bruce Catton described these and many other features of modern warfare.

READING FOCUS
1. Why did Catton call the Civil War "the first modern war"?
2. How did the warfare in the Civil War differ from earlier warfare?

The Civil War was the first of the world's really modern wars. That is what gives it its terrible significance. For the great fact about modern war, greater even than its frightful destructiveness and its planned, carefully applied inhumanity, is that it never goes quite where the people who start it plan it to go. People do not control modern war; it controls them. It destroys the old bases on which society stood. Because it does, it forces us to go on and find

Adapted from Bruce Catton, "The First Modern War," in America Goes to War, *1958.*

new bases, whether we want to or not. It has become so demanding that the mere act of fighting it changes the conditions under which we live. Of all the uncertainties people introduce into history, modern warfare is the greatest. If it says nothing else it says this to everyone involved in it, at the moment of its beginning: Nothing is ever going to be the same again.

Neither side in the Civil War was prepared to stop short of complete victory. In the old days, wars were formal. Two nations fought until it seemed to one side or the other that it would not be worthwhile to fight any longer. Then some sort of agreement would be reached. In the end nothing would have been changed very much.

But in the Civil War it was all or nothing. The southern states wanted absolute independence. The northern states wanted absolute union. Once a little blood had been shed, there was no halfway point at which the two sides could get together and make a compromise. So the stakes were greatly increased. This too affected the way in which people fought. If you are fighting a total war, the enemy's army is not your own target. What you are really shooting at is the ability to carry on the fight. This means you will hit wherever you can with any weapon that comes into your hand.

Probably it is this more than any other thing that distinguishes modern war: anything goes. The old "rules of civilized warfare" simply disappear. Making war becomes a matter of absolutes. You cannot stop anywhere short of complete victory. Your enemy's army remains one of your targets, to be sure. But if you can destroy the social and economic supports of that army, and thereby cause the army itself to collapse, you have gone a long way toward reaching your goal.

Consider for a moment the logical end of this attitude. It is nothing less than the road to horror. It wipes out the restraints which we have so carefully built up through many generations. If it has any kind of rational base, it is nothing more than a belief that the end justifies the means. It can—and does—put an entire nation at the mercy of its most destructive instincts. What you do to your enemy is not limited by any reluctance to inflict pain, misery, and death, and not by any feeling that there are limits to the things which a civilized people may do. It is limited only by your technical ability to do harm. Without suffering any pangs of conscience, the group becomes prepared to do things which no single member of the group would think of for a moment.

It paid the North to tear up railway lines in the South, to destroy iron foundries and textile mills and machine shops, to cut off the sources of raw material which enabled the Confederacy to maintain the fight. It was necessary—using that word in its military meaning—to cripple the South's ability to feed its civilians and its armies. The farmer's property, in other words, was a military objective. To destroy barns and corncribs, to drive off herds of cattle and hogs, to kill horses and mules—these acts became desirable from a military point of view.

So we got, in that war, highly destructive raids which had much the same justification that the air raid has today. Sending a Sherman through Georgia with the objective of destroying the state's productive capacity was only a step from sending bomber planes to turn a manufacturing city to rubble.

In any case, fighting that kind of war leads you to objectives you did not have when the fighting began. This is exactly what happened in the Civil War. The Union troops, invading the South, had as one of their objectives the destruction of southern property. The most obvious, easily removed piece of property in all of the South was the Negro slave. Even northerners who believed in slavery came to see that. This bit of living property was an asset to the government that was trying to destroy the Union. Other kinds of property were to be destroyed. This particular kind could not be destroyed, but it could be taken away from its owners and thereby made useless.

It took the northern armies only a very short time to learn this lesson. As soon as they had learned it, they began to take the institution of slavery apart. They did so not because they had anything against it, but because they wanted to win the war.

When the northern government began to fight the Civil War, it said it had no intention of making war on slavery. Yet by the beginning of 1863 the northern government had proclaimed the emancipation of slaves. The war now was being fought for union and for freedom—a great broadening of its base.

So the Civil War, which began as a war to restore the Union, ended as a war to end human slavery. It was fought to a conclusion, the southern Confederacy dissolved in smoke, and slavery ended. Afterwards we would go

The ruins of Richmond, Virginia, after the Civil War

back and pick up the old ways of life and get on with the business of being Americans.

The only trouble with that point of view is that after a modern war you do not "go back to" anything at all. The mere act of war forces you to face the future, because war always destroys the base on which you have been resting. It is an act of violence which—whatever its dreadful cost, whatever its insane waste of life and treasure—means that in one way or another you are going to do something different from what you have done in the past. The Civil War was a beginning, rather than an end, simply because it ended, forever one of the things on which American society had been built.

READING REVIEW

1. According to Catton, what gave modern war its terrible significance?
2. What did Catton mean when he said, "wars were formal" in the old days?
3. What one thing distinguished modern war above all else?
4. What was the logical end of the all-or-nothing attitude?
5. What did Catton mean when he said that the Civil War was a "beginning, rather than an end"?

126 A Close-Up of "This Poor President"

When Lincoln was President, life in the White House was very different from the way it is today. Almost anyone could get into the White House to see the President. It was also easy for President Lincoln to leave the White House freely to visit people or just walk around the city of Washington, D.C. Of course, the office of the presidency was much simpler then. The President had fewer responsibilities, for the government was much smaller. But the necessity of making difficult, often unpopular, presidential decisions was much the same as today. This account of President Lincoln was from the diary of William Howard Russell, a newspaper reporter for the London *Times.*

READING FOCUS
1. Why did Russell pity the President?
2. What does this account tell you about the office of the presidency in the 1860's?

Then there entered—with a shambling, loose, almost unsteady walk—a tall, lean man. He

Abraham Lincoln, 1858

was well over six feet tall, with stooping shoulders and long arms ending in very large hands. (These, however, were far exceeded in size by his feet.) He was dressed in an ill-fitting, wrinkled black suit, like an undertaker at a funeral. Around his neck a rope of black silk was knotted in a large knot, with flying ends sticking up above his coat collar. He had a strong, muscular yellow neck. Above that, among a great black mass of hair, rose the strange, quaint face and head of President Lincoln.

The impression produced by the size of his hands and feet, and by his flapping ears, was overcome by the appearance of kindliness, wisdom, and awkward good nature of his face. The mouth is absolutely huge. The nose—a large feature. The eyes—dark, full, and deeply set—are penetrating, but full of an expression which amounts almost to tenderness. Above them is a shaggy brow. A person who met Mr. Lincoln in the street would not take him to be what—according to the usages of European society—is called a "gentleman." Since I came to the United States, I have heard Americans criticize him more on that account than I could have expected among simple republicans, where everyone should be equal. At the same time, however, it would not be possible for anyone to pass him in the street without noticing him.

[*October 9*]
Calling on General McClellan the other night, I was told by the orderly, who was closing the door, "The general's gone to bed tired, and can see no one. He sent the same message to the President, who came looking for him ten minutes ago."

This poor President! He is to be pitied. Surrounded by such scenes, and trying with all his might to understand strategy, naval warfare, big guns, the movements of troops, military maps, reconnaissances, occupations, interior and exterior lines, and all the technical details of the art of killing. He runs from one house to another, armed with plans, papers, reports, recommendations, sometimes good humored, never angry, occasionally dejected and always a little fussy.

The other night, as I was sitting in the parlor at headquarters, with an English friend who had come to see General McClellan, in walked a tall man. Papers and bundles stuck out of his pockets. "Well," said he to Brigadier

Adapted from William Howard Russell, My Diary North and South, *Vols. I and II. London, 1863.*

Van Vliet, who rose to receive him, "is George in?"

"Yes, sir. He's come back, but is lying down, very much tired. I'll send someone up, sir, and tell him you wish to see him."

"Oh, no; I can wait. I think I'll have supper with him. Well, and what are you now—I forget your name—are you a major, or a colonel or a general?"

"Whatever you like to make me, sir."

Seeing that General McClellan would be busy I walked out with my friend. He asked me when I got into the street why I stood up when that tall fellow came into the room. "Because it was the President." "The President of what?" "Of the United States." "Oh! come, now you're teasing me. Let me have another look at him." He came back more surprised than ever. When I assured him that I was quite serious, he exclaimed, "I give up on the United States after this."

But for all that, there have been many more courtly Presidents who, in a similar crisis, would have displayed less ability, honesty, and plain dealing than Abraham Lincoln.

READING REVIEW

1. **(a)** How did Russell describe the President? **(b)** Does his description of Lincoln seem accurate to you? Why or why not?
2. How is the President treated when he goes to see General McClellan?
3. Why does Russell feel sorry for the President?
4. After reading Russell's account, how would you describe the President?

127 Background of the Emancipation Proclamation

At first, Northerners were fighting the Civil War to save the Union, not to free the slaves. Lincoln had many doubts about outright emancipation of the slaves. He favored compensated emancipation— that is, paying the slaveowners money for the freed slaves. He also thought that former slaves should be sent to Africa, to settle colonies and live there. But as the war continued the situation changed, and the war became a crusade to free the slaves. In this reading, historian John Hope Franklin gave the background of Lincoln's decision to issue the Emancipation Proclamation.

READING FOCUS

1. Why did Lincoln feel that emancipation would hurt the Union cause?
2. What was Lincoln's chief objective of this war?
3. What kinds of pressure were put on Lincoln to issue a proclamation?

Lincoln's reluctance to take positive action against slavery during his first year in office did not result from his affection for slavery. As a new member of the Illinois legislature in 1837, he declared that "slavery is founded both on injustice and bad policy." He had not changed his mind. In 1861, however, he realized that emancipation would bring on a crisis in the border states and that many Union soldiers were unwilling to fight to free the slaves. He also doubted that outright emancipation of slaves was legal, especially without compensation for the owners. He also doubted that whites and freed Negroes could live together in peace, and this led him to favor colonization. Compensation and colonization dominated his thinking as he moved slowly toward a policy of emancipation.

In March 1862 the President sent to Congress a special message on compensated emancipation. He urged the members to provide support for states that might want to free their slaves. He asked Congress to adopt a resolution to aid states that ended slavery. His personal appeals persuaded Congress to pass the resolution, but compensated emancipation was making no headway in the states.

The pressures of the generals and Congress were enough to give President Lincoln a clear understanding of the relationship of slavery to the war—if he lacked it. The pressures of individuals and groups added to the President's problems without contributing to a practical solution of the problem.

The war had hardly begun before the senior Senator from Massachusetts, Charles Sumner, began to urge upon the President outright emancipation of the slaves. After the disaster at Bull Run in July, Sumner went to the White House. Until midnight he discussed emancipation with Lincoln. He told Lincoln that the moment had come. The President could not agree.

Adapted from The Emancipation Proclamation *by John Hope Franklin, 1963.*

A poster celebrates President Lincoln's Emancipation Proclamation.

Sumner was not discouraged. He felt that it was his duty to keep the matter before the President. He continued to press the President. On December 27, 1861, he had a long talk with Lincoln and was delighted with the outcome.

On July 4, 1862, he was back at the White House with a tempting challenge to the President. "You can make this day more sacred and more historic than the Continental Congress." On this occasion the President did not tell Sumner that he was moving swiftly toward an emancipation policy. He said simply, "I would do it if I were not afraid that half the officers would throw down their arms and three more states would rise." This greatly upset Sumner. "He is hard to move. He is honest but unexperienced."

Among the abolitionists, Negro leader Frederick Douglass was the most outspoken in urging on President Lincoln the necessity of turning the war into a crusade against slavery. In the columns of his paper, in speeches, and in letters to friends at home and abroad he argued that the "Union cause would never prosper till the war took on an antislavery attitude, and the Negro was enlisted on the loyal side."

As the war moved into its second year, the pressure on the President to free the slaves increased. On June 20, 1862, a delegation of Quakers called on him and presented a petition praying for the emancipation of the slaves.

Other religious groups besieged the President. In July a committee of Presbyterians presented a copy of resolutions on slavery. On this occasion the President assured the committee that there was no difference between him and them regarding the moral character of the institution of slavery. The problem was how to get rid of it. "If a person were asked whether he would wish to have a growth on his neck, he could only answer no. But if we ask whether such a person should at once have it removed by the surgeon's knife, there might be a difference of opinion. Perhaps the person might bleed to death as the result of such an operation."

By this time Lincoln had decided to issue the Emancipation Proclamation at some date still not fixed. But he continued to give the impression that no decision had been reached. It was *after* he had reached the important decision that the most widely publicized demand for emancipation was made. Horace Greeley, the editor of the *New York Tribune,* had long been against slavery. Although generally friendly to the administration, he did not agree with Lincoln's view that emancipation would hurt the Union cause. He told him so in a moving editorial, "The Prayer of Twenty Million."

Many of Lincoln's supporters, Greeley told the President, were "sorely disappointed and deeply pained by the policy you seem to be following with regard to the slaves of rebels. . . . We think you are strangely and disastrously lacking in doing your official duty." He went on: "As one of the millions who would gladly have avoided this struggle at any sacrifice but that of principle and honor, but who now feel that the triumph of the Union is necessary not only to the existence of our country, but to the well-being of humankind, I beg you to give hearty obedience to the law of the land."

Lincoln could not ignore Greeley's biting criticism. The *Tribune* was widely read and greatly respected. Its editor was one of the strongest supporters of the Union cause. In a reply, which Greeley printed on August 25, the President said that he would not try to disprove any of Greeley's statements that he knew to be wrong. He briefly stated the policy he was following.

My chief object in this struggle *is* to save the Union, and *is not* either to save or to destroy slavery. If I could save the Union without freeing *any slave* I would do it, and if I could save it by freeing *all* the slaves I would do it; and if I could save it by freeing some and leaving others alone I would also do that. What I do about slavery, and the colored race, I do because I believe it helps to save the Union; and what I withstand, I withstand because I do *not* believe it would help save the Union. . . . I shall try to correct errors when they are shown to be errors; and I shall adopt new views as fast as they appear to be true views.

I have here stated my purpose according to my view of *official* duty; and I intend no change in my often-expressed *personal* wish that all people everywhere could be free.

One of the most imposing anti-slavery delegations called on the President on September 13, a delegation from Chicago that included Christians of all denominations. The President assured them that he had given much thought to emancipation, and indicated that the pressures on him were enormous.

Lincoln then asked the men from Chicago what good a proclamation of emancipation would do. "I do not want to issue a document that the whole world will see is useless. Would *my word* free the slaves, when I cannot even enforce the Constitution in the rebel states?" He expressed other doubts. What should be done with the slaves if they were freed? How could the Union feed and care for them? Lincoln said that he saw no legal or constitutional objections to a proclamation of emancipation, for as commander-in-chief he had a right "to take any measure which may best overcome the enemy." The delegation argued that nothing could be lost by proclaiming emancipation, even if it could not now be enforced. It would aid the war effort and win the sympathy of Europe and the whole civilized world.

In ending the interview, the President tried to comfort his visitors. He said that he hoped he had not been misunderstood because he had outlined the difficulties connected with issuing a proclamation to free the slaves. "I have not decided against a proclamation of liberty to the slaves, but hold the matter under consideration." He assured them that the matter was on his mind day and night, "more than any other."

READING REVIEW

1. Why did Lincoln decide not to take action on slavery during the first year of the war?
2. Why did Lincoln feel that outright emancipation of slaves may not be legal?
3. Name three groups that pressured Lincoln to issue a statement of emancipation.
4. Once the President issued a proclamation freeing all of the slaves, could he enforce it? Explain.
5. Why do you think Lincoln kept secret his decision to issue an emancipation proclamation?

128 Three Soldiers at Gettysburg

Part of the South's strategy in the Civil War was to strike into vital areas of the North and thus demoralize the Union army. The first attempt occurred at the Battle of Antietam in 1862, but it failed. In 1863 Southern troops under General Robert E. Lee marched across Maryland into Pennsylvania. There they met the Northern army at the small town of Gettysburg.

The Battle of Gettysburg lasted for three days—July 1–3, 1863—and it was the turning point of the Civil War. On the third day, Lee made a last desper-

READING FOCUS

1. What did each account have in common?
2. How did each account differ?

Haskell's Account

[Frank Haskell was a Union lieutenant from Wisconsin. Haskell was later promoted to colonel. He died at the Battle of Cold Harbor, Virginia, in June 1865.]

None on the hill needs to be told that *the enemy is advancing*. Every eye could see the troops advancing upon us! Regiment after regiment and brigade after brigade move from the woods and rapidly take their places in the lines forming the assault. More than half a mile [.8 kilometer] their front extends; more than a thousand yards [914 meters] the dull gray masses spread out. The red flags wave, their horsemen gallop up and down. The weapons of 18,000 men gleam in the sun. Right on they move, in perfect order, over ridge and slope, through orchard and meadow and cornfield, magnificent, grim, irresistible.

All was orderly and still upon our hill—no noise and no confusion. The men had little need of commands.

Our skirmishes open a spattering fire along the front. Then the thundering noise of our guns shake and echo and their sounding shells strike the enemy. All our available guns are now firing. But without wavering or stopping, the brave lines of the enemy continue to move on. The Rebel guns do not answer ours, and no charging shout rings out today, as is the Rebel custom. But the courage of these silent men amid our shots seems not to need other noise.

And so across all that broad open ground they have come, nearly half the way, with our guns roaring in their faces, until now only a hundred yards [91 meters] divide our ready left from their advancing right. The eager men on our left are impatient to begin. Let them.

I was wondering how long the Rebel ranks, deep though they were, could stand our volleys, when—great heaven! were my senses mad? The larger part of General Webb's brigade [northern troops]—heaven, it was true—there by the group of trees and the wall, was breaking from the cover and, without orders or reason, with no one to stop them, was falling back in fearful confusion! The fate of Gettysburg hung upon a single thread! A great emotion overwhelmed me at that instant. I drew my sword, which had always hung idle by my side, the symbol of command. All rules were forgotten. I ordered these men to "halt," and "face about" and "fire," and they heard my voice and gathered my meaning, and obeyed my commands. General Webb soon came to my assistance. He was on foot, but he was active, and did all that one could do to repair the break in the line. The men who had fallen back, facing the enemy, soon got back their confidence and became steady.

"How is it going?" Colonel Hall asked me, as I rode up. "Well, but Webb is under heavy attack and must have support, or he will be overpowered. Can you assist him?" "Yes." "You cannot be too quick." "I will move my brigade at once." "Good." He gave the order. The movement attracted the enemy's fire and was difficult. But in reasonable time and good order, Hall's men were fighting gallantly side by side with Webb's before the all-important point. From my position on horseback I could see that the enemy's right, under Hall's fire, was beginning to break. "See," I said to the men, "See the gray-backs run!" The men saw, and as they swept to their places by the side of Hall and opened fire, they roared—*"the hill is safe!"*

Dooley's Account

[John Dooley was a Confederate soldier in a Virginia regiment. He was taken prisoner at the Battle of Gettysburg. After the war he became a Jesuit priest.]

Abridged/adapted from The Battle of Gettysburg *by Frank Haskell, edited by Bruce Catton.*

Dooley's account adapted from John Dooley, Confederate Soldier, *Joseph T. Durkin, ed. 1945.*

Our artillery has now stopped and the enemy has checked its fury, too. The time set for our charge has come.

I tell you, there is no romance in making one of these charges. When you rise to your feet as we did today, I tell you the enthusiasm *ain't there.* Instead of burning to avenge the insults to our country, families, altars, and firesides, the thought is most frequently, *Oh,* if I could just come out of this charge safely, how thankful *I would be!*

We rise to our feet—but not all. There is a line of men still on the ground with their faces turned, men affected in four different ways. There are the gallant dead who will never charge again. There are the helpless wounded, and the men who have charged on many a battlefield but who are now helpless from the heat of the sun. Finally, there are the men who do not have enough courage to rise—but of these there are few.

Up, brave men! Some are actually *fainting* from the heat and dread. They have fallen to the ground overpowered. Onward—steady, not too fast—steady—keep well in line—there is the line of guns we must face—right in front but how far they appear! Nearly one third of a mile [.5 kilometer], off on Cemetery Ridge. Upon the center of this we must march. Behind the guns are strong lines of infantry. You may see them plainly and now they see us perhaps more plainly.

To the right of us and above the guns we are to capture, black heavy monsters fire forth their flame and smoke and storms of shot and shell upon our advancing line. Directly in front, breathing flame in our very faces, the long range of guns which must be taken thunder on our ranks. Now truly does the dying begin. The line becomes unsteady because at every step a hole in the line must be closed. Thus from left to right much ground is often lost.

Close up! Close up the ranks when a friend falls, while his blood falls on your cheek or throws a film over your eyes! Turn to left or right, while the bravest of the brave are sink-

Confederate soldiers break through the Northern lines.

Detail from Paul Philippoteaux's painting, "The Battle of Gettysburg"

ing to rise no more! Still onward! So many men have fallen now. Still we press on—oh, how long it seems before we reach those blazing guns! Our men are falling faster now, for the deadly guns are at work. Volley after volley mows us down.

On! men, on! Thirty more yards [27 meters] and the guns are ours! But who can stand such a storm of lead and iron? What a relief if the earth would open now and give us a safe way to retreat!

Just here—from right to left what remains of our men pour in their long reserved fire. Until now no shot had been fired, no shout of triumph had been raised. But now the well known southern battle cry burst wildly over the bloodstained field and *all that line of guns is ours.*

Shot through both legs, I fall about 30 yards [27 meters] from the guns. I fear I shall bleed to death. The dead and dying are all around, while the division sweeps over the Yankee guns. Oh, how I long to know the result, the end of this fearful charge! We seem to have victory in our hands. But what can the poor remains of a shattered division do if they meet a stubborn resistance beyond the guns?

There—listen—we hear a new shout, and cheer after cheer fills the air. Are those fresh troops advancing to our support? No! no! That shout never came from southern lips. Oh God!

Virginia's bravest, noblest sons have died here today and died all in vain!

Pickett's Account

[George Pickett was the general who led the Confederate charge up Cemetery Ridge. He wrote this account of the battle to his wife.]

My brave boys were full of hope and confident of victory as I led them forward, forming them in columns of attack. Though officers and men alike knew what was before them—knew the odds against them—they eagerly offered their lives, believing they would meet with success.

Over on Cemetery Ridge the Federals saw a scene never before witnessed on this continent. It was a scene which never took place before and can never take place again—an army forming in line of battle in full view of the enemy, under their very eyes—charging across a space nearly a mile [1.6 kilometers] in length over fields of grain and then a smooth expanse—moving with the steadiness of a dress parade, the pride and glory soon to be crushed by an overwhelming heartbreak.

Well, it is all over now. The battle is lost, and many of us are prisoners, many are dead, many wounded, bleeding and dying. Your soldier lives and mourns. If it were not for you, my darling, he would rather, a million times rather, be back there with his dead, to sleep for all time in an unknown grave.

READING REVIEW

1. What aspects of the charge did Haskell stress?
2. What aspects did Dooley stress?
3. What was the feeling expressed by General Pickett in his account?
4. Which of these accounts seems more accurate? Why?
5. Which seems more vivid? Why?

129 Sherman's March: His Own View

The Civil War was the first modern war. The Civil War was also a total war. This meant that the war not only was fought between armies but also was brought directly to the people. Fierce fighting took place in the streets of towns and cities, and in barns and farmhouses in the countryside. The people of the North and the South suffered great hardships.

The most famous and devastating example of civilian destruction during the Civil War was Sherman's march from Tennessee to Atlanta, Georgia, and then northward to Richmond, Virginia. In Georgia, Sherman's troops left behind total destruction. In this selection, General Sherman described the march from Atlanta to Richmond.

READING FOCUS

1. Why was Sherman's campaign so successful?
2. What was Sherman's mood as he left Atlanta?

The march from Atlanta began on the morning of November 15. The right wing and cavalry followed the railroad southeast toward Jonesboro. Another force went east, through Decatur, toward Madison. These different routes were designed to threaten both Macon and Augusta at the same time, in order to prevent a concentration of Confederate forces at our objective—Milledgeville, the capital of Georgia—about 100 miles [160 kilometers] away.

About 7 A.M. on November 16 we rode out of Atlanta. From the nearby hills, we paused to look back upon the scenes of our past battles. Behind us lay the city, smoking and in ruins, the black smoke rising high and hanging over the ruined city. Right before us was the Fourteenth Corps, marching steadily and rapidly, with a cheery look and fast stride that seemed to ignore the 1,000 miles [1,600 kilometers] that lay between us and Richmond. Some band struck up the anthem of "John Brown's soul goes marching on." The men caught up the song, and never before or since have I heard the chorus of "Glory, glory, hallelujah!" done with more spirit, or in a better setting of time and place.

The first night out we camped by the roadside. The whole horizon glowed from the bonfires made from railroad ties. All night groups of men were carrying the heated rails to the nearest trees and bending them around the trunks. Colonel Poe had provided tools for ripping up the rails and twisting them when red hot. But the best and easiest way was to heat the middle of the iron rails on bonfires made of

Adapted from William T. Sherman, Memoirs, Vol. II, 1875.

crossties, and then wind them around a telegraph pole or tree trunk. I placed great importance on this destruction of the railroad, gave it my personal attention, and issued several orders on the subject.

We found a good deal of corn, molasses, meal, bacon, and sweet potatoes. We also took many cows and oxen and a large number of mules. In all these the countryside was quite rich, never before having been visited by a hostile army. The recent crop had been excellent. It had just been gathered, and was stored for the winter. As a rule, we destroyed none of the crops, but kept our wagons full and fed our teams well.

The skill and success of the men in collecting provisions was one of the features of this march. Each brigade commander had authority to have a company of men who foraged, or searched for food and provisions. Each usually had about 50 men, with one or two commissioned officers selected for their boldness and energy. This company would be told about the planned day's march and camp, and be sent out before daylight. They would walk five or six miles [8 or 9 kilometers] beyond the route to be traveled by their brigade and visit every plantation and farm within that distance. They would usually find a wagon or family carriage and load it with bacon, cornmeal, turkeys, chickens, ducks, and everything that could be used as food or supply. Then they would go back to the main road, usually in advance of their wagon train. When it arrived, they would deliver the supplies they had gathered.

Often I would pass these foraging parties along the roadside, waiting for their wagons to come up, and I was amused at their strange collections—mules, horses, even cattle, packed with old saddles and loaded with hams, bacon, bags of cornmeal, and poultry of all kinds. Although this foraging involved great danger and hard work, there seemed to be something about it that attracted the soldiers. To them, it was a privilege to be a part of such a party. Each day they returned riding on all sorts of animals, which were taken from them at once and turned over for general use. But the next day they would start out again on foot, only to repeat the actions of the day before.

No doubt many acts of looting, robbery, and violence were committed by these parties of foragers, usually called "bummers." I have since heard of jewelry being taken from women, and other articles being taken that never reached the commissary. But these acts were not the general practice. No army could have carried sufficient food and supplies for a march of 300 miles [483 kilometers]; therefore, foraging of some sort was necessary. It enabled our men to be well supplied with all the things essential for life and good health. It meant the wagons had enough supplies in case of unexpected delay, and that our animals were well fed. Indeed, when we reached Savannah, experts said that our wagon trains were the finest they had ever seen with any army.

On November 23 we rode into Milledgeville, the capital of the state. The Twentieth Corps had entered before us. During that day the left wing was all united, in and around Milledgeville. The first stage of the journey was therefore complete, and absolutely successful.

READING REVIEW

1. Why did Sherman place great importance on the destruction of the railroads?
2. According to Sherman, what was one of the significant features of his march?
3. Why did the soldiers consider being part of the foraging parties a privilege?
4. What was Sherman's attitude toward the foraging parties?

130 Sherman's March: A Southern View

The soldiers who took part in Sherman's march northward to Richmond treated South Carolina harshly because they regarded it as the state most responsible for causing the war. When they marched out of Columbia, the capital of South Carolina, the city was in flames. Sherman always claimed that the fires had been started by Confederate troops withdrawing from the city. However, southern authorities said that they had set fire to military supplies, but not to the city itself. They claimed that Union troops had started the fires.

Emma LeConte, who wrote this account, was the daughter of a professor at South Carolina State University. During the war the university was turned into a hospital and she helped care for wounded Confederate soldiers there. She was 16 when Sherman's army marched into Columbia. Here, she gives her view of the "Yankees" coming to the city and the burning of Columbia.

READING FOCUS

1. How did the writer's mood change in these ten days?
2. What did she think of the Union troops?

An artist's view of General Sherman's troops and their "March to the Sea"

February 14, 1865

What a panic the whole town is in! I have not been out of the house myself, but Father says there is the greatest excitement. The Yankees are reported only a few miles away from the city, on the other side of the river. How many there are no one seems to know. Some people think Sherman will burn the town, but we can hardly believe that. Although these buildings are state property [South Carolina State University], the fact they are used as a hospital will, it is thought, protect them. I have been busily making large pockets to wear under my hoopskirt to hide my most valuable things.

February 15

Oh, how is it possible to write amid this excitement and confusion! They tell me the streets in town are lined with panic-stricken crowds trying to escape. All is confusion and turmoil. All day we have been listening to the booming of cannon—receiving conflicting reports of the fighting. All day wagons and ambulances have been bringing in the wounded along the muddy streets and through the rain.

Night. Nearer and nearer, clearer and louder, sound the cannon. Oh, it is heart-sickening to listen to it! Just now as I stood on the porch listening, the explosions sounded so frightfully loud and near that I could not help shuddering at each one. And the horrible uncertainty of what is before us!

February 16

How can the terror and excitement of today be described! About nine o'clock we were sitting in the dining room. "Wouldn't it be dreadful if they should shell the city?" someone said. "They would not do that," replied mother, "for they have not demanded its surrender." Just then, Jane, the nurse, rushed in crying out that they were shelling. We ran to the front door just in time to hear a shell go past. It fell and exploded not far off. This was so unexpected. I do not know why, but in all my list of expected horrors I somehow had not thought of a bombardment. We went to the basement, where we sat listening as the shells now fell nearer, and now farther off. The firing stopped about dinner time.

Adapted from Heroines of Dixie, *edited by Katherine M. Jones, 1955.*

February 17

At about six o'clock while it was still quite dark, we were suddenly awakened by a terrific explosion. The house shook—broken window-panes clattered down, and we all sat up in bed, for a few seconds silent with terror. Then all was quiet. We decided that the authorities had blown up some supplies before leaving town. After breakfast the cannons opened fire again and were so near that every blast shook the house. I think it must have been to cover our soldiers' retreat. It did not continue very long.

One o'clock P.M. Well, they are here. I was sitting in the back parlor when I heard the shouting of troops. I was at the front door in a moment. Jane came running and crying, "O Miss Emma, they've come at last!" She said they were marching down Main Street. Before them ran a panic-stricken crowd of women and children who seemed nearly crazy.

I ran upstairs to my bedroom windows just in time to see the U.S. flag run up over the State House. O what a horrid sight! What shame! After four long bitter years of bloodshed and hatred, now to wave there at last! I do not think I could possibly describe my feelings. I know I could not look at all.

Later. Gen. Sherman has assured the mayor "that he and all the citizens may sleep as securely and quietly tonight as if under Confederate rule. Private property will be carefully respected." Some public buildings have to be destroyed, but Sherman will wait until tomorrow when the wind has died down.

February 18

What a night of horror, misery, and agony! It makes one sick to think of writing down such scenes. Until dinnertime we saw little of the Yankees, except the guard on the campus, and the officers and men galloping up and down the street. The devils as they marched past looked strong and well dressed in dark, dirty-looking blue. The wagon trains were immense. Night came on. Of course we did not expect to sleep, but we looked forward to a peaceful night. At about seven o'clock I was standing on the back porch. Before me the whole southern horizon was lit up by campfires which dotted the woods. We could watch the wretches walking—shouting—hurrahing—cursing South Carolina—swearing—singing songs.

A fire on Main Street was raging, and we anxiously watched it from the upper front windows. In a little while the flames broke forth in every direction. The poor people rushing from their burning homes were not allowed to keep even the few necessities they gathered up in their flight—even blankets and food were taken from them and destroyed. The fire fighters attempted to use their engines, but the fire hose was cut to pieces and their lives were threatened.

The wind blew the flames from house to house with frightful rapidity. By midnight the whole town (except the outskirts) was ablaze. Still the flames had not come near enough to us to threaten our immediate safety, and for some reason not a single Yankee soldier had entered our house.

Everywhere the fires walled the streets with solid masses of flames as far as the eye could see—filling the air with its terrible roar. On every side the fire blazed, while every instant came the crashing of timbers and the thunder of falling buildings.

The college buildings caught on fire. All the doctors and nurses were on the roof trying to save the buildings. The poor wounded patients were left to themselves. Those who could crawled out, while those who could not move waited to be burned to death. The state house of course is burned.

We dread tonight. O, the sorrow and misery of this unhappy town! From what I can learn, the Yankees' chief aim has been to "humble our pride—southern pride."

Sunday, February 19
The day has passed quietly as regards the Yankees.

February 20
Shortly after breakfast—O joyful sight—the soldiers camped behind the campus marched by with all their immense wagon trains on their way out of Columbia. They tell us everyone will be gone by tomorrow evening.

February 21
A heavy curse has fallen on this town—from a beautiful city it is turned into a desert. How desolated and dreary we feel—how completely cut off from the world. No longer the shrill whistle of the engine—no daily mail—the morning brings no paper with news from the

Fire-gutted Columbia, South Carolina, after Sherman's troops have left

outside—there are no lights—no people in the streets. One feels still greater fear if the terrible stillness is broken by a laugh or too loud a voice.

February 22

I have seen it all. It is even worse than I thought. The place is in ruins. The entire heart of the city is in ashes—only the outer edges remain. Poor old Columbia—where is all its beauty—so admired by strangers, so loved by its children!

Everything is gone—stores, merchants, customers—all the eager faces gone—only three or four gloomy-looking people to be seen picking their way over heaps of ruins, brick, and timbers. The wind moans among the bleak chimneys and whistles through the gaping windows of some hotel or warehouse. The market is a ruined shell supported by crumbling arches—its spire has fallen and with it the old town clock whose familiar stroke we miss so much.

February 23

Somehow I feel we cannot be conquered. We have lost everything, but if all this—Negroes—property—could be given back a hundred times over I would not be willing to go back to them. I would rather stand any poverty than live under Yankee rule. I would much rather have France or any other country for a ruler—anything but live as one nation with the *Yankees*—that word in my mind stands for all that is mean, despicable, and hateful.

READING REVIEW

1. Why did Emma think that it was the Yankees' chief aim to "humble our pride—Southern pride"?
2. How did she describe Columbia after the Yankee troops moved on?
3. What did she think about living as one nation with the Yankees?

131 My Surrender to Lee

By the spring of 1865, Sherman's army was approaching Virginia and General Grant's army was already in Richmond. After four long, bitter years of fighting, the end of the war was in sight.

General Lee left Richmond hoping to get to North Carolina, but he was unabe to escape Grant and his army. Finally, realizing all was lost, Lee surrendered to Grant. The surrender came on April 9, 1865, at Appomattox Court House in Virginia. The Civil War was over.

The following selection is Grant's description of his meeting with Lee at Appomattox. It is taken from his memoirs, which he wrote many years later.

READING FOCUS

1. What was Grant's attitude toward Lee during this meeting? toward the Southern cause?
2. How would you describe General Lee? General Grant?

I had known General Lee in the old army, and had served with him in the Mexican War. I did not suppose, because of the difference in our age and rank, that he would remember me. I would more naturally remember him, because he was General Scott's chief of staff in the Mexican War.

When I had left camp that morning I had not expected the surrender to take place so soon, and so I was not in dress uniform. I was without a sword, as I usually was when on horseback in the field. I wore a soldier's tunic for a coat, with the shoulder straps of my rank to indicate to the army who I was.

When I went into the house I found General Lee. We greeted each other, and after shaking hands took our seats.

What General Lee's feelings were I do not know. He was a man of much dignity, without expression on his face. It was impossible to say whether he felt inwardly glad that the end had finally come, or felt sad over the result, and was too manly to show it. Whatever his feelings, they were entirely hidden from me.

My own feelings, which had been joyful when I received his letter, were sad and depressed. I felt like doing anything but celebrating the downfall of a foe who had fought so long and bravely, and had suffered so much for a cause—though that cause was, I believe, one of the worst for which a people ever fought. I do not question, however, the sincerity of the great majority of those who were opposed to us.

Adapted from Personal Memoirs of U.S. Grant, *Vol. II, 1886.*

The "Surrender of General Lee to General Grant"

General Lee was dressed in a full uniform which was completely new, and was wearing a sword of considerable value, very likely the sword which had been given him by the State of Virginia. In my rough traveling uniform, that of a private with the straps of a lieutenant-general, I must have contrasted very strangely with a man so handsomely dressed, six feet tall, and of such complete dignity. But this was not a matter that I thought of until afterwards.

We soon started to talk about old army times. He said that he remembered me very well in the old army. I told him that I remembered him perfectly, but from the difference in our rank and years (he was about 16 years older than I), I had not expected him to remember me. Our talk was so pleasant that I almost forgot the reason for our meeting. General Lee called my attention to it, and said that he had asked for this interview to find out the terms I proposed to give his army. I said that I meant only for his army to give up their weapons and not to use them again. He said that he had understood this from my letter.

Then we gradually started to talk again about matters which had nothing to do with the subject which had brought us together. This continued for some time. General Lee again interrupted the talk by suggesting that the terms I proposed to give his army ought to be written out. I then wrote out the following terms:

Appomattox, C.H., Va.
Apl. 9th, 1865

Gen. R. E. Lee,
    Com'g C. S. A.

GEN: In accordance with my letter to you of the 8th, I propose to receive the surrender of the Army of North Virginia on the following terms, to wit: lists of all the officers and men to be made. One copy to be given to an officer chosen by me, the other to be kept by such officer or officers as you may choose. The officers to give their individual words not to take up arms against the government of the United States, and each company or regimental commander to sign a like guarantee for the men of his command. The arms, artillery, and public property to be stacked and turned over to the officer appointed by me to receive them. This will not include the sidearms of the officers, nor their private horses or baggage. This done, all officers and men will be allowed to return to their homes, not to be disturbed by United States authority so long as they observe their words and the laws in force where they may live.

Very respectfully,
U.S. Grant,
Lt. Gen.

When I put my pen to the paper I did not know the first word that I should use in writing the terms. I only knew what was in my mind, and I wished to express it clearly, so that there could be no mistaking it. As I wrote on, the thought occurred to me that the officers had their own private horses and other possessions, which were important to them, but of no value to us. I also felt that it would be an unnecessary disgrace to ask them to give up their sidearms.

General Lee seemed to have no objections to the terms first proposed. When he read over the part about sidearms, horses, and private property of the officers, he said—with some feeling, I thought—that this would have a happy effect upon his army.

Then, after a little further talk, General Lee said to me that their army was organized a little differently from the army of the United States (still implying that we were two countries). In their army the members of the artillery owned their own horses. He asked if they could keep them.

I then said to him that I thought this would be about the last battle of the war—I sincerely hoped so. I said further that I thought that most of the men in the ranks were small farmers. The whole countryside had been so raided by the two armies that it was doubtful whether they would be able to put in a crop to get themselves and their families through the next winter without the help of the horses they were then riding. The United States did not want them. I would, therefore, instruct my officers to let every man of the Confederate army who claimed to own a horse or mule take the animal home. Lee said that this would have a happy effect. He then sat down and wrote out the following letter:

> Headquarters Army of Northern Virginia,
> April 9, 1865
>
> Lieut.-General U.S. Grant.
>
> General: I received your letter of this date containing the terms of the surrender of the Army of Northern Virginia as proposed by you. As they are much the same as those expressed in your letter of the 8th, they are accepted. I will proceed to choose the proper officers to carry out the terms.
>
> R.E. Lee, General.

READING REVIEW

1. Why did Grant feel General Lee would not remember him?
2. Why did Grant's feeling of joy upon receiving the letter of surrender change to one of sadness and depression?
3. List three terms of the surrender agreement.
4. Do you think Grant was fair in his requests? Why or why not?
5. (a) What were the three additional terms Grant added to the surrender agreement? (b) Why were they added?
6. How does the surrender compare to the way recent wars have ended?

132 The Anguish of the Wounded

The Civil War took a terrible toll. Over 600,000 men died during this terrible, bloody war. During each battle, hundreds—even thousands in the larger battles—were wounded. Often they were left to suffer or to die on the battlefield. The luckier ones were taken to nearby farms, homes, or open-air "hospitals" to be treated. There were never enough doctors to care for them and often not enough drugs, bandages, or medical supplies. Here Carl Schurz, a Union general at Gettysburg, described the treatment of the wounded.

READING FOCUS

1. What elements of the situation impressed Schurz the most?
2. Under what conditions did the surgeons have to perform operations?

To look after the wounded soldiers under my command, I visited the places where the surgeons were at work. At the Battle of Bull Run I had seen only on a very small scale what I was now to see. At Gettysburg the wounded—many thousands of them—were carried to the farms behind our lines. The houses, the barns, the sheds, and the open barnyards were crowded with moaning and screaming human beings. Still an unending parade of stretchers and ambulances was coming in from all sides with more wounded.

A heavy rain set in during the day and large numbers of men had to remain unprotected out in the open. I saw long rows of men lying on the ground as the water poured down upon them. Most of the operating tables were placed in the open where the light was best, some of them partly protected against the rain by canvas coverings or blankets stretched upon poles.

There stood the surgeons. Their sleeves were rolled up to the elbows. Their bare arms as well as their linen aprons were smeared with blood. They often held their knives between their teeth while they were helping a patient on or off the table. Around them lay pools of blood and amputated arms and legs.

Adapted from F. Bancroft and W. A. Dunning, eds., The Reminiscences of Carl Schurz, *1908.*

As surgeons operate, citizen volunteers assist the wounded.

Antiseptic methods were still unknown at that time. As a wounded man was lifted on the table, often screaming with pain, the surgeon quickly examined the wound. If he decided to cut off the injured limb, some ether was given and the body was put in position in a moment. The surgeon grabbed the knife from between his teeth, wiped it rapidly once or twice across his bloodstained apron, and began the cutting. After the operation, the surgeon would look around with a deep sigh, and then—"Next!"

And so it went on, hour after hour. The number of patients seemed never to lessen. Now and then one of the wounded men would call attention to the fact that his neighbor lying on the ground had died while waiting for his turn. The dead body was then quietly removed. Or a surgeon, having been long at work, would put down his knife, exclaiming that his hand had grown unsteady, and that this was too much for any human being to stand. Often tears streamed down his face.

Many of the wounded men suffered with silent bravery. Some would even force themselves to joke grimly about their situation or about the "skedaddling of the rebels." But there were, also, heart-rending groans, sharp cries of pain, and despairing exclamations—"Oh Lord! Oh, Lord!" or "Let me die!" or softer murmurings in which the words "mother" or "father" or "home" were often heard.

I saw many of my men among the sufferers, faces I well remembered. They greeted me with a look or even a painful smile and usually asked what I thought of their chances, or whether I could do anything for them. Sometimes they asked whether I thought the enemy was well beaten. I sadly realized that many of the words of cheer and encouragement I gave them were just empty sounds, but they might offer at least some comfort for the moment.

READING REVIEW
1. How did Schurz help his men?
2. Do you think there was anything else Schurz could have done?
3. How do you think the situation affected Schurz? the surgeons?

133 The Death of a President

The assassination of Abraham Lincoln is one of the tragedies of American history. News of the President's death was greeted with sorrow throughout the North. Even many Southerners expressed sadness when they heard that Lincoln was dead.

Gideon Welles, Lincoln's Secretary of the Navy, was present when Lincoln died. The following excerpt from Welles' diary gives his moving account of the death of the President.

I had retired to bed about half past-ten on the evening of the 14th of April, and was just getting asleep when Mrs. Welles, my wife, said some one was at our door. I arose at once and raised the window, when my messenger, James Smith, called to me that Mr. Lincoln, the President, had been shot. "Where," I inquired, "was the President when shot?" James said he was at Ford's Theatre on 10th Street.

The President had been carried across the street from the theatre, to the house of Mr. Peterson. We entered by going up a flight of steps above the basement and passing through a long hall to the rear, where the President lay extended on a bed, breathing heavily.

Several surgeons were present, at least six, I should think more. Among them I was glad to observe Dr. Hall, who, however, soon left. I inquired of Dr. Hall, as I entered, the true condition of the President. He replied the President was dead to all intents, although he might live three hours or perhaps longer.

The giant sufferer lay extended diagonally across the bed, which was not long enough for him. He had been stripped of his clothes. His large arms, which were occasionally exposed, were of a size which one would scarce have expected from his slender appearance. His slow, full breathing lifted the clothes with each breath he took. His features were calm and striking.

Senator Sumner, Speaker Colfax, Mr. Secretary McCulloch, and the other members of the Cabinet were there with the exception of Mr. Seward. A double guard was stationed at the door and on the sidewalk, to hold back the crowd, which was of course highly excited and anxious. The room was small and overcrowded. The surgeons and members of the Cabinet were as many as should have been in the room, and the hall and other rooms in the front or main house were full. One of these rooms was occupied by Mrs. Lincoln and her attendants. About once an hour Mrs. Lincoln would come to the bedside of her dying husband and with sobbing and tears remain until overcome by emotion.

(April 15.) It was dark, cloudy, and damp, and about six a.m. it began to rain. I remained in the room until then without sitting or leaving it, listening to the heavy groans, and witnessing the wasting life of the good and great man who was dying before me.

About 6 a.m. I experienced a feeling of faintness and for the first time after entering the room, I left it and the house, and took a short walk in the open air. It was a dark and gloomy morning, and rain set in before I returned to the house, some fifteen minutes later. Large groups of people were gathered every few yards, all anxious and concerned. Some one or more from each group stepped forward as I passed, to inquire into the condition of the President, and to ask if there was no hope. Grief was on every face when I replied that the President could survive but a short time. The colored people especially—and there were at this time more of them, perhaps, than of whites—were overwhelmed with grief.

A little before seven, I went into the room where the dying President was rapidly drawing near the closing moments. His wife soon after made her last visit to him. Robert, his son, stood with several others at the head of the bed. He bore himself well, but on two occasions gave way to overpowering grief and sobbed aloud. The breathing of the President became suspended at intervals, and at last entirely ceased at twenty-two minutes past seven. . . .

I went after breakfast to the Executive Mansion. There was a cheerless cold rain and everything seemed gloomy. On the Avenue in front of the White House were several hundred colored people, mostly women and children, weeping and wailing their loss. This crowd did not appear to diminish through the whole of that cold, wet day; they seemed not to know what was to be their fate since their great friend was dead, and their hopeless grief affected me more than almost anything else, though strong and brave men wept when I met them.

From Diary of Gideon Welles, *1911.*

READING REVIEW

1. **(a)** How did Welles describe the reaction of people to Lincoln's assassination? **(b)** Why were blacks especially saddened by the death of Lincoln?
2. What was the mood of Welles' description of Lincoln's death? Cite passages from the reading to explain your answer.

UNIT SIX READINGS

Rebuilding the Nation

CHAPTER 19
Restoring the South to the Union
(1865–1900)

134 A Policy for Reconstruction

Many people have wondered if the reconstruction period might have been different if Lincoln had lived. They wonder if Lincoln, who was more flexible and tactful than Andrew Johnson, might have been better able to deal with the Radical Republicans who wanted to punish the South. Of course, it is not possible ever to know, but we do know that Lincoln wanted to follow a moderate policy in restoring the South to the Union.

In this speech, delivered on April 11, 1865, just four days before he was assassinated, Lincoln explained the reconstruction policy he favored. In it he explained why he believed Louisiana had met the conditions necessary to restore it to the Union.

READING FOCUS

1. What were Lincoln's main arguments for readmitting Louisiana to the Union?
2. What was his viewpoint about giving blacks the right to vote?

Fellow citizens: We meet this evening not in sorrow, but in gladness of heart. The surrender of the principal Confederate army gives hope of a righteous and speedy peace.

Because of these recent successes, we must think more than ever about re-establishing national authority—about reconstruction. This task is filled with great difficulty. Unlike a war between independent nations, there is no authorized group for us to negotiate with. No one person has authority to surrender on behalf of any other person. We simply must begin with and help bring together the disorganized elements. And we, too—the loyal people—differ among ourselves about the methods and measures of reconstruction.

We all agree that the seceded states are out of their proper practical relationship with the Union. We also agree that the only object of the government, civil and military, in regard to those states, is to get them back into their proper practical relationship with the Union. I believe that it is not only possible, but in fact

The Reconstruction Constitution of Louisiana

Adapted from Arthur Brooks Lapsley, ed., The Writings of Abraham Lincoln.

easier, to do this without deciding or even considering whether those states have ever been out of the Union. Finding them safely at home, it would be completely useless to worry about whether they had ever been gone.

The number of voters on which the Louisiana government rests would be more satisfactory to all if it totaled 50,000, or 30,000, or even 20,000, instead of 12,000, as it does. It is also unsatisfactory to some that the vote is not given to colored people. I would myself prefer that it were now given to the very intelligent, and those who serve our cause as soldiers.

Still, the question is not whether the Louisiana government, as it stands, is quite all that is desirable. The question is, Will it be wiser to take it as it is and help to improve it, or reject it? Can Louisiana be brought into proper practical relation with the Union sooner by keeping or by getting rid of its new state government? Some 12,000 voters in the state have sworn loyalty to the Union. They have held elections, organized a state government, and adopted a free-state constitution. This gives the benefit of public schools equally to black and white, and gives the legislature the power to grant the vote to the colored people. This legislature has already voted to ratify the Thirteenth Amendment, recently passed by Congress abolishing slavery throughout the nation. These 12,000 persons are thus fully committed to the Union and to maintaining freedom in the state. They are committed to the very things, and nearly all the things, the nation wants. They ask the nation's recognition and its assistance to make good this commitment.

Now if we reject them, we do our utmost to disorganize them. We, in fact, say to the white people: You are worthless or worse. We will neither help you nor be helped by you. To the black people we say: This cup of liberty which these, your old masters, held to your lips, we will take from you. We will leave you to gather the spilled and scattered contents in some way. If this course, discouraging and paralyzing to both white and black, helps in any way to bring Louisiana into a proper practical relationship with the Union, I have so far not been able to see it.

If, on the contrary, we recognize and support the new government of Louisiana, the opposite is true. We encourage the hearts of 12,000 to stick to their work and fight for it, and feed it, and grow it, and ripen it to a complete success. The colored people, too, in seeing all united for them, are inspired with energy and courage. Grant that they get the vote. Will they not gain it sooner by saving the steps already taken toward it? Granted that the new government of Louisiana is related to what it should be only as the egg is to the chicken, we shall have the chicken sooner by hatching the egg than by smashing it.

READING REVIEW

1. According to Lincoln, would the task of reconstruction be "filled with great difficulty"?
2. Why did Lincoln feel it would not be beneficial to discuss "whether those states have ever been out of the Union"?
3. List three reasons why Louisana should have been readmitted to the Union.
4. According to Lincoln, how would the citizens of Louisiana have reacted if their request for readmission were rejected?
5. What did Lincoln mean when he said," We shall have the chicken sooner by hatching the egg than by smashing it."?

135 A Northern Teacher in Georgia

By the end of the war large parts of the South were in ruins and many southerners suffered great hardships. Things were especially difficult for the freed slaves. Many suffered from disease and hunger, and many died. Few had job skills or were able to read or write. They lacked jobs and land and often even homes. Something had to be done to help the freed slaves adjust to a new way of life.

Even before the end of the Civil War, many northerners—especially New England abolitionists—had gone into Union-occupied areas of the Confederacy to help the former slaves. They established schools and helped the freed slaves to find homes and jobs. Among these were Sarah Chase, a Quaker from Worcester, Massachusetts, and her sister Lucy, who went to the South early in 1863. They helped to establish schools and taught in various parts of the South for the next seven years.

READING FOCUS

1. What was Sarah Chase's attitude toward the people in Columbus, Georgia? toward her pupils?

Many blacks received their first lessons in schooling from teachers sent by the Freedmen's Bureau.

2. What was the attitude of southerners towards the Freedmen's Bureau? the attitude of northerners?
3. What future did Chase see for families in the South who favored the Union?

When I last wrote we had just opened a school at Savannah: There were already several schools there and Colonel Sickles [the military governor of the Carolinas] was managing the affairs of the Freedmen's Bureau in a most admirable manner. So it did not seem right to stay in that charming city, though we could have found enough important work there to fill every moment. Wishing to work where there was the most need—there are so many places where nothing has been done for the freedmen, and where they are sorely persecuted—we came here. A schoolhouse built by the soldiers had just been destroyed by the

From Dear Ones at Home, *edited by Henry L. Swint.*

citizens. The feeling is intensely bitter against anything northern. The affairs of the Bureau have been very much mismanaged in Columbus, and our government has been disgraced by the troops who were stationed here. Now the troops have been withdrawn, and the people are annoyed by the presence of the Bureau and "a few pious and enthusiastic northeastern schoolteachers." "Both must be cleared out of the place," says the daily press. We have never been treated rudely by any of the citizens, but we know that we are generally discussed, and that many plans are proposed for "getting rid" of us.

We have glorious schools, and I am so satisfied with the work here that nothing in the world could make me wish to be in another place, or doing anything else. In my own day school and night school, I have 140 pupils. They have made truly wonderful progress in the five weeks I have been teaching.

How much I wish you could see my school! A more earnest, fine-looking group of students could not be found. I find the people here more tidy and thrifty than in any other place I know, even though many are very poor and nothing has been given them from the North. They are always cheerful and hopeful, ever anxious to improve.

How I wish I were rich! For the first time in my life I say it, for I have so much need of money here. We are too far from the North to make it worthwhile to send any boxes here because it costs too much. But I ought to have money to buy a piece of cloth, or drugs or a splint for a broken limb, or a piece of bedding for some good old soul—someone who has "raised eight children for missus as if they were my own; and nursed master so well the doctor said I saved his life; and now I'm too old to work—I'm turned out to die like a dog." Though I receive money from home, the expense of living is very great. And no individual's funds are enough for everything that is needed.

There are a number of colored people in this place who are very well-off. They cheerfully do what they can, but in a population of about 8,000, they can do little. I shall organize mutual help societies in the Negro churches (Baptist and Methodist) as soon as possible. Large numbers of black people are working for their food alone, and the white people tell them that they are not free yet. Across the river, in

Alabama, several Negroes have been shot *because* they were free!

Union! I can more easily believe in the lion and the lamb lying down together than in a union of the North and South. In all the counties around here, the Union families are being persecuted. People here say that those who favor the North cannot live in their communities. We now have with us a family who fled for their lives from their plantation 14 miles [22 kilometers] away. They have never owned slaves and have always been loyal. Consequently the neighbors have been killing their cattle and taking their farm tools and doing many things to make them leave their place. A few nights ago, a regular armed force from the county surrounded their house. They were going to kill the whole family but, finding that one of the sons was not there, they left to decide whether to put it off for another time. During that time a part of the family escaped to the woods.

Such things happen all the time. But it is not a good idea to write North about them. If they get in print, it gives encouragement to many communities who are ready to act in the same way. Now that the military courts are withdrawn, I see only two alternatives for southerners who favor the Union in many parts of the South—either enduring constant persecution, or moving to the North.

READING REVIEW

1. What hardships did the freed slave encounter after the war?
2. Why did Sarah Chase wish she were rich?
3. Give two reasons why southerners felt "intensely bitter against anything northern."
4. How were the southern families that favored the Union treated?
5. How important was the Freedmen's Bureau in the assimilation of the former slave into white society?

136 A Radical Republican View

President Johnson and the Radical Republicans in Congress had very different ideas about reconstruction. Even so, for a time most of President Johnson's version of Lincoln's moderate reconstruction program was followed. Then in 1866, the Radical Republicans won control of Congress. With a majority large enough to override President Johnson's veto, Congress took control of reconstruction.

One of the leaders of the Radical Republicans was Thaddeus Stevens, who favored a harsh reconstruction program. This selection is a part of Stevens' speech of January 3, 1867, in favor of such a reconstruction program, which Congress passed over President Johnson's veto on March 2, 1867.

READING FOCUS

1. What view did Stevens have about the legal position of the Confederacy during the Civil War?
2. What was Stevens' view after the Civil War?
3. What reasons did Stevens give to claim that the President had no authority to reconstruct the Union?

Since the surrender of the armies of the Confederate States of America, a little has been done toward establishing this government upon the true principles of liberty and justice. But it will be only a little if we stop here. We have broken the chains of four million slaves. We have allowed them to walk about—so long as they do not walk in paths which are walked on by white people. We have allowed them the privilege of attending church—if they can do so without offending the sight of their former masters. We have even given them that highest and most agreeable proof of liberty—the right to work.

But how have we added to their liberty of thought? In what way have we taught them about and granted them the privilege of self-government? We have forced upon them the privilege of fighting our battles, of dying in defense of freedom, and of bearing their equal share of taxes. But where have we given them the privilege of taking part in the formation of the laws for the government of their native land? By what laws have we made them able to defend themselves against oppression and injustice?

Do you call this liberty? Do you call this a free republic, where four million people are subjects but not citizens? Twenty years ago I spoke against this—the tyranny in my native land. Then, twenty million white people held four million black people in slavery. I say it is

Adapted from Congressional Globe, *39th Congress, 2nd Session Part I, January 3, 1867.*

no nearer a true republic. Now, twenty-five million of a privileged class keep five million from taking part in the rights of government.

Nearly six years ago a bloody war started between different sections of the United States. Eleven states having a very large territory, and ten or twelve million people, aimed to break their connection with the Union. They wanted to form an independent empire, founded on the principle of human slavery and excluding every free state. They did not aim to reform the government of the country, but they claimed their independence of that government and of all obligations to its laws. The "Confederate States" had as perfect and absolute control over those eleven states as the United States had over the other twenty-five.

The two powers prepared to settle the question by arms. They each raised armies of more than half a million men. The war was regarded by other nations as a public war between independent enemies. The two sides regarded each other as such, and claimed to be governed by the laws of war in their treatment of each other. On the result of the war depended the fate of the warring parties.

The Union armies triumphed. The Confederate armies and government surrendered unconditionally. The law of nations then fixed their condition. They were subject to the controlling power of the conquerors. No former laws, no former treaties existed to bind opposing sides. They had all been melted and destroyed in the fierce fires of the terrible war.

In a monarchy, the king would have fixed the condition of the conquered provinces. He might have extended the laws of the empire over them, allowed them to keep some of their old institutions, or have enforced new laws.

In this country, sovereignty rests with the people, and is exercised through Congress. The legislative power is the only protector of that sovereignty. No other branch of the government, or other department, no other officer of the government, holds one single part of the sovereignty of the nation. No government official, from the President and Chief Justice down, can take any action which is not directed by the legislative power.

Since the President is only the servant of the people, who issue their commands to him through Congress, where does he obtain the constitutional power to create new states? Where does he get the power to remake old ones, to establish laws, to fix the qualification of voters, to declare that states have the right to command Congress to admit their Representatives?

To reconstruct the nation, to admit new states, to guarantee republican governments to old states—these are all legislative acts. The President claims the right to make use of them. Congress denies it and claims the right to belong to the legislative branch. This I take to be the great issue between the President and Congress.

The President wants to pardon the conquered rebels from all the expense and damages of the war. He insists that those of our people who had property burned or destroyed by rebel raiders shall not be paid back, but shall bear their own loss. He desires that the states created by him shall be accepted as valid states. At the same time he declares that the old rebel states are still in existence, and always have been, and have equal rights with the loyal states. He is determined to force a solid rebel delegation into Congress from the South.

In opposition to these things, a part of Congress seems to desire that the conquered side shall, according to the law of nations, pay at least a part of the expenses and damages of the war. The loyal people who were plundered and ruined by rebel raiders should be paid back in full. A majority of Congress desires that treason shall be made hateful, not by bloody executions, but by other adequate punishments.

There are several good reasons for the passage of this bill [the reconstruction program]. In the first place, it is just. I am now speaking of granting the vote to Negroes in the rebel states. Have not loyal blacks as good a right to choose rulers and make laws as rebel whites? In the second place, it is a necessity in order to protect the white people who are loyal to the Union in the seceded states. The white Union people are in a great minority in each of those states. With them the blacks would act together as a group. In most states they would form a majority, control the states and protect themselves.

Another good reason is, it would insure the power of the Republican Party. I believe that the safety of this great nation depends upon the continuing power of the Republican Party.

For these, among other reasons, I am for

Ticket to the "Impeachment of the President" trial

rebel state.
…ied. If it is
…it is a pun-
…t.
…said, "This
…ro equality
…honest Re-
…nore: Every
…ace or color,
…mortal soul,
…sty, and fair
…e rights for
…emns or ac-
…cquit white
…a verdict in
…a verdict in
…same set of
…such ought

…slaves were

…n of the Fed-
…construct the

…give to sup-
…construction
…ese reasons?

…why or why not?

---

137   Johnson's Acquittal

President Johnson's policies, his inflexible stand on reconstruction, and his vetoes of Congressional reconstruction bills made him a hated enemy to the Radical Republicans. They became determined to remove him from office, since they were convinced that Johnson would not enforce their reconstruction program. The House of Representatives impeached Johnson in February of 1868, and he was brought to trial in the Senate in March. In this selection, the Senate trial was described by William H. Crook, a White House guard.

READING FOCUS

1. Why was the trial so important?
2. How was the trial conducted by the prosecution? by the defense?
3. What was the outcome of the trial?

On the 23rd of March, when the actual trial began, the President said good-by to three of his lawyers, who had come to the White House for a final discussion. I was near them as they stood together on the porch. Mr. Johnson's manner was calm and unconcerned. He shook hands with each of them in turn, and said:

"Gentleman, my case is in your hands. I feel sure that you will protect my interests." Then he returned to his office. I went off with the lawyers. At the President's request, I went with them to the Capitol every day.

When, from my seat in the gallery, I looked down on the Senate chamber, I almost had a moment of terror. It was not because of the gathering. It was rather in the thought that one could feel in the mind of every man and woman there: For the first time in the history of the United States, a President was on trial for more than his life—his place in the judgment of his country's people and history.

The trial lasted three weeks. The President, of course, never appeared. In that respect the proceedings lacked the spectacular interest they might have had. Every day the President had a meeting with his lawyers. Otherwise, he attended to the routine work of his position. He was absolutely calm through it all.

As the trial went on, the belief grew with me—I think it did with everyone—that the weight of evidence and constitutional principle lay with the defense. There were several clever lawyers on the prosecution side, but most of the proceedings showed personal feeling and prejudice rather than proof. Every appeal that

---

Adapted from Through Five Administrations: Reminiscences of Colonel William H. Crook, *edited by Margarita Spalding Gerry.*

could be made to the passions of the time was used. By comparison, the calm, ordered, masterly reasoning of the defense must have made everyone believe in the truth of its cause.

But the legal struggle, after all, was hardly the contest that counted. The debate was for the benefit of the country at large. While the legal experts argued, the enemies of the President were working in other ways. The Senate was thoroughly checked for votes. Personal appeals and influence were constant. Every personal motive, good or bad, was used. Long before the final vote, it was known how most of the men would probably vote. Toward the end, only one doubtful vote remained—that of Senator Ross of Kansas. It looked as if Kansas—which had been the fighting ground of rebel guerrillas and northern abolitionists—was to have the determining vote.

Kansas was, from the beginning, abolitionist and Radical. It would have been supposed that Senator Ross would vote with the Radicals.

Then the Radical forces in the Senate and the House put pressure on the Senator from Kansas. Party discipline was used, and then ridicule. Either from uncertainty, or policy, or a desire to keep his associates in uncertainty, Ross refused to say how he would vote. In all probability he was honestly trying to decide for himself.

The last days before the vote was to be taken were breathless ones. The country was paralyzed. Business in Washington was almost at a standstill.

On May 16th the vote was taken. Everyone who by any possible means could get a ticket of admission to the Senate chamber arrived early that morning at the Capital. The floor and galleries were crowded.

The journal was read. The House of Representatives was told that the Senate, "sitting for the trial of the President upon the articles of impeachment," was ready to receive the other house in the Senate chamber. The question of voting first upon the eleventh article was decided.

The clerk read the legal statement of those crimes of which, in the opinion of the House of Representatives, the President was guility. At the end, the Chief Justice directed that the roll be called. The clerk called out:

"Mr. Anthony." Mr. Anthony rose.

"Mr. Anthony"—the Chief Justice looked at the Senator—"how say you? Is the respondent, Andrew Johnson, President of the United States, guilty or not guilty of a high misdeanor as charged in this article?"

"Guilty," answered Mr. Anthony.

A sigh spread round the room. Yet Mr. Anthony's vote was not in doubt. A two-thirds vote of 36 to 18 was necessary to convict. Thirty-four of the Senators were pledged to vote against the President. Although there was some doubt, it was thought that Mr. Fowler of Tennessee would most likely vote for the President. Senator Ross was the only one whose vote was really in doubt. No one knew his position. When Fowler's name was reached, everyone leaned forward to hear his answer.

"Not guilty," said Senator Fowler.

The tension grew. There were many names called before that of Senator Ross was reached. When the clerk called it, and Ross stood up, the crowd held its breath.

"Not guilty," replied the Senator from Kansas.

The Radical Senators, who had been with Ross only a short time before, turned to him in a rage. All over the hall people began to stir. The rest of the roll call was listened to with lessened interest, although there was still the chance of a surprise. When it was over, and the result—35 to 19—was announced, there was a wild outburst, chiefly groans of anger and disappointment, for the friends of the President were in the minority.

I did not wait to hear the verdict read—it would be no surprise to me, as I had been keeping a list of the votes on a slip of paper— I ran downstairs at top speed. In the corridor of the Senate I came across a curious group. In it was Thaddeus Stevens, now completely disabled, whose two attendants were carrying him high on their shoulders. All around him, the crowd, unable to get into the courtroom, was calling out: "What was the verdict?" Thad Stevens' face was filled with rage and disappointment. He waved his arms in the air and shouted in answer:

"The country is going to the devil!"

I ran all the way from the Capitol to the White House. I was young and strong in those days, and I made good time. When I burst into the library , where the President sat with three other men, they were quietly talking. There were no signs of excitement.

"Mr. President," I shouted, too excited and

filled with delight to stop myself, "you are acquitted!"

Everyone stood up. I made my way to the President and took hold of his hand. The other men surrounded him, and began to shake his hand. The President responded to their congratulations calmly enough for a moment, and then I saw that tears were rolling down his face.

READING REVIEW

1. Why did the Radical Republicans dislike President Johnson?
2. What kind of presssure did the Radical Republicans put on Senator Ross to vote their way?
3. Why did Ross refuse to say how he was going to vote?
4. Why do you think Ross voted for acquittal?

138 Launching the "New South"

In 1886, a group of New York business leaders asked Henry W. Grady, the editor of the Atlanta newspaper the *Constitution,* to come to New York to speak before their group. In his speech, Grady spoke of the "New South" and described the many changes that had taken place during the years following the war. Afterward, the speech became well known, and the term "New South" became famous. It convinced many people that the South had changed.

And indeed, by the 1880's, the South had changed in many ways. Many large plantations were broken up, and many small farms were started. Improved farming methods were used, and crops other than cotton were grown. Industry began to develop, and with industry came the growth of cities.

READING FOCUS

1. What were the conditions of the South when the Confederate soldier returned?
2. According to Grady, what were the characteristics of the "New South" in regard to the blacks? in regard to black-white relations?

Dear to me is the home of my childhood and the traditions of my people. I would not, if I

Adapted from Daniel J. Boorstin, ed., An American Primer, *Vol. I.*

could, dim the glory they won in peace and war. Nor would I by word or deed take anything from the splendor and grace of their civilization—never equaled before and perhaps never to be equaled again. There is a New South, not the result of protest against the old, but the result of new conditions, new adjustments, new ideas, and new hopes.

Dr. Talmadge [the previous speaker] has drawn for you the picture of your returning armies. He has told you how they came back to you, marching with proud and victorious step, reading their glory in a nation's eyes! Will you be patient while I tell you of another army that returned home at the close of the war. This army marched home in defeat and not in victory, in sorrow and not in splendor, but in glory that equaled yours, and to hearts just as loving. Let met picture for you the footsore Confederate soldier, as he turned his face southward from Appomattox in April 1865. Think of him as ragged, half-starved, heavy-hearted, weak from want and wounds. Having fought to the point of exhaustion, he surrenders his gun, shakes the hands of his comrades in silence, and—lifting his tear-stained, pale face for the last time to look at the graves that dot the old Virginia hills—pulls on his gray cap and begins the slow and painful journey home. What does he find when he reaches the home he left so prosperous and beautiful? He finds his house in ruins, his farm destroyed, his slaves free, his animals killed, his barns empty, his trade destroyed, his money worthless. His social system has been swept away. His people are without law or legal status. Crushed by defeat, his very traditions are gone. He has no money, credit, job, material, or training. Besides all this, he is faced with the problems of establishing a status for the freed slaves.

What does he do—this hero in gray with a heart of gold? Does he sit down in gloom and despair? Not for a day. The soldier stepped from the trenches into the fields. Horses that had charged Union guns now marched before the plow. Fields that ran red with human blood in April were green with the harvest in June. There was little bitterness in all this. Cheerfulness and frankness were widespread.

But in all this what have we accomplished? What is the sum of our work? We have found out that, in general, the free Negro counts more than he did as a slave. We have built schools and made them free for white and black. We have built towns and cities and put business above politics. We have challenged your spinners in Massachusetts and your iron-makers in Pennsylvania. We have established thrift in city and country. We have fallen in love with work. We have restored comfort to homes from which culture and elegance never left. Above all, we know that we have achieved in these times of peace a fuller independence for the South than that which our fathers sought to win in the political arena by their words or on the battlefield by their swords.

It is a great privilege to have had a part, however small, in this work. Never was a nobler duty given to human hands than the uplifting and rebuilding of the fallen and bleeding South, misguided perhaps, but beautiful in its suffering, and honest, brave, and generous always.

But what of the Negroes? Have we solved the problem they present, or progressed in honor and fairness toward the solution? Let the record speak. No section shows a more prosperous working population than the Negroes of the South. They share our schools, have the fullest protection of our laws and the friendship of our people. Self-interest, as well as honor, demands that they should have this. Our future, our very existence, depends upon our working out this problem in full and exact justice. We understand that when Lincoln signed the Emancipation Proclamation, your victory was assured. For he then committed you to the cause of human liberty, which weapons cannot overcome. Those of our leaders who pledged to make slavery the cornerstone of the Confederacy doomed us to defeat, committing us to a cause that reason could not defend or the sword maintain.

The relations of the southern people with the Negroes are close and friendly. We remember how for four years they guarded our defenseless women and children, whose husbands and fathers were fighting against their freedom. Whenever they struck a blow for their own liberty they fought in open battle. When at last they raised their hands so that the chains might be struck off, those hands were innocent of any wrong against their helpless charges, and worthy to be taken in loving grasp by every person who honors loyalty and devotion. Ruffians have mistreated them, rascals have misled them. But the South, with the North, protests against injustice to this simple and sincere people.

Law can bring the Negro only liberty and the vote. The rest must be left to conscience and common sense. It should be left to those among whom the Negroes' lot is cast, with whom they are closely connected. Their prosperity depends upon having intelligent sympathy and confidence. Faith has been kept with the Negroes in spite of statements to the opposite by those who claim to speak for us or by our enemies. Faith will be kept with them in the future.

But have we kept faith with you? In the fullest sense, yes. We fought hard enough to know that we were beaten. The chains that had held the South in narrow limitations fell forever when the chains of the Negro slave were broken. Under the old system the Negroes were slaves to the South and the South was a slave to the system.

The old South based everything on slavery and agriculture. The new South presents a perfect democracy. Its social system is less splendid on the surface but stronger at the center. It has a hundred farms for every plantation, fifty homes for every mansion, and industry that meets the complex needs of this complex age.

The new South loves its new work. Its soul is stirred with the breath of a new life. It is thrilled by the realization of growing power and prosperity. It understands that its emancipation came because in the wisdom of God its honest purpose was crossed and its brave armies were beaten.

The **Atlanta Constitution** — *an influential Southern newspaper*

This is said in no spirit of apology. The South has nothing for which to apologize. It believes that the late struggle between the states was war and not rebellion, and that its convictions were as honest as yours.

READING REVIEW

1. Describe the conditions of the South at the end of the war.
2. How did Grady explain the position of blacks in the "New South"?
3. (a) Grady spoke of "faith being kept." With whom had the "New South" kept faith? (b) Do you agree with Grady's views? Why or why not?

Booker T. Washington

139 Emphasizing Hard Work

By the 1880's black southerners were segregated from white southerners in schools and public facilities. Also, black Americans were now denied their political and civil rights. Some black leaders spoke out against this discrimination and urged blacks to struggle for their rights; other leaders disagreed.

In a speech in 1895 at the Atlanta Exposition, Booker T. Washington suggested that black Americans should follow a moderate course. His speech became known as the Atlanta Compromise because it seemed to indicate that black Americans should accept segregation. In actuality, Washington believed that if blacks gained job skills and training they would become necessary to the South's economy, and thus would become respected and regain their civil rights.

READING FOCUS

1. What advice did Washington give to blacks? to whites?
2. What did Washington say about demonstrating for social equality?

One third of the population of the South is of the Negro race. No project seeking the material, civil, or moral welfare of this section can ignore this part of our population and reach the highest success. I bring to you the feeling of the masses of my race when I say that in no way have the value and manhood of the American Negro been more fittingly and generously recognized than by the managers of this magnificent Exposition. It is a recognition that will do more to strengthen the friendship of the two races than any happening since the dawn of our freedom.

Not only this, but the opportunity given here will awaken among us a new era of industrial progress. We were ignorant and inexperienced, and it is not strange that in the first years of our new life we began at the top instead of at the bottom. A seat in Congress or the state legislature was more sought than land or industrial skill. The political convention or election speeches had more attraction than starting a dairy farm or truck garden.

A ship lost at sea for many days suddenly sighted a friendly ship. From the mast of the unfortunate ship was seen a signal, "Water, water; we die of thirst!" The answer from the friendly ship came back at once, "Cast down your bucket where you are." A second time the signal, "Water, water; send us water!" ran up from the distressed ship. It was again answered, "Cast down your bucket where you are." And a third and fourth signal for water was answered, "Cast down your bucket where you are." The captain of the distressed ship, at last listening to the advice, cast down his bucket, and it came up full of fresh, sparkling water from the Amazon River. To those of my race who depend on bettering their condition in a foreign land or who don't realize the importance of developing friendly relations with southern whites, who are their next-door neighbors, I would say: "Cast down your bucket where you are." Cast it down in making friends of the people of all races by whom we are surrounded.

Cast it down in agriculture, in industry, in commerce, in domestic service, and in the professions. In this connection it is well remembered that whatever other signs the South may have, when it comes to business it is in the

---

Adapted from Booker T. Washington, Up from Slavery: An Autobiography.

South that the Negro is given a chance in the commercial world. Our greatest danger is that in the great leap from slavery to freedom we may overlook the fact that most of us are to live by the productions of our hands and fail to keep in mind that we shall prosper as we learn to dignify and glorify common labor and put brains and skill into our occupations. We shall prosper if we learn to draw the line between the superficial and the substantial, the ornamental things of life and the useful things. No race can prosper till it learns that there is as much dignity in tilling a field as in writing a poem. It is at the bottom of life we must begin, not at the top. Nor should we permit our problems to overshadow our opportunities.

To those of the white race who look to the immigrants of foreign lands for the prosperity of the South, I would repeat what I say to my own race, "Cast down your bucket where you are." Cast it down among the eight million Negroes whose habits you know, whose loyalty and love you have tested. Cast down your bucket among these people who have, without strikes and labor wars, tilled your fields, cleared your forests, built your railroads and cities, and brought forth treasures from the earth. Casting down your bucket among my people, helping and encouraging them, you will find they will buy your extra land, grow crops in the waste places in your fields, and run your factories. While doing this, you can be sure in the future, as in the past, that you and your families will be surrounded by the most patient, faithful, law-abiding, and unresentful people that the world has seen. We have proved our loyalty to you in the past, nursing your children, watching by the sickbeds of your mothers and fathers, and often following them with tear-filled eyes to their graves. So in the future, we shall stand by you with a loyalty that no foreigner can equal. We are ready to lay down our lives, if need be, in defense of yours. We shall join our industrial, commercial, civil, and religious life with yours in the way that shall make the interests of both races one. In all things that are purely social we can be as separate as the fingers, yet one as the hand in all things essential to mutual progress.

The wisest among my race understand that demonstrating on questions of social equality is foolish. Progress in enjoying all the privileges that will come to us must be the result of severe and constant struggle rather than of forcing. No race that has anything to contribute to the markets of the world is banished for long. It is important and right that all privileges of the law be ours. But it is much more important that we be prepared for making use of these privileges. The opportunity to earn a dollar in a factory just now is worth much more than the opportunity to spend a dollar in an opera house.

READING REVIEW

1. (a) What did Washington mean when he advised blacks to "cast down your bucket"? (b) Why did he advise whites to do the same?
2. In Washington's viewpoint, how could blacks make the greatest progress?
3. (a) How did Washington try to encourage his black listeners? (b) How did he try to reassure his white listeners?

140   A Protest Against the Atlanta Compromise

Booker T. Washington was the best known leader of black Americans in the late 1800's and early 1900's. Other black leaders, however, disagreed with Washington's emphasis upon job training and vocational education for black Americans. Among those who disagreed was W. E. B. Du Bois, a Harvard-educated black scholar. He felt that talented blacks should go to colleges and universities. He also came to believe that only strong protests against inequality and discrimination could bring about change. In 1903 Du Bois singled out Washington and his Atlanta speech for criticism, and he made his own suggestions for the advancement of black people.

READING FOCUS

1. What did W. E. B. Du Bois single out as the main element of Booker T. Washington's "Atlanta Compromise"?
2. How did radicals and conservatives view this compromise?
3. How did Du Bois view Washington's compromise?

Easily the most striking thing in the history of the American Negro since 1876 is the im-

Adapted from W. E. B. Du Bois, The Souls of Black Folk, *6th ed.*

portance of Mr. Booker T. Washington. It began at the time when war memories and ideals were rapidly passing. A time of astonishing commercial development was beginning. A sense of doubt and hesitation overtook the freedmen's sons—it was then that his leadership began. Mr. Washington appeared with a simple, definite program, at the moment when the nation was a little ashamed of having given so much sentiment to Negroes, and was concentrating its energies on dollars. His program involved industrial education, pleasing the South, and acceptance and silence as to civil and political rights.

It startled the nation to hear a Negro proposing such a program after many years of bitter complaint. It startled and won the applause of the South. It interested and won the admiration of the North. And after a confused murmur of protest, it silenced if it did not convert the Negroes themselves.

To gain the sympathy and cooperation of the white South was Mr. Washington's first task. At the time Tuskegee [the school started by Booker T. Washington] was founded, this seemed, for a black person, almost impossible. And yet ten years later it was done in the words spoken at Atlanta: "In all things purely social we can be as separate as the five fingers, and yet one as the hand in all things essential to mutual progress." This "Atlanta Compromise" is the most notable thing in Mr. Washington's career. The South judged it in different ways. The radicals saw it as a complete surrender of the demand for civil and political equality. The conservatives regarded it as a working basis for joint understanding. So both approved it. Today its author is certainly the most distinguished southerner since Jefferson Davis, and the one with the largest personal following.

Mr. Washington represents in Negro thought the old attitude of adjustment and giving in, but adjustment at such a time as to make his program unique. This is an age of unusual economic development, and Mr. Washington's program naturally has an economic basis. It becomes a gospel of work and money and almost completely forgets the higher aims of life. Moreover, this is an age when the more advanced races are coming in closer contact with the less developed races, and race feeling is therefore stronger. Mr. Washington's program, for all practical purposes, accepts the

W. E. B. Du Bois

inferiority of the Negro race. Again, a reaction against wartime feelings has led to race prejudice against Negroes, and Mr. Washington withdraws many of the high demands of Negroes as American citizens. In other periods of prejudice all the Negro's tendency to self-assertion has been called forth. At this period a policy of giving in is advised. In the history of nearly all other races and peoples, the policy suggested for such crises has been that self-respect is worth more than lands and houses. And that a people who on their own surrender such respect, or stop struggling for it, are not worth civilizing.

In answer to this, it has been claimed that the Negro can survive only through giving in. Mr. Washington asks that black people give up, at least for the present, three things—

First, political power,

Second, demand for civil rights,

Third, higher education of Negro youth. They should concentrate all their energies on industrial education, on gaining wealth, and on pleasing the South. This policy has been courageously and insistently encouraged for over fifteen years, and has been triumphant for perhaps ten years. What has been the result? In these years there have occurred:

1. The disfranchisement [taking away the vote] of the Negro.

2. The legal creation of a separate status of civil inferiority for the Negro.

3. The steady withdrawal of aid from institutions for the higher training of the Negro.

These movements are not, to be sure, direct results of Mr. Washington's teachings. But his propaganda has, without a shadow of doubt, helped speed them up. The question then arises: Is it possible, and probable, that nine

203

million people can make effective progress along economic lines if their political rights are taken away, and they are made an inferior group and allowed only the smallest chance of developing their outstanding people? If history and reason give any distinct answer to these questions, it is *No*.

In failing to declare plainly and without doubt the demands of their people, even at the cost of opposing an honored leader, the thinking classes of American Negroes would be avoiding a heavy responsibility. They would be avoiding a responsibility to themselves, to the struggling masses, to the darker races of people whose future depends so largely on this American experiment, and especially to this nation. It is wrong to aid a national crime simply because it is unpopular not to do so. The growing spirit of kindliness and understanding between the North and South after the differences of a generation ago ought to make everyone happy, especially those whose mistreatment caused the war. But if that understanding is to be marked by the industrial slavery and civic death of those same black people, then those black people should oppose such a course by all civilized methods—even though it involves disagreement with Mr. Booker T. Washington.

READING REVIEW

1. Why did Du Bois object to Washington's advice to blacks to "give in"?
2. What consequences did Du Bois think would result from Washington's advice?

CHAPTER
20 Severe Trials for Democracy
(1865–1897)

---

141 Keeping Public Servants on Their Toes

The years after the Civil War were years of graft and corruption at all levels of American government. As a result, many writers and journalists tried to make Americans aware of the dishonesty in their governments, in the hopes of ridding the nation of dishonest officials. These writers often used humor to show the faults of government officials. Thomas Nast's famous cartoons of Boss Tweed and the Tammany Ring were examples; so were the books of David R. Locke, a favorite humorous writer of this period. Lincoln said of one of Locke's earlier books, "For the genius to write such things, I would gladly give up my office." In a later book, Locke wrote down the saying of "a wise Persian man living in New Jersey." The following excerpt is from this book.

READING FOCUS

1. Was Abou Ben Adhem a real or an imaginary person?
2. What question did the legislator ask Ben Adhem?
3. What advice did Ben Adhem give to the legislator in response to his question?

Abou Ben Adhem was not in a good mood. He had put a large sum of money in a bank in New York. The bank had failed because of the strong desire of its cashier to view the sights of the Old World. As the cashier took with him over half a million dollars, the bank had to close. The directors were very sorry, but Abou's money was gone. He was not in a good mood.

At this point a man from Albany approached, bowing deeply three times. "Mighty Abou," said he, "I am a member of the New York legislature."

"Away, man! I want no favors. I have no need of votes. I have no money to spend. I have no desire to be severe, but, sir, whenever I see a member of a legislature, I think that Nature is wasteful. There is a great deal of lightning wasted. Away!"

"Mighty Abou, you mistake me. I am, it is true, a member of that legislature. But I am an honest man. If you will take the trouble to remember, you will remember that there are two or three such as I."

Abou looked at him with a long stare of painful astonishment, ending with a long whistle of disbelief.

Adapted from David R. Locke, The Morals of Abou Ben Adhem.

"I am an honest member of the legislature of the state of New York," continued this man, "and I desire advice and enlightenment so that I may be of some use to my fellow citizens. Tell me, what can we do in the way of lawmaking that will get rid of all crime in the country? Is there no cure for it?"

Abou looked at him closely.

"I will trust you," he said. "I will believe that you are an honest man, despite the position you hold. And I will give you the information you desire.

"Sweet sir," continued Abou, "three hundred years ago there was a kingdom to the north of what is now Persia in which these things of which you complain did not happen very often. In that blessed land there was almost no crime—no accidents, no mistakes, no nothing. Life there was like a calmly flowing river. The people lived happily and died regretfully. I helped to organize that community. I was the author of the system that brought it about. I—"

"Three hundred years ago?" asked the stranger.

"Three hundred years ago,—did I not say so?"

"I beg your pardon; but, give me, oh give me, the system by which this most desirable state of things was achieved."

"I will. We had in Koamud, which was the name of the kingdom, no prisons, no reform schools, no civil-service examinations, no boards of any kind—nothing of the sort. If the government wanted a postmaster, for example, it did not go foolishly talking about qualifications or anything of that sort. It simply posted on the door of the post office a printed statement of what would be required of the postmaster. Then the first man who said he wanted the position was appointed."

"Were no bonds required of him?"

"No. He took the position, and undertook his duties."

"But suppose he stole money?"

"He was immediately caught and hanged."

"Hung for stealing?"

"Certainly, and for a mistake as well. If there was an error in his accounts by so much as a pound of twine, he was hung immediately."

"But suppose such irregularities were the result of bad business habits?"

"Then he was hung for being a bad busi-nessman. What we wanted was honesty and ability. We treated everyone else the same way. Suppose a railroad train ran off the track. Suppose we discovered that a rail was out of order, or that the roadbed was not properly kept up. We hung the president, directors, and superintendent. If the accident was caused by any slip on the part of the conductor, he was hung.

"Once we hung all the officials of the Teheran and Ispahan Railroad, and from that time there were no accidents on that line. Their successors were very careful. The superintendent slept very little. The company hung up a small gallows in the cab of every locomotive to remind the engineer of his fate in the event of trouble.

"Then we carried the same rule into everything. The people put their money into the First National Bank of Picalilly. Very good. The bank failed one morning. The authorities took the president, cashier, and board of directors out and hung them all, because they had been guilty of letting the bank fail.

" 'I didn't steal a dollar of this money,' said the president.

" 'Makes no difference,' said the judge, 'where it was lost. You haven't got it.'

" 'But you won't hang a man who has not stolen, will you?' said the president.

" 'I will hang you for being an idiot. I shall hang you for risking money that was not yours to risk.'

"And up he went.

"In fact, they hung them more mercilessly

The power of Boss Tweed

for being fools than for any other crime. If a man said, 'I stole it,' they felt a sort of pity for him. If he said, 'I lost it,' they felt none at all, and hung him up in a minute."

"What was the effect of this vigorous hanging?"

"Splendid. Bank officials made no mistakes in their figures and none in their business. The officers of the government were rather careful about their accounts, for they were hung for mistakes as well as for stealing. The presidents and directors of railroads took care of their tracks, and a more watchful and careful set of men than the conductors, engineers, and switchmen you never saw.

"The effect was good in another way. This system reduced the population greatly, but it made a magnificent race of men and women. You see, the vicious and the careless were all hung, leaving only the industrious and clear-headed to live. Consequently, it was a splendid people. I am, perhaps, a fair example. There were no lunatics, idiots, triflers, or dishonest people left to spread mischief and danger."

"Is that government still in existence?"

"Alas! no. There sprang up a class of people who began to feel sorry for criminals. They got into the habit of visiting them just before they were hanged, and sending them flowers, and begging the governor to pardon them. They created sympathy for them, and finally some escaped. Then it was all over. The moment there was any doubt as to the certainty of punishment, people became almost as bad as they are here. Then I left the country.

"Go to Albany, my friend, and make but one penalty—hanging—for all crimes or mistakes, in public or private. True, it would cause a heavy expense on each county for a gallows. It would probably make New York one of the smallest states, as far as population, in the country. In a week you probably couldn't get a quorum in the New York legislature. But the final effect would be splendid. The next generation would be fifty percent better than this, and the improvement would go on and on to the end of time. I have spoken. Leave me, for I am tired."

The stranger went away sorrowful.

"The idea is good," said he to himself, "but I dare not urge it. If hanging were the rule for crimes or mistakes, how long would my children have a father?"

READING REVIEW

1. **(a)** What remedy did Locke suggest to cure political graft and corruption? **(b)** What point do you think Locke was really making?
2. How applicable is this selection to American politics today? Explain your answer.

142 An English Reformer at a Political Convention

In the 1870's George Holyoake, a social reformer from England, visited the United States. He was interested in visiting and studying the cooperatives formed by American farmers.

Holyoake was also very curious about American politics, and he admired "the republican equality and the republican freedom of America." He wrote: "The minds of the people, like keyless watches, wind themselves up and always keep going." Because of this interest in politics, he attended a Republican Party convention in 1879 at Saratoga, New york. This was his description of that meeting.

READING FOCUS

1. What complaints did Holyoake have about Republican convention procedures?
2. What had Holyoake heard about the conduct at Democratic conventions?
3. What remarks did he make about equality?

The object of the convention, called by the Republican leaders, was to choose a candidate for governor of New York and other state officers. My wish was to see not only what was done, but also how it was done and where it was done.

The convention was held in the Town Hall. It was not bad inside. There was more space than we reserve for speakers in England. But in the center of the stage was a small, ugly desk. The president hit its hollow top with a pitiful wooden hammer, setting off weak echoes within it. Nobody had thought that the grandest use of a public hall is a public meeting.

Adapted from Among the Americans *by George Jacob Holyoake.*

Republican nominating convention, Saratoga, New York, 1876

I had heard a good deal in England about American political organization. It did not appear in the physical arrangements of the meetings though it showed in the proceedings. The names of the candidates for the chief office were read over. The popular name was that of "Alonzo B. Cornell," the son of the founder of the Cornell University. Mr. Cornell received the nomination for governor of New York State. That day I heard his name said a thousand times. Each delegate was called upon to announce aloud the name of the candidate he was voting for. There was only one Cornell, yet nobody answered as we would do in England—"Cornell." Each said, "Alonzo B. Cornell," or "Jehosophat P. Squattles," or whatever was the name of the other candidate.

An hour was spent over that new governor's name, yet if "Alonzo B." had been eliminated the business would have been finished in a third of the time. (Mr. Cornell himself was a modest, pleasant gentleman, with a businesslike method of speech.)

The character of every people, like that of every individual, is made up of contradictions. The Americans, as a rule, catch on to things quickly. Their conversation is clear, bright, and precise. Their understanding is direct. Yet these quick-witted listeners will tolerate speakers who are long-winded, indirect, and speak endlessly. They will sit and listen to them for long periods of time.

At the New York convention a "program of principles" called a "platform"—was read. No one could make sure what was meant, and a professor of memory could not remember half of what was written. All I remember was that the platform ended with some statements about things in general. Yet there were parts of it which showed intelligence—if only the writer had known when to stop.

I regretted not being able to go to Syracuse to see the Democratic convention. I was told the Democratic conventions were marked by great activity and disorder. The *New York Tribune* said that there would be many "large heads" at Syracuse. I wanted to see "large heads," as I had no idea what a political "large head" was. I was told that the Democrats are more boisterous in their meetings than Republicans. The Democrats seem to be like our Tories at home—indignant at any dissent at their meetings, but persistent in interrupting the meetings of others.

The Saratoga convention was characterized by great order and attention to whoever desired to speak. If anyone had a question, the answer was "The Chair takes a contrary view; the Chair decides against you." The chairman was an institution, or a court of authority. This I found to be a rule in America. The immediate attention given to anyone who wanted to speak was greater than in England. In England the theory of a public meeting is that anyone present may speak, but we never let them do it. If the chairman is willing the audience is not. At several public meetings that I attended in America the right of a person on the floor seemed equal to that of those on the platform. Citizens seemed to recognize the equality of each other. In England there is no public sense of equality. There is always somebody who is supposed to be better than anybody.

READING REVIEW

1. What evidence did Holyoake provide to back up his assertion that "the character of every people . . . is made up of contradictions"?
2. In Holyoake's view, how did public meetings in America differ from those in England?

143 Growing Up Republican

In the years after the Civil War, loyalties to political parties became especially strong. The party that a person supported was often the result of tradition and family upbringing. For example, a person who was brought up in a family that supported the Democratic Party would almost never vote for a Republican candidate. And a person raised in a family that supported the Republican Party would not vote for a Democratic candidate.

In these years, there were few Americans who were "independents." Most people supported either the Republican or Democratic Party, or perhaps a smaller third party. And there was very little "ticket splitting," or voting for some of the candidates of both major parties, as there is today. In this selection, Sarah Smith Pratt told what it was like to grow up in a Republican home in Indiana.

READING FOCUS

1. How did the writer characterize her father?
2. What event deepened the author's respect for the Republican Party?

The Republican Party Platform, 1868

Although we lived in a Democratic stronghold, our family happened to be Republican. I realize now that the great shaping force of Republicanism in my youth was my father. He was a perfect example of the "waving-the-bloody-shirt" type—intolerant of everything he did not approve of. He was of that great group of good men who are upset by wrongdoing, but are never willing to hold office. He had great influence throughout the county we lived in because of his education, moral courage, and ability to speak well. He was listened to with respect by a large group of farmers. Nick Smith's [the author's father] opinions were quoted all over the county. He was the delight of the virtuous and the terror of the wrong-doer. He loved to criticize liquor-sellers and Democrats.

He had come from Baltimore and settled in Indiana about 1836, bringing a stock of farm tools, roofing materials, vats, tanks, and hydraulic rams, all greatly needed in that new country.

I was surrounded with Republicanism from the very minute I was born. Editorials read aloud from the newspapers of that day, explained loudly to my mother and filled with criticisms of the "jackasses" and "natural-born fools" who headed the other party—these stamped themselves forever on the well-behaved children who sat and listened.

And yet my father's hunting friend and the companion of his long Sunday walks was Walter Beach, a strong, outspoken Democrat.

My first knowledge of the word "Democrat" came because of Dash, my dog. One night he was found near the kitchen door of the editor of the *Times*. The *Times* was the Democratic newspaper—the *Journal,* the Republican. This editor, because he was short and somewhat pompous, was called "Whistlebreeches."

"Whistlebreeches shot Dash last night. He's lying dead in their yard," my brother came and told us as we were at breakfast.

"Get the wheelbarrow, Lutie, and get him and bury him in the yard—that—that Democrat," my father said as he gulped down his coffee.

Adapted from Sarah S. Pratt, The Old Crop in Indiana.

When I saw this editor go past our house on his way home at noon, despite my grief I was interested in the name I had heard my father call him: Democrat!

"What *is* a Democrat, Papa? I think it is such a pretty word."

"Democrat," exploded by father, "a Democrat is a man—" he said, too mad to know just what to say. "A man who—who—"

"Now, Nicholas, be careful before the children. Don't say anything mean. You know our minister is a Democrat and so is our doctor."

My father, feeling a little ashamed by this time, said nothing, but he had left a bad impression of the party started by Jefferson. I still think "Democrat" is a great word. It is perhaps the most important of human meanings and—in its perfection—the most unreachable.

An event which deepened my respect for the party in power [the Republican Party] occurred right after the war when a Methodist conference was to be held in Delphi. Brother Sims and Brother McIntosh asked our parents to entertain some of the visiting clergy. We were Episcopalians, but joyfully opened our doors to the visitors. Three of their most interesting men stayed at our house. Two of them were celebrities. The third was a professor from New Orleans. These good-humored men were soon well liked by the whole household. One of them was Elder John L. Smith, a noted man in his day. Another was John Hogarth Lozier—called Chaplain Lozier because of his work in the army, and admired by hundreds of soldiers. The third was a brown-eyed professor.

All the men were strong Republicans. My father, pleased beyond measure to find his own feelings backed up by three such men, showed them the greatest hospitality. There never were more cheerful or wittier talks than those that lasted these three days at our home.

Chaplain Lozier was a writer of verses, many of which had been set to music. Some of them described political events. He had a popular song set to the tune of "Wait for the Wagon." He would recite this line by line and we would all sing it:

In Uncle Sam's dominions in 1861
The fight between the Union and secession was begun

The South declared they'd have the rights
That Uncle Sam denied
Or in his Union wagon they would not longer ride.

Wait for the wagon, the old Union wagon,
Wait for the wagon and we'll all take a ride.

This visit served to deepen my belief that the Republican Party was even greater than I had thought it was. Of course, there were good Democrats—old Dr. Blanchard and Lawyer Sims and plenty of good people who were our neighbors. But to think that from the outside world had appeared Elder Smith wearing a long black coat and silk hat, carrying a gold-headed cane, and having elegant manners. He was a Republican. And there was Chaplain Lozier, who could make poems and have them printed and sung. He too was a Republican. And there was Professor Henry Jackson, who could write in French and teach in a young woman's school. And he too was a Republican. Altogether, the greatness of the Republican party was increased in my mind by this visit of these loyal Methodists.

READING REVIEW

1. What did the author mean by a "waving-the-bloody-shirt" type?
2. What did the author think about the term "Democrat"?
3. Why did the author's encounter with the visiting Methodists deepen her respect for the Republican Party?
4. Do you think party loyalty is as strong today as it was in the Smith family?

144 Why Great Men Are Not Chosen Presidents

Many historians believe that there have been very few great American Presidents—perhaps seven or eight at most. In his book *The American Commonwealth*, James Bryce, an English scholar, tried to explain why Americans have elected so many ordinary Presidents. This work has been called "the greatest book written about this country." Bryce visited the United States three times before he wrote his study. And he later served as the British ambassador to Washington. Although this selection may seem critical, Bryce actually had a favorable opinion of the American system of government.

READING FOCUS

1. According to Bryce, why are great men not chosen as Presidents?
2. Acording to Bryce, what were the characteristics necessary to be a good President?

Europeans often ask, and Americans do not always explain, how it happens that this great office—to which any man can rise by his own merits—is not more frequently filled by great men. In America, which is a country where political life is unusually keen, it might be expected that the Presidency would always be won by a man of brilliant gifts. But since the heroes of the Revolution died out with Jefferson and Adams and Madison some sixty years ago, no person except General Grant has reached the office whose name would have been remembered if he has not been President. No President except Abraham Lincoln has shown rare or striking qualities in the office. Who now knows or cares to know anything about the personality of James K. Polk or Franklin Pierce? The only thing remarkable about them is that, being so ordinary, they should have climbed so high.

Several reasons may be suggested for this fact, which Americans are themselves the first to admit.

One is that the number of people with great abilities drawn into politics is smaller in America than in most European countries. In France and Italy, half-revolutionary conditions have made public life exciting and easy to enter. In Germany, a well-organized civil service develops the art of government with unusual success. In England, many persons of wealth and leisure seek to enter politics, while vital problems touch the interests of all classes and make people eager observers of the political scene. In America, many able men rush into a field which is comparatively small in Europe, the business of developing the material resources of the country.

Adapted from The American Commonwealth *by James Bryce.*

Another reason is that the methods and habits of Congress, and indeed of political life generally, seem to give fewer opportunities for personal distinction. There are fewer ways in which a man may win the admiration of his countrymen by outstanding thought, speech, or ability in administration.

A third reason is that important men make more enemies than less well-known men do. They are therefore less admirable candidates. It is true that the important man has also made more friends, that his name is more widely known, and that he may be greeted with louder cheers. Other things being equal, the famous man is preferable. But other things never are equal. The famous man has probably attacked some leaders in his own party, has replaced others, has expressed his dislike of some group, has perhaps committed errors which can be turned into offenses. No man can be in public life for long and take part in great affairs without causing criticism. People constantly search out all the corners of a Presidential candidate's past life. Therefore, when the choice lies between a brilliant man and a safe man, the safe man is preferred. Party feeling, strong enough to support a man without positive merits, is not always strong enough to gain forgiveness for a man with positive faults.

A European finds that this needs to be explained. For in the free countries of Europe, brilliance or some striking achievement is what makes a leader triumphant. Why should it be different in America? Because in America party loyalty and party organization have been so perfect that anyone chosen as a candidate by the party will get the full party vote if his character is good and his "record," as they call it, is unstained. The safe candidate may not receive quite so many votes from the moderate people of the other side as the brilliant one would, but he will not lose nearly so many from his own party. Even those who admit he is only ordinary will vote for him when the moment for voting comes. Besides, most American voters do not object to ordinary candidates. They have a lower idea of the qualities necessary for a statesman than those who direct public opinion in Europe. They like their candidates to be sensible, vigorous, and, above all, what they call "magnetic." They do not value, because they see no need for, originality or profundity, a cultured background or great knowledge. Candidates are selected by small groups of persons who run the political party but are usually commonplace men.

It must also be remembered that the merits of a President are one thing and those of a candidate another thing. An important American is reported to have said to friends who wished him to be a candidate, "Gentlemen, let there be no mistake. I would make a good President but a very bad candidate." Now to a party it is more important that its choice should be a good candidate than that he should turn out to be a good President. It will be a misfortune to the party, as well as to the country, if the candidate elected proves to be a bad President. But it is a greater misfortune to the party if it is beaten, for it will then lose four years of national patronage.

After all—and this is a point much less obvious to Europeans than to Americans—a President need not be brilliant. Englishmen, imagining him as something like their Prime Minister, assume that he ought to be a great speaker, having also the power to propose a great policy or write a good law. They forget that the President does not sit in Congress. His main duties are to promptly and effectively carry out the laws and maintain public order, and choose the executive officials of the country. Firmness, common sense, and, most of all, honesty are the qualities which the country needs in its chief executive.

So far we have been considering personal merits. But in the selection of a candidate many other considerations have to be regarded. The chief of these is the amount of support which can be secured from different states or regions of the Union. State feeling and sectional feeling are powerful factors in a Presidential election. The Northwest, including the states from Ohio to Dakota, is now the most populous region of the Union, and therefore counts for most in an election. Thus a northwestern man makes the best candidate. A large state casts a greater vote in the election, and every state is of course more likely to be carried by one of its own citizens than by a stranger. Therefore a man from a large state is preferable as a candidate. The problem is further complicated by the fact that some states are already safe for one or the other party, while others are doubtful. Most of the Northwestern and New England states are certain to go Republican. All of the Southern states are (at present) certain to go Demo-

cratic. It is more important to please a doubtful state than one you have already. Thus a candidate from a doubtful state, such as New York or Indiana, is to be preferred.

READING REVIEW

1. What were the three main reasons Bryce gave for the lack of "great men" who have held the office of President?
2. (a) List three qualities which Bryce said a good President should possess. (b) Do you think that American Presidents still have the characteristics Bryce described?
3. According to Bryce, what was the difference between a "good candidate" and a "good President"?

CHAPTER
21 Settling the Last Frontier
(1865–1900)

145 A Sioux Chief's Speech on Whites

Many Indian leaders became well known during the long period of conflict between the Indians and white settlers on the Great Plains. One of the most famous of these leaders was Sitting Bull, a chief of the Sioux. Although he became well known as a great warrior and war chief, he also was respected as a religious leader or "medicine man."

In the first selection, Sitting Bull spoke of the relationship between Indians and white people. In the second reading, he talked about Custer's "last stand." Most people at the time thought that Sitting Bull was one of the chiefs who led the Sioux at Little Big Horn. Sitting Bull, however, did not take part in that battle.

READING FOCUS

1. What wrongs did Sitting Bull accuse the whites of committing against the Indians?
2. How did Sitting Bull justify the Indians' actions?

What treaty that the whites have kept has the red man broken? Not one. What treaty that the whites ever made with us red men have they kept? Not one. When I was a boy the Sioux owned the world. The sun rose and set in their lands. They sent ten thousand horsemen to battle. Where are the warriors today? Who killed them? Where are our lands? Who owns them?

What white man can say I ever stole his lands or a penny of his money? Yet they say I am a thief. What white woman taken as captive was ever insulted by me? Yet they say I am a bad Indian. What white man has ever seen me drunk? Who has ever come to me hungry and gone without food? Who has ever seen me beat my wives or abuse my children? What law have I broken? Is it wrong for me to love my own? Is it wicked in me because my skin is red? Because I am a Sioux? Because I was born where my fathers lived? Because I would die for my people and my country?

*   *   *   *

The palefaces had things that we needed in order to hunt. We needed ammunition. Our interests were in peace. I never sold that much

land. [Here Sitting Bull picked up with his thumb and forefinger a little dirt, lifted it, and let it fall and blow away.] I never made or sold a treaty with the United States. I came in to claim my rights and the rights of my people. I was driven by force from my land. I never made war on the United States government. I never stayed in the white man's country. I never committed any robberies in the white man's country. I never made the white man's heart bleed. The white man came onto my land and followed me. The white man made me fight for my hunting grounds. The white man made me kill him or he would kill my friends, my women, and my children.

We have all fought hard. We did not know Custer. There were not as many Indians as the white man says. There were not more than two thousand. I did not want to kill any more men. I did not like that kind of work. I only defended my camp. When we had killed enough, that was all that was necessary.

READING REVIEW

1. According to Sitting Bull, what were the two most important wrongs the white man committed against the Indians?
2. What crimes was he accused of by whites?
3. How did he defend his own actions?

Adapted from Cry of the Thunderbird: The American Indian's Own Story, *edited and with an Introduction and Commentary by Charles Hamilton. New edition copyright © 1972 by the University of Oklahoma Press. Reprinted by permission of the University of Oklahoma Press.*

Sitting Bull, Chief of the Sioux

146   A Proposed Solution to the "Indian Problem"

The "Indian problem" had begun when the Europeans first settled in America. Conflict between the two groups centered largely on the concept of land ownership and differing ideas and ways of life. For the Indians, the problem was how to remain on the land where they had lived and hunted for centuries. For the white settlers, the problem was how to get the land and what to do with the Indians.

During the late 1860's, a long period of conflict began. As white settlers began to move beyond the Mississippi River, they came into conflict with the Indians who lived and hunted on the Great Plains. Thoughtful Americans wondered how the Indians could be removed from these lands without violating ideals of justice and humanity. General Nelson A. Miles, an Army officer with expe-

READING FOCUS

1. Did Miles think that the Indians are equals of the whites?
2. What were the major features of the plan that Miles proposed?

Strange as it may seem, after nearly 400 years of conflict between the European and American races on this continent—a conflict in which war and peace have alternated almost as frequently as the seasons—we still must ask the question, What is to be done with the Indians?

The real issue is this: Shall we continue the uncertain and expensive policy that has hurt our name as a nation and a Christian people? Or shall we work out some practical and just system by which we can govern one quarter of a million of our people? Can we secure and maintain their loyalty, raising them from the darkness of barbarism to the light of civilization? Can we put an end to these endless and expensive Indian wars?

In considering the subject, it might be well to examine first the causes of the present situation. If we dismiss from our minds the prejudice we have against the Indian, we can understand more clearly the feelings of both races.

The Indians have the same motives that govern all other people. The lack of confidence and the bitter hatred now existing between the two races have been caused by the warfare that has lasted for centuries. And stories of bad faith, cruelty, and wrong have been handed down by tradition from father to son among both groups of people. It is unfair to suppose that one side has always acted rightly, and that the other is responsible for every wrong that has been committed. We might speak of the treachery of the red man, the violence of his crimes, the cruelties of his tortures, and the hideousness of many of his savage customs. We might try to estimate the number of his victims. Yet at the same time the other side of the picture might appear equally black with injustice.

Adapted for Nelson A. Miles, "The Indian Problem," North American Review, March 1879.

One hundred years before the Pilgrims landed at Plymouth, the Spanish government issued a decree which allowed American Indians to be made slaves. Later they were sold into slavery in Massachusetts, Rhode Island, Pennsylvania, Virginia, the Carolinas, Georgia, and Louisiana, and hunted with dogs in Connecticut and Florida. They were, for all practical purposes, disfranchised by our original Constitution. By either war or treaty, nearly every tract of land which was desirable to them and valuable to the white settler was taken away. Step by step, they were driven back from the Atlantic to the Far West. Now there is scarcely a spot of ground upon which the Indians have any certainty of remaining permanently.

It may be well to remember that for the most part Europeans were treated kindly by the Indians when they first landed on American shores. When Europeans came to make permanent settlements, they were supplied with food, which enabled them to last through the long and cheerless winters. For a time during the early settlement of this country, peace and good will existed, only to be followed by warfare.

The available land that can be given to the Indians is being rapidly decreased. They cannot be moved farther west. Some political party or administration must take the responsibility of protecting their rights of person and property.

The advantage of placing the Indians under some government strong enough to control them and just enough to command their respect is clear. It is therefore suggested that a system which has proved to be practical should receive at least a fair trial. The government employs army officers who, by long and faithful service, have established reputations for integrity, character, and ability. These officers have commanded armies, reconstructed states, and controlled millions of dollars' worth of public property. During years of experience on the frontier, they have opened the way for civilization and Christianity. The services of these officials could prevent war and uplift the Indian race.

Allowing the civilized and semicivilized Indians to remain under the same supervision as at present, the President of the United States should have power to place the nomadic, or wandering, tribes under the control of the War

Department. Officers of known character and experience, who would be interested in improving the Indians' condition, should be placed in charge of the different tribes. One difficulty in the past has been that they have been managed by officials too far away, who knew nothing of the people they were dealing with. The Indians, as far as possible, should be kept in sections of the country to which they have already adapted.

Every effort should be made to locate the Indians by families. The ties of relationship among them are much stronger than is generally supposed. By this means, the Indians will become independent of their tribal relations, and will not be found crowded together in large and unsightly camps, as are common now.

The officers in charge should have enough force to preserve order, patrol the reservations, recover stolen property, arrest the lawless, and keep the Indians upon their reservations and within the limits of their treaties. The officer in charge should have the power to control or prevent the sale of ammunition, as well as to stop the sale of liquor among the Indians. Many thousands of Indian ponies, useful only for war or hunting, should be sold and the money used to buy domestic animals.

The warriors may be made to care for their flocks and herds. The work of the Indians that is now wasted can be used for peaceful and useful pursuits. Yet the great work of reform must be mainly with the young people of the different tribes.

Several years ago I suggested that our unoccupied military posts be used as schools. As many Indian youths as can be gathered voluntarily should be placed at these schools, especially the sons of chiefs who will in a few years govern the different tribes. They should be taught the English language, habits of work, the benefits of civilization, and the power of the white race. After a few years, they would return to their people with some education, with more intelligence, and with their ideas of life entirely changed for the better. They would, in turn, be able to educate their own people. Their influence for good could not be estimated. The expense of educating them would be less than at present, and thousands would benefit. The Indians, as they become civilized and educated, as they acquire property and pay taxes toward the support of the government, should have the same rights of citizenship as all other men enjoy.

A race of savages cannot by any human means be civilized and Christianized within a few years of time. Neither will 250,000 people with their descendants be destroyed in the next 50 years. The white man and the Indian should be taught to live side by side, each respecting the rights of the other. Both should live under wholesome laws, enforced with authority and justice. Such a government would be most helpful to the Indians. It would also be satisfactory to three other groups: (a) people who have invested their capital and are developing the wealth that for ages has lain in the Western mountains; (b) people who have left the overcrowded centers of the East, and whose homes are now on the plains and valleys of the Far West; and (c) the soldiers who are called upon every year to withstand greater exposure and suffering than is required by the troops of any other nation on the globe.

An attempt to merge two cultures

READING REVIEW

1. What evidence was there to support the conclusion that Miles felt the Indians were the equals of the whites?
2. (a) How did Miles summarize the relationship between Indians and whites? (b) Cite evidence to prove or disprove the fairness of his summary.
3. List the three major features of the plan that Miles proposed.

147 Resisting "Americanization"

After many years of conflict on the Great Plains, the Indians were defeated and forced to live on reservations. Even so, many Americans still felt that the "Indian problem" had not been solved. They believed that the Indians had to be "Americanized."

As a result, the United States government tried to "Americanize" the Indians in various ways. Education was considered especially important in this effort. Consequently, many Indian children were sent to boarding schools many miles away from their homes. By 1898 some day schools had been built near the reservations. In this selection, Helen Sekaquaptewa, a Hopi Indian born in Arizona, told of her experiences at a day school in the early 1900's.

READING FOCUS

1. What Hopi traditions were practiced in regard to schooling?
2. Who were the "Progressives"? the "Traditionals"?

By the time I was old enough to go to school, a day school had been built near the village. Children up to the third grade could go to school by day and live at home. This was a favor to the Hopi parents. Still, many of them tried to prevent their children from attending the day school.

When we were five or six years old, we and our parents became involved with the school officials—assisted by the Navajo police officers—in a serious and rather desperate game of hide-and-seek. Every day the school principal sent out a truant officer, and many times he himself went with the officer. They went to Hopi homes to take the children to school.

When September came, there was no peace for us. Early in the morning, from our houses, we could see the principal and the officer start out from the school, walking up the trail to "get" the children. Parents tried every day in different ways to hide us from them, for once you were caught, you had lost the game. You were discovered and listed and you had to go to school and not hide any more.

Adapted from Me and Mine: The Life Story of Helen Sekaquaptewa, *as told to Louise Udall.*

Sometimes, after a very early breakfast, somebody's grandmother would take a lunch and go with a group of eight to twelve little girls and hide them in the cornfields away from the village. On another day another grandmother would go in the other direction over the hills among the cedar trees. We would play in a narrow valley, have our lunch, and come back home in the afternoon. Men would be out with little boys playing this game of hide-and-seek.

A place where one or two small children could be hidden away quickly was the rabbit blanket. A rabbit blanket is made by cutting dressed rabbit skins in two-inch strips and weaving them together with wool thread. When not in use, in warm weather, this blanket is hung by the four corners from a hook in the rafter beam. But once it was discovered, this hiding place was out. The school officer would feel the rabbit blanket first thing when he came into the room.

Most houses have a corn storage cupboard in a wall. A cloth covered the front, making a good place to keep the corn dry and clean. One day the officers were only two doors away from our home when my mother became aware of their presence. She grabbed her young son Henry and put him in the cupboard just in time to win the game—that day.

Our houses were two and three stories high. When a lower room became old and unsafe, it was used as a dumping place for ashes, peach stones, melon and squash seeds, and bits of discarded corn. Anything that could be eaten was preserved in the ashes, and the room was gradually filled. In time of famine these bits of food could be dug out and eaten. In my home such a room was about three-fourths filled. One September morning my brother and I were hidden there. We lay on our stomachs in the dark, facing a small opening. We saw the feet of the principal and police officers as they walked by, and heard their big voices as they looked about wondering where the children were. They didn't find us that day.

I don't remember for sure just how I came to be "caught." Maybe both my mother and I got a little tired of getting up early every morning and running off to hide all day. She probably thought to herself, "Oh, let them get her. I am tired of this. It is wearing me down." The hide-and-seek game continued through September. But when October came, the colder weather was on the school's side.

So one morning I was "caught." Even then, it was the rule among mothers not to let the child go voluntarily. As the police officer reached out to take me by the arm, my mother put her arm around me. Tradition required that it appear that I was forced into school.

I was taken from the village to the schoolhouse, along with several other children. First, each of us was given a bath by one of the Indian women who worked at the school. Then we were dressed in cotton underwear, cotton dresses, and long black stockings and heavy shoes supplied by the government. Each week we had a bath and a complete change of clothing. We were allowed to wear the clothes home each day, but my mother took off the clothes of the hated white man as soon as I got home, until it was time to go to school the next day.

Names were given to each child by the school. Mine was "Helen." Each child had a name card pinned on for as many days as it took the teacher to learn and remember the name she had given us. Our teacher was Miss Stanley. She began by teaching us the names of objects around the room. We read a little from big charts on the wall later on, but I don't remember ever using any books.

A feud developed over the years as the people were divided into sides for and against those who came from the outside. These two factions were known as the "Friendlies" (to the government) and the "Hostiles" (to the government). Later these groups were known as the "Progressives" and the "Traditionals."

Those who put their children into school voluntarily were given an ax, a hoe, a shovel, or a rake. (Stoves and wagons they had to work for.) "Hostile" parents scornfully rejected these tools even though they would have served them better than the tools they made of wood or stone. These gifts were looked upon only as a bait that would end in no good to the Indians. "Hostile" parents warned their children, when they were leaving for school, "Don't take the pencil in your hand. If you do, it means you agree to what they want you to do. Don't do it."

The attitude of the parents carried over to their children, as was shown on the school grounds. The children of the "Friendlies" made fun of us, calling us "Hostiles," and they would not let us join with them in their play. Going back up the trail after school was often a skirmish. The "Friendly" children often ran ahead up the trail and gathered rocks and threw them down at us when we came to the bottom of the steep rocky ledge. Sometimes we would try another way up to avoid being hit by rocks.

I liked school. It was pleasant and warm inside. I liked to wear the clothes they gave us at school; but when I learned that the kids were "hostile" to us, I didn't want to go to school. Everyone, even the principal and the teachers and employees, were more or less against us.

The Mennonites had a church in Old Oraibi, but our parents would not let us go even to their Sunday School. We wanted to go, and sometimes we went to Sunday School by a back path. They would give us a little ticket each time we came, and on Christmas they gave a big prize to the one who had the most tickets. We did not understand much of what they said, but it was nice to be there. I received a few tickets but gave them away. I did not dare accept a present.

READING REVIEW

1. Why did the Hopi parents try to prevent their children from attending day school?
2. Cite evidence from the reading that showed how the Hopi parents resisted "Americanization."
3. What effect do you think the hide-and-seek game had on the "Americanization" of the Hopi children?

148 A Letter Home from a Norwegian Farmer

Pioneering farmers followed the miners and cattle raisers toward the "last frontier" as they settled and farmed the land on the Great Plains. Although plains farming was difficult, backbreaking work, thousands of families moved to the plains. Many were immigrants, especially from the countries of Scandinavia.

Gro Svendsen and her husband, Ole, left Norway in 1862 to settle in Iowa. Her life on the Great Plains was far from easy, and she died in 1878 after giving birth to her tenth child. But in this letter written in 1873 to her parents, she tried to tell of the good things in her life on the plains.

READING FOCUS

1. What did Gro Svendsen's letter tell you about the lives of pioneer farmers on the Great Plains?
2. What were the hardships and rewards of life on the Great Plains?

December 6, 1873

My beloved Parents:

I am writing you, my dear parents, in the hope that you are still living and in good health. I should have written you a long time ago. At least I should have thanked you, Father, for your last letter dated the first of March.

I must tell you first of all that we are all well. My health is not always of the best, but so far God has spared me from any long illness, and so I feel that I cannot complain. Rather I should thank God for His infinite goodness.

The children have always been in good health. They are growing strong and healthy. Little Bergit was small and frail for a long time, but this summer she has grown plump and fat. Steffen is very healthy looking, chubby and fat; his cheeks are pink and white like a rose. I wish his grandmother could see him. I am sending you pictures of Svend and Niels and Carl and Albert so now you can see what they look like. Ole was not at home when the pictures were taken, so he was left out. Niels is just as tall as Svend, but not so fat. Many who do not know them think they are twins.

My four oldest children have been attending Norwegian school this fall, but I must sadly confess that they are far behind in their studies. If they were at home in Norway, I know full well that they would have learned a great deal more. We so seldom have Norwegian school, and it is slow work to try to teach the boys at home.

When I wrote you last spring I told you that we were very much concerned about Ole's father, who had been kicked by a horse and was very ill. However, when Ole arrived there, his father had gotten well again.

Store-Ole was here a couple of weeks ago. He stayed a little over a week. His family is well. They like their new home very much and are more than happy over having moved there, in spite of the fact that their harvest will be poor this year because of the locusts that attacked their grain.

Here, also, the crops will be poor. This spring the locusts destroyed our fields, too. In many places there will be no harvest. We did get a little, enough for our own living, but none to sell. So it will be difficult to pay our many debts. We were forced to buy our land for $480. Since we had no money, we had to borrow. Then we had other bad luck. One of our horses had a sore leg this summer. At the time when there was most work to be done we couldn't use him, so we had to buy another horse that cost $150. The sick horse is well again, and now we have three draft horses and one colt. We still owe for the new horse. His name is Jack.

Times have been hard this fall—much harder than any since we came to this land. The future is uncertain. No one knows what tomorrow will bring.

We have been thinking of selling this land and moving up to Rock County [Minnesota] in order to be near Store-Ole. If the opportunity should come, we might move. If we did sell, we should have to get enough for our land so that we would have a few hundred dollars to start all over again in our new home. In the meantime we shall await whatever life may bring.

From what I have said you will see that we are not rich. But though we have no material wealth, we have nevertheless possessions of greater worth—a quiet and peaceful home with many children, all normal, gifted with health and intelligence, spirited, cheerful, and happy. We have other possessions, too. I could not name them all, but all these blessings seem to be of far greater value than money. I am more than satisfied and thankful to God for all His goodness toward His unworthy children.

This letter, which should reach you before Christmas, will be short. But I wanted you to know that we are all well.

A joyous Christmas and a blessed New Year to you, my dear parents, sisters, and brothers.

With love from
Ole and Gro

READING REVIEW

1. Describe the life of a pioneer farmer on the Great Plains during the 1870's.
2. How do you think you would have liked living on the plains in the 1870's?
3. **(a)** What things in life made Gro Svendsen happy? **(b)** What were her chief worries?

Adapted from Frontier Mother: The Letters of Gro Svendsen, *translated and edited by Pauline Farseth and Theodore C. Blegen.*

The Rise of Industrialism

CHAPTER
22 The Growth of American Industry
(1860's–1890's)

149 Life Behind a Toy Counter

What was it like to work as a salesperson in a department store? In the late 1800's, a Canadian sociologist wanted to find out more about the lives and working conditions of sales clerks in large stores. As a result, she decided to take a job as a saleswoman. For several days during the Christmas season she worked in a New York department store. For one week's work she earned $2.00 in wages and $3.25 in commissions. However, 30 cents was taken from her salary for the three times she arrived late for work. (Every time sales clerks were late, 10 cents was deducted from their weekly salary.)

READING FOCUS
1. What was it like to work as a salesperson in a large department store?
2. How did the store treat their employees?

The hurried breakfast, the rush out into the street crowded with people carrying their lunches, and the streetcar packed with pale-faced sleepy-eyed men and women made the

Adapted from Annie M. MacLean, "Two Weeks in Department Stores," American Journal of Sociology, Vol. IV, May 1899, in Neil Harris, ed., The Land of Contrasts.

working world seem very real. Hurrying workers filled the center of the city. No one was stirring. I reached the store promptly at eight, the time of opening. The manager said he would give me two dollars a week plus 5 percent commission on sales. I was then given a number, and by "424" I was known during my stay there.

I was sent to the toy department, where I found sixty-seven other people who were to work with me. The place was filled with all kinds of toys, from a monkey beating a drum to a doll that said "mamma." Our business was first to dust and arrange the stock. Then we stood ready for customers. Our business was to see that no one escaped without buying something. The confusion can be readily imagined. As soon as the elevators emptied themselves on the floor, there was one mad rush of clerks with a quickly spoken, "What would you like, madam?" or, "Something in toys, sir?" The majority of answers were rude. Some people were amused, and a few were alarmed at the urgency of the clerks. One young boy, on being asked by half a dozen clerks at once, threw up his hands in horror, and said, "For God's sake, let me get out of here!" He ran down the stairs, not even waiting for the elevator. The cause of such wasteful activity on the part of so many employees was the 5 percent commission, which could add two or three dollars a week to one's salary.

One of the difficult things at first was trying to remember the prices, for they were frequently changed during the day, and the penalty for selling something at a lower price was that one was immediately fired. Selling above price, however, met with no disapproval. Every morning there were special sales. Sometimes articles that had sold for one dollar would be reduced to ninety-eight cents. Again, twenty-five-cent articles would be offered at a bargain for forty cents "today only." The manager's brief instructions each morning kept us aware of the bargains. The charms of the bargain counter disappear when one has been behind the scenes and learned something of its history. The humor of it seemed to impress the clerks, for often they would exchange knowing winks when some customer was being victimized.

Oh, that first morning! The hours seemed days. "Can I possibly stand up all day?" was my main thought, for I soon learned that anyone who was found sitting down would be harshly criticized. Later in the week, one of the girls who was exhausted sat for a moment on a little table that was for sale—there was not a seat of any kind in the rooms, and the only way one could get a moment's rest was to sit on the children's furniture that was for sale on one part of the floor. The manager came along and found the poor girl resting. He called out in rough tones: "Get up out of that, you lazy hussy; I don't pay you to sit around all day!" By night the men as well as the women were limping wearily across the floor. Many sales were made under positive physical agony.

How well I remember my first sale there! The people were slow to arrive that morning; in fact, they were slow every morning. We hardly ever had any business until eleven o'clock, and the greatest rush came about six. From twelve thirty to two was a busy time also. My first two customers were types that were common. First a woman with a business-like expression came to me and demanded that I show her building blocks. They were shown, but proved unsatisfactory. The dolls' buggies, boys' sleds, laundry sets, and skates were examined in slow succession. I was asked about the prices and merits of everything. Then she looked at me and said: "I do not intend to buy today; I just wished to examine your goods." Still I had not a sale on my book and she had taken half an hour of my time.

The next customer was a man who wanted a boy's sled at a cost of one dollar and a half. Now, we had none at that price, but we had them at one dollar and thirty-five cents, and one dollar and sixty-five cents, either of which I thought would suit him. But I was mistaken. He gave me a look of utter scorn, and then criticized me for advertising things we did not have in stock. I meekly suggested that I was

A nineteenth century store

not responsible for the ads that appeared in the morning papers. But he was not at all pleased by this. I felt rather upset, but the comforting voice of a cashier said "Don't mind him, he's only a cheapskate."

Thus encouraged I started out on another sale. This time it was a small boy who wanted to buy, and the bright-faced little fellow did me good. He had eighty cents, he said, and he wanted presents for the baby, and Tom, and Freda, and Cousin Jack, and several others. I suggested one thing after another, till finally he had spent his money.

The boy was happy, and so was I. I looked admiringly at the eighty cents set down on my sales sheet. It meant that I had earned four cents in commission. After that the sales came frequently. They were all small, of course, and amounted to only $14.98 for the day. But this was more than I sold any day after that. It has often been noticed that new clerks do better at first than they do later. With me, freshness and interest in the novelty helped to take away my tiredness, and thus invited sales.

My first day ended at six thirty. I went wearily to the coat-room and more wearily to my boarding place. When I arrived there, I could only throw myself upon my small white cot in the dormitory and wonder if it would be all right for a working girl to cry. Presently I was dreaming that blows from an iron hammer were falling upon me. In a little while it was morning, and another day had begun.

READING REVIEW

1. What challenges were presented to the sociologist in her job as a salesperson?
2. (a) How would you characterize the store's attitude toward its employees? (b) toward the public?
3. What changes have probably taken place in the operations of department stores?

150 A Trust Is Born

In the 1870's and 1880's, the rapid growth of American industry was greatly spurred by the trend toward business consolidation, or combination. Companies used this form of business organization to gain control of a large part of the market in a certain industry—for example, oil. When the corporations in an industry joined together into one large trust, they gained many advantages. The large size of the trust enabled it to take advantage of the money-saving techniques of mass production and cheap marketing. The trust also could limit production, fix prices, and secure lower railroad rates. Trusts were so effective that they were able to drive out most competition and establish a monopoly or near-monopoly. The American tobacco trust, formed by James Buchanan Duke, was a good example of how such a giant business combination worked.

READING FOCUS

1. What methods did Duke use to make his business successful?
2. After the trust was formed, what techniques were used to dominate the market?

It became evident that any business that might develop a wide market for its product would end up in a financier's hands. Entrepreneurs themselves might become financial tycoons, as was the case with James B. Duke. For if money could be made by supplying consumers with goods and services, much more could be made by controlling stocks and bonds. Duke and his tobacco empire are striking not so much for size or importance of product, but because they show the methods that were used in bringing together various branches of a new industry and the way in which a new technology—mechanized cigarette-making—could promote consolidation.

Tobacco had been an important plantation crop before the Civil War. After the war, John Ruffin Green sold tobacco under the trade name of "Bull Durham." (It was named after Durham, North Carolina, the town in which it was processed.) The picture of the bull became a well-known trademark that Blackwell and

Carr, who took over after Green, fought to protect. They learned quickly that testimonials and advertising were essential in convincing the consumer to smoke their tobacco or buy their chewing plug. By 1884 the Blackwell and Carr factory had become the largest in the world. Soon many brands of tobacco were being produced in Durham. Those who processed the tobacco were determined to make the city the tobacco capital of the South.

However, the North Carolina town of Winston, near the sleepy village of Salem, soon began to rival Durham as a center for manufacturing tobacco products. One of the aggressive young salesmen in that area was R. J. Reynolds, who headed a family firm there. Lewis Ginter and John Allen had a thriving business in Richmond. Liggett and Myers was a growing firm in St. Louis. There was a great demand for tobacco all over the nation. Chewing and smoking brands were produced in ever-increasing quantities to satisfy it. Concerned with the protection of their trademarks, which clearly distinguished one brand from another, manufacturers passed out premiums and coupons. They gave rebates to dealers, and paid bribes to put their brands in certain stores.

It was not long, however, before Buck Duke would take over all the others. Born in 1856, James Buchanan Duke was named after the Democratic President elected in that year. Duke's father had been a small farmer before the Civil War. Afterward he returned to the land to grow and sell tobacco. His little tobacco curing factory grew steadily. By 1872 it was producing 125,000 pounds [577,000 kilograms] of tobacco a year. In 1874 the elder Duke and his two sons, James and Ben, moved the factory to Durham. The elder Duke took both boys in as partners to form W. Duke & Sons. To obtain more capital, several partners from outside the firm were brought in.

Cigarettes had been popular in Europe for many years, though in America they could not yet compete with plug and smoking tobacco. But Duke felt that he was hitting his head against the stone wall of Bull Durham. Blackwell and Carr had moved far ahead of their rivals in selling plug and smoking tobacco. Duke knew that he could not compete with them, and so he decided on cigarettes. But these had to be rolled by hand. Although Duke had some of the best workers in the business,

From The Potentates by Ben B. Seligman.

their output was still too small for an expanding market. Then the Dukes obtained a cigarette machine, which could turn out 120,000 cigarettes a day. Realizing that cigarettes were popular in cities, Duke set up a branch in New York. He successfully competed with the better-known firm of Ginter and Allen. He gave premiums and matched Ginter ad for ad. A favorite selling method was to place a picture of a pretty girl in each package of cigarettes. He sent clever salespeople on the road to find business. People were hired to go from store to store asking only for Duke's product. Incoming immigrants were given free cigarettes at ports of entry. By 1890 W. Duke and Company had become first in the tobacco industry.

Meanwhile, Duke was watching developments in oil, steel, whisky, and sugar. All were being combined through trusts. Why not tobacco? But first one had to get into the good graces of financiers. Duke began to negotiate for small thirty-day or sixty-day loans with New York bankers, always paying them back promptly. Soon Duke had established a line of credit with the powers that counted.

Finally, Duke was able to convince four other large companies that they all ought to get together. In 1890 the American Tobacco Company was started, a combination of Duke, Ginter, and three others. This was 90 percent of the cigarette industry. Capitalization was set at $25,800,000, though the combined tangible assets were just slightly over $3,000,000. Eight years later another company was formed to handle plug tobacco. Dealers were forced to take other items through tie-in sales. If they wanted cigarettes, they had to also take the trust's tobacco plug.

American Tobacco continued to expand by all means available, some fair, many unfair. Almost absolute control over cigarette-making machinery was worked out. Dealers refusing to take the trust's products were blacklisted and subjected to ruinous price wars. Through all these operations, Buck Duke ruled with an iron hand. He fired his star salesman, Edward Small, when he refused to move his family to Cincinnati. By 1905 American Tobacco and its related Consolidated Tobacco Company, both headed by Duke, controlled three fourths of the smoking-tobacco, and over nine tenths of the snuff, in addition to having almost complete control of the cigarette market.

Four other firms were taken over in the

An advertisement for James Duke's "Trust"

early 1890's. Liggett and Myers was then taken over. In 1899 it was R. J. Reynolds' turn to join the trust.

Stocks and bonds were controlled to yield a profit to insiders. Operations were always carried out in secret. Duke used several techniques to dominate the market. One was price-cutting. Another was to form phony "independent" companies to make it look as though there were competition. Duke also offered premiums and rebates, created rival brands to confuse consumers, and took over more competitors. Once a market had been won, retail prices were kept at the same level, while the jobber was squeezed with higher wholesale prices.

Nor was the foreign market neglected. Duke tried to get his products into Japan, but the government there decided to set up its own monopoly. He bought a factory in England, but the Imperial Tobacco Company was formed so British manufacturers could protect English people against American cigarettes. After several years of conflict, the usual cartel agreement [a cartel is an international trust] was reached. The United States and Cuban markets were given to Duke, Great Britain was given to Imperial, and the rest of the world was shared through the British-American Tobacco Company. The entire industry, with the exception of cigar-making, was now controlled by the "Tobacco Trust."

READING REVIEW
1. Why was the cigarette-making machine so crucial to James Duke's business success?
2. List the steps and decisions that led to the establishment of the "trust".

151 On Business Success

In the years after 1870, as industry grew rapidly in the United States, several business leaders came to control entire industries and became enormously wealthy. One of them, Andrew Carnegie, was a Scottish immigrant who settled in the city of Pittsburgh. He studied and worked hard and eventually gained control of many steel mills. Carnegie's steel mills were Pittsburgh's most important industry.

In the following selection from Carnegie's autobiography, he described what he thought were the main reasons for business success. He also told about an early business deal he took part in.

READING FOCUS

1. What were the main reasons for business success?
2. What were the characteristics of a good business leader?

The Keystone Bridge Works have always been a source of satisfaction for me. Almost every company that had tried to build iron bridges

---

Adapted from Autobiography *by Andrew Carnegie.*

A cartoonist's version of Andrew Carnegie

ANDREW
CARNEGIE

ALBERT
LEVERING

LIFE

in America had failed. Many of the bridges that they built had fallen. Some of the worst railway disasters in America were caused that way. But nothing has ever happened to a Keystone bridge, and some of them have stood where the winds were strong.

Luck had nothing to do with it. We used only the best material and enough of it, making our own iron and later our own steel. We inspected everything very carefully, and would build a safe structure or none at all. When asked to build a bridge which we knew was not strong enough or was poorly designed, we refused. We guaranteed any piece of work that had the stamp of the Keystone Bridge Works (and there are few states in the Union where they are not to be found).

This policy is the true secret of success. It will be uphill work for a few years until your work is proven, but after that it is smooth sailing. Instead of objecting to inspectors, all manufacturing companies should welcome them. A high standard of excellence is easily maintained, and people are educated in the effort to reach excellence. I have never known a company that became successful unless it did good, honest work. Even in these days of the fiercest competition, when price is very important, at the root of great business success there still lies the much more important factor of quality. The effect of attention to quality upon everyone in the firm, from the president of the concern down to the lowest worker, cannot be overestimated.

The president of an important manufacturing work once boasted to me that their workers had chased away the first inspector who had appeared, and that they had never been troubled with another since. This was said as if it ought to be a matter of sincere congratulation, but I thought to myself: "This concern will never stand the strain of competition; it is sure to fail when hard times come." The result proved the correctness of my belief. The surest basis for a manufacturing concern is quality. After that, and a long way after, comes cost.

I have a great deal of personal attention for some years to the affairs of the Keystone Bridge Works, and when important contracts were involved often went myself to meet the parties. On one such occasion in 1868, I visited Dubuque, Iowa, with our engineer, Walter Katte. We were competing for the contract to build the most important railway bridge that had been built up to that time, a bridge across the Mississippi.

That visit proved how success often depends upon small and unimportant things. We found we were not the lowest bidder. Our chief rival was a bridge-building company in Chicago to which the board of directors who were in charge of building the bridge had decided to give the contract. I stayed and talked with some of the directors. They knew nothing about the advantages and disadvantages of cast-iron and wrought-iron. We had always made the upper part of the bridge with wrought-iron, while our rivals' was made of cast-iron. I explained the result of a steamer striking against the one and against the other. In the case of wrought-iron, it would probably only bend. In the case of cast-iron, it would certainly break and down would come the bridge. One of the directors was able to back up my argument. The other night, he said, he had run his buggy in the dark into a cast-iron lamppost, which had broken to pieces.

"Ah, gentlemen," I said, "there is the point. A little more money and you could have had the indestructible wrought-iron and your bridge would stand against any steamboat. We never have built and we never will build a cheap bridge. Ours don't fall."

There was a pause. Then the president of the bridge company asked if I would excuse them for a few moments. I left the room. Soon they called me back and offered the contract, provided we built the bridge at the lower price, which was only a few thousand dollars less. I agreed to this. That cast-iron lamppost so conveniently smashed gave us one of our most profitable contracts. What is more, it obtained for us the reputation of having won the Dubuque bridge against all competitors.

The moral of that story lies on the surface. If you want a contract, be on the spot when it is given. A smashed lamppost or something equally unthought of may secure the prize if the bidder is there. And if possible stay until you can take the written contract home in your pocket.

READING REVIEW

1. According to Carnegie, what policy was "the true secret of success"?
2. Do you agree with Carnegie's assessment of what makes a business successful? Why or why not?

152 Rockefeller's Achievements

Probably no single business leader of the late 1800's received more praise or criticism than John D. Rockefeller. Born into a poor family, in time he came to control the nation's oil industry. In 1870 he organized the Standard Oil Company and located his oil refineries in Cleveland.

Like many other industrial leaders of the time, Rockefeller used unfair business methods. For example, at times he would cut prices until competing companies went bankrupt or sold out to him.

By 1882 the Standard Oil Trust had been formed. Just five years later, in 1887, Rockefeller controlled 95 percent of the oil refineries in the nation.

In this selection, historian Allan Nevins gave his analysis of Rockefeller and his methods. He described Rockefeller's innovations, or the changes he introduced to American industry.

READING FOCUS

1. What did Nevins say was the dominant ideal of pioneering America?
2. What did Nevins mean when he called Rockefeller a "great innovator"?

It is plain that the place Rockefeller holds in American industrial history is that of a great innovator. Early on, he saw the advantage of combination and order in an industry that was bloated, lawless, and chaotic. Following this vision, he formed a scheme of industrial organization which, magnificent in its harmony and strength, world-wide in its scope, possessed a striking novelty. He met great opposition. Producers, rival manufacturers, courts, legislatures, presidents, and public opinion fought him at every step. He and his partners marched from investigation to investigation, from lawsuit to lawsuit, under a growing load of criticism. But they moved forward. They believed that the opposition was mistaken and irrational. They felt that the full victory of competitive laissez-faire individualism would mean a step backward, confusion, and general loss.

Adapted from John D. Rockefeller, *Vol. II, by Allan Nevins.*

The Standard Oil Trust, likened to a thief

The dominant ideal of pioneering America was one of complete independence and self-sufficiency. Long after the new industrial era was far advanced, people held on to the old faith in a self-balancing system of private ownership, small-unit enterprise, and free competition. They believed that this system would give every person a reward roughly equal to his or her work, integrity, and ability. They were slow to see that the industrial system was not self-balancing, that it grew less so decade by decade. They were slow to see that people were less and less independent, more and more interdependent. They were reluctant to admit that free competition was steadily becoming more restricted, and that its character was changing. It was no longer a competition of small business and individual firms. It was becoming a competition organized by great corporations.

Rockefeller was a realist. Partly by intuition, partly by hard thought, he understood the real nature of economic forces and the real motives behind American industry. He and the other leaders of the "heroic age" in American business development were the guiding forces of our industrial society. Many of the forces and elements in that society were unreasonable and wasteful. Rockefeller wished to bring about a more reasonable and efficient pattern.

Behind this desire he placed a good mind, a skill in organization, and a dynamic personal force which were not surpassed, and possibly not equaled, by those of any other industrial captain in history.

Rockefeller's economic foresight, and the courage he showed in sticking to it, deserve praise. He knew that he was carrying through a great experiment, and he believed the experiment to be sound and wise. Any careful analysis of the work of the best leaders shows that money was not the central object, but a by-product. Greedy people exist, but they seldom obtain great fortunes, for greed tends to defeat itself in complex business operations. Those who built the really great economic structures were not thinking mainly of dollars, or they would have stopped after their first great business successes.

One great fact to be remembered when studying Rockefeller and other captains of industry is that American business has typically been a more optimistic, lighhearted undertaking than business in other lands. The best business people have been great adventurers. The giants of the "heroic age" of industry can be compared with the famous Elizabethan captains—with Drake, Hawkins, Cavendish, Frobisher, Cabot (some of whom were good business people, too). In business, Americans of the nineteenth century found the Great Game. They played it with enjoyment and enthusiasm, they enjoyed it even when it was dangerous, and they took its ups and downs calmly. Of all its leaders, none showed more boldness or swiftness than Rockefeller, and none more balance in accepting defeats and victories. Love of the game was one of the motives, particularly as his keen eye saw a pattern in the game that less intelligent people missed.

READING REVIEW

1. According to Nevins, what important characteristic of the new industrial era did many people fail to see?
2. What methods did Rockefeller use to obtain his goal?
3. (a) Why did Nevins compare industrial leaders with historical figures? (b) Do you agree or disagree with this comparison?

153 "It Is All Wrong To Be Poor"

During the years of the late 1800's, some Americans became very wealthy by amassing fortunes in business and in the stock market. Newspapers and magazines told of the fabulous fortunes that were being made and how the rich lived. Many Americans soon began to envy the lives of the very wealthy. The great American dream of becoming rich was shaped during these years.

Russell Conwell, a Union army officer turned preacher, said that there was no point in envying the rich. Instead he suggested that everyone should settle down and make money where he or she lived. He preached this message more than 6,000 times all over the United States in a famous speech called "Acres of Diamonds." The title of the speech came from its opening story, which told of a rich Arab who sold his lands to go in search of diamonds. The new owner of the Arab's land then found these same riches on the very property that the Arab had sold. The excerpt below is from this speech.

READING FOCUS
1. What was the main thrust of Conwell's Speech?
2. What definition did Conwell give for greatness?

Now then, I say that the opportunity to get rich, to obtain great wealth, is here in Philadelphia now, within the reach of almost every man and woman who hears me speak tonight. I mean just what I say. I have come here to tell you what in God's sight I believe to be the truth. If my years have been of any value in teaching me common sense, I know I am right. The men and women sitting here, who found it difficult perhaps to buy a ticket to this talk, have within their reach "acres of diamonds," opportunities to get wealthy. There never was a place on earth more suited to this purpose than the city of Philadelphia today. Never in the history of the world did a poor person without money have such an opportunity to get rich quickly and honestly as he or she has now in our city.

Adapted from Acres of Diamonds *by Russell H. Conwell.*

I say that you ought to get rich. It is your duty to get rich. How many of my religious brothers and sisters say to me, "Do you, a Christian minister, spend your time going up and down the country advising young people to get rich, to get money?" "Yes, of course I do." They say, "Isn't that awful!" Why don't you preach the gospel instead of preaching about people making money?" "Because to make money honestly is to preach the gospel." That is the reason. The people who get rich may be the most honest people you find in the community.

"Oh," but says some young man here tonight, "I have been told all my life that if a person has money he is very dishonest and dishonorable and mean and contemptible." My friend, that is the reason you have none, because you have that idea of people. The foundation of your faith is altogether false. Let me say here clearly, and say it briefly—ninety-eight out of one hundred of the rich people of America are honest. That is why they are rich. That is why they are trusted with money. That is why they carry on great enterprises and find plenty of people to work with them. It is because they are honest.

Says another young man, "I hear sometimes of people who get millions of dollars dishonestly." Yes, of course, you hear this, and so do I. But such people are so rare a thing in fact that the newspapers talk about them all the time as a matter of news until you get the idea that all the other rich people get rich dishonestly.

My friends, drive me out into the suburbs of Philadelphia, and introduce me to the people who own their homes around this great city, those beautiful homes with gardens and flowers. I will introduce you to the very best people in character as well as in enterprise in our city. A man is not really a true man until he owns his own home. Those who own their homes are made more honorable and honest and pure, and true and economical and careful, by owning their homes.

Money is power, and you ought to be reasonably ambitious to have it. You ought to because you can do more good with it than you could without it. Money printed your Bible, money builds your churches, money sends your missionaries, and money pays your preachers. (You would not have many of them if you did

A display of wealth

you wish to be great at all, you must begin where you are and with what you are, in Philadelphia, now. He that can give to this city any blessing, he who can be a good citizen while he lives here, he that can make better homes, he that can be a blessing whether he works in the shop or sits behind the counter or keeps house—whatever be his life, he who would be great anywhere must first be great in his own Philadelphia.

READING REVIEW

1. Why did Conwell say that it is a person's duty to get rich?
2. According to Conwell, what made a great man?
3. What effect might Conwell's speech have had on his listeners? Explain your answer.

not pay them.) The person who gets the largest salary can do the most good with the power that is given to him or her.

I say, then, you ought to have money. If you can honestly obtain riches in Philadelphia, it is your Christian and godly duty to do so. It is an awful mistake of these religious people to think you must be awfully poor in order to be religious.

Some people say, "Don't you sympathize with the poor people?" Of course I do, or else I would not have been speaking all these years. I sympathize with the poor, and the number of poor who are to be sympathized with is very small. While we should sympathize with God's poor—that is, those who cannot help themselves—let us remember there is not a poor person in the United States who was not made poor by his or her own shortcomings, or by the shortcomings of someone else. It is all wrong to be poor, anyhow.

Greatness consists not in the holding of some office. It consists in doing great things with little means and in the accomplishment of great purposes from the private ranks of life. To be great at all one must be great here, now, in Philadelphia. He who can give to this city better streets and better sidewalks, better schools and more colleges, more happiness and more civilization, more of God, he will be great anywhere. Let every man or woman here, if you never hear me again, remember this. If

CHAPTER
23 The Struggle to Organize Workers
(1860's–1890's)

154 Changing Labor Conditions

Walter Wyckoff wanted to find out how other people in the United States lived. Consequently, soon after he graduated from Princeton University, he decided to travel across the country.

Along the way, Wyckoff worked at many different jobs. One of his jobs was construction work for the World's Columbian Exposition in Chicago in 1892. In this selection he wrote of the working conditions at the Exposition.

READING FOCUS

1. Who was "Mr. Ford," and what kind of worker did he symbolize?
2. What new kind of worker had arisen with the development of unions and impersonal corporations?

Our work was the general care of all the plank roads on the grounds. They had been put in fairly good condition, but they received hard use, and constant repairs were necessary. We were, therefore, to give our attention, up to five o'clock in the afternoon, to those sections of the road which most needed repairs. After five, when the work for the day was over, our duty was to go over all the roads and see that they were in good condition for the next morning.

Our job is not easy. The roads constantly need to be repaired. A good deal of hard work is necessary to keep them in order. It is mostly pick and shovel work, the hardest kind of work as far as my experience goes. The old trenches must be kept open and new ones dug, and sometimes the sides of long sections of the road must be buried under a layer of earth to prevent the bare planks from twisting out of shape in the sun.

Among the workers on the grounds, none has interested me more than an American carpenter with whom I sometimes spend an evening. The man is lonely and uncomfortable in his new surroundings. The conditions he faces as a worker are as disturbing to him as the unfamiliar surroundings of his daily life. He holds on to his individuality, but the new things which face him here make that difficult.

The man is a master carpenter from a village home in Ohio. But the certainty of steady work for many months at four dollars a day was tempting enough to cause him to leave his family behind and come here. He had arrived a few days ago and had found work right away.

Seeing the man, a tall, fine-looking, self-respecting American worker, and hearing him speak, and learning even this little of his history, you could see his past. You could almost see a comfortable wooden cottage, which he had built himself, with a garden plot about it and flower beds in front, standing on a well-shaded village street. He owns the cottage and the plot of land, and his children were born there. He is an officer of the village church and has been justice of the peace, and more than once he has served as school trustee. The idea of social inequality is new to him, and it makes

him self-conscious. In his home village his family and the families of all his neighbors are all equals. The only exceptions are the minister, the doctor, the village lawyer, and the schoolmaster, because of their special education. His children study and play at school with the children of all his neighbors, and meet with them at church and elsewhere.

But here things are new and strange. He is no longer a man with a name to distinguish him, but has become a worker with a number on his jacket. He goes to work as just one in an army of ten thousand numbers. Home has changed to a barrack. There he, a number, sleeps in a numbered bunk, and eats as one of half a thousand men. His comfort and convenience are not considered, and his views have no bearing whatever on the course of things.

The superintendent of the building upon which he works, whose energy and skill he admires, shifts him about with dozens of other men, having no more regard for him as an individual than if he were a piece of wood. Once he spoke to his superintendent about some detail of the work and found him a most appreciative listener. Then he started to talk about a subject of general interest, only to find that by some mysterious change he was speaking to a stone wall.

And now something else faces him which he regards as another loss of his individuality. He is urged to agree to this loss, and it gives him some concern. He knows very little about labor unions, and now he is bombarded with appeals to join one.

Management does not discriminate between union and nonunion workers in employing people at the Exposition. But many of the union workers here are making the most of the present opportunity. They want to publicize their principles and bring desirable non-union workers into their organization. My carpenter friend, whom I shall call Mr. Ford, has received much attention.

Two or three times he has asked me to go with him in the evening to meetings which are held near the fairgrounds, and hear speeches from delegates from the Central Labor Union. These we have not found very helpful. There has been a good deal of beer-drinking and much useless speech, which has grown heated at times. Now and then a plain, matter-of-fact worker has given us an interesting talk on the history of unionism and on the need of orga-

Adapted from Walter A. Wyckoff, The Workers.

nization among workers as the only means of safeguarding their interests.

Mr. Ford, much confused, has listened to all this. We have talked it over together on the way back to our rooms, and sometimes late into the night. I have tried to explain to him, as well as I understand it, the idea for labor organization, and the necessity for it which has grown out of the great industrial change since the middle of the 1800's. But Mr. Ford, for all practical purposes, belongs to another period. The industrial change has hardly affected him. He served his apprenticeship, and then was a journeyman and then a master carpenter in due course. In his experience, work has always had its basis in a personal relation, as, for example, between himself as a contractor and the person whose job he undertook and from whom he received payment. A similar personal relation has always existed between himself and the people he has employed.

This new relation between a worker and an impersonal corporation which hires him is one that he does not readily understand. And this merging of one's individuality in an organization which attempts to regulate hours, wages, and employers is a thing he hates.

"Why," he said to me, "I give up my independence, and I'm no better than the worst carpenter in the group. We all get union wages alike. There's no reason for a man to do his best. He ain't a man any more, anyway. He's only a part of a machine. Why, such work as some I see done here, I'd be ashamed to do by moonlight, with my eyes shut. But it makes no difference in the union, you're all on the same level, as nearly as I can make out."

READING REVIEW
1. Contrast Mr. Ford's relation toward work with that of the new relationship established by corporations.
2. What was Mr. Ford's viewpoint about unions?

155 A Disillusioned Immigrant

During the late 1800's and the early 1900's, millions of immigrants from many countries came to America. This huge group of newcomers to the United States is often referred to as the "New Immigration." It consisted mainly of immigrants from nations in southern and eastern Europe. For the most part, the newcomers were unskilled workers who had no choice but to live crowded together in slum neighborhoods in the large cities of the East.

During the New Immigration, for the first time, large numbers of Jews from eastern Europe, especially Russia and Poland, came to America. One of these immigrants was Anzia Yezierska, a sixteen-year-old girl who arrived in New York in 1901. In this selection she told of her dreams and expectations before her arrival and her reactions to what she found.

READING FOCUS
1. What expectations did Anzia Yezierska and her family have?
2. Why did she have doubts about America?

We traveled in steerage [the section of the ship where those who paid the cheapest fares were crowded together under the decks]—dirty bundles—foul odors—seasick people—but I saw and heard nothing of the stinking dirtiness and ugliness around me. I seemed to float in showers of sunshine. Sight after sight of the new world were in my imagination. From everyone's lips flowed the golden legend of the golden country:

"In America you can say what you feel—you can join your friends in the open streets without fear."

"In America there is a home for everyone. The land is your land. Not like in Russia where you feel yourself a stranger in the village where you were born and lived—the village in which your father and grandfather lie buried."

"Everyone is like everybody else in America."

"All people can do what they want with their lives in America."

"Plenty for all. Learning flows free like milk and honey."

"Learning flows free."

The word painted pictures in my mind. I saw before me free schools, free colleges, free libraries, where I could learn and learn and learn and keep on learning.

In our village there was a school, but only for Christian children. In the schools of Amer-

Adapted from Hungry Hearts *by Anzia Yezierska.*

ica I'd lift up my head and laugh and dance—
a child with other children. Like a bird in the
air, from sky to sky, from star to star, I'd soar
and soar.

"Land! Land!" came the joyous shout.

"America! We're in America!" cried my
mother, almost crushing us in her happiness.

Everyone crowded and pushed on deck.
They strained and stretched to get the first
glimpse of the "golden country," lifting their
children on their shoulders that they might
see beyond them.

Men fell on their knees to pray. Women
hugged their babies and wept. Children
danced. Strangers hugged and kissed like old
friends. Old men and women had in their eyes
a look of young people in love.

Age-old visions sang themselves in me—
songs of freedom of an oppressed people.

America! America!

An immigrant neighborhood

*　　*　　*　　*

Between buildings that rose up like mountains, we struggled with our bundles. Up
Broadway, under the bridge, and through the
crowded streets of the ghetto, we followed our
friend, Gedalyeh Mindel.

I looked about the narrow streets of
squeezed-in stores and houses, ragged clothes,
dirty bedding hanging out of the windows, ash-
cans and garbage cans piled up on the sidewalks. A sadness pressed down my heart—the
first doubt of America.

"Where are the green fields and open spaces
in America?" cried my heart. "Where is the
golden country of my dreams?"

A loneliness for the sweet-smelling silence
of the woods that lay beyond our mud hut built
up in my heart, a longing for the soft earth of
our village streets. All around me was the
hardness of brick and stone, the stinking
smells of crowded poverty.

"Here's your house with separate rooms
like in a palace." Gedalyeh Mindel opened the
door of a dingy, airless apartment.

"Where's the sunshine in America?" my
mother cried in dismay.

She went to the window and looked out at
the wall of the next house. "Like in a grave so
dark."

"It ain't so dark, it's only a little shady."
Gedalyeh Mindel lighted the gas. "Look only."
He pointed with pride to the dim gaslight. "No

candles, no kerosene lamps in America, you
turn on a screw and put to it a match and you
got light like with sunshine."

Again the shadow fell over me, again the
doubt of America!

In America there were rooms without sunlight, rooms to sleep in, to eat in, to cook in,
but without sunshine. And Gedalyeh Mindel
was happy. Could I be satsfied with just a place
to sleep and eat in, and a door to shut people
out—to take the place of sunlight? Or would I
always need the sunlight to be happy?

And where was there a place in America
for me to play? I looked out into the alley below
and saw pale-faced children running in the
street.

"Where is America?" cried my heart.

*　　*　　*　　*

My eyes were shutting themselves with
sleep—the dead-weight sleep of complete
exhaustion.

"Heart of mine!" my mother's voice moaned
above me. "Father is already gone an hour.
You know how they'll squeeze from you a
nickel for every minute you're late. Quick
only!"

I grabbed my bread and herring and ran
down the stairs and out into the street. I ate
running, blindly pushing through the hurrying crowds of workers—my haste and fear
choking each mouthful.

I felt a strangling in my throat as I neared the sweatshop [the factory where she worked]. All my nerves screwed together into iron hardness to withstand the day's torture.

For an instant I hesitated as I faced the window of the old building—dirt and decay cried out from every crumbling brick.

In the shop, raging around me the roar and the clatter, the clatter and the roar, the grind of the pounding machines. Half maddened, half deadened, I struggled to think, to feel, to remember—what am I—who am I—why was I here?

I struggled in vain—confused and lost in the noise.

"America—America—where was America?" it cried in my heart.

The factory whistle—the slowing-down of the machines—the noon hour had come.

I woke as from a nightmare—a tired waking to pain.

In my brain reason began to dawn. In my heart feelings began to pulse. The wound of my wasted life began to hurt and ache. My childhood ended by work—must my youth die too—unlived?

The odor of herring and garlic—the hungry eating of food—laughter and loud, vulgar jokes. Was it only I who was so unhappy? I looked at those around me. Were they happy or only not aware of their slavery? How could they laugh and joke? Why were they not torn with rebellion against this grind—the crushing, deadening movements of the body, where only hands live and hearts and brains must die?

A touch on my shoulder. I looked up. It was Yetta Solomon from the machine next to mine.

"Here's your tea."

I stared at her, half hearing.

"Ain't you going to eat nothing?"

"Yetta! I can't stand it!" The cry broke from me. "I didn't come to America to turn into a machine. I came to America to make from myself a person. Does America want only my hands—only the strength of my body—not my heart—not my feelings—my thoughts?"

READING REVIEW

1. Name three things Anzia Yezierska and her family expected when they came to America.
2. What caused her first doubts about America?
3. What advice might Mr. Conwell (Reading 20) have given to Anzia?

156 An Italian Boy's Name Change

In 1896, when he was nine years old, Leonard Covello came to American with his mother and two younger brothers. (His father had made the trip earlier to earn money for their passage.) Like thousands of other "New Immigrants," the Covellos came from Italy. And like thousands of other immigrants, they found that becoming American brought both pleasure and pain.

Many years later, Covello wrote of his experiences as a newcomer. He stressed the culture conflict that developed between immigrant parents and their children. Covello wrote: "We soon got the idea that "Italian' meant something inferior, and a barrier was erected between children of Italian origin and their parents. This was the accepted process of Americanization. We were becoming Americans by learning how to be ashamed of our parents."

READING FOCUS

1. In what ways were the immigrants being Americanized?
2. Why was Leonard Covello's father so upset by the family's name change in school?

Every day in school before receiving our bowl of soup we recited the Lord's Prayer. I had no idea what the words meant. I only knew that I was expected to bow my head. I looked around to see what was going on. Swift and simple, the teacher's blackboard pointer brought the idea home to me. I never looked around again after that.

I learned arithmetic and penmanship and spelling—every misspelled word had to be written ten times or more in my notebook. I do not know how many times I wrote "I must not talk." In this same way I learned how to read in English, learned geography and grammar, the states of the Union, all the capital cities and choice bits of poetry and sayings. Most learning was done in unison. That is, all the children recited to the teacher while they stood at attention. Repetition. Repetition until

---

Adapted from The Heart is the Teacher *by Leonard Covello and Guido D'Agostino.*

the things you learned beat in your brain even at night when you were falling asleep.

Silence! Silence! Silence! This was the characteristic feature at school. You never made an unnecessary noise or said an unnecessary word. Outside in the hall we lined up by size, girls in one line and boys in another, without a sound, to go to the assembly. Eyes front and at attention. Lord help you if you broke the rule of silence. I can still see a distant relative of mine, a girl named Miluzza, who could never stop talking. She stood in a corner behind Mrs. Cutter [the teacher] throughout an entire assembly with a spring-type clothespin fastened to her lower lip as punishment. Not at all frightened, instead defiant—Miluzza with that clothespin hanging from her lip. . . .

The piano struck up a march and from the hall we paraded into assembly—eyes straight ahead in military style. Mrs. Cutter was there on the platform, her eyes reaching every corner of the assembly hall. It was always the same. We stood at attention as the Bible was read and at attention as the flag was waved back and forth, and we sang the same song. I didn't know what the words meant, but I sang it loudly with all the rest, in my own way, "Three Cheers for de Red Whatzam Blu!"

One day I came home from school with a report card for my father to sign. I remember that my friend Vito Salvatore happened to be there, and Mary Accurso had stopped in for a moment to see my mother. With a tired look my father looked over the marks on the report card and was about to sign it. However, he paused with the pen in his hand.

"What is this?" he said. "Leonard Covello! What happened to the *i* in Coviello?"

My mother stopped sewing. Vito and I just looked at each other.

"Well?" my father insisted.

"Maybe the teacher just forgot to put it in," Mary suggested. "It can happen." She was going to high school now and spoke with an air of authority, and people always listened to her. This time, however, my father didn't even hear her.

"From Leonardo to Leonard I can follow," he said, "a perfectly natural process. In America anything can happen and does happen. But you don't change a family name. A name is a name. What happened to the *i*?"

"Mrs. Cutter took it out," I explained. "Every time she pronounced Coviello it came

Students in a New York City School

out Covello. So she took out the *i*. That way it's easier for everybody."

My father hit the table with his fist. "And what has this Mrs. Cutter got to do with my name?"

"What difference does it make?" I said. "It's more American. The *i* doesn't help anything." It was one of the very few times that I dared oppose my father. But even at that age I was beginning to feel that anything that made a name less foreign was an improvement.

Vito came to my rescue. "My name is Victor—Vic. That's what everybody calls me now."

"Vica. Sticka. Micka. You crazy in the head!" my father yelled at him.

For a moment my father sat there, bitter rebellion building in him. Then, with a shrug of giving up, he signed the report card and shoved it over to me. My mother now suddenly entered the argument. "How is it possible to do this to a name? Why did you sign the card? Narduccio, you will have to tell your teacher that a name cannot be changed just like that."

"Mamma, you don't understand."

"What is there to understand? A person's life and his honor is in his name. He never changes it. A name is not a shirt or a piece of underwear."

My father got up from the table, lighted the twisted stump of a cigar and moved out of the argument. "Honor!" he muttered to himself.

"You must explain this to your teacher," my mother insisted. "It was a mistake. She will know. She will not let it happen again. You will see."

"It was no mistake. It was done on purpose. The *i* is out, and Mrs. Cutter made it Covello. You don't understand!"

"Will you stop saying that!" my mother insisted. "I don't understand. I don't understand. What is there to understand? Now that you have become Americanized you understand everything and I understand nothing."

With her in this mood I dared not answer. Mary went over and put her hand on my mother's shoulder. I called to Vito and together we walked out of the apartment and downstairs into the street.

"She just doesn't understand," I kept saying.

"I'm gonna take the *e* off the end of my name and make it just Salvator," Vito said. "After all, we're not in Italy now."

Vito and I were standing unhappily under the gas light on the corner. Somehow or other the joy of childhood had left us. We were only boys, but a sadness that we could not explain pressed down upon us. Mary came and joined us. She had a book under her arm. She stood there for a moment, while her dark eyes looked at us questionably.

"But they don't understand!" I insisted.

Mary smiled. "Maybe some day, you will realize that *you* are the only one who does not understand."

READING REVIEW

1. Why did Leonard Covello's teacher change the spelling of his last name?
2. (a) Why did Leonard Covello's parents object to the change in the spelling of their family name? (b) Do you agree or disagree with their objection? Explain.

Immigrants arrive in America.

157 Fear of the Immigrant

For the millions of immigrants who came to America in the late 1800's and early 1900's, their first sight of their new land was the Statue of Liberty. It stands on an island at the entrance of New York Harbor. And for most newcomers the statue with its uplifted torch was a wonderful and welcome sight.

However, not all Americans in these years welcomed the newcomers. Many Americans were worried by the "New Immigrants," whose ways of life and customs seemed so strange and foreign. Thomas Bailey Aldrich, a writer and editor of the *Atlantic Monthly* magazine, expressed the fears of many Americans in his poem "Unguarded Gates."

READING FOCUS

1. What were three phrases the poet used to describe America?
2. What were three phrases the poet used to describe immigrants?

Wide open and unguarded stand our gates,
    Named of the four winds, North, South,
    East, and West;
Portals [gates] that lead to an enchanted land
Of cities, forests, fields of living gold,
Vast prairies, lordly summits [mountains]
    touched with snow,
Majestic rivers sweeping proudly past . . .
A realm [land] wherein are fruits of every
    zone, . . .
A later Eden planted in the wilds. . . .
Here, it is written, Toil shall have its wage,
And Honor honor, and the humblest man
Stand level with the highest in the law.
Of such a land have men in dungeons dreamed.
    . . .

Wide open and unguarded stand our gates,
And through them presses a wild motley
    throng—
Men from the Volga and the Tartar steppes,
Featureless figures of the Hwang Ho,
Malayan, Scythian, Teuton, Celt, and Slav,
Flying the Old World's poverty and scorn;

From "Unguarded Gates" in The Works of Thomas Bailey Aldrich, Poems, Vol. II.

These bringing with them unknown gods and
    rites,
Those, tiger passions, here to stretch their
    claws.
In street and alley what strange tongues are
    loud. . . .

O liberty, white Goddess! is it well
To leave the gates unguarded?
Lift the down-trodden, but with hand of steel
Stay those who to thy sacred portals come
To waste the gifts of freedom. Have a care
Lest from thy brow the clustered stars be torn
And trampled in the dust. . . .

READING REVIEW

1. How did Aldrich picture the United States in the first stanza?
2. List two things the immigrants expected to find in America.
3. Where did members of the "motley throng" come from?
4. For whom did the poet say the gates should be shut?

158 The Need for Unions

In the late 1800's and early 1900's workers faced many problems that were the result of the new industrial age. In order to try to solve these problems, workers began to join together and to organize into unions. However, the right of workers to organize unions and to bargain collectively with employers became an important issue. At times, it seemed that most Americans and even state governments and the federal government were opposed to this effort. Union leaders often had great difficulty in persuading working people to join labor unions. In this selection John Mitchell, president of the United Mine Workers from 1896 to 1908, argued in favor of labor unions.

READING FOCUS

1. According to Mitchell, under what conditions did labor lose its value?
2. To what was trade unionism basically opposed?
3. What was the goal of trade unionism?

In its basic principle, trade unionism is plain and clear and simple. Trade unionism starts by recognizing that under normal conditions individual, unorganized workers cannot bargain advantageously with the employer for the sale of their labor. Since workers have no money saved, they must sell their labor immediately. Moreover, they have no knowledge of the market and no skill in bargaining. Finally, they have only their own labor to sell, while the employer uses hundreds or thousands of workers and can easily do without the services of any particular individual. Thus workers, if bargaining only for themselves, are at a great disadvantage.

Trade unionism recognizes the fact that under such conditions labor loses value. The labor which workers sell is, unlike other commodities, a thing which is of their very life and soul and being. In the individual contract between a rich employer and a poor worker, the laborer will get the worst of it. Workers are constantly weakened because of wages too low to buy nourishing food, hours too long for enough rest, working conditions that destroy moral, mental, and physical health, and dangers that may cause accidents and disease. The "individual bargain," or individual contract, between employers and workers means that the condition of the worst and lowest worker in the industry will be that which the best worker must accept.

From first to last, from beginning to end, always and everywhere, trade unionism is opposed to the individual contract. It is this principle, the absolute and complete end of contracts between employers and individual workers, upon which trade unionism is founded. There can be no lasting prosperity for the working classes, no real and lasting progress, until this principle is firmly and fully established.

Trade unions were founded to find a substitute for the individual bargain. A trade union, in its usual form, is an association of workers who have agreed among themselves not to bargain individually with their employer or employers, but to agree to the terms of a collective or joint contract between the employer and the union. The difference between the individual and the collective or joint bargain is simply this: In the individual contract one worker in a hundred refuses to accept

---

Adapted from John Mitchell, Organized Labor: Its Problems, Purposes, and Ideals.

work, and the employer keeps the service of ninety-nine. In the collective bargain the hundred employees act together and the employer keeps or fires all of them on the same terms. The ideal of trade unionism is to combine in one organization all the workers employed, or capable of being employed, at a given trade. And to demand and secure for each and all of the workers a definite minimum standard of wages, hours, and conditions of work.

To carry out a joint bargain, it is necessary to establish an accepted minimum of wages and conditions which will apply to all. This does not mean that the wages of all shall be the same, but only that equal pay shall be given for equal work. There cannot be more than one minimum wage in a given trade, in a given place, at a given time.

The recognition of the union is nothing more nor less than the recognition of the principle for which trade unionism stands—the right to bargain collectively and to insist upon minimum standards.

There are many employers who are willing to give up the principle of the individual bargain but do not accept the principle of the collective bargain. These employers state that they do not insist upon dealing with their employees as individuals, but that they must keep the right of dealing with "only their own employees." They say that they must not be forced to permit a worker who is not their own employee to interfere in their business.

The right to bargain collectively, however, or to take any other united action, necessarily involves the right to representation. Experience and reason both show that a person who is dependent on the good will of an employer is in no position to negotiate with him. If he insists on what he considers to be the rights of the workers represented by him he may be fired or at least lose his employer's favor. Not only should workers have the right of making collective contracts, but they should also have the right of being represented by whomever they wish. To deny the right of representation is tyranny.

READING REVIEW

1. Why was it impossible for an individual worker to bargain effectively with an employer?
2. What, according to Mitchell, was the basic principle of trade unionism?
3. Why was representation an important part of trade unionism?

CHAPTER

24 Farmers Revolt Against Big Business
(1860's–1890's)

159 Hardships of Rural Life

A world away from the rapidly growing, crowded cities of the East and Midwest, with their working-class slums and mansions of the rich, were the farmers of the Great Plains. Eugene V. Smalley, a well-known journalist in the years after the Civil War, traveled through the Great Plains, where he visited many of the farms. He wrote about the lives of the farm families on the plains. In this selection, he emphasized the isolation of farm life and suggested what could be done to make farm life more pleasant.

READING FOCUS

1. Why were American farmers so isolated?
2. What solution did Smalley suggest?

United Mine Workers membership certificate

In no civilized country have the farmers so poorly adapted their home life to the conditions of nature as have the people of our vast plains region. This is a strong statement, but I am led to this conclusion by ten years of observation. The European farmer lives in a village, where considerable social enjoyment is possible. The women talk together at the village well, and visit frequently at one another's homes. The children find playmates close to home. There is a school, and if the village is not a very small one, a church. The old men gather on summer evenings to smoke their pipes and talk of the crops. The young men play ball on the village green. In a word, something takes place to break the monotony or sameness of daily life. The houses, though small and with little furniture, have thick walls of brick or stone that keep out the summer's heat and the winter's cold.

Now contrast this life with the life of a poor settler in North or South Dakota or Nebraska. Every homesteader must live upon his claim for five years to confirm his title to it. If the country were so thickly settled that every quarter-section of land, or 160 acres [64.7 hectares], had a family upon it, each family would still be half a mile [.8 kilometer] from any neighbor. But many settlers own 320 acres [129.5 hectares] and a few have 640 acres [259 hectares]. Then there are sections of land set aside for schools and other sections that are not occupied at all. Thus the average space separating the farms is, in fact, always more than half a mile [.8 kilometer]. Many settlers must go a mile or two to reach a neighbor's house.

If there is any region in the world where the natural sociable instinct of people should be upheld, that region is our northwestern prairies. A short hot summer is followed by a long cold winter. The treeless plain stretches away to the horizon in every direction. In summer, it is covered with grain fields or grass and flowers, and is lovely in its color and vastness. But one mile of it is almost exactly like another. When the snow covers the ground it is bleak and depressing. There are no birds left after the wild geese and ducks have flown south. The silence of death rests on the vast

A sod house on the prairie

landscape, except when it is swept by cruel winds.

In such a region, you would expect the houses to be strongly built, but they are not. The new settlers are too poor to build a house of brick or stone. Instead, they haul a few loads of lumber from the nearest railway station. Then they put up a frail little house of two, three, or four rooms that looks as though the prairie winds would blow it away. The barn is often made of sod walls with a straw roof. A barbed-wire fence surrounds the barnyard. There are usually no trees.

In this small, cramped home, the farm family sees nothing more cheerful than the distant houses of other settlers, just as ugly and lonely, and stacks of straw and unthreshed grain. In the summer there is a school for the children, one, two, or three miles away. But in winter the distances across the snow-covered plains are too great for them to travel. Each family must live mainly to itself. A drive to the nearest town is almost the only pleasure. There are few social events in the life of these prairie farmers to liven up the monotony of the long winter evenings.

Visits from neighbors are few, because of the long distances which separate the farm-

Adapted from E. V. Smalley, "The Isolation of Life on Prairie Farms," Atlantic Monthly, *September 1893.*

houses. Another reason is the differences among the people. They have no common past to talk about. They were strangers to one another when they arrived in this new land, and their work and ways have not thrown them together much. Often the strangeness is increased by differences of national origin. There are Swedes, Norwegians, Germans, French Canadians, and perhaps even Finns and Icelanders. The Americans themselves come from many different states. It is hard to establish any social bond in such a mixed population.

An alarming amount of insanity occurs among farmers. In proportion to their numbers, the Scandinavian settlers send the most people to the insane asylums. The reason is easy to see. These people came from cheery little farm villages. Life in their homeland was hard and full of work, but it was not lonesome. Think for a moment how great the change must be from the white-walled, red-roofed village in Norway to an isolated cabin on a Dakota prairie. It is little wonder that so many Scandinavian farmers lose their mental balance.

There is only one solution for the dreariness of farm life on the prairies. The isolated farmhouse must be abandoned, and the people must draw together and live in villages. The peasants of the Russian steppes did this centuries ago, and so did those on the great plain of the Danube. In the older parts of our prairie states, titles to homestead claims are now nearly all confirmed, so farmers no longer have to live on the land they farm. They might go out with their teams to till their fields, and return at evening to village homes. It would be entirely possible to divide the land over again so that each settler would still have 160 acres [64.7 hectares], and no one would live more than a mile from the farthest limit of his farm. The homes of the families would surround a village green, where the schoolhouse would stand. There would probably be a store and a post office. An active social life would soon develop in such a community.

If the plains people were thus brought together into towns, some home industries might be established that would add to family incomes, or at least save expenses. The economic weakness of farming in the North is based on the idle period of the farmer and the work animals during the long winter. If it were possible to bring back to the farm some of the crafts that were carried on in the country thirty or forty years ago, there would be a great gain in comfort, intelligence, and happiness.

According to habit, American farmers feel they must live upon the land they till, and must have no near neighbors. This habit will be hard to break, but I believe it must in time give in to the advantages of living closer together. I have known instances, however, where efforts at more neighborly ways of living have been made on a small scale, and have failed. In the early settlement of Dakota, sometimes four families, each taking a quarter-section homestead, would build temporary houses at the quarter-sections' meeting line, in order to be near each other. But a few years later, when they were able to put up better buildings, they moved to the opposite sides of their claims. They did so, they said, because their chickens got mixed up with those of their neighbors. In these instances, I should add, the people were Americans. There is an individuality about the average American farmer, the result of generations of isolated living, that does not encourage living close to others.

I am aware that nothing changes so slowly as the customs of a people. It will take a long time to change the settled American habit of isolated farms. If it is ever changed, the new system will have to be introduced near the top of the rural social scale, and work down gradually to the masses. A group of farmers of superior intelligence and of above-average means must set an example and establish a model farm village. Such an experiment would be widely discussed by the newspapers. This extensive free advertising could hardly fail to interest other people in the idea.

The farmers of the West have thus far been engaged in a hard struggle to establish themselves on the soil, obtain the necessities of life, and pay off their mortgages. They are getting ahead year by year. In the older settled districts good houses are taking the place of the pioneer homes, and the towns show progress. Before long these prairie people will begin to try to solve the problems that come with a higher civilization. Then it will be found, I believe, that the first great step toward more comfortable living, intellectual development, and social enjoyment is the abandonment of the lonesome farmhouse and the establishment of the farm village.

READING REVIEW

1. What comparisons were made between the living conditions of American farmers and those of European farmers?
2. Cite three generalizations for which Smalley presented little or no evidence.
3. What, eventually, reduced the isolation of Great Plains farmers?

160 A Populist Analysis of Farmers' Problems

During the hard times of the 1880's and 1890's farmers throughout the country gathered in Grange halls and other meeting places to discuss their problems and to demand relief. As this happened, the Grange, a national farm organization founded to provide community activity for farm families, began to work for the improvement of farm conditions. The Grange established cooperatives, and its members went into politics. Then in the early 1890's members of the Grange and other farmers formed their own political party—the Populist Party.

In 1890, William Peffer, a Kansas lawyer and journalist, was elected to the Senate on the Populist Party ticket. In this selection, he summarized the farmers' complaints against the manufacturers, the banks, and the railroads.

READING FOCUS

1. What changes took place in the farmer's situation between the 1840's and the 1890's?
2. Why did the political power of farmers decline?

A hundred years ago 90 percent of our population lived on farms. Transportation was so expensive that surplus wheat and corn could not be sold 50 miles [80 kilometers] away from a market town. Now great cities have grown up, the market has expanded, and distance is practically meaningless. From a small area along the Atlantic coast, we have spread across

---

Adapted from William A. Peffer, The Farmer's Side: His Troubles and Their Remedy.

the continent. We travel by railroad from Boston to San Francisco in less than six days.

The American farmer of today is a completely different sort of person than he was 50 or 100 years ago. A great many men and women now living remember when farmers were largely manufacturers. That is, they made a great many tools and other things for their own use. Every farmer had tools with which he made wooden tools such as forks and rakes, handles for his hoes and plows, spokes for his wagon, and various other things.

Then the farmer produced flax and hemp and wool and cotton. These fibers were prepared on the farm. They were spun into yarn, woven into cloth, made into clothes, and worn at home. Upon every farm geese were kept. Their feathers were used in the home's beds and pillows, and the surplus was sold at the nearest market town.

When winter came, animals raised on the farm were butchered. Meat for family use during the next year was prepared and preserved in the smokehouse. The orchards supplied fruit for cider, for apple butter, and for preserves. Wheat was threshed, a little at a time, just enough to supply the needs of the family for money. Everything was saved and put to use.

One of the results of that sort of careful planning was that only a small amount of money was required to carry on the business of farming. A hundred dollars a year was probably as much as the largest farmers of that day needed to pay for workers, repairs of tools, and all other expenses, because so many things were paid for with farm crops.

Now we find that nearly everything has been changed. All over the West farmers thresh their wheat all at one time, get rid of it all at one time, and in a great many instances waste the straw. They sell their hogs, and buy bacon and pork. They sell their cattle, and buy fresh beef or canned beef or corned beef. They sell their fruit, and buy it back in cans. If they raise flax at all, they thresh it, sell the seed, and burn the straw. Instead of having clothing made on the farm or by a neighbor woman or country tailor a mile away, they either buy their clothing ready-made at the nearest town, or buy the cloth and have a city tailor make it.

Instead of making tools which they use on the farm, they go to town to purchase even a handle for an ax or a mallet. They purchase

237

twine and rope and all sorts of material made of fibers. Indeed, they buy nearly everything now that they once produced, and these things all cost money.

Besides all this, there is something even stranger. In earlier times the American home was a free home. There was not one case in a thousand where a home was mortgaged to secure the payment of borrowed money. Only a small amount of money was then needed to carry on the business of farming, and there was always enough of it to supply the demand. Now when at least ten times as much is needed, there is little or none to be obtained. Nearly half the farms are mortgaged for as much as they were worth, and interest rates are very high.

As to the cause of such changes in the condition of farmers, it is the railroad builder, the banker, the moneychanger, and the manufacturer who have hurt the farmer. The manufacturers came with their factories. The wagonmaker's shop in the neighborhood has given way to the large company in the city where people by the thousand work and where a hundred or two hundred wagons are made in a week. The shoemaker's shop has given way to large companies in the cities where most of the work is done by machines. The old smokehouse has given way to the packing house. The farmer now is forced to go to town for nearly everything. Even a hand rake to clean up the yard must be bought at the city store.

And what is worse, if they need a little more money, they are forced to go to town to borrow it. But they do not find the money there. In place of it they find an agent who will "negotiate" a loan. The money is in the East, at a distance of a thousand, three thousand, or five thousand miles [1,600, 4,830, or 8,050 kilometers]. The farmers of the country today are maintaining an army of distributors, loan agents, bankers, and others, who are absolutely worthless for all good purposes in the community.

These things, however, involve only the mechanics of farming. The farmers' territory has been invaded by people who buy large tracts of land and operate these large farms like factories. This is "bonanza" farming. The aim of some of the great "bonanza farms" of Dakota is to use machinery so effectively that farming one full section, or 640 acres [259 hectares], represents one year's work for only one person. Railroad companies gave special rates to the bonanza farmers. And while this disastrous competition was going on, ranchers too took possession of vast areas of the public lands and raised cattle by the million at no expense beyond the cost of herding.

These are some of the causes of the hard times in the farming industry. It was impossible for the average farmers to hold their own with such odds against them.

While these problems were increasing, other forces were operating to add to farmers' difficulties. The people were rapidly taking on debts, while prices of farm products fell very low. While one hundred dollars had the same value in 1889 as it did in 1869, lower farm prices made it worth more. It requires twice as many bushels of wheat or of corn or of oats, twice as many pounds of cotton or tobacco or wool, to pay off a debt in 1887 as it did to pay a debt of the same amount in 1867.

It is frequently said that the farmers themselves are to blame for all these problems, but that is not true. The farmer has been the victim of a gigantic scheme of plunder. Never before has such a vast combination of brains and money forced people into labor for the benefit of a few.

In the beginning of our history nearly all the people were farmers, and they made our

A Populist Party campaign poster

laws. But as the national wealth increased, they came to supply the needs of those who own or control large fortunes. Farmers worked while others reaped the harvest. It is greed that robbed the farmers. High interest rates took all their money. And now, when their problems are becoming worse and disaster overtakes them, they appeal to those they have made rich only to learn how poor and helpless they are.

From this testimony readers need have no difficulty in determining for themselves "how we got here." Money [bankers and financiers] rules our financial policy. Money controls the business of the country. Money is robbing the people. These people of Wall Street hold the bonds of nearly every state, county, city, and township in the Union. Every railroad owes them more than it is worth. Every trust and combine made to rob the people had its beginnings in the example of Wall Street dealers. This dangerous power which money gives is taking away the liberties of the people. It now has control of nearly half their homes, and is reaching out its clutching hands for the rest. This is the power we have to deal with.

READING REVIEW

1. According to Peffer, how had the farmers' situation changed between the 1840's and the 1890's in terms of self-sufficiency, competition, and cash?
2. On whom or what did Peffer place the blame for the farmers' changed situation?
3. Do you agree or disagree with Peffer's reasoning? Cite evidence from the reading to support your answer.

161 United Against a "Common Enemy"

All farmers faced the problems of debt, overproduction, and low prices during the hard times of the 1880's and 1890's. But these years were especially difficult for black farmers in the South. Some leaders hoped that poor blacks and whites could work together to solve their problems. One man who hoped this was possible was T. Thomas Fortune. Born a slave in Florida, Fortune attended Howard University after the Civil War. He later became the publisher of a newspaper, the New York Age.

READING FOCUS

1. (a) What did Fortune call "industrial slavery"?
   (b) What did he say were the characteristics of the "new slaveholder"?
2. What did Fortune say would be the future struggle in the South?

I know it is not fashionable for writers on economic questions to tell the truth. But the truth should be told. During the war the government confiscated the slave population of the South, but it left to the rebels a far more valuable kind of property. The slave, the perishable wealth, was taken by the government and then freed. But property in land, the wealth which does not perish, was left to the rebels.

The United States took the slave but left the thing which gave birth to *personal slavery* and is now fast giving birth to *industrial slavery*. The latter is more agonizing and much worse than that other slavery, which I once withstood. The old slaveholders had to feed, clothe, and house their property, and take care of it when disease or accident threatened its life. But industrial slavery requires no such care. The new slaveholder only wants to obtain the most labor for the least cost. He does not regard the worker as of any consequence when he can no longer produce. Having worked him to death, or ruined his health and robbed him of his labor, he turns him out upon the world to live upon the charity of people or to die of starvation. He knows that there is no profit in wasting time and money upon a disabled industrial slave. He makes wealth and death at one and the same time. He could not do this if our social system did not give him a monopoly of the soil from which a living must be obtained.

I think of the absolutely destitute condition of the colored people of the South at the close of the war. I remember the moral and intellectual harm slavery did them. Not only were they bankrupt, but they were absolutely cut off from the soil, with no right or title to it. Now they have already got a respectable slice of land. They have eagerly taken hold of the opportunities for educational development provided by good men and women. They have

Adapted from Black and White: Land, Labor and Politics in the South *by Timothy Thomas Fortune.*

A black sharecropper

The future struggle in the South will be, not between white people and black people, but between capital and labor, landlord and tenant. Already the armies are gathering on the field.

The same battle will be fought upon southern soil that is in preparation in other states where the conditions took longer to develop but are no more deep-rooted or harmful. The social problems in the South will be found to be the same as those in every other section of our country. Questions of "race," "condition," etc., will be properly adjusted as people become better off and forget the unhappy past.

The hour is coming when the working classes of our country, North, East, West, and South, will recognize that they have a *common cause,* a *common humanity,* and a *common enemy.* If they want to triumph over wrong, without distinction of race or previous conditions, *they must unite!* When the battle begins, the rich, be they black or be they white, will be found upon the same side. And the poor, be they black or be they white, will be found on the same side.

Necessity knows no law and discriminates in favor of no person or race.

READING REVIEW

1. Why did Fortune say that "industrial slavery" was worse than "personal slavery"?
2. (a) Which groups did Fortune think would be involved in the "future struggle in the South"? (b) Find evidence in your textbook to prove or disprove his prediction.

bought homes and supplied them with articles of convenience and comfort, often of luxury. I am surprised not at this progress, but that the race did not terrorize and rob society as society had for so long terrorized and robbed them. The thing is strange and marvelous, in the extreme. Instead of becoming outlaws, as the situation would seem to have indicated, the black men and women of the South went to work to better their own lives and the crippled condition of the country, which had been produced by the ravages of rebellion. Meanwhile, many white people of the South, the capitalists, the land-sharks, and the ruffians organized themselves into a band of outlaws. They deliberately murdered innocent men and women for political reasons, and robbed them of their honest labor because they were too lazy to work themselves.

But this highly abnormal, unnatural condition of things is fast passing away. White people, having asserted their superiority in matters of assassination and robbery, have settled down on a barrel of dynamite, as they did in the days of slavery. They will await the explosion with the same self-satisfaction true of them in other days.

CHAPTER
25 Life Styles in the New Industrial Age
(1860's–1890's)

162 The Making of a New Yorker

From 1865 to 1900, more and more Americans left farms and small towns to live in the cities. In 1869 no American city had a population of 1 million, but by 1890 New York, Chicago, and Philadelphia each had more than 1 million people.

What caused so many thousands of people to leave their homes and try to start a new life in the city? This great movement of people had many causes. People were attracted to the cities by hopes of jobs and high wages; many also came to escape the dullness of farm life. Cities were interesting places with their bright lights, tall buildings, and bustling activity. The largest American city was New York City. Its crowded streets and activity fascinated many people, especially writers like William Sydney Porter, better known as O. Henry. In this selection, O. Henry wrote about "the making of a New Yorker."

READING FOCUS

1. How did Raggles view the cities he had visited?
2. What event turned Raggles into a New Yorker?

Besides many other things, Raggles was a poet. He was called a tramp. But that was only a way of saying that he was a philosopher, an artist, a traveler, a naturalist, and a discoverer. But most of all he was a poet. In all his life he never wrote a line of poetry; he lived his poetry.

Raggles' specialty, had he used ink and paper, would have been sonnets to the cities. He studied cities. A city to Raggles was not only a pile of bricks and mortar, with a certain number of inhabitants. It was a thing with a characteristic and distinct soul, an individual life with its own special flavor and feeling. Two thousand miles [3,220 kilometers] to the north and south, east and west, Raggles wandered, studying cities. And when he found the heart of a city and listened to its secret confession, he went on to another.

Through the ancient poets [those of Greece and Rome] we have learned that cities are like women. So they were to poet Raggles. His mind carried a clear idea of the figure that symbolized and typified each one.

Chicago seemed to swoop down upon him with a breezy suggestion of plumes and perfume.

Pittsburgh impressed him as a royal and generous lady—homely, hearty, with a red

Adapted from "The Making of a New Yorker" from The Trimmed Lamp by O. Henry.

face, washing the dishes in a silk dress and white slippers, and telling Raggles to sit before the roaring fireplace and drink champagne along with his pigs' feet and fried potatoes.

New Orleans had simply looked down upon him from a balcony. He could see her thoughtful, starry eyes and catch the movement of her fan, and that was all.

Boston appeared to the poetic Raggles in an unusual way. It seemed to him that he had drunk cold tea and that the city was a white, cold cloth that had been wrapped tightly around his head to spur him to some unknown but tremendous mental effort.

One day Raggles came to the heart of the great city of Manhattan. She was the greatest of all. He wanted to classify and label her and arrange her with the other cities.

Raggles landed from a ferryboat one morning and walked into the center of the town confident and at ease. Without money—as a

Hester Street, New York City

241

poet should be—but with the excitement of an astronomer discovering a new star, Raggles wandered into the great city.

Late in the afternoon he came out of the roar and commotion with a look of terror on his face. He was defeated, puzzled, frightened. Other cities had been as easy to read and understand as a child's book. But here was one as cold, glittering, serene, and impossible as a four-carat diamond in a window to a young man in love looking at it and feeling his modest clerk's pay in his pocket.

The greetings of the other cities he had known—their homey kindliness, their rough charity, friendly curses, talkative curiosity, or indifference. This city of Manhattan gave him no clue. It was walled against him. Never an eye was turned upon him. No voice spoke to him.

On Broadway Raggles, the successful suitor of many cities, stood, shy, like any country youth. For the first time he experienced the sad humiliation of being ignored. And when he tried to understand this brilliant, swiftly changing, ice-cold city he failed completely. The houses were defensive walls. The people were bright but bloodless ghosts.

The thing that weighed heaviest on Raggles' soul was the spirit of absolute egotism that seemed to fill the people. Humanity was gone from them. They were like gods of stone, worshiping themselves. Frozen, cruel, cut to an identical pattern, they hurried on their ways like statues brought to life, while soul and feeling lay dead in the marble.

Gradually Raggles became aware of certain types. One was an elderly gentleman with a snow-white, short beard, pink, unwrinkled face and stony, sharp blue eyes. He seemed to personify the city's wealth and icy unconcern. Another type was a tall, beautiful woman, calm, dressed like the princesses of old, with eyes coldly blue. And another was a broad, swaggering, grim fellow, with large cheeks, a baby's skin, and the knuckles of a prize fighter. This type leaned against cigar signs and looked at the world with scorn.

Raggles got up his courage and begged for money. The people passed on without a wink of an eyelash to indicate that they were aware of him. And then he said to himself that this fair but pitiless city of Manhattan was without a soul, and that he was alone in a great wilderness.

Raggles started to cross the street. There was a blast, a roar, a hissing and a crash as something struck him and tossed him over and over six yards [5.5 meters] from where he had been.

Raggles opened his eyes. And then a hand soft as a falling petal touched his head. Bending over him was the woman dressed like a princess of old, with blue eyes, now soft with human sympathy. Under his head on the street were silks and furs. With Raggles' hat in his hand and with his face pinker than ever from an outburst against reckless driving, stood the elderly gentleman who personified the city's wealth. From a nearby cafe hurried the man with fat cheeks and baby skin, carrying a glass full of a red liquid.

"Drink dis, sport," he said, holding the glass to Raggles' lips.

Hundreds of people surrounded him in a moment, their faces wearing the deepest concern. Two policemen got into the circle and pressed back the crowd of people wanting to help. A newsboy slipped one of his papers beneath Raggles' elbow, where it lay on the muddy pavement. A brisk young man with a notebook was asking for names.

A bell clanged importantly, and an ambulance cleared an opening through the crowd. A cool surgeon said, "How do you feel, old man?" The princess of silks and satins wiped a red drop or two from Raggles' head.

"Me?" said Raggles, with an angelic smile, "I feel fine."

He had found the heart of his new city.

In three days they let him leave his bed for the convalescent ward in the hospital. He had been there an hour when the attendants heard sounds of a fight. They found that Raggles had assaulted and hit another patient.

"What's all this about?" asked the head nurse.

"He was speaking badly about me town," said Raggles.

"What town?" asked the nurse.

"Noo York," said Raggles.

READING REVIEW

1. Why might some readers today be offended by O. Henry's description of cities?
2. (a) What do you think was the main idea of O. Henry's story? (b) Do you agree or disagree with it? Explain.

An immigrant family does piece work at home.

163 New York: Another View

Although cities held great attractions for many Americans, the ugliness and the problems caused by rapid growth and by too many people could not be hidden. All large cities had slum areas, where people lived crowded together in dirty, foul-smelling dwellings. Many of these dwellings were airless and without plumbing.

In New York City thousands of people lived crowded together in such run-down tenements. Many of these tenement-dwellers died of disease and lack of proper food. These conditions in city slums alarmed many people. One of them, Jacob Riis, a newspaper reporter, wrote about slum neighborhoods in New York City and took pictures of the conditions there. This selection is from his most famous book, *How the Other Half Lives*, written in an effort to improve such conditions.

READING FOCUS

1. What was life in a tenement like, according to Riis' description?
2. Why were living conditions in such tenements especially hard on children?

There are tenements everywhere. Suppose we look into one on Cherry Street. Be a little careful, please! The hall is dark and you might fall over the children pitching pennies back there. Not that it would hurt them. Kicks and punches are their daily diet. They have little else. Here, where the hall turns into complete darkness, is a step, and another, and another. A flight of stairs. You can feel your way if you cannot see it. Stifling? Yes! What do you expect. All the fresh air that ever enters these stairs comes from the hall door that is forever slamming, and from the windows of dark bedrooms.

That was a woman filling her pail you just bumped against. The sinks are in the hallway, so that all the tenants may get to them—and all smell horrible in the summer. Hear the pump squeak! It is the lullaby of tenement-house babies. During the summer, when a thousand thirsty throats want a cooling drink in this block, the pump is worked in vain. But

―――――――――――――――

Adapted from Jacob Riis, How the Other Half Lives.

the saloon, whose open door you passed in the hall, is always there. The smell of it has followed you up.

Here is a door. Listen! That short hacking cough, that tiny, helpless cry—what do they mean? They mean that the soiled bow of white you saw on the door downstairs [when someone died, a bow was hung on the door—black for an adult, white for a child] will have another story to tell—oh, a sadly familiar story—before the day ends. The child is dying with measles. With half a chance it might have lived. But it had none. That dark bedroom killed it.

"It was took all of a sudden," says the mother, smoothing the little body with trembling hands. There is no unkindness in the rough voice of the man in overalls who sits by the window grimly smoking a clay pipe, while he watches his child die, bitter as his words sound: "Hush, Mary! If we cannot keep the baby, need we complain—such as we?"

"Such as we!" What if the words ring in your ears as you grope your way up the stairs and down from floor to floor, listening to the sounds behind the closed doors—some of quarreling, some of coarse songs, more of cursing. They are true. When the summer heat comes with its suffering, its meaning is more terrible than words can tell. Come over here. Step carefully over this baby—it is a baby, in spite of its rags and dirt—under these iron bridges called fire escapes. They are loaded down, despite the warnings of the firemen, with broken household goods, with washtubs and barrels, which no one could climb over to escape from a fire.

This gap between dingy brick walls is the yard. That strip of smoke-colored sky up there is the heaven of these people. Do you wonder that the name does not attract them to the churches? That baby's parents live in the back tenement here. This tenement is much like the one in front we just left, only fouler and darker. A hundred thousand people lived in back tenements in New York last year.

What sort of answer, do you think, would these tenement-dwellers give to the question, "Is life worth living?"

READING REVIEW

1. What were the worst features of tenements, as Riis described them?
2. Name two effects they had on children who lived in them.

3. Why do you think Riis wrote his article in such strong terms? Cite evidence from your textbook to support your answer.

164 How Much Progress for Women?

In 1876 Americans celebrated their centennial. One important feature of this celebration of the nation's first one hundred years was the Philadelphia Centennial Exposition. This huge exposition glorified human achievements and progress in many fields. However, there was at least one group of Americans who were not happy with the progress they had made. At this time, American women were still struggling to gain the right to vote and to be considered as social equals. In this selection Elizabeth Cady Stanton, a leader in the women's rights movement, told about the Woman's Pavilion, or building, at the Exposition.

READING FOCUS

1. What were Elizabeth Cady Stanton's objections to the Woman's Pavilion?
2. In Stanton's view, what were women's most fitting contributions to the Centennial Exposition?

The Woman's Pavilion on the centennial grounds was an afterthought, as religious philosophers claim woman herself to have been. The women of the country, after having contributed nearly $100,000 to the centennial, found that no provision had been made for the separate exhibition of their work. The centennial board then decided to raise funds to build a separate building, to be known as the Woman's Pavilion. It covered an acre of ground, and was built at a cost of $30,000—a small sum in comparison with the money which had been raised by women and spent on the other buildings.

The Pavilion was no true exhibit of woman's abilities. Few women are, as yet, owners of the businesses which their work makes profitable. Cotton factories, in which thousands of women work, are owned by men. The shoe

Adapted from Elizabeth Cady Stanton, Eighty Years and More.

business, in some branches of which women are doing more than half the work, is under the ownership of men. Rich embroideries from India, rugs of downy softness from Turkey, the muslin fabric of India, Waltham watches (whose finest mechanical work is done by women), and ten thousand other industries found no place in the pavilion. Said United States Commissioner Meeker of Colorado, "Woman's work makes up three fourths of the exposition; it is scattered through every building. Take it away, and there would be no exposition."

But this pavilion did one good service for the woman by showing her capabilities as an engineer. The boiler, which provided the force for operating the pavilion, was under the care of a young Canadian girl, Miss Allison. She had loved machinery from childhood, and had spent much time in her father's large mills. When she was chosen to run the pavilion machinery, it caused much opposition. It was said that the committee would, some day, find the pavilion blown to bits; that a woman engineer would spend her time reading novels instead of watching the steam gauge; that the idea was impractical. But Miss Allison soon proved both her abilities and the falseness of these statements by taking her place in the engine room and managing its workings with perfect ease. She declared that the work was cleaner, more pleasant, and much less tiring than cooking over a kitchen stove. "Since I have had to earn my own living," she said, "I have never done work I like so well. Teaching school is much harder, and one is not paid so well." She was confident that she could manage the engines of an ocean steamer. There were thousands of small engines in use in various parts of the country, she said. There was no reason why women should not be employed to manage them, following the profession of engineer as a regular business.

But the Woman's Pavilion would have been truly historic if some displays had hung upon its walls. These displays might have included the yearly protest of Harriet K. Hunt against taxation without representation. Another might have been the legal papers served upon the Smith sisters for their refusal to pay taxes while unrepresented. Still another might have been papers issued by the city of Worcester for the forced sale of the house and lands of Abby Kelly Foster, an abolitionist, because she re-

Elizabeth Cady Stanton

fused to pay taxes without representation. With these should have been exhibited framed copies of all the laws bearing unjustly upon women—those which rob her of her name, her earnings, her property, her children, her person. Another exhibit might have included the legal papers in the case of Susan B. Anthony, who was tried and fined for claiming her right to vote under the Fourteenth Amendment; and the decision of Mr. Justice Miller in the case of Myra Bradwell, denying national protection for woman's civil rights.

Woman's most fitting contributions to the Centennial Exposition would have been these protests, laws, and decisions, which show her political slavery. But all this was displayed in rooms outside the exposition grounds, where the National Woman's Suffrage Association raised its flag and made its protests.

To many thoughtful people it seemed unreasonable for women to complain of injustice in this free land, among such universal rejoicing. When the majority of women are seemingly happy, it is natural to suppose that the discontent of the minority is the result of unfortunate individual circumstances. But the history of the world shows that the great majority, in every generation, just accept the conditions into which they are born. Those who demand larger liberties are always a small minority, whose claims are made fun of and ignored. We would honor any Chinese woman who claimed the right to her own feet so that she could walk; the Hindu widow who refused to climb upon the funeral fire of her husband; and the Turkish woman who threw off her veil and left the harem.

Why not honor as well the intelligent minority of American women who protest against the false disabilities by which their freedom is limited and their development stopped? That only a few protest against the injustice of long-established laws and customs does not disprove the fact of the oppressions. The satisfaction of the many, if real, only proves their lack of concern. That a majority of the women of the United States accept, without protest, the disabilities which grow out of the fact that they cannot vote is simply an evidence of their ignorance and cowardice. The minority who demand a higher political standing clearly prove their greater intelligence and wisdom.

READING REVIEW

1. According to Stanton, what one good service for women did this pavilion provide?
2. What evidence did she offer to prove that the Woman's Pavilion was an afterthought?
3. What exhibits did she suggest should have been included in the pavilion to make it a "truly historic" exhibit?
4. How did Stanton describe the efforts of some American women to improve their lives?
5. If a Woman's Pavilion were set up today, what kinds of exhibits should it contain to show the contributions of women to society?

165 A Close-Up of Mark Twain

Two important writers of the late 1800's were Mark Twain and William Dean Howells. Twain described the new industrial age in his book *The Gilded Age,* but he was even more popular as a local-color writer who captured the frontier spirit and humor of the West. Howells was famous for his realistic writing. His best-known book, *Silas Lapham,* told about the lives of some newly rich Americans.

Howells and Twain were close friends. And when Twain died in 1910, Howells wrote a tribute to the man he called "the Lincoln of our literature." Although he called it *My Mark Twain,* he noted that he always called Twain by his real name, Samuel Clemens, because his pen name "seemed always somehow to mask him from my personal sense." In this selection, Howells spoke of visiting Twain at his home in Hartford, Connecticut.

READING FOCUS

1. Where did Twain do most of his writing?
2. What did Howells and Twain have in common?

Clemens and his architect had planned a luxurious study over the library in his new house. But as his children grew older, it was given to them to use as a schoolroom. He then used the room above his stable. There we used to talk together until he discovered that he preferred to use the large billiard room at the top of his house as a place to write and meet friends. It was pretty cold up there in the early spring and late fall weather. But by lighting all the gas burners and building a fire, we could keep it well above freezing. Here he wrote many of his tales and sketches, and for all I know, some of his books.

We took special pleasure in looking out of the high windows at the pretty Hartford landscape, and down to the tops of the trees covering the hillside near his house. We agreed that there was a charm in trees seen from such a point of view. He had not been a country boy or, rather, a village boy, for nothing. Nothing that nature can offer the young was lost on him. We were natives of the same vast Mississippi Valley. Missouri and Ohio were close enough so that we had learned many of the same ways of talking. I had outgrown mine because I read more, but I gladly recognized the phrases which he used for their lasting juiciness.

His natural use of words formed the backbone of his style. I may have read more, but he was always reading some vital book. It might be some out-of-the-way book, but it had

_____

Adapted from My Mark Twain *by William Dean Howells.*

the root of the human matter in it. Perhaps it was a book of great trials, an autobiography, a history, or a narrative of travel—something that showed him life at first-hand. As I remember, he did not care much for fiction, and he had certain distinct dislikes. One was for my dear and honored favorite, Jane Austen. As for plays, he hated the theater, and said he would rather add a list of numbers than follow a plot on the stage. Generally, I think his pleasure in poetry was not great, and I do not believe he cared much for the usual accepted masterpieces of literature. He liked to find out good things and great things for himself. Sometimes he would discover these in a masterpiece new to him alone.

Of all the literary men I have known he was the most unliterary in his background and manner. I do not know whether he knew any Latin, but I think not. German he knew pretty well, and enough Italian to have fun with it. But he used English in all its various forms as if it were native to his own air, as if it had come up out of American, out of Missourian ground. His style was what we know, for good and for bad. But his manner, if I may separate the two, was as entirely his own as if no one had ever written before. He was not enslaved to the consecutiveness in writing which the rest of us are chained to. That is, he wrote as he thought, as all people think, without sequence, without an eye to what went before or should come after. If something occurred to him beyond or beside what he was saying, he put it down on his page, and made it as much at home there as its nature would allow. Then, when he was through with this idea, he would go back to his original thoughts, and keep on with what he had been talking about. He followed this manner in the construction of sentences, and the arrangement of his chapters.

I helped him with a Library of Humor, which he once edited. When I had done my work according to tradition, with authors, times, and topics carefully studied in order, he tore it all apart, and threw in the pieces wherever he wanted to at the moment. He was right. We were not making a textbook, but a book for the pleasure rather than the instruction of the reader. He did not see why the principle on which he built his own tales and novels should not apply to it. On minor points he was, beyond any author I have known, without favorite phrases or pet words. He also

Mark Twain

was not against repeating words many times. If a certain word served him better than a substitute, he would use it on a page as many times as he chose.

READING REVIEW
1. What formed the backbone of Twain's writing style?
2. In two or three sentences, summarize the things that Howells admired most about Twain's writing.

166 Small-Town Pleasures

During the new industrial age, American customs and ways of life were changing. The rapid growth of industry and cities caused great changes in the way Americans acted, thought, and lived. The old customs gave way to the new, in recreation just as they did in everything else. Organized sports took the place of the simpler games of frontier days. The circus and "Wild West" show were new and popular forms of entertainment.

In small towns, however, recreation continued to follow the more traditional ways. Here, people played games rather than watched them, and they attended picnics and fairs. In this selection, writer Albert Britt, born in 1874, talked about his

247

A county fair in Indiana

boyhood on a farm in southern Illinois and the
pastimes he enjoyed.

READING FOCUS

1. What were the main amusements of Albert
   Britt's youth?
2. How were the forms of amusement enjoyed by
   Britt different from those enjoyed by people
   today?

Sunday was a day of rest for older people, and
the place to rest was a comfortable chair in-
doors. Only extreme heat could drive them outside to soft grass and the shade of convenient
trees. After I had become a city person, I
thought of a walk in the woods or through the
fields as a form of recreation and my divorce
from the farm was complete. Fields and woods
were for work and not for idle walking by
grown people.

Even mild games were thought to be beneath the dignity of adults, although croquet
was permissible. Tennis was unknown to us,
although it was creeping into the towns. There
was one exception in the case of tennis. Bill
Adcock, a prosperous farmer, liked what he

heard about this game and came home from
town one day with a full set of the necessary
equipment, net, rackets, and balls. My brother-
in-law Dan saw it and liked the game but not
enough to spend money for the equipment. A
long fishnet, which he tied himself, made a fair
net. He could make his own rackets, which he
did—wooden paddles of at least the right shape
and size. Balls of course he could not make, so
he had to buy them. The result was a game
that was a mockery of lawn tennis, even as it
was played in that early day. But Dan had an
idea. Paddle tennis is with us today.

Of course, being good Americans, we played
baseball, but no games on Sunday, although
batting and fielding practice were allowed.
Neighborhood baseball rose and fell as the
number of active young men varied. There
were two or three seasons when we Tylerville
players thought rather well of ourselves because of a young farmer nearby who could
manage to pitch a curve ball. Unfortunately,
his control was uncertain and our dream of a
township championship never got to first base.

Diamonds were set up whenever there was
a large enough stretch of level pastureland to
give the players at least a chance to field the
ball, although I remember one diamond where
a long hit into right field had a better than
even chance of rolling down a slope into a creek
at the bottom. There were bitter arguments

From An America That Was *by Albert Britt.*

over the scoring of such a hit. Some held the theory that a hit was a hit. Others maintained that such a performance was an act of God and not a home run. Umpires, when there were any, generally followed the rule of safety-first by balancing an outrageously wrong decision in favor of team A by an equally absurd error in behalf of team B at the first opportunity. There were few pitchers' battles, and scorers were kept busy. Thirty-two to twenty-five was thought of as a close game and was entirely satisfactory to those who were watching.

A small, coal-mining community ten or fifteen miles [16 or 24 kilometers] away in the next county went in strong for baseball and turned out a team that could give a busy afternoon to towns two or three times their size. Wherever they went, a crowd of rooters went with them, not only to cheer but also to bet. Those were good times for coal miners and pay was high by our standards. The rooters were well supplied with money. In the early stages of the game, the bettors walked up and down in front of the spectators showing their money and looking for customers. If there were local laws against public betting, they never applied inside the baseball field when the miners were playing.

When scores were close and hits were important, men who had bet money on the game pleadingly offered "A dollar for a hit!" and if a lucky batter got a hit he gathered in a small harvest of silver dollars from the dust at his feet. These miner-sportsmen were way over our heads and we watched them in silent awe and admiration.

Our money operations were limited to occasional collections to buy new balls. Players supplied their own bats and gloves, although most of us played barehanded. Charlie Glass was our most admired catcher because of his willingness to stand close behind the bat without mitt, mask, shinguard, or chest protector. It was not our courage but our lack of money that fixed the limit of our equipment. League balls cost a dollar or more, and a lost ball might throw us into bankruptcy. Unless it was lost, a ball stayed in play as long as the stitching held.

Picnics were favorite summer affairs, usually requiring an anniversary or some celebration for an excuse. Farmers were not likely to go on picnics for the mere joy of spending time with Nature. We were in close touch with Na-ture twelve months of the year and knew it for what it was, a cold-blooded creature who could deal blessing or blight with equal indifference. The Fourth of July was always a good time for a picnic, giving opportunity for a patriotic display and lots of good food at the same time. There were Sunday School picnics. Old Settlers' meetings, country school picnics, and sometimes political picnics.

A big social event was the county fair, which was usually held in early September. That was the week when rain was a catastrophe, however much it might be needed. The fair was a combination livestock show and exhibition of farm machinery and farm products, fruit, vegetables, grain, jams, jellies, preserves, pickles, rows of canned fruits from farm kitchens. Blue, red, and white ribbons, emblems of awards, were proudly displayed by the happy winners. There were side shows too—the fat, tattooed, or bearded lady, a snake charmer with a snake wound around her, the grisly bones found in a cellar somewhere that bore witness to a mysterious murder. In the afternoon there were running and trotting races.

One popular feature was the balloon lift. This always drew a crowd, from the building of the fire that heated the air to lift the big balloon to the moment when the daring pilot cut loose with his parachute and floated down, usually to land in the middle of a cornfield half a mile away.

For country people the fair was another and bigger picnic with fried chicken, lemon pie, and endless visiting. Farmers from all over the county met and gossiped around the pens of fat hogs or prize-winning cattle, and women made envious comments on the blue-ribbon peaches or the excellence of a patchwork quilt that the judges had ignored. There were exhibits of work done in country schools. One year our district walked off with some kind of ribbon. The reason for our achievement is forgotten, but it is certain that samples of my penmanship were not included in the exhibit.

READING REVIEW

1. List two amusements of Albert Britt's youth.
2. How did the way he played baseball differ from the way baseball is played today?
3. Which of the activities that Britt described are still enjoyed today?

UNIT EIGHT READINGS

The Arrival Of Reform

CHAPTER 26 The Square Deal and the New Freedom
(1897–1920)

167 How Tammany Hall Operated

By the end of the 1800's corrupt political machines controlled the governments of many large cities. Tammany Hall in New York City was one of the most powerful of these political machines. It stayed in power through graft, bought the votes of immigrants through favors, and set up a "balanced ticket" so that a member of each major ethnic group held a top position in city government. An important politician in Tammany Hall for many years was George Washington Plunkitt.

In 1905 a young newspaper reporter, William L. Riordan, wrote a book about Plunkitt. The book included an account, in Plunkitt's own words, on how he became a politician and a millionaire.

A cartoonist's impression of Tammany Hall

READING FOCUS
1. What was the basic philosophy on which Tammany Hall operated?
2. Why was Plunkitt so successful?

Everybody is talking these days about Tammany people growing rich on graft, but nobody thinks of drawing the distinction between honest graft and dishonest graft. There's all the difference in the world between the two. Yes, many of our people have grown rich in politics. I have myself. I've made a big fortune out of the game, and I'm getting richer every day. But I've not gone in for dishonest graft—blackmailing gamblers, saloon-keepers, and so on. And neither have any of the people who have made big fortunes in politics.

There's an honest graft, and I'm an example of how it works. I might sum up the whole thing by saying: "I seen my opportunities and I took 'em."

Just let me explain by examples. My party's in power in the city, and it's going to undertake a lot of public improvements. Well, I'm told ahead of time, say, that they're going to lay out a new park at a certain place.

I see my opportunity and I take it. I go to that place and buy up all the land I can in the neighborhood. Then the board of this or that makes its plan public, and there is a rush to get my land, which nobody wanted before.

Ain't it perfectly honest to charge a good price and make a profit on my investment and foresight? Of course, it is. Well, that's honest graft.

Adapted from William L Riordan, Plunkitt of Tammany Hall.

Or supposing it's a new bridge they're going to build. I find out and I buy as much property as I can that has to be used for the road approaches to the bridge. I sell the property at my own price later on and drop some more money in the bank.

Wouldn't you? It's like looking ahead in Wall Street or in the coffee or cotton market. It's honest graft and I'm looking for it every day in the year. I will tell you frankly that I've got a lot of it, too.

I'll tell you of another case. They were going to fix up a big park. I learned of it and went looking about for land in that neighborhood. I could get nothing at a bargain except a big piece of swamp, but I bought it right away and held on to it. What happened was just what I counted on. They couldn't make the park complete without Plunkitt's swamp, and so they had to pay a good price for it. Anything dishonest in that?

I don't own a dishonest dollar. If my worst enemy was given the job of writing an epitaph for my grave marker he couldn't do more than write:

"George W. Plunkitt. He Seen His Opportunities, and He Took 'Em."

What's important in holding your grip on your district is to go right down among the poor families and help them in the different ways they need help. I've got a regular system for doing this.

If there's a fire on Ninth, Tenth, or Eleventh Avenue, for example, any hour of the day or night, I'm usually there with some of my election district captains as soon as the fire engines arrive. If a family is burned out, I don't ask whether they are Republicans or Democrats. I don't refer them to the Charity Organization Society, which would investigate their case in a month or two and decide they were worthy of help about the time they are dead from starvation. I just get a place for them to live, buy clothes for them if their clothes were burned up, and fix them up till they get things running again. It's philanthropy, but it's politics, too—mighty good politics. Who can tell how many votes one of these fires brings me? The poor are the most grateful people in the world, and, let me tell you, they have more friends in their neighborhoods than the rich have in theirs.

If there's a family in my district that needs help, I know it before the charitable societies do. Me and my men are the first to help. I have a special group of people to look up such cases. The result is that the poor look up to George W. Plunkitt as a father, they come to him when they're in trouble, and they don't forget him on election day.

READING REVIEW

1. What did Plunkitt mean when he said, "I seen my opportunities and I took 'em"?
2. What methods did Plunkitt use to gain the support of his electorate?
3. (a) According to Plunkitt, what was the difference between honest and dishonest graft? (b) Do you think politicians today make this same distinction? Cite evidence from your textbook to support your opinion.

168 A Muckraker's Attack on City Corruption

By 1900 many Americans felt that something had to be done to reform American government and American life. This push toward reform was known as the Progressive movement. Some of the most important supporters of the Progressive movement were the writers and newspaper reporters who were making Americans aware of how widespread corruption in government and abuses of power had become in the United States.

These crusading, reform-minded writers were disliked by some Americans, including Theodore Roosevelt. In a speech in 1906, Roosevelt described the writers by referring to a character in the book *Pilgrim's Progress*—"the man with the muckrake." One writer, Lincoln Steffens, proudly adopted the term "muckraker" to refer to anyone who wanted to uncover, or rake up, corruption. Soon the term became very popular.

Steffens became famous because of his magazine articles on corruption in American cities. The following selections are from his book *The Shame of the Cities*.

READING FOCUS

1. Why, according to Steffens, did business leaders make bad politicians?
2. How did he propose to eliminate corruption?

Adapted from Lincoln Steffens, The Shame of the Cities.

There is hardly a government office from United States Senator down to alderman in any part of the country to which some business leader has not been elected. Yet politics remains corrupt and government pretty bad. Business leaders have failed in politics as they have in good citizenship. Why?

Because politics is business. That's what's the matter with everything—art, literature, religion, journalism, law, medicine. They're all business, and all as you see them.

Make politics a sport, as they do in England, or a profession, as they do in Germany. Then we'll have—well, something else than we have now—if we want it, which is another question. But don't try to reform politics with the banker, the lawyer, and the merchant. For they are business people and there are two things that make it very difficult for them to achieve reform: One is that they are different from, but no better than, the politicians. The other is that politics is not "their line."

There are exceptions both ways. Many politicians have gone into business and done well. (Tammany ex-mayors, and nearly all the old bosses of Philadelphia, are important financiers in their cities.) Business managers have gone into politics and done well. (Mark Hanna, for example.) The politician is a businessman with a specialty. When a businessman in some other line learns the business of politics, he is a politician, and there is not much reform left in him. Consider the United States Senate, and believe me.

The commercial spirit is the spirit of profit, not patriotism; of credit, not honor; of individual gain, not national prosperity; of trade, not principle.

We cheat our government and we let our leaders rob it. We let them persuade and bribe our power away from us. True, they pass strict laws for us, but we let them pass bad laws too,

Lincoln Steffens

giving away public property in exchange. Our good, and often impossible, laws we allow to be used for oppression and blackmail. And what can we say? We break our own laws and rob our own government—the woman at the tax office, the lyncher with his rope, and the captain of industry with his bribe and his rebate. The spirit of graft and of lawlessness is the American spirit.

The people are not innocent. This will not be news to many observers. It was to me. When I set out to describe the corrupt systems of certain typical cities, I meant to show simply how the people were deceived and betrayed. But in the very first study—St. Louis—the startling truth showed that corruption was not merely political. It was financial, commercial, and social. Its offshoots were so complex and far-reaching that one mind could hardly grasp them all.

The corruption of St. Louis came from the top. The best citizens—the merchants and big financiers—ruled the town, and they ruled it well. They set out to overtake Chicago. The commercial and industrial war between these two cities was a picturesque and dramatic spectacle such as is seen only in our country. Business leaders were not just merchants, and politicians were not just grafters. The two kinds of citizens got together and used the power of banks, railroads, factories, the prestige of the city, and the spirit of its citizens to gain business and population. And it was a close race. Chicago, having a head start, always led. But St. Louis had spirit, intelligence, and tremendous energy. It pressed Chicago hard. It excelled in a sense of civic beauty and good government. There are those who still think it might have won. But a change occurred. Public spirit became private spirit, and public enterprise became private greed.

Along about 1890, public franchises and privileges were sought, not only for legitimate profit and common convenience, but also for loot. Taking only slight but always selfish interest in the public councils, leading merchants and financiers misused politics. Other less important and even less honest men, catching the smell of corruption, rushed into the Municipal Assembly, drove out the remaining respectable leaders, and sold the city—its streets, its wharves, its markets, and all that it had—to the now greedy business people and bribers.

So gradually has this taken place that these same citizens hardly realize it. Go to St. Louis and you will find the habit of civic pride in them. They still boast. The visitor is told of the wealth of the residents, of the financial strength of the banks, and of the growing importance of the industries. Yet the visitor sees poorly paved streets full of garbage, and dirty or mud-filled alleys. He passes a broken-down firetrap of a building crowded with the sick, and learns that it is the city hospital.

In Pittsburgh graft falls into four classes: franchises, public contracts, vice, and public funds. There was, besides these, a lot of other loot—public supplies, public lighting, and the water supply. But I cannot go into these. Neither can I stop to discuss the details of the system by which public funds, earning no interest, were put in favored banks from which the city borrowed money at a high interest rate. All these things were managed well within the law. That was the great principle underlying the Pittsburgh plan.

The vice graft, for example, was not blackmail as it is in New York and most other cities. It is a legitimate business, conducted not by the police, but in an orderly fashion by syndicates. The leader of one of the parties at the last election said it was worth $250,000 a year. I saw a man who was laughed at for offering $17,500 for the slot-machine concession. He was told that it was leased for much more. "Speakeasies" [unlicensed drinking places] have to pay off so many people that even though they may earn $500 or more in 24 hours, their owners often just about make a living.

We Americans may have failed. We may be selfish and influenced by gain. Democracy with us may be impossible and corruption inevitable, but these articles, if they have proved nothing else, have shown that we can stand the truth. There is pride in the character of American citizenship. This pride may be a power in the land. So this record of shame and yet of self-respect, disgraceful confession, yet a declaration of honor, is dedicated, in all good faith, to the accused—to all the citizens of all the cities in the United States.

READING REVIEW

1. **(a)** What were two reasons Steffens gave to support his viewpoint that business leaders made bad politicians? **(b)** Do you think this premise is applicable to today's society? Why or why not?
2. Whom did Steffens blame for corruption?
3. Using information from your text, describe the role that "muckrakers" played in the Progressive movement.

169 Black Americans and Progressive Reforms

Although the reforms of the progressive movement brought important benefits to most Americans, the movement did little to improve the lives of black Americans.

When Theodore Roosevelt became President, many black Americans expected that they would be included in Roosevelt's progressive reforms. They remembered his praise of black troops during the Spanish-American War. They recalled how he stirred the hopes of black Americans by inviting Booker T. Washington to dinner at the White House and by condemning lynching. Yet during Roosevelt's Presidency, the earlier hopes of black Americans were not realized. Roosevelt and most progressive reformers ignored the need to improve conditions among blacks. In the following selection, a visiting English writer, H. G. Wells, told of the plight of black Americans.

READING FOCUS

1. What was the basic question that Wells asked about blacks for which he had received no answer?
2. Why did Wells admire blacks?

In regard to the colored population, just as in regard to the great and growing numbers of Jews, and the growing numbers of Roman Catholics, I have tried time after time to get some answer from Americans to the question that is to me the most obvious. "Your grandchildren and the grandchildren of these people will have to live in this country side by side. Do you think—do you believe it possible—that under the increasing pressure of population and competition, they will be living then in just the same relations that you and these people are living in now? If you do not, then what relations do you suggest should exist between them?"

Adapted from H. G. Wells, The Future in America.

It is not too much to say that I have never once had the beginning of an answer to this question. Usually one is told with great seriousness that the problem of color is one of the most difficult that we have to consider. The conversation then breaks up into long stories and unfavorable statements about black people.

Whatever America has to show in heroic living today, I doubt if it can show anything finer than the quality of will, the constant effort hundreds of black people are making today to live blamelessly, honorably, and patiently. They get for themselves what scraps of refinement, learning, and beauty they can. They keep their hold on a civilization they are begrudged and denied. They do it not for themselves only but for all their race. Each educated colored person is an ambassador to civilization. They know they have a handicap. Yet each one, I like to think, is aware of being a representative, fighting against injustice, insult, and the unspeakable meannesses of bigoted enemies. Every one of them who remains decent and honorable does a little to beat that opposition down.

But what patience the Negroes need! They cannot ever show contempt. They must regard as superior those whose daily conduct is clear evidence of moral inferiority. Negroes must go to and fro self-controlled, without all the equalities that the great flag of America proclaims—that flag for which black people fought and died. Negroes must take second place to the strangers who pour in to share the nation's wealth, strangers ignorant even of its language. That Negroes must do—and wait. The Welsh, the Irish, the Poles, the white South, and the Jews may have grievances and complain aloud. Negroes must keep still. The others may be hysterical, revengeful, threatening; their wrongs excuse them. For Negroes there is no excuse. And of all the races upon earth, which has suffered such wrongs as this Negro race? Those people who scorn them have sinned against them beyond all measure.

No, I can't help idealizing the dark submissive figure of the Negro in this spectacle of America. The Negro seems to me to sit waiting—and waiting with a marvelous and constant patience—for finer understanding and a nobler time.

READING REVIEW

1. **(a)** What was the important question that Wells asked about black people? **(b)** What kinds of answers did he receive?
2. Why did Wells admire black Americans?
3. According to Wells, what future did the black person have?
4. **(a)** What role did Wells see the educated black person playing? **(b)** Do you agree or disagree with the view expressed by Wells? Explain your answer.

A sharecropper family in Virginia, 1900

170   A Muckraker's Attack on Big Business

The muckrakers told Americans of the many abuses in their society. Their books and articles made many American readers deeply concerned about the consequences of the great industrial growth and business consolidation then taking place. The muckrakers brought many of the unfair business methods and practices of large industries to the attention of the public.

Probably the most famous of all muckraking reports about American industry was Ida Tarbell's *History of the Standard Oil Company.* In this series of newspaper articles, which later became a book, Tarbell exposed the practices and policies of that giant monopoly.

READING FOCUS

1. What practices have made Standard Oil a monopoly?
2. What solutions did Ida Tarbell suggest to eliminate monopolistic practices?

The profits of the present Standard Oil Company are enormous. For five years the dividends have been averaging about $45 million a year. When we remember that probably one third of this great yearly profit goes into the hands of John D. Rockefeller, that probably 90 percent of it goes to the few people who make up the "Standard Oil family," the Standard Oil Company becomes a much more serious public matter than it was in 1872, when it began to take over the oil business.

For, consider what must be done with the greater part of this $45 million. It must be invested. The oil business does not need it. It has money for all of its ventures. The money must go into other industries. Naturally, these other interests will be connected to oil. One such interest will be gas, and we have the Standard Oil people steadily taking over the gas interests of the country. Another will be railroads, for all industries depend on transportation. Besides, railroads are one of the great consumers of oil products and must be kept in line as buyers. So we have the directors of the Standard Oil Company acting as directors on nearly all of the great railways of the country. They will go into steel, and we have Mr. Rockefeller's great holdings in the steel trust. They will go into banking, and we have the National City Bank and its connected institutions in New York City and Boston, as well as a long chain running throughout the country.

No one who has followed this history can expect that these holdings will be bought on a rising market. Buy cheap and sell high is a rule of business. When you control enough money and enough banks, you can always work it out so that a stock you want will be temporarily cheap. No value is destroyed for you—only for the original owner. This has been one of Mr. Rockefeller's most successful maneuvers in doing business. The result is that the Standard Oil Company is probably in the strongest financial position of any organization in the world. And every year its position grows stronger, for every year another $45 million is poured into taking over the property most essential to keeping and broadening its power.

Adapted from Ida M. Tarbell, History of the Standard Oil Company.

Ida Tarbell

In spite of the Interstate Commerce Commission, the crucial question is still that of transportation. Until the people of the United States have solved the question of free and equal transportation, there will always be a trust question. As long as it is possible for a company to own the carrier on which a great natural product depends for transportation, and to use this carrier to limit a competitor's supply or to cut it off entirely, it is foolish to talk about constitutional amendments limiting trusts. As long as the Standard Oil Company can control transportation, as it does today, it will remain master of the oil industry. The people of the United States will pay a high price for oil because of their indifference in regard to transportation. And they will see an increasing amount of natural resources and transportation systems owned by the Standard Oil monopoly.

If all we suffered was limited business opportunities for a few hundred men and women and a constantly rising price for refined oil, the case would be serious enough. But there is a more serious side to it. The ethical cost of all this is the main concern. We are a commercial people. We cannot boast of our arts, our crafts, our culture. Our pride is the wealth we produce. As a consequence, business success is holy. We justify practically any methods to achieve it.

Very often people who admit the facts, who see that Mr. Rockefeller has employed force and fraud to obtain his ends, justify him by declaring, "It's business." That is, "It's business" has come to be a legitimate excuse for hard dealing, sly tricks, special privileges. It is a common enough thing to hear people arguing that the ordinary laws of morality do not apply in business.

Now, if the Standard Oil Company were the only company in the country guilty of the practices which have given it monopolistic power, this story never would have been written. But it is simply the most outstanding example of what can be done by these practices. The methods it uses with such skill, constancy, and secrecy are used by all sorts of business people, from corner grocers up to bankers. If exposed, they are excused on the ground that this is business. If the point is pushed, frequently the defender of the practice falls back on the Christian doctrine of charity, and points out that we are only human and must allow for each other's weaknesses! If this excuse were carried to its logical conclusion, our business people would be weeping on each other's shoulders over human weakness, while they picked each other's pockets.

And what are we going to do about it? For it is *our* business. We, the people of the United States, and nobody else, must cure whatever is wrong in the industrial situation, typified by this account of the growth of the Standard Oil Company. It is clear that our first task is to obtain free and equal transportation privileges by railroad, pipeline, and waterway. It is not an easy matter. It is one which may require severe methods. But the whole system of rate discrimination has been nothing but violence. Those who have profited by it cannot complain if curing the evils they have caused brings hardship to them. At all events, until the transportation matter is settled, and settled right, the monopolistic trust will be with us, a barrier to our free efforts.

As for the ethical side, there is no cure but in an increasing scorn of unfair play—an increasing sense that a thing won by breaking the rules of the game is not worth winning. The business person who fights to obtain special privileges, to crowd competitors off the track by unfair methods, should be treated just the way we treat the doctor or lawyer who is "unprofessional" or the athlete who abuses the rules. Then we shall have gone a long way toward making business a fit profession for our young people.

READING REVIEW

1. According to Ida Tarbell, how were the large profits of the Standard Oil trust being used?
2. (a) What was the key to Standard Oil's monopoly? (b) What evidence did Tarbell present to support her viewpoint?
3. What did Tarbell believe was the "ethical cost" of the oil industry monopoly?
4. List two solutions Tarbell suggested to break Standard Oil's monopoly.

171 On Trusts and Business Reform

President Theodore Roosevelt was a skilled politician whose bold acts and personality captured the imagination of Americans. His efforts to regulate the trusts made many Americans think of him as the leader of the progressive movement. In fact, he was less a crusader than many other progressive reformers. He believed that reform had to come slowly and had to be carefully planned.

However, Roosevelt did make an enormous contribution to the progressive movement. His popularity and his support of many of the progressive aims helped to publicize the movement and gained it widespread support. The following selection is from Roosevelt's first annual message to Congress in 1901.

READING FOCUS

1. Why did most Americans feel trusts were harmful?
2. Why did President Roosevelt urge caution in dealing with corporations?
3. What business reforms did President Roosevelt advocate?

The tremendous and highly complex industrial development which went on during the last half of the 1800's brings us face to face, at the beginning of the 1900's, with very serious social problems. Old laws and old customs were once quite enough to regulate the accumulation and distribution of wealth. They are no longer enough.

The growth of great industrial centers has meant a startling increase, not only in wealth itself, but in the number of very large individual and corporate fortunes. The creation of these great corporate fortunes has not been due to the tariff, nor to any other governmental action, but to natural causes in the business world, operating in other countries as they operate in our own.

The process has created much opposition, a great part of which is wholly without cause. It is not true that as the rich have grown richer the poor have grown poorer. On the contrary, never before has the average wage-earner,

Adapted from James D. Richardson (comp.), A Compilation of the Messages and Papers of the Presidents, *Vol. X 1789–1902.*

farmer, or small trader been so well-off as in this country at the present time. There have been abuses connected with the accumulation of wealth. Yet a fortune gained in legitimate business can be acquired only when the person doing so brings great benefits to others.

The captains of industry who have built the railway systems across this continent, who have developed our industry, have on the whole done great good to our people. Without them our development could never have taken place. Moreover, we should realize that it is important not to interfere any more than is necessary for the public good with the strong and forceful people upon whom the success of business operations rests.

Another reason for caution in dealing with corporations is to be found in international business. The richest concerns and those managed by the ablest people are naturally those that take the lead in the struggle for commercial supremacy among the nations of the world. America has only just begun to dominate the international business world. It is of the greatest importance that this position not be placed in danger.

Moreover, striking with ignorant violence at the interests of one set of people almost inevitably puts the interests of all in danger. The basic rule in our national life is that, on the whole, and in the long run, we shall go up or down together. Disaster to great business concerns never limits its effects to the people at the top. It spreads throughout, and while it is bad for everybody, it is worst for those farthest down.

All this is true. And yet it is also true that there are real and serious evils. A practical effort must be made to correct them.

There is a widespread belief among the American people that the great corporations known as trusts are harmful to the general welfare. This belief does not spring from a spirit of envy or lack of pride in the great industrial achievements. It does not rest upon ignorance of the fact that a good deal of capital is needed to accomplish great things. It is based upon the sincere belief that combination and concentration should be, not forbidden, but supervised and within reasonable limits controlled. In my judgment this belief is right.

It is no limitation upon property rights or freedom of contract to require that when people receive from the government the privilege of doing business under corporate form, they should be truthful as to the value of the property in which capital is to be invested. Corporations engaged in interstate commerce should be regulated if they harm the public. Great corporations exist only because they are created and safeguarded by our institutions. It is therefore our right and our duty to see that they work in harmony with these institutions.

The first essential in determining how to deal with the great industrial combinations is knowledge of the facts. In the interest of the public, the government should have the right to inspect and examine the workings of the great corporations engaged in interstate business. Publicity is the only sure remedy we now have. What further remedies are needed in the way of governmental regulation, or taxation, can only be determined after publicity has been obtained.

The large corporations, commonly called trusts, though organized in one state, always do business in many states. There is a complete lack of uniformity in the state laws dealing with them.

Therefore, in the interest of all the people, the nation should take over the supervision and regulation of all corporations doing an interstate business. There would be no hardship in such supervision; banks are subject to it, and in their case it is now accepted as a simple matter of course.

When the Constitution was adopted at the end of the 1700's, no human wisdom could foretell the sweeping changes which were to take place by the beginning of the 1900's. At that

President Theodore Roosevelt

time it was accepted as a matter of course that the states were the proper authorities to regulate the comparatively insignificant corporations of the day. The conditions are now wholly different. Wholly different action is called for.

READING REVIEW

1. **(a)** How would you describe Roosevelt's attitude toward the "captains of industry"? **(b)** Why did he recommend caution in dealing with them?
2. **(a)** What was the "widespread belief" among Americans about trusts? **(b)** Did Roosevelt agree with this belief?
3. Name two reforms President Roosevelt felt were necessary to regulate "big business."
4. Do you think Americans today regard trusts as harmful? Why or why not? Cite evidence from your textbook to support your conclusion.

172 The Growing Interest in Conservation

One of Theodore Roosevelt's most important achievements was the interest he helped create in the conservation of America's natural resources. In 1908 he held a White House conference on conservation. At this conference more than a thousand delegates listened to speeches expressing concern over how the nation's resources were being used and suggesting reforms. A few speakers such as George Kunz, a mineralogist, also stressed the need to protect America's natural beauty.

In his speech, from which this selection was taken, Kunz spoke of human beings as having passed through various stages of development—savagery, barbarism, and civilization. His remarks reflected the widely held theory of the time that all peoples had progressed through the same well-defined steps on their way to modern civilization.

READING FOCUS

1. According to Kunz, what was the relationship between preserving the beauty of nature and the development of civilization?
2. Why did he say it was necessary to have government impose regulations about the environment?

The great forces of nature have created the mineral wealth stored beneath the earth. They have carved the hollows and valleys in which our lakes lie and our streams flow. They have lifted up our mountain ranges and have made the soil that feeds our forests and crops. These same forces have made the various features called scenery, which delights the eye, and stirs the imagination. And scenery in turn has affected our movements, our life, and our development. Thus, for many reasons, human history has always been identified with the natural landscape.

In recommending to the conference the protection of American scenery, I deny that there is a conflict between the idea of preserving scenery and the idea of properly using our material resources. Every interest represented in this conference is looking forward to the same goal—the greatest happiness and good for the greatest number of people. That will be reached best by friendly cooperation, by mutual adjustments, and by reasonable concessions when necessary.

The purpose of our organization is to encourage the beautiful without preventing the development of forests, mines, railroads, or water power. But it must not be forgotten that there are many factors in reaching human happiness.

In the lowest status of savagery, when humans are nearest the beasts of the field, hap-

Yosemite National Park

Adapted from George F. Kunz in Proceedings of a Conference of Governors. *Washington: Government Printing Office, 1909.*

piness depends almost exclusively upon satisfying bodily needs. But as we lift ourselves up through the stages of savagery, and through barbarism into civilization, a new element of happiness becomes important. In this rise, with its accompanying intellectual development, our thoughts constantly range farther and farther from the narrow limits of our own bodies for satisfaction. While meeting physical wants is the first necessity, other needs must also be met.

The wholesome pleasure which one obtains from being in nature is a characteristic of our civilization. We cannot get rid of it even if we wanted to. It makes us better, happier, more efficient citizens. It is a fact of human nature to be honestly recognized. It should not be put aside as empty sentimentalism any more than using the physical resources of the land would be held in contempt as too commercial.

Our goal should therefore be to see how closely we can get together so as to join our interests for the common good. It is at this point that we need some judicial power higher than the individual to weigh the merits of conflicting interests. There are occasions, for instance, when the value to the community of damming a given stream at a given place may not be truthfully expressed in dollars and cents. When we balance all considerations, we may find that the location of the dam farther upstream or farther downstream, or on some other stream, or even preventing it from being built, may contribute to the greatest good for the greatest number. Thus, the necessity for regulation by some branch of government representing all interests is apparent. It is proper that the law should regulate the destruction of trees, rocks, river banks, and other notable features of the landscape.

Nothing is more valuable in creating a love of beauty in the average person than the scenic beauty of forests, mountains, and rivers. For this reason, such objects of natural beauty should be carefully guarded against injury or destruction.

READING REVIEW

1. How did Kunz link the appreciation of the beauty of nature and the development of civilization?
2. Why did Kunz believe that some higher judicial power must weigh the merits of "conflicting interests"?

3. **(a)** According to Kunz, what should government do in order to protect the environment for the "common good" of all citizens? **(b)** Do you agree or disagree with Kunz's opinion? Explain your answer.

173 The Birth of the Progressive Party

The summer of 1912 was an exciting time in American politics. After the Republicans nominated Taft for the Presidency, Roosevelt split with the party. He and a group of his supporters, together with a wide variety of reformers, joined together to form a third political party known as the Progressive (or "Bull Moose") Party. They held a convention in August at Chicago, where the delegates sang "Onward Christian Soldiers" and drafted a platform which they called "A Contract with the People." They nominated Roosevelt for President and Hiram Johnson of California for Vice President. In this selection Jane Addams, who took part in the convention, described it.

READING FOCUS

1. Why did people join the Progressive Party in 1912?
2. What was the platform of the Progressive Party?

From various directions, people were drawing toward a new political party. It was at first as if one heard in the distance the grave and measured step of history. But the pace increased during the first half of 1912, and became absolutely breathless by midsummer. It was in August 1912 that the Progressive Party was organized.

Suddenly, as if by magic, the city of Chicago became filled with men and women from every state in the Union who were moved by the same needs and hopes. They showed each other common sympathies and memories. They urged methods for righting old wrongs and establishing new standards. For three days they defined their purposes and joined their wills.

Among the members of the platform committee for the new party were social workers,

Adapted from The Second Twenty Years at Hull–House *by Jane Addams.*

others closely identified with religion, and still others who were scholars. Sometimes when we came across members of the American Economic Association, or of the Civil Service Reform League, or similar groups, we feared that a few people were trying through the new party to obtain measures which, although worthy, had only limited support. To me, this was very alarming. But I gradually discovered that the situation was in reality the very opposite of this. The dean of a university law school acted as head of the resolution committee, and others who knew law supplied information. But these people, together with the so-called "practical" members of the committee, were not representing the opinion of any individual nor the philosophy of any group. They were trying, as conscientious American citizens, to meet the basic duty of adapting the laws to the changed conditions of national life.

Delegates had all experienced the frustration and disappointment of individual effort. They had come to this first national convention of the Progressive Party not only to urge reform legislation, but to test its usefulness through the consent of their fellow citizens, to throw their measures into the life of the nation itself. They believed that the program of social legislation placed before the country by the Progressive Party was of great importance to the average voter regardless of party.

In the hope that the political organization of the nation might never again get so far away from the life of the people, the platform rec-

A Progressive Party campaign poster, 1912

ommended equal suffrage, direct primaries, and the initiative and referendum. We quoted to each other the saying of Walt Whitman, that it seemed to him unbearable that large groups of people should follow those who do not believe in people. We placed at the head of our precious new party two men of political wisdom who had shown an understanding not only of the social demands of the people but also of the people themselves. We realized that Colonel Roosevelt possessed a unique power. In spite of our belief in our leader, however, I was there—and I think the same was true of many others—because the platform expressed the social hopes so long ignored by the politicians.

Although we were all quite well aware that the convention was far from being united, it seemed to us at the moment as if it really were. Certainly, for the time being, all doctrines and group egotisms were dropped. Or rather, they were melted down by overwhelming good will and enthusiasm.

The Progressive convention has been described many times, perhaps never quite adequately. It was a curious moment of release from inhibitions. It did not seem in the least strange that quiet, reserved men and women should speak aloud of their religious and social beliefs, confident that they would be understood. Because we felt so at home in that huge Coliseum, there was a quick understanding of those hidden feelings which we were mysteriously moved to express.

During the three days of the Progressive convention, one could almost hear the breakdown of the well-worn slogans which had provided the old parties their election battle cries for half a century. The sound was not unlike the uproar which accompanies a great religious conference. The old-line politicians were as much surprised to find that politics had to do with the matters discussed at the Progressive convention as the social workers were delighted to discover that their long concern for human needs had come to be considered politics. Nevertheless, in spite of the careful platform building, the entire noisy convention was well described as the "barn raising of a new party."

READING REVIEW

1. List two reasons why people joined the Progressive Party and participated in their national convention.

2. Summarize the Progressive Party Platform in 1912.
3. (a) To Jane Addams, which was more important—having Roosevelt as party leader or having a reform platform? (b) From what you have read, do you think her judgment was correct?
4. Why did Jane Addams describe the convention as the "barn raising of a new party"?

174 A Program for Reform

President Woodrow Wilson was a progressive of a different sort from Theodore Roosevelt. Roosevelt distinguished between good and bad trusts. He declared that the government should not break up large corporations but regulate them. Wilson believed that all large trusts were bad. He felt that the trusts were too powerful to be controlled and that the antitrust laws should be used to break them up. Wilson used the phrase "a New Freedom" to describe his program of reform. He also wrote a book called *The New Freedom* in which he outlined his reform philosophy. The following selection is taken from that book.

READING FOCUS
1. What reforms did Wilson propose?
2. What basic philosophy underlined Wilson's "New Freedom" program?

We have entered a very different age from any that came before us. We have entered an age in which we do not do business the way we used to do business. We do not carry on any of the operations of manufacture, sale, transportation, or communication as people used to carry them on. There is a sense in which the individual has been submerged. In most parts of our country people work not for themselves, not as partners in the old way in which they used to work, but generally as employees of great corporations. There was a time when corporations played a very small part in our business affairs. Now they play the chief part, and most workers are the servants of corporations.

You know what happens when you are the servant of a corporation. Your individuality is

From Woodrow Wilson, The New Freedom *by William E. Leuchtenburg.*

swallowed up in the individuality and purpose of a great organization.

American industry is not free, as once it was free. American enterprise is not free. The person with only a little capital is finding it harder to get into the field, more and more impossible to compete with big business. Why? Because the laws of the country do not prevent the strong from crushing the weak. That is the reason. And because the strong have crushed the weak, the strong dominate the industry and the economic life of this country. What this country needs above everything else is laws which will look after the people who are striving to succeed rather than the people who are already successful.

Don't fool yourselves for a moment as to the power of the great interests which now dominate our development. They are so powerful that it is almost questionable whether the government of the United States can dominate them or not. Go one step further, make their organized power permanent, and it may be too late to turn back. The roads divide at the point where we stand. They stretch out to regions far separated from one another. At the end of one is the old, tiresome scene of government tied up with special interests. At the other shines the free light of individual freedom, the light of unrestrained enterprise.

I believe in human liberty as I believe in the wine of life. There is no salvation for workers in the small favors of industrial masters. Guardians have no place in a land of free people. Prosperity guaranteed by trustees has no prospect of lasting. Monopoly means the wasting away of enterprise. If monopoly continues, it will always control government. I do not expect to see monopoly hold back itself.

The government of our country cannot be placed in the hands of any special class. The policy of a great nation cannot be tied up with any particular set of interests. I want to say again and again that my arguments do not involve the *character* of the people to whom I am opposed. I believe that the very wealthy who got their money by certain kinds of corporate enterprise have closed in their horizon, and that they do not see and do not understand the people. It is for that reason that I want to break up the little group that has determined what the government of the nation should do. We must save our government from the domination of special classes, not because these special classes are necessarily bad, but because no special class can understand the interests of a great community.

The meaning of liberty has deepened. But it has not stopped being a demand of the human spirit, a basic necessity for the life of the soul. And the day is at hand when it shall be realized on this consecrated soil—a New Freedom. It will be a liberty widened and deepened to match the broadened life of the modern American, returning to us the control of our government. It will throw open all gates of lawful enterprise, releasing energies and warming the generous impulses of our hearts. It will be a process of freedom and inspiration, full of a breath of life as sweet and wholesome as the airs that filled the sails of Columbus, giving the promise and boast of magnificent opportunity in which America dare not fail.

READING REVIEW

1. (a) Name two special interests Wilson felt endangered the United States. (b) How could these groups prove harmful to America?
2. Why did Wilson feel that the trusts must be broken up?
3. Why did Wilson call his reform policies the "New Freedom"?

175   A Spaniard's Report on the 1916 Election

In the election of 1916, the Democrats nominated Woodrow Wilson for a second term. The Republicans chose Charles Evans Hughes, Chief Jus-

Wilson's campaign truck

tice of the Supreme Court, as their candidate. Theodore Roosevelt was again chosen by the Progressive Party. During the campaign, Americans were especially concerned with foreign affairs. With World War I raging in Europe, Wilson's slogan—"He kept us out of war"—attracted many voters. Other issues, of course, were important in the campaign. A Spanish writer, Julio Camba, was in the United States at the time of the election and wrote this account of the campaign.

READING FOCUS

1. According to Camba, what were the "basic tendencies" in American life?
2. What did Camba say was the significance of the election of 1916?

The battle has already taken shape. The Republican and Progressive parties have met in Chicago to nominate candidates. Soon the Democratic Party will meet. Afterwards, in the month of November, will come the elections, first for the electoral college, then for the President. The names which are most often heard now are Wilson, who is now President, Roosevelt, and Hughes.

We must prepare to see one of the most picturesque spectacles in the world—that is, a Presidential election in the United States. To give you an idea of the sporting spirit with which the people regard such equal contestants, it is necessary to quote the following paragraph from the *Evening Post:* "It is a pity that two men as famous as Wilson and Hughes could not appear together on the same platform! That would be a sensational match, and spectators would pay a fabulous price for admission."

Hughes holds over Wilson the enormous advantage of the offensive. The ex-justice can attack all the Presidential acts of Wilson, who will have to make great efforts to defend them. In his turn, Hughes will have to show how he would have acted if he had been President. Hughes can depend on a greater number of personal sympathizers than Wilson, who seems to make enemies of his friends. Wilson, in turn, enjoys great intellectual prestige. He

Adapted from "Un Año en el otro mundo" by Julio Camba from This Was America *by Oscar Handlin.*

writes very well, speaks well, and is considered a most honorable and well-intentioned man.

The candidates are ready. The boxers have put on their gloves. The first round is about to begin.

There are two basic tendencies in the life of this country. One is an idealistic and humanitarian tendency with a great moral content, which reaches from William James, the philosopher, to Henry Ford, the manufacturer of automobiles. The other is a materialistic tendency without any content of idealism, a tendency of capitalism and imperialism. The two tendencies, as may be seen in this election, are now in a state of balance.

It is certain that Hughes and Roosevelt, as against Wilson, represent the second of those tendencies. Hughes stands for the Wall Street capitalists, who gained him the nomination. He speaks for the trusts. He represents the scorn of money for moral values. His friends have put signs all over New York which read: "We don't want professors meddling in our affairs," and "What's the use of democracy in business?" Hughes, in short, represents the materialism of a civilization in which quality counts for nothing. What counts are dollars, many dollars, business, bridges, telephones, cranes, skyscrapers, noise, speed.

If matters continue as they have until now, and if Hughes does not win this time, he (or someone else who represents the same things) will win in four years. The second tendency is steadily winning out over the first. By the same degree that a people enriches itself with material possessions, it also loses some of its spiritual content. The 1800's are dying in the trenches of Europe. At the end of the war, France, Germany, England, and Italy will face in the United States a people whose ideals are those of the corporation—to do business. And *what is the use of democracy in business!* What help is democracy in making money?

This moral difference between that which Hughes represents and that which Wilson represents is, without doubt, much more important for the relations of North America with the rest of the world than the possible difference of opinion between those two men on the European war. One must, moreover, be aware of the position of the President of the United States to understand the importance of the election. The President of the United States is a kaiser [emperor]. He is elected, by a demo-cratic process, a kaiser for four years; yet he is a kaiser who gets what he wishes.

READING REVIEW

1. **(a)** What according to Camba, were the "two basic tendencies" in American life? **(b)** Which of these philosophies did Wilson stand for? Hughes?
2. How did the election match them against each other?
3. **(a)** Camba called the American President a "kaiser" (German for "emperor"). **(b)** Do you think the use of the term is accurate? Why or why not?
4. **(a)** Why did Camba compare the presidential election to a sporting event? **(b)** Do you think this is an appropriate analogy? Why or why not?
5. Why was the difference between Wilson's and Hughes' philosophy important for the relations of North America with the rest of the world?

176 What the Progressives Achieved

The progressive movement came to an end when the United States entered World War I. It had started to slow down with the outbreak of war in Europe in 1914. With their attention now on foreign affairs, many Americans became less interested in reform. A great many Americans also felt that the progressive movement had achieved its aims and that further reform was not needed. Then, too, many Americans were tired of the endless talk about reforming the ills of society. What had the reform movement of the early 1900's accomplished, they wondered? Richard Hofstadter, a leading modern historian who has studied this period, gave his answer to this question. The following selection is from the introduction to his book *The Progressive Movement: 1900–1915.*

READING FOCUS

1. What were the characteristics of the Progressive movement?
2. What did the Progressives accomplish?

For a long time historians have written of the period between 1900 and 1914 as the Progres-

From The Progressive Movement 1900–1915, *edited by Richard Hofstadter.*

sive era, and of its variety of reform agitations as the Progressive movement. In using these terms, historians have followed the example of many of the period's leading figures. They liked the ring of the word "Progressive" as applied to themselves. The people of that age were proudly aware, even as they were fighting their battles, that there was something distinctive about the political and social life of their time which sharply marked it off from the era of materialism and corruption.

From the end of the Civil War to the close of the 1800's, the physical energies of the American people had been organized for a remarkable burst of material development. But their moral energies were relatively inactive. Certain moral aspects of the American character had become all but invisible. It was as though the controversy over slavery, the Civil War itself, and the difficulties and failures of Reconstruction had exhausted the moral and political capacities of the people. They abandoned crusades and reforms and jumped instead into the rewarding tasks of material achievements.

During this period Americans had filled up a vast area of land between the Mississippi River and California. They had crossed the country with a railroad network of more than a quarter of a million miles. Still more impressive was the growth of the urban and industrial part of the economy. Whole systems of industry and whole regions of industrial production were created. The urban population jumped from 9.9 million to 30.1 million. Thoughtful observers could see that the day was not very far off when the rural population would be outnumbered and the characteristic

A hopeless effort

problems of the nation would be city problems.

By 1900 it became increasingly evident that all this material growth had been achieved at a terrible cost in human values and in the waste of natural resources. The land and the people had been robbed. Farmers had received small returns for their work. They had had little or no protection against exploitation by the railroads, against the high cost of credit, or against an unjust burden of taxation. At the same time the cities that grew with American industry were themselves industrial wastelands—centers of illegal activities and poverty, ugly, full of crowded slums, badly managed. Industry, after a period of great competition, was rapidly becoming concentrated. Big business choked free competition and concentrated political power in a few hands. Moreover, business, great and small, had lowered the character and quality of politics. Working with powerful bosses, business had won favors and privileges in return for its grants of money to corrupt political machines. Domination of the nation's affairs by political bosses and business organizations was now seen to be a threat to democracy itself.

What had happened, as a great many people saw it at the beginning of the Progressive era, was that in the extraordinary outburst of productive energy of the past few decades, the nation had not developed at the same time the means of meeting human needs or controlling or reforming the evils that come with any such rapid change. The Progressive movement, then, may be looked upon as an attempt to develop the moral will, the intellectual insight, and the political and administrative agencies to remedy the evils of a period of industrial growth. Since the Progressives did not believe in revolution, it was also an attempt to work out a strategy for orderly social change.

What were the main qualities of Progressivism? The name itself may be slightly misleading. Of course, the Progressives believed in progress. But so did a great many conservatives. The distinguishing thing about the Progressives was something else, which for lack of a better term might be called "activism." They argued that social evils will not remedy themselves, and that it is wrong to sit by without doing anything and wait for time to take care of them. As one writer put it, they did not believe that the future would take care of itself. They believed that the people of the country should be stimulated to work energetically to bring about social progress. Progressives believed in energy and governmental action.

If the people were sufficiently aroused, they would grab power away from city and state bosses and millionaire senators and take it back into their own hands. Having done so, they would use their regained power—through the city, state, or federal governments—to solve social and economic problems. Tenements would be gotten rid of. The labor of women and children would be forbidden. The Negro race would be supported in the struggle for its rights. High tariffs and monopoly prices would be regulated out of existence. Social legislation would protect the working classes from the terrible dangers of industry. Dangerous foods and falsely advertised drugs would be driven off the market. Unfair competition by the great corporations would be subject to constant government control. The concentration of business control in the hands of a few powerful banking interests would be broken up. Better credit would be provided for farmers and small business owners. The commercial exploitation of vice and drink would be reduced or eliminated.

The Progressive movement depended on the civic alertness and the aroused mood of a great part of the public. Such a mood cannot last forever. Perhaps what was most remarkable about the Progressives was their ability to maintain enthusiasm for reform as long as they did.

Despite the briefness of many of its achievements, the heritage of the Progressive movement cannot be considered small or unimportant. The Progressives developed for the first time on a large scale a type of realistic journalism and social criticism that has become a permanent quality of American thinking. They gave a new strength to a climate of opinion hostile to monopoly. They forced big business to operate carefully and even to exercise some self-restraint. The traditions of responsible government and forceful leadership of men like Theodore Roosevelt and Woodrow Wilson established unforgettable high points in American leadership. Finally, the reforms of the Progressive era established a basis for further reforms to be passed when the need for them was felt.

The men and women of the Progressive movement must be considered the pioneers of the welfare state. This was not because they sought to promote the growth of big government for its own sake. But they were determined to remedy the most pressing and dangerous social ills of industrial society. In the attempt they quickly learned that they could not achieve their aims without using the power of government. Moreover, they declared—and they were the first in our history to do so with real practical success—the idea that government cannot be seen only as a cold and negative policing agency. Instead it has a wide responsibility for the welfare of its citizens, and for the poor and powerless among them. For this, Progressivism must be understood as a major part in the history of the American conscience.

READING REVIEW

1. According to Hofstadter, what did the Progressives accomplish during the period from 1865 to 1900?
2. What price did the Progressives pay for these accomplishments?
3. What were the chief characteristics of the Progressive movement?

CHAPTER
27 New Directions in American Life
(1900–1920)

177 The All-Powerful Telephone

In the early 1900's, many great changes took place in the United States. These changes were the result of new inventions and new methods of industrial production. One of the important inventions of this period was the telephone. In 1911 Arnold Bennett, an English writer, visited the United States. He was both fascinated and terrified by the widespread use of the telephone and he wrote the following selection about this "evil" invention. In fact, he became so interested in this new device that he took a tour of the New York City phone company to learn more about how the telephone system worked.

READING FOCUS

1. What characteristics of the telephone appealed to American society?
2. How did the American and European opinions of the telephone differ?

What strikes and frightens the backward European as much as anything in the United States is the efficiency and fearful common use of the telephone. I think of the big cities as great heaps pierced everywhere by elevator shafts full of movement. I think of them too as being threaded, under pavements and over roofs and between floors and ceilings and walls, by millions upon millions of live threads that unite all the privacies of people—and destroy them in making them public! I do not mean that Europe has failed to adopt the telephone, nor that in Europe there are no hotels with the dreadful curse of an active telephone in every room. But I do mean that the European telephone is a toy, and a somewhat clumsy one, compared with the serious American telephone. Many otherwise highly civilized Europeans are shy when speaking into a telephone, as they would be in speaking to a king or queen. Average middle-class Europeans still speak of their telephone, if they have one, in the same falsely casual tone as Americans tend to speak of their motor-car. It is nothing—but somehow it comes into the conversation!

"How odd!" you exclaim. And you are right. It is we Europeans who are wrong, through no particular fault of our own.

The American is ruthlessly logical about the telephone. The only occasion on which I was in really serious danger of being taken for a madman in the United States was when, in a Chicago hotel, I permanently removed the receiver from the telephone in my room. The whole hotel was horrified. Half of Chicago shuddered. In response to a request from the management, I put the receiver back. On the horrified face of the manager I could read the

Adapted from Your United States *by Arnold Bennett.*

unspoken question: "Is it possible that you have been in this country a month without understanding that the United States is primarily a vast collection of telephone booths?" Yes, I gave in and admired! And I predict that on my next visit I shall find a telephone on every table of every restaurant that respects itself.

It is the efficiency of the telephone that makes it irresistible to a great people whose passion is to "get results"—the speed with which the communication is given, and the clear loudness of the telephone's voice in reply to yours. These things are completely unknown in Europe. If I were to live in the United States, I too should become a victim of the telephone habit, as it is practiced in its most advanced form in suburban communities. There a person takes to the telephone as people in more decadent lands take to drugs. You can see them in the morning at their bedroom window, pouring confidences into their telephone, thus combining the joy of an innocent vice with the healthy freshness of breeze and sunshine.

Now it was obvious that behind the apparently simple outer aspects of any telephone system there must be a complex and marvelous secret organization. In Europe my curiosity would probably never have been excited by the thought of that organization. At home one accepts everything as a matter of course. But in the United States, partly because the telephone is so much more wonderful and terrible there, and partly because in a foreign land one often has whims, I wanted to see the mysteries hidden at the other end of all the wires. Thus, one day, I paid a visit to a telephone exchange in New York. There I saw what nine hundred and ninety-nine out of every thousand of the most eager telephone users seldom think about and will never see.

My first impression was a murmuring sound, as of hundreds of scholars in a school learning their lessons, and a row of young women seated on stools before a long machine of holes and pegs and pieces of elastic cord— all looking extremely serious. One saw at once that none of these young women had a single moment to spare. They were all involved in the tremendous machine, were part of it, keeping up with it and in it, and not daring to take their eyes off it for a moment. What they were saying it was impossible to guess. If one placed oneself close to any particular young woman, she seemed to utter no sound, but simply and without stopping, pegged and unpegged holes at random among the thousands of holes before her. She apparently did this in obedience to the signaling of tiny lights that continually went on and off.

We who had entered were ignored. We might have been ghosts, invisible and silent. Even the supervisors did not turn to look at us as they moved restlessly behind the stools. And yet somehow I could hear the delicate shoulders of all the young women saying, without speaking: "Here come these tyrants again, who have invented this exercise which nearly but not quite cracks our brains for us! They know exactly how much they can get out of us, and they get it. They are cleverer and more powerful than we are, and we have to give in to their discipline. But —" And afar off I could hear: "What are you going to wear tonight?" "Will you dine with me tonight?" "I want two seats." "Very well, thanks, and how is Mrs. . . .?" "When can I see you tomorrow?" "I'll take your offer for those bonds." . . . And I could see the inside of endless offices and living rooms. But of course I could hear and see nothing really except the low, serious voices and quick movements of those completely absorbed young women on stools exactly alike.

I understood why the telephone service was so efficient. I understood not only from the conduct of the long row of young women, but from everything else I had seen in the precise and evilly clever arrangement of the whole establishment.

READING REVIEW

1. How do you think Bennett really felt about the telephone? Cite evidence from the reading to support your conclusion.
2. **(a)** What characteristics of the telephone operators did Bennett admire? **(b)** To whom did he compare them?

178 Ford's First Assembly Line

American business and industry continued to expand rapidly during the early years of the 1900's. One of the most far-reaching developments in industry before America's entry into World War I was the introduction of the modern assembly line, pioneered by Henry Ford in the production of automobiles. In this selection, Ford described how the idea for the assembly line came about.

READING FOCUS

1. What were the advantages of assembly line production?
2. How did the assembly line method of production change the role of workers?

A Ford car contains about 5,000 parts, counting screws, nuts, and everything. Some parts are fairly large, and others are hardly larger than watch parts. In our first assembling, we simply started to put a car together at a certain spot on the floor. Workers brought to it the parts as they were needed in exactly the same way that one builds a house.

When we started to make parts, it was natural to create a single department of the factory to make each one. Usually one worker performed all of the operations necessary on a small part. But the rapid speedup of production made it necesary to work out some plans of production so that workers would not be falling over one another.

The first step forward in assembly came when we began taking the work to the workers instead of the workers to the work. We now have two general principles in all operations—that a worker should never have to take more than one step, if it can possibly be avoided, and that no worker need ever bend over.

The principles of assembly are these:

1. Place the tools and the workers in the sequence of the operation so that each part used in making the automobile will travel the least possible distance while in the process of finishing.

2. Use work slides or some other form of carrier so that when a worker completes his operation he drops the part always in the same place. That place should always be the most convenient to his hand. And if possible have gravity carry the part to the next worker for his operation.

Adapted from My Life and Work *by Henry Ford in collaboration with Samuel Crowther.*

3. Using moving assembling lines by which the parts to be assembled are delivered at convenient distances.

The result of the application of these principles is the reduction of the necessity for thought on the part of the workers and the reduction of their movements to a minimum. They do as nearly as possible only one thing with only one movement.

Along about April 1, 1913, we first tried the experiment of an assembly line on a small generator. We try everything in a small way at first. We will rip out anything once we discover a better way, but we have to know absolutely that the new way is going to be better than the old before we do anything drastic.

I believe that this was the first moving line ever installed. The idea came in a general way from the overhead cable that the Chicago packers use in cutting up beef. We had previously assembled the generator in the usual way. With one worker doing a complete job, he could turn out from thirty-five to forty pieces in a nine-hour day, or about twenty minutes for each assembly. What he did alone was then divided into twenty-nine operations. On an assembly line, that cut down the time for each assembly to thirteen minutes, ten seconds. Then we raised the height of the line eight inches [20 centimeters]—this was in 1914—and cut the time to seven minutes. Further experimenting with the speed cut the time down to five minutes.

In short, the result is this: with the aid of scientific study one worker is now able to do somewhat more than what four workers did only a few years ago. That line established the efficiency of the method and we now use it everywhere. The assembling of the motor, formerly done by one person, is now divided into eighty-four operations—those workers do the work that three times their number used to do.

READING REVIEW

1. How did the idea for the assembly line come about?
2. (a) What were some advantages of an assembly line? (b) Some of its disadvantages?
3. Do you think that a worker would have shared Ford's enthusiasm for this new production method? Why or why not?
4. (a) How did this lead to specialization of jobs? (b) What significance did this have for the future of laborers?

179 Why a Minimum Wage?

Henry Ford also brought great changes in the field of labor relations. In 1914 the Ford Motor Company astonished the business world by voluntarily reducing the weekly hours of work and providing a minimum daily wage of $5 for each of its workers. The $5-a-day wage was nearly double what Ford and other automobile companies had been paying. In the following selection Ford explained the philosophy behind this policy.

READING FOCUS

1. What was the proper relationship of a business and its employees?
2. On what basic philosophy did Ford base his decision to establish a mimimum wage?
3. How did Ford bring about a change in labor relations?

What good is industry if it is so unskillfully managed that it does not return a living to everyone concerned? No question is more important than that of wages—most of the people of the country live on wages. The scale of their living—the rate of their wages—determines the prosperity of the country.

It is not usual to speak of employees as partners, and yet what else are they? Whenever people find the management of a business too much for their own time or strength, they call in assistants to share the management with them. Why, then, if people find the production part of a business too much for their own hands, should they deny the title of "partner" to those who come in and help them produce? Every business that employs more than one person is a kind of partnership. The moment a person calls for assistance in business—even though the assistant be but a child—that moment the person has taken a partner.

No person is independent as long as he or she has to depend on another's help. It is a mutual relation. The boss is the partner of the worker; the worker is partner of the boss. It is useless for one group or the other to think that it is the one necessary unit. Both are neces-

Adapted from My Life and Work *by Henry Ford in collaboration with Samuel Crowther.*

sary. They are partners. When they pull and push against each other, they simply hurt the organization in which they are partners and from which both draw support.

It ought to be the employer's ambition, as leader, to pay better wages than any similar line of business, and it ought to be the workers' ambition to make this possible. Of course, there are workers in all factories who seem to believe that if they do their best, it will be only for the employer's benefit—and not at all for their own. It is a pity that such a feeling should exist. But it does exist and perhaps it has some justification. If an employer encourages workers to do their best, and the workers learn after a while that their best does not bring any reward, then they naturally drop back into "getting by." But if they see the profit of hard work in their pay envelope—proof that harder work means higher pay—then they also begin to learn that they are a part of the business, and that its success depends on them and their success depends on it.

"What ought the employer to pay?" "What ought the employee to receive?" These are minor questions. The basic question is, "What can the business stand?" Certainly no business can stand to pay out more than it makes. When you pump water out of a well at a faster rate than the water flows in, the well goes dry.

Employers can gain nothing by looking over the employees and asking themselves, "How little can I get them to take?" Nor can employees gain much by glaring back and asking, "How much can I force them to give?" In time, both will have to turn to the business and ask, "How can this industry be made safe and profitable, so that it will be able to provide a sure and comfortable living for all of us?"

It ought to be clear that the high wage begins down in the factory. If it is not created there, it cannot get into pay envelopes. There will never be a system invented which will do away with the necessity of work. Nature has seen to that. Idle hands and minds were never intended for any one of us. Work is our sanity, our self-respect, our salvation. So far from being a curse, work is the greatest blessing. True social justice flows only out of honest work. The worker who contributes much should take away much. Therefore no element of charity is present in the paying of wages.

The kind of workers who give the business the best that is in them are the best kind of workers a business can have. And they cannot be expected to do this indefinitely without proper recognition of their contribution. People who come to the day's job feeling that no matter how much they may give, it will not give them enough of a return to keep them from being poor are not in shape to do a day's work. But if people feel that their day's work is not only supplying basic needs, but is also giving them a margin of comfort and making them able to give their families opportunities and pleasure, then their job looks good to them and they are free to give it their best.

I have learned through the years a good deal about wages. I believe in the first place that, all other considerations aside, our own sales depend in a measure upon the wages we pay. If we can distribute high wages, then that money is going to be spent. It will serve to make storekeepers and distributors and manufacturers and workers in other lines more prosperous. Their prosperity will show up in our sales.

We announced and put into operation in January 1914, a kind of profit-sharing plan. The minimum wage for any class of work and under certain conditions was $5 a day. At the same time we reduced the working day to eight hours—it had been nine—and the week to forty-eight hours. This was entirely a voluntary act. It was to our way of thinking an act of social justice, and in the last analysis we did it for our own satisfaction. There is a pleasure in feeling that you have made others happy—that you have lessened in some degree the burdens of other people—that you have provided something out of which may be had pleasure and saving. Good will is one of the few really important assets of life. Determined people can win almost anything they go after, but unless they gain good will, they have not profited much.

READING REVIEW

1. According to Ford, what was the relationship between a business and its employees?
2. What mistakes could employers make in determining wages?
3. (a) On what basis should wages be determined? (b) Is this philosophy still applicable to today's workplace? Why or why not?
4. (a) Why, in Ford's view, did his company establish its minimum wage? (b) How did the establishment of a minimum wage by Ford affect other businesses?

UNIT NINE READINGS

Becoming a World Power

<table>
<tr><td>

CHAPTER

28

American Expansion Overseas

(1898–1914)

180

America's "Anglo-Saxon" Mission

A great change took place in American foreign policy in the late 1800's. The nation's traditional isolationist policy was replaced by a policy of expansionism. During these years a number of writers developed arguments in favor of American expansion overseas as well as in the Western Hemisphere.

One of the most influential of these writers was Josiah Strong, a Congregational minister. His arguments in favor of American expansion were based, however, on two false beliefs. One was the concept of an Anglo-Saxon "race," which to Americans meant the people of Great Britain and their descendants. The other belief, called social Darwinism, applied the theories of scientist Charles Darwin—especially the theory of the "survival of the fittest"—to peoples and nations. Many Americans misused Darwin's theories to claim that the earth should belong to the energetic, the strong, and the fit—that is, to the American people.

READING FOCUS

1. According to Strong, what "great ideas" form the basis of civilization?
2. What is America's Anglo-Saxon mission?

</td><td>

Every race which has deeply impressed itself on the human family has been the representative of some great idea—one or more—which has given direction to the nation's life and form to its civilization. The Anglo-Saxon is the representative of two great ideas, which are closely related. One of them is that of civil liberty. Nearly all of the civil liberty in the world is enjoyed by Anglo-Saxons: the English, the British colonists, and the people of the United States. Some peoples, such as the Swiss, are allowed by their neighbors to maintain it. Others, such as the French, have experimented with it. But, in modern times, the peoples whose love of liberty has won it, and whose genius for self-government has preserved it, have been Anglo-Saxons.

The other great idea represented by the Anglo-Saxon is that of a pure, spiritual Christianity.

It is not necessary to argue that the two great needs of human beings are, first, civil liberty, and second, a pure, spiritual Christianity. These are the forces which, in the past, have contributed most to advancing the human race. They must continue to be, in the future, the most efficient aids to its progress. It follows, then, that Anglo-Saxons, as the great representative of these two ideas, have a special relationship to the world's future. They are divinely commissioned to be, in a sense, their brother's keeper.

Another important fact is the Anglo-Saxon's rapidly increasing strength in modern times. In 1700 this race numbered less than 6

Adapted from Josiah Strong, Our Country: Its Possible Future and Its Present Crisis.

</td></tr>
</table>

million persons. In 1800, Anglo-Saxons (I use the term somewhat broadly to include all English-speaking peoples) had increased to about 20 million. In 1880 they numbered nearly 100 million, having increased almost five times over in 80 years.

In 100 years the United States has increased the size of its territory ten times. There can be no reasonable doubt that North America is to be the great home of the Anglo-Saxons, the principal seat of their power, the center of their life and influence. Our continent has room and resources and climate, it lies in the pathway of the nations, and it belongs to the zone of power. Already, among Anglo-Saxons, we lead in population and wealth.

Moreover, our social institutions are stimulating. In Europe the various classes of society are, like the layers of the earth, fixed and rigid. There can be no great change without a terrible upheaval, a social earthquake. Here, society is like the waters of the sea, constantly moving. All people are free to become whatever they can make of themselves. They are free to transform themselves from rail-splitters or tanners into the nation's President. Our aristocracy, unlike that of Europe, is open to all comers. Wealth, position, influence, are prizes offered for energy. Every farmer's child, every apprentice and clerk, every friendless and penniless immigrant, is free to enter the contest. Thus many causes combine to produce here the most forceful and tremendous energy in the world.

What is the significance of such facts? It seems to me that God, with great wisdom and skill, is training the Anglo-Saxon race for an hour sure to come in the world's future. Up until now in the history of the world there has always been unoccupied land westward. Into this the crowded countries of the East have poured their surplus populations. But there are no more new worlds. The unoccupied farmlands of the earth are limited, and will soon be taken.

The time is coming when the pressure of population on the means of subsistence will be felt here as it is now felt in Europe and Asia. Then the world will enter upon a new stage of its history—the final competition of races. The Anglo-Saxon is being trained for this. Long before our numbers reach a billion, the expansionist tendency inherited by this race, and strengthened in the United States, will assert

One view of America's "Anglo-Saxon Mission"

itself. Then this race of unequaled energy, with all its numbers and the might of wealth behind it—the representative of liberty and Christianity—having developed aggressive traits to force its institutions upon all people will spread itself over the earth. If I predict correctly, this powerful race will move down upon Mexico, down upon Central and South America, out upon the islands of the sea, over upon Africa, and beyond. And can anyone doubt that the result of this competition of races will be the "survival of the fittest"?

Is there room for reasonable doubt? This race, unless weakened by alcohol and tobacco, is destined to drive out many weaker races, absorb others, and mold the remainder, until, in a very true and important sense, it has Anglo–Saxonized humankind.

READING REVIEW

1. **(a)** Name the two great ideas that Strong said formed the basis of civilization. **(b)** According to Strong, how did the Anglo-Saxons represent these ideas?
2. What evidence did Strong offer to support his prediction that Americans would "Anglo-Saxonize" the human race?

181 An American Soldier's Memory

Americans entered the Spanish-American War in 1898 with great enthusiasm. But the Americans were almost as unprepared for war as the Spaniards. American soldiers were sent off to war without proper equipment. In a climate where temperatures often were above 100 degrees Fahrenheit (38° Celsius), American forces were issued heavy woolen uniforms. Their weapons were outdated Springfield rifles that were almost useless, and their food supplies often consisted of spoiled canned meat. Diseases such as malaria, typhoid, dysentery, and yellow fever were widespread.

Of the 5,400 men who died in the war, over 5,000 died from disease. Only 400 lost their lives in battle. Jacob Judson, an Illinois militia officer who received his training for combat near Tampa, Florida, wrote this account of the war more than fifty years later.

READING FOCUS

1. Why did American soldiers suffer so many unnecessary hardships during the Spanish-American war?
2. How did Judson feel about his experience in the Spanish-American war?

We of the Spanish War who are still living can look back on our war experience, and can thank our Heavenly Father for being alive today. It's remarkable what our bodies can stand, when I think back on our Picnic Island days

Adapted from a letter by Jacob Judson, Illinois National Guard, April 15, 1956; now in the Manuscript Collection of the Chicago Historical Society.

Army training camp in Tampa, Florida, 1898

in Tampa, Florida—untrained men in a heavy rain, a fierce storm blowing our tents out into the sea, no protection, our clothing soaked to the skin. At sea they gave us canned corned beef that stunk so we had to throw it overboard. Then our landing at Sebony in Cuba, camping at the foot of a hill, with large land crabs crawling over us at night. After that our long march toward San Juan Hill through jungles and swamps, joining up with Rough Riders on Kettle Hill, heavy rains pouring down, no tents for cover, every man for himself, standing in trenches in a foot of water and mud, day and night. When off duty, we massaged our feet to get them back in shape. When the sun came out, our boys would help each other by wringing out wet clothes and blankets, quickly cutting down branches from trees, and constructing an overhead protection by laying on palm leaves. Abel Davis and I found a spot under a tree not far from Teddy Roosevelt's tent.

For lack of proper food men grew weak. Our food ration consisted of a slice of salt pork, hardtack, and some grains of coffee that we had to crack between stones or rocks. Then came the issue of wool-lined underwear in a tropical climate, and orders to burn the underwear we brought from home. After that, you would see the boys in the river streams, their backs covered with boils. Wool-lined underwear and salt pork do not go in a tropical climate.

Then came malaria. It was my duty in the mornings to take our sick boys to the division hospital. There were no doctors in attendance, just a hospital corps sergeant who issued pills out of one bottle for all sicknesses. Sick men lay on cots, their mouths, ears, and noses full of flies. I would go over to these poor boys and with my finger clear their mouths of flies—not so much as a piece of paper to cover their faces. Other boys lay day and night on the edge of the sinks; because of malaria they had no control of their bowels. Morning sick detail would come along and take away any that had died. Their bodies would be buried on a hillside. If heavy rains washed away the soil, a second burial was necessary.

I was one of the fortunate boys. It had been my privilege to train Abel Davis when he joined up with the First. We were very close pals. Abel Davis had a brother who was a doctor in Chicago. This doctor gave Abel a box containing medicines for malaria and other tropical sicknesses, so when I came down with malaria Abel took care of me. There were very few doctors; most of them were down with malaria themselves. Abel pulled me through. Then he came down with the malaria himself, and I used his medicines until he got better. If it was not for that box of medicines, I think both Abel's bones and mine would lie in Cuban hills today.

Colonel Teddy Roosevelt said "The Spanish War was but a drop in the bucket as compared with the war following." This statement was no doubt true. The next war had troops spread all over Europe. But the soldier [in World War I] had full modern equipment, proper clothes, healthy, nourishing food, and the very best medical care, none of which was given the Spanish War soldier.

When the war ended and we landed at Montauk, Long Island, our boys were thin, underweight, and yellow as lemons. It took us years to recover. So I say: Let us thank God for taking care of us all these years.

READING REVIEW

1. **(a)** From Judson's account, what hardships could have been prevented? **(b)** What could have been done by the United States government and military to alleviate some conditions which distressed the American soldiers?
2. What was Judson's attitude toward his experiences in the army?
3. Do you think that his description was accurate? Cite evidence from the reading to support your opinion.

182 In Defense of Imperialism

The success of the United States in the Spanish-American War led some Americans to dream of a colonial empire. Leading the enthusiasm for overseas possessions was Albert J. Beveridge, a young lawyer from Indiana. In the following speech, delivered in 1898 during his campaign for the Senate, he made a strong appeal for action. After his election, he continued to favor and encourage a policy of expansionism.

READING FOCUS

1. Why did Beveridge favor expansion?
2. What methods did he use to gain support for his ideas?
3. According to Beveridge, why did "Imperialism" appeal to many Americans?

It is a noble land that God has given us—a land that can feed and clothe the world; a land set like a guard between the two oceans of the globe. It is a mighty people that God has planted on this soil. It is a people descended from the most masterful blood of history and constantly strengthened by the strong working folk of all the earth. It is a people imperial by virtue of their power, by right of their institutions, by authority of their heaven-directed purposes.

It is a glorious history our God has given His chosen people. Its keynote was struck by the Liberty Bell, and is heroic with faith in our mission and our future. It is a history of leaders who expanded the boundaries of the republic into unexplored lands and savage wildernesses. It is a history of soldiers who carried the flag across blazing deserts and through hostile mountains. It is a history of a multiplying people who overran a continent in half a century. It is a history of prophets who saw the consequences of evils inherited from the past, and of martyrs who died to save us from them.

Therefore, in this campaign, the question is larger than a party question. It is an American question. It is a world question. Shall the American people continue their restless march toward the commercial supremacy of the world? Shall free institutions extend their blessed reign until the empire of our principles is established over the hearts of all humankind?

Have we no mission to perform, no duty to discharge to our fellow humans? Has the Almighty Father given us gifts and marked us with His favor, only to rot in our own selfishness? This happens to people and nations who are cowardly and self-absorbed—China, India, and Egypt.

Adapted from Modern Eloquence, *Vol. 10, by Albert J. Beveridge, edited by Ashley H. Thorndike.*

Uncle Sam takes a look at the menu.

Shall we be as the man who had one piece of gold and hid it, or as he who had ten pieces of gold and used them until they grew to riches? And shall we gather the reward for carrying out our high duty as the sovereign power of earth? Shall we occupy new markets for what our farmers raise, new markets for what our factories make, new markets for what our merchants sell? Shall we take advantage of new sources of supply for what we do not raise or make, so that what are luxuries today will be necessities tomorrow? Shall our commerce be encouraged until American trade is the imperial trade of the entire globe?

The opposition tells us that we ought not to govern a people without their consent. I answer: The rule of liberty, that all just government takes its authority from the consent of the governed, applies only to those who are capable of self-government. I answer: We govern the Indians without their consent, we govern our territories without their consent, we govern our children without their consent. I answer: How do you assume that our government would be without their consent? Would not the people of the Philippines prefer the just, humane, civilizing government of this republic to the savage, bloody rule of plundering from which we have rescued them?

Shall we turn these people back to the bloody hands from which we have taken them? Shall we abandon them to their fate, with the wolves of conquest all about them—with Germany, Russia, France, even Japan, hungering for them? Shall we save them from those nations, to give them a self-rule of tragedy? It would be like giving a razor to a baby and telling it to shave itself.

They ask us how we will govern these new possessions. I answer: Out of local conditions and necessity. If England can govern foreign lands, so can America. If Germany can govern foreign lands, so can America. If those nations can supervise protectorates, so can America. Why is it more difficult to govern Hawaii than New Mexico or California? Both had a foreign population. Both were more distant from the seat of government when they came under our control than Hawaii is today.

Will you say by your vote that American ability to govern has decayed, that a century's experience in self-rule has failed? Will you show by your vote that you do not believe in American vigor and power and practical sense? Or will you say that we are of the ruling race of the world—that ours is the blood of government, the heart of authority, the brain and genius of administration? Will you remember that we do only what our fathers did—we simply pitch the tents of liberty farther westward, farther southward. We only continue the march of the flag.

There are so many real things to be done—canals to be dug, railways to be laid, forests to be felled, cities to be built, fields to be tilled, priceless markets to be won, ships to be launched, peoples to be saved, civilization to be proclaimed, and the flag of liberty flung to the eager air of every sea.

We cannot escape our world duties. We must carry out the purpose of a fate that has driven us to be greater than our small intentions. We cannot retreat from any soil where Providence has placed our flag. It is up to us to save that soil for liberty and civilization. For liberty and civilization and God's promise fullfilled, the flag must from now on be the symbol to all humankind.

READING REVIEW

1. What were Beveridge's arguments in favor of expansion?
2. (a) How did Beveridge support his case by appealing to his listeners' pride? (b) To their feelings of competition? (c) To their sense of duty?
3. Do you think these methods of persuasion would be effective today? Why or why not?

183 A Criticism of Imperialism

Not all Americans favored the United States' new policy of overseas expansion. Many well-known Americans spoke out against expansionism. After the Spanish-American War, Carl Schurz, a liberal reformer, became a leading opponent of American expansion. Schurz, who had originally come to the United States from Germany, had been a lawyer, an abolitionist, a Senator from Missouri, and Secretary of Interior in President Hayes' cabinet.

Schurz was especially opposed to the American annexation of the Philippines. The following are selections from a speech he gave on the subject in 1899.

READING FOCUS

1. How did America's earlier territorial gains differ from those of the 1890's?
2. Why did Schurz object to the process of "Americanization"?

According to the solemn proclamation of our government, the Spanish-American War was undertaken only for the liberation of Cuba, as a war of humanity and not of conquest. But our easy victories put conquest within our reach. When our troops took over foreign territory, a loud demand arose that, pledge or no pledge, the conquests should be kept, including even the Philippines on the other side of the globe.

Why not? was the cry. Has not the career of the Republic almost from its very beginning been one of territorial expansion? Has it not acquired Louisiana, Florida, Texas, the vast areas that came to us through the Mexican War, and Alaska? Has it not digested them well? Were not those acquisitions much larger than those now thought of? If the Republic could digest the old, why not the new? What is the difference?

Look with a clear eye, and you will soon discover differences that should warn you to look out. There are five of great importance.

1. All the former acquisitions were on this continent and, except for Alaska, on our borders.

2. They were located not in the tropical but in the temperate zone, where democratic institutions do well, and where our people could move in great numbers.

3. They were very thinly settled—in fact, without any population that would have been in the way of new settlements.

4. They could be organized as territories in the usual manner. It was expected that they would presently come into the Union as self-governing states with populations much like our own.

5. They did not require an increase in our army and navy, either to subject them to our rule or to protect them from foreign attack.

Compare now our old acquisitions on all these important points with the ones now under discussion.

They are not continental, not bordering our present land, but are overseas—the Philippines are many thousand miles distant from our coast. They are all located in the tropics, where people of the Northern races, such as Anglo-Saxons, have never moved in large numbers. They are more or less densely populated, parts of them as densely as Massachusetts. Their populations consist almost exclusively of races to whom the tropical climate is well suited—Spanish mixed with Negroes in the West Indies, and Malays, Tagals, Filipinos, Chinese, Japanese, Negritos, and various more or less barbarous tribes in the Philippines.

The question is asked whether we may hope to adapt those countries and populations to our system of government. At this, those who favor annexation answer cheerily that when they belong to us, we shall soon "Americanize" them. This seems to mean that Americans in sufficiently large numbers will move there to change the character of the people until they are more like us.

This is a false belief. If we go honestly about it, we may indeed accomplish several helpful things in those countries. But one thing we cannot do. We cannot strip the tropical climate of those qualities which have kept people of the Northern races, to which we belong, from moving and settling there in large numbers. It is true that you will find in towns of tropical regions a few persons of Anglo-Saxon or of other Northern origin—merchants, railroad builders, speculators, professional

Adapted from Frederick Bancroft, ed., Speeches, Correspondence and Political Papers of Carl Schurz, *Vol. 6.*

A political cartoon about American imperialism

people, and mechanics. But their number is small, and most of them expect to go home as soon as they make some money.

The scheme of Americanizing our "new possessions" in that way is therefore absolutely hopeless. The forces of nature are against it. Whatever we may do for their improvement, the people of the Spanish islands will outnumber us. The vast majority are completely alien to us, not only in origin and language, but in habits, traditions, ways of thinking, principles, ambitions—in short, in most things that are of the greatest importance in human and political cooperation.

What, then, shall we do with such peoples? Shall we organize those countries as territories with a view to their eventual admission as states? If they become states on an equal footing with the other states, they not only will govern themselves, but will take part in governing the whole Republic. They will share in governing us, by sending Senators and Representatives into our Congress to help make our laws, and by voting for President and Vice-President. The prospect of such consequences is so alarming that you may well pause before taking the step.

But this may be avoided, it is said, by governing the new possessions as mere dependencies, or subject provinces. This would be a most serious departure from the rule that governed our former acquisitions. It is useless to speak of the District of Columbia and Alaska as proof that we have done such things before and can do them again. Every honest person will at once admit the great difference between those cases and the permanent establishment of arbitrary government over large territories with millions of inhabitants. The question is not only whether we can do such things, but whether having the public good at heart, we *should* do them.

If we adopt such a system then we shall, for the first time since the abolition of slavery, again have two kinds of Americans. There will be Americans of the first class, who enjoy the privilege of taking part in the government in accordance with our Consitutional principles. And there will be Americans of the second class, who are to be ruled by the Americans of the first class.

This will be a difference no better—rather somewhat worse—than that which existed 125 years ago between English people of the first class and English people of the second class. The first were represented by King George and the British Parliament. The second group consisted of the American colonists. This difference led to the American Declaration of Independence—a document which, I regret to say, seems to have lost much of its charms among some of our citizens. Its basic principle was that "governments derive their just powers from the consent of the governed."

We are now told that we have never fully lived up to that principle. Therefore, we may now throw it aside altogether. But I say to you that, if we are true believers in democratic government, we should move in that direction and not away from it. If you tell me that we cannot govern the people of those new possessions in accordance with that principle, then I answer that this is a reason we should not attempt to govern them at all.

If we do, we shall change the government of the people, for the people, and by the people into a government of one part of the people, the strong, over another part, the weak. Abandoning such a basic principle may at first seem to involve only distant lands, but it can hardly fail to affect democratic government at home. And I warn the American people that a democracy cannot deny its faith in a vital principle—it cannot long play the role of king over subject populations without creating in itself ways of thinking and habits of action most dangerous to its own vitality.

READING REVIEW

1. According the Schurz, how did earlier American territorial gains differ from those of the 1890's?
2. Why did he oppose the American annexation of the Philippines?
3. How did Schurz regard the effort to "Americanize" foreign peoples?
4. (a) Do you think Schurz was more concerned about the effects of expansion on people in the territories or their effects on Americans? (b) Cite evidence from the reading to support your conclusion.

184 The White Man's Burdens

In 1899 Rudyard Kipling, a British writer, wrote a poem called "The White Man's Burden." The poem, written and published in the United States, immediately became a popular defense of expansionism and imperialism. Kipling wrote that the "white man's burden," or responsibility, was to take up the task of governing what Kipling described as childlike and untamed people. He argued that it was the duty of more advanced nations to bring civilization to the backward peoples of the earth.

The poem was imitated and made fun of by many Americans, especially those who were against expansion in the Philippines. The first stanza of Kipling's seven-stanza poem appears here. Following it are poems which are imitations of and answers to his poem.

READING FOCUS

1. What was Kipling's opinion of the conquered people?
2. What was the purpose of the poems which follow the Kipling poem?

Take up the White Man's burden—
    Send forth the best ye breed—
Go bind your sons to exile
    To serve your captives' need;
To wait in heavy harness,
    On fluttered folk and wild—
Your new-caught sullen peoples,
    Half-devil and half-child.

*   *   *   *

Pile on the brown man's burden
    To gratify your greed;
Go, clear away the Negroes
    Who progress would impede;
Be very stern, for truly
    'Tis useless to be mild
With new-caught sullen peoples,
    Half devil and half child.
Pile on the brown man's burden,
    And if ye rouse his hate,
Meet his old-fashioned reasons
    With Maxims up-to-date;
With shells and dum-dum bullets,†
    A hundred times make plain
The brown man's loss must ever
    Imply the white man's gain.

*   *   *   *

Take up the sword and rifle,
    Send forth your ships with speed,
To join the nations' scramble,
    And vie with them in greed;
Go find your goods a market;
    Beyond the western flood,
The heathen who withstand you
    Shall answer it in blood.

† A Maxim was a machine gun; dum-dum bullets expanded on impact.

First poem from "The White Man's Burden" by Rudyard Kipling, 1899. Second, third, and fourth poems adapted from Little Brown Brothers *by Leon Wolff.*

Take up the sword and rifle,
    Still keep your conscience whole—
So soon is found an unction [remedy]
    To soothe a guilty soul.
Go with it to your Maker,
    Find what excuse ye can—
Rob for the sake of justice,
    Kill for the love of man.

*   *   *   *

We've taken up the white man's burden
    Of ebony and brown;
Now will you tell us, Rudyard,
    How we may put it down?

READING REVIEW

1. What was Kipling's attitude toward the conquered people?
2. (a) What was the point of the first poem that imitated the Kipling poem? (b) of the second? (c) of the last, four-line poem?
3. Cite two examples from the poems which satirized the white man's reasons for continuing to follow an expansionist policy.

185   From The Hawaiian Viewpoint

By the late 1800's Americans owned most of the sugar plantations in Hawaii and had obtained a treaty that allowed Hawaiian sugar to enter the United States duty free. However, the McKinley Tariff Act of 1890 threatened the Hawaiian sugar planters by allowing all foreign sugar to enter the United States duty free and by giving a two-cent per pound subsidy to American sugar producers. Shortly afterward the planters asked that Hawaii be annexed by the United States, believing this was the only way to save their sugar industry.

Queen Liliuokalani, who was supported by the Hawaiian people, opposed annexation. And in 1893, because of her efforts against them, the planters and other Americans in Hawaii revolted against her rule and set up their own government. In this selection, the queen told what happened in Hawaii before the annexation.

READING FOCUS

1. Why did the Hawaiians allow Americans to take over their government?
2. What actions of the United States did Queen Liliuokalani criticize?

It has been said that the Hawaiian people under the rule of the chiefs were harshly ruled. Under the monarchy, it was held, their condition greatly improved, but the native government in any form finally became intolerable to the better informed part of the community. I shall not examine such statements in detail. But I do feel called upon to make a few remarks from my own—that is to say, the native Hawaiian—viewpoint.

I shall not claim that in the days of Captain Cook our people were civilized. I shall not claim anything more for their progress in civilization and Christian morality than missionary writers have. Perhaps I may safely claim even less, admitting the criticism of some intelligent visitors who were not missionaries. In other words, the habits and prejudices of New England Puritanism were not well adapted to a tropical people, and could not be thoroughly absorbed by them.

But they have accepted Christianity in substance. I know of no people who have developed a tenderer Christian conscience, or who have shown themselves more ready to obey its commands. And where else in the world's history have savage people, pagan for ages, with fixed customs and beliefs, made equal progress in civilization and Christianity in the same amount of time?

Does it say nothing for us that we have always recognized our Christian teachers as worthy of authority in our councils? That while four fifths of the population of our islands were killed by diseases introduced by foreigners, the ruling class held on to Christian morality, and gave its strong support and service to the work of saving and civilizing the masses? Has not this class loyally held on to the brotherly alliance made with the better group of foreign settlers, giving freely of its authority and its substance, its sons and daughters, to cement and prosper it?

Why should it be thought strange that education and knowledge of the world have made us able to see that as a race we have some special mental and physical requirements not shared by other races? That certain habits and ways of living are better for our health and happiness than others? And that a separate nationality and a particular form of govern-

Adapted from Hawaii's Story by Hawaii's Queen *by Liliuokalani.*

Americans owned the first large sugar plantations in Hawaii.

ment, as well as special laws, are, at least for the present, best for us? These things were ours until the pitiless and tireless "annexation policy" was effectively backed by the naval power of the United States.

Before this we had allowed foreigners to give us a consitution and control the offices of government. Not without protest, indeed, for this grabbing of power caused us much humiliation and distress. But we did not resist it by force. It had not entered our hearts to believe that these friends and allies from the United States would ever go so far as to overthrow our form of government, grab our nation by the throat, and turn it over to a foreign power.

Perhaps there is a kind of right, known as the "Right of Conquest," under which robbers may take whatever they are strong enough to grab from others. I will not pretend to decide how far civilization and Christian teachings have outlawed this right.

If we have been friendly to those who sought our ruin, it was because they were Americans, like those whom we believed to be our dearest friends and allies. If we did not resist their final outrage by force, it was because we could not do so without striking at the military might of the United States. The conspirators, having actually gained possession of the government, refused to give up their conquest. So it happens that the people of the islands have no voice in determining their future, but are in a condition like that of the American Indians.

It is not for me to consider this matter from the American point of view. The current question of annexation, however, involves a departure from the established policy of that country and a dangerous change in its foreign relations. I am able to say, with absolute authority, that the native people of Hawaii are entirely loyal to their own chiefs, and are deeply attached to their own customs and government. They either do not understand, or bitterly oppose, the scheme of annexation.

Perhaps I may say here a final word about the Americans who favor this annexation of Hawaii. I observe that it is pretty much a party matter, favored chiefly by Republican leaders and politicians. But is it really a matter of party interest? Is the American Republic to decline and become a colonizer and a land-grabber? And is this prospect acceptable to a people who depend upon self-government for their liberties? There is little question but that the United States could become a successful rival of the European nations in the race for conquest and could create a great military and naval power if such is its ambition. But is such an ambition praiseworthy? Is such a departure from established principles patriotic or wise?

READING REVIEW

1. According to Queen Liliuokalani, why did the Hawaiians let the Americans take control of their government?
2. For what actions did Queen Liliuokalani criticize the Americans?
3. (a) What special interests did some Americans have in the Hawaiian islands? (b) How did this affect the United States policy with regard to establishing a new government for Hawaii?

Expansion in the Caribbean
(1898–1914)

186 A Canal Builder at Work

Americans in the early 1900's were proud of their great achievement in building the Panama Canal. Much of the credit for this feat belonged to Colonel Goethals, who was appointed chief engineer by Theodore Roosevelt in 1907. Goethals had to deal with a labor force of 30,000 workers, overcome landslides that delayed the work, and solve enormous engineering problems. Offices, schools, houses, recreation centers, machine shops, and dining halls—all had to be built. Goethals spent time each day listening to workers' complaints, and he soon won the respect and dedication of the workers. In this section Arthur Bullard, who traveled to Panama in 1909, told about the building of the canal.

READING FOCUS
1. Why was Goethals a successful leader?
2. What was Bullard's opinion of Goethals?

"Tell me something about Colonel Goethals." My friend was a keen observer who had already given me much information about life and work in the Canal Zone.

"You want to know about the old man?" he said after a moment's thought. "Well, the most distinctive picture of him I have is this. I used to live at Culebra. One night I was sitting out on the porch, smoking. There were only a few lights here and there in the Administration Building. One by one they went out, all except that in the old man's office. It was almost ten o'clock when his light went out. It was the dry season. A full moon, as big as a dining-room table, was out—a gorgeous night. The old man

Adapted from Arthur Bullard, Panama: The Canal, the Country and the People.

came out and walked across the grass to his house. He didn't stop to look up at the moon; he just walked along, his head a little forward, still thinking. And he hadn't been in his own house ten minutes before all the lights were out there. He'd gone to bed. The only time the colonel isn't working is from 10 P.M. to 6 A.M., when he's asleep."

That seems to be the thing which impresses our men down here most of all about the boss. He is always on the job.

Just what is the job?

Strictly speaking, it is administrative, rather than constructive, engineering. The type of the canal was decided upon before the present commission was installed. They have had but few changes of importance to make: widening the channel in the Cut, increasing the size of the locks, and moving the Pacific locks inland, beyond the range of a hostile fleet. Their work has been the perfecting of details and the carrying out of what had been already determined.

Colonel George Washington Goethals, the Chief Engineer and Chairman of the Panama Canal Commission, is now at the head of this great national job of ours. A visitor to the Isthmus who has not included the colonel among the sights has missed more than half of what there is to see down here. You will not have to wait long before you are brought into the throne room, and are face to face with the most absolute autocrat in the world.

Many people have described Colonel Goethals as having a boyish face. But they must have seen him with his hat on, for his hair is white. If, as they say, his face looks 20 and his hair 60, I could not see it, for his eyes—which dominate—look 40. He is broad-shouldered and erect. Above everything, he looks alert and fit. Although he does not spare himself, he has not lost a day from malaria.

Of course, the first thing you do will be to hand him your perfectly useless letter from your representative in Congress. Useless, because even if you have no letter he will show you every courtesy he can without interfering with the job. And he will not interfere with the job even if you bring letters from all the members of Congress.

Like every man who accomplishes a great amount of work, he believes in routine.

Six mornings a week he is "out on the line." He took me along on one of these inspection trips. It was before seven when we reached Pedro Miguel, and we walked back through the Cut to Empire. It was four hours of bitter hard walking, for the colonel kept to no well-worn path. Whatever interested him he wished to see close up. The colonel said, "The only way to keep your health in this climate is to take a little exercise every morning." Doubtless it is true, but I had rather die quickly than keep alive at that rate.

He spends his afternoons on routine desk work, signing papers, approving reports, and so forth. It is part of his system that he discourages oral reports. Everything comes to him on paper. If he wants to talk with any of his subordinates, he generally does it during his morning trips—on the spot. Perhaps the phrase he uses most frequently is, "Write it down."

The afternoon office work is often interrupted by callers. The stream of tourists grows steadily, and the colonel realizes that it is we, the people of the United States, who are doing this canal job. Anyone who is sufficiently interested to come down and look it over is welcome.

The most remarkable part of Colonel Goethals' routine is his Sunday Court of Low, Middle, and High Justice. The colonel holds a session every Sunday morning. I had the good fortune to be admitted one Sunday morning to the audience chamber.

The first callers were a Negro couple from Jamaica. They had a difference of opinion as to the ownership of $35 which the wife had earned by washing. Colonel Goethals listened until the fact was established that she had earned it, then ordered the man to return it. He started to protest something about a husband's property rights under the English law. "All right," the colonel said, decisively. "Say the word, and I'll deport you. You can get all the English law you want in Jamaica." The husband decided to pay and stay.

Then came a Spanish worker who had been hurt in an accident. The colonel called in his chief clerk and told him to help the unfortunate man prepare his claim. "See that the papers are prepared correctly and have them pushed through."

A man came in who had just been thrown out of the service for brutality to the men under him. This action was the result of an investigation before a special committee. The man wanted his job back. The colonel read over the papers in the case, and when he spoke, his language was vigorous. "If you have any new evidence, I will instruct the committee to re-open your case. But as long as this report stands against you, you will get no mercy from this office. If the men had broken your head with a crowbar, I would have stood up for them. We don't need slave drivers on this job."

Then a committee from the Machinists' Union wanted an opinion on some new shop rules. A nurse wanted a longer vacation than the regulations allow. A man and his wife were dissatisfied with the house they had been given. A supervisor of steam shovels came in to ask advice about applying for another job under the Panama government. The end of the canal work is approaching and the farsighted men are beginning to look into the future. "Of course I can't advise you," the colonel said. "You know I would hate to see you go. But if you decide that it is wise, come in and see me. I may be able to give you some introductions which will help you." (And, as everyone knows that a letter of introduction from the chairman of the commission would look like an order to the Panama government, there is another man who will want to vote for Goethals for President in 1916!)

An American Negro introduced some humor. He was convinced that his services were of more value than his foreman felt they were. The colonel preferred to accept the foreman's judgment in the matter. The dissatisfied worker announced that he was the best blacksmith's helper on the Isthmus and that he planned to appeal this decision. The colonel's eyes twinkled. "To whom are you going to ap-

Construction of the Panama Canal

One view of America's role in Colombia's affairs

peal?" he asked. For the fact is that the decisions made in these Sunday sessions will not be changed before the Day of Judgment.

The procession kept up till noon—pitiful, patience-trying foolishness, with occasional humor. "Once in a while," the colonel said, "something turns up which is really important for me to know. And, anyway, they feel better after they have seen me, even if I cannot help them. They feel that they got a fair chance to state their troubles. They are less likely to cause discontent. But it is a strain."

READING REVIEW

1. Why was it necessary for Goethals to be an "absolute autocrat" in supervising the construction of the Panama Canal?
2. **(a)** What phrase did Goethals use most frequently? **(b)** Why did he require his subordinates to do this?
3. **(a)** What was the purpose of the Sunday Court of Low, Middle, and High Justice? **(b)** How did this practice speed up the ultimate completion of the Panama Canal?

187 Colombia's Protest on America's Actions

The actions taken by the United States to obtain the right to build a canal across the Isthmus of Panama increased the Latin American nations' distrust of their neighbor to the north. Colombia, which was forced to give up the territory of Panama, felt especially threatened. However, that small nation realized that it could not resist the power of the United States. Consequently, lead-ers of Colombia's government, who were seeking payment for their former territory of Panama, appealed to world opinion for support.

The following selections are from a pamphlet written by Colombia's foreign minister, Francisco José Urrutía, to present his nation's case. A year after the canal was officially opened in July 1920, the United States paid $25 million to Colombia, which in turn recognized the independence of Panama.

READING FOCUS

1. Why was Colombia angered by America's action in 1903?
2. What did Urrutía suggest the United States do to insure the safety of the Panama Canal?

Until 1903 the relations between Colombia and the United States were most friendly. Good will toward Colombia was always recognized by the United States, not only in negotiations about the Panama Canal but in all matters.

The statement that Colombia ever opposed the opening of the Panama Canal is absolutely untrue. On the contrary, the entire diplomatic history of Colombia, from the time of its freedom from Spain, shows how great was its desire to see the canal built. Out of regard for self preservation, it did try to bring this about without harming its own sovereignty.

With the canal now open, Colombia cannot ignore the fact that this great work is one of the chief factors in the future material development of the world. But as long as the agreement giving a lawful title to the United States is not carried out, Colombia will also maintain that the work, great as it is, stands as a monument to an even greater crime. It will insist that Colombia and Colombia alone is the lawful owner of the Isthmus of Panama. If the formal opening of the canal should take place before a final settlement is arrived at, Colombia will be forced once more to protest to the other nations of the world, against the violation of its sovereignty.

In the eyes of the people of Colombia and of all America, the Panama Canal stands for the victory of might over right, the triumph of

---

Adapted from Francisco José Urrutía. A Commentary on the Declaration of the Rights of Nations. *Washington, D.C.: 1916.*

force over law. It stands for this far more than it does for the splendid conquest of tropical nature by the science and energy of the people of the United States. The United States has the power to remove this feeling, to change this state of affairs, and to insure that the canal shall be what it would have been without the crime committed in 1903—a great and powerful link uniting Colombia and the United States.

Reference has been made to the danger threatening the canal if it were attacked from Colombian territory, and of the necessity of preventing an alliance between Colombia and any other nation. If any such danger or any such necessity exist, the best guarantee of the safety of the canal lies in an agreement with Colombia. Fear that the Panama Canal might be attacked some day from Colombian territory may be avoided by the United States. This cannot be through a policy of force, but through a policy of friendship and justice. Such a policy calls for returning—by means of payment for past grievances—the ancient and traditional good will and friendship between Colombia and United States.

If the safeguarding of the Panama Canal enters into the scheme of the national defense of the United States, it is natural to suppose that that protection would be sought in an honest and loyal manner by encouraging the friendship of Colombia and by respecting its sovereignty. It can never be reached by returning to a policy already disapproved by both the American continents.

READING REVIEW

1. Summarize the relationship between Colombia and the United States prior to 1903.
2. What did Urrutía mean by "the crime committed in 1903"?
3. **(a)** What action did Urrutía threaten to take against the United States? **(b)** Do you think this was a serious threat? Why or why not?

188 An American in Mexico, 1914

After a revolution broke out in Mexico in 1910, relations between Mexico and the United States became troubled. At first President Wilson, who was anxious not to intervene in Mexico, followed a policy of "watchful waiting." However, in 1914 several American sailors were arrested in Tampico. When the Mexican government refused to apologize by firing a 21-gun salute, Wilson sent American troops to take Veracruz.

The anxious days that followed are described in the following selection by Edith O'Shaughnessy, the wife of Nelson O'Shaughnessy, American charge d'affaires at the United States embassy in Mexico City. Although O'Shaughnessy had to support Wilson's actions, in later years he declared that Wilson's Mexican policy was "brutal, unwarranted, and stupid."

READING FOCUS

1. What was Edith O'Shaughnessy's opinion of President Huerta?
2. Why did President Wilson send American troops to Mexico in 1914?
3. How did Edith O'Shaughnessy assess America's role in the Mexican Revolution?

April 18th. 6:30 p.m.
It makes me sick with dread to think of the probable fate of Americans in the deserts and mountains of Mexico. Someone has made a mistake, somewhere, somehow, that we should come in to give the final blow to this distracted nation, which still holds on, and rightly, to the little sovereignty we have left it. The foreign powers think we are playing the most cold-blooded, most cruel game of grab in history.

10 p.m.
If we get through this, the next incident will mean war. I hope that the leaders in Washington will appreciate some of the difficulties Nelson has to meet, and act accordingly. How glad I am that I haven't sent my son or my jewels with various terror-stricken friends who have fled. War hasn't come yet. After everything is said and done, everything depends on the life of that wise and patient old Indian [Huerta], who—whatever his sins—is legally president of Mexico. Chase legality out of Latin America and where are you? After him will come anarchy, chaos, and finally intervention—the biggest police job ever undertaken in the Western Hemisphere, however one may feel like making little of it from a military standpoint.

Adapted from A Diplomat's Wife in Mexico *by Edith O'Shaughnessy.*

American troops in Mexico.

April 19th. 2:30 a.m.
I can't sleep. National and personal problems keep running through my brain. Three railroad men came to the embassy this evening. They brought reports of a plan for the massacre of Americans in the street tonight. But, strange and wonderful thing, a heavy rain is falling. It is my only experience of a midnight rain in Mexico, except that which fell upon the mobs crying "Death to Diaz," nearly three years ago. As all Mexicans hate to get wet, rain is as effective as shellfire in clearing the streets, and I don't think there will be any trouble. Fate seems to keep an occasional unnatural shower on hand for Mexican crises.

Had this war been started by a great incident or for a great principle, I could stand it. But because the details of a salute could not be decided upon, we cause ourselves, and inflict on others, the horrors of war. It is no situation for amateurs. The longer I live the more respect I have for technical training. Every foreign office in Europe or any other continent keeps experts for just such cases. I may become an interventionist, but *after* Huerta. He has proved himself greatly superior, in executive ability, to any leader Mexico has produced since Diaz, in spite of his lack of balance and his surprising childishness. He would have sold his soul to please the United States and gain recognition. [Wilson refused to recognize the Huerta government.] In that small, soft hand (doubtless bloody, too) were possibilities of bringing back prosperity.

April 20th
My heart is sick. Wednesday that great fleet arrives. What is it going to fight? It can't bombard Veracruz. The streets are full and the houses overflowing with fleeing people. It can't climb the mountains and protect the countless Americans living inland. Huerta's army is engaged in the north in a death struggle against enemies of the government, armed with our guns. Oh, the pity of it!

And this city, beautiful Mexico City, so wonderfully located in the very center of the Western Hemisphere, a great continent to the north and the south, halfway between immense oceans, and lifted nearly 8,000 feet [2,400 meters] up to the heavens!

April 21st
We are at war. American and Mexican blood flowed in the streets of Veracruz today. The story that reaches us is that the captain of the German ship *Ypiranga* tried to land 17 million rounds of ammunition. Admiral Fletcher protested. The captain of the *Ypiranga* insisted on doing it. The admiral prevented him by force, and they say, took the town—thus putting us on a war basis. Whether this is a true version of what has happened I don't know. It

has been many a year since American blood flowed in the streets of Veracruz. General Scott took it in 1847. The endless repetitions of history!

April 22nd
The newspapers are rather fierce this morning. One headline in the *Independiente* says that "the Mexican bullets will no longer spill brothers' blood, but will hit blond heads and white breasts swollen with vanity and cowardice." The newspapers add that the Americans landed "without a declaration of war, like criminals." It is impossible to expect the Mexicans to grasp the idea that the landing of our troops was a simple police measure. In the face of the facts, I am sure such distinctions will be overlooked. At 7:30 an officer appeared in the drawing-room, saying that President Huerta was outside. There was no time to ring for servants. I went to the door and waited while the fearless old Indian, in his gray sweater and soft hat, came quickly up the steps. It was his first and last visit to the embassy during our stay there.

I led him into the drawing-room, where we had a strange and moving conversation. I could not, for my country's sake, speak the endless regret that was in my heart for the official part we had been forced to play in the action carried out by us to his country's undoing. He greeted me calmly.

"Señora, how do you do? I fear you have had many annoyances."

Then he sat back, quietly in a big armchair, impersonal and mysterious. I answered as easily as I could that the times were difficult for everyone. I said that we were very grateful for what he had done for our personal safety and that of other Americans. I asked him if there was anything we could do for him. He gave me a long, piercing look, and after a pause, answered:

"Nothing, Señora. All that is done I must do myself. Here I must remain. The moment has not come for me to go. Nothing but death could remove me now."

I felt the tears come to my eyes, as I answered—"Death is not so terrible a thing."

He answered again, very quietly, "It is the natural law, to which we must all give in. We were born into the world according to the natural law, and must leave according to it—that is all."

He does not want us to leave by way of Guadalajara and Manzanillo. He is giving us his train tomorrow night to take us to Veracruz. There will be a full escort, including three officers of high rank.

I was dreadfully keyed up. I felt the tears come to my eyes. He seemed to think that it was fear that moved me, for he told me not to be anxious.

I said, "I am not weeping for myself, but for the tragedy of life."

And, indeed, since seeing him I have been in a sea of sadness, personal and impersonal—impersonal because of the crushing destiny that can overtake a strong man and a country, and personal, because this many-colored, vibrant Mexican experience of mine is drawing to a close. Nothing can ever be like it.

As we three [Huerta, Edith, and Nelson] stood there together he said, very quietly, his last word:

"I hold no ill will toward the American people, nor toward President Wilson." And, after a slight pause, he added, "He has not understood."

It was the first and last time I ever heard him speak the President's name. I gave him my hand as he stood with his other hand on Nelson's shoulder, and knew that this was indeed the end. I think he realized that my heart was warm and my sympathies rushing out to beautiful, agonizing Mexico. For, as he stood at the door, he suddenly turned and made me a deep bow. Then, taking Nelson's arm, he went out into the starry, perfumed evening, and I turned back into the house I was so soon to leave, with the sadness of life like a hot point, deep in my heart. So is history written. So do circumstances and a man's will seem to raise him up to great ends, and so does destiny crush him.

I am sad, very sad, tonight. Whatever else life may have in reserve for me, this last conversation with a strong man of another temperament than mine will remain on my heart—his calm, his philosophy on the eve of a war he knows can only end in disaster.

READING REVIEW

1. What incident provoked American intervention in Mexico?
2. **(a)** What did Edith O'Shaughnessy think of America's intervention in Mexico? **(b)** Based on this reading do you think America's actions were justified? Why or why not?

3. What were Edith O'Shaughnessy's feelings toward President Huerta?
4. How did President Huerta feel toward President Wilson and the United States? Cite evidence from the reading which supports your answer.

CHAPTER
30 Involvement in World War I
(1914–1920)

189 Wilson's "War Message"

After World War I broke out in Europe in 1914, the United States managed to keep out of the war for nearly three years. During this period both sides—the Allies and the Central Powers—violated American neutrality. American ships bound for Europe were stopped by both Great Britain and Germany. However, in 1917 Germany sharply increased submarine warfare against the United States.

After months of growing tension over German submarine warfare and its violation of the rights of neutral shipping, President Wilson asked Congress to declare war on Germany. On April 2, 1917, Wilson went before Congress and delivered his "War Message." It was passed by the Senate two days later, by a vote of 82 to 6, and by the House on April 6, by a vote of 375 to 50.

READING FOCUS
1. Why should the United States declare war?
2. According to Wilson, what were America's war aims?

I have called the Congress into special session because there are serious, very serious, choices of policy to be made, and made immediately.

Adapted from A Compilation of the Messages and Papers of the Presidents, *Vol. XVII. New York: Bureau of National Literature, Inc.*

It was neither right nor constitutional that I should take the responsibility of making them.

On February 3rd, 1917, I officially informed you of the announcement of the Imperial German Government that on and after February 1st, it would put aside all restraints of law or humanity and use its submarines to sink every ship that tried to approach the ports of Great Britain and Ireland, the western coast of Europe, or any of the ports controlled by the enemies of Germany within the Mediterranean.

The new policy has swept every restriction aside. Ships of every kind, whatever their flag, type, cargo, destination, or errand, have been ruthlessly fired on and sent to the bottom of the sea without warning and without thought of help or mercy for those on board. Even hospital ships and ships carrying relief to the stricken people of Belgium have been sunk with the same reckless lack of sympathy or of principle.

I was for a little while unable to believe that such things would, in fact, be done by any government that considered itself civilized. International law had its origin in the attempt to set up some laws which would be respected and observed upon the seas, where no nation had the right of control. That law has been built up by painful stage after stage, always with a clear view of what the heart and conscience of humanity demanded.

I am not now thinking of the loss of property involved, great and serious as that is, but only of the reckless and wholesale destruction of the lives of noncombatants, men, women, and children, engaged in activities which have always, even in the darkest period of modern history, been regarded as innocent and legitimate. Property can be paid for; the lives of peaceful, innocent people cannot be.

The present German submarine warfare against commerce is a warfare against humankind. It is a war against all nations. American ships have been sunk, American lives taken in ways that have stirred us very deeply. But the ships and people of other neutral, friendly nations have been sunk in the same way. There has been no discrimination. The challenge is to all people. Each nation must decide for itself how to meet it.

When I addressed Congress on February 26th, I thought that it would be enough to assert our neutral right with arms; our right to use the sea against unlawful interference;

our right to keep our people safe against unlawful violence. But armed neutrality, it now appears, will not work. Because submarines are, in effect, outlaws when used as the German submarines have been used against merchant shipping, it is impossible to defend ships against their attacks. (The law of nations has assumed that merchant ships would defend themselves against cruisers or visible ships chasing them upon the open sea.) Under the present circumstances, we have to destroy the ships on sight.

The German government denies the right of neutrals to use arms at all within certain areas of the sea. The Germans say that the armed guards which we have placed on our merchant ships will be treated as outside the protection of law and dealt with as pirates would be. Armed neutrality is weak enough at best. In such circumstances it is likely only to produce what it was meant to prevent—it is practically certain to draw us into the war without either the rights or the effectiveness of belligerents.

There is one choice we cannot make, that we are incapable of making. We will not choose the path of submission and suffer the most sacred rights of our nation and our people to be ignored or violated. The wrongs against which we now array ourselves are no common wrongs; they cut to the very roots of human life.

With a strong sense of the solemn and even tragic character of the step I am taking and of the grave responsibilities it involves, but in unhesitating obedience to what I see as my constitutional duty, I advise that the Congress declare the recent course of the Imperial German Government to be, in fact, nothing less than war against the government and people of the United States. I advise that it formally accept the status of belligerent which has thus been thrust upon it. I advise that it take immediate steps not only to put the country in a more thorough state of defense, but also to use all its power and resources to defeat the German empire and end the war.

We are now about to accept battle with this natural foe of liberty and shall, if necessary, spend the whole force of the nation to end its power. We are glad, now that we see the facts with no veil of false pretense about them, to fight thus for the ultimate peace of the world and for the liberation of its peoples, the Ger-

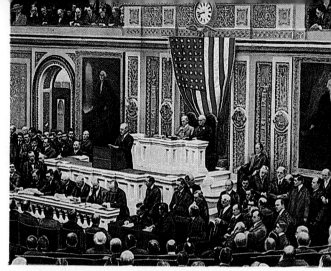
President Wilson addresses Congress.

man peoples included; for the rights of nations great and small and the privilege of human beings everywhere to choose their way of life and obedience. The world must be made safe for democracy. Its peace must be planted upon the tested foundations of political liberty.

We have no selfish ends to serve. We desire no conquest, no dominion. We seek no payment for ourselves, no material compensation for the sacrifices we shall freely make. We are but one of the champions of the rights of humans. We shall be satisfied when those rights have been made as secure as the faith and the freedom of nations can make them.

Just because we fight without hatred and without selfish objectives, seeking nothing for ourselves but what we wish to share with all free peoples, we shall, I feel confident, conduct ourselves without passion and observe the principles of right and fair play we are fighting for.

It is a distressing and oppressive duty which I have performed in thus speaking to you. There may be many months of fiery trial and sacrifice ahead of us. It is a fearful thing to lead this great peaceful people into war, into the most terrible and disastrous of all wars, with civilization itself in the balance. But the right is more precious than peace. We shall fight for the things which we have always carried nearest our hearts—for democracy, for the right of those who submit to authority to have a voice in their own governments, for the rights and liberties of small nations, for such a universal domination of right as shall bring peace and safety to all nations and make the world itself at last free.

To such a task we can dedicate our lives and our fortunes, everything that we are and everything that we have. We can do this with the pride of those who know that the day has come when America is privileged to spend its blood and its might for the principles that gave it birth, happiness, and peace. God helping us, we cannot do otherwise.

READING REVIEW

1. **(a)** List two reasons why Wilson felt the United States should declare war in 1917. **(b)** Do you agree with Wilson? Why or why not?
2. What did Wilson advise the country to do?
3. What were America's objectives upon entering World War II?

190 Women Unite to Support the War

American women made a great contribution to the war effort. Many of them took over jobs in factories and industry. Many others did volunteer work for organizations such as the Red Cross. They spent many hours preparing bandages to be used in hospitals and first-aid stations. Mary Carolyn Davies, an American writer, described this experience in a poem she called "Fifth Avenue and Grand Street." In the poem, Fifth Avenue stands for wealth and fashion, while Grand Street, on New York's Lower East Side, was a low-income area where many immigrants lived.

Factory workers, 1920

READING FOCUS

1. What was the purpose of this poem?
2. What common element brought the women together?

I sat beside her, rolling bandages.
I peeped. "Fifth Avenue," her clothes were
    saying.
It's "Grand Street," I know well, my shirt-
    waist [a kind of dress] says,
And shoes, and hat, but then, she didn't hear,
Or she pretended not, for we were laying
Our coats aside, and as we were so near,
She saw my pin like hers. [Many women dur-
    ing the war wore a star-shaped pin to
    show that someone close to them was
    serving in the armed forces.]
And when girls are
Wearing a pin these days that has a star,
They smile out at each other. We did that,
And then she didn't seem to see my hat.

I sat beside her, handling gauze and lint,
And thought of Jim. She thought of someone
    too;
Under the smile there was a little glint
In her eyelashes, that was how I knew.
I wasn't crying—but I haven't any
Pride in it; we've a better chance than they
To take blows standing, for we've had so
    many.
We two sat, fingers busy, all that day.

I'd spoken first, if I'd known what to say.
But she did soon, and after, told of him.
The man she wore the star for, and the way
He'd gone at once. I bragged a bit of Jim;
Who wouldn't who had ever come to know
Him? When the girls all rose to go,
She stood there, shyly, with her gloves half
    on,
Said, "Come to see me, won't you?" and was
    gone.

I meant to call, too, I'd have liked it then
For we'd a lot in common, with our men
Across. But now that peace is here again
And our boys safe, I can't help wondering—
    Well,

"Fifth Avenue and Grand Street" by Mary Carolyn Davies.

Will she forget, and crawl back in her shell
And if I call, say "Show this person out"?
Or still be friendly as she was? I doubt
If Grand [Street] will sit beside Fifth Avenue
Again, and be politely spoken to.

We're sisters while the danger lasts, it's true;
But rich and poor's equality must cease
(For women especially), of course, in peace.

READING REVIEW

1. What do you think the writer was trying to say in this poem?
2. **(a)** Why did it apply especially to women? **(b)** Do you think the writer was right? Why or why not?
3. **(a)** Do you think the two women described in the poem will meet and be friends after the war is over? **(b)** Which stanzas in the poem support your conclusion?

191   Action at the Front

During World War I, about 8 million soldiers were killed and about 20 million were wounded in the fighting. It was the first war in which tanks, dirigibles, and airplanes were used. And it was the first war in which submarines and machine guns were used on a large scale. The use of these weapons, and of poison gas, for mass killing greatly increased the horrors of the fighting. On the western front, soldiers spent weeks in muddy, rat-filled trenches facing steady artillery bombardments and the threat of poison gas.

Eldon Canright, a private from Wisconsin, spent 180 days in the trenches along the western front. In this letter home, he told his family what the fighting there was like.

READING FOCUS

1. How did Canright feel about fighting?
2. What aspects of war did he find exciting?

Somewhere in France
July 8, 1918

My Dear Folks:
I believe I have told you in another letter that because of the fine record we have made since we have been at the front, we have been chosen as "shock troops." Well, we sure are being shocked!

Try and picture the very worst thunderstorm you have ever heard. Then multiply it by about 10,000 and you will get some idea of the battle that has been and still is raging along this front and in which we are taking a very active part!

The battle started shortly after midnight a few days ago and has been raging ever since! It started with a very heavy bombardment all along the front, and as the country here is very flat, you can see for a long way. I can tell you that it is some sight at night to see the blinding flashes of the guns all along the line. Even far off on the horizon you can see the pink glow flare up and die down and flare up and die down again—very much like a city burning in the distance. The roar and crash of the guns just seems to tear the air into pieces, and explosions shake the ground. To add to the confusion you have the whine and shrieks of the shells, some coming and some going! And signal rockets of all colors are constantly shooting up into the air, and that is the way the army "talks" at night. It's a wonderful sight! The first night, a shell struck an ammunition supply and rockets went shooting in every direction. It lasted for several minutes and was very thrilling!

Of course every so often the Germans send over poison gas. We have to be constantly on the alert for it and wear our gas clothes most of the time, and carry our gas masks all the time!

We all have cotton in our ears. Still, the noise of the guns has made some of us temporarily deaf. We have not taken off any of our clothes or gone to bed since the battle started. When it slows up a little we just lie down on the ground, right by the guns, and get what little rest and sleep we can. Our meals are brought to us, as we may not leave the position long enough to go and get them!

The first day they shot down an observation balloon right near us. A pilot attacked it and hit it with his machine gun. The balloon came down in flames, but the observer jumped out and landed with a parachute! However, about a minute later, even before the observer had

---

Adapted from "Some War-Time Letters" by Eldon J. Canright in the Wisconsin Magazine of History, V: 192–195 (1921–1922).

hit the ground, another airplane had rushed up after the plane that "got" the balloon. The second plane shot him down and he came tumbling out of the clouds with his plane in flames. That happened three days ago, and the burned and broken airplane is still lying there, and so are the two pilots. They are an awful sight. And when the wind is in the right direction (or rather wrong direction) we get a very disagreeable odor, and there are several dead horses, etc., lying out there, too. No one has had time to bury them yet!

During the daytime there are a great many airplanes flying overhead, constantly trying to "see" what the other side is doing. We have seen some very exciting air battles. It is nothing unusual to see anywhere from two to two dozen airplanes fighting and chasing each other in and out of the clouds as they try to get into position to fire—we can hear the "spitting" of their machine guns as they fire. Sometimes you can hear them fighting when they are above the clouds, too! And twice a very daring German pilot flew down over our position and turned his machine gun on us! We could hear the "whang and spit" of the bullets as they struck the ground within a few feet of us! He flew so low that we could see the black cross on the plane and see the pilot shooting at us! But they didn't stay long. They would just shoot down and fire and then away they'd go before we had a chance to shoot back at them.

You see, we are right out in the open with no trenches to protect us, and so we are an easy mark for anything like that! And the Germans have been sending over many shells, too! So the field around our position is all torn up with shell holes—some big ones, too. One of those big shells makes a noise like the rumble and roar of a freight train going about 1,000 miles [1609 kilometers] an hour! When we hear them coming we say, "Here comes another of the devil's fast freights!" And when they burst, a mountain of rocks and dirt shoots up in the air higher than the trees! They make a hole about eight feet [2.5 meters] deep and about fifteen feet [4.5 meters] in diameter. And shell fragments scatter for about 300 feet [91 meters]. A shell fragment makes an awful wound, too, as it just tears a great hole in you, while a bullet just drills a clean round hole! So you can imagine what would happen if one of those shells should make a "direct hit" on our position!

There is, or rather was, a little town over in a clump of trees near here—now there isn't even a wall or a piece of a house standing. There are just broken bricks and pieces of plaster scattered around.

Another thrilling sight is to see the ammunition caissons [wagons] bringing up ammunition. Each caisson is drawn by six horses hitched in teams of two, and a man rides the left horse of each team. They generally come up just before dark and you can see the long line of caissons stretching away down the road and coming at a gallop. The horses are covered with sweat and lather when they get here! We unload the caissons in a hurry and then they

Action on the front lines during World War I

start back again, at a gallop, as the Germans are apt to shell the road at any time—so they are running for their lives! In fact the other night the road was shelled when they were bringing up ammunition! The driver swung off the road and came through the fields, spurring the horses to even greater speed!

This kind of warfare means a great many killed and wounded. But I prefer it, as it is the only way to end the war—just kill off all the Germans!

I have given you details and described disagreeable things, but I just want you to know what war is and what it means for us and for everyone!

But I think it's great sport and certainly am glad I'm here and taking part in this—one of the greatest battles the world has ever known.

Love,
E. J. Canright,
Medical Department
149th Field Artillery
A.E.F.,
A.P.O. No. 715

READING REVIEW

1. How would you describe Canright's attitude toward the fighting?
2. What hardships did the soldiers on the front line face?
3. (a) Did Canright seem to share the war aims that Wilson outlined for the nation? (b) Give two pieces of evidence in the reading which supports your conclusion.
4. Do you think other soldiers shared Canright's feeling about the "sport" of war? Why or why not?

192 Celebrating the Armistice—in France

For Americans the end of the war came less than two years after they entered the conflict. For Europeans the agony of the war had lasted longer—for four long years. During this time, millions of people had died and millions of others had suffered great hardships.

Mildred Aldrich, an American news reporter and writer, spent the war years living in France. She had worked for several years as a reporter and editor in Boston, then had moved to France in 1898 and bought a small house in the country near the Marne River. The Battle of the Marne in 1914 was fought in the area near her house. In this selection, she told of the end of the war and how she and her French neighbors reacted to the news of peace.

READING FOCUS

1. What were the terms of the armistice?
2. How did the French react to the news of peace?

Saturday morning [November 9] we read about the armistice in the newspapers. Stiff as the terms were, we knew that Germany could not hesitate, just as we knew that the French would not discuss. I had only to look at the two maps I had studied two days before to know that Germany was forced to accept even if the terms had been harder. Yet I could have cried to think it had come so soon. I knew that once Germany had, with Wilson's aid, been allowed to talk, the armistice was inevitable. Beaten to the point where its case was hopeless, and where the final surrender of its army was in sight, it could save itself from invasion only by accepting any terms proposed. As for the Allies, no matter how they felt, they could hardly go on with the fighting once Germany gave in. Much as one grieved that the surrender was made with Germany still the invader, the order to "cease firing" meant the saving of thousands of lives.

The expected news came early Monday morning. As we expected, the Germans had accepted the hard terms of the "unconditional surrender," and the order had been given to "cease firing" at eleven. We had known it would come, but the fact that the order had been given rather surprised us. To realize that it was over! How could one in a minute?

I was up early to wait for the papers. It was a perfectly white day. The whole world was covered with the first frost and wrapped in a deep white fog, as if the huge flag of truce were wound around it. I went out on the lawn and looked toward the north. The fog was so thick,

Adapted from Mildred Aldrich, When Johnny Comes Marching Home. *Boston: Small, Maynard and Company, 1919.*

The French and Americans celebrate Armistice Day in the streets of Paris.

I could not see as far as the hedge. Yet out there I knew the guns were still firing. Between them and me lay such devastation as even the imagination cannot exaggerate, and such suffering and pain as human understanding can but partly understand. Four years and four months—and how much is still before us? The future has its job laid out for it. Are ordinary humans capable of handling it?

Later, as I stood near the road, I heard footsteps running toward me on the frozen ground. Out of the fog came Marin, the town crier, with his drum on his back. He waved his drumsticks at me as he ran, and cried, "I am coming as fast as I can, Madame. We are ringing our bells at four—at the same time Clemenceau reads the terms in the Chamber of Deputies and Lloyd George reads them in London." As he reached the corner just above my gate he swung his drum round and beat it like mad.

It did not take two minutes for all our little village to gather about him. In a loud, clear voice he read the order of the day, which officially announced that the war had ended at eleven o'clock. The inhabitants of the town were authorized to hang out their flags, light up their windows, and join in a dignified celebration of the liberation of France. Then he slowly lifted his cap in his hand as he read the last phrase, which begged them not to forget to pray for the brave soldiers who had given their lives that this day might be, and not to forget that to many among us this day of rejoicing was also a day of mourning.

There was not a cheer.

Amelie told the whole story when she dropped on a bench at the kitchen door, and with dry eyes and tightened lips exclaimed, "Finally! It's over. We beat them!"

After all, that was the important thing. It was not what we hoped for, or what we wanted, but the killing was over. I don't see how the French, on whose bodies and souls the burden had fallen, can, even in their disappointment, have any other thought just now.

Less than an hour after Marin passed over the hill, the mayor and his associates arrived to present me formally with the thanks of the town for the part I had taken in sharing the hard days with them. I did so wish again for some magic means by which every one of the American women who had stretched out generous helping hands across the sea to this little place could have seen the scene, and heard me try to make a French speech. I stumbled a bit, but the French are good at understanding. As far as their faces went I might have been rivaling the best French speaker. I put the honors where they were due. But in spite of all I said for the moment I was to them—America.

They all went out on the lawn before leaving to look off toward the battlefield. It was still covered with fog, although the mist had thinned. "There," said the mayor, making a sweeping gesture toward the north, "there after all it was decided, perhaps, right under our eyes. Without that victory, all the aid the States sent us later would have been in vain." Perhaps. At any rate that is still the opinion of everyone.

Then we all shook hands at the gate, and they hurried back to ring the church bells to salute the victory. I did not go with them, as they suggested. I was content to sit here on the spot where I had watched in those hot days of September 1914.

The mist was lifting slightly. All along the valley the bells rang for hours, cut at regular intervals by the booming of the guns at the forts.

I sat on the lawn alone, thinking that all over France—wherever the bells had not been destroyed—this same scene was being carried out. I was sure that in Paris, where Clemenceau was standing before the deputies, his reading of the terms of the armistice was being emphasized by guns saluting the victory and by cheers in the streets.

READING REVIEW

1. (a) Summarize the terms of the armistice. (b) What did Mildred Aldrich think about the armistice terms?
2. Describe the French reaction to the news of peace.
3. (a) Would you say that Mildred Aldrich's outlook is more French than American? (b) more American than French? (c) a mixture of both?

193 In Defense of the League

At the end of World War I, President Wilson attended the Versailles Conference, where he helped to write the peace treaty. When he returned home in 1919, he asked Congress to ratify the treaty. However, there was a bitter debate in the United States over whether the Senate should ratify the Treaty of Versailles, and thus approve America's joining the League of Nations. Many Senators were opposed to the United States' joining the League. They feared that membership in the League would involve America too deeply in European politics—perhaps even lead the nation into another war.

President Wilson, however, believed strongly in the League. As a result he decided to appeal directly to the American people for support. On a cross-country speaking tour in the fall of 1919, he made thirty-seven speeches in twenty-nine cities. But the tour ended suddenly when Wilson suffered a stroke. The following selection is from a speech Wilson gave on September 4, at the beginning of his speaking tour.

READING FOCUS

1. Why did President Wilson support the League of Nations?
2. What were some of the unique characteristics of the League of Nations?

After all the discussion of the Treaty of Versailles, perhaps you would like to know what is in it. I find it very difficult in reading some of the speeches that I have read to form any idea about that great document. It is a document unique in the history of the world for many reasons. I think I cannot do you or the peace of the world a better service than by pointing out to you what this treaty contains and what it seeks to do.

In the first place, my fellow Americans, it seeks to punish one of the greatest wrongs in history, the wrong which Germany sought to do to the world and to civilization. Germany attempted an intolerable thing, and it must be punished for the attempt. The terms of the treaty are severe, but they are not unjust.

Adapted from War and Peace: The Public Papers of Woodrow Wilson, *Vol. 1. Published by Harper & Row, Publishers, 1927.*

Wilson (front left) with Taft (front right)

I can state that the people associated with me at the Peace Conference in Paris had it in their hearts to do justice and not wrong. But they knew, perhaps with a greater sense of what had happened than we could possibly know, the many solemn agreements which Germany had disregarded, the long preparation it had made to defeat its neighbors, and the complete disregard it had shown for human rights. They had seen their lands destroyed by an enemy that devoted itself not only to the effort at victory, but to the effort at terror. There is a method of adjustment in that treaty by which the reparation shall not be pressed beyond the point which Germany can pay. But it will be pressed to the greatest point that Germany can pay—which is just, which is righteous. For, my fellow citizens, this treaty is not meant only to end this single war. It is meant as a notice to any government which in the future may attempt such a thing that humanity will unite to inflict the same punishment on it.

There is no national triumph sought in this treaty. There is no glory sought for any particular nation. The thought of the leaders collected around that peace table was of their people, of the sufferings that they had gone through, of the losses they had suffered. Let us never forget the purpose—the high purpose, the disinterested purpose—with which America lent its strength not for its own glory but for the defense of humanity.

As I said, this treaty was not intended only to end this war. It was intended to prevent any similar war. I wonder if some of the opponents of the League of Nations have forgotten the promises we made our people before we went to that peace table. We had taken men from every household, and we told mothers and fathers and sisters and wives and sweethearts that we were taking those men to fight a war which would end all wars. If we do not end wars, we are unfaithful to the loving hearts who suffered in this war.

That is what the League of Nations is for— to end this war justly, and then to serve notice on other governments which might consider trying to do the same things that Germany attempted. The League of Nations is the only thing that can prevent another dreadful catastrophe and fulfill our promises.

When people tell you, therefore, that the League of Nations is intended for some other purpose than this, answer: If we do not do this thing, we have neglected the central promise we made to our people. The rivalries of this world have not cooled. They have been made hotter than ever. The harness that is to unite nations is more necessary now that it ever was before. Unless there is this assurance of combined action before wrong is attempted, wrong will be attempted just as soon as the most ambitious nations can recover from the financial stress of this war.

Now, look at what else is in the treaty. It is unique in the history of humankind, because the heart of it is the protection of weak nations. There never was a congress of nations before that considered the rights of those who could not enforce their rights. There never was a congress of nations before that did not seek to bring about some balance of power by means of serving the strength and interest of the strongest powers concerned. This treaty says people have a right to live their own lives under the governments which they themselves choose to set up. That is the American principle, and I was glad to fight for it. If there is no League of Nations, the military point of view will win out in every instance, and peace will not last.

Some people have feared with regard to the

League of Nations that we will be forced to do things we do not want to do. If the treaty were wrong, that might be so. But if the treaty is right, we will wish to preserve right. I think I know the feelings of our great people better than do some others I hear talk.

The heart of this treaty then, my fellow citizens, is not even that it punishes Germany. That is a temporary thing. It is that it corrects the age-old wrongs which characterized the history of Europe. There were some of us who wished that the treaty also would reach some other age-old wrongs. It was a big job. I do not say that we wished that it were bigger. There were other wrongs elsewhere than in Europe which, no doubt, ought to be righted, and some day will be righted, but which we could not include in the treaty because we could deal only with the countries that the war had affected.

Have you ever thought, my fellow citizens, about the real source of revolution? Revolutions do not spring up overnight. Revolutions come from the long suppression of the human spirit. Revolutions come because people know that they have rights and that they are disregarded. When we think of the future of the world in connection with this treaty, we must remember that one of the chief efforts of those who made it was to remove that anger from the heart of great peoples who had always been suppressed, who had always been the tools in the hands of governments not their own. The makers of the treaty knew that if these wrongs were not removed, there could be no peace in the world. This treaty is an attempt to right the history of Europe.

If I were to state what seems to me the central idea of this treaty, it would be this: Nations do not consist of their governments but of their people. That is a simple idea. It seems to us in America to go without saying. But, my fellow citizens, it was never the leading idea in any other international congress made up of the representatives of governments. They were always thinking of national policy, of national advantage, of the rivalries of trade, of the advantages of territorial conquest. There is nothing of those things in this treaty.

I have not come to debate the treaty. It speaks for itself, if you will let it. The arguments against it are directed against it with a great misunderstanding of it. Therefore, I am not going anywhere to debate the treaty. I am going to explain it. And I am going, as I do here today, to encourage you to assert the spirit of the American people in support of it. Do not let people pull it down. Do not let them misrepresent it. Do not let them lead this nation away from the high purposes with which this war was fought. When this treaty is accepted, soldiers will not have to cross the seas again. That is the reason I believe in it.

I say "when it is accepted," for it will be accepted. I have never had a moment's doubt of that. The only thing I have been impatient of has been the delay. Do you realize, my fellow citizens, that the whole world is waiting on America? The only country in the world that is trusted at this moment is the United States. The peoples of the world are waiting to see whether their trust is justified or not. That has been the reason for my impatience. I knew their trust was justified, but I resented the time that certain people wish to take in telling them so. We shall tell them so in a voice as true as any voice in history. In the years to come, people will be glad to remember that they had some part in the great struggle which brought about the fulfillment of the hopes of humankind.

READING REVIEW

1. What arguments did Wilson offer to urge the United States Congress to ratify the treaty?
2. Why, according to Wilson, was the League "unique in the history of humankind"?

194 An Attack on the League

The bitter debate over ratification of the Treaty of Versailles and joining the League of Nations lasted for many months. By the time the Senate voted in November 1919, forty-five amendments and three "reservations," or special clauses to protect American interests, had been added to the treaty. When the final vote was taken on November 19, the Senate rejected the treaty, and thus refused to have the United States join the League of Nations.

One of the leading foes of the treaty, Republican Senator William E. Borah of Idaho, delivered the following speech during the Senate debate

Senator William E. Borah

READING FOCUS

1. Why did Borah oppose the League of Nations?
2. What did Borah say about "entangling alliances with Europe"?

What is the result of this Treaty of Versailles? We are in the middle of all of the affairs of Europe. We have entangled ourselves with all European concerns. We have joined in alliance with all the European nations which have thus far joined the League, and all nations which may be admitted to the League. We are sitting there dabbling in their affairs and meddling in their concerns. In other words—and this comes to the question which is fundamental with me—we have surrendered, once and for all, the great policy of "no entangling alliances" upon which the strength of this Republic has been based for 150 years.

Adapted from American Problems: A Selection of Speeches and Prophecies by William E. Borah, *edited by Horace Green.*

Will my friends who talk of reservations tell me where is the reservation in these articles which protects us against entangling alliances with Europe?

Will those who are differing over reservations tell me which one protects the doctrine laid down by our first President? That fundamental proposition is surrendered, and we are a part of European turmoils and conflicts from the time we enter this League.

You have put in here a reservation concerning the Monroe Doctrine. I think that, as far as language could protect the Monroe Doctrine, it has been protected. But as a practical matter, tell me honestly, as people familiar with the history of your country and of other countries, do you think that you can meddle in European affairs and keep Europe from meddling in your affairs?

There is another and even more pressing reason why I shall vote against this treaty. It endangers what I believe to be the underlying, the very first principles of this Republic. It is in conflict with the right of our people to govern themselves free from all restraint, legal or moral, by foreign powers. It challenges every principle of my political faith. If this faith were mine alone, you could accuse me of arrogance. But I am only being faithful to American ideals as they were created by those who built the Republic and as they have been extended throughout the years.

I will not, I cannot, give up my belief that America must, not alone for the happiness of its own people, but for the moral guidance and greater happiness of the world, be permitted to live its own life. Next to the tie which binds a person to his or her God is the tie which binds a person to his or her country. All schemes, all plans, however ambitious and fascinating they seem, which would compromise our country's freedom of action, I reject absolutely.

Senators, we should not close our eyes to the fact that democracy is something more than just a form of government by which society is restrained into free and orderly life. It is a moral and spiritual force as well. And these are things which live only in the air of liberty. The foundation upon which democracy rests is faith in the moral instincts of the people. Its ballot boxes, the vote, its law and constitutions are but the outward sign of the deeper and more essential thing—a continuing trust in the moral purposes of the average man and woman.

When this is lost, your outward forms, however democratic in terms, are a mockery. You cannot mix the distinguishing virtues of a real republic with the destructive forces of the Old World and still preserve them. You cannot tie a government whose fundamental principle is that of liberty to a government whose first law is that of force and hope to preserve the former. These things are in constant conflict. One must in time destroy the other.

We may become one of the four dictators of the world, but we shall no longer be master of our own spirit. And what shall it profit us as a nation if we share with others the glory of world control but lose that fine sense of confidence in the people, the soul of democracy.

Look upon the scene as it is now presented. Behold the task we are to take on. Then think of the method by which we are to deal with this task. When this League is formed, four great powers representing the dominant people will rule half of the inhabitants of the globe as subject peoples—rule them by force, and we shall be a party to the rule of force. There is no other way by which you can keep people in subjection. You must either give them independence, recognize their rights as nations to live their own life and set up their own form of government. Or you must deny them these things by force. That is the scheme, the method proposed by the League.

We are told that this treaty means peace. Even so, I would not pay the price. Would you buy peace at the cost of any part of our independence? We could have had peace in 1776. The price was high, but we could have had it. James Otis, Sam Adams, John Hancock, and Joseph Warren were surrounded by those who encouraged peace and British rule. All through that long and trying struggle, there was a cry of peace—let us have peace.

We could have had peace in 1860. Lincoln was advised by people of great influence and wisdom to let our brothers—and, thank heaven, they are brothers—leave in peace. But the tender, loving Lincoln, bending under the fearful weight of almost certain civil war, an apostle of peace, refused to pay the price. A united country will praise his name forevermore—bless it because he refused peace at the price of national honor and national integrity. Peace upon any other basis than national in-

dependence, peace bought at the cost of any part of our national integrity, is fit only for slaves.

But your treaty does not mean peace—far, very far, from it. If we are to judge the future by the past, it means a war. Is there any guarantee of peace other than the guarantee which comes from the control of the war-making power by the people? Yet the people at no time and in no place have any voice in this scheme for world peace.

Can you hope for peace when love of country is disregarded in your scheme, when the spirit of nationality is rejected, even scoffed at? Your treaty in a dozen instances breaks the divine law of nationality. Peoples who speak the same language, kneel at the same ancestral tombs—moved by the same traditions and common hopes—are torn apart, broken in pieces, divided, and given to hostile nations. And this you call justice. No, your treaty means injustice. It means slavery. It means war. And to all this you ask this Republic to become a party. You ask it to abandon the principles under which it has grown to power and accept the principles of repression and force.

I turn from this scheme based upon force to another scheme, planned 143 years ago in old Independence Hall, in the city of Philadelphia, based upon liberty. I like it better. I have become so used to believing in it that it is difficult for me to reject it.

America will live its own life. The independence of this Republic will have its defenders. Thousands have suffered and died for it, and their sons and daughters will not be betrayed into the hands of foreigners. The noble face of our first President, so familiar to every boy and girl, looking out from the walls of the Capitol in stern reproach, will call those who come here for public service to a reckoning. The people of our beloved country will finally speak, and we will return to the policy which we now abandon. America, free in spite of all these things, will continue its mission in the cause of peace, of freedom, and of civilization.

READING REVIEW

1. Why did Borah believe that the treaty represented a danger to the United States?
2. To what American tradition did Borah appeal?
3. How did Borah use American history to strengthen his case against the treaty?

The Golden Twenties and the New Deal

CHAPTER

31 A Decade of Prosperity Ends in a Crash

(1920–1932)

195 Stock Market Fever

During the 1920's, more and more Americans invested their money in stocks. So many people were buying and selling stocks that the New York Stock Exchange had to close down several times during its regular Saturday trading sessions. This was the only way that the brokers' clerks could catch up each week with all the paper work required by the enormous volume of stocks being bought and sold. It seemed at times that everyone was speculating in the stock market.

In this selection, newspaper writer Franklin P. Adams made fun of the frenzied stock buying in a poem called "American Bores Common."

READING FOCUS

1. Why was the author critical of the great increases in buying and selling stocks?
2. Did the author invest in the stock market? Why or why not?

In days of not so very old
Bores did I know a million fold.
They used to tell me this or that:

From Christopher Columbus and Other Patriotic Verses *by Franklin P. Adams.*

How cheap—or dear—they'd leased a flat;
They used to tell me of That Kid—
What little Elsie said or did;
They used to tell me of the trains
Between New York and Tiger Plains,
And of how fast they made the trip
From house to office—zippety zip!
Of girls they used to talk—and boast.
Of games, perhaps, they talked the most;
Of fights and baseball games they'd seen;
Of single strokes from tee to green;
Of backhand drives and passing shots;
Of hands that won stupendous pots.
They used to tell, with silly pride,
How yesterevening they were Fried.
They used to tell, the bores supreme,
Of this or that Uncanny Dream.
But nowadays the bores I find
Are of a single, standard kind:
For every person I may meet
At lunch, at clubs, upon the street,
Tells me, in endless wordy tales,
Of market purchases and sales;
Of how he bought a single share
Of California Prune and Pear;
Or how he sold at 33
A million shares of T. & T.
How McAvoy and Katzenstein [stock market brokers]
Told him to sell at 99;
Of thousands lost and millions made
In this or that egregious trade;
How bright he was to buy or sell
EP, GM, X, or GL.
In herds, in schools, in droves, in flocks
The men and women talk of stocks.
They talk in couples and in crowds,
And I, whose head is in the clouds,
Who hold that Mind is more than Matter,
Am bored by all this market patter.

How long can any land be sane
With all its mind on moneyed gain?
And whither, prithee, do we drift
Whose port is Gain instead of Thrift?
It makes me ill, and even sicker
To see so many watch the ticker.
To Mammon bends the national knee;
What fools these stock-mad mortals be!
Ill fares, as Goldsmith [a British writer of
    the 1700's] used to gab it,
The land where everyone's a Babbitt [a per-
    son who strives for money and success, ig-
    noring artistic and intellectual values].
But what a zob they made of me!
I sold a stock at 43
A month ago, and up to date
It's selling at 388.

Ill fares the land, as said before
Where everyone's a stock-mad bore.

READING REVIEW

1. According to the author, what was wrong with the nation's preoccupation with the stock market?
2. (a) What evidence was there that the author invested in the stock market? (b) Why did he regret his decision?
3. Do you think this poem is applicable to today's society? Why or why not?

196 What Caused the Depression?

The stock market crash of October 1929 was the beginning of the Great Depression that lasted through the 1930's. During this period of hard times, banks and businesses closed down and many millions of Americans were forced out of work.

What caused the depression? Economists have developed many conflicting theories about the direct and indirect causes of the depression. Some blame the lack of prosperity in American agriculture during the 1920's and the farmers' reduced buying power. Some blame the unequal distribution of income. Others blame overinvestment in the stock market. Still others feel that the huge government debts among nations put too much pressure on the world economy.

The following selection was written by John Kenneth Galbraith, a present-day economist. In it he gave his explanation of this crisis in America's economy.

The New York Stock Exchange

READING FOCUS

1. In Galbraith's view, what caused the depression?
2. Why did he say that the economy in 1929 was "basically unsound"?

The collapse of the stock market in the autumn of 1929 was a natural result of the speculation that went before. The only question about that speculation was how long it would last. Sometime, sooner or later, confidence in increasing stock values would weaken. When this happened, some people would sell. There would be a rush to unload. This was the way past spec-

Adapted from The Great Crash *by John Kenneth Galbraith.*

ulative orgies had ended. It was the way the end came in 1929. It is the way speculation will end in the future.

We do not know why a great speculative orgy occurred in 1928 and 1929. The long accepted explanation that credit was easy and so people were forced to borrow money to buy common stocks on margin is obviously nonsense. On many occasions before and since, credit has been easy, and there has been no speculation whatever. Furthermore, much of the 1928 and 1929 speculation occurred using money borrowed at interest rates which for years before, and in any period since, would have been considered exceptionally high. Money, by ordinary standards, was tight in the late 1920's.

Far more important than the rate of interest and the supply of credit is the mood. Speculation on a large scale requires a sense of confidence and optimism. People must also have faith in the good intentions of others, for it is through others that they will get rich. When people are cautious, questioning, or suspicious, they resist speculative enthusiasms.

Savings must also be plentiful. Speculation, however it may rely on borrowed funds, must be nourished in part by those who participate. If savings are growing rapidly, people will be willing to risk some of it against the prospect of a good return. . . .

A great many people have always felt that a depression was inevitable in the 1930's. There had been (at least) seven good years; now, by a law of compensation, there would have to be seven bad ones.

There is also the belief that economic life is governed by an inevitable rhythm. After a certain time, prosperity destroys itself and depression corrects itself. In 1929 prosperity, in accordance with the law of the business cycle, had run its course.

Neither of these beliefs can be seriously supported. The 1920's, by being comparatively prosperous, did not call for the 1930's to be depressed. In the past, good times have given way to less good times and less good or bad to good. But change is normal in a capitalist economy. No inevitable rhythm required the collapse of 1930–40.

Finally, the high production of the 1920's did not, as some have suggested, outrun the wants of the people. During these years people were indeed being supplied with an increasing volume of goods. But there is no evidence that they had no more desire for automobiles, clothing, travel, recreation, or even food. On the contrary, all later evidence showed (given the income to spend) a capacity for a large further increase in consumption.

What, then, were the causes of the depression?

There seems little question that in 1929 the economy was fundamentally unsound. This is a circumstance of first-rate importance. Many things were wrong, but five weaknesses seem to have had an especially close bearing on the disaster. They are:

1. *The bad distribution of income.* In 1929 the rich were clearly rich. It seems certain that the 5 percent of the population with the highest incomes in that year received approximately one third of all personal income. The proportion of personal income received in the form of interest, dividends, and rent—the income, broadly speaking, of the well-to-do—was about twice as great as in the years following World War II.

This highly unequal distribution of income meant that the economy was dependent on a high level of investment or a high level of luxury consumer spending or both. The rich cannot buy great quantities of bread. If they are to get rid of what they receive it must be on luxuries or through investment in new plants and new projects. Both luxury and investment spending are subject to wider changes than the bread and rent outlays of the $25-a-week worker. This high-bracket spending and investment was especially open, one may assume, to the crushing news from the stock market in October of 1929.

2. *The bad corporate structure.* . . . American business in the 1920's had opened its hospitable arms to an exceptional number of promoters, grafters, swindlers, imposters, and frauds. In the long history of such activities, there was a kind of flood tide of corporate theft.

3. *The bad banking structure.* The banking structure of the United States was weak. When one bank failed, the assets of others were frozen while depositors elsewhere had a warning to go and ask for their money. Thus one failure led to other failures, and these spread with a domino effect. Even in the best of times local misfortune or isolated mismanagement could start such a chain reaction. (In the first six months of 1929, 346 banks failed in various

People crowd Wall Street as they rush to the New York Stock Exchange.

parts of the country; their deposits totaled nearly $115 million.) When income, employment, and values fell as the result of a depression, bank failures could quickly become an epidemic.

4. *The doubtful state of the foreign balance.* During World War I, the United States became a creditor nation, rather than a debtor nation. In the ten years following the war, the surplus of exports over imports, which once had paid the interest and principal on loans from Europe, continued. The high tariffs, which restricted imports and helped to create this surplus of exports, remained.

Before the war, payments on interest and principal had in effect been deducted from the trade balance. Now that the United States was a creditor, they were added to this balance. During most of the 1920's, the difference was covered by cash—that is, gold payments to the United States—and by new private loans by the United States to other countries. But countries could not make up for their bad trade balance with increased payments of gold, at least not for long. This meant that they had to increase their exports to the United States, reduce their imports, or not pay their past loans. President Hoover and the Congress moved quickly to get rid of the first possibility—that the accounts would be balanced by larger imports—by sharply increasing the tariff. Accordingly, debts, including war debts, were not paid and there was a decline in American exports. The reduction was not great in relation to the total output of the American economy, but it contributed to the general suffering and was especially hard on farmers.

5. *The poor state of economic knowledge.* . . . It seems certain that the economists of the late 1920's and early 1930's were almost determined to be wrong. In the months and years following the stock market crash, they gave advice that was constantly on the side of measures that would make things worse. Asked how the government could best help economic recovery, the sound and responsible adviser suggested that the budget should be balanced. Both political parties agreed on this. . . .

A commitment to a balanced budget meant there could be no increase in government spending to expand purchasing power and relieve suffering. It meant there could be no further tax reduction. But taken in the strictest sense it meant much more. From 1930 on the budget was far out of balance. Balance, therefore, meant an increase in taxes, a reduction in spending, or both. The balanced budget was not the only restraint on government policy. There was also the fear of "going off" the gold standard and, most surprisingly, of risking inflation. . . .

It is in light of the above weaknesses of the economy that the role of the stock market crash in the great tragedy of the 1930's must be seen. The collapse in securities values affected first the wealthy and the well-to-do. In the world of 1929 this was an important group. Its members spent a large proportion of the consumer income. They controlled the greatest share of personal saving and investment. Anything that struck at the spending or investment by this group would of necessity have broad effects on spending and income in the economy at large. . . .

The stock market crash was also an exceptionally effective way of exploiting the weaknesses of the corporate structure. Many companies were forced by the crash to cut down on spending. Their later collapse destroyed both the ability to borrow and the willingness to lend for investment.

The crash was also effective in bringing to an end the foreign lending by which international accounts had been balanced. Now the accounts had, in the main, to be balanced by reduced exports. . . .

Finally, when the misfortune had struck, the attitudes of the time kept anything from being done about it. This, perhaps, was the worst feature of all. Some people were hungry in 1930 and 1931 and 1932. Others feared that they might go hungry. Everyone suffered from a sense of complete hopelessness. Nothing, it seemed, could be done. And given the ideas which controlled policy, nothing could be done.

If the economy had been basically sound in 1929, the effect of the great stock market crash might have been small. But business in 1929 was not sound. On the contrary, it was exceedingly fragile. It was open to the kind of blow it received from Wall Street. . . .

READING REVIEW

1. List four reasons why America experienced a depression.
2. What evidence did Galbraith offer to support his statement that the economy in 1929 was "basically unsound"?
3. According to Galbraith, why did the attitudes of the time prevent anything from being done about the depression?

197 Hoover's "American Plan"

As the United States sank deeper and deeper into the worst depression in its history, Americans searched for workable solutions to their economic problems. The nation had never before faced such widespread poverty and so much suffering. But President Hoover believed the nation was suffering only from "frozen confidence" and that prosperity was "just around the corner." Because of this outlook, Hoover tried to use traditional methods to deal with the crisis. Although he realized that some government action was necessary, he was willing to take only limited measures, such as helping to provide some new jobs and making loans to businesses.

In the following speech of June 1931, Hoover outlined his views on how to deal with this crisis.

READING FOCUS

1. What was the "American Plan"?
2. According to Hoover, what role should the United States government take in planning for the future development of the country?

We have many citizens insisting that we produce an advance "plan" for the future development of the United States. They demand that we produce it right now. I presume the "plan" idea is an infection from the slogan of the "five-year-plan" through which Russia is struggling to save itself from ten years of starvation and misery.

I am able to propose an American plan to you. We plan to take care of a 20 million increase in population in the next twenty years. We plan to build for them 4 million new and better homes, thousands of new and still more beautiful city buildings, thousands of factories. We plan to increase the capacity of our railways, to add thousands of miles of highways and waterways, to install 25 million electrical horsepower, to grow 20 percent more farm products. We plan to provide new parks, schools, colleges, and churches for these 20 million people. We plan more leisure for men and women and better opportunities for its enjoyment.

We not only plan to provide for all the new generation. We shall, by scientific research and invention, lift the standard of living of the whole population. We plan to secure a greater distribution of wealth, a decrease in poverty, and a great reduction in crime. And this plan will be carried out if we just keep on giving the American people a chance. Its moving force is in the character and spirit of our people. They have already done a better job for 120 million people than any other nation in all history.

Some groups believe this plan can only be carried out by a fundamental, a revolutionary, change of method. Other groups believe that

Adapted from "Address to the Indiana Editorial Association" in State Papers and Other Public Writings of Herbert Hoover, *Vol. I*, edited by William Starr Myers.

any system must be the outgrowth of our character and traditions. They believe that we have established certain ideals over 150 years, upon which we must build rather than destroy.

If we analyze the ideas which have been put forward for handling our great national plan, they fall into two main types. The first holds that the major purpose of a nation is to protect the people and to give them equality of opportunity. It holds that the basis of all happiness is in the development of the individual, and that we should steadily build up cooperation among the people themselves to this end.

The other idea is that we shall, directly or indirectly, regiment the population into a bureaucracy to serve the state. It holds that we should use force instead of cooperation in planning, and thereby direct every person as to what may or may not be done.

These ideas present themselves in practical questions which we have to answer. Shall we abandon the philosophy and beliefs of our people for 150 years by turning to a belief that is foreign to our people? Shall we establish a giveaway from the federal treasury? Shall we undertake federal ownership and operation of public utilities instead of regulating them? Shall we protect our people from the lower standards of living of foreign countries? Shall the government, except in temporary national emergencies, enter into competition with its citizens? Shall we regiment our people by extending the arm of bureaucracy into a great many affairs?

Our immediate task as a people is to defeat the forces of economic disruption and pessimism that have swept over us. The duty of government in these times is to use its agencies and influence to strengthen our economic institutions; to inspire cooperation in the community so as to keep up good will and keep our country free from disorder and conflict; to cooperate with the people so that the deserving shall not suffer; and to strengthen the foundations of a better and stronger national life. These have been the objectives of my administration in dealing with this, the greatest crisis the world has ever known. I shall stick with them.

READING REVIEW

1. According to Hoover, what was the proper role of the government in dealing with the depression?

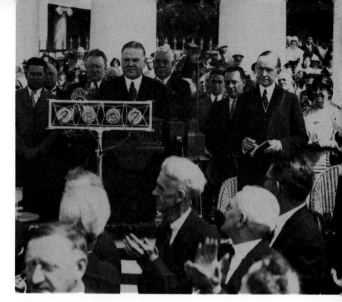

President Herbert Hoover

2. **(a)** Did Hoover favor or oppose increased government planning for the future development of the United States? **(b)** List two arguments he used to support his position.

CHAPTER

32 The Great Depression and the New Deal
(1933–1941)

198 On Government and the Economy

In 1932 the Democratic Party nominated Franklin D. Roosevelt as its candidate for President. Roosevelt had served as Assistant Secretary of the Navy under President Wilson and had become governor of New York in 1928. But he was not well known to many Americans when he began his Presidential election campaign. His campaign travels to all parts of the nation and his speeches promising to act immediately to end the depression won him victory in the 1932 election.

In his Inaugural Address, Roosevelt promised "a new deal for the American people," and he

READING FOCUS

1. According to Roosevelt, what were the basic economic rights of all Americans?
2. What role should the federal government play in ending the economic crisis?

I want to speak not of politics but of government. I want to speak not of parties but of universal principles. They are not political, except in that larger sense in which a great American once defined politics—that nothing in all of human life is unrelated to the science of politics.

A look at the situation today indicates only too clearly that equality of opportunity as we have known it no longer exists. Our industrial system is built. The problem just now is whether under existing conditions it is not overbuilt. Our last frontier has long since been reached. There is practically no more free land. More than half of our people do not live on farms, and they cannot make a living by cultivating their own property. There is no safety valve in the form of a Western frontier to which those thrown out of work by the Eastern economic machines can go for a new start. We are not able to invite immigrants from Europe to share our endless plenty. We are now providing a drab living for our own people.

Our system of constantly rising tariffs has at last reacted against us. It has closed our Canadian frontier on the north, our European markets on the east, many of our Latin-American markets to the south, and a sizable part of our Pacific markets on the west.

Just as freedom to farm has ended, so also opportunity in business has narrowed. It still is true that people can start small businesses, trusting their own shrewdness and ability to keep ahead of competitors. But area after area has been taken over altogether by the great corporations. Even in the fields which still have no large companies, the small operator starts under a handicap. The statistics of the past 30 years show that the independent business owner is running a losing race. Perhaps he is forced into bankruptcy. Perhaps he cannot get credit. Perhaps he is "squeezed out" by highly organized corporate competitors—as your corner grocery store owner can tell you.

Recently a careful study was made of the concentration of business in the United States. It showed that our economic life is dominated by some 600 corporations that control two thirds of American industry. The other third is shared by 10 million small businesses. More striking still, it appears that if the process of concentration goes on at the same rate, at the end of another century all American industry will be controlled by a dozen corporations, run by perhaps a hundred people.

Clearly, all this calls for us to think over our values. A builder of more industrial plants, a creator of more railroad systems, an organizer of more corporations, is as likely to be a danger as a help. The day of the great financial promoters to whom we granted anything if they would build or develop is over. Our task now is not discovery or exploitation of natural resources or producing more goods. It is the less dramatic task of managing resources and businesses already in existence. We need to get back foreign markets for our surplus production, and solve the problem of underconsumption. We must adjust production to consumption, distribute wealth and products more fairly, and adapt existing economic organizations to the service of the people. The day of enlightened management has come.

In older times the central [national] government was first a place of refuge, and then a threat. In the same way, in our present economic system the huge corporation is no longer a servant but a danger. I would draw the parallel one step farther. We did not think, when national government became a threat in the 1700's, that we should abandon the principle of national government. Nor today should we abandon the principle of corporations, just because their power can be abused. In other times we dealt with the problem of an overly ambitious central government by changing it gradually into a constitutional democratic gov-

Adapted from The Public Papers and Addresses of Franklin D. Roosevelt, Vol. I, published by Random House, Inc.

ernment. So today we are changing and controlling our economic units.

As I see it, the task of government in its relation to business is to help in developing an economic declaration of rights, an economic constitutional order. Happily, the times indicate that to create such an order not only is the proper policy of government, but is the only line of safety for our economic structures as well. We know now that these economic units cannot exist unless prosperity is uniform. Purchasing power must be well distributed throughout every group in the nation. That is why even the most selfish corporations would be glad to see wages raised and unemployment ended, and the Western farmer restored to prosperity. That is why some enlightened industries themselves try to limit the freedom of action of each business group within the industry in the common interest of all.

I feel that we are coming to see that private economic power is a public trust. I believe that in order to keep that power any individual or group must fulfill that trust. The people who have reached the top of American business life know this best. Happily, many of them urge that we adopt this greater social contract.

The terms of that contract are as old as the Republic, and as new as the new economic order.

Every person has a right to life. This means the right to make a comfortable living, a right that may not be denied. We have no actual famine. Our industrial and agricultural systems can produce enough and still have capacity to spare.

Every person has a right to individual property. This means a right to be assured of the safety of one's savings. In all thought of property, this right is supreme. All other property rights must give way to it.

These two requirements must be satisfied chiefly by the individuals who control the great industrial and financial concerns which dominate our industrial life. They are not business leaders, but rather princes of property. I am not prepared to say that the system which produces them is wrong. But I do say that they must take the responsibility which goes with the power. Many enlightened business leaders know this.

The responsible heads of finance and industry, instead of acting alone, must work together to achieve the common good. They must, where necessary, sacrifice this or that personal advantage and seek a general advantage. It is here that government comes in. Whenever the dishonest competitor or the reckless promoter refuses to join in achieving a goal recognized as being for the public welfare, the government may properly be asked to apply restraint. Likewise, if the group should ever use its collective power against the public welfare, the government must be swift to protect the public interest.

The government should take over the function of economic regulation only as a last resort when private initiative has finally failed. As yet there has been no final failure, because there has been no attempt.

The final goal of the Declaration of Independence was liberty and the pursuit of happiness. We have learned a great deal about both in the past hundred years. We know that individual liberty and individual happiness mean nothing unless both are achieved without one man's meat being another man's poison. We know that liberty which robs others of basic rights cannot receive governmental protection.

All this is a long, slow task. Human endeavor is not simple. Government includes the art of making a policy, and using political techniques to secure as much of that policy as will receive general public support. We must build toward the time when a major depression cannot occur again. If this means sacrificing the easy profits of inflationary booms, then let them go, and good riddance.

Faith in America, faith in our tradition of personal responsibility, faith in our institutions, faith in ourselves, demand that we recognize the new terms of the old social contract. We shall fulfill them. We must do so. Otherwise, a rising tide of misery, caused by our common failure, will swamp us all. But failure is not an American habit. In the strength of great hope we must all share our common responsibility.

READING REVIEW

1. List the two economic rights of all Americans.
2. (a) How can the economic rights of Americans be guaranteed by business? (b) by government?
3. How did the government help end the crisis?
4. Do Americans still adhere to this basic economic philosophy?

199 WPA and the Arts

Enormous problems faced President Roosevelt when he took office in March of 1933. Millions of Americans were unemployed, thousands stood in "bread lines" for food every day. As part of the New Deal, Roosevelt planned programs to provide direct relief for the unemployed. Several government agencies also were set up to provide work for jobless Americans.

One of these agencies was the Works Progress Administration (WPA). The WPA provided jobs not only for unemployed factory and office workers but also for artists, writers, musicians, and actors. Through the Arts Projects, the WPA decorated post offices and other government buildings with murals. It performed free concerts, staged plays and musicals, and wrote a set of guidebooks about America. In this selection, writer Robert Bendiner described the WPA Arts Projects.

READING FOCUS

1. What were the main types of Arts Projects?
2. How did the Arts Projects sponsored by the W.P.A. help America and Americans during the depression?

In the history of the world, few depression governments have given housewives free piano lessons. Fewer still have put thousands of artists to work. And before the 1930's probably none had given stage people an annual wage, even a small one, to put on free puppet shows and classical plays. But the New Deal did all of these things. In addition, it paid $90 a month to unemployed reporters, unpublished writers, skilled researchers, and others to prepare some 250 books about America.

It has been pointed out over and over that the Arts Projects, as these operations of the Works Progress Administration were known, produced no Mozarts or Da Vincis. Neither did they produce lasting works of drama or fiction.

Adapted from pp. 178–200 in "WPA, Willing Patron of the Arts" in Just Around the Corner *by Robert Bendiner.*

What they did do was to help many talented people through the hard times. And they exposed to those talents millions of Americans who would otherwise never have known their charms. This introduction of struggling artists helped to destroy in four years certain American myths that had been around for a hundred years—that painting had to be European to have merit, and required wealth to be appreciated; that all concerts except those by the town band were in the nature of good works to which dutiful women dragged long-suffering husbands; and that except for four or five cities the American people required no theater at all.

Statistics are no key to quality, but they *can* point to a highly stimulated interest in music, painting, and plays. By the end of the 1930's, nearly 70 art centers were flourishing in communities where many art teachers had never before seen a professional painting. Some 60,000 Americans had taken painting lessons from government-paid artists. Offices and lobbies in government buildings across the land boasted murals and new paintings. Audiences estimated at 100 million people had heard some 150,000 free concerts, most of them by three dozen newly created symphony orchestras. And a half-million Americans each month had enrolled in free music classes, 40,000 in New York City alone.

A visiting English critic was amazed. "Accidentally WPA has dug up an extraordinary amount of talent," said Ford Madox Ford. "Art in America is being given its chance, and there has been nothing like it since before the Reformation."

Certainly a Renaissance was not what Harry Hopkins [head of the WPA] and his aides had in mind when they thought of the Arts Projects. What interested them was the hope of creating a whole new idea of government relief. In three years the country had come a long way from the Hoover view that direct aid to the victims of flood or earthquake was right and proper but not aid to the victims of human-made economics. For a time, welfare was the answer, then work of any kind for any purpose. Now the time had come for "maintaining the morale and skills" of the unemployed by paying them to perform the work they could do best until the private sector was ready to rehire them or pay for their works.

While the Public Works Administration went on with its building, the newly planned

Works Progress Administration would serve human beings. WPA funds would be spent on people, not things. What they were to do would be determined by what they *could* do, not by what the community might lack in the way of parking lots or sewage disposal plants.

Carrying the idea further, WPA proposed to help *all* the jobless artists who might come to it for help, rather than just the truly gifted, who would most likely be the least in need. For years government agencies had hired the best artists, or those it considered such, to do murals and sculpture for its buildings. Now the problem was to employ not just the best, but also those who were merely good—in practice even those who were mediocre and sometimes those who were not very good, but who also had to eat.

Of all Americans engaged in the arts in the 1930's, the worst off by far were show people [entertainers]. Some 40,000 show people were extremely poor. So it was that, of all the good works of the WPA, the Federal Theater Project had the greatest opportunity, made the biggest splash, and left the most vivid memories.

One of the great charms of the Federal Theater was that it really covered the country. WPA shows were not just for New York, Chicago, and San Francisco. They were also for Tacoma (Washington), Reading (Pennsylvania), and Timberline Lodge (Oregon), not to mention Gary (Indiana), Peoria (Illinois), and Red Bank (New Jersey). They brought theater to towns in the United States that had not seen live actors for years. And they were received with great enthusiasm.

Three other WPA efforts in the arts left more visible reminders than the Federal Theater. About the Music Project I know little beyond the story of a violinist in a WPA orchestra in Florida. He apologized to the audience, on behalf of himself and the other musicians, for the quality of their concert. Their hands were still stiff, he explained, from their previous relief job, which was building a highway. The lasting work that the Music Project did was to search out and record the real folk music of America—the songs of the Southern mountaineers, the Indian-flavored songs of early Oklahoma, the Cajun songs of Louisiana, and the African-inspired songs of the Mississippi bayous.

On the Art Project, as the painters' and sculptors' unit was called, nobody pretended

Murals by WPA artists adorn many public buildings.

that the quota of genius was high. Considering the varied talents it had to work with, the Art Project sensibly made no attempt to have everyone paint. Of the 4,000 to 5,000 federally enrolled artists, far fewer than half were engaged in painting pictures or sculpturing or doing murals. Many taught free art classes. Some took photographs of old and decaying American houses. Others worked on posters and stage sets for the Federal Theater.

But the Art Project's real monument was the Index of American Design. For this magnificent work, still widely used, some 500 people reproduced in oil and watercolor the native art with which Americans, from early settlers to late Victorians, had decorated their homes, their possessions, and themselves. Here appeared in all their brightness the scarlet tulips that enlivened the coffeepots of the Pennsylvania Dutch, the embroidery of seventeenth-century Massachusetts, and the wonderful carved figureheads from New England ships. It was this great work, with its 7,000 skillful illustrations, that convinced many Americans that we had a native art after all.

It was charged that the fourth of the federal projects in the arts, the WPA Writers' Project, had little to do with writing. True, the memorable names connected with it can be counted on the fingers. What passed for a Writers' Project was essentially what writer Bernard DeVoto called it, "a project for research workers." Happily, good writers and skilled journalists, headed by Henry Alsberg, its first national director, turned out the most colorful series of guides a nation could ask for. A one-time newspaper reporter, Alsberg felt that Americans might want to know more about places, people, and things in the United States than they could get from filling-station maps. There had not been a guide to America since 1909.

Alsberg's feeling was right. It fitted in, moreover, with the concept that ran through all the Arts Projects—namely, that given the talent available and the controversy that creative work might involve, their best contribution would be to expose Americans for the first time to true, detailed, and vivid information about America. The result was that the guides—one for each of the 48 states, 30 for major cities, and 20 others for great travel arteries like *U.S. One* and *The Oregon Trail*—were remarkably rich.

It was, all in all, a magnificent experiment and one that went far to support sculptor Gutzon Borglum's letter when the WPA was still a developing idea of Harry Hopkins: "I want to suggest that you make your aid to the creative ones among us greater, more effective in scope. You are not after masterpieces, and you should not be discouraged if you have many failures. The real success will be in the interest, the human interest, which you will awaken, and what that does to the nation's mind. I believe that's the door through which you can coax the soul of America back to interest in life." It certainly coaxed it over to a somewhat *different* life.

READING REVIEW

1. **(a)** What were the four main types of Arts Projects? **(b)** List major accomplishments of each.
2. Why did the federal government offer aid to America's museums, theaters, and other cultural centers?
3. **(a)** Does the federal government offer this type of aid today? **(b)** Do you think it should? Explain.
4. In what way did the Arts Projects help in the psychological healing of America during and after the depression?
5. According to the author, what was the real success of the Arts Project?

200   How Social Security Was Born

Today, Americans take for granted many of the economic and social benefits provided by the federal government. Many of these programs began during the New Deal. One of the most significant programs was social security.

The idea of old-age and unemployment insurance had first been suggested during the progressive era. But the depression brought new demands for such a program. After two years of planning with members of Congress, the Roosevelt administration set up a program of old-age and unemployment insurance. This program, spelled out in the Social Security Act, was passed by Congress in 1935. In this selection, Frances Perkins—Secretary of Labor in President Roosevelt's cabinet and the first woman to serve in the cabinet—outlined how the social security law came about.

READING FOCUS

1. What factors influenced the passage of the Social Security Act through Congress?
2. What was President Roosevelt's attitude toward the social security legislation?

Before his inauguration in 1933, Roosevelt had agreed that we should explore at once methods for setting up unemployment and old-age insurance in the United States. Therefore, early in 1933, the President encouraged Senator Robert F. Wagner and Representative David J. Lewis, who were both deeply interested in the subject, to go ahead with their bill on unemployment insurance. The bill, in a rough draft, was offered frankly for educational purposes. It was hoped that in the course of holding hearings the Congressional committees and the introducers of the bill would work out a satisfactory unemployment insurance law.

The President asked me to discuss the matter in as many groups as possible. I began in the cabinet. I made a point of bringing it up at least at every second meeting. In time, the other cabinet members became sincerely and honestly interested.

Adapted from The Roosevelt I Knew *by Frances Perkins.*

Hearings were held before Congress. Effective people were invited to testify before the Congressional committees. I myself made over a hundred speeches in different parts of the country that year. I always stressed social insurance as one of the methods for helping the unemployed in times of depression and for preventing depressions. We encouraged others to talk and write about the subject.

The Wagner-Lewis bill in Congress covered only unemployment insurance, but there was a great demand for old-age insurance also. It was easy to add this feature—and politically almost necessary. The President began telling people he was in favor of adding old-age insurance clauses to the Wagner-Lewis bill and putting it through as one program.

A great deal of educational work was done in 1933. But by June 1934 the Wagner-Lewis bill had not reached committee agreement. There had been differences of opinion in the testimony and recommendations to Congress. We began to see that there must be further study and a more complete plan before the bill could be presented to Congress for action.

The President had put the program on the must list. But the weather grew hot and Congress was very tired. Roosevelt decided that it might be better to tell Congress that he would be happy to agree to their adjourning if they understood that he would have a study made during the summer and would present a full program on economic security on January 1 when Congress met again. Congress gladly agreed.

Since members of the cabinet had developed great interest in the social security program, I suggested that it might be well to have the study made by a cabinet committee. The President readily agreed. He saw at once that a program developed by a committee of the cabinet would be under his control. It would not be likely to get off into the kind of political discussion and publicity that might cause doubt and delay.

The members of the cabinet Committee on Economic Security appointed by the President were the Secretary of Labor [Frances Perkins], chairman; Secretary of Agriculture Henry Wallace; Secretary of the Treasury Henry Morgenthau; and Attorney General H. S. Cummings. Harry Hopkins was added because of his vital experience as administrator of the relief program.

Frances Perkins

It was evident to us that any system of social insurance would not relieve all poverty. Nor would it relieve the sufferings of the presently old and needy. Nevertheless, it was also evident that this was exactly the right time to look ahead to future problems of unemployment and unprotected old age. It was never, I think, suggested by any reasonable person that relief should be abandoned in favor of unemployment and old-age insurance, but it was thought that there could be a blend of the two.

I took pains to make certain that Roosevelt understood and pledged himself to support the program as we worked it out. It must be made clear that this technique of using a cabinet committee to develop the program for him did not mean that he was evading the great issue. I had more than one special conference with him about the subjects we would have to consider in the cabinet committee.

I asked him if he thought it best for me to be chairman, since the public knew I favored the general idea. Perhaps it would be better, from the point of view of Congress and the public, if the Attorney General were chairman.

He was quick in his response. "No, no. You care about this thing. You believe in it. Therefore I know you will back it more than anyone else, and you will drive it through. You will see that something comes out, and we must not delay. I am convinced. We must have a program by next winter and it must be in operation before many more months have passed."

I indicated to him that there were sound arguments, advanced by many thinkers, that since we were in the midst of deflation [a decline in prices, caused by a decrease in the supply of money, or in spending] the collection of any money for reserves, no matter by what method, would be further deflationary.

"We can't help that," he answered. "We have to get it started or it never will start."

He was aware that 1936 was not too far away, that there might be a change of administration, and that this program, which in his own mind was *his* program, would never be accomplished, or at least not for many years, if it were not put through immediately.

By the time the study was fully started, the President's imaginative mind had begun to work on it. At cabinet meetings and when he talked privately with a group of us, he would say, "You should make it simple—very simple. So simple that everybody will understand it. And what's more, there is no reason why everybody in the United States should not be covered. I see no reason why all children, from the day they are born, shouldn't be members of the social security system. When they begin to grow up, they should know they will have old-age benefits direct from the insurance system to which they will belong all their life. If they are out of work, they get benefits. If they are sick or disabled, they get benefits.

"And there is no reason why only the industrial workers should get the benefit of this. Everybody ought to be in on it—the farmer and his wife and his family.

"I don't see why not," he would say, as I began to shake my head. "I don't see why not. Cradle to the grave—from the cradle to the grave they ought to be in a social insurance system."

It was not that I did not admire his bold idea of including every person. But I felt that it was impractical to try to develop and manage so broad a system before we had some experience and machinery for the first and most pressing steps.

Moreover, I felt sure that the political climate was not right for such a universal approach. I may have been wrong. Having the administrative responsibility, I was more alarmed than he about how we were going to achieve it. The question of financing was most important. Roosevelt, because he was looking at the broad picture, could skip over that difficult problem.

It is difficult now to understand fully the doubts and confusions in which we were planning this great new undertaking in 1934. The problems of constitutional law seemed almost impossible to overcome. I drew courage from a bit of advice I got accidentally from Supreme Court Justice Harlan Stone. I had said to him, at a social occasion a few months earlier, that I had great hope of developing a social insurance system for the country, but I was deeply uncertain of the method. I said laughingly, "Your Court tells us what the Constitution permits."

Stone had whispered, "The taxing power of the federal government, my dear. The taxing power is sufficient for everything you want and need."

This was a windfall. I told the President but bound him to secrecy as to the source of my sudden superior legal knowledge. I insisted in the cabinet committee that the taxing power was the method for building up the fund and determining its expenditure for unemployment and old-age benefits to be paid in the future.

The bill with the cabinet committee's recommendations was prepared the first week in January 1935. We took it to the President to see how it should be introduced in Congress. We thought it would be wise to have it referred to a special committee on social security, if possible a joint committee of the Senate and House. Since the measure rested primarily upon the constitutional taxing power of the federal government, it would have gone ordinarily to the Ways and Means Committee.

The news got around that a special committee was being recommended. Representative Robert L. Doughton of North Carolina, chairman of the Ways and Means Committee, went to see the President. He was angry that anyone had thought of bypassing him, though he had never made a speech in the House that had indicated he had any interest in social security. It was a surprise to find out that he cared.

As a result the President said to me, "No, no, it will never do. We will have to put it through the Ways and Means Committee. It is the only thing to do. You will hurt Bob Doughton's feelings if you don't."

The Ways and Means Committee had a number of able members. They put their minds to this new problem not only of finances but of social and economic policy for the whole United States.

The House Committee and other members of Congress began to hear from the voters in favor of the social security bill. It was soon clear that it was going to be moved along. In August 1935 Republicans as well as Democrats voted for the bill. There were only a very few who had the courage to vote against it.

I remember that when I appeared before the Senate Committee old Senator Thomas Gore raised a sarcastic objection. "Isn't this socialism?" he asked me.

My answer was, "Oh, no."

Then, smiling, leaning forward and talking to me as though I were a child, he said, "Isn't this a teeny-weeny bit of socialism?"

When the law was signed by the President [on August 14, 1935], we had a little ceremony in his office and he gave out the usual pens. I had brought in not only Congressman Doughton, but also Senator Wagner and Congressman Lewis, and one or two other members of Congress, and had provided the pens for them. As he was signing the copies of the bills with pens that would be given to its sponsors, the President looked up at me. "Frances, where is your pen?" he asked.

"I haven't got one," I replied.

"All right," he said to his secretary, "give me a first-class pen for Frances." And he insisted I was responsible for the bill and thanked me personally in very appreciative terms.

READING REVIEW

1. (a) Cite two examples of how personal influence affected the passage of the social security bill. (b) How did public opinion aid in the passage of this legislation?
2. Describe President Roosevelt's attitude concerning social security.
3. Based on what you have read, do you think social security is a good program? Cite evidence from this reading and your textbook to support your conclusion.

201 Winning a Sit-Down Strike

By the middle of 1934, after some improvement in the economy, American business and industry again began to slow down. As a result, some Americans began to criticize many of Roosevelt's policies, and their opposition increased during Roosevelt's second term. However, organized labor, especially the members of the newly formed CIO union, continued to support President Roosevelt. They believed that the New Deal's labor policy had brought great benefits and greater economic freedom to working people.

In this selection, Bob Stinson, an auto worker, told of the first sit-down strike in the General Motors plant at Flint, Michigan, in 1936. When interviewed by writer Studs Terkel many years later, Stinson clearly recalled the day he and the other workers won their strike.

READING FOCUS

1. What was the objective of a sit-down strike?
2. How did this sit-down strike change the relationship between employer and employee?

Everybody has to have something they're really sold on. Some people go to church. If I'd had anything I'm really sold on, it's the UAW [United Automobile Workers].

I started working at Fisher Body in 1917 and retired in '62, with 45 years service. Until 1933, no unions, no rules: you were at the mercy of your foreman. I could go to work at seven o'clock in the morning, and at seven fifteen the boss'd come around and say: come back at three o'clock. If he preferred somebody else over you, that person would be called back earlier, though you were there longer.

I left the plant so many nights hostile. If I were a fella big and strong, I think I'd a picked a fight with the first fella I met on the corner. It was lousy. You might call yourself a man if you was on the street, but as soon as you went through the door and punched your card, you was nothing more or less than a robot. Do this, go there, do that. You'd do it.

We got involved in a strike in Detroit, and we lost the strike. Went back on our knees. That's the way you learn things. I got laid off in the fall of '31. I wasn't told I was blackballed, but I was told there was no more jobs at Fisher Body for me. So I came to Flint and was hired right off the bat.

Condensed from Hard Times: An Oral History of the Great Depression by Studs Terkel.

Employees of General Motors participate in a sit-down strike.

We had a Black Legion in this town made up of stool pigeons and bigotty kind of people. They got themselves in good with the management by puttin' the finger on a union organizer. Once in a while, a guy'd come in with a black eye. You'd say, "What happened?" He'd say, "I was walking along the street and a guy come from behind and knocked me down."

The Black Legion later developed into the Flint Alliance. It was supposed to be made up of good solid citizens, who were terrorized by outside agitators, who had come in here to take over the plant. They would get schoolkids to sign these cards, [and] housewives. Every shoe salesman downtown would sign these cards. Businessmen would have everyone in the family sign these cards. They contended they had the overwhelming majority of the people of Flint.

Most people in town was hopin' the thing'd get solved. They had relatives and friends that they knew working in the plant; [it] was no bed of roses. They did accept some of this outside agitator stuff that got in the paper. I think anybody who reads this stuff day after day accepts a little bit of it. The great majority of the people was neutral.

There was fear. You kept your mouth shut when you was in strange company. Every time you put a union button on, you were told to leave the plant. You were fired so fast, it made your head spin.

The Flint sit-down happened Christmas Eve, 1936. I was in Detroit. When I came back, the second shift [the men who worked from 4:30 P.M. to 12:30 A.M.] had pulled the plant [struck]. It took about five minutes to shut the plant

line down. The foreman was pretty well astonished.

The boys pulled the switches and asked all the women who was in Cut-and-Sew to go home. They informed the supervisors they could stay, if they stayed in their office. They told the plant police they could do their job as long as they didn't interfere with the workers.

We had guys patrol the plant, see that nobody got involved in anything they shouldn't. If anybody got careless with company property—such as sitting on an automobile cushion without putting burlap over it—he was talked to. You couldn't paint a sign on the wall or anything like that. You used bare springs for a bed. 'Cause if you slept on a finished cushion, it was no longer a new cushion.

Governor [Frank] Murphy said he hoped he would never have to use National Guard against people. But if there was damage to property, he would do so. We invited him to the plant and see how well we were taking care of the place.

They'd assign roles to you. When some of the guys at headquarters wanted to tell some of the guys in the plant what was cookin', I carried the message. I was a scavenger, too.

The merchants cooperated. There'd be apples, bushels of potatoes, crates of oranges that was beginnin' to spoil.

The soup kitchen was outside the plant. The women handled all the cooking, outside of one chef who came from New York. He had anywhere from ten to twenty women washing dishes and peeling potatoes in the strike kitchen. Mostly stews, pretty good meals. They were put in containers and hoisted up through the window. The boys in there had their own plates and cups and saucers.

Most of the men had their wives and friends come down, and they'd stand inside the window and they'd talk. Find out how the family was. If the union supplied them with enough coal.

We had a ladies' auxiliary. They'd visit the homes of the guys that was in the plant. They would find out if there was any shortage of coal or food. Then they'd maneuver around amongst themselves until they found some place to get a ton of coal.

Some of 'em would have foremen come to their homes: "Sorry, your husband was a very good operator. But if he don't get out of the plant and away from the union, he'll never again have a job at General Motors." If this woman was the least bit scared, she'd come down and cry on her husband's shoulder. He'd more than likely get a little disturbed, get a hold of his strike captain. Sometimes you just had to let 'em go. Because if you kept them in there, they'd worry so much over it, that'd start ruinin' the morale of the rest of the guys.

Morale was very high at the time. It started out kinda ugly because the guys were afraid they put their foot in it and all they was gonna do is lose their jobs. But as time went on, they begin to realize they could win this darn thing, 'cause we had a lot of outside people comin' in showin' their sympathy.

Nationally known people contributed to our strike fund. Mrs. Roosevelt for one. We even had a member of Parliament come from England and address us.

Lotta things worked for the union we hadn't even anticipated. Company tried to shut off the heat. It was a bluff. Nobody moved for half an hour, so they turned it back on again. They didn't want the pipes to get cold. If the heat was allowed to drop, then the pipes will separate—they were all jointed together—and then you got a problem.

Some of the time you were scared, because there was all kinds of rumors going around. We had a sheriff—he came in one night and read the boys the riot act. He told 'em they had to leave. He stood there, looked at 'em a few minutes. A couple of guys began to curse 'im, and he turned around and left.

The men sat in there for forty-four days. Governor Murphy was trying to get both sides to meet on some common ground. I think he lost many a good night's sleep. We wouldn't use force. Mr. Knudsen was head of General Motors and, of course, there was John L. Lewis [founder of the CIO]. They'd reach a temporary agreement and invariably the Flint Alliance or GM headquarters in Detroit would throw a monkey wrench in it. So every morning, Murphy got up with an unsolved problem.

John L. [Lewis] was as close to a Shakespearean actor as any I've ever listened to. He had more command of language. He made a speech that if they shoot the boys out at the plant, they'd have to shoot him first.

Finally, we got the word: THE THING IS SETTLED. My, you had to send about three people, one right after the other, down to some of those plants because the guys didn't believe it. Finally, when they did get it, they marched out of the plants with the flag flyin' and all that stuff.

When Mr. Knudsen put his name to a piece of paper and says that General Motors recognizes the UAW-CIO—until that moment, we were non-people, we didn't even exist. That was the big one.

READING REVIEW

1. Describe the working conditions which existed in Flint before the strike.
2. Give two reasons why the strikers made a special effort to take care of the company property.
3. What type of outside help or encouragement did the strikers receive?
4. In what ways did the strike alter the employer-employee relationship at General Motors?

202 The New Deal in History

For decades now, Americans have been thinking, talking, and writing about the New Deal. During the 1930's—the years of the New Deal—people's feelings were especially strong. Some Americans in those years thought that the New Deal was a radical threat to the American way of life. Others believed that the New Deal programs were moderate reforms necessary to help the nation recover from the depression.

Like other Americans, historians, too, have held strong opinions about the New Deal. In 1945 historian Henry Steele Commager reviewed the record of the New Deal and summed it up in a magazine article. In the following selection,

READING FOCUS

1. What were the major achievements of the New Deal?
2. Why did Commager say that the New Deal "is here to stay"?

Now that the bitter quarrels over New Deal policies have been drowned out by the war [World War II], it is possible to evaluate those policies in some historical perspective. Those policies have been decisively voted for four times by large popular majorities. They have been turned into reality so fully that controversy about them is almost irrelevant. It should be possible to fix, with some degree of accuracy, the place occupied by Roosevelt in American history.

We can see now that the "Roosevelt revolution" was no revolution. Rather it was the high point of 50 years of historical development. Roosevelt himself, though clearly a leader, was an instrument of the people's will rather than a creator of, or a dictator to, that will. Indeed, the issue of the expansion of government control for democratic purposes began in the 1890's. A longer perspective will see the 50 years from the 1890's to the present as a historical unit. The roots of the New Deal go deep down into our past. It is not understandable except in terms of that past.

What was really only a new deal of the old cards looked, to startled and troubled Americans at the time, like a revolution for two reasons. It was carried through with breathless rapidity. And, in spirit at least, it contrasted sharply with what came immediately before it. But if the comparison had been made, not with the Coolidge-Hoover era, but with the Wilson, the Theodore Roosevelt, even the Bryan era, the contrasts would have been less striking than the similarities.

Actually, the precedents for the major part of the New Deal legislation were to be found in these earlier periods. Regulation of rail-

roads and of business dated back to the Interstate Commerce Act of 1887 and the Sherman Act of 1890. The farm relief program of the Populists and of Wilson anticipated much that the Roosevelt administration passed into law. The beginnings of conservation can be traced to the Carey Act of 1894 and the Reclamation Act of 1902.

Power regulation began with the Water Power Act of 1920. Supervision over securities exchanges began with laws of the Harding and Coolidge administrations. Regulation of money is as old as the Union. The fight which Bryan and Wilson waged against the "money power" and Wall Street was more bitter than anything that came during the New Deal. Labor legislation had its beginnings in such states as Massachusetts and New York over 50 years ago. Much of the program of social security was worked out in Wisconsin and other states early in the 1900's.

There is nothing remarkable about this. Nor does it lessen in any way the significance of President Roosevelt's achievements and contributions. It is to the credit of Roosevelt that he worked within the framework of American history and tradition.

What, then, are the major achievements, the lasting contributions, of the first three Roosevelt administrations? First, perhaps, comes the restoration of self-confidence, the reassertion of faith in democracy. Those who lived through the electric spring of 1933 will remember the change from depression and discouragement to excitement and hope. Those able to compare the last decade with previous decades will agree that interest in public affairs has rarely been as widespread, as alert, or as responsive.

All this may seem indefinite. If we look to more definite things, what does the record show? Of primary importance has been the physical rebuilding of the country. It became clear, during the 1920's and 1930's, that the natural resources of the country—its soil, forests, water power—were being destroyed at a dangerous rate. The development of the Dust Bowl, and the migration of farmers to the Promised Land of California, the tragic floods on the Mississippi and the Ohio, dramatized to the American people the urgency of this problem.

Roosevelt tackled it with energy and boldness. The Civilian Conservation Crops enlisted

---

Adapted from "Twelve Years of Roosevelt" by Henry Steele Commager in The American Mercury, *April 1945, pp. 391–401.*

almost 3 million young men. They planted 17 million acres in new forests, built over 6 million small dams to stop soil erosion, and fought forest fires and plant and animal diseases. To check erosion, the government organized a cooperative program which obtained the help of over one fourth of the farmers of the country. More important than all this was the TVA, a gigantic laboratory for regional rebuilding.

Equally important has been the New Deal achievement in human rehabilitation. Roosevelt came into office at a time when unemployment had reached perhaps 14 million, and when private solutions had failed. It was perhaps inevitable that he should sponsor a broad program of government aid. More important than relief was the acceptance of the principle that the government was responsible for the welfare and security of its people.

That this principle was bitterly opposed now seems hard to believe. Its establishment must stand as one of the main achievements of the New Deal. Beginning with emergency legislation for relief, the Roosevelt program in the end included the whole field of social security—unemployment assistance, old-age pensions, aid to women and children, and public health. It involved programs of rural rehabilitation, the establishment of maximum hours and minimum wages, the prohibition of child labor, and reform in housing.

In the political field the achievements of the New Deal were equally notable. First we must note the steady trend toward the strengthening of government and the expansion of government activities—whether for good or bad only the future can tell. As yet no better method of dealing with the problems of a modern economy and society has shown itself. It can be said that though government today has, quantitatively, far greater responsibilities than it had a generation ago, it has, qualitatively, no greater power. For our constitutional system remains as it always was. All power still resides in the people and their representatives in Congress. They can at any moment take from their government any power.

We seem to have overcome our traditional distrust of the government and realized that a strong state could be used to benefit and advance the nation. That is by no means a New Deal achievement. But it is a development which has gained much from the experience of

Unemployed, but still resourceful

the American people during the Roosevelt administrations.

It has meant, of course, a marked federal centralization. Along with this has come a great increase in the power of the President. The charge that Roosevelt has been a dictator can be dismissed, along with charges that Jefferson, Jackson, Lincoln, Theodore Roosevelt, and Wilson were dictators. American politics simply doesn't run to dictators. But Roosevelt has been a "strong" executive—as every great democratic President has been a strong executive. There is little doubt that Roosevelt accepted this situation cheerfully.

The New Deal, as far as can be foreseen, is here to stay. There seems no chance of a reversal of any of the major developments in politics in the last twelve years. This was recognized by the Republicans in 1940 and again in 1944. Both platforms endorsed all the essentials of the New Deal.

And what, finally, of Roosevelt himself? It may seem too early to fix his position in our history. Yet that position is reasonably clear. He takes his place in the great tradition of American liberalism, along with Jefferson, Jackson, Lincoln, Theodore Roosevelt, and Wilson. Coming to office at a time when the very foundations of the republic seemed threatened, he restored confidence and proved that democracy could act as effectively in crisis as could totalitarian governments.

A liberal, he put government clearly at the service of the people. A conservative, he pushed through reforms designed to strengthen the natural and human resources of the nation, restore agriculture and business to their former prosperity, and save capitalism. He saw that problems of government were primarily political, not economic. He saw that politics should control the economy, not the other way around.

"The only sure defense of continuing liberty," Roosevelt said, "is a government strong enough to protect the interests of the people, and a people strong enough and well enough informed to maintain its sovereign control over its government." The Roosevelt administration proved once more that it was possible for such a government to exist and such a people to flourish, and restored to the United States its position as "the hope of the human race."

READING REVIEW

1. According to Commager, what were the three major accomplishments of the New Deal?
2. Cite two pieces of evidence which Commager used to support his conclusion that the New Deal "is here to stay."
3. Why did Commager reach a favorable conclusion about President Roosevelt and his New Deal policies?

203 A Critic on the New Deal

The verdict of history about the New Deal has not been all favorable. Some critics of the New Deal charge that it expanded the authority of the federal government by taking away powers of state governments. They point out that the New Deal programs greatly increased the national debt. Critics also argue that the Roosevelt administration helped labor unions to become much too powerful.

John T. Flynn was one of these critics who believed that Roosevelt's New Deal policies were disastrous for the nation. Flynn was particularly worried about the growth of the government bureaucracy and its increasing power. In this selection from his book *The Roosevelt Myth,* written in 1948, Flynn also bitterly attacked Roosevelt himself as well as his policies.

READING FOCUS

1. What lasting changes did Roosevelt's policies have on American economic and political systems?
2. Why did Flynn feel Roosevelt's New Deal policies were disastrous for the nation?

Many good people in America still cherish the false idea that Roosevelt performed some amazing achievement for this country. They believe he took our economic system when it was completely broken down and restored it to vitality. They think he took over our political system when it was weakest and restored it to its full strength. He put himself on the side of the underprivileged masses. He transferred power from the great corporation executives to the simple working people of America. He controlled the adventurers of Wall Street, and gave security to the humble men and women of the country.

But not one of these claims is true. He did not restore our economic system to vitality. He changed it. The system he so stupidly moved us into is more like the bureaucracy of Germany before World War I than our own traditional order.

Before his regime we lived in a system which depended for its expansion upon private investment in private enterprise. Today [1948] we live in a system which depends for its expansion and vitality upon the government. This is a prewar European importation. And it was imported at the moment when it had fallen apart in Europe. In this system the government takes by taxes or by borrowings the savings of all the citizens and invests them in non-wealth-producing undertakings in order to create work.

Behold the picture of the American economy today. In America today every fourth person depends for a livelihood upon employment either directly by the government or indirectly in some industry supported by government funds. There is a public debt of $250 billion, compared to a pre-Roosevelt debt of $19 billion, and a government budget of $40 billion instead of $4 billion before Roosevelt. Inflation has doubled prices and reduced the lower-paid employed workers to a state of poverty as bad as that of the unemployed in the depression. More

Adapted from The Roosevelt Myth *by John T. Flynn.*

people are on various kinds of government relief than when we had 11 million unemployed. Bureaucrats are in every field of life. And the President is calling for more power, more price-fixing, more regulation, and more billions. Does this look like the traditional American scene?

No, Roosevelt did not restore our economic system. He did not construct a new one. He substituted an old one which lives upon permanent crises and an armament economy. And he did not by a process of orderly design and building, but by a series of mistakes. He moved one step at a time, in flight from one problem to another. Now we have a state-supported economic system that will continue a little at a time to destroy the private system until it disappears altogether.

Roosevelt did not restore our political system to its full strength. One may like the shape into which he battered it, but it cannot be called a repair job. He changed our political system with two weapons—blank-check congressional appropriations and blank-check congressional legislation. In 1933 Congress gave up much of its power when it put billions into his hands. It gave him a blanket appropriation to be spent at his own will. And it passed general laws leaving it to him, through great government bureaus that he set up, to fill in the details of legislation.

These two mistakes gave Roosevelt a power which he used ruthlessly. He used it to break down the power of Congress and concentrate it in the hands of the executive. The result of these two betrayals—the smashing of our economic system and the twisting of our political system—can only be the planned economic state. This, in the form of either communism or fascism, dominates the entire continent of Europe today. The capitalist system cannot live under these conditions. Free representative government cannot survive a planned economy. Such an economy can be managed only by a dictatorial government. The only result of our present system—unless we reverse the drift—will be the gradual disappearance of the system of free enterprise under a free representative government.

There are people who honestly defend this change. They at least are honest. They believe in a planned economy. They believe in a highly centralized government operated by a powerful executive. They do not say Roosevelt saved our system. They say he has given us a new one. That is logical. But no one can praise Roosevelt for doing this and then insist that he restored our traditional political and economic systems to their former vitality.

Roosevelt's star was sinking sadly in 1938 when he had 11 million unemployed and when Hitler made his first war moves in Europe. The cities were filling with jobless workers. Taxes were rising. The debt was soaring. The war rescued him and he seized upon it like a drowning man. By leading his country into the fringes of the war at first and then deep into its center all over the world he was able to do the only things that could save him—spend billions to spread the hot flames of war hysteria and put every man and woman into the war mills. Under the pressure of patriotism, he could silence criticism and work up the illusion of the war leader.

On the moral side, I have barely touched that subject. It will all still be told. But go back through the years, read the speeches and platforms and judgments Roosevelt made, and consider them in the light of what he did. Look up the promises of thrift in public office, of balanced budgets and lower taxes, of honesty in government, and of security for all. Read the speeches he made promising never, never again to send our sons to fight in foreign wars. He broke every promise. He betrayed all who trusted him.

The figure of Roosevelt exhibited before the eyes of our people is false. There was no such being as that noble, selfless, hard-headed, wise, and farseeing combination of philosopher, philanthropist, and warrior. It has been created out of pure propaganda. A small collection of dangerous people in this country are using it to advance their own evil purposes.

READING REVIEW

1. (a) Name two myths about Roosevelt. (b) What evidence did Flynn offer to support his conclusion that these were untrue?
2. Describe the changes Roosevelt made in our economic and political systems.
3. According to Flynn, what was the result of a "planned economy"?
4. Why do you think Roosevelt provoked such strong feelings?
5. What do you think of Flynn's criticism of President Roosevelt?

33 Decades in Contrast
(1920–1939)

204 A Revolution in Manners and Morals

In many ways, the society we live in today took shape after World War I. Cities and suburbs began to look the way they do now. Things we take for granted, such as automobiles and canned foods, first came into wide use in the 1920's. And along with these material changes came changes in the way people lived, acted, and thought. One writer, Frederick Lewis Allen, described these changes in people's lives as a revolution in manners and morals. In the following selection from a well-known book he wrote about the 1920's, Allen tells about the revolution that took place during those years in the lives of American women.

READING FOCUS

1. Why did women's attitudes change during the 1920's?
2. According to Allen, why were these changes "revolutionary"?

A revolution in manners and morals was beginning to affect men and women of every age in every part of the country. A number of forces were working together to make this revolution inevitable.

First of all was the state of mind brought about by the war and its conclusion. A whole generation had been affected by the eat-drink-and-be-merry-for-tomorrow-we-die spirit which accompanied the departure of the soldiers to the training camps and fighting front. It was impossible for this generation to return unchanged when the war was over. They found

Adapted from Only Yesterday *by Frederick Lewis Allen.*

themselves expected to settle down into the dull routine of American life as if nothing had happened. They couldn't do it, and they said so.

The revolution was speeded up by the growing independence of the American woman. She won the vote in 1920. She seemed, it is true, to be very little interested in it once she had it. She voted mostly as the men about her did. Few of the younger women had even a slight interest in politics. To them it was a low and useless business, without flavor and without hope. Nevertheless, winning the vote had its effect. It greatly strengthened woman's position as man's equal.

Even more marked was the effect of women's growing independence from housekeeping. Smaller houses were being built, and they were easier to take care of. Families were moving into apartments, and these required even less of the housekeeper's time and energy. Women were learning how to make lighter work of the preparation of meals. Much of what had once been housework was now either moving out of the home entirely or being made easier by machinery. Women were slowly becoming freed from routine to "live their own lives."

And what were these "own lives" of theirs to be like? Well, for one thing, they could take jobs. Up to this time girls of the middle classes who had wanted to "do something" had been largely restricted to school-teaching, social-service work, nursing, stenography, and clerical work in business firms. But now they poured out of the schools and colleges into all kinds of new occupations. They crowded the offices of publishers and advertisers. They sold antiques and real estate, opened little shops, and invaded the department stores. Married women who had children and could not seek jobs cheered themselves with the thought that homemaking and child-rearing were really "professions," after all. No topic was so furiously discussed at luncheon tables from one end of the country to the other as the question whether the married woman should take a job, and whether the mother had a right to. And as for the unmarried woman, she no longer had to explain why she worked in a shop or an office. It was not working that now had to be defended.

With the job—or at least the sense that the job was a possibility—came a feeling of economic independence. With the feeling of economic independence came a weakening of husbandly and parental authority. Unmarried women were leaving the shelter of the family home and getting apartments of their own. Yet even the job did not provide the American woman with the complete satisfaction which the management of a mechanized home no longer provided. She still had energies and emotions to burn; she was ready for the revolution.

Like all revolutions, this one was helped by foreign propaganda. It came, however, not from Moscow, but from Vienna. Sigmund Freud had published his first book on psychoanalysis at the end of the 1800's. But it was not until the war that Freudian ideas began to circulate widely among the American public.

The principal forces which stimulated the revolution in manners and morals were all 100 percent American. They were prohibition, automobiles, confession and other popular magazines, and the movies.

When the Eighteenth Amendment was ratified, prohibition seemed to have an almost united country behind it. Evasion of the law began immediately, however. Strong and sincere opposition to it quickly gathered force. The results were the bootlegger, the speakeasy, and a spirit of deliberate revolt which in many communities made drinking "the thing to do." From these facts in turn flowed further results: the cocktail party, and the general transformation of drinking from a men's pastime to one shared by both men and women together. Meanwhile a new sort of freedom was being made possible by the enormous increase in the use of the automobile. The automobile offered an easy way of escaping temporarily from the supervision of parents and chaperons, or from the influence of neighborhood opinion.

Finally, as the revolution began, its influence led to confession magazines and sensational motion pictures. These in turn had their effect on a vast number of readers and moviegoers who had never heard and never would hear of Freud.

The most obvious sign of what was taking place was the great change in women's dress and appearance. Skirts became shorter and shorter, until they finally reached the knee. With the short skirt went an extraordinary change in the weight and material and amount

Cover page of Life *magazine, 1926*

of women's clothing. The boyishly slender figure became the aim of every woman. The flesh-colored stocking became as standard as the short skirt. Petticoats almost disappeared from the American scene. In fact, the tendency of women to do away with one layer of clothing after another became so great that in 1928 the *Journal of Commerce* estimated that in the previous 15 years the amount of material required for a woman's complete outfit (except for her stockings) had declined from 19¼ yards to 7 yards [17.6 meters to 6.4 meters].

Not satisfied with the freedom of short and skimpy clothes, women sought, too, the freedom of short hair. During the early years of the decade, the bobbed head became increasingly frequent among young girls, chiefly on the ground of convenience. In the late 1920's bobbed hair became almost universal among girls in their twenties, very common among women in their thirties and forties, and by no means rare among women of sixty. Women universally adopted the small cloche hat which fitted tightly on the bobbed head.

The manufacturers of cosmetics and the owners of beauty shops made enormous profits. The popularity of rouge and lipstick spread swiftly to even the smallest village. Women who in 1920 would have thought the use of makeup immoral were soon applying it regularly and making no effort to hide the fact.

Beauty shops had sprung up on every street to give "facials," to make war against the wrinkles and sagging chins of age, to pluck and trim and color the eyebrows, and otherwise to heighten and restore the bloom of youth.

These changes in fashion—the short skirt, the boyish figure, the straight, long-waisted dresses, the use of makeup—were signs of a real change in the American feminine ideal (as well, perhaps, as in men's idea of what was the feminine ideal). Women were determined to have freedom—freedom to work and to play without the restrictions that had bound them before to lives of comparative inactivity. But what they sought was not the freedom from men which had put the suffragists of earlier years into hard straw hats and mannish suits and low-heeled shoes. The women of the 1920's wanted to be able to attract men even on the golf links and in the office. Nor was the postwar feminine ideal one of maturity or wisdom or grace. On the contrary: the search for slenderness, and the boyish figure, the popularity of short skirts—all were signs that, consciously or unconsciously, the women of this decade worshiped youth. They wanted to be—or thought men wanted them to be—men's casual and light-hearted companions. Youth was their pattern.

READING REVIEW

1. Why did Allen call this change in manners and morals "revolutionary"?
2. What were the four principal forces which stimulated this revolution?
3. What were the four conditions which Allen concluded made this revolution inevitable?
4. How did the "American feminine ideal" change?
5. (a) What are some changes in society in recent years that have affected women's lives? (b) Do you consider these changes "revolutionary"? Why or why not?

205 Trying To Be a Career Woman

Though women in the 1920's had many new freedoms, they did not always find their new freedom an easy experience. Should a married woman work? What was a suitable career for a woman? These were questions women faced.

Elisabeth Stern, a writer, was trained as a social worker. After her marriage—to her supervisor—she stayed home to raise a family. However, during the flu epidemic of World War I, her husband became ill and she supported the family by working in a department store. After her husband recovered, she continued to work but as his assistant. In this selection she told of a new job opportunity and the many problems it presented.

READING FOCUS

1. What challenges did Elisabeth Stern encounter as a "career woman"?
2. How did the interview board discriminate against Elisabeth Stern?

One day in late winter, a long, important-looking envelope came to the office with the name of a well-known woman in the corner. "For you, Mrs. Morton" [Elisabeth Stern's married name], said the typist.

The letter told me they were planning to open a "health center" in the industrial neighborhood where the Hungarians lived. What they thought of was a place where clinics would be held and free medical treatment given, and where, during the summer, clubs, classes, and community activities would be developed. In time, they would open a camp for children. The president of a large business had signed the letter as chairman of the committee.

They knew, he said, that I had done this sort of work. They wanted me to talk the matter over with them. There were a number of candidates for the position, but they had written to three they particularly wished to have as "first choice." The salary was almost as much as my husband was making.

This was not "just writing." It was not "assisting my husband."

This was a real job for me to do myself, one requiring training, certain special abilities, and experience.

Had I been gathering that experience in the years when I was simply meeting each problem of our life as it came along? I thought over my teaching, my work in the department store, my work with my husband. Curious. I had been an "executive"—why, for years.

Adapted from I Am a Woman—and a Jew *by Elisabeth G. Stern.*

Here was an opportunity that any man could be satisfied to have, and at a salary equal to a man's. We had friends teaching in the university who were earning $2,500 a year as heads of their departments. We knew a minister whose parish paid him $1,800 a year, and he was an old man with four degrees.

My husband, whose work this was, who was my chief, received only $700 a year more than this letter offered me.

Could a woman—I—be worth this much? The war had created new conditions, of course. Before, when a woman asked for work, she understood she must expect at least $1,000 a year less than a man, even as an "executive" in a business or profession. I had women friends teaching in colleges and doing social work, who held positions exactly equal with men, and who cheerfully accepted salaries less than half those of the men.

But every woman I knew who had outstanding work, a "big job," was an unmarried woman, or a widow. Married women, at the head of a work as important as a *man's*—and well-paid—were still practically unknown.

What would our friends and neighbors say if I went away every day to the office—to another office than my husband's? When I had worked at the store my husband was ill. He had been home, and the children had been under his care part of the time. What would people say if I left my children—to do work that was not my husband's, but my own entirely?

If I took this new job, I would be away from nine to five daily, six days a week. My work would be more exacting than my husband's. I would have to leave my children completely in the care of strangers.

The community felt itself very broadminded when it said, "Oh, she's not an old maid, she's an unmarried woman with a lot of brains who hasn't found a man big enough for her to marry." But the married woman who went to work had to prove that her husband was a man big enough for her to have married. She could not be "bigger" than he. She could not really be as "big."

All these things went through my mind. It will seem strange to women today, but I was afraid to take the work offered me.

Days passed, almost a week, and I could not make a decision. One laughs at these things later. I smile, too, to think now of my fear and hesitation. But I smile as one does at something done by a younger sister.

One morning I turned to my husband and told him of the new offer, of the letter that had been lying under my pillow for almost a week now.

"Do you want me to do this?" I asked.

He sat thoughtful, silent, a while. "I do not know," he said finally. "It means a great responsibility. It means a real opportunity. It's a really excellent salary." His grave eyes came to mine, worried then. "It is so big a salary that I am troubled by it. It will mean that you must give yourself completely to your work. You'll have to work so hard! I've hoped that after—that store work—you'd never do anything except what you felt you might drop when you wished. I want you to feel that you are free to do anything you like. Do you want to give up writing?"

I think, if he had not said that, I should never have answered the letter. But I understood what he wished to tell me. He wanted me to have a sheltered life, with the responsibility of earning our income on him and the pleasure of economic freedom for me—the fun of writing whenever I wanted to stop working, instead of the serious job of the daily task, the concrete thing, with monthly salary and hourly duties.

"I'd like to do—this," I said.

I met my board one Thursday morning, five people who met in the office of the chairman. Two were women. Of the men one was young and enthusiastic and impractical, and the other was an older man with quiet voice and movement. They had heard of me, knew my work and my husband. They spoke well of my husband.

We discussed the plans they had in mind, and the work done in the past. We decided

Careers outside the home

what activities it might be practical for us to begin with.

Then there was a pause.

"Mrs. Morton," came the voice of the chairman, "this work we are planning will take all your time and all your energy. We know you are a married woman, and we believe, at least I do," and he smiled in a very kind, fatherly way, "that married women are going to become more and more important in all kinds of work in the future, in professions and business equally. We're employing numbers of women in our bank every day. But I want to ask you two questions now. The first is this: you have children, have you not?" I nodded. He went on, slowly, "We did not know you had a family when we first began to consider you. That I will tell you frankly, Mrs. Morton. How will that fit in with your work? Will your husband agree to your giving all your time to this work?"

The other four waited, with him, for me to answer. I understood that these two questions had been discussed before I came in. They had been objections raised by someone.

I thought of the children. Had I neglected them? I wanted to smile, openly, at the question. What work would I do which I could promise to put first, before them? The fact that I was their mother answered that question. I could only work harder, give myself doubly. Nothing would ever come that could stand before them in my thought.

"I held a professional job even when my little daughter was a baby," I answered, letting that speak for me.

The larger of the two women shook her head. "But that's it, Mr. Blank," she said. "Let us be frank, Mrs. Morton. I've heard a great deal about you from Mr. Blank. I think this is your work. But I'm an old-fashioned woman," she admitted. "I do not feel quite easy about seeing young wives and mothers leave their homes. I was a schoolteacher myself, and I gave up my work as soon as I married. However, I am willing to keep up with the times," and she smiled to Mr. Blank. "I feel we ought to be intelligent. It is not clear to me, though," she confessed, "that your children do not suffer by having their mother away on other interests. I can understand that writing would not interfere so with your home. Please do not think I am being too personal, but we have to be in this matter. Can you give your children

the proper care if you come to us—and are you doing social work because you want to, or just as a stop-gap?"

It was shrewd of her. She was more acute about me than was I myself.

But at the time I did not think of her shrewdness. I thought only how unfair her questions were. I thought that if I were an unmarried woman, I would never have been asked if my dependents were cared for. I would not have been asked to assure them that I would not neglect the work I was paid to do for some other interest. It was because I was a married woman, a mother, that I was in this undignified position and questioned in this way.

"I do not think," I said, "I wish to speak about my children and the care I give them. It seems to me that if a woman is capable of arranging for the lives of several hundred people, she is equally able to arrange the lives of those dearest to her. I do not wish to discuss how I plan to do so. That seems to be my personal business."

The large lady grew red. She did not answer. The chairman sat back, too. I had been "independent" to the board. I had not been polite and respectful. In other words, I had destroyed my opportunity.

I said good-by, and said good-by to $2,800 a year as I went out.

The house was empty and still when I came in, for my husband was away, the children were at school. I had to get rid of some of the disappointment that I felt. I set to work, scrubbed and washed and swept. I tore through that house with broom and mop. This is what "they" thought I ought to do!

My husband listened to the account of the meeting quietly. "You were right," he said finally. "You could never have started the job under such conditions. Your board would have said that you were giving only part of your attention to the work, that you were thinking of your children and your home. It would have been an impossible situation."

It was true, and I knew it. But still, disappointment ate at me. I had thrown it all away. A man would never have done it. He would have known how to speak, how to smooth things out. Only women were emotional and hasty.

"A man wouldn't have had to meet such a situation," my husband said. "Do you think he would be asked, even if he were a widower, how he planned to take care of his children?"

I looked at him. "Did you want me to have that job?" I asked, for the second time. "Did you really want me to have it?"

He did not answer immediately. "I don't know," he said slowly. "I don't really care what you do, just so it makes you happy. I would prefer you not to have burdens to weigh you down, like, I suppose, a man carries. That's not because I don't believe you can carry them. It is just that I prefer to do that for us."

"Do you think of me," I asked then, "just as a—well, little girl? Don't you think—well, that I am as mature as you, as capable?"

At that he laughed, his rare, deep laugh. "I know that is disturbing you," he answered. "You want to be thought 'just as good as a man'—in anything. You feel unhappy because you are afraid I do not regard you so. I suppose you are just as mature as a man, as capable. But," and here he smiled at me again, "it is not because you are capable and a good executive that I love you, my darling."

He did not say quite what I wanted him to say. He did not say I was as capable as a man. But I was satisfied.

"There'll be other opportunities," he said. "Meanwhile, let's get back to my work."

READING REVIEW

1. Give two reasons why Elisabeth Stern was reluctant to accept the new job?
2. (a) What benefits did the new job offer? (b) How did her husband react to the job offer?
3. (a) What did the board ask her in their interview? (b) Do you think the board's questions to her were fair? Why or why not?
4. Discuss three ways in which conditions for working women have changed since the 1920's.

206 An Age of Hero-Worship

Throughout the history of the United States, certain men and women have become heroes to the American people. In earlier times these heroes were often famous generals or politicians. Americans also seemed greatly to admire men and women known for outstanding individual achievements. In this selection, writer Bruce Bliven suggested that in the 1920's such hero-worship seemed more intense and involved more people.

One of the most popular heroes of the period was Charles Lindbergh, but many other Americans also became objects of national hero-worship.

READING FOCUS

1. Why, according to Bliven, did Americans worship heroes so much in the 1920's?
2. What "hero-making machinery" existed in the United States today

For some years past, the most persecuted man in the world has undoubtedly been Charles A. Lindbergh, the American flyer. For a long time, he never dared to appear in public without a police guard, lest his clothes be torn from his back and his life put in danger by frenzied hero-worshipers.

He was driven nearly to desperation by the crowds which gathered at every landing field where his airplane was expected. These crowds, in their eagerness to be near him, refused to leave a clear space in which he could land. When he toured the United States to increase interest in flying, he was driven through the streets of each city in an automobile. Several of his friends had to catch as best they could the heavy packages of candy and the wreaths of flowers which lovesick women tossed at him from the crowd.

Hero-worship is not a new phenomenon in American life. But like many other things nowadays, it is speeded up and achieved on a larger scale. Thirty years ago, after the Spanish-American War of 1898, Admiral Dewey was the subject of equal worship. It ended overnight, however, when he hurt the country's feelings by making a technical transfer to his wife of a house which had been presented to him by the people. Another hero of the same war, Richmond Person Hobson, became the target of masses of strange young women who insisted, one after another, on kissing him in public.

As we have it today, however, hero-worship is a product of our times, especially of the movies and the radio. For twenty-five years movies were silent. A deep psychological need grew among most people to see in person, and to

Adapted from "An Age of Hero-Worship" by Bruce Bliven in America as Americans See It, *edited by Fred J. Ringel.*

Charles A. Lindbergh and the Spirit of St. Louis

hear the voices of, those whom they had so often followed as gray shadows on a silver screen. The popular movie star dared not appear in public without a disguise, and counted his or her fan mail by hundreds of thousands of letters each year. Then came the radio and it reversed the process. Millions wanted to see the owner of the voice to whose tones, musical or otherwise, they responded night after night. There are several persons, quite unknown a few years ago, who now receive a fee as high as $1,000 a performance just to stand upon a stage.

Americans' love of sport, and their admiration of athletics, of course, accounts for much of the present hero-worship. The typical American attitude toward athletics is still one of spectatorship rather than participation. The outstanding figures in sports—"Babe" Ruth in baseball, Bobby Jones in golf, W. T. Tilden in tennis, Red Grange or Albie Booth in football—are the objects of the greatest public interest. They can, and some of them do, earn large sums of money by endorsing certain advertised products, by writing for the press, and by appearing in vaudeville theaters. For that matter, anyone who has become somewhat known, by whatever means, can take advantage of it to some extent. The woman who shoots her husband or boyfriend writes her life story from her prison cell for some sensational newspaper. The winner of an endurance contest, who has rocked in a rocking chair, or ridden a bicycle, or sat in a tree, longer than anyone else, is an outstanding hit in a theater, though often completely forgotten soon afterward.

What we have seen in recent years is the creation of a vast new machinery for making everyone aware of any new person or idea. Of this machinery the movies and the radio are but a part, although an important one. Let anyone say or do anything interesting, and within a week everyone in America has heard his voice on the radio, seen his photograph and read his interviews in the newspapers, seen and heard him in the movies. This fact has a double result. It not only creates heroes by magic, but it guarantees that people will tire of them with equal speed. Just as a popular song now runs its course and dies in half the time it did a few years ago, there is no one so completely forgotten as the person in the spotlight last year.

The movie is the deadliest of all enemies of these soon-forgotten celebrities. They are now required to make a speech before the camera, and rarely do they come through this ordeal well. They have trouble talking, they perspire, make mistakes in grammar, or what is worse, read a speech which was obviously prepared for them by someone else. It seems probable that when television comes along, only the very sturdiest of our heroes will be able to last.

Are Americans more interested in hero-worship than the people of other countries? Or is it just that the hero-making machinery exists here in more complete form than elsewhere? Certainly hero-worship is not unknown in Europe. American movie stars are mobbed more mercilessly in London than they are in New York. Lindbergh was never in greater danger from the bear-like affection of the mob than at Le Bourget airport in Paris. The making of mob-idols is neither uniquely an American phenomenon nor one of the present age alone. In explanation of America's attitude there are several things to be said, though I can hardly do more than suggest them here.

1. The Americans are only very partially believers in the theory of democracy. While their politics are republican, their business life—which is to them far more important—is conducted on strictly autocratic lines. In this country, as elsewhere, the mob desires ruthless leaders whose strength and success make up for their own weakness and failure.

2. A common error is to suppose that the American temperament is like the English, or that of other North European peoples. It is not. In its intensity, violence of thought and action,

and changeability, it is much more Latin than Nordic.

3. It must be remembered, moreover, that America is not so much a nation as a parliament of nations. It has become a commonplace to point out that New York City alone has more Irish than Dublin, more Italians than Naples, more Jews than Jerusalem. Not only in New York but throughout America, these groups with their various racial backgrounds and cultural heritages are vaguely conscious of their differences from one another. They do what they can to find a common meeting ground. It is not too fanciful to say that when they all worship the same hero at the same moment, they feel a sense of kinship to each other which they can acquire in no other way.

4. Most important of all, however, is a feeling at which I have already hinted. Americans, like other Western peoples, feel an uneasy, increasing sense of insecurity in the modern world, where they seem more and more to be the puppets of great economic forces which are beyond anyone's power to control. In this predicament they turn with relief to anyone who, in any field, appears to stand out beyond everyone else. They feel that the world needs giants—as perhaps it does. When they find them, they pretend that they are even taller than in fact they are.

READING REVIEW

1. (a) Name four reasons why hero-worship was so prevalent in America during the 1920's. (b) Do you agree with these reasons? Why or why not?
2. According to Blivens, what was the "deadliest" of the hero-making machinery? Why?
3. Why do you think none of the "heroes" Blivens mentioned was a woman?
4. (a) Who are some people that you especially admire today? (b) Why do you admire them?

207 A Teenager on the Soup Line

Many Americans today sometimes wonder what life was like during the Great Depression. They have seen movies and read stories about people standing in soup lines or bread lines, about people going hungry, about jobless people hitchhiking around the nation looking for work. But do these movies and stories give a true picture of the times? What was life like during the 1930's?

In the late 1960's, writer Studs Terkel decided to find out about American life during the Great Depression by interviewing people who remember those times and asking them how the depression had affected them. He spent months interviewing people and used their conversations in his book *Hard Times*. In this selection, Peggy Terry told about her experiences as a teenager from Oklahoma during the depression.

READING FOCUS

1. How did the author describe life during the depression?
2. According to the author, what was the difference between poor people today and poor people then?

I first noticed the difference when we'd come home from school in the evening. My mother'd send us to the soup line. And we were never allowed to curse. If you happened to be one of the first ones in line, you didn't get anything but water that was on top. So we'd ask the guy that was putting the soup into the buckets—everybody had to bring their own bucket to get the soup—he'd dip the greasy watery stuff off the top. So we'd ask him to please dip down to get some meat and potatoes from the bottom of the kettle. But he wouldn't do it. So we learned to curse.

Then we'd go across the street. One place had bread, large loaves of bread. Down the road just a little way was a big shed, and they gave milk. My sister and me would take two buckets each. And that's what we lived off for the longest time.

I can remember one time, the only thing in the house to eat was mustard. My sister and I put so much mustard on biscuits that we got sick. And we can't stand mustard till today.

There was only one family around that ate good. Mr. Burr worked at the ice plant. Whenever Mrs. Burr could, she'd feed the kids. But she couldn't feed 'em *all*. They had a big tree that had fruit on it. She'd let us pick those. Sometimes we'd pick and eat 'em until we were sick.

Adapted from Hard Times: An Oral History of the Great Depression *by Studs Terkel.*

Her two daughters got to go to Norman to college. When they'd talk about all the good things they had at the college, she'd kind of hush 'em up because there was always poor kids that didn't have anything to eat. I remember she always felt bad because people in the neighborhood were hungry. But there was a feeling of together. . . .

When they had food to give to people, you'd get a notice and you'd go down. So Daddy went down that day and he took my sister and me. They were giving away potatoes and things like that. But they had a truck of oranges parked in the alley. Somebody asked them who the oranges were for, and they wouldn't tell 'em. So they said, well, we're gonna take those oranges. And they did. My dad was one of the ones that got up on the truck. They called the police, and the police chased us all away. But we got the oranges.

It's different today. People are made to feel ashamed now if they don't have anything. Back then, I'm not sure how the rich felt. I think the rich looked down on the poor as much as they do now. But among the people that I knew, we all had an understanding that it wasn't our fault. It was something that had

A soup line during the depression

happened to the system. Most people blamed Hoover, and they cursed him—it was all his fault. I'm not saying he's blameless, but I'm not saying either it was all his fault. Our system doesn't run by just one person, and it doesn't fall by just one person, either.

Did I feel a sense of shame? I remember it was fun. It was fun going to the soup line. 'Cause we all went down the road, and we laughed and we played. The only thing we felt is that we were hungry and we were going to get food. Nobody made us feel ashamed. There just wasn't any of that.

Today you're made to feel that it's your own fault. If you're poor, it's only because you're lazy and you're ignorant, and you don't try to help yourself. You're made to feel that if you get a check from Welfare that the bank at Fort Knox is gonna go broke.

Then I got married. My husband and me just started traveling around, for about three years. It was a very nice time, because when you're poor and you stay in one spot, trouble just seems to catch up with you. But when you're moving from town to town, you don't stay there long enough for trouble to catch up with you. It's really a good life, if you're poor and you can manage to move around.

I was pregnant when we first started hitch-hiking, and people were really very nice to us. Sometimes they would feed us. I remember one time we slept in a haystack, and the lady of the house came out and found us and she said, "This is really very bad for you because you're going to have a baby. You need a lot of milk." So she took us up to the house.

She had a lot of rugs hanging on the clothesline because she was doing her house cleaning. We told her we'd beat the rugs for her giving us the food. She said, no, she didn't expect that. She just wanted to feed us. We said, no, we couldn't take it unless we worked for it. And she let us beat her rugs. I think she had a million rugs, and we cleaned them. Then we went in and she had a beautiful table, full of all kinds of food and milk. When we left, she filled a gallon bucket full of milk and we took it with us.

You don't find that now. I think maybe if you did that now, you'd get arrested. Somebody'd call the police. The atmosphere since the end of the Second War—it seems like the minute the war ended, the propaganda started. In making people hate each other.

READING REVIEW

1. How did Peggy Terry feel about the soup line?
2. What did Peggy Terry mean when she talked about that "feeling of together"?
3. (a) How did Peggy Terry compare the poor people today with poor people during the depression? (b) Do you agree or disagree with her?

208 Fleeing the Dust Bowl

American farmers in the plains states were hit by a terrible drought during the 1930's. This lack of rain caused large areas of the Great Plains to dry up and turn into what came to be called "the Dust Bowl." The situation in Oklahoma and other states of the Great Plains was so serious that thousands of farm families were forced to leave their farms. Many of them headed west to California to look for jobs as migrant farm workers.

These poor and desperate Americans were models for the characters in a famous novel written by John Steinbeck, *The Grapes of Wrath.* Woody Guthrie, a song writer, also told of the lives of these people in some of his folk songs. The following selection includes Guthrie's memory of wandering across America in the 1930's.

READING FOCUS

1. What was Guthrie's point in the song "Do Re Me"?
2. To whom was Guthrie speaking in "Pastures of Plenty"?

I got a few little jobs—helping a water-well driller, hoeing figs, irrigating strawberries in the sandy land, laying roofs, hustling sign jobs with a painter.

I followed the oil towns and found myself as far west as Hobbs, New Mexico. I'd learned how to play a guitar, a few of the easy chords, and was making saloons like a preacher changing from street corner to street corner.

I hit Pampa in the Panhandle of Texas, and stuck there a while. Then the dust storms begun blowing blacker and meaner, and the rain was getting less, and the dust more and more. I made up a little song that went:

'37 was a dusty year
And I says, Woman, I'm leavin' here.

Do Re Mi *and* Pastures of Plenty *words and music by Woody Guthrie.*

And on one dark and dusty day, I pulled out down the road that led to California.

The further west you walk, the browner, hotter, stiller and emptier the country gets.

I met the hard-rock miners, old prospectors, desert rats, and whole swarms of hitchhikers, migratory workers—squatted with their little piles of belongings in the shade of the big sign boards, out across the flat, hard-crust, gravelly desert. Kids chasing around in the blistering sun. Ladies cooking scrappy meals in sooty buckets, scouring the plates clean with sand. All waiting for some kind of a chance to get across the California line.

*   *   *   *

Do Re Me

Lots of folks back east, they say,
Is leavin' home every day,
Beatin' a hot old dusty way to th' California line.
'Crost th' desert sands they roll
Gettin' outta that old dust bowl,

They think they're a-goin' to a sugar bowl
But here's what they find:

Oh, the police at the port of entry say,
"You're number Fourteen Thousand for to-day! Oh!

"If you ain't got th' do re me, folks,
If you ain't got th' do re me,
Why, ya better go back t' beautiful Texas,
Oklahoma, Kansas, Georgia, Tennessee;
    California is a garden of Eden,
    A paradise to live in or see;
    But, believe it or not,
    You won't find it so hot
    If you ain't got th' do re me!"

If you wanta buy a home or farm,
That cain't do nobody harm,
Or take your vacation by the mountains or sea,
Don't swap your old cow for a car,
Ya better stay right where you are;
Ya better take this little tip from me.

Cause I look thru the want ads every day
But the headlines in the papers always say:

Chorus: "If you ain't got. . . ."

An artist's impression of the "Dust Bowl"

Yes, guess I'm what you'd call a migrant worker. Guess you had to think up some kind of name for me. I travel, yes, if that's what you mean in your red-tape and your scary offices, but you can just call me any old word you want to. You just set and call me off a whole book full of names, but let me be out on my job while you're doing the calling. Thataway, we can save time and money and get more work turned out.

I ain't nothing much but a guy walking along. You can't hardly pick me out in a big crowd, I look so much like everybody else. Streets. Parks. Big places. I travel . . . yes, I travel. Ain't you glad I travel and work? If I was to stop, you'd have to up and leave your job and start traveling, because there's . . . a lot of traveling that's got to be done.

*   *   *   *

Pastures of Plenty

It's a mighty hard row that my poor hands has
    hoed;
My poor feet has traveled a hot, dusty road;
Out of your dust bowl and westward we rolled;
And your deserts was hot and your mountains
    was cold.

I worked in your orchards of peaches and
    prunes;
Slept on the ground in the light of your moon;

On the edge of your city you'll see us and then
We come with the dust and we go with the
    wind.

California, Arizona, I make all your crops,
Then, it's north up to Oregon to gather your
    hops,
Dig the beets from your ground, cut the grapes
    from your vine,
To set on your table your light sparkling wine.

Green pastures of plenty from dry desert
    ground
From that Grand Coulee dam where the water
    runs down;
Ever' state in this union us migrants has been;
We'll work in this fight and we'll fight till we
    win.

Well, it's always we rambled, that river and I,
All along your green valley I will work till I
    die;
My land I'll defend with my life if it be,
'Cause my pastures of plenty must always be
    free.

READING REVIEW

1. What did Guthrie say about the opportunities in California?
2. To what group was he speaking in "Pastures of Plenty"?
3. Based on the reading selection, make two generalizations about the life of migrant workers during the depression.

209 The Golden Age of Radio

Although Americans underwent many hardships during the Great Depression of the 1930's, not all was gloom and misery. The entertainment industry did a thriving business. Hollywood, for example, turned out such all-time movie favorites as "Gone With the Wind" and "The Wizard of Oz." Over 60 percent of all Americans went to the movies every week. (It was possible to see a double feature for as little as ten cents.)

Even cheaper was radio. The 1930's were the heyday of this medium, and many different types of shows were broadcast live from stations all over the country. Families gathered around the radio to relax, much as they watch television today.

Joseph Julian, the author of this account, began his radio career as a bit actor and sound-effects man in 1932, in the depths of the depression. Here he talked about some of his experiences in the mid-1930's.

READING FOCUS

1. What was the standard form of network programming during the late 1930's?
2. How did radio of the "Golden Age" differ from radio today?

Gradually, I began getting more auditions— and winning a few now and then. I picked up isolated jobs on shows like *Flash Gordon; Inner Sanctum; Joyce Jordan, Girl Interne;* and *Renfrew of the Mounted.*

Waiting in the studio for a *Renfrew* rehearsal to start, I got into a conversation with a tall, distinguished-looking gentleman named Brad Barker. In the middle of a discussion, he suddenly excused himself, walked over to a large cardboard cylinder mounted on a metal frame, put his mouth to one end, and emitted the blood-curdling howl of a timber wolf. This was the opening signature of *Renfrew of the Mounted,* a weekly series of half-hour stories of manhunts and battles between the good guys and bad guys in the Canadian wilderness.

Barker (what's in a name?) was one of a small group of specialists who made a good living doing animal sounds, baby noises, and screams—which were always in demand.

The animal imitators could come up with just about anything asked of them, from the

chirp of a canary (any age) to the roar of a rhinoceros.

Donald Bain, one of the best, could meow and bark and spit, as both characters of a cat and dog fight. Some actors once played a dirty trick on him. They accompanied him to the Automat, where he regularly had lunch, then one telephoned from the outside and had him paged. Pretending to be the director of a radio show, he told Bain he needed someone in a hurry who could do a good cat and dog fight, and that he had been recommended. Would he be willing to do a short audition over the phone? Whereupon Bain furiously snarled and meowed and spat and barked into the receiver, while everyone in the restaurant roared at the antics of this seemingly crazy little man.

The baby criers were usually women, who carried a small pillow around with them, into which they gurgled, whined and bawled. Sometimes they would also lisp the words of a young child.

The screamers? You might think anyone can scream? Not so. 'Tis an art. There are all kinds of screams: some that are short and eerie, others that are long and shrill. And screams you might hear in a Gothic tale, of the victim before the kill. Some screamers were better than others, but they all saved the throats of the actors for whom they doubled, enabling them to continue the performance without hoarseness.

The most powerful casting director at that time was Frances von Bernhardi, who worked for Frank and Anne Hummert, an incredibly successful husband-and-wife team that dominated the field of radio drama. Former journalists, they pioneered the format of the daily series and filled them with the same low common denominator—sentimentality.

The Hummerts themselves usually dreamed up a show's original concept, building it around a folksy or easily identifiable character. They employed a large stable of writers. One group worked exclusively at developing story lines and plots. When approved by the Hummerts, the scripts were passed along to the dialogue writers. There were many do's and don't's. For instance, all characters had to be constantly identified by name:

JOHN: Why, hello, Henry!
HENRY: Hello, John.
JOHN: Haven't seen you in a long time, Henry.

From This Was Radio: A Personal Memoir *by Joseph Julian.*

HENRY: Yes, that's true, John.

JOHN: How about joining me for a drink, Henry?

HENRY: Why, I'd like to, John.

Unnatural? Yes, but they felt it was essential to know who was talking to whom at all times. They must have thought their listeners were pretty stupid not to be able to tell from the dialogue itself.

Plot lines were often altered by a performer's real-life situation. Some contracts provided they be written out of the show for a few weeks in order to rehearse a Broadway play. The writers would then invent a reason for the character's disappearance. Perhaps he would be sent on a journey abroad, or to a rest home, or, perhaps, to jail. The same when an actor took sick. And, if he suddenly quit or was fired, there were always easy ways of killing him off—a heart attack, an auto accident, a murder.

Long pauses could never be indicated in a script. "Dead air" was forbidden. The theory was that during even a five-second silence, a hundred thousand listeners might be just tuning in. Hearing nothing, they'd turn to another station, losing all those customers for the sponsor's product.

A family enjoys listening to the radio.

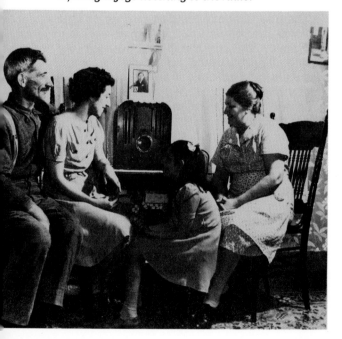

To snag new listeners, and for those who may have missed a chapter, each episode of a serial had to be preceded by a short summary of the plot:

ANNOUNCER: Yesterday, we left Alice in her living room, along with John Hennesy, her sister Gwendolyn's husband. John had just confided that he had always been in love with Alice, and had made a terrible mistake in marrying Gwendolyn. Gwendolyn, who had left the house moments before, suddenly remembered she had forgotten some books she wanted to return to the library. As she reentered the living room, John had just put his arms around Alice's waist. Gwendolyn froze as she heard John say:

JOHN: Darling, I love you more than anything in this world!

This would be followed by a music sting (*sharp chord*), the organ music would fade, and the announcer would come in with the first commercial. Generally there was an opening, middle, and closing commercial—a terrible price that listeners didn't seem to mind paying for their addiction to "soaps."

*   *   *   *

By the late thirties network programming had pretty well standardized its form. Its main categories—drama, comedy, and music—were served up in quarter-, half-, and one-hour slices of time.

Most of the dramas were, of course, the daytime "soaps"—so called because they were listened to mostly by women while doing their washing and cleaning, who were thus presumably vulnerable to sales pitches by the soap company sponsors.

In the evenings dramas were always on the menu, but the emphasis was on comedy and music.

Most of the important comedians sprang full-blown from vaudeville—especially those whose specialty was essentially non-visual, such as the joke tellers. But these comics paid a price for their new popularity. In vaudeville, a comedy routine lasted for years; in radio, it was consumed in a night. The strain of building a new show every week took its toll, and there were many breakdowns and retirements and comebacks among the nation's top funny men.

There was also a kind of humor special to radio. Mock insults and feuds between two leading comedians would boost each other's ratings, and sometimes could be kept running for months, such as the one between Jack Benny and Fred Allen, in which Allen kept finding new ways to describe Benny's stinginess. One evening a sketch had Benny being held up by a thief who snarled, "Money or your life!" The long, long period of dead air that followed became hilarious, and was topped by Benny finally saying petulantly, "I'm thinking it over." This just couldn't be as funny in any other medium. And there was Allen's classic retort to an insult by Benny: "If I had my writers here you wouldn't talk to me like that and get away with it!"

Speaking of comedy, probably the most unique comedy performance in radio history occurred in 1937 when, during a newspaper strike, the mayor of New York City, Fiorello H. La Guardia, took to the air to read funny papers to the children. The kids "didn' wanna know from nothin" about wages and working conditions—they missed their funnies! La Guardia, mayor of *all* the people, understood what that deprivation meant. Every evening for as long as the strike lasted, he would act out all the parts in his high squeaky voice and slight lisp, gesturing dramatically as he described the pictures and read the ballooned dialogue of the comic strips that regularly appeared in the New York papers. It was something to hear—and behold.

READING REVIEW

1. List the three main categories of standardized network programming.
2. How did radio as Julian described it differ from radio today?

210 Black America's Great Migration

For black Americans, the war years and the period following World War I were a time of tremendous change. During these years, black families in ever-increasing numbers moved from the South to the cities of the North. Nearly one million black Americans took part in this so-called "Great Migration."

Why did so many people leave the South? Crop failures caused by floods and the boll weevil (an insect that destroys cotton) led to great hardships, especially for farm workers. At the same time, northern factories needed workers to replace those who had left to serve in World War I. Thus the hope of greater opportunities, higher wages, and a better life caused more and more black Americans to move to the North. In this selection, Charles Johnson, a black sociologist, tells us about the Great Migration.

READING FOCUS

1. According to Johnson, what caused the "Great Migration"?
2. How did the Great Migration affect Negro culture in the North? How did it affect race relations in the North?

The cities of the North—stern, impersonal, and enticing—needed people with strong muscles. Europe, suddenly at war, had stopped supplying them, when thousands of blacks came from the South like a silent shadow. There were 500,000 people in the first three-year period. They had come first to the little towns of the South, then to the cities near the towns. Sooner or later, they boarded a special train bound for the North, to go to the cities which attracted them, to their bright lights and high wages, crowds, excitement, and struggle for life.

There was Chicago in the West, known far and wide for its great stockyards; Chicago, remembered for the fairyland wonders of the World's Fair; home of mills yelling for workers.

And there was Pittsburgh, gloomy and cheerless, and the nearby towns of Bethlehem, Duquesne, and Homestead. One railroad line brought in 12,000 new laborers free. The railroads, the vast construction projects of the state, and the large mills wanted workers.

And there was New York City, with its Harlem—the Mecca of Negroes the country over. Old families, brownstone mansions, a step from Broadway. It had factories and docks, large clothing industries, and buildings to be "superintended." It was a land of opportunity for musicians, actors, and those who wanted to

Adapted from Charles S. Johnson, "The New Frontage on American Life," in Alain Locke, ed., The New Negro. New York: Albert and Charles Boni, 1925.

Black Americans work in northern factories.

succeed, and the national headquarters of everything but the government.

And there was Cleveland, with a faint southern feeling but with iron mills; St. Louis, with great foundries, brick and pottery works; Detroit, the automobile center, with its high wages reflecting the daring economic policies of Henry Ford; Akron and its rubber; Philadelphia, with its comfortable old traditions; and the many little industrial towns where fabulous wages were paid.

Migrations, says one expert, are nearly always due to the influence of an idea. In the case of the Negroes, it was not just an idea, but an idea that was made possible. By tradition, Negroes are rural types. Their usual occupation is agriculture. Their mental and social habits have been adjusted to such an economy.

The South has few cities. The life of the section is based not on manufacturing but on the soil—and more than anything else, the fluffy white bolls of cotton. Cotton is King. When it lives and does well, there is comfort for the owners. When it fails, as is most often the case, a heavy heel twists on the neck of the black tenant farmer. The sharecropping system causing dishonesty and holding Negroes always in debt and almost in slavery; the fierce hatred of poor whites in frightened and desperate competition; the cruelty of the masters; the dullness of rural life; the hope for something better; distant flashes of a new country, calling—these were the soil in which

the idea of migration took root and flowered. There was no slow, deliberate making of plans, or inspired leadership, or forces dark and mysterious. To each person in his or her setting came an impulse and an opportunity.

There was Jeremiah Taylor, of Bobo, Mississippi, old and worn out and resigned to his farm. One of his sons came in one morning with the report that folks were leaving "like Judgment day." He had seen a labor man who promised a free ticket to a railroad camp up north. Jeremiah went to town, half doubting, and came back excited and decided. His son left, he followed. In four months his wife and two daughters packed their possessions, sold their chickens, and joined them.

Into George Horton's barber shop in Hattiesburg, Mississippi, came a white man from the North. Said he: "The colored folks owe a debt to the North because it freed them. The North owes a debt to the colored folks because after freeing them it took away their living. Now, this living is offered with interest and a new birth of liberty. Will the colored people live up to their side of the bargain?" The deciding argument was free transportation. Hattiesburg contributed forty men.

And there was Joshua Ward, who had prayed for these times and now saw God cursing the land and stirring up his people. He would ask for his anger no longer.

Rosena Shephard's neighbor's daughter went away. Silence for six weeks. Then she wrote that she was earning $2 a day packing sausages. "If that lazy, good-for-nothing gal can make $2 a day, I can make $4," and Mrs. Shephard left.

Clem Woods could not tolerate any fellow's getting ahead of him. He did not want to leave his job and couldn't explain why he wanted to go North. His boss proved to him that his chances were better at home. But every person who left added to his restlessness. One night a train passed through with two coaches of men from New Orleans. Said one of them: "Good-by, I'm bound for the promised land," and Clem got aboard.

Mrs. Selina Lennox was slow to do anything, but she was a friendly person. The emptiness of her street wore upon her. No more screaming, darting children, no more bustle of men going to work or coming home. The familiar greetings of women who were shopping, the smell of boiled food—all of these were gone.

Mobile Street, once noisy, was now very quiet, as if some disaster threatened. Now and then the Italian storekeeper, confused and sad, would walk to the middle of the street and look first up and then down and walk back into his store again. Mrs. Lennox left.

George Scott wanted more "free liberty" and accepted a railroad ticket from a stranger who always talked in whispers and seemed to have plenty of money.

Dr. Alexander H. Booth's practice declined. Some of his patients who had left and had owed him money for a long time paid up with an air of superiority that made him very angry. In their letters they said such things as "home ain't nothing like this" or "nobody who has any grit would stay." The doctor left.

Jim Casson in Grabor, Louisiana, had paid his poll taxes, his state and parish taxes. And yet there was no school for his children.

Miss Jamesie Towns taught fifty of the colored tenants' children for four months, out near Fort Valley, Georgia. Her salary was reduced from $16.80 to $14.40 a month.

*   *   *   *

There is a new type of Negro—a city Negro. He is being shaped out of strangely different elements of the general background. This is a fact overlooked by students of human behavior. In ten years, Negroes have been actually transplanted from one culture to another.

Once there were personal and close relations, in which individuals were in contact most of their lives. Now there are group relations, in which the whole structure is broken, and people are in contact at only one or two points of their lives. The old controls are no longer expected to operate. The newcomers are forced to change their lives.

With Negroes in more industrial contact and competition with white workers of greater experience and numbers, bad feelings build up. The fierce economic fears of workers in competition are increased by racial differences. Beneath the disastrous East St. Louis conflict was a boiling anger toward southern Negroes coming in to "take white people's jobs."

Here lies one of the points of highest tension in race relations. White workers have not, except in a few instances, overcome hatred based on race enough to allow Negro workers the same privileges they themselves enjoy.

While refusing Negroes admission to their unions, they grow furious over their dangerous borings from the outside. Where there is agitation and unrest, there is change. Old traditions are being shaken and rooted up by new ideas. In this the year of our Lord 1925, extending across the entire country, seventeen cities are in violent agitation over Negro residence areas. Once Negroes were silent. Now they are more apt to act with conviction. Claude McKay, the young Negro poet, caught the mood of the new Negro in this, and he turned it into fiery verse which Negro newspapers copied and recopied:

> If we must die, let it not be like hogs,
> Hunted and penned in an inglorious spot.

Less is heard of the two historic "schools of thought" clashing over the question of industrial training versus higher education for the Negro. Both are, sensibly, now taken for granted as quite necessary. The industrial schools are concerned with adjusting their courses to the new fields of industry in which Negro workers will play an increasing role. The universities must meet the demand for trained Negroes in business, the professions, and the arts. The level of education has been raised through the work of both types of schools.

Thus the new frontier of Negro life is spread out in a jagged, uneven, but progressive pattern. For a group historically kept back and not readily assimilated, contact with its surrounding culture causes uneven results. There is no fixed racial level of culture. There are as many differences in culture, education, and sophistication among Negroes as between the races. It is likely that the culture which has both nourished and abused Negro strivings will, in the end, be enriched by them.

READING REVIEW

1. List three reasons why the Negro migrated to the North.
2. What ways did the Negro culture in the North differ from that of the South?
3. (a) What was a "city Negro?" (b) How did this characterization of the Negro reflect the change in cultures?
4. (a) According to Johnson, what increased racial tensions throughout this period? (b) Do you think this is a problem in today's society? Why or why not?

211 A Black Writer on the Harlem Renaissance

During the 1920's, there was a cultural renaissance, or rebirth, in black culture that came to be known as the "Harlem Renaissance." An extremely talented group of writers and poets began to speak out against injustices in America and to write of the joys, sorrows, and hopes of black Americans.

Black pride was aroused by these writers and by America's growing interest in black music, art, and entertainment, especially in the Harlem area of Manhattan in New York City. Jazz music became the rage, and many black entertainers became extremely popular and famous, as did many nightclubs in Harlem. In this selection, Langston Hughes, one of the leading black writers of that time, wrote about the Harlem Renaissance.

READING FOCUS

1. What effect did white audiences have on black entertainers?
2. According to Hughes, what was the "Harlem Renaissance" really like?
3. What effect did the Harlem Renaissance have on the "ordinary" Negro?

The 1920's were the years of Manhattan's black Renaissance. It began with the musical revue *Shuffle Along*. It reached its peak just before the crash of 1929, the crash that sent Negroes, white folks, and all rolling down the hill.

Shuffle Along was a honey of a show. Swift, bright, funny, carefree, and gay, with a dozen danceable, singable tunes. Everybody was in the audience—including me. People came back to see it many times. It was always packed.

To see *Shuffle Along* was the main reason I wanted to go to Columbia. When I saw it, I was thrilled and delighted. From then on I was in the gallery of the Cort Theatre every time I got a chance. *Shuffle Along* gave just the proper push—a pre-Charleston kick—to that Negro vogue of the 1920's that spread to books,

---

Adapted from "When the Negro Was in Vogue" in The Big Sea *by Langston Hughes.*

African sculpture, music, and dancing.

The 1920's brought the rise of Roland Hayes, who packed Carnegie Hall; the rise of Paul Robeson in New York and London; the booming voice of Bessie Smith on thousands of records; and the rise of that grand comedienne of song, Ethel Waters. The 1920's brought Louis Armstrong and Josephine Baker.

White people began to come to Harlem in large numbers. For several years they packed the expensive Cotton Club on Lenox Avenue. But I was never there, because the Cotton Club was a Jim Crow club for gangsters and rich whites. They did not want Negro customers, unless you were someone famous like Bojangles [a dancer]. So Harlem Negroes did not like the Cotton Club and never appreciated its Jim Crow policy in the very heart of their dark community. Nor did ordinary Negroes like the growing numbers of whites in Harlem after sundown, filling the little cabarets and bars. Formerly only colored people laughed and sang there. Now strangers were given the best ringside tables to sit and stare at the Negro customers—like amusing animals in a zoo.

The Negroes said: "We can't go downtown and sit and stare at you in your clubs. You won't even let us in your clubs." But they didn't say it out loud—for Negroes are practically never rude to white people. So thousands of whites came to Harlem night after night, thinking the Negroes loved to have them there. They firmly believed that all the people who lived in Harlem left their houses at sundown to sing and dance in nightclubs, because most of the whites saw nothing but the nightclubs, not the houses.

Some of the small clubs had people like Gladys Bentley, who was something worth discovering in those days, before she got famous. For two or three amazing years, Miss Bentley sat and played a big piano all night long, without stopping. She slid from one song to another, with a powerful and continuous underbeat of jungle rhythm. Miss Bentley was an amazing exhibition of musical energy—a large, dark, masculine woman, whose feet pounded the floor while her fingers pounded the keyboard—a perfect piece of African sculpture, made alive by her own rhythm.

But when the place where she played became too well known, she began to sing with an accompanist, became a star, moved to a larger place, then downtown, then to Hollywood. The old magic of the woman and the piano and the night and the rhythm are gone. But everything goes, one way or another. The 1920's are gone and lots of fine things in Harlem night life have disappeared like snow in the sun—since it became completely commercial, planned for the downtown tourist trade, and therefore dull.

The dancers at the Savoy even began to practice acrobatic routines. They did absurd things for the entertainment of whites that probably never would have entered their heads to attempt just for their own amusement.

Some critics say that that is what happened to certain Negro writers, too. They stopped writing to amuse themselves and began to write to amuse and entertain white people. In so doing they distorted their material and left out their American brothers of a lighter complexion. Maybe it's true, since Negroes have writer-racketeers like any other race. But I have known almost all of them, and most of the good ones have tried to write honestly and express their world as they saw it.

All of us know that the happy, sparkling life of the so-called Negro Renaissance of the 1920's was not so happy and sparkling beneath the surface. But it was a period when, at almost every Harlem uppercrust dance or party, one would be introduced to various distinguished white celebrities who were there as guests. It was a period when preachers opened up shouting churches as sideshows for white tourists. It was a period when every season there was at least one hit play on Broadway acted by a Negro cast. And when books by Negro authors were being published with much greater frequency and given much more publicity then ever before or since. It was a period when white writers wrote about Negroes more successfully (commercially speaking) than Negroes did about themselves. It was the period when Ethel Barrymore appeared in blackface in *Scarlet Sister Mary* It was the period when the Negro was in vogue.

I was there. I had a swell time while it lasted. But I thought it wouldn't last long. For how could a large and enthusiastic number of people be crazy about Negroes forever? But some people in Harlem thought the race problem had at last been solved. They were sure the New Negro would lead a new life from then on in green pastures of tolerance created by Countee Cullen, Ethel Waters, Claude McKay,

Langston Hughes

Duke Ellington, Bojangles, and Alain Locke.

I don't known what made any Negroes think that—except that they were mostly intellectuals doing the thinking. The ordinary Negroes hadn't heard of the Negro Renaissance. And if they had, it hadn't raised their wages any. As for all those white folks in the speakeasies and night clubs of Harlem—well, maybe a colored man could find *some* place to have a drink that tourists hadn't yet discovered.

READING REVIEW

1. **(a)** What if any effect did white audiences have on the work of the black writers and entertainers? **(b)** What evidence did Hughes present to support his conclusion?
2. **(a)** What was Hughes' attitude toward black intellectuals? **(b)** toward the ordinary people of Harlem?
3. **(a)** Why did some people feel the race problem had been solved? **(b)** Did Hughes agree with this assumption? Why or why not?

Isolation Through World War II

CHAPTER **The Nation**
34 **Moves Toward**
Isolationism
(1920–1932)

212 **Hope for a**
Rich Future

In the 1920's, Congress passed several laws to limit immigration into the United States. These laws reflected a widespread feeling of prejudice and intolerance toward the large groups of immigrants who came from southern and eastern Europe in the late 1800's and early 1900's.

Not all Americans felt this way about the newcomers. Many Americans believed that the vitality and strength of the United States were based on the great diversity of its people, cultures, and ideas. They did not view their nation as a "melting pot," where people's differences were "melted down" and everyone was "Americanized." Horace Kallen, a scholar and writer, held this view, suggesting that the ideal nation was one in which each group maintained its identity and contributed its special talents to society.

READING FOCUS

1. Why did some Americans fear the immigrants?
2. What "social alternatives" did Kallen say that America faced?

Today the descendants of the colonists appear to be making a new Declaration of Indepen-

Adapted from Culture and Democracy in the United States *by Horace M. Kallen.*

dence. Again, as in 1776, Americans of British background fear that certain possessions of theirs, which may be lumped under the word "Americanism," are in danger. The danger comes, once more, from a force across the ocean. But this time the force is regarded not as superior, but as inferior. The relationships of 1776 are thus reversed. To save the unalienable rights of the colonists of 1776, it was necessary to declare all people equal. To save the unalienable rights of their descendants in the 1900's, it becomes necessary to declare all people unequal. In 1776 all people were as good as their betters. In 1920 people are permanently worse than their betters.

In 1776 most white people in the colonies *were* actually rather free and rather equal with respect to each other. I speak not so much of the absence of great differences in wealth, as of the fact that the white colonists were similar to each other. They had ethnic and cultural unity and the same background and ideals. Their 150-year-old tradition as Americans blended with their older traditions as Britons. They did not, until the quarrel with the mother country began, regard themselves as anything but English subjects, sharing England's dangers and England's glories.

In time, the nation created by the Declaration of Independence gained all the continental area known as the United States. The French in Louisiana and the Germans in Pennsylvania remained at home. But the descendants of the British colonists traveled across the continent, founding new settlements. If the population of these settlements had continued to grow in the same proportion as it did between 1810 and 1820, Americans of British background would have totaled over 100 million today. The inhabitants of the country today do number over 100 million. But they are not the children of the colonists and pioneers. They are later immigrants and the children of later immigrants, and they are not only British but of all the other European backgrounds.

First came the Irish. They are ethnically different from the British and Catholic in religion. They came seeking food and freedom. Their area of settlement is chiefly the East.

Behind the Irish came large numbers of Germans, quite different in speech and customs. They were culturally and economically far better off than the Irish. They settled inland, over a stretch of territory extending from western New York to the Mississippi.

Beyond the Germans, in Minnesota and the Dakotas, are the Scandinavians. Beyond these, in the mountain and mining regions, are central and southern Europeans—Slavs of various stocks, Magyars, Finns, Italians. Across the Rockies, a group of Americans of British background balances the small group on the Atlantic seacoast. They are flanked on the south by Latins—Spaniards, Mexicans, Italians—and scattered groups of Asiatics—and on the north by Scandinavians. The distribution of the population along the two coasts is similar. On the Atlantic shore French-Canadians, Irish, Italians, Slavs, and Jews alternate with the British-American population and each other.

Of all these immigrant peoples, most were of peasant stock. They were unable to read or write, surviving on a minimum of food and a maximum of work. The fearful Americans think that their coming to the United States was determined not by any spiritual reason, but because of the steamship agencies and economic need or greed. This opinion ignores four significant exceptions and one notable one. The significant exceptions are the Poles, the Finns, the Bohemians, the Slovaks. Political and religious and cultural persecution plays a large role in their movement here. The notable exception is the Jews. The Jews, more than any other people, come with the attitude of the earliest settlers. For they come because of persecution and disaster and are in search of economic opportunity, liberty of conscience, and civil rights.

All immigrants and their children undergo "Americanization" if they remain in one place in the country long enough—say six or seven years. In general, "Americanization" seems to mean the adoption of the American kind of English speech, American clothes and manners, and the American attitude in politics. "Americanization" means, in short, the disappearance of the outward differences upon which so much race prejudice is based. It appears to mean the blending together, by "the miracle of assimilation," of Jews, Slavs, Poles, French, Germans, Hindus, Scandinavians, and so on. They all are to become similar in background, tradition, outlook, and spirit to the descendants of the British colonists—the "Anglo-Saxon" stock.

Broadly speaking, these elements of Americanism are somewhat outward, the effect of environment. Along with them go American individualism, the American tendency to look on the bright side of things, and the other "pioneer" virtues. They are purely reactions to the country's natural wealth. As such they are common to all societies where the relation between population and resources is similar.

America is at the parting of the ways. Two genuine social alternatives face Americans, either of which they may achieve if they wish. What do Americans want to make of the United States—a unison, singing the old British theme "America," the America of New England? Or a harmony, in which that theme shall be dominant perhaps, but one among many, and not the only one?

In the United States, the whole social situation is favorable to the idea of unison—everything is favorable except the basic law of America itself and the spirit of American institutions. To achieve unison would require vi-

The Statue of Liberty welcomes immigrants.

olating them. Fundamentally it would require completely nationalizing education, doing away with every form of parochial and private school, ending instruction in all languages except English, and concentrating on the teaching of history and literature based on the English tradition.

Achieving the other alternative, a harmony, also requires united public action. But this action would not go completely against the ideals of America's fundamental law or the spirit of American institutions. It would seek simply to eliminate the waste and the stupidity in the society's organization, by way of freeing and strengthening those strong forces now at work. Taking the existing ethnic and cultural groups, it would seek to provide conditions under which each group might attain cultural perfection that is *proper to its kind*. All of the various nationalities which make up the American nation must first of all be taught this fact. Perhaps it used to be, to patriotic minds, the outstanding idea of "Americanism"—that democracy means self-realization through self-control and self-discipline.

What is essential in the life of humankind is its inborn positive quality—its inner inheritance. People may change their clothes, their politics, their religions, their philosophies, to a greater or lesser degree. They cannot change their grandparents. Jews or Poles or Anglo-Saxons, in order to stop being Jews or Poles or Anglo-Saxons, would have to cease to be. They inherit their selfhood and the kind of happiness they pursue. This is what, in fact, democracy in operation assumes. There are human capacities which it is the function of the nation to liberate and protect.

As intelligence and wisdom gain over "politics" and special interests, the outlines of a possibly great and truly democratic nation can be seen. Its form would be a federal republic. It would be a democracy of nationalities, cooperating voluntarily through common institutions. Thus "American civilization" may come to mean the perfection of the cooperative harmonies of "European civilization"—an orchestration of humankind. As in an orchestra, every type of instrument has its specific tone and its proper theme and melody in the whole symphony. So in society, each ethnic group is like a natural instrument. The harmony and discords of them all make the symphony of civilization.

READING REVIEW

1. **(a)** List the two alternatives Kallen believed Americans faced. **(b)** Which one did he favor? Why?
2. What did Kallen mean by "Americanization"?
3. Would you say that American society today has become either of Kallen's alternatives? Explain.

---

213 Two British Views of American Isolation

Right after World War I, the European nations believed that the United States would join the League of Nations and use its influence and power to help keep the peace in Europe. These hopes ended with the Senate's rejection of the Treaty of Versailles. How did Europe react to America's refusal to join the League? For the most part, Europeans were quite critical of it.

Some Europeans, however, tried to analyze more thoughtfully the reasons behind America's return to its traditional policy of isolation. Among them were two British writers, J. A. Spender and Collinson Owen. The first selection is taken from a book by Spender; the second is from a book by Owen.

READING FOCUS

1. According to the authors, what were the main reasons for America's return to a policy of isolation?
2. How did America's contradictory actions influence the British view on American isolation?

The first thing, it seems to me, is for Europeans to realize that the United States is not a European power. The habit of treating it as if it acted from the same motives, sympathies, and dislikes as European nations has been the source of much misunderstanding. Most Americans still think they are lucky not to be in Europe and not to be forced to mix themselves in its very tangled affairs. To these—the vast majority of Americans—participation in the war to meet the German challenge was a break, but not a change, in their traditional policy. They regard it as common sense to keep out of Europe if they can.

Adapted from Through English Eyes *by J. A. Spender.*

But this is not the only opinion in America. A large minority of important and politically knowledgeable people have a generous desire to do what they think is their duty to the world. And the whole business community wants to trade with Europe, lend it money, and get back from it what it owes. This "common sense," this idealism, and this commercial ambition are all factors in American policy. We have to consider their interaction in attempting to judge any particular part of its policy.

At the present moment America is seeking a compromise which it hopes will give it the best of all possibilities. It will trade in Europe, maintain its claims on Europe, and shout "Hands off Europe." This annoys and confuses the Europeans. It involves America in such apparent contradictions as starting an enormous program of naval construction at the same time it is proposing a plan for all nations to give up war. There is, nevertheless, a search for the right and wise policy going on all the time, and to treat it with distrust would be a great mistake. It is better to consider what has happened and why it has happened.

The British people should not hastily condemn American policy. The American state of mind corresponds almost exactly to that of the British until quite recently. For a large part of my life—roughly from the year 1880 to the year 1904—it was the aim of both British political parties to stay clear of "continental entanglements." We said to ourselves that the sea made us safe and that we should be able to sit quietly on our island. Why, we asked, should we meddle in quarrels which did not concern us when we had the whole British Empire demanding our extra energy and capital?

It was not argument but events which drove us out of our "splendid isolation." Very reluctantly we came to the conclusion that we must either help to control events on the continent or be controlled by them. Whether we chose rightly or wrongly history must decide. But by the beginning of the 1900's we had discovered that nonintervention was not, as we had supposed, an easy and simple solution, but the most difficult and complicated of all foreign policies. As much as Great Britian might have wished to turn its back on its neighbors, they could not or would not turn their backs on it. Every year these points of contact and friction seemed to increase.

The nation's isolation policy under fire

I am not suggesting that American policy will follow the same or a parallel course. Their 3,000 miles [4,830 kilometers] of ocean seem to make it even more obvious common sense for Americans to stand apart than our 21 miles [34 kilometers] of English Channel made it for us. The possibilities of meeting between the United States and other nations are fewer than those between the British Empire and other nations. An attack on the United States from Europe would be far more difficult than an attack on the British Isles from the continent. But Americans too discovered in 1917 that it was impossible for them to remain outside a great European struggle. At the end of it, their President said that there would be no neutrals in another war. Thus he proposed a League of Nations to keep the peace. Europeans accepted it and America rejected it. Europe is thus left with an American institution which America refused to accept—an American orphan left on Europe's doorstep. The United States still believes, in spite of its experiences of 1917, that nonintervention is a possible policy. At all events the United States is determined that it alone will decide whether, when, and how it will intervene.

The real cause of all this misunderstanding of America is the Great War. Before then all the European nations were aware of the United States, but not obsessed by it.

the workers and farmers of these countries may have dreamed of America as the great land of opportunity. But most accepted America much as America thought of itself: a very great country, but a country still in the making. It was a country which had made remarkable progress considering the short time it had been a nation. But it was a country which still had a very long way to go before it could be regarded as a nation as European nations thought of the term. It was not even a real naval or military power, in days when to be a great naval or military power was one of the proofs of civilization.

But the war changed all that. While all Europe was locked in its four years' struggle, America stole up on us like a bill collector in the night. The war changed us, and seemed to change America. But the fact is that, riches apart, America was exactly the same country after the war that it was before it. Essentially it still remained the same partly developed community. In many ways frontier conditions still ruled, side by side with great material prosperity.

*   *   *   *

Perhaps the most startling discovery one can make in the United States is the fact that many Americans have come to the conclusion that they really won the war.

When this rumor first began, some two or three years after the war was over, no sensible person in Europe paid any real attention to it. No doubt that attitude was then correct. But things have changed very much since then. There are many individuals in the United States who are much too fair and sane to believe in any such fantastic idea. But the people as a whole, aided by the superpatriots, part of the press, the politicians, the movies, and that curious belief that everything American is necessarily best, have now convinced themselves that it was what America did that really mattered. The years 1914-17 are forgotten. Everyone's memory is concentrated on 1918.

This false idea shared by a very large part of a vast nation is not just something to be made fun of. It has its direct effect on inter-national politics. The more firmly America believes this idea, the more likely it is to feel strengthened in its official attitude toward Europe as a continent of warring barbarians, full of old-fashioned treaties and secret diplomacy.

It is a difficult subject to discuss even with some of the best and most open-minded Americans. Although they know that such a claim is absurd, on the whole they would like to feel that America's participation was the really deciding factor.

If the war was really a fight to maintain what we call civilization, against the scientific, military barbarism of the Germany of 1914, then in upholding civilization, the Allies by the middle of 1917 were almost bled to death. The war by that time had become a blood tax on those nations which believed in upholding this civilization. America believed in this ideal, as it assured us both before and after its participation. The blood tax it was called upon to pay in saving it was very, very small. That is the only point of view that needs to be presented in any discussion of whether or not America won the war.

But it would be useless to present such a view to most Americans. They have become convinced of their comforting false idea. And they believe that the soldiers who crossed the Atlantic to Europe were noble crusaders such as the world had never seen before. It is the habit, of course, of every nation to praise the courage of its own soldiers in war. But though this is a tendency common to all nations, the United States—so far as the last war is concerned—easily goes beyond any other in praising its soldiers. If ever there was a sort of inferiority complex about America's late entrance in the war, it has long since been forgotten, and has been replaced by a mass-produced self-satisfaction and pride concerning the events of 1914-18.

It is a self-satisfaction which has a very definite business as well as patriotic value. So long as America feels like this, there can be no uneasiness of mind concerning Europe's war debts. "Those Europeans" may be feeling the pinch a bit, but they're always getting into wars anyhow, and don't known how to finish them when they begin. America had to do that for them, spending a lot of its own best blood and its own good money in the process. Too much talk about generosity to France and the rest of them becomes tiresome after that.

Adapted from The American Illusion *by H. Collinson Owen.*

1. What did Spender think was the main reason for American isolation?
2. In Owen's analysis, what incorrect belief did he think helped to explain America's actions since the war?
3. In your opinion, do these two articles agree or disagree about the causes of American isolationism? Explain. **(a)** What two actions did America take which were contradictory to this policy? **(b)** How did the British react?

214 Lobbying for Disarmament

After World War I, the major military powers of the world held a series of conferences aimed at limiting the naval armaments race. At the Washington Naval Conference of 1921, the United States, Great Britain, and Japan agreed to a ten-year "naval holiday." During this time they would build no new warships.

In 1930, as this period was drawing to a close, these same nations, plus France and Italy, met in London to renegotiate. Now Great Britain and France went further, urging the abolition of battleships and submarines. The Americans objected, arguing instead for parity (that is, equality). This would allow the United States to build *more* warships, since it had had fewer than the British to begin with.

Earlier, President Herbert Hoover had pledged to reduce American naval strength. What was happening now? To many, it seemed that the United States was opposing real disarmament. One critical group was the Women's International League for Peace and Freedom. It sent the President a strongly worded letter of complaint. The next day Dorothy Detzer, executive director of the league (referred to here as the W.I.L.), was asked to visit the President.

READING FOCUS

1. What was the position of the Women's International League in regard to disarmament?
2. Why was Hoover hesitant to ask for total naval disarmament?

The President spoke about the contents of the letter. He said he knew that the public was

---

Adapted from Appointment on the Hill *by Dorothy Detzer.*

disturbed by "rumors" from London that the naval conference was deadlocked, and that the U.S. delegation was in great part responsible for this situation. He recognized, too, the sincerity of the W.I.L. in pressing for more affirmative action. But he felt sure, he said, that we would not be so vocal and persistent if we knew all the facts.

In our letter, he reminded me, we had pointed out that private citizens were not always in a position to know the facts. He knew our interest, respected our energy. Therefore, he had decided to take me into his confidence. If I understood the real situation, he hoped the situation itself would persuade me to divert the present flood of W.I.L. criticism into equally vigorous public support for the government's undertaking at London.

At this point, Mr. Hoover took from his pocket a key and unlocked a deep drawer in the desk. From the drawer, he drew out a bulky package of dispatches. "These," he said, placing

Dorothy Detzer

the package on his desk, "are the decoded cables sent to me by the U.S. delegation in London. I want you to read them. For I am sure when you have done so, you will agree with me that your letter was based on a misunderstanding.

I picked up the first cable and began to read. The President picked up a pencil and began to "doodle." It took me almost an hour to read through the thick pile of confidential dispatches. In that hour, there unfolded before me the whole inside story of that naval conference.

When I laid down the last decoded cable, dated only that day, the President looked up from the paper he was covering with elaborate patterns of intricate circular designs.

"Well," said the President gently as he smiled across the desk at me, "don't you agree now that your letter was based on a misunderstanding?"

I hesitated. I liked this shy, gray President. There was something strangely appealing about his very shyness. He did not seem like the controversial storm center of editorials and cartoons, or even the formal official who received White House delegations. He was just a man in a blue serge suit with very kind, tired eyes. My immediate instinct was a protective one. Who was I to add even a fraction to the heavy burden he carried? Yet I knew integrity demanded my first loyalty.

"No, Mr. President," I said after the momentary pause. "To me, those dispatches only confirm the rightness of our letter."

"What do you mean?" he asked, swinging his chair about in a motion of impatience. "Can't you see all the complications—all the difficulties?"

"Yes, I think I do," I answered. "They are even worse than I had imagined."

"Then why do you say those dispatches confirm the rightness of your letter?"

"Because," I answered, "these dispatches have convinced me that the U.S. delegation is allowing the difficulties to block the achievement of your announced policies."

Mr. Hoover made another gesture of impatience.

"Why do you say that?" he asked.

"Mr. President, I didn't have to read these dispatches to know that the U.S. delegation in London is concentrating all its effort on the principle of parity, and not on reduction," I answered. "That certainly is no secret; the press reports that fact every day. Yet you stated publicly, before the conference convened, that our country was prepared to reduce its naval strength in proportion to any other nation, and that it only remained for the other nations to say how low they would go—they couldn't go too low for us. But our delegation, instead of supporting the proposals now before the conference for the abolition of battleships and submarines, blocks those proposals by its demands for parity. And won't parity mean a new super battleship for us as well as an extension of our cruiser program? That, it seems to me, contradicts your pledge that the United States would go as low as any other nation. Therefore, if the conference fails, why won't the fault lie with the United States, Mr. President?"

"But since reading those dispatches," said the President, "you certainly must see that there are other factors which must be considered in this situation also; and because of those factors, you should realize that if the conference fails the responsibility will not rest on the United States."

"Mr. President," I said, "I'm sorry, but I can't understand what you mean. The factors you refer to certainly complicate the problems. I can't, of course, know all that is involved by just reading those dispatches. But in spite of such limited knowledge, what I *do* know convinces me that the United States will be responsible for the outcome of the conference. And as we suggested in our letter, it would seem that that responsibility is yours, Mr. President."

Mr. Hoover looked as though I had struck him. He swung his chair around in a half circle so that his back was partly toward me. He gazed silently out of the window across Executive Avenue. Opposite, the White House grounds lay lovely and serene in the gathering spring twilight. Inside the room, there was only a prolonged silence, and the pallid dusk of early evening. What should I do? Should I leave? But one didn't just leave a President; one had to be dismissed. I must wait; his was the next move. Yet after what seemed to be an endless time, I half rose in my chair.

"Mr. President," I asked quietly, "do you want me to leave?"

The President turned slowly in his chair. "No, sit down," he said wearily. "I want to ask you a question." There was a long pause. Then looking up he said, "What would you do now if you were the President of the United States?"

This time, I felt as if the President had struck me.

"Mr. President," I said, trying to make my tone as light as possible, "I don't suppose a President of the United States will ever ask me that question again. And perhaps you will think that only arrogance or ignorance would lead me to answer it. I hope it is neither; for I want to answer it.

"Go on," he said. "I want to hear what you would do."

"Mr. President," I began, "you don't know it, but in one sense we have shared a tremendous experience. Only you were the chief of the American Relief Administration in Europe [after World War I], and I was only an ordinary relief worker with the Friends' Mission. But however different our status in that work, we both know what war means to all the little people. If I were President of the United States, I would never forget for one moment all those little people. Remembering them, I would discard all ideas of 'parity' and 'limitation' and 'reduction,' and I would offer at London a program so daring and inspiring that the world would rise up and call me blessed. You can do that; you have the power. You would be opposed and attacked, of course, by the vested interests in war, but those are the ones who are never shot at or starved." I paused. "Why can't you do that?"

"I can't," said the President, swinging his chair around toward the window again. "I can't. Besides, you forget this is not a disarmament conference. This is a conference on limitation."

"I haven't forgotten that, Mr. President," I said. "But certainly you can 'limit' things down to nothing. And what other nation has such an opportunity as the United States now? We have two big oceans on either side of us, friendly neighbors to the north and south. Who threatens us? We are powerful, and rich, and safe. We could go farther than any other nation. If you would offer a program of real naval disarmament, supplemented perhaps with a positive economic program, think what that would mean for peace. Why can't you do something like that before it is too late?"

"I can't," he said. "I can't."

"Well, if you can't do all of that," I pursued, "why can't you accept the proposals for the abolition of battleships and submarines? If the other nations are making those proposals just as a bluff, why don't you call their bluff? But if they are honest, what a good start that would be. If the United States doesn't respond now, it may be forever too late."

The President was silent for a long moment; then he raised his hands in a gesture of futility, and dropped them on the desk. "I can't," he fairly whispered. "I can't."

I looked at the weary profile silhouetted against the window. In it was sadness, and worry, and frustration. "He's trapped," I said to myself, "trapped. He holds the most powerful position in the most powerful nation in the world, and yet for some reason the President of the United States is not a free agent."

I looked at my watch; it was six o'clock. I had been there two hours. I rose to my feet. "It is six o'clock, Mr. President. Don't you want me to go?" Mr. Hoover's eyes never moved from the window. It was a moment before he jerked slightly, as though aware that someone had just spoken.

"What did you say?" he asked.

"Perhaps you would like me to go," I said.

"Oh, yes—yes," he answered. "Yes, of course."

"Thank you very much for letting me talk to you," I said, feeling a little at a loss to know how to end such an interview.

I got my coat off the rack and went out into the lovely April evening. I would go to the office now and type a memorandum while the events of the last two hours were still fresh in my mind. Tomorrow I would take it to the bank and place it in my safety deposit box. This was a memorandum which could not be dictated to a secretary nor put in the office files. For I was burdened with a secret: the naval conference would fail.

READING REVIEW

1. What did the League want the American delegation to do?
2. How did Hoover respond to the Women's International League's proposal?
3. (a) Why did Hoover take Detzer into his confidence? (b) Did Detzer change her opinion after her meeting with the President? Why or why not?
4. How did Detzer explain Hoover's reluctance to "offer a program of real naval disarmament"?

CHAPTER 35 From Isolationism to War

(1932–1941)

215 A "Bug's-Eye" View of Europe

Don Marquis, a newspaper writer, became famous as the creator of an imaginary insect named Archy. Archy, a cockroach, was a shrewd observer of people and events, and he did not hesitate to express his opinions on any subject. He had very strong viewpoints, especially about American society.

Each night, Archy used Marquis' office typewriter to write down his ideas about what was happening in the world. Archy supposedly operated the typewriter keys by jumping on them head first. Because he was unable to move the shift key on the typewriter, he was not able to use capital letters or punctuation. In this selection, you will read Archy's view of "post war europe."

if the league of nations
can survive the mutual animosities
of the powers which belong to it
it is safe from the activities
of the countries which stayed outside of it
it furnishes a wonderful mechanism
with which to do what the powers
want to do if they only knew
what they wanted to do
incidentally i wonder why europe of today
is always referred to by highbrow writers
as post war europe
they seem to think that the war
which started in nineteen fourteen
is over with whereas there have been
merely a few brief truces
that war is merely worrying through
its first half century
and will only cease permanently
when a generation comes along
which has forgotten all the old feuds

archy the cockroach

"the league" from the lives and times of archy and mehitabel *by don marquis.*

READING FOCUS

1. Why did Archy the cockroach favor the League of Nations?
2. Did the author believe the war was really over?

READING REVIEW

1. To what "mutual animosities," or hatreds, was Archy referring?
2. (a) According to Archy, when would wars cease permanently? (b) Do you agree with him? Why or why not?
3. (a) Why did the author use a make-believe character to express his opinions about "post war europe"? (b) Do you think that using a make-believe character was effective? Explain.

Don't bring the League home!

216 The Menace of Hitler

Many Americans were deeply concerned about events in Europe in the late 1930's. They were disturbed by the rise of dictators in some European nations and the aggressive ambitions of these dictators. With each new act of aggression by Germany, Italy, and Japan, some Americans feared that war was certain.

One person who was especially concerned about these events was Dorothy Thompson, a famous journalist whose newspaper and magazine writings were well known to Americans. During these years, it was said that she was "the equivalent of a troop of tanks in the prewar skirmishing with Adolf Hitler." The following selection was written on February 18, 1938, shortly after Austrian chancellor Kurt von Schuschnigg had met with Hitler and agreed to admit Nazi members into the Austrian cabinet. Still not satisfied with this agreement, Hitler sent an army into Austria a few weeks later. Austria then came under the total control of Germany.

READING FOCUS

1. Why did Hitler want Austria?
2. What did Dorothy Thompson see for the future of Europe?

Write it down. On Saturday, February 12, 1938, Germany won the world war, and dictated, at Hitler's mountain retreat, a peace treaty to make the Treaty of Versailles look like one of the great humane documents of the ages.

Write it down. On Saturday, February 12, 1938, Nazism started on the march across all of Europe east·of the Rhine.

Write it down that the world revolution began in earnest—and perhaps the world war.

From Let the Record Speak *by Dorothy Thompson.*

Write it down that the democratic world broke its promises and gave in, not in the face of strength, but of terrible weakness, armed only with ruthlessness and daring.

What happened?

On February 4, Hitler ousted his chief of staff and fourteen other generals. Why? Because the army leadership refused to move against an unarmed, friendly country—their German-speaking neighbor, Austria. Why did they refuse? Because of squeamishness? Hardly. Because they thought that Britain and France would interfere? Perhaps. Or because they themselves feared the ultimate catastrophe the future would bring as a result of this move? I think this is the best guess.

A week later, Hitler, with his reorganized army, made his move. How did he make it? He called in the chancellor of Austria, Doctor von Schuschnigg, and gave him an ultimatum. Sixty-six million people against six million people. German troops were ready at Austria's borders. Hitler's generals stood behind him as he interviewed the Austrian chancellor. Hitler taunted his victim. "You know as well as I know that France and Britain will not move a hand to save you." Hitler will doubtless hail this meeting as a friendly reconciliation between two German-speaking peoples and the strengthening of peace in eastern Europe.

What does the chancellor of Austria really think about Nazism?

He expressed himself hardly more than a month ago, on January 5, in the *Morning Telegraph* of London.

War rumblings from Europe

345

This is what he said:

"There is no question of ever accepting Nazi representatives in the Austrian cabinet. An enormous distance separates Austria from Nazism. We do not like arbitrary power, we want law to rule our freedom. We hate terror. Austria has always been a humanitarian state. As a people, we are tolerant by nature. Any change now in our *status quo* could only be for the worse."

Why does Germany want Austria? For raw materials? It has none of any importance. To add to German prosperity? Austria is a poor country with serious problems. But strategically it is the key to the whole of central Europe. Czechoslovakia is now surrounded. The wheat fields of Hungary and the oil fields of Rumania are now open. Not one of them will be able to withstand the pressure of German domination.

It is horror walking. Not that "Germany" joins with Austria. We are not talking of "Germany." We see a new Crusade, under a pagan symbol, worshiping "blood" and "soil," preaching the holiness of the sword and glorifying conquest. It hates the Slavs, whom it thinks to be its historic "mission" to rule. It subjects all of life to a militarized state. It persecutes men and women of Jewish blood. Now it moves into the historic stronghold of Catholic Christianity, into an area of mixed races and mixed nationalities, which for a thousand years the Austro-Hungarian Empire could rule only with tolerance. Adolf Hitler's first hatred was not communism, but Austria-Hungary. Read *Mein Kampf* [Hitler's book]. And he hated it for what? For its tolerance? He wanted 80 million Germans to rule with an iron hand an empire of 80 million "inferiors"—Czechs, Slovaks, Magyars, Jews, Serbs, Poles, and Croats.

Today, all of Europe east of the Rhine is cut off completely from the western world. The swastika banner, we are told, is the crusader's flag against Bolshevism [Communism]! Madness! Only the signs on the flags divide them [Germany and the Soviet Union].

And it never needed to have happened. One strong voice of one strong power could have stopped it.

Tomorrow, one of two things can happen. Despotism can stop where it is, through the lack of real leadership and creative brains. For the law of despotisms is that they kill off the good, and the brave, and the wise. Perhaps all of Europe east of the Rhine will become, eventually, a no-man's land of poverty, militarism, and despair. But nonetheless a plague spot.

More likely the other law of despotism's nature—the law of constant aggressiveness—will cause it to move farther and onward, made bolder and stronger by each success.

To the point where civilization will take a last stand. For take a stand it will. Of that there is not the slightest doubt.

Too bad that it did not take it this week.

READING REVIEW

1. Why, as Dorothy Thompson saw it, did Germany want Austria?
2. (a) According to Thompson, who or what could have stopped Hitler? (b) Do you agree or disagree with the author? Explain your answer.
3. (a) What two alternatives did Thompson predict for the future? (b) Was her prediction correct?

217 London During the Blitz

After Hitler's invasion of Poland in September 1939, Great Britain and France went to war against Germany. By June 1940 Hitler's blitzkrieg warfare had been so successful that only Great Britain was left to fight Nazi Germany. Then Hitler decided to try to bomb Great Britain into surrender.

All during these long months of war, foreign correspondents, or reporters stationed abroad, kept the American people informed about the war. One of these correspondents was Edward R. Murrow. He was in England during the Battle of Britain, and his radio reports of the nightly Nazi air raids made him famous. Night after night he told Americans of the courage of the British people, the daring of the Royal Air Force pilots, and the horrors they faced. The following are selections from Murrow's broadcasts during the Battle of Britain.

READING FOCUS

1. How did the nightly air raids affect the British?
2. What difficulties did Murrow encounter in trying to report the war?

September 10, 1940
This is London. And the raid which started about seven hours ago is still in progress. Larry LeSueur [a fellow correspondent] and I

have spent the last three hours driving about the streets of London and visiting air-raid shelters. We found that like everything else in this world the kind of protection you get from the bombs on London tonight depends on how much money you have. On the other hand, the most expensive dwelling places here do not necessarily provide the best shelters, but certainly they are the most comfortable.

We looked in on a renowned hotel tonight and found many old dowagers [women] and retired colonels settling back on the overstuffed settees [couches] in the lobby. It wasn't the sort of protection I'd seek from a direct hit from a half-ton bomb, but if you were a retired colonel and his lady, you might feel that the risk was worth it because you would at least be bombed with the right sort of people.

Only a couple of blocks away we pushed aside the canvas curtain of a trench cut out of a lawn of a London park. Inside were half a hundred people, some of them stretched out on the hard wooden benches. The rest huddled over in their overcoats and blankets. Dimmed electric lights glowed on the whitewashed walls, and the cannonade of anti-aircraft and reverberation of the big stuff the Germans were dropping rattled the boards underfoot at intervals. One woman was saying sleepily that it was funny how often you read about people being killed inside a shelter. Nobody seemed to listen. Then over to the famous cellar of a world-famous hotel, two floors underground. On upholstered chairs and lounges there was a cosmopolitan crowd. But there wasn't any sparkling conversation. They sat, some of them with their mouths open. One of them snored. King Zog [the former king of Albania] was over in a far corner on a chair, the porter told me.

The number of planes tonight seems to be about the same as last night. Searchlight activity has been constant, but there has been little gunfire in the center of London. The bombs have been coming down at about the same rate as last night. It is impossible to get any estimate of the damage. Darkness prevents observation of details. The streets have been deserted, save for a few clanging fire engines during the last four or five hours. The planes have been high again tonight, so high that the searchlights can't reach them.

Adapted from In Search of Light *by Edward R. Murrow.*

Once tonight an anti-aircraft battery opened fire just as I drove past. It lifted me from the seat and a hot wind swept over the car. It was impossible to see. When I drove on, the streets of London reminded me of a ghost town in Nevada—not a soul to be seen. A week ago there would have been people standing on the corner shouting for taxis. Tonight there were no people and no taxis. Earlier today there were trucks delivering mattresses to many office buildings. People are now sleeping on those mattresses, or at least they are trying to sleep.

And so London is waiting for dawn. We ought to get the all clear in about another two hours. Then those big German bombers that have been lumbering and mumbling overhead all night will have to go home.

September 13, 1940
This is London at 3:30 in the morning. This has been what might be called a "routine night"—air-raid alarm at about nine o'clock and intermittent bombing ever since. I had the impression that more high explosives and fewer incendiaries [fire bombs] have been used tonight. Only two small fires can be seen. Again the Germans have been sending their bombers in singly or in pairs. The anti-aircraft barrage has been fierce but sometimes there have been periods of twenty minutes when London has been silent. Then the big red buses would start up and move on till the guns started working again. That silence is almost hard to bear. One becomes accustomed to rattling windows and the distant sound of bombs, and then there comes a silence that can be felt. You know the sound will return. You wait, and then it starts again. That waiting is bad. It gives you a chance to imagine things.

The scale of this air war is so great that reporting it is not easy. Often we spend hours traveling about this sprawling city, viewing damage, talking with people and occasionally listening to the bombs come down, and then more hours wondering what you'd like to hear about. We've told you about the bombs, the fires, the smashed houses and the courage of the people. We've read you the communiques and tried to give you an honest estimate of the wounds inflicted upon this, the best bombing target in the world. But the business of living

Nightly bombings devastate London.

and working in this city is very personal—the little incidents, the things the mind retains, are in themselves unimportant, but they somehow weld together to form the hard core of memories that will remain when the last all clear has sounded. That's why I want to talk for just three or four minutes about the things we haven't talked about before; for many of these impressions it is necessary to reach back through only one long week. There was a rainbow bending over the battered and smoking East End of London just when the all clear sounded one afternoon. One night I stood in front of a smashed grocery store and heard a dripping inside. It was the only sound in all London. Two cans of peaches had been drilled clean through by flying glass, and the juice was dripping down onto the floor.

Today I went to buy a hat—my favorite shop had gone, blown to bits. The windows of my shoe store were blown out. I decided to have a haircut; the windows of the barbershop were gone, but the Italian barber was still doing business. Someday, he said, we smile again, but the food doesn't taste so good since being bombed. I went to another shop to buy flashlight batteries. I bought three. The clerk said, "You needn't buy so many. We'll have enough for the whole winter." But I said, "What if you aren't here?" There were buildings down in that street, and he replied, "Of course we'll be here. We've been in business here for a hundred and fifty years."

September 18, 1940

There are no words to describe the thing that is happening. Today I talked with eight American correspondents in London. Six of them had been forced to move. All had stories of bombs, and all agreed that they were unable to convey through print or the spoken word an accurate impression of what's happening in London these days and nights.

I may tell you that Bond Street has been bombed, that a shop selling handkershiefs at $40 the dozen has been wrecked, that these words [of the broadcast] were written on a table of good English oak which sheltered me three times as bombs tore down in the vicinity. But you can have little understanding of the life in London these days—the courage of the people, the flash and roar of guns rolling down streets where much of the history of the English-speaking world has been made, the stench of air-raid shelters in the poor districts. These things must be experienced to be understood.

September 22, 1940

I'm standing again tonight on a rooftop looking out over London, feeling rather large and lonesome. In the course of the last fifteen or twenty minutes there's been considerable action up there, but at the moment there's an ominous silence hanging over London. But at the same time a silence that has a great deal of dignity. Just straightaway in front of me the searchlights are working. I can seen one or two bursts of anti-aircraft fire far in the distance. Just on the roof across the way I can see a man wearing a tin hat, a pair of powerful night glasses to his eyes, scanning the sky. Again, looking in the opposite direction, there is a building with two windows gone. Out of one window there waves something that looks like a white bed sheet, a window curtain swinging free in this night breeze. It looks as though it were being shaken by a ghost. There are a great many ghosts around these buildings in London. The searchlights, miles in front of me, are still scratching that sky. There's a three-quarter moon riding high.

Down below in the streets I can see just that red and green wink of the traffic lights, one lone taxicab moving slowly down the street. Not a sound to be heard. As I look out across the miles and miles of rooftops and chimney pots, some of those dirty-gray buildings look almost snow-white in this moonlight here tonight. And the rooftop spotter across the way swings around, looks over in the direction of the searchlights, drops his glasses and just stands there. There are hundreds and hundreds of men like that standing on rooftops in London tonight watching for fire bombs, waiting to see what comes out of this steel-blue sky. The searchlights now reach up very, very faintly on three sides of me. There is a flash of a gun in the distance but too far away to be heard.

READING REVIEW

1. How did Murrow describe the air raids?
2. According to Murrow, what was a "routine night"?
3. Why was Murrow's reporting job so difficult?
4. What opinions do you think Americans formed from these broadcasts?

218 America, "The Arsenal of Democracy"

When World War II broke out in Europe in 1939, the United States faced the problem of what role, if any, it would take in the conflict. During the following year, as Hitler's armies defeated one country after another, the debate over what course of action America should take became increasingly heated.

At first, most Americans wanted to remain out of the war. But by 1940, with Great Britain the only nation left in the struggle against Nazi Germany, many Americans became deeply concerned.

Some Americans began to question whether neutrality was a wise policy for the nation. Then, near the end of 1940, President Roosevelt dramatically declared that he favored aiding Great Britain with weapons and military supplies. In a historic "fireside chat," broadcast to the American people over radio on December 29, 1940, President Roosevelt argued that the United States could not remain neutral.

READING FOCUS

1. Why did Roosevelt say the United States could not remain neutral?
2. What actions did Roosevelt urge the United States to take?

This is not a fireside chat on war. It is a talk on national security. The whole purpose of your President is to keep you now, and your children later, and your grandchildren much later, out of a last-ditch war for the preservation of American independence and all of the things that American independence means.

Never before since Jamestown and Plymouth has our American civilization been in such danger as now.

For, on September 27, 1940—by an agreement signed in Berlin—Germany, Italy, and Japan [the Axis powers] joined together. They threatened that if the United States interfered with their expansion program—a program aimed at world control—they would unite against us.

The United States has no right or reason to encourage talk of peace until there is a clear intention on the part of the aggressor nations to give up all thought of dominating or conquering the world.

Some of our people like to believe that wars in Europe and in Asia are of no concern to us. But it is a matter of most vital concern to us that European and Asiatic war makers should not gain control of the oceans which lead to this hemisphere.

Does anyone seriously believe that we need to fear attack while a free Britain remains our most powerful naval neighbor in the Atlantic? Does anyone seriously believe, on the other hand, that we could rest easy if the Axis powers were our neighbors there?

Adapted from "Fireside Chat," December 29, 1940, by Franklin D. Roosevelt, from the National Archives and Record Service, Franklin D. Roosevelt Library.

President Franklin D. Roosevelt

If Great Britain goes down, the Axis powers will control the continents of Europe, Asia, Africa, and Australia, and the oceans as well. They will be able to throw enormous military and naval resources against this hemisphere. It is no exaggeration to say that all of us in the Americas would be living at the point of a gun—a gun loaded with explosive bullets, economic as well as military.

We would enter upon a new and terrible period in which the whole world, our hemisphere included, would be run by threats of brute force. To survive in such a world, we would have to convert ourselves permanently into a militaristic power with a war economy.

Some of us like to believe that even if Great Britain falls, we are still safe because of the Atlantic and the Pacific oceans. But the width of these oceans is not what it was in the days of clipper ships. At one point between Africa and Brazil, the distance is less than from Washington to Denver, Colorado—five hours for the latest type of bomber. And at the north of the Pacific Ocean, America and Asia almost touch each other.

Frankly and definitely there is danger ahead—danger against which we must prepare. But we well know that we cannot escape danger, or the fear of it, by crawling into bed and pulling the covers over our heads.

There are those who say that the Axis powers would never have any desire to attack the Western Hemisphere. This is the same dangerous form of wishful thinking which has destroyed the powers of resistance of so many conquered peoples. The plain facts are that the Nazis have said, time and again, that all other races are their inferiors and therefore subject to their orders. And most important of all, the vast resources and wealth of this hemisphere make up the most tempting loot in all the world.

The experience of the past two years has proven beyond doubt that no nation can appease [make concessions to] the Nazis. No one can tame a tiger into a kitten by stroking it. There can be no appeasement with ruthlessness. There can be no reasoning with a bomb. We know now that a nation can have peace with the Nazis only at the price of total surrender.

The American appeasers ignore the warning to be found in the fate of Austria, Czechoslovakia, Poland, Norway, Belgium, the Netherlands, Denmark, and France. They tell you that the Axis powers are going to win anyway. They argue that the United States might just as well use its influence to achieve a dictated peace and get the best out of it that we can.

They call it a "negotiated peace." Nonsense! Is it a negotiated peace if a gang of outlaws surrounds your community and, on threat of death, makes you pay tribute to save your own lives?

The British people are conducting an active war against an unholy alliance. Our own future security is greatly dependent on the outcome of that fight. Our ability to keep out of war is going to be affected by that outcome.

I make this direct statement to the American people. There is far less chance of the United States getting into war if we do all we can now to support the nations defending themselves against attack by the Axis than if we go along with their defeat, then wait our turn to be attacked.

If we are to be completely honest with ourselves, we must admit there is risk in any course we may take. But I believe that most of our people agree that the course I suggest involves the least risk now and the greatest hope for world peace in the future.

The people of Europe who are defending themselves do not ask us to do their fighting. They ask us for the implements of war—the planes, the tanks, the guns, the freighters which will enable them to fight for their liberty and our security. We must get these weapons to them in sufficient volume and quickly enough so that we and our children will be saved the agony and suffering of war which others have had to endure.

There is no demand for sending American military force outside our own borders. There is no intention by any member of your government to send such a force.

Our national policy is not directed toward war. Its only purpose is to keep war away from our country and our people.

Democracy's fight against world conquest is being greatly aided, and must be aided still more, by the rearmament of the United States and by sending every ounce of munitions and supplies that we can possibly spare to help the defenders who are in the front lines. It is no more unneutral for us to do that than it is for Sweden, Russia, and other nations to send steel and ore and oil into Germany every day.

This is not a matter of feelings or of controversial personal opinion. It is a matter of realistic military policy, based on the advice of our military experts. These experts and the members of Congress and the Administration have one single purpose—the defense of the United States.

I want to make it clear that it is the purpose of the nation to build now with all possible speed every machine and factory that we need to manufacture our defense material. We have the people—the skill—the wealth—and above all, the will.

We must be the great arsenal of democracy. For us this is an emergency as serious as war itself. We must apply ourselves to our task with the same determination, the same sense of urgency, the same spirit of patriotism and sacrifice as we would show if we were at war.

READING REVIEW

1. According to Roosevelt, in what danger was the United States?
2. What reasons did Roosevelt give for supporting his position that the United States could not remain neutral?
3. What would happen if Great Britain was defeated?
4. (a) What two actions did Roosevelt suggest the United States take? (b) Do you agree with his suggestions? Why or why not?

219 A Famous Flyer on Neutrality

In March 1941 Congress passed the Lend-Lease Act, which permitted the United States to send unlimited weapons and military equipment to Great Britain. But even after passage of the law, Americans continued to debate the nation's role in the European war. On one side were the interventionists, who wanted the United States to enter the war on the side of the Allies. On the other side were the isolationists, who thought Americans should keep completely out of Europe's affairs.

One of the best-known isolationists was the famous American flyer Charles A. Lindbergh. He became a leading member of America First, a nationwide organization that favored arming for defense but argued that the United States could not save the Allies. Lindbergh made the following speech at an America First meeting in New York City on April 23, 1941.

READING FOCUS

1. Why did Lindbergh urge neutrality?
2. How did Lindbergh justify his position?

I know I will be severely criticized by the interventionists in America when I say we should not enter a war unless we have a reasonable chance of winning. That, they will claim, is far too materialistic a view. But I do not believe that our American ideals and our way of life will gain through an unsuccessful war. And I know that the United States is not

Adapted from "We Cannot Win This War for England" by Charles A. Lindbergh, in Vital Speeches of the Day, *1941.*

Charles A. Lindbergh

prepared to wage war in Europe successfully at this time.

I have said it before, and I will say again, that I believe it will be a tragedy for the entire world if the British empire collapses. That is one of the main reasons why I opposed this war before it was declared, and why I have constantly favored a negotiated peace. I did not feel that England and France had a reasonable chance of winning. France has now been defeated. Despite the propaganda and confusion of recent months, it is now obvious that England is losing the war. I believe this is realized even by the British government. But they have one last desperate plan remaining. They hope that they may be able to persuade us to send troops to Europe and to share with England militarily, as well as financially, the fiasco of this war.

I do not blame England for this hope, or for asking for our assistance. But we now know that it declared a war under circumstances which led to the defeat of every nation that sided with it, from Poland to Greece. We know that in the desperation of war England promised to all these nations armed assistance that it could not send. We know that it misinformed them as it has misinformed us about its military preparations, its military strength, and the progress of the war.

In time of war, truth it always replaced by propaganda. I do not believe we should be too quick to criticize the actions of a warring nation. But we do have a right to think of the welfare of America first, just as the people in England thought first of their own country when they encouraged the smaller nations of Europe to fight against hopeless odds. When England asks us to enter the war, it is considering its own future, and that of its empire. In making our reply, I believe we should consider the future of the United States and that of the Western Hemisphere.

It is not only our right, it is our duty as American citizens to look at this war objectively and to weigh our chances for success if we should enter it. I have attempted to do this, especially from the standpoint of air power. I have been forced to the conclusion that we cannot win this war for England, no matter how much aid we send.

I ask you to look at the map of Europe today and see if you can suggest any way in which we could win this war if we entered it. Suppose we had a large army in America, trained and equipped. Where would we send it to fight? The campaigns of the war show only too clearly how difficult it is to force a landing, or to maintain an army, on a hostile coast.

Suppose we took our navy from the Pacific, and used it to convoy [to provide naval protection to] British shipping. That would not win the war for England. It would, at best, permit it to exist under the constant bombing of the Germans. Suppose we had an air force that we could send to Europe? Where could it operate? Some of our squadrons might be based in the British Isles. But it is physically impossible to base enough aircraft in the British Isles alone to equal in strength the aircraft that can be based on the continent of Europe.

I have asked these questions on the assumption that we had an army and an air force large enough and well enough equipped to send to Europe, and that we would dare remove our navy from the Pacific. But the fact is that none of these assumptions is correct. Our army is still untrained and inadequately equipped for foreign war. Our air force lacks modern fighting planes because most of them have already been sent to Europe. We have only a one-ocean navy.

When these facts are stated, the interventionists shout that we are defeatists, that we are undermining the principles of democracy, and that we are giving comfort to Germany by talking about our military weakness. But everything I mention here has been published in our newspapers, and in the reports of congressional hearings in Washington. Our military position is well known to the governments of Europe and Asia. Why, then, should it not be brought to the attention of our own people?

I say it is the interventionists in America, as it was in England and in France, who give comfort to the enemy. I say it is they who are undermining the principles of democracy when they demand that we take a course to which more than 80 percent of our citizens are opposed. [According to public opinion polls, by December 1941 only 20 percent of the American people were in favor of declaring war on Germany.] I charge them with being the real defeatists, for their policy has led to the defeat of every country that followed their advice since this war began. There is no better way to give comfort to an enemy than to divide the people of a nation over the issue of foreign war. There is no shorter road to defeat than by entering a war with inadequate preparation. Every nation that has adopted the interventionist policy of depending on someone else for its own defense has met with defeat and failure.

There is a policy open to this nation that will lead to success—a policy that leaves us free to follow our own way of life and to develop our own civilization. It is not a new and untried idea. It was favored by Washington. It was incorporated in the Monroe Doctrine. Under its guidance the United States has become the greatest nation in the world.

It is based upon the belief that the security of a nation lies in the strength and character of its own people. It recommends the maintenance of armed forces sufficient to defend this hemisphere from attack by any foreign powers. It demands faith in an independent American destiny. It is a policy not of isolation, but of independence; not of defeat, but of courage. It is a policy that led this nation to success during the most difficult years of our history, and it is a policy that will lead us to success again.

We have weakened ourselves for many months by dabbling in Europe's wars. While we should have been concentrating on American defense, we have been forced to argue over foreign quarrels. We must turn our eyes and our faith back to our own country before it is too late. And when we do this, a different outlook opens before us. Practically every difficulty we would face in invading Europe becomes an asset to us in defending America. Our enemy, and not we, would then have the problem of transporting millions of troops across the ocean and landing them on a hostile shore. They, and not we, would have to provide the convoys to transport guns and trucks and munitions and fuel across 3,000 miles [4,800 kilometers] of water. Our battleships and submarines would then be fighting close to their home bases. We would then do the bombing from the air and the torpedoing at sea. And if any part of an enemy convoy should ever pass our navy and our air force, they would still be faced with the guns of our coast artillery and behind them the divisions of our army.

The United States is better situated from a military standpoint than any other nation in the world. Even in our present condition of unpreparedness, no foreign power is in a position to invade us today. If we concentrate on our own defenses and build the strength that this nation should maintain, no foreign army will ever attempt to land on American shores.

War is not inevitable for this country. Such a claim is defeatism in the true sense. No one can make us fight abroad unless we ourselves are willing to do so. No one will attempt to fight us here if we arm ourselves as a great nation should be armed. Over 100 million people in this nation are opposed to entering the war. If the principles of democracy mean anything at all, that is reason enough for us to stay out. If we are forced into a war against the wishes of an overwhelming majority of our people, we will have proved democracy such a failure at home that there will be little use fighting for it abroad.

READING REVIEW

1. Give three reasons why Lindbergh opposed America's entry into the war.
2. Why did Lindbergh think his position was wise?
3. (a) Compare Lindbergh's position regarding American neutrality to that of President Roosevelt's (Reading 218). (b) Which position do you agree with? Why?

220 An Editorial on the Danger of Neutrality

Charles Lindbergh, America's flyer-hero and a leader of the isolationist America First Committee, attracted nationwide attention with the speech he made on April 23, 1941, urging that the United States should stay out of the war in Europe. A week later, on April 30, *The New York Times,* one of the nation's most influential newspapers, published a strong editorial challenging Lindbergh's point of view. The *Times* editorial, which follows, argued forcefully that the United States had no choice but to aid England in its fight against Nazi Germany.

READING FOCUS

1. According to *The New York Times,* why was it dangerous to take a neutral position?
2. What would happen if England was defeated?

Those who tell us now that the sea is still our certain bulwark [defense], and that the tremendous forces sweeping the Old World threaten no danger to the New, give the lie to their own words in the precautions they would have us take.

They favor an enormous strengthening of our defenses. Why? Against what danger would they have us arm if none exists? To what purpose would they have us spend these almost incredible billions upon billions for ships and planes, for tanks and guns, if there is no immediate threat to the security of the United States? Why are we training the youth of the country to bear arms? Under pressure of what fear are we racing against time to double and quadruple our industrial production?

No man in his senses will say that we are arming against Canada or our Latin-American neighbors to the south, against Britain or the captive states of Europe. We are arming solely for one reason. We are arming against Hitler's Germany—a great predatory [warlike] power in alliance with Japan.

It has been said that if Hitler cannot cross the English Channel he cannot cross 3,000 miles [4,800 kilometers] of sea. But there is only one reason why he has not crossed the English Channel. That is because 45 million determined Britons, in a heroic resistance, have converted their island into an armed base, from which proceeds a steady stream of sea and air power. As Secretary [of State Cordell] Hull has said: "It is not the water that bars the way. It is the resolute determination of British arms. Were the control of the seas by Britain lost, the Atlantic would no longer be an obstacle—rather, it would become a broad highway for a conqueror moving westward."

That conqueror does not need to attempt at once an invasion of the continental United States in order to place this country in deadly danger. We shall be in deadly danger the moment British sea power fails; the moment we are compelled to divide our one-ocean Navy between two oceans simultaneously.

The combined Axis fleets outmatch our own: they are superior in numbers to our fleet

___

From "Editorial Challenging Lindbergh's Views on Entry into World War II" in The New York Times, *April 30, 1941.*

The New York Times *response to Charles Lindbergh's speech*

THE NEW YORK TIMES, WE

LET US FACE THE TRUTH

In New York Harbor, on an island close to the steamship lanes, stands the most famous statue in the world. It is not the most beautiful statue but to many millions of passengers coming up the bay it has seemed to be. It stands for one of the dearest dreams in human history—Liberty.

The millions who pursued that dream began to come before there was a statue to greet them. They came first when the shores were lined with solemn woods. They came in sailing ships when the voyage required two months or more. They came in crowded steamship steerage under hardships not much

five million determined Britons in a heroic resistance have converted their island into an armed base from which proceeds a steady stream of sea and air power. As Secretary Hull has said: "It is not the water that bars the way. It is the resolute determination of British arms. Were the control of the seas by Britain lost, the Atlantic would no longer be an obstacle—rather, it would become a broad highway for a conqueror moving westward."

That conqueror does not need to attempt at once an invasion of continental United States in order to place this country in deadly danger. We shall be in deadly danger the moment British sea power fails; the moment the eastern gates of the Atlantic are open to

moral and spiritual values which make life worth living. This def means many things. It means, i first instance, a clear recognition the most dangerous of all courses could follow in this hour of decisi a policy of drift: of do-nothing w there is still time to act effecti of letting hesitancy ripen into disa ment, and disagreement curdle factions which will split the count

It means strong leadership in W ington: a willingness to forego methods of indirection and surprise veiled hints and innuendo, and to the plain facts of the situation b It means leadership which is as erous as it is strong: leadership w is willing to forget old quarrels, r in every category of vessel, from warships and aircraft carriers to destroyers and submarines. The combined Axis air strength will be much greater than our own if Hitler strikes in time— and when has he failed to strike in time? The master of Europe will have at his command the resources of 20 conquered nations to furnish his materials, the oil of the Middle East to stoke [run] his engines, the slave labor of a continent to turn out his production.

Grant Hitler the gigantic prestige of a victory over Britain, and who can doubt that the first result, on our side of the ocean, would be the prompt appearance of imitation Nazi regimes in a half-dozen Latin-American nations, forced to be on the winning side, begging favors, clamoring for admission to the Axis? What shall we do then? Make war upon these neighbors, send armies to fight in the jungles of Central or South America; run the risk of outraging native sentiment and turning the whole continent against us? Or shall we sit tight while the area of Nazi influence draws ever closer to the Panama Canal, and a spreading checkerboard of Nazi airfields provides ports of call for German planes that may choose to bomb our cities?

But even if Hitler gave us time, what kind of "time" would we have at our disposal?

There are moral and spiritual dangers for this country as well as physical dangers in a Hitler victory. There are dangers to the mind and heart as well as to the body and the land.

Victorious in Europe, dominating Africa and Asia through his Axis partners, Hitler could not afford to permit the United States to live an untroubled and successful life, even if he wished to. We are the arch enemy of all he stands for: the very citadel [stronghold] of that democracy which he hates and scorns. As long as liberty and freedom prevailed in the United States, there would be constant risk for Hitler that our ideas and our example might infect the conquered countries which he was bending to his will. In his own interest he would be forced to harry [harass] us at every turn.

Who can doubt that our lives would be poisoned every day by challenges and insults from Nazi politicians; that Nazi agents would stir up anti-American feeling in every country they controlled; that Nazi spies would overrun us here; that Hitler would produce a continual series of lightning diplomatic strokes—alliances and "nonaggressions pacts" to break our will; in short, that a continuous war of nerves, if nothing worse, would be waged against us?

And who can doubt that, in response, we should have to turn our nation into an armed camp, with all our traditional values of culture, education, social reform, democracy, and liberty subordinated to the single, all-embracing aim of self-preservation? In this case we should indeed experience "regimentation." Every item of foreign trade, every transaction in domestic commerce, every present prerogative [right] of labor, every civil liberty we cherish, would necessarily be regulated in the interest of defense.

READING REVIEW

1. **(a)** What reasons did *The New York Times* give to explain why the United States must aid England against Germany? **(b)** Do you agree with these reasons? Why or why not?
2. What did the paper claim would happen if England was defeated?
3. Do you think the arguments in the editorial were effective or not? Why?

CHAPTER
36 Americans in World War II
(1941–1945)

221 An Army Nurse in The Philippines

After the Japanese attack on Pearl Harbor in December 1941, the United States entered World War II. The early months of the war were a disaster for the United States. The Japanese armed forces moved steadily through Southeast Asia, conquering nation after nation and invading island chains in the Pacific Ocean. American and Filipino troops under General Douglas MacArthur struggled to defend the Philippine Islands. But early in January 1942 Manila, capital of the Philippines, was forced to surrender. American forces then retreated to the Bataan Peninsula and the island of Corregidor. There they fought heroically, until Bataan was conquered on April 9 and Corregidor finally fell on May 6.

Thousands of American soldiers, including many sick and wounded, were trapped in the Philippines. In this selection, an army nurse at Bataan and Corregidor described the last weeks.

READING FOCUS

1. What were the conditions at the hospital?
2. How did the people react to the bombings?

Conditions at Hospital Number 1 were not too good during the last few weeks we spent there. Patients were flooding in. We increased from 400 to 1,500 cases in two weeks' time. Most of them had serious wounds, but nine out of ten patients had malaria or dysentery besides.

We were out of quinine [a drug used in treating malaria]. There were hundreds of gas gangrene cases, and our supply of vaccine had run out months before. There were no more sulfa drugs. There weren't nearly enough cots, so triple-decker beds were built from bamboo, with a ladder at one end so we could climb up to take care of the patients. They had no blankets or mattresses.

There was almost no food except carabao [water buffalo]. We had all thought we couldn't

Adapted from "An Army Nurse at Bataan and Corregidor," as told to Annalee Jacoby in History in the Writing *by Gordon Carroll.*

eat carabao, but we did. Then came mule, which seemed worse, but we ate that too. Most of the nurses were wearing government-issue heavy-laced men's shoes. [From the term "government issue" came the name for American soldiers in World War II—GI's.] We had to keep our feet taped up to walk in them. Our uniforms had been gone for a long time, so we mostly wore size 32 air corps coveralls. We carried steel helmets and gas masks even in the wards, but we didn't expect to use them.

We went about our work feeling perfectly safe because of the Red Cross markings on the roof. When bombers came overhead on April 4, we hardly noticed them. Then suddenly incendiary [fire] bombs dropped. They hit the receiving wards, mess hall, doctors' and officers' quarters, and the steps of the nurses' dormitory, setting fire to all the buildings but luckily not hitting the wards. Several people walking outside were killed. The patients were terrified, of course, but behaved well. The Japanese prisoners were perhaps the most frightened of all. Everything was a blur of taking care of patients, putting out fires, straightening overturned equipment.

We remained frightened until two hours later when someone heard the Japanese radio in Manila announce that the bombings had been an accident and wouldn't happen again. After that, we wouldn't even leave the hospital for a short drive. We felt safe there and nowhere else.

The morning of April 7 we were all on duty when a wave of bombers came over. The first

An army hospital in the Philippines

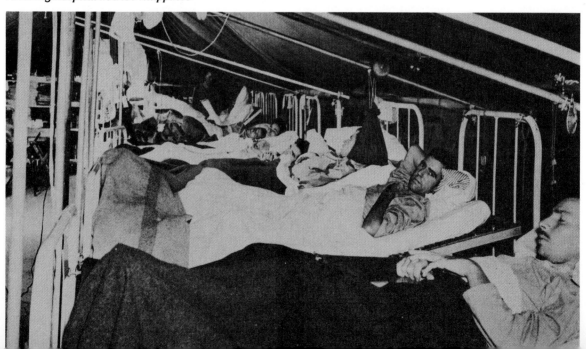

bomb hit near the Filipino mess hall and knocked us down before we even knew planes were overhead. An ammunition truck was passing the hospital entrance. It got a direct hit. The boys on guard at the gate were shell-hocked, smothered in the dirt thrown up by the explosion.

Hospital patients picked us up and we began caring for patients hurt by shrapnel [bomb fragments]. Everything was terror and confusion. Patients, even amputation cases, were falling and rolling out of the triple-decker beds. Suddenly a chaplain, Father Cummings, came into the ward, threw up his hands for silence and said: "All right boys, everything's all right. Just stay quietly in bed, or lie still on the floor. Let us pray." The screams stopped instantly. He began the prayer just as a second wave of planes came over.

The first bomb hit near the officers' quarters, the next struck the patients' mess hall just a few yards away. The shock waves bounced us three feet of the cement floor and threw us down again. Beds were tumbling down. Flashes of heat and smoke burned our eyes. But through it all we could hear Father Cummings' voice reciting the Lord's Prayer. He never stopped, never even fell to the ground, and the patients never moved. Father Cummings' clear voice went through to the end. Then he turned quietly and said: "All right, you take over. Put a tourniquet on my arm, will you?" And we saw for the first time that he'd been badly hit by shrapnel.

The next few hours were a nightmare, except for the way everyone behaved. We were afraid to move, but realized we had to get to work. One Filipino with both legs amputated— he'd never gotten out of bed before by himself—rolled onto the ground and said: "Miss, are you all right, are you all right?" The ward boys all told us, "You go on outside—don't stay here any longer. We'll take care of everything." We tried to care first for the patients most seriously hurt. A great many all over the hospital were bleeding badly. We went to where the bomb had hit the ward and began pulling patients from the crater. I saw Rosemary Hogan, head ward nurse, and thought for a moment her face had been torn off. She wiped herself with a sheet, smiled and said: "It's nothing, don't bother about me. Just a nose bleed." But she had three shrapnel wounds.

It would be hard to believe the bravery after that bombing if you hadn't seen it. A soldier had risked his life by going directly to the traction wards where patients were tied to beds by wires. He thought it was better to hurt the men temporarily than to leave them tied helpless above ground where they'd surely be hit by shrapnel, so he cut all tractions and told the patients: "Get under the bed, Joe."

We began immediately to move patients to another hospital. We were so afraid the Japanese would be back again the next day that even the most serious cases were moved, because giving them any chance was better than none. There were only 100 patients left the next morning. We worked all that day making up beds to admit new patients. It never occurred to anyone that we wouldn't go on as usual. Suddenly, after dark, we were told we were leaving in 15 minutes—that we should pack only what we could carry. Then we heard that the Japanese had broken through and the Battle of Bataan was over. The doctors all decided to stay with the patients, even doctors who had been told to go to Corregidor.

We left the hospital at 9 that night—got to Corregidor at 3 in the morning. The trip usually took a little over an hour. As we drove down to the docks, the roads were jammed. Soldiers were tired, aimless, frightened. Cars were overturned. There were bodies in the road. Clouds of dust made it hard to breathe. At midnight on the docks we heard that the Japanese had burned our hospital to the ground.

Bombers were overhead, but we were too tired to care. We waited on the docks while the navy tunnel and ammunition dump at Marivales were blown up. Blasting explosions, blue flares, red flares, shrapnel, tracers, gasoline exploding—it was like a hundred Fourths of July all at once, but we were too frightened to be impressed. As we crossed the water with Corregidor's big guns firing over our heads and shells from somewhere landing close by, the boat suddenly shook and the whole ocean seemed to rock. We thought a big shell had hit the water in front of us. It wasn't until we landed that we learned that an earthquake had hit just as Bataan fell.

Corregidor seemed like heaven that night. They fed us and we slept, two to an army cot. We went to work the following morning. Months before, patients on Corregidor had filled a few side tunnels only. Now they were in doubledecker beds all along the halls and in the main tunnel. There was constant bombing and shelling—sometimes shock waves from a bomb outside would knock people down at the opposite end of the tunnel. Emperor Hirohito's birthday, April 29, was a specially bad day. The bombing began at 7:30 in the morning and never stopped. Shelling was heavy; soldiers counted over 100 explosions per minute. Dive bombers were going after the gun on the hill directly above our heads and the shock waves inside were terrific.

The worst night on Corregidor was when a bomb hit outside the tunnel entrance. A crowd had gone outside for a cigarette and many were sleeping on the ground at the foot of the cliff. When the first shell hit nearby, they all ran for the tunnel, but the iron gate was shut and it opened outward. As more shells landed, they smashed men against the gate and twisted off arms and legs. All the nurses got up and went back to work—the operating room was overflowing until 5:30 in the morning. There were many amputations.

At 6 o'clock one evening, after the usual bombing and shelling, 21 of us were told we were leaving Corregidor by plane. We don't know how we were selected. Everyone wanted to leave, of course, but morale was splendid. Everyone realized the end was getting close, but none gave up hope.

Now we're safe in Australia. But the only reaction we notice is wanting to make up somehow, anyhow, for those who didn't get away.

READING REVIEW

1. Describe the conditions at Hospital Number 1 on Bataan.
2. (a) What was the mood of the patients? (b) of those working in the hospital?

---

222 Women and War

Although there were great changes in America during World War II, for most Americans the wartime years did not bring the severe hardships and widespread destruction endured by the peoples of Europe. Americans experienced rationing and shortages of food and other supplies, but they did not have to face enemy bombs or advancing armies.

One of the greatest changes in the United States was the profound effect the war had on the lives of American women. With millions of men in the armed forces, women took over many of the jobs in the nation's factories, farms, and businesses. Many women also now had to take care of their homes and their families alone. In this selection, written shortly after World War II, anthropologist Margaret Mead told of some of these changes in women's lives.

READING FOCUS

1. How did the war change women's role?
2. Why did the American soldiers worry about the women on the home front?

In wartime, men and women get out of step and begin to wonder about each other. "What will he be like after all those years in the army?" "What will she be like after all those years alone at home?" "I do hope he won't have changed too much." "I hope she will look the same."

All this is natural enough. Boys and girls grow up together in the same world, seeing a lot of each other, each knowing what the other is thinking. Husbands are used to coming home at night and telling their wives what they think of the news in the paper, and having their wives tell them they are exactly right— or exactly wrong. Either way, they know what's going on. Dramatic news, quintuplets and quads, double murders and triple suicides, all fall into place in peacetime. They are events that spice the usual events of life, in which most babies are born one at a time and husbands and wives may sometimes feel like murdering each other but hardly ever do. But in wartime, boys and girls, men and women, separated in time and in space, aren't in step any more, and both begin to wonder what the other one will be like . . . after the war.

The man overseas reads his paper or his magazines filled with news that women are doing new and therefore, by definition, "unwomanly" jobs. (A womanly job is just a job that everybody is used to seeing women do.) He reads about the mannish clothes women are wearing, the welding outfits they are

---

Adapted from "Women and War" by Margaret Mead in While You Were Gone, *edited by Jack Goodman.*

wielding, and he worries. What's happening to women anyway? What will be the use of winning the war if when you go back home all the girls' heads are filled with a lot of strange and unwelcome nonsense?

The newspapers are full of wild stories: bobby soxers [a term for teenagers in the 1940's, since many of them wore heavy white socks called "bobby socks"] wandering about Times Square or storming a performance by Frank Sinatra; the riotous living of war workers. If the man overseas were at home, all this would make sense. He'd have a chance to see that being a woman worker means long hard hours doing unfamiliar work, cramped and difficult living conditions, hours of standing in line waiting for food. He'd know that for every straying bobby soxer there are a hundred youngsters who are working in factories or doing their absent brothers' work on the farm.

Besides the bobby soxers and the quadruplets in the newspapers, there has been continuous writing on the theme: "Will women be willing to return to the home?" This worrying question is often inspired by those in whose interest it will be to discharge women workers as soon as the war is over.

Statistics on how many women are working and plan to work appear in headlines which add, "Eight out of every ten women asked say they will work after the war." Most of those women who say they will go on working are the women who would have been working anyway. The number of American women who work has been rising from 2.5 million in 1880 to over 5 million in 1920 and to 11 million in 1940. In 1950—if you ask for official estimates—you'll find that about 16 million women will be working in the United States. That's the kind of society we have, one in which many men aren't paid enough to support their wives, one in which women without husbands are expected to support themselves, one in which very few brothers are willing to support their unmarried sisters. In back of the headlines and the statistics and the threatening questions in the newspapers there lies the simple fact that more women in the United States have to work each year. And that more women than ever before will be working at some time in their lives.

This needn't worry the returning men very deeply. It was part of the America they left, and it's part of the America they are coming back to. The war has speeded things up a little, that's all. After the war, just as it would have been if there had been no war, most girls will plan to work between school and marriage. Many will plan to work until the first baby. Some will go back to work when their children are grown. And an increasing number will work because they have no husbands and no other means of support.

However, some striking things have happened during the war which are due to the war. During the war, over 3 million women have gone to work who would *not* have worked if there had not been a war. A million girls between 14 and 18 who would ordinarily have been in school have been working part or full time. A million young married women, with and without children, have gone to work. Many of them are wives of men in the armed forces. The remainder of the 3 million women include many women who have worked before and have gone back to work. Some are mothers who cannot stand waiting for the mail to bring news of their sons. Some are mothers who already know that their sons will never return.

There are several ways of looking at these things which have been happening to women. Some people find it more interesting that women have done jobs which no one thought they could do—become welders and machine setters, railroad conductors, and taxi drivers. Most of these are strictly wartime shifts and will become men's jobs again after the war.

To some, the fact that we have women in the armed forces in this war is the most striking thing that has happened. There are only a little over a quarter of a million women in the services. They have joined up in the face of a great deal of disapproval from brothers and boy friends and fathers. They have been given, for the most part, dull and inglorious jobs to do.

What do these figures mean? What will it mean to men that women who wouldn't otherwise have worked now have worked? That their wives have been working while they were gone? That their mothers and their mothers-in-law have worked?

It means, for one thing, that women, as a group, are better informed than they were before. They understand what a time clock is and what a checkoff is. Farm women have learned a great deal more about the drudgery and techniques of farm life. Women in homes which

"THE GIRL HE LEFT BEHIND" IS STILL BEHIND HIM She's a WOW
WOMAN ORDNANCE WORKER

WOW — Women Ordnance Worker

used to employ servants will know a great deal more about housework. Women who have left housework for the factory will come back with some new ideas of what it means to work definite hours. Millions of women will understand more of what their husbands are talking about, when their husbands talk sense, and will have a sounder idea of when they are talking nonsense. A great many more women will understand more about money, how hard it is to make, as well as how hard or easy it is to spend. Here, perhaps, is one of the places where the experience of women in wartime America will be a useful supplement to the men's. While the men have had four or five years less of dealing with money, the women have had that much more.

The second important experience women have had, while the men were away, is moving about. Small-town girls have gone to cities, city girls to little country towns, factory and office girls to pick beets and milk cows. Northern girls have gone south, and eastern girls have gone west. Some of this moving-about experience will match the men's. Men have lived abroad, but mostly in camps. Women have not had such strange ways of life, but they have actually had to cope with things more—buy and prepare food and convert trailers into homes.

And most of all women have waited. Many of them—those who have worked and traveled—have waited by doing something. Others have just waited. In their minds has been the echo of his "I want to find you just the same." Many women have sensibly interpreted this to mean that he wants her to be as good a 1945 model as she was a 1940 model, as smart a 23-year-old as she was an 18-year-old.

But others, less realistic, have taken boy friends and husbands at their word and tried not to change at all. They have tried to keep their minds, if not their hats, just as they were when their men left. Many of these girls, instead of moving out into the wartime world, have gone home to Mother. They have slipped back into dependent, little-girl positions, stayed 18 years old or even slipped back a little. Getting to know a wife who has tried to stay the same is really going to be more difficult than getting acquainted with a wife who has driven a truck or worn a uniform.

When the returning man looks his wife or sweetheart in the eye, between them will stand his years of danger and hardship which she cannot share or even properly imagine, her flat, empty years which she could not value because he was away. In peacetime, men and women count upon living side by side, watching children grow and gardens flower and houses go up and bank accounts increase and chins get double or beards get stubbier and life flow more quietly—together. All of our patterns for the relations between men and women were based on this simple expectation. This generation will have to make new patterns.

Last of all, the man who left the country in 1941–42 will come back to a new generation of girls. These girls will be, inevitably, a new kind of girl, girls brought up on the war years, on a different sort of romance. They don't expect as much of boys as their older sisters did who grew up when dates were commoner. They will have practically no memory of the depression years. War has stood at the beginning of their young girlhood; war did not crash rudely into the middle of it, finding them unprepared. They will be standing on tiptoe waiting for the postwar world.

READING REVIEW

1. (a) According to Margaret Mead, what worries did American servicemen have about women on

the home front? **(b)** Do you think their worries were justified? Why or why not?

2. How did women working during wartime affect women's perception of their "traditional" role in American society?

3. **(a)** What did the author think women's roles would be in the future? **(b)** Was she correct? Explain.

---

223 Life in a Relocation Camp

After the Japanese attack on Pearl Harbor, many American government officials believed that Japanese Americans were a danger to the nation's security. As a result, about 112,000 Japanese Americans were placed in detention or relocation camps. Most of these Japanese Americans were not allowed to leave the relocation camps until January of 1945. Despite the federal government's internment program, over 17,000 Japanese Americans served in the American armed forces, many winning military awards for bravery.

Monica Sone, a Nisei, or Japanese American born in the United States, wrote the following account of life in a relocation camp. She was a college student in Seattle, Washington, when the war broke out and she and her family were sent to a relocation camp in Idaho.

Today, most Americans view the wartime treatment of Japanese Americans as unfair. But during World War II most Americans accepted it as necessary.

READING FOCUS

1. Why did the American government send the Japanese Americans to relocation camps?
2. How did Japanese Americans react when the United States government asked for volunteers?

Camp Minidoka was located in the south-central part of Idaho, north of the Snake River. It was a semidesert region. When we arrived I could see nothing but flat prairies, clumps of greasewood shrubs, and jack rabbits. And of course the hundreds and hundreds of barracks, to house 10,000 of us.

Adapted from Nisei Daughter *by Monica Sone. Copyright © 1953, 1981 by Monica Sone.*

Our home was one room in a large army-type barracks, measuring about 20 by 25 feet [6 by 7.5 meters]. The only furnishings were an iron pot-belly stove and cots.

On our first day in camp, we were given a rousing welcome by a dust storm. We felt as if we were standing in a gigantic sand-mixing machine as the gale lifted the loose earth up into the sky, hiding everything. Sand filled our mouths and nostrils and stung our faces and hands like a thousand darting needles.

Just as suddenly as the storm had broken out, it died away. We walked out of the mess hall under a pure blue sky, startling in its peacefulness. In the deepening blue shadows, people hurried here and there, preparing for their first night in camp. The Issei [Japanese Americans born in Japan] men stomped along in their wooden *getas* (high sandals). The Issei women in cool cotton print *yukatas* (Japanese house kimonos) slipped along noiselessly. They bowed to each other, murmuring "*Oyasumi nasai. Rest well.*" These familiar words in the alien darkness of the prairie were welcome sounds. I suddenly saw that these people were living through difficult circumstances with simple dignity and patience, and I felt ashamed of my own strong emotions. That night we let ourselves sink deep into the yawning silence of the prairie, which was shattered only by the barking of the coyotes.

Idaho summer sizzled on the average of 110 degrees [43 degrees Celsius]. For the first few weeks I lay on my cot from morning till night, not daring to do more than go to the mess hall three times a day.

When September came we slowly emerged from our stupor. The sun no longer stabbed the backs of our necks. Now when I awoke in the mornings, the air felt cool and crisp.

The momentum of the change carried me along into a job at the camp hospital as ward secretary. Henry [her brother] had already been working at the hospital for weeks. Sumi [her sister] and her young friends signed up as nurse's aides. Father finally settled on becoming a member of the internal security staff— a policeman, complete with an olive-drab uniform. Mother, who was not well, stayed home to mop the floor, wash the family laundry, iron and mend our clothes, and attend the English language class, choir practice, prayer meetings, and a Japanese doll-making class.

Japanese Americans in a relocation camp

By fall, Camp Minidoka has bloomed into a full-grown town. Children went to school in the barracks, taught by professional teachers among the evacuees and people hired from the outside. Except for the members of the administration staff, the evacuees themselves supplied the entire labor force in the camp. All church activities were in full session.

During our spare hours, we confiscated scrap lumber, piece by piece, from a lumber pile. Tables and chairs gradually made their appearance in our tiny apartment. Rows of shelves lined the bare walls. We bought gallons of shellac, and white paint, yards of white organdy for curtains, and blue damask for the cots and clothes closet. We had a living room, powder room, three bedrooms, a study, storage room, and a kitchen all in one. It had everything except the kitchen sink and privacy.

Winter in Minidoka was as intense an experience as summer had been. We gave a strong cheer for the government when we were told that they would provide winter clothing for those who needed them. Mother was the first to go after her clothing. When she came

home with the bundle, we all gathered around her excitedly to see what she had. She held up a pair of longjohns [men's underwear], olive-drab trousers, and a navy pea coat [jacket].

"They're good quality woolens," she said calmly, " and they'll certainly keep me warm. Only thing, it's too bad we aren't all males."

Sumi and I protested hysterically that we were all going to look like members of the internal security staff, since these clothes were exactly what Father and his friends wore on patrol duty. It was only after a man living in our block became lost one night in a snowstorm and died from exposure that we finally gave in. We ran to the clothing office. The man gave us what was left—size 40 longjohns, sleeveless, collarless vests which hung down to our knees, and wonderful thick, bear-sized pea coats. That taught us a lesson that a man, or at any rate, a woman, cannot live on pride alone.

We had lived in camps through four seasons, and each season had served as a challenge to us. In the meantime we had drifted farther and farther away from the American scene. We had been set apart, and we had become adjusted to our existence. The great struggle in which the world was engaged seemed far away.

Then one day a group of army personnel marched into our camp on a special mission. They made a startling announcement. "The United States War Department has decided to form a special combat unit for the Nisei. We have come to recruit volunteers."

We gasped and we tried to speak. Dunks Oshima, who had brought the news to us, eyed us fiercely as he cried, "What do they take us for? Saps? First, they change my army status to 4-C because of my ancestry, and run me out of town. Now they want me to volunteer for a suicide squad so I could get killed for democracy. That's going some for sheer nerve!"

That was exactly the way most of us felt, but the recruiting officers were well prepared to cope with our emotional explosion. They called meetings and we flocked to them with an injured look.

An officer spoke to us. "You're probably wondering why we are here, recruiting for volunteers from your group. I think that my explanation is best expressed in the statement recently issued by our President, regarding a citizen's right and privilege to serve the country. I want to read it to you:

"No loyal citizens of the United States should be denied the democratic right to exercise the responsibilities of their citizenship, regardless of their ancestry. The principle on which this country was founded and by which it has always been governed is that Americanism is a matter of the mind and the heart. Americanism is not, and never was, a matter of race or ancestry. All loyal American citizens should be given the opportunity to serve this country wherever their skills will make the greatest contribution, whether it be in our armed forces, war production, agriculture, government service, or other work essential to the war effort."

It all sounded very well. It was the sort of declaration which rang true and clear in our hearts. But there were questions in our minds which needed answering. The speaker threw the meeting open for discussion. We said we didn't want a separate Nisei combat unit because it looked too much like segregation. We wanted to serve in the same way as other citizens, in a mixed group with the other Americans.

The man answered: "But if the Nisei men were to be scattered throughout the army, you'd lose your significance as Nisei. Maybe you want it that way, because in the past you suffered with your Japanese faces. Well, why not accept your Japanese face? Why be ashamed of it? Why not take advantage of it for a change? There are powerful organizations now campaigning on the [West] Coast to deport you all to Japan, citizens and residents alike. But there're also men and women who believe in you, who feel you should be given the chance to stand up and express yourselves. They thought that a Nisei combat unit would be just the thing. Whatever you accomplish, whatever you achieve, will be yours and yours alone."

We saw that the speaker was sincere and believed earnestly in this cause. Then we asked him another burning question. "Why had the government ever put us here in the first place? Why? Why? Why?"

The man looked at our wounded faces and said: "I can't answer that question. I can only repeat what you already know, that the government thought evacuation was necessary. The evacuation took place, and right or wrong, it's past. Now we're interested in your future. The War Department is offering you a chance to volunteer and to distinguish yourselves as Japanese-American citizens in the service of your country. Believe me, this combat unit is not segregation in the sense you think it is."

The tension in the mess hall eased, and questions and answers came more naturally. After the meeting we returned to our barracks to continue the debate. Dunks came with us.

"What's a fellow to do?" Dunks said wryly. "They've got us over a barrel. If we don't do our bit, you can bet your boots there won't be much of a future for us here. Those on the Coast who want to deport us will see to that."

I put in, "I'll bet, though, that some of those characters will be totally against a Nisei combat team."

Henry snorted, "Those scrooges will be against anything which might make us look good."

Dunks said, "It's the general public I'm thinking about. They're the ones who count. They want proof of our loyalty. Okay, I'm giving it to them, and maybe I'll die for it if I'm unlucky. But if after the war's over and our two cents don't cut any ice with the American public, well, to blazes with them!"

The next day Henry announced, "Tomorrow I'm going down to volunteer." No one said a word. Father stared down at his veined hands. Mother's face turned into a white mask.

"Please don't feel so bad, Mama."

Mother smiled thinly. "I don't feel bad, Henry. In fact, I don't feel anything just now."

Father spoke to her tenderly, "Mama, if Henry had been born in Japan, he would have been taken into the army and gone off to war long ago."

"That's right. And I guess it's about time we all stopped thinking about the past. I think we should go along with our sons from now. It's the least we can do."

Father said, gratefully, "That's what I wanted to hear. At least we're together on this matter. Imagine what Dunks must be going through."

Mrs. Oshima had refused to speak to her son ever since he had decided to volunteer. "Is this what we deserve from our children," she said, "after years and years of work and hardship for their sake? Ah, we've brought up nothing but fools! They can be insulted, their parents insulted, and still they volunteer."

Early the next morning, Dunks, and George and Paul, sons of Mr. Sawada, the clothing salesman, came into our apartment on their way to the camp hospital for their physical.

"Let's go, Hank, before the crowd gets there."

They left with a great clatter and loud shouting. Father, Mother, Sumi, and I sank to our cots feeling as if we had come out of a turbulent storm which had been raging steadily in our minds since Pearl Harbor. The birth of the Nisei combat team was the climax to our evacuee life, and the turning point. It was the road back to our rightful places.

READING REVIEW

1. What was life like in a relocation camp?
2. Give two reasons why Japanese Americans were sent to relocation camps.
3. (a) Why did the government establish a seperate Nisei combat unit? (b) Do you think it was fair to segregate Nisei soldiers? Why or why not?
4. (a) If you had been a Japanese American during the war, how would you have felt about being placed in a relocation camp? (b) Would you have volunteered to serve in the armed forces? Explain.

224 Bravery at the Bulge

During World War II the United States armed forces continued their traditional policy of separate units for black Americans. Moreover, a large number of black Americans were put in service units—doing work in supply depots, driving trucks, doing repair and maintenance jobs. But some black units were assigned to combat. And for a brief period, late in the war, the barriers of racial segregation were broken down.

When the Germans broke through the Allied lines in December 1944, in their counterattack at the Battle of the Bulge, the Allies desperately needed fighting units. As a result, black units and white units fought together to stop the German advance. In this selection Walter White, who was secretary of the NAACP, told of this history-making event of black and white Americans fighting together.

READING FOCUS

1. Why were black soldiers asked to volunteer?
2. How did white and black soldiers react to fighting alongside each other?

One of the most dramatic examples of the abandonment of interracial antagonisms in combat by troops themselves—and a tragic reversal by the army high command—occurred during and after the Battle of the Bulge.

The Germans' sudden, effective breakthrough threatened disaster. The tide of war might have been changed at that point. At the very least, the war would have been longer if this daring maneuver had succeeded, even though more men and war materials would probably have brought Allied victory. Many Americans now alive would have died in the meantime.

Every available man was thrown into the fight to stop the German advance. But even then there were not enough. Desperate appeals were sent to the United States to rush more combat troops as quickly as possible. Many were sent by plane, but even these were not enough. It was at this point, during some of the fiercest fighting, that General John C. H. Lee issued an appeal to colored Service of Supply troops to volunteer for combat.

"It is planned to assign you without regard to color or race to units where assistance is most needed," General Lee promised. He made no effort to minimize the desperate nature of the fighting nor the great number of casualties caused by the German breakthrough. He pointed out that all noncommissioned officers would have to give up their ratings to qualify for service as combat troops.

Great numbers of volunteers answered General Lee's appeal. In some units 80 percent of the soldiers offered their services. In one engineer unit, 171 out of 186 men volunteered. One private in an ordnance company declared: "We've been giving a lot of sweat. Now I think we'll mix some blood with it!"

Negroes were delighted at this first opportunity to function as "real" soldiers. The response was so great that the army had to set up a quota to prevent complete disorganization of its service units.

Generals George Patton, Omar Bradley, and Courtney Hodges gave their approval to the use of Negro soldiers in completely unsegregated combat units. General Eisenhower

Adapted from A Man Called White *by Walter White.*

was enthusiastic. But Eisenhower's chief of staff, W. Bedell Smith, insisted that the plan be submitted to General George C. Marshall, army chief of staff.

Washington was alarmed at the idea of an unsegregated, genuinely democratic army. It ordered the plan abandoned. But the need for combat troops was so critical that the high command in Washington was forced to agree to a compromise—the use of all-Negro platoons in white regiments, instead of a mixture of whites and Negroes throughout the regiments. Although Negro soldiers felt that they had been let down, they were still enthusiastic. The Negro platoons were distributed among eleven combat divisions of the First and Seventh Armies. They fought in the crucial stages of the Battle of the Bulge and through the later Allied drive across Germany.

Several of the Negro volunteers won the Distinguished Service Cross or Silver Star. Others were cited for bravery beyond the call of duty.

The army took a poll among the white officers and soldiers who had fought with Negro troops. The results are to me a striking example of the fact that race prejudice is not as stubborn as some people imagine. The army poll showed that after having served in the same unit with black combat soldiers, 77 percent of the officers favored integration, as contrasted with 33 percent before the experience. The figures among enlisted men were 77 percent and 35 percent, after and before serving with Negroes.

A white South Carolina sergeant was quoted by the army as saying, "When I heard about it, I said I wouldn't wear the same shoulder patch they did. After that first day, when we saw how they fought, I changed my mind. They are just like any of the other men to us."

Another sergeant from Alabama, after telling how bitterly he had opposed serving with Negroes at first, confessed a total change of attitude. "I used to think they would be cowards in combat, but I saw them work."

Some 84 percent of white company officers and 81 percent of white platoon sergeants declared that Negro troops had fought superbly, and 17 percent of officers and 9 percent of enlisted men even went so far as to say that Negroes fought better than white troops.

General Patton highly praised the black volunteers. General Eisenhower declared: "All

Black soldiers in World War II

my commanders reported that these volunteers did excellent work." General Charles Lanham of the 104th Division, presenting combat decorations to eleven Negroes, went even further to declare: "I have never seen any soldiers who have performed better in combat than you have."

But Eisenhower, to the dismay of many of us who had faith in him, testified before the Senate armed services committee in 1948 that he believed racial segregation in the army should continue at the platoon level. And in April 1948 the Secretary of War bluntly told a distinguished group of 15 Negro leaders that the army would continue segregation.

READING REVIEW

1. Name two reasons why the army asked black soldiers to volunteer.
2. (a) How did black soldiers react to their recruitment for a fighting unit? (b) Why did black Americans respond as they did?
3. What was the attitude of white officers and soldiers who fought with black soldiers?

225 Dive Bombers Over Italy

Americans eagerly followed the war news on radio and in the press. Often they learned about the land campaigns and air and sea battles by reading the newspaper stories written by foreign correspondents. These American reporters covered every phase of World War II on every one of the many battle fronts. Many of these brave reporters went with the American units into battle. They shared the soldiers' daily hardships and dangers, and many of them lost their lives in battle.

Ernie Pyle, one of the most outstanding foreign war correspondents, spent many months at the battle fronts with American troops. His name and his stories were well known to most Americans by the time he died during the fighting on the Pacific island of Ie Shima in April 1945. In this selection, he wrote about the war in Europe, describing American dive bombers and their crews fighting in Italy during 1943.

READING FOCUS

1. What was the primary function of dive bomber squadrons?
2. What were the most striking features of dive bombing?

I spent some time with a dive-bomber squadron of the 12th Air Support Command. There were about 50 officers and 250 enlisted men in each squadron. They all lived in a big apartment house built by the Italian government for war workers and their families. It was out in the country at the edge of a small town.

In the dive-bomber groups in Italy, pilots and mechanics believed that the dive bomber was the most wonderful machine produced in this war. Certainly, those dive-bomber boys were a spectacular part of our air force.

Their function was to work in extremely close support of our infantry. For instance, suppose there was a German gun position just over a hill which was holding us up because our troops couldn't get at it with their guns. They called on the dive bombers and gave them the

---

Adapted from Brave Men *by Ernie Pyle.*

location. Within an hour, and sometimes much quicker, bombers would come screaming out of the sky right on top of that gun and blow it up.

They could do the same thing to bunched enemy troops, bridges, tank columns, convoys, or ammunition dumps. Because of their great accuracy they could bomb much closer to our own troops than other kinds of planes would dare. Most of the time they worked less than a thousand yards [914 meters] ahead of our front lines—and sometimes even closer than that.

The group I was with had been in combat six months. During that time they had flown 10,000 missions, fired more than 1 million rounds of 50-caliber ammunition, and dropped 3 million pounds [1.4 million kilograms] of bombs. That's more than the entire Eighth Air Force in England dropped in its first year of operation.

Those boys dived about 8,000 feet [2,440 meters] before dropping their bombs. Without brakes their speed in such a dive would ordinarily build up to around 700 miles [1,125 kilometers] an hour, but the brakes held them down to about 390 miles [625 kilometers].

The dive bombers approached their target in formation. When the leader made sure he had spotted the target he wiggled his wings, raised his diving brakes, rolled on his back, nosed over, and down he went. The next man behind followed almost instantly, and then the next, and the next—not more than 150 feet [45 meters] apart. There was no danger of their running into each other, for the brakes held them all at the same speed.

At about 4,000 feet [1,220 meters] the pilot released his bombs. Then he started his pullout. The strain was terrific, and all the pilots would "black out" a little bit. It was not a complete blackout, and lasted only four or five seconds. It was more a heaviness in the head and a darkness before the eyes, the pilots said.

If you ever heard a dive bombing by our planes you'd never forget it. Even in normal flight those planes made a sort of screaming noise. In a dive, the wail could be heard for miles. From the ground it sounded as though they were coming directly down on us. It was a horrifying thing.

For several months the posting period back to America [the number of missions a pilot had to fly before being sent home on leave] was set

P52 Mustangs were converted into "dive bombers."

at a certain number of missions. Then it was suddenly increased by more than 20. When the order came, there were pilots who were within one mission of going home. So they had to stay and fly a few more months. Some of them never lived to finish the new allotment.

There is an odd psychological factor in the system of being sent home after a certain number of missions. When pilots got to within three or four missions of the finish, they became so nervous they almost jumped out of their skins. A good many were killed on their last mission. The squadron leaders wished there were some way they could surprise a man and send him home with six or eight missions still to go, thus sparing him the agony of those last few trips.

Nowhere in our fighting forces was cooperation closer or friendship greater than between Americans and British in the air. I never heard an American pilot make a critical remark about a British flier. Our pilots said the British were cooler under fire than we were. The British attitude and manner of speech amused them, but they were never scornful.

They liked to listen in on their radios as the British pilots talked to each other. For example, one day they heard one pilot call to another, "I say, old chap, there is a Jerry [the English nickname for Germans during the war] on your tail."

To which the pilot in danger answered, "Quite so, quite so, thanks very much, old man."

And another time, one of our dive bombers got shot up over the target. His engine was smoking and he was losing altitude. He made for the coast all alone, an easy target for any German fighter that might come along. He was just barely staying in the air, and he was a sad and lonely boy indeed. Then suddenly he heard over his earphones a distinctly British voice saying, "Cheer up, chicken we have you."

He looked around and two Spitfires [British fighter planes], one on either side, were leading him back to his home field.

READING REVIEW

1. How did the dive bomber groups support the army infantry?
2. List two striking features of dive bombing.
3. How did the British and American pilots assist each other?

226 Dropping the Atomic Bomb

When President Roosevelt died in 1945, Vice-President Harry Truman became President. The new President now faced the tremendous task of ending the war and planning for the peace.

After the war in Europe ended, Truman and the other Allied leaders met at Potsdam, Germany, in July 1945. At the meeting they agreed to demand that Japan surrender unconditionally. Japan refused. President Truman, who had been in office less than four months, now had to make the awesome decision of whether to drop an atomic bomb on Japan. Fearing that an attack on the Japanese mainland by American warships and planes would cost as many as a million American lives, Truman decided to approve the use of the atomic bomb. In this selection, taken from President Truman's memoirs, the President explained his decision to use the atomic bomb at Hiroshima.

Nagasaki after the atomic bomb

READING FOCUS

1. Why did Truman decide to drop the atomic bomb on Japan?
2. How did Truman feel about his decision?

The idea of the atomic bomb had been suggested to President Roosevelt by the famous and brilliant Dr. Albert Einstein. Its development turned out to be a vast undertaking. It was the achievement of the combined efforts of science, industry, labor, and the military, and it had no parallel in history. The people in charge and their staffs worked under great pressure. The whole enormous task required the services of more than 100,000 people and immense quantities of material. It required over two and a half years and the spending of $2.5 billion. Only a few of the thousands of people who worked in these plants knew what they were producing. So strict was the secrecy that even some of the highest-ranking officials in Washington did not have the slightest idea of what was going on. I did not.

Before 1939 it had been generally agreed among scientists that in theory it was possible to release energy from the atom. In 1940 we had begun to share with Great Britain all scientific knowledge useful to war, although Britain was at war at that time and we were not. Following this—in 1942—we learned that the

Adapted from Memoirs, Vol. I, Year of Decisions *by Harry S Truman.*

Germans were at work on a method to harness atomic energy for use as a weapon of war.

It was under the general policy of sharing knowledge between our nation and Great Britain that research on the atomic bomb started in such feverish secrecy. American and British scientists joined in the race against the Germans. Working together with the British, we thus made it possible to achieve a great scientific triumph in the field of atomic energy. Nevertheless, basic and historic as this event was, it had to be considered at the time as relatively unimportant to the far-flung war we were fighting in the Pacific at a terrible cost in American lives.

We could hope for a miracle, but the daily tragedy of a bitter war was always with us. We worked to construct a weapon of such overpowering force that the enemy could be forced to give in swiftly once we could use it. This was the primary aim of our secret and vast effort. But we also had to carry out the enormous effort of our basic and traditional military plans.

My own knowledge of these developments had come only after I became President, when Secretary of War Henry Stimson had given me the full story. He had told me at the time that the project was nearing completion and that a bomb could be expected within another four months. It was at his suggestion, too, that I had then set up a committee of top people and had asked them to study with great care the possibilities the new weapon might have for us.

It was their recommendation that the bomb be used against the enemy as soon as it could be done. They recommended further that it should be used without warning and against a target that would clearly show its devastating strength. I had realized, of course, that an atomic bomb explosion would cause damage and causalties beyond imagination. On the other hand, the scientific advisers of the committee reported, "We can propose no technical demonstration likely to bring an end to the war; we see no acceptable alternative to direct military use." It was their conclusion that no technical demonstration they might propose, such as dropping the bomb on a deserted island, would be likely to bring the war to an end. It had to be used against an enemy target.

The final decision of where and when to use the atomic bomb was up to me. Let there be no mistake about it. I regarded the bomb as a military weapon and never had any doubt that it should be used. My top military advisers recommended its use. When I talked to Churchill, he told me that he favored the use of the atomic bomb if it might help end the war.

In deciding to use this bomb, I wanted to make sure that it would be used as a weapon of war in the manner set down by the laws of war. That meant that I wanted it dropped on a military target. I had told Stimson that the bomb should be dropped as nearly as possible upon a war production center of prime military importance.

Stimson's staff had prepared a list of cities in Japan that might serve as targets. Kyoto, though favored as a center of military activity, was eliminated when Secretary Stimson pointed out that it was a cultural and religious shrine of the Japanese.

Four cities were finally recommended as targets: Hiroshima, Kokura, Niigata, and Nagasaki. They were listed in that order as targets for the first attack. The order of selection was in accordance with the military importance of these cities. But allowance would be given for weather conditions at the time of the bombing. Before the selected targets were approved as proper for military purposes, I personally went over them in detail with Secretary Stimson, General Marshall, and General Arnold, and we discussed the matter of timing and the final choice of the first target.

General Spaatz, who commanded the Strategic Air Forces, which would drop the bomb, was given some independence as to when and on which of the four targets the bomb would be dropped. That was necessary because of weather and other operational considerations. In order to get preparations under way, the War Department instructed General Spaatz that the first bomb would be dropped as soon after August 3 as weather would permit.

A specialized B-29 unit had been selected for the task. Seven modified B-29's, with pilots and crews, were ready and waiting for orders. Meanwhile ships and planes were rushing the materials for the bomb and specialists to assemble them to the Pacific island of Tinian in the Marianas.

On July 28 Radio Tokyo announced that the Japanese government would continue to fight. There was no choice now. The bomb was scheduled to be dropped after August 3 unless Japan surrendered before that day.

On August 6, the fourth day of my journey home from Potsdam, came the historic news that shook the world. I was eating lunch with members of the *Augusta*'s crew when I was handed the following message:

TO THE PRESIDENT
FROM THE SECRETARY OF WAR

BIG BOMB DROPPED ON HIROSHIMA AUGUST 5 AT 7:15 P.M. WASHINGTON TIME. FIRST REPORTS INDICATE COMPLETE SUCCESS WHICH WAS EVEN MORE CONSPICUOUS THAN EARLIER TEST.

I was greatly moved. I said to the group of sailors around me, "This is the greatest thing in history. It's time for us to get home."

A few minutes later a second message was handed to me. It read as follows:

FOLLOWING INFORMATION REGARDING MANHATTAN† RECEIVED. "HIROSHIMA BOMBED VISUALLY. THERE WAS NO FIGHTER OPPOSITION AND NO FLAK. PARSONS REPORTS 15 MINUTES AFTER DROP AS FOLLOWS: 'RESULTS CLEAR CUT SUCCESSFUL IN ALL RESPECTS. VISIBLE EFFECTS GREATER THAN IN ANY TEST. CONDITIONS NORMAL IN AIRPLANE FOLLOWING DELIVERY.'"

When I had read this I signaled to the crew in the mess hall that I wished to say something. I then told them of the dropping of a powerful new bomb which used an explosive twenty thousand times as powerful as a ton of TNT. I went to the wardroom, where I told the officers, who were at lunch, what had happened. I could not hide my expectation that the Pacific war might now be brought to a speedy end.

† The bomb's development was called the Manhattan Project.

READING REVIEW

1. Summarize the steps the President went through in making the final decision to drop the bomb.
2. What factors led to the decision on where to drop the first bomb?
3. What was President Truman's feeling about his decision to drop the bomb?
4. (a) Based on the evidence provided in the reading, do you think that President Truman made the right decision? (b) Why or why not?

Reshaping the Postwar World

CHAPTER 37 Responsibilities of World Leadership (1945–1960)

227 Organizing the United Nations

Eleanor Roosevelt was one of the most active First Ladies in the nation's history. She took a special interest in New Deal programs to help young Americans and in efforts to improve the lives of minority groups. And she continued to play an important role in American political life after President Roosevelt's death.

One of Eleanor Roosevelt's greatest contributions was her work with the United Nations. In late 1945 she was appointed by President Truman as a member of the United States delegation to the organizing meeting of the UN General Assembly. At this meeting, held in London in 1946, she served on the committee formed to deal with humanitarian, educational, and cultural matters. In the following account, from her autobiography, she told about her work as a delegate.

READING FOCUS
1. What was Eleanor Roosevelt's role in establishing the United Nations?
2. Why was it important for the organizational meeting of the United Nations to be successful?

In December of 1945 I received a message from President Truman. He reminded me that the

Adapted from On My Own *by Eleanor Roosevelt.*

first organizing meeting of the United Nations General Assembly would be held in London, starting in January 1946. He asked me if I would serve as a member of the United States delegation.

"Oh, no! It would be impossible," was my first reaction. "How could I be a delegate to help organize the United Nations when I have no background or experience in international meetings?"

My secretary, however, urged me not to refuse without giving the idea careful thought. I knew in a general way what had been done about organizing the United Nations. After the San Francisco meeting in 1945, when the Charter was written, it had been accepted by the various nations, including our own. I knew, too, that we had a group of people headed by Adlai Stevenson working with representatives of other member nations in London to prepare for the formal organizing meeting. Then, as I thought about the President's offer, I knew that I believed the United Nations to be the one hope for a peaceful world. I knew that my husband had placed great importance on the establishment of this world organization. So I felt a great sense of responsibility. Finally I decided to accept.

Members of the delegation sailed on the *Queen Elizabeth* in January 1946. The dock was crowded with reporters and news photographers who surrounded the Senators and the members of the House of Representatives on the delegation. I was feeling rather lost and quite uncertain about what lay ahead. But as it turned out there was plenty to do even for a confused beginner in such affairs. The first thing I noticed in my stateroom was a pile of blue sheets of paper on the table. These blue sheets turned out to be documents—most of them marked "secret"—that apparently related to the work of delegates. I had no idea where they had come from but assumed they were meant for me, so I looked through them. They obviously contained background information on the work to be taken up by the General Assembly as well as statements of our government's position on various problems.

So, I thought, somebody is putting me to work without delay. I sat down and began reading—or trying to read. It was dull and very hard work. I had great difficulty in staying awake, but I knew my duty when I saw it and read them all. By the time I finished I supposed that the Department of State had no more secrets from me. But I would have found it hard to reveal anything because I was seldom really sure of the exact meaning of what was on the blue sheets. At the time, I feared this was because I couldn't understand plain English when it concerned State Department matters. Later I changed my mind on this, because others seemed to have the same difficulty.

People on the *Queen Elizabeth* were very kind to me. Nevertheless I felt much alone at first. One day, as I was walking down the passageway to my room, I met Senator Arthur H. Vandenberg.

"Mrs. Roosevelt," he said in his rather deep voice, "we would like to know if you would serve on Committee 3."

I had two immediate and rather contradictory reactions to the question. First, I wondered who "we" might be. Was a Republican Senator deciding who would serve where? And why, since I was a delegate, had I not been consulted about committee assignments? But my next reaction crowded these thoughts out of mind. I suddenly realized that I had no idea what Committee 3 might be. So I kept my thoughts to myself and humbly agreed to serve where I was made to serve.

"But," I added quickly, "will you or someone kindly see that I get as much information as possible on Committee 3?"

The Senator promised and I went on to my room. The truth was that at that time I did not know whom to ask for information or guidance. As I learned more about my work, I realized why I had been put on Committee 3, which dealt with humanitarian, educational, and cultural questions. There were many committees dealing with the budgetary, legal, political, and other questions. I could just see the

Signing the United Nations Charter

members of our delegation puzzling over the list and saying:

"Oh, no! We can't put Mrs. Roosevelt on the political committee. What could she do on the budget committee? Does she know anything about legal questions? Ah, here's the safe spot for her—Committee 3. She can't do much harm there!"

Oddly enough, I felt very much the same way about it. On the ship coming over, however, State Department officials held briefings [information meetings] for the delegates. We listened to experts on various subjects explain the problems that would be brought up, give the background on them, and then state the general position of the United States. I attended all these sessions. Discovering that there also were briefings for newspaper people aboard the ship, I went to all their meetings, too. As a result of these briefings and various discussions, I began to realize that Committee 3 might be much more important than had been expected. And, in time, this proved to be true.

At the early sessions in London, which were largely concerned with organization, I got the strong impression that many of the old-timers in the field of diplomacy were very doubtful about the new world organization. They had seen so many failures, they had been through the collapse of the League of Nations, and they seemed to doubt that we would achieve much. The newcomers, the younger people in most cases, were the ones who showed the most enthusiasm and determination.

I might point out here that during the entire London session of the Assembly, I was very uneasy. I knew that as the only woman on the delegation I was not very welcome. Moreover, if I failed to be a useful member, it would not be considered only that I as an individual had failed, but that all women had failed. There would be little chance for others to serve in the near future.

As a normal thing, the important—and I might say, the hard—work of any organization such as the United Nations is not done in the big, public meetings of the General Assembly, but in the small and almost continuous meetings of the various committees. It was while working on Committee 3 that I really began to understand the inner workings of the United Nations. It was ironical perhaps that one of the subjects that created the greatest political heat of the London sessions came up in this "unimportant" committee to which I had been assigned.

The issue arose from the fact that there were many war refugees in Germany when the armistice was signed—Ukrainians, Poles, Czechoslovaks, Latvians, Lithuanians. Estonians and others. A great number of them were still living there in temporary camps because they did not want to return to live under the Communist rule of their own countries. There also were the Jewish survivors of the German death camps.

This situation flared up in Committee 3. It was raised originally by the Yugoslav representative, Leo Mates. The Yugoslav—and, of course, the Soviet Union—position that Mates put forward was that any war refugees who did not wish to return to their countries were traitors to their countries. He argued that the refugees in Germany should be forced to return home and to accept whatever punishment might be given to them. This position was strongly supported by the Soviet representative.

The position of the Western countries, including the United States, was that large numbers of the refugees were not traitors. We felt that they must be guaranteed the right to choose whether they would return to their homes. Since the London sessions were largely technical rather than political debates and since Committee 3 was the scene of one of the early clashes between the Soviet Union and the West, the newspapers carried much of the controversy.

I felt very strongly on the subject, as did others. We spent many hours trying to write some kind of resolution on which all could agree. We never did. Our chairman had to present a majority report to the General Assembly which was immediately challenged by the USSR. In the Assembly the minority position was handled, not by the Soviet representative on Committee 3, but by the head of the Soviet Union's delegation, Andrei Vishinsky. Vishinsky was one of the Russians' great legal minds, a skilled debater, a man with ability to use the weapons of wit and ridicule. It was clear that in view of the importance of the issue someone would have to speak for the United States. The question of who this was to be made our delegation extremely anxious. There was a hurried consultation among the male members. When they broke up, John Foster Dulles approached me rather uncertainly.

"Mrs. Roosevelt," he began, rather lamely, "the United States must speak in the debate. Since you are the one who has carried on for us in this controversy in the committee, do you think you could say a few words to the Assembly? I'm afraid nobody else is really familiar with the subject."

"Why, Mr. Dulles," I answered as meekly as I could manage, "in that case I will do my best."

Actually, I was badly frightened. I trembled at the thought of speaking against the famous Mr. Vishinsky. But when the time came I walked, tense and excited, to the platform and did my best. The hour was late and we knew the Russians would delay a vote as long as possible on the theory that some of our allies would get tired and leave. I knew we must, if possible, hold the South American delegates until the vote was taken because their votes might be decisive. So I talked about Simon Bolivar and his stand for the freedom of the people of Latin America. I talked and watched the delegates. To my joy the South American representatives stayed with us to the end and, when the vote came, we won. This vote meant that the Western nations would have to worry about the ultimate fate of the refugees for a long, long time, but the principle of the right of an individual to make his or her own decisions was a victory well worth while.

The final night the vote on Committee 3's report was taken so late that I did not get back to the hotel till about one o'clock. I was very tired. As I walked wearily up the stairs, I heard two voices behind me. Turning around, I saw Senator Vandenberg and Mr. Dulles. They obviously had something to say to me, but for the life of me I can't remember which one of them said it. Whichever it was, he seemed to be speaking for both.

"Mrs. Roosevelt," he said, "we must tell you that we did all we could to keep you off the United States delegation. We begged the President not to nominate you. But now that you are leaving we feel we must admit that we have worked with you gladly and found you good to work with. And we will be happy to do so again."

I don't think anything could have made the weariness disappear as did those words. I shall always be grateful for the encouragement they gave me.

READING REVIEW

1. **(a)** How did Eleanor Roosevelt feel about serving as a member of the United States delegation? **(b)** About the committee on which she served?
2. What factors contributed to Mrs. Roosevelt's "uneasy" feeling during the London session?
3. Why was the issue of refugees important?
4. How did Eleanor Roosevelt contribute to the success of the first United Nations meeting?
5. Why was Eleanor Roosevelt's participation at this international meeting significant?

228 Beginnings of the Cold War

Many Americans hoped that the Western powers and the Soviet Union would continue their wartime cooperation after World War II. But by 1946 the Soviet Union and the United States were sharply divided over such issues as the postwar boundaries of Eastern Europe, disarmament, and the international control of atomic energy. The so-called "Cold War" between the Western powers and the Soviet Union had now begun. It was clear that the Soviet Union was determined to maintain its influence in Eastern Europe and expand it into others areas of the world. It was equally clear that the United States was determined to stop the further expansion of Communism by the Soviet Union.

Exactly how the Cold War began and whose fault it was is a subject of continuing controversy among many historians. In the following selection, historian John Lewis Gaddis gave his analysis of how the Cold War began.

READING FOCUS

1. How did World War II revolutionize American foreign policy?
2. How did ideological differences between the United States and the Soviet Union contribute to the "Cold War"?

American leaders did not want a Cold War, but they wanted insecurity even less. By early 1946 President Truman and his advisers had reluctantly concluded that recent actions of the Soviet Union endangered the security of the United States. In order to understand how the

Adapted from The United States and the Origins of the Cold War 1941–47 *by John Lewis Gaddis.*

The Cold War "heats up."

leaders who made American foreign policy came to this conclusion, it is necessary to view the situation as they saw it, not as it appears today in the light of historical hindsight.

World War II had produced a revolution in United States foreign policy. Before that conflict, most Americans believed that their country could best protect itself by staying out of political entanglements overseas. The events of 1939–40 persuaded leaders of the Roosevelt administration that they had been wrong. The bombing of Pearl Harbor convinced others in the United States. From then on, American policy-makers would seek security through involvement, not isolation. They believed that to prevent new wars the whole system of relations between nations would have to be changed. They felt that only the United States had the power and influence to carry out this task. As a result, United States officials set to work, even before entering into the war, to plan a peace settlement which would accomplish such a change in relations between nations.

Lessons of the past greatly influenced how American leaders saw the future. Determined to avoid mistakes which, in their view, had caused World War II, American planners sought to disarm defeated enemies, give peoples of the world the right to shape their own future, revive world trade, and replace the League of Nations with a new and more effective organization. But without victory over the Axis, the United States would never be able to carry out its plan for peace. Given the realities of the military situation, victory depended upon cooperation with the Soviet Union, an ally whose commitment to American postwar ideals was, at best, questionable.

The leaders of the Soviet Union also looked to the past in planning for the future. But their very different experiences led them to conclusions that did not always agree with those of their American allies. For Stalin, the key to peace was simple: keep Russia strong and keep Germany weak. He showed little interest in Washington's plans for collective security [a policy designed to keep world peace by having nations join together to guarantee the security or safety of all nations], the reduction of tariff barriers, and reform of the world money system. Self-determination for the people in Eastern Europe, however, he would not allow. This region was vital to Soviet security, but the people who lived there were bitterly anti-Russian. Nor could Stalin agree with Allied efforts, also growing out of lessons of the past, to limit reparations [payments for war damages] paid by Germany. These two conflicts—Eastern Europe and Germany—became major areas of disagreement in the emerging Cold War.

Moscow's position would not have seemed so alarming to American officials, however, if it were not for the Soviet Union's continued belief in an ideology favoring the overthrow of capitalism throughout the world. Hopes that the United States might cooperate successfully with the Soviet Union after the war had been based on the belief, encouraged by Stalin himself, that the Soviets had given up their former goal of spreading communism. Soviet expansion into Eastern Europe in 1944 and 1945 caused Western observers to fear that they had been misled. Just at the moment of victory over the Axis, the old fear of world revolution reappeared.

It seems likely that American foreign policy-makers mistook Stalin's determination to ensure Russian security through spheres of influence for a new effort to spread communism outside the borders of the Soviet Union. The Russians did not immediately set up Communist governments in all the countries they occupied after the war. And Stalin showed very little interest in promoting the fortunes of Communist parties in areas beyond his control. Historians now generally agree on the limited nature of Stalin's objectives. But the Soviet leader failed to make the limited nature of his objectives clear. Having just defeated one dictator, Americans could not regard the emergence of another one without the strongest feelings of alarm and anger.

Nor did they see any reason to give in to what Stalin seemed to be doing. The United States had come out of the war with complete control over the world's most powerful weapon, the atomic bomb. It also had a near-monopoly over the productive facilities which could make possible quick reestablishment of war-shattered economies. Convinced that technology had given them the means to shape the postwar world to their liking, American officials assumed that these instruments would leave the Russians no choice but to go along with American peace plans.

Frustrated in their efforts to work out an

acceptable settlement with the Soviet Union, under strong pressure from Congress and the public to make no further compromises, American leaders started on a new Russian policy during the first months of 1946. From now on, expansionist moves by the Soviet Union would be resisted, even at the risk of war. Negotiations would continue, but future concessions would have to come from Moscow. Meanwhile, the United States would begin rebuilding its military forces, now badly decreased by demobilization. It would also begin an ambitious program of economic assistance to nations threatened by communism.

It is easy for historians, writing twenty-five years later, to suggest ways in which the United States might have avoided, or at least lessened, the dangers of a postwar confrontation with the Soviet Union. President Roosevelt could have eased Russia's military burden by launching a second front in Europe in 1942 or 1943. He could have removed Eastern Europe from the provisions of the Atlantic Charter, thereby recognizing the Soviet sphere of influence in that part of the world. American officials could have helped in the giant task of repairing Russian war damage by granting a generous reconstruction loan, and by allowing extensive reparations from Germany. Finally, the United States could have attempted to lessen Soviet distrust by voluntarily giving up its monopoly over the atomic bomb.

But these were not workable alternatives at the time. An early second front would have greatly increased American casualties and might have weakened support for the war effort. Recognition of the Soviet position in Eastern Europe would have caused opposition in the Senate to American membership in the United Nations, and might have endangered Roosevelt's reelection. Economic concessions to the Russians, in the form of either a reconstruction loan or a more flexible attitude on reparations, would have created a storm of protest from a Congress still largely isolationist in its approach to foreign aid. A decision to give up the atomic bomb would have so alienated the American people and their representatives on Capitol Hill as to weaken the very functioning of the government.

Historians have debated at length the question of who caused the Cold War, but without shedding much light on the subject. Too often they view that event only as a series of actions by one side and reactions by the other. In fact, policy-makers in both the United States and the Soviet Union were constantly weighing each other's intentions, as they understood them, and modifying their own courses of action accordingly. In addition, officials in Washington and Moscow brought to the task of policy making a variety of fixed ideas, shaped by personality, ideology, political pressures, even ignorance and irrationality, all of which influenced their behavior. Once this complex interaction of stimulus and response is taken into account, it becomes clear that neither side can take complete responsibility for the Cold War.

But neither should the conflict be seen as predetermined if for no other reason than the impossibility of "proving" inevitability in history. The power vacuum in central Europe caused by Germany's collapse made a Russian-American confrontation likely. It did not make it inevitable. People as well as circumstances make foreign policy, and through such drastic methods as war, appeasement, or resignation, policy-makers can always change the difficult situations in which they find themselves. One may legitimately ask why they do not choose to go this far, but to view their actions as predetermined by blind, impersonal "forces" is to deny the complexity and particularity of human behavior, not to mention the ever-present possibility of accident. The Cold War is too complicated an event to be discussed in terms of either national guilt or inevitability.

If one must assign responsibility for the Cold War, the most meaningful way is to ask which side had the greater opportunity to adapt itself, at least in part, to the other's position, given the range of alternatives as they appeared at the time. Revisionists [those historians who hold America more responsible than the Soviet Union for causing the Cold War] have argued that American policy-makers had greater freedom of action. But this view ignores the restrictions enforced by domestic politics. Little is known even today about how Stalin determined his choices, but it does seem safe to say that the very nature of the Soviet system gave him a larger selection of alternatives than were open to leaders of the United States. The Russian dictator was free from pressures of Congress, public opinion, or the press. Even ideology did not restrict him: Stalin was the master of Communist doctrine, not a prisoner of it, and could modify or suspend Marxism-Leninism whenever it suited him. This is not to say that Stalin wanted a Cold War—he had every reason to avoid one. But his absolute powers did give him more chances to overcome the internal restraints on his policy than were available to democratic leaders in the West.

The Cold War grew out of a complicated interaction of external and internal developments inside both the United States and the Soviet Union. The external situation—circumstances beyond the control of either power—left Americans and Russians facing one another across a helpless Europe at the end of World War II. Internal influences in the Soviet Union—the search for security, the role of ideology, massive postwar reconstruction needs, the personality of Stalin—together with those in the United States—the ideal of self-determination, fear of communism, the illusion of unlimited power fostered by American economic strength and the atomic bomb—made the resulting confrontation a hostile one. Leaders of both superpowers sought peace, but in doing so gave in to considerations which, while they did not cause war, made a resolution of differences impossible.

READING REVIEW

1. How did "lessons of the past" influence American foreign policy in 1946?
2. How did Gaddis feel one should approach the study of the Cold War?
3. (a) Which nation did Gaddis think had the primary responsibility for the Cold War? (b) What evidence did he offer to support his claim?
4. (a) Why did Gaddis say the Cold War was inevitable? (b) Do you agree? Why or why not?

229 A Report on the Korean Conflict

In June 1950, Communist-ruled North Korea began an invasion of South Korea. The United States immediately pledged aid to South Korea, and, with the support the United Nations, helped to organize an army to defend South Korea. American military forces formed the largest part of this United Nations army, but Canada, Australia, New Zealand, and other nations also provided troops.

During the Korean War many news reporters, or correspondents, went along with American troops to report on the war in Asia. One of the most famous of these war correspondents was Marguerite Higgins, who wrote for the New York *Herald Tribune*. In this selection from her book about the war in Korea, she described an unexpected enemy attack on American headquarters (located in a schoolhouse) in July 1950.

READING FOCUS

1. How did the reporter react to the attack?
2. Why did correspondents risk their lives to report on the war in Korea?

Half a dozen officers, myself, and Harold Martin [of the *Saturday Evening Post* magazine], were finishing breakfast in the schoolhouse at seven in the morning when suddenly bullets exploded from all directions. They crackled through the windows, splintered through the thin walls. A machine-gun burst slammed the coffeepot off the table. A grenade exploded on the wooden frame on which I had been sleeping, and another grenade sent fragments flying off the roof.

"Where is the little beauty who threw that?" asked Captain William Hawkes, an intelligence officer, as he grabbed at his bleeding right hand, torn by a grenade splinter.

We tried to race down the hall, but we had to hit the floor fast and stay there. We were all bewildered and caught totally by surprise. It was impossible to judge what to do. Bullets were spattering at us from the hill rising directly behind us and from the courtyard on the other side.

Thoughts tumbled jerkily through my mind—"This can't be enemy fire . . . we're miles behind the front lines . . . that grenade must have been thrown from 15 or 20 yards [between 13 and 18 meters] . . . how could they possibly get that close? . . . if they are that close, they are right behind the schoolhouse . . . they can be through those windows and on top of us in a matter of seconds . . . nobody in here even has a carbine [rifle] . . . well, it would be too late anyway . . . why did I ever get myself into this? . . . I don't understand the [weapons] fire coming from the courtyard . . .

From War in Korea *by Marguerite Higgins.*

American troops defend a South Korean village.

what has happened to our defense? . . . could it possibly be that some trigger-happy GI started all this? . . ."

There was soon no doubt, however, that it was enemy fire. We were surrounded. During the night the Reds [Communists] had sneaked past our front lines, avoiding the main roads and traveling over mountain trails. In camouflaged uniforms, they crept onto the hillside behind the schoolhouse. Others, circling around, set up machine guns in a rice paddy on the other side of the schoolyard. This accounted for the vicious cross fire.

They had managed to get by our defenses for several reasons. The GIs were completely exhausted from a long patrol into enemy territory. Some of the guards fell asleep. And at least one column of the enemy was mistaken, by those officers awake and on duty, for South Korean police.

We had been warned the night before that South Koreans were helping us guard our exposed right flank. This was only one of the hundreds of cases in which confusion in identifying the enemy lost us lives. It is, of course, part of the difficulty of being involved in a civil war.

I learned all of this, of course, much later. On the schoolhouse floor, with our noses scraping the dust, the only thought was how to get out of the bullet-riddled building without getting killed in the process. The bullets cutting through the cardboard-thin walls ripped the floor boards around us, and we all kept wondering why one of us didn't get hit.

I mumbled to Harold that it looked as if we would have a very close blow-by-blow account of battle to give to the American public. But

he didn't hear me because one of the officers suddenly said, "I'm getting out of here," and dove out the window into the courtyard in the direction away from the hill. We all leaped after him and found a stone wall which at least protected us from the rain of fire from the high ground.

In the courtyard we found an uproar of officers and noncoms attempting to dodge the incoming fire and at the same time trying to find their men and produce some order out of the chaos. Some of the soldiers in the courtyard, in their confusion, were firing, without aiming, dangerously close to the GIs racing in retreat down the hill.

Colonel Michaelis, his executive officer, Colonel Farthing, and company commanders were booting reluctant GIs out from under jeeps and trucks and telling them to get to their units up the hill.

A lot of yelling was coming from the opposite corner of the courtyard. I turned my head around in time to see an officer taking careful aim at one of our machine gunners. He winged him. It was a good shot, and an unfortunate necessity. The machine gunner had gone crazy in the terror of the surprise attack and had started firing on our own vehicles and troops with the machine gun.

An officer came up with the gloomy information that several hundred Koreans had landed on the coast a thousand yards [914 meters] to the north.

I started to say something to Martin as he kneeled methodically recording the battle in his notebook. My teeth were chattering uncontrollably, I discovered, and in shame I broke off after the first disgraceful squeak of words.

Then suddenly, for the first time in the war, I experienced the cold, awful certainty that there was no escape. My reactions were commonplace. As with most people who suddenly accept death as inevitable and about to happen, I was simply filled with surprise that this was finally going to happen to me. Then as the conviction grew, I became hard inside and fairly calm. I stopped worrying. Physically the result was that my teeth stopped chattering and my hands stopped shaking. This was a relief, as I would have been extremely embarrassed had anyone caught me in that state.

Fortunately, by the time Michaelis came around the corner and asked, "How are you doing, kid?" I was able to answer in a respectably self-contained tone of voice, "Just fine, sir."

A few minutes later Michaelis, ignoring the bullets, moved suddenly into the middle of the courtyard. He yelled for a cease-fire.

"Let's get organized and find out what we're shooting at," he shouted.

Gradually the scramble in the courtyard turned into a pattern of resistance. Two heavy machine-gun squads crept up to the hill under cover of protecting rifle fire and fixed aim on the enemy trying to swarm down. Platoons and then companies followed. Light mortars were dragged up. The huge artillery guns lowered and fired point-blank at targets only a few hundred yards away.

Finally a reconnaissance officer came up and reported that the soldiers landing on the coasts were not a new enemy force to overwhelm us but South Korean allies. On the hill, soldiers were silencing some of the enemy fire. It was now 7:45. It did not seem possible that so much could have happened since the enemy had struck.

As the intensity of fire let up slightly, soldiers started bringing in the wounded from the hills, carrying them on their backs. I walked over to the aid station. Because of the sudden rush of casualties, everyone was frantically busy.

One medic was running short of plasma but did not dare leave his patients long enough to try to round up some more. I offered to administer the remaining plasma and passed about an hour there, helping out as best I could.

My most vivid memory of the hour is Captain Logan Weston limping into the station with a wound in his leg. He was patched up and promptly turned around and headed for the hills again. Half an hour later he was back with bullets in his shoulder and chest. Sitting on the floor smoking a cigarette, the captain calmly said, "I guess I'd better get a shot of morphine now. These last two are beginning to hurt."

It was at the aid station that I realized we were going to win after all. Injured after injured came in with reports that the North Koreans were "being murdered" and that they were falling back. There was a brief lull in the fighting. Then the enemy, strengthened with fresh reinforcements, struck again. But Michaelis was ready for them this time. At 1:30 in the afternoon, when the last attacking force had been driven back, more than 600 dead North Koreans were counted in the hills behind the schoolhouse. We really had been lucky.

After the schoolhouse battle I usually took a carbine along in our jeep. I'm a lousy shot, but I know I duck when bullets start flying my way. I reasoned that the enemy had the same reaction and that my bullets, however wild, might at least scare him into keeping his head down or might throw his aim off.

Most correspondents carried weapons of some kind. The enemy did not care if they shot unarmed civilians. And the fighting line changed so often that no place near the front lines was safe from sudden enemy attack.

In those days the main difference between a news reporter and a soldier in Korea was that the soldier in combat had to get out of his hole and go after the enemy, whereas the correspondent had the privilege of keeping his head down. It was commonplace for correspondents to be at the company and platoon level, and many of us frequently went on patrol. We felt it was the only honest way of covering the war. The large number of correspondents killed or captured in Korea is testimony of the dangers to which many willingly subjected themselves.

READING REVIEW

1. What were Marguerite Higgins' reactions to the surprise attack?
2. Should correspondents be allowed on the front lines with fighting troops? Why or why not?
3. What effect might first hand news reports about the war have had on the American public?

CHAPTER 38
Returning to Peace and Prosperity
(1945–1960)

230 Truman on the Railroads

With the end of World War II in 1945, the United States began to make the change from a wartime to a peacetime economy—a change known as reconversion. A smooth transition was one of the major goals of Harry S Truman, who became President when Roosevelt died in the spring of the year. As this account indicated, President Truman's task was not an easy one.

READING FOCUS
1. Why was the union threatening to strike?
2. How did Truman propose to settle the railroad strike?

The labor-management pot came to a boil late in 1945. The dire forecasts of massive unemployment had not materialized. But wave upon wave of strikes shut down one major segment of industry after another. Workers battled management for peacetime wages to match their wartime earnings and for pensions, welfare funds, union security, and other fringe benefits.

As the new year of 1946 opened, 900,000 workers, led by Walter Reuther's auto workers, were already on strike. Within weeks they were followed by 700,000 steel workers, 263,000 packinghouse workers, 200,000 electrical workers, 50,000 communications workers. Never before had the nation been faced with such a workers' revolt. The year was to register a total of 116,000,000 man-days of work lost due to strikes, which was three times

Adapted from The Truman Presidency *by Cabell Phillips.*

higher than it ever had been before (and twice as high as in any year since then). In February, an even more menacing prospect darkened the picture—a general strike on the nation's railroads.

Months of fruitless negotiation between the twenty powerful rail brotherhoods and railroad management reached a final dead end on April 18. An arbitration board had proposed to settle the unions' demand for a $2.20-a-day wage increase at $1.28 and to put off a decision on work rules for a year. The carriers accepted and the unions rejected the proposal. Eighteen of the brotherhoods agreed to further negotiation, but the Brotherhood of Locomotive Engineers, headed by Alvaney Johnston, and the Brotherhood of Railroad Trainmen, whose president was A. F. Whitney, said they were through with negotiation. They called a strike of their members in thirty days—for May 18.

Both Johnston and Whitney, paunchy, shrewd old veterans of the labor wars going

President Harry S Truman

back to the turn of the century, were old political friends of the President. They had given him a boost in his 1940 campaign for reelection to the Senate and were among his strongest backers for the Vice Presidential nomination. Until April 18, their defiance of Truman's arm's-length effort to settle their differences with the carriers had been conducted in good spirits. Now their attitude was to stiffen in cold hostility.

With the collapse of bargaining negotiations in April, President Truman took the rail dispute into his own hands and put John R. Steelman to work on the problem as his personal representative. Weeks of consultation and wheedling followed, but to no avail. On Wednesday, May 15, three days before the strike deadline, the President summoned the management representatives and the leaders of the twenty brotherhoods to his office. He talked to them and found that leaders of eighteen of the unions were willing to settle on the basis of the $1.28 arbitration award. But not Whitney and Johnston. Between them, they could bring every wheel on the railroads to a stop, and that was what they proposed to do. Peering coldly through his thick glasses at his two old friends, the President said:

"If you think I'm going to sit here and let you tie up this whole country, you're crazy."

"We've got to go through with it, Mr. President," Whitney said. "Our men are demanding it."

Truman got up from his desk, ending the conference. "All right, I'm going to give you the gun. You've got just 48 hours—until Thursday at this time—to reach a settlement. If you don't, I'm going to take over the railroads in the name of the government."

By now, an angry uproar from Congress and the press was arising from all across the country. The threat of paralysis in the transportation system seemed intolerable.

When the Thursday deadline came without a break in the deadlock, Truman called the railroad leaders again to his office to watch—and to be on public view to the news photographers—as he signed an executive order carrying out his threat of seizure of the railroads. Whitney and Johnson grudgingly agreed to postpone their strike for five days, but not an instant longer. That made the new and final deadline 4 o'clock on the afternoon of Saturday, May 25. On Thursday, Steelman called the

leaders in for another all-day session at the White House. When it was over, Whitney and Johnston continued to hold out. That night they wrote the President a curt letter saying: "We have told you many times that the present agitation among the men is extremely serious and their demands cannot be abandoned. Therefore your offer is unacceptable."

When Harry Truman's mad is up, his eyes glint coldly behind his spectacles and his mouth is a thin, hard line pulled down at the corners. This was the image as he stalked into a specially called meeting of his Cabinet that Friday morning. In the manner of Lincoln and the Emancipation Proclamation, he had summoned them not to ask their views but to tell them what he was going to do. He was going to Congress in person the next day and demand the stiffest labor law in history—one that would give him authority to draft strikers into the armed services without respect to age or dependency when their strike threatened to bring on a national emergency. When the Attorney General raised a question about the constitutionality of such a move, the President brushed him aside. "We'll draft 'em first and think about the law later," he said.

Next, he turned to Charley Ross, his press secretary, and told him to arrange a coast-to-coast radio hookup for him that night so that he could explain to the people what he was about to do.

"Here's what I'm going to say," he snapped. "Get it typed up. I'm going to take the hide right off those so-and-so's."

Ross's blood pressure rocketed as he read what possibly will stand for all time as the angriest public message ever written in a President's own hand. It accused the labor leaders of having tried to sabotage the war effort while America's young men faced death on the battlefield. Now they were sabotaging the peace by "holding a gun to the head of the government." He called on the ex-soldiers who had been his comrades in arms to help "eliminate the Whitneys and the Johnstons," and to "hang a few traitors and make our country safe for democracy."

It is hard to guess what might have happened if this blast had reached the public. Happily, Charley Ross was the kind of old friend who could go to the President and say, "Look, Harry, this just won't do." Which is basically what he did, and with the help of Clark Clifford a greatly toned-down version of the speech was hammered out before the President went on the air at 10 o'clock that night.

Even so, that speech was one of the sharpest attacks on a group of individuals by a President that has ever been uttered. In it Mr. Truman said:

My fellow countrymen—I come before the American people tonight at a time of great crisis.

The crisis of Pearl Harbor was the result of action by a foreign enemy. The crisis tonight is caused by a group of men within our own country who place their private interests above the welfare of the Nation. . . .

I assume that these two men [Johnston and Whitney] know the havoc which their decision has caused, and the even more extreme suffering which will result in the future. . . . This is no contest between labor and management. This is a contest between a small group of men and their government. . . .

If sufficient workers to operate the trains have not returned by 4 P.M. tomorrow, as head of your government I have no alternative but to operate the trains by using every means within my power. . . .

Saturday—the next day—was as packed with drama as a Hollywood cliffhanger. Steelman was locked in a room at the Statler Hotel with Whitney and Johnston in a last-ditch effort to make them relent. Clifford and Sam Rosenman, in the Cabinet room at the White House, were battling against both time and uncertainty trying to draft the President's speech to Congress. Would, or would not, the strike be settled by the time the President got to the Capitol? Steelman telephoned Clifford that an agreement might be signed any minute, but he couldn't be certain.

"That was going to put us in a fix if it were settled at the last minute, and we had this speech," Clifford recalled. So he and Rosenman wrote out a couple of alternative pages that might be substituted at the last minute. The President had already left for the Capitol with the original text when they finished. Hatless, Clifford set out in pursuit, only to find on arrival at the office of Speaker Sam Rayburn that the President had already entered the House Chamber and was about to begin his speech.

Five minutes later, Clifford got a call through to Steelman at the Statler, who told

him breathlessly: "It's signed!"

Clifford scribbled a note on a scrap of paper: "Mr. President, agreement signed, strike over," and gave it to the Secretary of the Senate who scurried across the corridor and into the House Chamber and thrust the note on top of the text from which the President had already begun to read. Truman halted in midsentence and then looked up with a grin:

"Gentlemen, the strike has been settled," he said. There was an outbreak of applause and shouts from the packed Chamber.

READING REVIEW

1. List two reasons why the railroad workers were going to strike.
2. (a) What proposal did President Truman offer to end the railroad strike? (b) How did Congress react to Truman's proposal?
3. In what way did President Truman's actions set a precedent for future negotiations?

231 The Middle of the Road

The election of Dwight D. Eisenhower to the presidency in 1952 brought a Republican to the White House for the first time in twenty years. This victory did not mean, however, that all the programs of the previous Democratic administrations were to be discarded. Instead, Eisenhower and his advisers followed a middle-of-the-road approach, maintaining many New Deal policies but modifying others. They called their philosophy Modern, or New, Republicanism.

The meaning of New Republicanism is outlined here by Arthur Larson, who was Eisenhower's Undersecretary of Labor. He placed New Republicanism midway between two outlooks of the past: the probusiness approach of 1896 (when Republican William McKinley was elected President) and the prolabor approach of 1936 (when Democrat Franklin D. Roosevelt won a second, overwhelming victory).

READING FOCUS

1. According to Larson, what were the characteristics of New Republicanism?
2. How did President Eisenhower establish the "Authentic American Center in politics"?

AMERICA NEEDS

EISENHOWER

An Eisenhower campaign poster

In the nineteenth century, there was not enough government regulation and not enough labor strength and freedom. Result: unruly business expansion at the expense of the rights of people. In the nineteen-thirties there was too much government regulation and not enough business incentive and freedom. Result: deadened business activity and a long depression, accompanied by much humanitarian concern for the victims of the depression.

Now we have as much government activity as is necessary, but not enough to stifle the normal motivations of private enterprise. And we have a higher degree of government concern for the needs of people than ever before in our history. At the same time, the government is pursuing a policy of restoring responsibility to individuals and private groups. This balance, together with the restoration of a better balance between federal and state governments, is allowing all these elements in our society to make their maximum contribution to the common good.

Adapted from A Republican Looks at His Party *by Arthur Larson.*

By bringing together these best forces in American life, President Eisenhower and his associates have, for the first time in our history, discovered and established the Authentic American Center in politics. This is not a Center in the European sense of an uneasy mid-point between large and powerful left-wing and right-wing elements of varying degrees of radicalism. It is a Center in the American sense of a common meeting-ground of the great majority of our people on our own issues. [It is set] against a backdrop of our own history, our own current setting and our own responsibilities for the future.

What are the reasons for this recent emergence of the American Consensus? There are at least five.

First should be noted the common social and historical background which makes this high degree of agreement possible. We have not entered this period trailing centuries of class consciousness and class warfare. We did not, as a nation, start from a beginning-point in which people were divided into aristocrats and serfs, or into rich capitalists and propertyless laborers. Of course, during Revolutionary times there were some "aristocrats" of a sort, but they did their best to play down that fact. And there were struggling laborers, but they in turn never thought of themselves as a fixed "lower class." Above all, the great majority of people, whether farmers, pioneers, or workers, largely identified themselves in the one great enterprise of making their fortunes in a young and expanding country.

Reenforcing this common social origin was an ideological position. The American Revolution was part of a period of brilliant thought on political philosophy. The nation's leaders, in the *Federalist Papers,* the Constitution, and the Declaration of Independence, laid down a solid platform upon which all later American thought could build.

A third reason for the appearance of the Consensus is the gradual moving-together of the interests which have provided our principal conflicts. Responsible labor and business leaders are proclaiming the doctrine that labor and management have far-reaching interests in common. The business community has come to accept a wide range of governmental measures, formerly opposed as "interference," as highly helpful to business. The antagonism between farmers and "Eastern bankers," which loomed so large some years ago, seems to have dissolved. [This may be due to] the increase of ownership by farmers of their own farms, and with agreement on the need for special measures to protect farm income.

These are factors of a long-term or gradual kind which have made the Consensus possible. But why has it appeared just now?

For this there are two main reasons.

One is that there is arisen in the world an ideology—that of the Communists—which actively challenges and menaces almost everything we stand for. Principles that we have always taken for granted as the air we breathe are now denounced and denied over a large part of the world. We may even have allowed ourselves at times to think of these principles as trite—suitable perhaps for a fourth-grade civics course, but not the sort of thing you would make the subject of serious discussion among adults.

Now we suddenly find these familiar ideas to be our rallying-point in a grim struggle for the highest stakes in history. A common danger has forced us all to think about what we really think. In doing so, we are finding that we think more like each other than we ever realized, because the essential alikeness of our thoughts shines out against the looming black cloud of a system of thought we hate.

The second reason why the American Consensus has now so clearly emerged, is that the Eisenhower Administration has defined it, given voice to it and put it into practice.

This point is of crucial importance. If one were to go no further than to show that a wide area of agreement on fundamentals had been achieved, this would no doubt provide an interesting contribution to the history of political science. But it would have no practical impact on current political events. Under our two-party system, the decisive issue becomes: under which party banner does this American Center rally to carry forward these agreed principles?

The answer here given is: the New Republicanism as exemplified by the Eisenhower Administration.

The primary reason is that it is the Eisenhower Administration that "invented" the successful formula, the genius of which lies in bringing together all that is best in American life, whatever its origin.

Historians may someday very well con-clude that the Democratic Party was the party adapted to radical reform and free-wheeling experimentation at a time when things were badly out of joint [during the Great Depression]. They may find that the Republican Party was the party designed to carry a more mature America forward on a course of steady progress and expansion, backed by the broad support of the American Consensus.

Given the continued existence of the two-party system, then, the Center will have to express itself in much the way it did in electing President Eisenhower in 1952. That is, [it will have to add] to the vote of one party both the independent vote and a considerable portion of the vote of the other party.

To summarize: in politics—as in chess—the man who holds the center holds a position of almost unbeatable strength.

READING REVIEW

1. What were characteristics of New Republicanism as stated by Larson?
2. What reasons did Larson give for the emergence of the "American Consensus"?
3. Why, as Larson saw it, was the Democratic Party unable to be the party of the center?

232 McCarthy's Anticommunist Crusade

In the years immediately after World War II, communism was expanding aggressively in Europe and Asia. Was the same thing happening in the United States? Many Americans were afraid of Communist subversion, and their fears were stimulated by Senator Joseph McCarthy of Wisconsin. He accused the government itself of employing "known Communists."

Political reporter Richard Rovere here summarized McCarthy's career as a crusader against communism. He called the Senator a demagogue, meaning a political leader who appealed to people's prejudices and hatreds.

READING FOCUS

1. What did "McCarthyism" mean?
2. How did McCarthy influence politics in America?

At the start of 1950, Senator Joseph McCarthy was unknown to the general public outside Wisconsin. Then, on February 9, 1950, he made a speech in Wheeling, West Virginia. In it he said that the Department of State was full of Communists and that he and the Secretary of State knew their names. Later there was some dispute (there was always dispute whenever he said anything) as to whether he had stated that there were 205, 81, 57, or "a lot" of Communists. But the number was of slight importance. The fact was, he insisted, that Communists "known to the Secretary of State" were "still working and making policy."

A Senate committee was immediately appointed to look into his startling claims. It was the first of five investigations, held by four different committees. They were concerned exclusively with the problem of whether Senator McCarthy was telling the truth about others or others were telling the truth about Senator McCarthy. In the spring of 1950, when Com-

Adapted from "McCarthy's Anti-Communist Crusade" in Senator Joe McCarthy, by Richard Rovere.

Senator Joseph McCarthy

munist power in the Far East was being mobilized for the war in Korea, political life in the United States seemed largely a matter of determining whether American diplomacy was in the hands of traitors.

Barely a month after Wheeling, "McCarthyism" was coined by Herbert Block, the cartoonist who signs himself "Herblock." The word was an oath at first—a synonym for the hatefulness of mudslinging. Later it became, for some, an affirmation, nothing more or less than a militant patriotism.

McCarthyism managed, for a time, to make politics in America seem almost entirely a matter of idiotic chatter about "loyalty risks" and "security risks." A visitor from another civilization would have been forced to conclude that in the United States the measure of political virtue was the number of unworthy civil servants a government managed to dismiss.

The parties seldom argued over the number of gifted people brought into the government. The test was how many rotten apples each had been able to find. "We're kicking the Communists and fellow travelers and security risks out of the Government . . . by the thousands," the Vice-President of the United States said. It happened to be a fact that not one certifiable Communist had been disclosed as working for the government—though quite possibly there were a few. But this was not the worst of it. The worst was that McCarthyism had led us to think that the health of the nation was war against clerks of doubtful patriotism.

McCarthyism was, among other things, a flight from reality. It elevated the ridiculous and ridiculed the important. It outraged common sense and held common sense to be outrageous. It made sages of screwballs and accused wise men of being fools. It diverted attention from the moment and fixed it on the past, which it distorted almost beyond recognition.

The reality it fled, while madly professing to be the only doctrine that faced it, was a terrible one. Only a Communist or an idiot could have denied that the Communist threat to the United States was real and great. The whole Western world was endangered, in those days as in these, by the thrust of Soviet power. Just before McCarthy erupted, it had been increased by the emergence of China as an ally of the Soviet Union and by the Russian mastery of nuclear weapons.

In the early part of the decade, the threat seemed more directly a military one than it does today. Within a few months of McCarthy's first appearance as a national figure, it was established by shellfire and tramping armies in Korea that communism was willing to risk military aggression and war. Communist power in the world was the central reality for the United States in early 1950. The problem we faced was to form and lead an alliance capable of resisting the Soviet thrust and to find strategies of resistance that would not lead to general war and universal destruction.

McCarthyism ignored this reality. "There is only one real issue for the farmer, the laborer, and the businessman—the issue of communism in government," McCarthy said in a campaign speech in 1952. He even insisted that the struggle against world communism was a diversion from the struggle against the domestic conspiracy. Speaking, in 1951, of our intervention in Korea, he said, "So the administration which would not fight communism at home undertook to prove to the American people that it was willing to fight communism abroad."

This sort of talk would have been nonsense at any time. In 1951 and 1952, it was stupid. In the 1930's and early 1940's there had been a strong Communist movement in this country, and Communists within the government. It was unquestionably the government's business to combat the movement. By 1950, this had been fairly effectively done—if, in fact, it had not been overdone. The FBI had just about abandoned its concern with bank robbers to turn its full force on communism. The Communist Party, moreover, was in an advanced state of disintegration—partly because of a spreading disillusionment among its members, partly because the government was locking up its leaders. If the conspiracy was still in any way effective, its effectiveness eluded McCarthy. He could find nothing more exciting than an army dentist [who might be a Communist], a novel by a Communist on a library shelf, and an ex-Communist here and there in some minor agency. He did no better than that.

Here and there, no doubt, there were (and probably still are) Communist agents in the government. Communism is, after all, an international conspiracy. It would be astonishing if a government employing two or three million people harbored no Communists at all.

But the damage that agents can do is limited in any case. In our particular case steps had been taken long before McCarthy came along to uncover as many agents as possible and further to limit the damage any remaining ones could do.

Even if McCarthy had done far better, McCarthyism would still have been trading in dangerous illusions. It was insisting that communism was a danger, not to the United States, but in the United States. In truth it was just the other way about. It was focusing attention on the spy rather than on the power for whom the spy spies. It concentrated on the Communist or ex-Communist dentist in the United States Army rather than on the Red [Soviet] Army, combat-ready and nuclear-armed. We were supposed to dread not Stalin and Khrushchev with their armies and their satellites, not the gathering economic strength of communism, not the appeal of its propaganda in those parts of the world where bread is still scarce—we were to dread the dentist and his promotion to major.

READING REVIEW

1. What did the term "McCarthyism" mean?
2. Cite two ways McCarthy affected politics in America.
3. (a) According to Rovere, what reality did McCarthy ignore? (b) Why was this dangerous?

CHAPTER **Age of**
39 Advancement
(1945–1960)

233 A Critical Look at Television

Television was shown to the public at the New York World's Fair of 1939–40, but the new medium was little more than a curiosity until after World War II. Even in 1947 there were only 10,000 sets and very few hours of programs. Then the industry boomed. By 1957 there were 40 million sets in use, and over 450 television stations.

At first the very existence of television seemed so extraordinary that audiences were content to sit for hours watching dancing cigarette packages and old movies. By the end of the 1950's, however, some people were taking a closer look. One man who didn't like what he saw was Newton Minow, who became chairman of the Federal Communications Commission in 1961. In an address to the National Association of Broadcasters, he broke precedent by criticizing the industry. His speech is remembered for his description of television as "a vast wasteland."

READING FOCUS

1. What aspects of television did Minow criticize?
2. What recommendations did Minow make?

In today's world . . . the old complacent, unbalanced fare of action-adventure and situation comedies is simply not good enough.

Your industry possesses the most powerful voice in America. It has an inescapable duty

---

Adapted from Equal Time: The Private Broadcaster and the Public Interest *by Newton N. Minow, edited by Lawrence Laurent.*

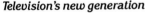

Television's new generation

to make that voice ring with intelligence and with leadership. In a few years this exciting industry has grown from a novelty to an instrument of overwhelming impact on the American people. It should be making ready for the kind of leadership that newspapers and magazines assumed years ago, to make our people aware of their world.

Ours has been called the jet age, the atomic age, the space age. It is also, I submit, the television age. And just as history will decide whether the leaders of today's world employed the atom to destroy the world or rebuild it for mankind's benefit, so will history decide whether today's broadcasters employed their powerful voice to enrich the people or debase them.

Like everybody, I wear more than one hat. I am the Chairman of the FCC. I am also a television viewer and the husband and father of other television viewers. I have seen a great many television programs that seemed to me eminently worthwhile. When television is good, nothing—not the theater, not the magazines or newspapers—nothing is better.

But when television is bad, nothing is worse. I invite you to sit down in front of your television set when your station goes on the air and stay there without a book, magazine, newspaper, profit-and-loss sheet or rating book to distract you—and keep your eyes glued to that set until the station signs off. I can assure you that you will observe a vast wasteland.

You will see a procession of game shows, violence, audience participation shows, formula comedies about totally unbelievable families, blood and thunder, mayhem, violence, sadism, murder, Western badmen, Western good men, private eyes, gangsters, more violence and cartoons. And, endlessly, commercials—many screaming, cajoling and offending. And most of all, boredom. True, you will see a few things you will enjoy. But they will be very, very few. And if you think I exaggerate, try it.

Is there one person in this room who claims that broadcasting can't do better?

Well, a glance at next season's proposed programming can give us little heart. Of seventy-three and a half hours of prime evening time, the networks have tentatively scheduled fifty-nine hours to categories of "action-adventure," situation comedy, variety, quiz and movies.

Is there one network president in this room who claims he can't do better?

Why is so much of television so bad? I have heard many answers: demands of your advertisers; competition for ever higher ratings; the need always to attract a mass audience; the high cost of television programs; the insatiable appetite for programming material—these are some of them. Unquestionably these are tough problems not susceptible to easy answers.

But I am not convinced that you have tried hard enough to solve them.

I do not accept the idea that the present overall programming is aimed accurately at the public taste. The ratings tell us only that some people have their television sets turned on, and of that number, so many are tuned to one channel and so many to another. They don't tell us what the public might watch if they were offered half a dozen additional choices. A rating, at best, is an indication of how many people saw what you gave them. Unfortunately, it does not reveal the depth of the penetration, or the intensity of reaction. And it never reveals what the acceptance would have been if what you gave them had been better—if all the forces of art and creativity and daring and imagination had been unleashed. I believe in the people's good sense and good taste, and I am not convinced that the people's taste is as low as some of you assume.

My concern with the rating services is not with their accuracy. Perhaps they are accurate. I really don't know. What, then, is wrong with the ratings? It's not been their accuracy—it's been their use.

Certainly I hope you will agree that ratings should have little influence where children are concerned. The best estimates indicate that during the hours of 5 to 6 P.M., 60 per cent of your audience is composed of children under twelve. And most young children today, believe it or not, spend as much time watching television as they do in the schoolroom. I repeat—let that sink in—most young children today spend as much time watching television as they do in the schoolroom. It used to be said that there were three great influences on a child: home, school and church. Today there is a fourth great influence, and you ladies and gentlemen control it.

If parents, teachers, and ministers conducted their responsibilities by following the ratings, children would have a steady diet of ice cream, school holidays and no Sunday School. What about your responsibilities? Is there no room on television to teach, to inform, to uplift, to stretch, to enlarge the capacities of our children? Is there no room for programs deepening their understanding of children in other lands? Is there no room for a children's news show explaining something about the world to them at their level of understanding? Is there no room for reading the great literature of the past, teaching them the great traditions of freedom? There are some fine children's shows, but they are drowned out in the massive doses of cartoons, violence and more violence. Must these be your trademarks? Search your consciences and see if you cannot offer more to young beneficiaries, whose future you guide so many hours each and every day.

What about adult programming and ratings? You know, newspaper publishers take popularity ratings too. The answers are pretty clear; it is almost always the comics, followed by the advice-to-the-lovelorn columns. But, ladies and gentlemen, the news is still on the front page of all newspapers, the editorials are not replaced by more comics, the newspapers have not become one long collection of advice to the lovelorn. Yet newspapers do not need a license from the government to be in business—they do not use public property. But in television—where your responsibilities as public trustees are so plain—the moment that the ratings indicate that Westerns are popular, there are new imitations of Westerns on the air faster than television can switch us from Hollywood to New York. Broadcasting cannot continue to live by the numbers. Ratings ought to be the slave of the broadcaster, not his master. And you and I both know that the rating services themselves would agree.

Let me make clear that what I am talking about is balance. I believe that the public interest is made up of many interests. There are many people in this great country, and you must serve all of us. You will get no argument from me if you say that, given a choice between a Western and a symphony, more people will watch the Western. I like Westerns and private eyes too—but a steady diet for the whole country is obviously not in the public interest. We all know that people would more often prefer to be entertained than stimulated or informed. But your obligations are not satisfied if you look only to popularity as a test of what to broadcast. You are not only in show business; you are free to communicate ideas as well as relaxation. You must provide a wider range of choices, more diversity, more alternatives. It is not enough to cater to the nation's whims—you must also serve the nation's needs.

And I would add this—that if some of you persist in a relentless seach for the highest rating and the lowest common denominator, you may very well lose your audience. Because the people are wise, wiser than some of the broadcasters—and politicians—think.

READING REVIEW

1. What did Minow dislike about television?
2. (a) According to Minow, what did the television rating procedure indicate? (b) How did he think ratings should be used?
3. (a) What would Minow have done to improve television programming? (b) Do you agree with his proposals? Why or why not?

234 The Other America

The United States in the 1950's experienced greater prosperity than ever before. By 1956, for example, the average family had one and a half times the purchasing power it had had in 1929. Times were good for the majority of the American people. Things were very different, though for a large minority. These were the people Michael Harrington called "the other America"—the poor.

READING FOCUS

1. Why did Harrington say poor people were "invisible"?
2. What did Harrington propose to solve the problem of poverty?

There is a familiar America. It is celebrated in speeches and advertised on television and

Adapted from The Other America *by Michael Harrington.*

in the magazines. It has the highest mass standard of living the world has ever known.

In the 1950's this America worried about itself, yet even its anxieties were products of abundance. There was worry about Madison Avenue and [the role of advertising]. There was discussion of the emotional suffering taking place in the suburbs. In all this, there was an assumption that the basic grinding economic problems had been solved in the United States. In this theory the nation's problems were no longer a matter of basic human needs, of food, shelter, and clothing. Now they were seen as a question of learning to live decently amid luxury.

While this discussion was carried on, there existed another America. In it dwelt somewhere between 40,000,000 and 50,000,000 citizens of this land. They were poor. They still are.

To be sure, the other America is not poor in the same sense as those poor nations where millions cling to hunger as a defense against starvation. This country has escaped such extremes. That does not change the fact that tens of millions of Americans are, at this very moment, maimed in body and spirit, existing at levels beneath those necessary for human decency. If these people are not starving, they are hungry, and sometimes fat with hunger, for that is what cheap foods do. They are without adequate housing and education and medical care.

The millions who are poor in the United States tend to become increasingly invisible. Here is a great mass of people, yet it takes an effort of the intellect and will even to see them.

The other America, the America of poverty, is hidden today in a way that it never was before. Its millions are socially invisible to the rest of us. One must begin a description of the other America by understanding why we do not see it.

Poverty is often off the beaten track. It always has been. The ordinary tourist never left the main highway, and today he rides interstate turnpikes. He does not go into the valleys of Pennsylvania. He does not see the company houses in rows, the rutted roads (the poor always have bad roads whether they live in the city, in towns, or on farms), where everything is black and dirty. And even if he were to pass through such a place by accident, the tourist would not meet the unemployed men in the bar or the women coming home from a sweat-shop.

Then, too, beauty and myths are perennial masks of poverty. The traveler comes to the Appalachians in the lovely season. He sees the hills, the streams, the foliage—but not the poor. Or perhaps he looks at a run-down mountain house and decides that "those people" are truly fortunate to be living the way they are and that they are lucky to be exempt from the strains and tensions of the middle class. The only problem is that "those people" are under-educated, underprivileged, lack medical care, and are in the process of being forced from the land into a life in the cities, where they are misfits.

These are normal and obvious causes of the invisibility of the poor. They operated a generation ago; they will be functioning a generation hence. It is more important to understand that the very development of American society is creating a new kind of blindness about poverty. The poor are increasingly slipping out of the very experience and consciousness of the nation.

If the middle class never did like ugliness and poverty, it was at least aware of them. "Across the tracks" was not a very long way to go. Occasionally, almost everyone passed through the Negro ghetto or the blocks of tenements, if only to get downtown to work or to entertainment.

Now the American city has been transformed. The poor still inhabit the miserable housing in the central area, but they are increasingly isolated from contact with, or sight of, anybody else. The failures, the unskilled, the disabled, the aged, and the minorities are right there, across the tracks, where they have always been. But hardly anyone else is.

In short, the very development of the American city has removed poverty from the living, emotional experience of millions upon millions of middle-class Americans. Living out in the suburbs, it is easy to assume that ours is, indeed an affluent society.

This new segregation of poverty is compounded by a well-meaning ignorance. A good many concerned and sympathetic Americans are aware that there is much discussion of urban renewal. Suddenly, driving through the city, they notice that a familiar slum has been torn down and that there are towering, modern buildings where once there had been tene-

An "America" familiar to too many

ments or hovels. There is a warm feeling of satisfaction, of pride in the way things are working out: the poor, it is obvious, are being taken care of.

The irony in this is that the truth is nearly the exact opposite to the impression. The total impact of the various housing programs in postwar America has been to squeeze more and more people into existing slums.

Clothes make the poor invisible too: America has the best-dressed poverty the world has ever known. For a variety of reasons, the benefits of mass production have been spread much more evenly in this area than in many others. It is much easier in the United States to be decently dressed than it is to be decently housed, fed or doctored. Even people with terribly depressed incomes can look prosperous.

Then, many of the poor are the wrong age to be seen. A good number of them (over 8,000,000) are sixty-five years of age or better; an even larger number are under eighteen. The aged members of the other America are often sick, and they cannot move. Another group of them live out their lives in loneliness and frustration. They sit in rented rooms, or else they stay close to a house in a neighborhood that has completely changed from the old days. Indeed, one of the worst aspects of poverty among the aged is that these people are out of sight and out of mind, and alone.

The young are somewhat more visible, yet they too stay close to their neighborhoods. Sometimes they advertise their poverty through a newspaper story about a gang killing. But generally they do not disturb the quiet streets of the middle class.

And finally, the poor are politically invisible. It is one of the cruelest ironies of social life in advanced countries that the dispossessed at the bottom of society are unable to speak for themselves. The people of the other America do not, by far and large, belong to unions, to fraternal organizations, or to political parties. They are without lobbies of their own; they put forward no legislative program. They have no face; they have no voice.

Thus, there is not even a cynical political motive for caring about the poor, as in the old days. Because the slums are no longer centers of powerful political organizations, the politicians need not really care about their inhabitants. The slums are no longer visible to the middle class, so much of the idealistic urge to fight for those who need help is gone. Only the social agencies have a really direct involvement with the other America, and they are without any great political power. . . .

Only the larger society, with its help and resources, can really make it possible for these people to help themselves. Yet those who could make the difference too often refuse to act because of their ignorance and smugness. They view the effects of poverty—above all, the warping of the will and spirit that is a consequence of being poor—as choices. Understanding is an important step in breaking down this prejudice.

The United States contains an affluent society within its borders. Millions and tens of millions enjoy the highest standard of life the world has ever known.

But when all is said and done, after one reads the facts, either there are anger and shame, or there are not. And, as usual, the fate of the poor hangs upon the decision of the better-off. If this anger and shame are not forthcoming, someone can write a book about the other America a generation from now and it will be the same, or worse.

READING REVIEW

1. According to Harrington, what was the "other America"?
2. Name three reasons why Harrington thought the poor in the United States tended to be increasingly "invisible."
3. What solution did Harrington offer to eliminate poverty in the United States?
4. What do you think of Harrington's solution?

235 Desegregation: On the Front Lines

A landmark in the history of American civil rights was the 1954 Supreme Court decision, *Brown v. Board of Education of Topeka.* The judges ruled that segregating black students from white students in public education was unconstitutional. They urged that schools should be desegregated "with all deliberate speed."

Desegregation went smoothly in some communities, but elsewhere it was accompanied by protests and violence. One such place was Little Rock, Arkansas. When nine black students attempted to enter Central High School in the fall of 1957, Governor Orval Faubus brought in troops to keep them out, and screaming mobs kept the town in an uproar. The students were able to go to school only when President Eisenhower federalized the National Guard—that is, brought it under federal control—and sent in paratroopers.

The story of the students' first day in school—September 25, 1957—is told here by Daisy Bates, then president of the Arkansas chapter of the National Association for the Advancement of Colored People. Although the students did enter the school, the struggle was far from over. The next year Little Rock's schools were closed down entirely. It was a long time before desegregation was an accomplished fact in the city.

READING FOCUS

1. What was the significance of this event for American history?
2. How did the black students feel about their long awaited "victory"?

In midafternoon [of September 24] the city was electrified by the news that President Eisenhower had federalized all ten thousand men of the Arkansas National Guard units. . . . The Secretary of Defense ordered 1,000 paratroopers to Little Rock from Fort Campbell, Kentucky. The soldiers were part of the 101st Airborne "Screaming Eagle" Division of the 327th Infantry Regiment.

When the Negro and white paratroopers arrived at Camp Robinson, an Army base in the suburb of North Little Rock, there was a general exodus of newsmen from our house. One reporter called back to me, "Come on, Mrs. Bates, aren't you going to see the troops enter the city?"

"No," I replied, "but thank God they're here."

After the newsmen were gone, I walked out onto the lawn. I heard the deep drone of big planes, and it sounded like music to my ears. I walked around the yard. I saw other women standing in their yards, looking upward, listening. I heard the subdued laughter of children and realized how long it had been since I'd heard that sound. Kept within doors in recent days, they now spilled out onto yards and driveways. From an open kitchen doorway Mrs. Anderson was heard singing, "Nobody knows the trouble I've seen . . ." A fear-paralyzed city had begun to stir again.

Around 6 P.M., the long line of trucks, jeeps, and staff cars entered the heart of the city to the wailing sound of sirens and the dramatic flashing of lights from the police cars escorting the caravan to Central High School. The "Battle of Little Rock" was on.

*   *   *   *

I knew the parents [of the schoolchildren were] waiting to hear from me, [to find out if] the children would be going back to Central tomorrow. I delayed calling them. I was awaiting a call from Superintendent [of Schools Virgil T.] Blossom. Finally, about 10 P.M., I called the parents to tell them I had not heard from Mr. Blossom. I assumed that the mob would be at the school the next morning and therefore decided that the children could not be sent to Central the next day, troops or not.

From The Long Shadow of Little Rock *by Daisy Bates.*

Shortly after midnight Mr. Blossom telephoned. "Mrs. Bates, I understand you instructed the children that they were not to go to Central in the morning."

"That is correct."

"But General Walker said that he is here to put the children in school. So you must have them at your house by eight thirty in the morning." Major General Edwin A. Walker, chief of the Arkansas Military District, had been put in command of the 101st Airborne Division and newly federalized Arkansas militia.

"I can't," I said. "I can't reach them. We have an agreement that if I want them, I will call *before* midnight. In order to get some sleep and avoid the harassing calls, they take their phones off the hook after midnight." How I wish I had done the same, I thought wearily, as I listened to the Superintendent's urgent tones. "I suppose I could go to each home, but I can't go alone," I said.

"I'll call Hawkins and Christophe and ask them to accompany you," Mr. Blossom said. "You may expect them shortly." Edwin Hawkins was Principal of Dunbar Junior High School and L. M. Christophe was Principal of Horace Mann High School, both Negro schools.

At about 1 A.M. the three of us set out. Our first stop was some eight blocks away, the home of fifteen-year-old Gloria Ray. We knocked for what seemed ten minutes before we got an answer. The door opened about three inches exposing the muzzle of a shotgun. Behind it stood Gloria's father.

"What do you want now?" was his none-too-cordial greeting, as he looked straight at me. He forgot—I hope that was the reason—to remove his finger from the trigger or at least to lower the gun.

My eyes were fixed on the muzzle, and I could sense that Hawkins and Christophe, standing behind me, were riveted in attention. In my most pleasant, friendliest voice, and trying to look at him instead of the gun, I said that the children were to be at my house by eight thirty the next morning, and that those were the instructions of Superintendent Blossom.

"I don't care if the President of the United States gave you those instructions!" he said irritably. "I won't let Gloria go. She's faced two mobs and that's enough."

Both Mr. Christophe and Mr. Hawkins assured him that with the Federal troops there, the children would be safe. We all, of course, added that the decision was up to him. At this point I asked if he wouldn't mind lowering his gun. He did. I told him if he changed his mind to bring Gloria to my house in the morning. Somewhat shakily we made our way to the car.

"Good Lord," sighed Mr. Christophe, "are we going to have to go through this with all nine sets of parents?"

The children's homes were widely scattered over Little Rock, and so our tour took better than three hours. Our encounter with Mr. Ray impressed on our minds the need to identify ourselves immediately upon entering the grounds of each home. But the cautious parents still greeted us with gun in hand although they were a little more calm than Mr. Ray, and accepted the change in plans without objection.

At eight twenty-five the next morning, all the children except Gloria had arrived. My phone rang. "What time are we to be there, Mrs. Bates?" It was Gloria.

"They're all here now."

"Wait for me!" she said. "I'll be right over!"

In less than ten minutes, Mr. Ray, shy and smiling, led Gloria into the house. He looked down at his daughter with pride. "Here, Daisy, she's yours. She's determined to go. Take her. You seem to have more influence over her than I have, anyhow."

No sooner had Gloria joined the group than I was called to the telephone. A school official wanted to know whether the children were there. "All nine," I answered. I was told that a convoy for them was on its way.

*   *   *   *

Soon jeeps were rolling down Twenty-eighth Street. Two passed our house and parked at the end of the block, while two remained at the other end of the block. Paratroopers quickly jumped out and stood across the width of the street at each end of the block—those at the western end standing at attention facing west, and those at the eastern end facing east.

An Army station wagon stopped in front of our house. While photographers, perched on the tops of cars and rooftops, went into action, the paratrooper in charge of the detail leaped out of the station wagon and started up our driveway. As he approached, I heard Minni-

The Arkansas National Guard escorts black students into Central High School.

392

jean say gleefully, "Oh, look at them, they're so—so soldierly! It gives you goose pimples to look at them!" And then she added solemnly, "For the first time in my life, I feel like an American citizen."

The officer was at the door, and as I opened it, he saluted and said, his voice ringing through the sudden quiet of the living-room where a number of friends and parents of the nine had gathered to witness this moment in history: "Mrs. Bates, we're ready for the children. We will return them to your home at three thirty o'clock."

I watched them follow him down the sidewalk. Another paratrooper held open the door of the station wagon, and they got in. Turning back into the room, my eyes none too dry, I saw the parents with tears of happiness in their eyes as they watched the group drive off.

* * * *

Tense and dramatic events were taking place in and around the school while the Negro pupils were being transported by the troops from my home to Central High.

A block from the school, a small group of hardcore segregationists ignored Mayor James Meyers' orders to disperse peacefully and return to their homes. The major [in charge of the troops] repeated the command when the surly, angry crowd refused to disperse. He was forced to radio for additional help. About thirty soldiers answered the emergency call "on the double," wearing steel helmets, carrying bayonet-fixed rifles, their gas masks in readiness, and "walkie-talkies" slung over their shoulders.

The soldiers lowered their rifles and moved slowly and deliberately into the crowd. The mob quickly gave way, shouting insults at the troops in the process. In a matter of minutes the streets, which for days had been littered with hate-filled mobs, cigarette butts, half-eaten sandwiches, and used flash bulbs, were strangely quiet.

At 9:22 A.M. the nine Negro pupils marched solemnly through the doors of Central High School, surrounded by twenty-two soldiers. An Army helicopter circled overhead. Around the massive brick schoolhouse 350 paratroopers stood grimly at attention. Scores of reporters, photographers, and TV cameramen made a mad dash for telephones, typewriters, and TV studios. Within minutes a world that had been holding its breath learned that the nine pupils, protected by the might of the United States military, had finally entered the "never-never land."

When classes ended that afternoon, the troops escorted the pupils to my home. Here we held the first of many conferences that were to take place during the hectic months ahead.

I looked into the face of each child, from the frail ninety-pound Thelma Mothershed with a cardiac condition, to the well-built, sturdy Ernest Green, oldest of them all. They sat around the room, subdued and reflective—and understandably so. Too much had happened to them in these frenzied weeks to be otherwise.

I asked if they had a rough day. Not especially, they said. Some of the white pupils were friendly and had even invited them to lunch. Some were indifferent, and only a few showed open hostility.

Minnijean Brown reported that she had been invited by her classmates to join the glee club.

"Then why the long faces?" I wanted to know.

"Well," Ernest spoke up, "you don't expect us to be jumping for joy, do you?"

Someone said, "But Ernest, we *are* in Central, and that shouldn't make us feel sad exactly."

"Sure we're in Central," Ernest shot back, somewhat impatiently. "But how did we get in? We got in, finally, because we were protected by paratroops. Some victory!" he said sarcastically.

"Are you sorry," someone asked him, "that the President sent the troops?"

"No," said Ernest. "I'm only sorry it had to be that way."

READING REVIEW

1. How did Daisy Bates react to President Eisenhower sending the National Guard to escort the black students to Central High?
2. How did she describe the students before and after their first day?
3. How did this event change the course of black–white relations in America?
4. Why did Ernest feel that finally getting to Central High was a hollow victory? Do you agree with him? Why or why not?

Into a New Era

CHAPTER
40 Domestic Developments
(1960 to the Present)

236 An Appraisal of Kennedy

Young, handsome, and well-educated, President Kennedy inspired many Americans to take an active interest in government and politics. His energy and idealism also made many Americans believe that the increasingly serious problems facing the nation in the 1960's could and would be solved. Thus President Kennedy's tragic death in 1963 seemed, for a time, to mark an end to many of America's hopes and dreams.

Theodore Sorensen, one of the President's advisers, tried to analyze the special appeal that Kennedy had for so many Americans. Part of the President's popularity was based on Kennedy's "style," or way of doing things. In his book about Kennedy, from which the following selection is taken, Sorensen wrote: "The Kennedy style was special—the grace, the wit, the elegance. . . . But what mattered most to him, and what in my opinion will matter most to history, was the substance—the strength of his ideas and ideals, his courage and judgment."

READING FOCUS

1. How did Kennedy's death affect historians' perception of his presidency?
2. How was Kennedy different from the other Presidents?

How will history judge him? It is too early to say. I am too close to say. But history will surely record that his achievements were beyond his years. In an eloquent letter to President Kennedy on nuclear testing, Prime Minister Harold Macmillan of Britain once wrote: "It is not the things one did in one's life that one regrets, but rather the opportunities missed." It can be said of John Kennedy that he missed very few opportunities.

In less than three years he presided over a new era in American race relations, a new era in American-Soviet relations, a new era in our Latin-American relations, a new era in fiscal and economic policy, and a new era in space exploration. His Presidency helped start the longest and strongest period of economic expansion in our peacetime history. It helped start the largest and swiftest build-up of our defensive strength in peacetime history. And it brought new and enlarged roles for the federal government in higher education, mental illness, civil rights, and the conservation of human and natural resources.

Some moves were dramatic, such as the Cuban missile crisis, the Test Ban Treaty, the Peace Corps, and the Alliance for Progress. Some were small day-by-day efforts on Berlin or Southeast Asia, where no real progress could be claimed. Some were simply holding our own. No nation slipped into the Communist orbit, no nuclear war raised havoc on our planet, no new recession set back our economy. But generally Kennedy was not content to hold his own. His efforts were devoted to turning the country around, starting it in new direc-

---

Adapted from Kennedy *by Theodore C. Sorensen.*

President John F. Kennedy delivers his Inaugural Address.

tions, getting it moving again. "He believed," said his wife, "that one man can make a difference and that every man should try." He left the nation a whole new set of basic propositions—on freedom now instead of someday for the black American—on winding down instead of "winning" the Cold War—on the unthinkability instead of the inevitability of nuclear war—on cutting taxes in times of deficit—on battling poverty in times of prosperity.

For the most part, on November 22, these problems had not been solved and these projects had not been completed. Even most of those completed will impress historians a generation from now only if this generation makes the most of them.

But I suspect that history will remember John Kennedy for what he started as well as for what he completed. The forces he released in this world will be felt for generations to come. The standards he set, the goals he outlined and the talented people he attracted to politics and public service will influence his country's course for at least ten years.

People will remember not only what he did but what he stood for. This, too, may help the historians assess his Presidency. He stood for excellence in an era of indifference—for hope in an era of doubt—for placing public service ahead of private interests—for understanding between East and West, black and white, labor and management. He had confidence in people and gave them confidence in the future.

It will not be easy for historians to compare John Kennedy with those who came before him and after him. He was unique in his effect on the office. He was the first to be elected at so young an age, the first of the Catholic faith, the first to reach for the moon and beyond, the first to announce that all racial segregation and discrimination must be abolished as a matter of right, the first to meet our enemies in a potentially nuclear confrontation, and the first to take a solid step toward nuclear arms control. And he was the first to die at so young an age.

All his life he was a winner until November 1963. In battle he became a hero. In literature he won a Pulitzer Prize. In politics he reached the Presidency. His inaugural address, his wife, his children, his policies, his conduct of crises, all reflected his pursuit of excellence.

History and the future must decide. Usually they reserve greatness for those who win great wars, not those who prevent them. But in my unobjective view I think it will be difficult to measure John Kennedy by any ordinary historical yardstick. For he was an extraordinary man, an extraordinary politican, and an extraordinary President. It is my belief that no scale of good and bad Presidents can rate John Fitzgerald Kennedy. A mind so free of fear and myth and prejudice, so opposed to clichés, so unwilling to fool or be fooled, to accept or reflect mediocrity, is rare in our world—and even rarer in American politics.

Without lessening any of the great men who have held the Presidency in this century, I do not see how John Kennedy could be ranked below any one of them.

His untimely and violent death will affect the judgment of historians. The danger is that it will turn his greatness into legend. Even though he was himself almost a legendary figure in life, Kennedy was a constant critic of the myth. It would be an ironic twist of fate if his martyrdom should now make a myth of the mortal man.

In my view, the man was greater than the legend. His life, not his death, created his greatness. In November 1963, some saw it for the first time. Others realized that they had too casually accepted it. Others mourned that they had not admitted it to themselves before.

READING REVIEW

1. What two events of Kennedy's Presidency did Sorensen feel were the most dramatic? Why?
2. According to Sorensen, what accomplishments of President Kennedy's administration would historians remember? Why?
3. (a) Why did Sorensen say it would not be easy for historians to compare Kennedy to other Presidents? (b) Do you agree with Sorensen's analysis? Why or why not?

237 Johnson on Equal Rights for All

When Lyndon Johnson became President after President Kennedy's assassination, he promised the nation he would continue President Kennedy's programs. Almost immediately he called on Congress to pass the civil rights bill that Kennedy had proposed. After a bitter struggle in the Senate, the Civil Rights Act of 1964 was passed into law in July of 1964. Now, for the first time, all black Americans were guaranteed the right to register to vote.

However, some voter registration drives in the South led to violence. In Selma, Alabama, a Unitarian minister was killed in March 1965 after he had taken part in a protest march. A week later, on March 15, Johnson spoke before Congress, proposing a second civil rights bill. The following selection is taken from that speech—a moving statement of Johnson's belief in American democracy.

READING FOCUS

1. Why did President Johnson feel the right to vote is the most important right of Americans?
2. What were President Johnson's goals?

I speak tonight for the dignity of all human beings and the destiny of democracy. I urge every member of both parties, Americans of all religions and of all colors, from every section of this country, to join me in that cause.

At times, history and fate meet at a single time in a single place to shape a turning point in people's unending search for freedom.

So it was at Lexington and Concord. So it was a hundred years ago at Appomattox. So it was last week in Selma, Alabama.

There, long-suffering men and women peacefully protested the denial of their rights as Americans. Many were brutally assaulted. One good man—a man of God—was killed.

There is no cause for pride in what has happened in Selma. There is no cause for self-satisfaction in the long denial of equal rights of millions of Americans. But there is cause for hope and for faith in our democracy in what is happening here tonight.

For the cries of pain and the hymns and protests of oppressed people have brought together all the majesty of this great government—the government of the greatest nation on earth.

Our mission is at once the oldest and the most basic of this country—to right wrong, to do justice, to serve people.

In our time we have come to live with the moments of great crisis. Our lives have been marked with debate about great issues, issues of war and peace, issues of prosperity and depression.

But rarely in any time does an issue show the secret heart of America itself. Rarely do we meet a challenge, not to our growth or abundance, our welfare or security, but rather to the values, purposes, and meaning of our beloved nation.

The issue of equal rights for American Negroes is such an issue.

Adapted from "The Right to Vote" by Lyndon B. Johnson, in Vital Speeches of the Day, April 1, 1965.

There is no Negro problem. There is no southern problem. There is no northern problem. There is only an American problem.

And we meet here tonight as Americans—not as Democrats or Republicans—to solve that problem.

This was the first nation in the history of the world to be founded with a purpose. The great statements of that purpose still sound in every American heart, North and South: "All men are created equal." "Govenment by consent of the governed." "Give me liberty or give me death."

Those are not just clever words. Those are not just empty theories. In their name Americans have fought and died for two hundred years.

Those words are promised to all citizens so they can share in the dignity of all human beings. This dignity cannot be found in people's possessions. It cannot be found in their power or in their position. It really rests on their right to be treated as a person equal in opportunity to all others.

It says that they shall share in freedom. They shall choose their leaders, educate their children, and provide for their family according to their ability and their merits as human beings.

To apply any other test, to deny people their hopes because of their color, race, religion, or place of birth is not only to do injustice. It is to deny America and to dishonor the dead who gave their lives for American freedom.

Our forebears believed that if this noble view of the rights of people was to flourish it must be rooted in democracy. The most basic right of all was the right to choose your own leaders.

The history of this country in large part is the history of the expansion of that right to all of our people. Many of the issues of civil rights are very complex and most difficult. But about this there can and should be no argument. Every American citizen must have an equal right to vote.

There is no reason which can excuse the denial of that right. There is no duty which weighs more heavily on us than the duty we have to insure that right. Yet the harsh fact is that in many places in this country men and women are kept from voting simply because they are Negroes.

This bill will establish a simple, uniform standard for voting. It will provide for citizens to be registered by officials of the United States government, if state officials refuse to register them.

It will eliminate tiresome, unnecessary lawsuits which delay the right to vote.

Finally, this legislation will insure that properly registered individuals are not prohibited from voting.

There is no constitutional issue here. The command of the Constitution is plain. There is no moral issue. It is wrong—deadly wrong—to deny any of your fellow Americans the right to vote in this country.

There is no issue of state's rights or national rights. There is only the struggle for human rights.

On this issue, there must be no delay, no hesitation, no compromise with our purpose.

We cannot, we must not, refuse to protect the right of every American to vote in every election that he or she may desire to participate in.

But even if we pass this bill the battle will not be over.

What happened in Selma is part of a far larger movement which reaches into every section and state of America. It is the effort of American Negroes to secure for themselves the full blessings of American life.

Their cause must be our cause too. Because

President Lyndon B. Johnson

it's not just Negroes, but really it's all of us, who must overcome the crippling legacy of bigotry and injustice.

And we shall overcome.

As a man whose roots go deeply into southern soil, I know how agonizing racial feelings are. I know how difficult it is to change the attitudes and the structure of our society. But a century has passed—more than a hundred years—since the Negroes were freed.

And they are not fully free tonight.

Negroes are not the only victims. How many white children have gone without an education? How many white families have lived in poverty? How many white lives have been scarred by fear, because we wasted energy to maintain the barriers of hatred and terror?

And so I say to all of you here and to all in the nation tonight that those who appeal to you to hold on to the past do so at the cost of denying you your future. This great, rich, restless country can offer opportunity and education and hope to all—all, black and white, all, North and South, sharecropper and city dweller.

These are the enemies: Poverty, ignorance, disease. They are our enemies, not our fellow humans, not our neighbors. And these enemies too—poverty, disease, and ignorance—we shall overcome.

There is really no part of America where the promise of equality has been fully kept. In Buffalo as well as in Birmingham, in Philadelphia as well as in Selma. Americans are struggling for their freedom. This is one nation. What happens in Selma and Cincinnati is a matter of concern to every American.

At the real heart of the battle for equality is a deep-seated belief in the democratic process. Equality does not depend on the force of arms or on tear gas. It depends upon the force of moral right, on respect for law and order.

The bill I am presenting to you will be known as a civil rights bill.

But in a larger sense, most of the program I am recommending is a civil rights program. Its object is to open the city of hope to all people of all races. All Americans must have the right to vote. And we are going to give them that right.

All Americans must have the privileges of citizenship, regardless of race. And they are going to have those privileges.

I would like to remind you that to exercise these privileges takes much more than just legal right. It requires a trained mind and a healthy body. It requires a decent home and the chance to find a job and the opportunity to escape from poverty.

Of course people cannot contribute to the nation if they are never taught to read or write; if their bodies are stunted from hunger; if their sickness goes uncared for; if their life is spent in hopeless poverty, just drawing a welfare check.

So we want to open the gates to opportunity. But we're also going to give all our people, black and white, the help that they need to walk through those gates.

My first job after college was as a teacher in Cotulla, Texas, in a small Mexican-American school. Few of my students could speak English and I couldn't speak much Spanish.

My students were poor and they often came to class without breakfast. They knew, even in their youth, the pain of prejudice. They never seemed to know why people disliked them, but they knew it was so, because I saw it in their eyes.

I often walked home late in the afternoon, after classes were finished, wishing there was more that I could do. But all I knew was to teach them the little that I knew, hoping that it might help them against the hardships that lay ahead.

Somehow you never forget what poverty and hatred can do when you see its scars on the hopeful face of a young child.

I never thought then, in 1928, that I would be standing here in 1965. It never occurred to me that I might have the chance to help the sons and daughters of those students, and to help people like them all over this country.

But now I do have that chance. And I'll let you in on a secret—I mean to use it.

And I hope that you will use it with me. This is the richest, most powerful country which ever occupied this globe. The might of past empires is little compared to ours. But I do not want to be the President who built empires, or sought grandeur, or extended authority. I want to be the President who educated young children to the wonders of their world.

I want to be the President who helped to feed the hungry and to prepare them to be taxpayers instead of tax eaters.

I want to be the President who helped the

poor to find their own way and who protected the right of every citizen to vote in every election.

I want to be the President who helped to end hatred among people and who promoted love among the people of all races, all regions, and all parties.

READING REVIEW

1. **(a)** Why did Johnson believe voting is the most basic right of all Americans? **(b)** Do you agree? Why or why not?
2. Summarize President Johnson's goals.
3. **(a)** Do you think that Johnson achieved his goals? **(b)** Cite evidence from the textbook to support your opinion.

238 The Moon Landing

One of the proudest American achievements of the 1960's was the successful flight of Apollo 11, which carried the first astronauts to the moon. The project had been started under President Kennedy in 1961. Several Apollo flights had taken place during the Presidency of Lyndon Johnson. And it was President Nixon who called the astronauts after the flight of Apollo 11 to congratulate them on their accomplishment. "For one priceless moment," he said, "all the people on earth are truly one."

Apollo 11 was launched from Cape Canaveral, Florida, on July 15, 1969. On board were Neil Armstrong, Edwin Aldrin, and Michael Collins. On July 20, Armstrong and Aldrin, in a detachable lunar module, landed on the surface of the moon. In the following selection, Armstrong discussed the flight and landing.

READING FOCUS

1. According to Armstrong, what were the most significant aspect of the Apollo 11 mission?
2. What features of the moon impressed Armstrong most?

Our goal, when we were assigned to this flight last January, seemed almost impossible. There

Adapted from "The Moon Had Been Awaiting Us a Long Time" by Neil Armstrong in Life, *August 22, 1969.* © *1969*

Apollo II astronauts on the surface of the moon

were a lot of unknowns, unproved ideas, unproved equipment. The lunar module had never flown. There were many things about the lunar surface we did not know. It remained to be seen whether it was possible for the ground to communicate simultaneously with two vehicles up there. I honestly suspected, at the time, that it was unlikely that Apollo 11 would make the first lunar landing flight. There was just too much to learn—too many chances for problems.

Then came the flights of Apollo 9 and 10, which were so magnificently successful. It began to seem that we really would get a chance at a landing. From that point on, preparations became relentless.

We were not concerned with safety, specifically, in these preparations. We were concerned with mission success, with the accomplishment of what we set out to do. I felt a successful lunar landing might inspire people around the world to believe that impossible goals really are possible, that there really is hope for solutions to humanity's problems.

We were very conscious of the symbolism of our exploration, and we wanted the small things which go along with a flight to reflect our very serious approach to the business of flying the lunar mission.

The patch we designed was meant to symbolize the peaceful American attempt at a lunar landing. We wanted the names we chose for communication to have both dignity and symbolism. The name Eagle [for the lunar module] was intended to reflect a degree of national pride in the enterprise. The name Columbia [for the space capsule] is also a national symbol. It reflected, too, the aura of adventure, exploration, and seriousness with which Columbus took on his assignment.

The day of the lunar landing was a long one and there was a lot to do every minute. We got up at 5:30 that morning and touched down about 3:20 P.M. Houston time. Our ignition for powered descent was smooth and right on time. But at about 30,000 feet [9,144 meters] we began to have computer problems. They seem to have come from overloading the computer. Mission Control analyzed the problem and the cause, and advised us promptly that we could safely override the alarms and continue our descent.

From about 30,000 feet [9,144 meters] down to 5,000 feet [1,524 meters] we were totally absorbed in analyzing and dealing with this problem, and checking our instruments. Our attention was thus taken away from the windows and from identification of landmarks outside. The first chance we had to spend some time looking out was from below 3,000 feet [914.4 meters]. It was difficult at that height to see very far ahead. The only landmark we could see was a very large, very impressive crater.

At first we considered landing just short of it. That location seemed clearly to be where our automatic guidance system was taking us. By the time we were down around 1,000 feet [305 meters], however, it was quite obvious that Eagle was attempting to land in a most undesirable area. I had an excellent view of the crater and the boulder field out of the left window. There were boulders as big as Volkswagens all around.

The rocks seemed to be coming up at us awfully fast. We reduced our descent rate from 10 to 3 feet [3 to .9 meters] per second. It would have been interesting to land in that boulder field from a scientific point of view. I was tempted, but my better judgment took over. We pitched forward to a level altitude, and scanned the surface to the west for a better touchdown area. The one we chose was only a couple of hundred feet square, about the size of a big house lot. It was ringed on one side by some fairly good-sized craters and on the other with a field of small rocks, but it still looked as if we could live with it. I put Eagle down there.

I am told that my heartbeat increased noticeably during the lunar descent, but I would really be disturbed with myself if it hadn't. During the final seconds of descent, our engine kicked up a substantial amount of lunar dust which blew out almost parallel to the surface, at very high speeds. Normally on earth if you kick up dust it hangs in the air and settles back to the ground very slowly. But since there is no atmosphere on the moon, dust sails away in a flat, low path, leaving a clear space behind it. The dust we kicked up probably still hadn't settled on the lunar surface by the time we landed, but it was a long way away from us and going fast. It was possible to see through it—I could make out rocks and craters—but its movement was distracting. It made it difficult to pick out the speeds for a smooth touchdown. It was much like landing in a very fast-moving ground fog.

Buzz [Aldrin] and I had about 12 minutes of very post-touchdown [after landing] work, and then we could relax enough to have a sense of relief, of elation.

It took us somewhat longer to come out from Eagle than we had anticipated. It wasn't until after landing that I made up my mind what to say: "That's one small step for a man, one giant leap for mankind." Beyond those words I don't recall any particular emotion or feeling other than a little caution, a desire to be sure it was safe to put my weight on that surface outside Eagle.

From inside Eagle the sky was black, but it looked like daylight out on the surface and the surface looked tan. There is a very peculiar lighting effect on the lunar surface which seems to make the colors change. I don't understand this completely. If you look down along your own shadow, or into the sun, the moon is tan. If you look straight down at the surface, particularly in the shadows, it looks very, very dark. When you pick up material in your hands it is also dark, gray or black. The material is of a generally fine texture, almost like flour, but some coarser particles are like sand. Then there are, of course, scattered rocks and rock chips of all sizes. My only real problem on the surface was that there were so many places that I would like to have investigated.

All the things we left on the moon are pretty well known by now. We were particularly pleased to leave the patch of Apollo 1 in memory of our friends and fellow astronauts Gus Grissom, Ed White, and Roger Chaffee [three astronauts who lost their lives during an on-ground training accident in 1967] and the medals in memory of Gagarin and Komarov [two Soviet astronauts]. I believe that the Russians share our own dreams and hopes for a better world.

Looking back, touchdown was for me the most striking achievement in the flight. Liftoff was the next most striking. I thought quite a bit about that single ascent engine and how much depended upon it. When the moment came it was perfection. It gave us not only a very pleasant ride but also a beautiful, final view of our moon base as we lifted up and away from it.

My overwhelming impression of the moon as I walked on it and photographed it was that I was taking pictures of a steady-state process, a process in which some rocks are being worn down continually on the surface and other new ones are being thrown out on top by new events occurring either near or far away. In other words, no matter when humans first reached this spot—a thousand years ago or 100,000 years ago or even a million years from now—it would look generally the same. The only difference would be that at each period in time one would see slightly different rocks, slightly different surfaces, all influenced by the same processes. From what I saw I believe that most of the processes are external (that is, things like meteorite impact). But some materials indicate that there may have been internal processes on the moon at some time.

The most dramatic memories I have now are the sights themselves, those magnificent visual images. They go far beyond any other visual experiences I've had in my life. Of all the spectacular views we had, the most impressive to me was on the way toward the moon, when we flew through its shadow. We were still thousands of miles away but close enough so that the moon almost filled our circular window. It was eclipsing the sun, from our position, and the corona [the outermost part of the atmosphere] of the sun was visible around the moon. It was magnificent, but the moon itself was even more so. We were in its shadow so there was no part of it lit by the sun. It was lit only by the earth, by earthshine. This made the moon appear blue-gray. The entire scene looked three-dimensional.

I was really aware, visually aware, that the moon was in fact a sphere, not a disk. It seemed almost as if it were showing us its roundness, its similarity in shape to our earth, in a sort of welcome. I was sure then that it would be a hospitable host. It had been awaiting its first visitors for a long time.

READING REVIEW

1. According to Armstrong, why was the moon landing so important?
2. What was the most striking achievement of the flight? Why?
3. What characteristics of the moon impressed Armstrong most? Why?
4. Cite three ways in which Armstrong used symbolism to reflect the seriousness surrounding the lunar landing mission.

239 The Meaning of Watergate

In June of 1972, five men were arrested as they attempted to break into Democratic National Committee headquarters at the Watergate building in Washington, D.C. It was soon discovered that they were working for the campaign committee to reelect President Nixon. Although President Nixon declared that he knew nothing about the burglary, news reporters discovered evidence that pointed to a White House cover-up of the burglary as well as other possible criminal activities.

The Watergate scandal soon became a national crisis, as more and more Americans came to believe that the President was covering up a crime and lying about his activities. After many months of Congressional investigations into the Watergate scandals, President Richard M. Nixon resigned from office in August 1974.

In this selection, Theodore White, the author of several best-selling books on recent Presidential election campaigns, expresses his opinion about how and why Watergate happened.

Senators Howard Baker and Sam Ervin, Watergate committee

READING FOCUS

1. What did White say was the role of myths in American civilization?
2. How did the Watergate crisis affect Americans?

The true crime of Richard Nixon was simple. He destroyed the myth that binds America together. For this he was driven from power.

The myth he broke was critical—that somewhere in American life there is at least one person who stands for law, the President. That faith overcomes all distrust all evidence or suspicion of wrongdoing by lesser leaders, all corruptions. That faith holds that all people are equal before the law and protected by it. It holds that no matter how the faith may be betrayed elsewhere, at one particular point— the Presidency—justice will be done. It was that faith that Richard Nixon broke.

All civilizations rest on myths. But in America myths have exceptional meaning. A myth is a way of giving meaning to the raw

<hr>

Adapted from Breach of Faith *by Theodore H. White.*

and contradictory evidence of life. It lets people make patterns in their own lives, within the larger patterns.

There is, however, an absolutely vital political difference between the mythology of other nations and the mythology of America. Other nations may fall or last. They may change their governing myths. But French people will always remain French people, Russians will be Russians, Germans remain Germans, and English people—English people. But America is different. It is the only peaceful civilization in the world made up of many races. Its people come from such diverse heritages of religion, language, habit, and color that if America did not exist it would be impossible to imagine that such a grouping could ever behave like a nation. It would be impossible unless its people were bound together by a common faith.

Politics in America is the binding faith. That begins with the founding faith of the Declaration of Independence: "We hold these truths to be self-evident: that all men are created equal, that they are endowed by their Creator with certain unalienable rights, that among these are life, liberty, and the pursuit of happiness."

Of all the political myths out of which the Republic was born, none was more hopeful than the myth of the Presidency—that the people, in their shared wisdom, would be able to choose the best person to lead them. From this came a related myth—that the Presidency, the supreme office, would make noble any person who held its responsibility. The office and its duties would, by their very weight, make an individual a superior person, wise enough to resist the clash of all selfish interests.

Richard Nixon behaved otherwise. His lawlessness exploded the myths. He left a nation approaching the 200th anniversary of its glorious independence with a President and a Vice-President neither of whom had been chosen by the people. The faith was shattered. Being shattered, it was to leave American politics more confused than ever since the Civil War.

What Richard Nixon left us is best understood as a set of questions—questions about ourselves and what we seek from government.

The simplest set of questions can be asked and answered in the formula of popular detective stories: Who did it?

Like any popular detective story, this is a story of bungling criminals. It begins with the circumstance, very difficult for Richard Nixon's enemies to accept, that most of the top people involved were strong patriots, convinced that what they were doing was best for their country. Men like Ehrlichman and Haldeman [Nixon's two most important aides] were true believers in the purpose of America as they saw it. They sought nothing for themselves. Beneath came all the others, people of little patriotism and no principle.

They entered into government, all of them, with no greater knowledge of how power worked than the intrigues of political campaigning. They could not understand the essential balance there must always be in the nation's affairs between distrust and suspicion on the one hand and faith and trust on the other. A naive politician gets nowhere. A successful politician must be something of a hypocrite, promising all to all, knowing that, if elected, he or she must inevitably sacrifice the interests of some for others. But people in government must know when to choose trust and faith over political need. The people must trust their words at whatever cost—or they cannot govern. In the Presidency, above all, it is essential to recognize the moment for truth.

From mid-April of 1973 to his end in 1974, the President lied, lied again, and continued to lie. His lying not only added to the anger of those who were on his trail. It slowly destroyed the faith of Americans in that President's honor. He knew what he was doing, for he consciously relied on the mystique of the Presidency to carry him through what lay ahead.

If Nixon had committed a historic crime—treason, or accepting graft, or knowingly twisting American national policy for personal or partisan ends—the detective story would be enough. Its answer to the question is that the criminals were caught because they were bunglers.

But the initial crime [the Watergate break-in] was commonplace. Nixon might have erased it easily by acting as Presidents must act against lawbreakers. Instead he made it a disaster by trying to cover it up. So another set of questions arose—not how the criminals were caught, but why Nixon did what he was caught doing.

"Why?" is a political question and one that will hang over American politics for years to come. Nixon was not a stupid man. What did he think he was defending beyond his own skin and reputation?

To trace the answers to the question of "Why?" one must accept the political reality that Richard Nixon and his aides were, for the first time in American politics since 1860, carrying on an ideological war [a struggle between differing sets of ideas]. Because they felt their purpose was high and necessary and the purpose of their enemies dangerous or immoral, he and his aides believed that the laws did not bind them—or that the laws could legitimately be bent.

Again one must go back to a set of American myths to explain the intensity of the ideological war that began in the 1960's.

Wrapped around the original political myths of America—of liberty, of equality, of a government-of-laws-not-people—had been a culture, long since destroyed, with a set of social myths now twisted by time into the rigid political principles of today.

The old social myths rested on the belief that free citizens were able to control their own futures by their own efforts. In the original American community of farmers 200 years ago, it was considered a matter of thrift and constant work and planning whether a person made it or did not. But in corporate America, since the beginning of the 1900's, fewer and fewer people have been able to control their own future by their own efforts. Now, in present-day America, everyone was locked up—in corporations, in unions, in organizations, in schools, in draft boards, in the tax net—and group pressure was the thing. Nixon and his men believed in the old social myths and the old culture. His opponents believed in mobilizing group pressure to force the federal government to do their will or to protect their future.

The old myths glorified self-government. The states and the federal government originally agreed that each had separate responsibilities. But in practice, by the 1960's the heart of the problem lay in the cities and suburbs.

But the most deceptive inherited social myth was that of American power. That myth was recent. It rested on the brief dominance of American arms as they spread triumphant over the entire globe in 1945. What had happened, however, by the 1960's, was that the myth of American power had been weakened by the revolutions of the postwar world. Americans were faced with a new reality—they were engaged in the first major war that they would not win. By the time Nixon came to power, that realization had split the country at every level. Resentment at the waste and killing in Vietnam had spilled out into the streets in sputtering violence and frightening bloodshed.

Nixon had to be sure, recognized the weakening of American power abroad. As soon as he took office in 1969, he had begun to end the war in Vietnam. But he clung to the old doctrine that the President alone could make the decisions and arrange the timing for a withdrawal from Asia that would bring peace with honor. Those who opposed him, whether in the streets or in the news system, he would treat with moral fierceness.

The political detective story of Nixon's crime begins there—with his belief that he, as President, was the only caretaker of America's power. The Nixon aides saw themselves as waging war in Vietnam to make peace. They had no doubt that national security required them to carry on that war by all means possible until peace with honor had been won. If the end was good then the means, however brutal, must also be good. And from this idea of the President's authority came most of the early illegalities, the buggings, the wire-taps, the surveillances, the minor crimes. Until finally the President's aides saw no distinction between ends and means. They were making war not just in Vietnam but all across the home front, too. All the disputes over home issues, as well as foreign issues, became part of the ideological war.

But the political story does not quite answer the "Why?" or explain the particular fierceness of behavior of the men at the White House.

To explain the spite and hatred of their struggle, one must add one more condition—the change of culture that was taking place all over America in the 1960's. The Nixon aides were people of the embattled old culture. As such, they believed the new culture was not only undermining the authority of their President to make war-and-peace, but striking into their homes, families, and schools, too. It was undermining the values with which they had grown up and still held dear.

This conflict of the two cultures far surpassed in emotion the traditional American political struggle between "conservatives" and "liberals." The two cultures clashed in every form of expression—in language, in costume, in slogans. They clashed over important matters—civil rights, "law-and-order," safety in the streets, drug abuse, the dignity of women. The line of clash between the two cultures ran through families as well as communities. Fathers against sons, mothers against daughters, students against teachers, arguing over such matters as dress and manners and morals, and sex and drugs and rioting. This clash of culture and personal values was taking place at the same time as the political clash over the hard issues. And the two added to each other.

One must see all three wars—the war abroad, the ideological war, the cultural war—as crossing each other in the agony of an unstable personality in order to answer the personal "Why?" of Richard Nixon's collapse. The answer can come only by imagining that here was a man who could not, in his waking moments, accept the man he recognized in his own nightmares—the outsider, the loner, the loser.

Throughout his career, except for a few brief years in 1971 and 1972, that had been his inner roles—the outsider, the loser. "They" were against him, always. His authority as President was being challenged by the news system, the rioters, the Congress, the intellectuals. The culture, the manners, the beliefs of his lonely life of striving were being wiped out by the fashions of the new culture. Losers play dirty. He, too, would change the rules. His ruthlessness, vengefulness, nastiness were the characteristics of a man who has seen himself as underdog for so long that he cannot distinguish between real and fancied enemies, a man who does not really care whom he hurts when pressed, who cannot accept or understand when or what he has won.

Always, in the crisis, he reacted as the cornered loser. He could not shake that characteristic. In 1972 he had won so largely that he could misread his victory. It was a victory for his ideas and politics. But he saw it as personal, as a loner. It was not simply an election he had won. He had conquered a land. Its citizens were the occupied. And he could use the law as he wished, however much a hostile Congress, the news system, or intellectuals protested.

READING REVIEW

1. According to White, what was the "true crime" of Richard Nixon?
2. Why did White say that myths were especially important to American society?
3. How did President Nixon's administration shatter Americans' faith in the Presidency?
4. (a) According to White, how did the Watergate crisis affect American politics and society? (b) Do you agree with White's assessment? Why or why not?

240 A New Direction Under Reagan

When Ronald Reagan became President in 1981, the United States was facing serious problems abroad. American citizens were being held hostage in Iran. The Soviet Union was moving troops into Afghanistan, increasing international tensions.

As serious as these problems were, the crises the nation faced at home were even more severe. Inflation rates were soaring. Economic productivity was declining. Some citizens were losing confidence in the government's ability to deal with these problems.

In his Inaugural Address, President Reagan tried to reassure Americans that they could handle any present and future challenges. One way of getting the nation moving again, he declared, was to limit the growth of federal government.

READING FOCUS

1. Why did Reagan say that "government is the problem?"
2. What was Reagan's solution to this problem?

In this present crisis, government is not the solution to our problem; government is the problem.

From time to time we've been tempted to believe that society has become too complex to be managed by self-rule, that government by an elite group is superior to government for, by and of the people.

From Ronald Reagan, "Inaugural Address," in The New York Times, Jan. 21, 1981.

But if no one among us is capable of governing himself, then who among us has the capacity to govern someone else?

All of us together—in and out of government—must bear the burden. The solutions we seek must be equitable with no one group singled out to pay a higher price.

We hear much of special interest groups. Well, our concern must be for a special interest group that has been too long neglected.

It knows no sectional boundaries, or ethnic and racial divisions and it crosses political party lines. It is made up of men and women who raise our food, patrol our streets, man our mines and factories, teach our children, keep our homes and heal us when we're sick.

Professionals, industrialists, shopkeepers, clerks, cabbies and truck drivers. They are, in short, "We, the people." This breed called Americans.

Well, this Administration's objective will be a healthy, vigorous, growing economy that provides equal opportunities for all Americans with no barriers born of bigotry or discrimination.

Putting America back to work means putting all Americans back to work. Ending inflation means freeing all Americans from the terror of runaway living costs.

President Ronald Reagan delivers his 1981 Inaugural Address.

All must share in the productive work of this "new beginning," and all must share in the bounty of a revived economy.

With the idealism and fair play which are the core of our system and our strength, we can have a strong, prosperous America at peace with itself and the world.

So as we begin, let us take inventory.

We are a nation that has a government—not the other way around. And this makes us special among the nations of the earth.

Our government has no power except that granted it by the people. It is time to check and reverse the growth of government which shows signs of having grown beyond the consent of the governed.

It is my intention to curb the size and influence of the Federal establishment and to demand recognition of the distinction between the powers granted to the Federal Government and those reserved to the states or to the people.

All of us—all of us need to be reminded that the Federal Government did not create the states; the states created the Federal Government.

Now, so there will be no misunderstanding, it's not my intention to do away with government.

It is rather to make it work—work with us, not over us; to stand by our side, not ride on our back. Government can and must provide opportunity, not smother it; foster productivity, not stifle it.

If we look for the answer as to why for so many years we achieved so much, prospered as no other people on earth, it was because here in this land we unleashed the energy and individual genius of man to a greater extent than has ever been done before.

Freedom and dignity of the individual have been more available and assured here than in any other place on earth. The price of this freedom at times has been high, but we have never been unwilling to pay that price.

It is no coincidence that our present troubles are parallel and are proportionate to the intervention and intrusion in our lives that result from unnecessary and excessive growth of government.

It is time for us to realize that we are too great a nation to limit ourselves to small dreams. We're not, as some would have us believe, doomed to an inevitable decline. I do not believe in a fate that will fall on us no matter what we do. I do believe in a fate that will fall on us if we do nothing.

So, with all the creative energy at our command let us begin an era of national renewal. Let us renew our determination, our courage and our strength. And let us renew our faith and our hope. We have every right to dream heroic dreams.

READING REVIEW

1. What evidence did President Reagan offer to support his claim that government is the nation's biggest problem?
2. (a) What were the objectives of Reagan's administration? (b) Do you think Reagan accomplished these objectives? Cite evidence from your textbook to support your viewpoint.

241 The Shaping of The Presidency, 1984

Many issues disrupted traditional politics in the 1984 presidential election. Historian Theodore H. White identifies the issues which he claims divide American society: women's quest for equality, a transformation in the objectives of the traditional civil rights movement, the reawakening of ethnic awareness, and the continuing debate on the proper relationship between church and state. White states that each of these issues will have to be addressed through a system of presidential politics that he contends is outdated and dangerous.

In the following excerpt, White describes President Reagan's response to each issue and also discusses the effects of money power and television power on democracy and American politics in 1988 and beyond.

READING FOCUS

1. According to White, why is the current system of presidential politics dangerous?
2. How has President Reagan responded to each of the issues White has identified?

The last legacy of the 1984 election to the election of 1988 is that all the new underswells

Adapted from "The Shaping of the Presidency 1984" by Theodore H. White in TIME Magazine, November 19, 1984.

and surges will have to find their way to a decision through a system of presidential politics now grown so obsolete as to be dangerous.

Simply put, somewhere in the past 20 years the U.S. political system became entangled in rules and customs that make it more vulnerable to special-interest groups than ever before, and television makes this even worse.

The primary system, where the choice of candidates begins, bounces crazily from state to state, hobbled by bizarre party regulations, dominated by the dramatic needs of television. Few except scholars understand the complicated rules that govern the sequence of nomination. New York has changed its nominating rules four times in the past four elections. In California, once a winner-take-all state, no candidate now runs statewide. One could go on to more outlandish and contradictory rules, laws, regulations. This unworkable system leaves both the parties and the candidates prey to local pressure groups.

What emerges is political bedlam and national boredom. But there are other more troubling results: not least the total exhaustion of the candidates, who must perform as political athletes, operating by glands, not by reason; and just as important—the inability of any schoolteacher to tell students approaching voting age how the nation chooses its leaders.

Many professional politicians will say, off the record, that our system of politics is too important to be left to self-chosen politicians and that Congress must step in and act, by law, to make the process reasonable. Perhaps the best current proposal is that the long run of primaries be sliced into four separate Tuesdays, one month apart, set not by regions but by time zones. Time zones run from north to south, so parochial regional interests would be blurred. Time-zoned primaries would force all national candidates to address themselves once a month to a full cross section of the nation, less fettered by special interests, ethnic or racial groups.

By 1988 it is certain that both parties will be holding primaries simultaneously in a free-for-all that will confuse everyone. New public laws, not new party regulations, are needed.

The conventions are the next step in choice. But the conventions have also changed; they no longer choose, they only ratify the primaries. They are spectacles into which television tries to inject drama; even television's own leaders feel too much power has been placed in their hands. One veteran television producer said, "Let's give the conventions back to the politicians. Give the parties control of the two hours of prime time we allot. Let them fill it as they want. If we think there's any news, we can tack it on afterward as commentary. But the conventions should be their show, not ours."

The national contest that follows the conventions is soiled by two intertwined circumstances: money power and television power. The flood of money that gushes into politics today is a pollution of democracy. Money buys television time, buys Election Day "expenses," buys access to decision makers. Most candidates now control personal political action committees that let them mobilize allies long before an election.

More important even than money power is the power of television. Television is the main battleground for public opinion in our time. Television reaches its climax in the so-called great debates. They are vital as a display of contending personalities, but they have turned into quiz shows where candidates stuffed with facts try to outdo each other.

Much can be done to restrain both money power and television power. Wise laws can forbid the contribution of money to any candidate in one state from sources in any other state. Wise laws can require time from the networks to be shared evenly between the major candidates. New laws can and must help. Yet, in the end, politics is the entry way to power, and in our system, politics delivers power into the hands of the most potent constitutional leader in the world. It is into Ronald Reagan's hands, instincts, purposes that this election has delivered us.

Much will depend on how Ronald Reagan interprets the vote. Landslides give Presidents enormous authority, but they can lead either to disasters, as did the landslides of Herbert Hoover, Lyndon Johnson and Richard Nixon, or to profound redefinitions of American life, as Franklin Roosevelt engineered. Of course, squeakers too can change American life, as Lincoln and Kennedy proved. What is critical in both landslides and squeakers is the ability of a President to read the tides, the yearnings that went into his victory, to distinguish between his own campaign rhetoric and the reality he must force his people to face.

Geraldine Ferraro (left) meets with astronaut Sally Ride (center) and Coretta Scott King (right).

With re-election, Reagan has been handed enormous authority to make the Soviets face U.S. strength and truly negotiate, with some hope of realism on both sides. What is less sure is whether his victory will give him sufficient new vigor to reorganize his discordant White House staff, his Cabinet and his Pentagon.

More important than anything else is how an aging but renewed Ronald Reagan reads his own country. Every great President has been a great politician—Jefferson, Lincoln, Theodore Roosevelt, Franklin Roosevelt, Kennedy—even George Washington, who lived before the age of party politics. They could tell by political instinct how far and how fast they could lead their own people. This will be the test of a second Reagan Administration: its reading of the forces that underlay its election.

Reagan will probably be forced to recognize the pressure of women, but not as a group, rather as individuals displaying talents hitherto unused. Both women in the outgoing Senate were Republicans, so were nine Representatives, so were two Cabinet members. Can Reagan stretch to find more?

On blacks, Reagan, a man without prejudice, may yield a little, but only if he can find blacks of merit, and certainly not enough to satisfy black Democrats. He will not meet Jesse Jackson's demands, those he will willingly leave to the Democrats.

The new President will have it in his power to mold the takeover generation. Its leaders were the managers of his campaign, and they expect their share of the rewards. Politics is where the jobs are, and command too, and rewards in wealth follow. Reagan can by appointment and preference choose from those who pursue his aims with intelligence and give them importance by public notice. He can set them against the hot eyes who see him (and George Bush) as the eldering generation to be discarded in the struggle for power in 1988. Abraham Lincoln left no young men behind to pursue his purposes; he was too busy with war, and cut short by assassination. Franklin Roosevelt did seek out young men— and left behind the generation that was to dominate his party for years after his death.

Most of all, Reagan will write his mark on American life by how he shapes the issues of values and moralities. He is on record as supporting a school-prayer amendment and a right-to-life amendment and opposing a women's Equal Rights Amendment; on all these Mondale differed. This may have been only the rhetoric of the Republican campaign: words blown away by the winds. It is the push the President puts behind such matters of manners and morals, both at the highest court level and the lowest congressional level, that will shape the takeover generation in the Republican Party and set its members against the Democrats' takeover generation.

If Reagan recaptures his old vigor to forge a policy that wisely harnesses all the new forces in the nation, his election could prove to be one of historic reorientation, the long-awaited realignment of American politics.

If he does not, the campaign of 1984 will have led to just one more election of passage, and the last word will be left to others in 1988—or beyond.

READING REVIEW

1. **(a)** According to White, what is wrong with the presidential primary system? **(b)** What solutions did he offer to improve the system?
2. **(a)** Why have money and television power been so important in elections? **(b)** What did White say can be done to restrain the influence of money and television power?
3. How did White feel about the presidential debates? Do you agree or disagree? Why?
4. According to White, on what important area in American history could President Reagan leave his mark?

CHAPTER **A New Role in World Affairs**
(1960 to the Present)

242 The Missile Crisis in Cuba

In October of 1962, President Kennedy learned from American intelligence reports that the Soviet Union was building powerful missile bases in Cuba. These bases posed so great a danger to the United States' security that Kennedy decided to act immediately. Kennedy communicated with the leaders of the Soviet government and demanded that the Soviet Union dismantle and remove these missile sites. For the next few days, war seemed possible.

Several years later Robert Kennedy, the President's brother, as well as his Attorney General, wrote a detailed account of the Cuban missile crisis. In this selection, Robert Kennedy described what happened on October 27 and 28—the most crucial and dangerous days of the missile crisis.

READING FOCUS
1. What was Robert Kennedy's role in the Cuban missile crisis?
2. How was the Cuban missile crisis resolved?

[Saturday, October 27]
The President ordered the Ex Comm [the Executive Committee for National Security, which included Secretary of State Dean Rusk, several other members of the Cabinet, and military officials] to meet again at 9:00 P.M. in the White House. While the letter was being typed and prepared to be sent, he and I sat in his office. [This was the letter President Kennedy sent to Khrushchev on October 27, requesting that the missiles in Cuba be dismantled. In return, the United States would end its naval "quarantine."] He talked about Major Anderson and how it is always the brave and the best who die. [Anderson, a U-2 pilot, had been killed the day before by missile fire while on a reconnaissance mission over Cuba.] He talked

Adapted from Thirteen Days, A Memoir of the Cuban Missile Crisis *by Robert F. Kennedy.*

about the mistakes that lead to war. War is rarely planned. The Russians don't wish to fight any more than we do. They do not want to go to war with us nor we with them. And yet if events continue as they have in the last several days, that struggle—which no one wishes, which will accomplish nothing—will engulf and destroy humanity.

He wanted to make sure that he had done everything in his power, everything possible, to prevent such a catastrophe. Every opportunity was to be given to the Russians to find a peaceful settlement which would not decrease their national security or be a public humiliation. It was not only for Americans that he was concerned, or primarily the older generation of any land. The thought that disturbed him the most, and that made the prospect of war much more fearful than it would otherwise have been, was the possibility of the death of the children of this country and all the world—the young people who had no role, who had no say, who knew nothing even of the confrontation, but whose lives would be ended like everyone else's. They would never have a chance to make a decision, to vote in an election, to run for office, to lead a revolution, to determine their own futures.

It was this that troubled him most, that gave him such pain. And it was then that he and Secretary Rusk decided that I should visit with [Soviet] Ambassador Dobrynin and personally make known the President's great concern.

I telephoned Ambassador Dobrynin about 7:15 P.M. and asked him to come to the Department of Justice. We met in my office at 7:45. I told him first that we knew that work was continuing on the missile bases in Cuba and that in the last few days it had been speeded up. I said that in the last few hours we had learned that our reconnaissance planes flying over Cuba had been fired upon and that one of our U-2's had been shot down and the pilot killed. That for us was a most serious turn of events.

President Kennedy did not want a military conflict. He had done everything possible to avoid a military engagement with Cuba and with the Soviet Union, but now they had forced our hand. Because of the deception of the Soviet Union, our photographic reconnaissance planes would have to continue to fly over Cuba. If the Cubans or Soviets shot at these planes, then we would have to shoot back. This would inevitably lead to further incidents and to escalation of the conflict.

He said the Cubans resented the fact that we were violating Cuban air space. I replied that if we had not violated Cuban air space, we would still be believing what Khrushchev had said—that there would be no missiles placed in Cuba. In any case, I said, this matter was far more serious than the air space of Cuba—it involved the peoples of both of our countries and, in fact, people all over the globe.

The Soviet Union had secretly established missile bases in Cuba while at the same time claiming privately and publicly that this would never be done. We had to have a commitment by tomorrow that those bases would be removed. I was not giving them an ultimatum but a statement of fact. He should understand that if they did not remove those bases, we would remove them. President Kennedy had great respect for the ambassador's country and the courage of its people. Perhaps his country might feel it necessary to take action. But before that was over, there would be not only dead Americans but dead Russians as well.

He asked me what offer the United States was making, and I told him of the letter that President Kennedy had just sent to Khrushchev. He raised the question of our removing our missiles from Turkey. I said that there could be no arrangement made under this kind of threat or pressure. In the last analysis this was a decision that would have to be made by NATO. However, I said President Kennedy had been anxious to remove those missiles from Turkey (and Italy) for a long period of time. He had ordered their removal some time ago. It was our judgment that, within a short time after this crisis was over, those missiles would be gone.

I said President Kennedy wished to have peaceful relations between our two countries. Time was running out. We had only a few more hours—we needed an answer immediately from the Soviet Union. I said we must have it the next day.

I returned to the White House. The President was not optimistic, nor was I. He ordered twenty-four troop-carrier squadrons of the Air Force Reserve to active duty. They would be necessary for an invasion. He had not given up hope, but what hope there was now rested with Khrushchev's changing his course within the next few hours. It was a hope, not an expectation. The expectation was a military confrontation by Tuesday and possibly tomorrow.

[Sunday, October 28]

I had promised my daughters for a long time that I would take them to the horse show. Early Sunday morning I went to the Washington Armory to watch the horses jump. In any case, there was nothing I could do but wait. Around 10:00, I received a call at the horse show. It was Secretary Rusk. He said he had just received word from the Russians that they had agreed to withdraw the missiles from Cuba.

I went immediately to the White House, and there I received a call from Ambassador Dobrynin, saying he would like to visit with me. I met him in my office at 11:00 A.M.

He told me that the message was coming through that Khrushchev had agreed to dismantle and withdraw the missiles under adequate supervision and inspection; that everything was going to work out satisfactorily; and that Mr. Khrushchev wanted to send his best wishes to the President and to me.

It was quite a different meeting from the night before. I went back to the White House and talked to the President for a long time. While I was there, he placed telephone calls to former Presidents Truman and Eisenhower. As I was leaving, he said, making reference to Abraham Lincoln, "This is the night I should go to the theater." I said, "If you go, I want to go with you." As I closed the door, he was seated at the desk writing a letter to Mrs. Anderson [wife of the U-2 pilot killed on a flight over Cuba a few days earlier].

READING REVIEW

1. What troubled President Kennedy most on the evening described here?
2. How would you describe Robert Kennedy's meeting with the Soviet ambassador?
3. How did Khrushchev respond to President Kennedy's letter?
4. (a) According to Robert Kennedy, what action was the United States prepared to take if the Soviet Union refused to remove the missiles in Cuba? (b) Do you think the United States was prepared to go to war over this issue? Cite evidence from the reading to support your conclusion.

243 The War in Vietnam

American involvement in the Vietnam War began in 1962 when President Kennedy sent 8,000 military "advisers" to help train the South Vietnamese army. Then, in 1964, President Johnson began to send American combat troops. And in 1965, the United States began the bombing of North Vietnam.

Almost from the beginning, American opinion on the Vietnam War was divided. Some American leaders, known as "hawks," supported the war because they felt the Untied States had promised to protect South Vietnam and that America's honor and world leadership role were at stake. Other leaders, called "doves," opposed the war, believing that the United States could not create a stable, democratic government in South Vietnam nor instill within the South Vietnamese people the will to fight. As the war continued and more American troops were sent to Vietnam, this debate over the role of the United States in Vietnam continued and grew more bitter.

In the following selection, President Johnson offered a defense of the war. In response, Senator William Fulbright suggested that American involvement in Vietnam was a mistake.

READING FOCUS

1. According to President Johnson, why did the United States become involved in Vietnam?
2. Why did Fulbright say American involvement in Vietnam was a mistake?

[PRESIDENT JOHNSON]

Tonight Americans and Asians are dying for a world where each people may choose its own path to change.

Why must we take this painful road?

Why must this nation endanger its ease, and its interest, and its power for the sake of a people so far away?

We fight because we must fight if we are to live in a world where every country can shape its own destiny. And only in such a world will our own freedom be finally secure.

President Johnson's speech adapted from "Peace Without Conquest," an address by Lyndon B. Johnson at Johns Hopkins University, April 7, 1965.

The first reality is that North Vietnam has attacked the independent nation of South Vietnam. Its object is total conquest.

Of couse, some of the people of South Vietnam are participating in an attack on their own government. But trained men and supplies, orders, and arms, flow in a constant stream from north to south.

This support is the heartbeat of the war.

Over this war—and all Asia—is another reality: Communist China. The rulers in Hanoi are urged on by Peking. This is a government which has destroyed freedom in Tibet, which has attacked India, and has been condemned by the United Nations for aggression in Korea. It is a nation which is helping the forces of violence in almost every continent. The contest in Vietnam is part of a wider pattern of aggressive purposes.

Why are we in South Vietnam?

We are there because we have a promise to keep. Since 1954 every American President has offered support to the people of South Vietnam. We have helped to build, and we have helped to defend. Thus over many years we have made a national pledge to help South Vietnam defend its independence.

And I intend to keep that promise.

United States troops in Vietnam

To dishonor that pledge, to abandon this small and brave nation to its enemies, and to the terror that must follow, would be an unforgivable wrong.

We are also there to strengthen world order. Around the globe, from Berlin to Thailand, are people whose well-being rests, in part, on the belief that they can count on us if they are attacked. To leave Vietnam to its fate would shake the confidence of all these people in the value of an American commitment and in the value of America's word. The result would be increased unrest and instability, and even wider war.

We are also there because there are great stakes in the balance. Let no one think for a moment that retreat from Vietnam would bring an end to conflict. The battle would be started again in one country and then another. The central lesson of our time is that the appetite of aggression is never satisfied. To withdraw from one battlefield means only to prepare for the next.

Our objective is the independence of South Vietnam, and its freedom from attack. We want nothing for ourselves—only that the people of South Vietnam be allowed to guide their own country in their own way.

We will do everything necessary to reach that objective. And we will do only what is absolutely necessary.

We hope that peace will come swiftly. But that is in the hands of others besides ourselves. And we must be prepared for a long continued conflict. It will require patience as well as bravery, the will to endure as well as the will to resist.

I wish it were possible to convince others with words of what we now find it necessary to say with guns and planes: Armed hostility is useless. Our resources are equal to any challenge. Because we fight for values and we fight for principles, rather than territory or colonies, our patience and determination are unending.

Once this is clear, then it should also be clear that the only path for reasonable people is the path of peaceful settlement.

Such peace demands an independent South Vietnam—securely guaranteed and able to shape its own relationships to all others—free from outside interference—tied to no alliance—a military base for no other country.

These are the essentials of any final settlement.

[SENATOR FULBRIGHT]

We are now in a war to "defend freedom" in South Vietnam. The official war aims of the United States government, as I understand them, are to defeat what is regarded as North Vietnamese aggression, to demonstrate the uselessness of what the Communists call "wars of national liberation" and to create conditions under which the South Vietnamese people will be able freely to determine their own future.

I have not the slightest doubt of the sincerity of the President and the Vice-President and the Secretaries of State and Defense in putting forward these aims. What I do doubt, and doubt very much, is the ability of the United States to achieve these aims by the means being used. I do not question the power of our weapons and the efficiency of our military plans; they are certainly impressive. What I do question is the ability of the United States or any other Western nation to go into a small, alien, undeveloped Asian nation and create stability where there is chaos, the will to fight where there is defeatism, democracy where there is no tradition of it, and honest government where corruption is almost a way of life.

Sincere though it is, the American effort to build the foundations of freedom in South Vietnam is having an effect quite different from the one intended.

One wonders how much the American commitment to Vietnamese freedom is also a commitment to American pride—the two seem to have become part of the same package. When we talk about the freedom of South Vietnam, we may be thinking about how disagreeable it would be to accept a solution short of victory. We may be thinking about how our pride would be injured if we settled for less than we set out to achieve. We may be thinking about our reputation as a great power, fearing that a compromise settlement would shame us before the world, marking us as a second-rate people with failing courage and determination.

Such fears are senseless. They are unworthy of the richest, most powerful, most productive, and best educated people in the world.

The cause of our difficulties in Southeast Asia is not a lack of power but too much of the wrong kind of power. We are trying to remake Vietnamese society, a task which certainly

Adapted from The Arrogance of Power *by J. William Fulbright.*

cannot be accomplished by force and which probably cannot be accomplished by any means available to outsiders. The objective may be desirable, but it is not practical.

With the best intentions in the world the United States has involved itself in the affairs of developing nations in Asia and Latin America, practicing what has been called a kind of "welfare imperialism." Our honest purpose is the advancement of development and democracy. To achieve this purpose, it has been thought necessary to destroy ancient and unproductive ways of life. In this latter goal we have been successful, perhaps more successful than we know. Bringing skills and knowledge, money and resources in amounts unknown in traditional societies, the Americans have overcome native groups and interests and become the dominant force in a number of countries. Far from being bumbling, wasteful, and incompetent, as critics have charged, American government officials, technicians, and economists have been very successful in breaking down the barriers to change in ancient but fragile cultures.

Here, however, our success ends. Traditional rulers, institutions, and ways of life have crumbled under the fatal impact of American wealth and power. But they have not been replaced by new institutions and new ways of life, nor has their breakdown brought about an era of democracy and development. It has rather brought an era of disorder and demoralization because, while destroying old ways of doing things, we have also destroyed the self-confidence and self-reliance which a society needs to build its own institutions. We have reduced those peoples we intended to help to a condition of dependency. We have done this for the most part without meaning to. With every good intention we have intruded on fragile societies. Although we have been successful in uprooting traditional ways of life, we have been unsuccessful in planting the democracy and advancing the development which are the honest aims of our "welfare imperialism."

READING REVIEW

1. List two reasons why the United States fought in Vietnam.
2. Why did Senator Fulbright believe that American involvement in South Vietnam was a mistake?

Johnson reacts to news of the Vietnam War.

244   Lessons from a Lost War

Ten years after the fall of Saigon, many Americans are still reluctant to discuss the war in Vietnam. Despite divided sentiments concerning United States involvement in Southeast Asia, historians have speculated about the legacy of Vietnam.

The question that Americans—foreign-policy makers and war veterans alike—are asking is: What did Vietnam teach us? The following excerpt offers an analysis of the lack of public support for the Vietnam War.

READING FOCUS

1. What was the most important dilemma raised by the Vietnam War?
2. What lessons did the United States learn as a result of the Vietnam War?

The most bedeviling of all the dilemmas raised by Viet Nam concerns the issue of public support. On the surface it might seem to be no issue at all: just about everybody agrees that Viet Nam proved the futility of trying to fight a war without a strong base of popular support. But just how strong exactly? [Walt] Rostow*

---

* President Johnson's national security adviser.

From Time *magazine, April 15, 1985.*

Americans protest the Vietnam War.

argues that the only U.S. war fought with tremendous public backing was World War II. He points out that World War I "brought riots and splits," the War of 1812 was "vastly devisive" and even during the War of Independence one-third of the population was pro-revolution, one-third pro-British and one-third "out to lunch." Rostow proposes a 60–25–15 split as about the best that can be expected now in support of a controversial policy: a bipartisan 60% in favor, 25% against and 15% out to lunch.

A strong current of opinion holds that Lyndon Johnson guaranteed a disastrously low level of support by getting into a long, bloody war without ever admitting (perhaps even to himself) the extent of the commitment he was making. Colonel [Harry] Summers†, who considers Viet Nam a just war that the U.S. could and should have won, insists that any similar conflict in the future ought to be "legitimized" by a formal, congressional declaration of war. Says Summers: "All of America's previous wars were fought in the heat of passion. Viet Nam was fought in cold blood, and that was intolerable to the American people. In an im-

† Author of *On Strategy: A Critical Analysis of the Vietnam War.*

mediate crisis the tendency of the American people is to rally around the flag. But God help you if it goes beyond that and you haven't built a base of support."

At the other extreme, former Secretary of State Dean Rusk defends to this day the Johnson Administration's effort "to do in cold blood at home what we were asking men to do in hot blood out in the field." Rusk points out that the war began with impressive public and congressional support. It was only in early 1968, says Rusk, that "many at the grass-roots level came to the opinion that if we didn't give them some idea when this war would come to an end, we might as well chuck it." The decisive factor probably was the defection of middle-class youths and their parents, a highly articulate segment that saw an endless war as a personal threat—though in fact the burden of the draft fell most heavily on low-income youths.

Paradoxically, though, Johnson might well have been able to win public support for a bigger war than he was willing to fight. As late as February 1968, at the height of the Tet offensive, one poll found 53% favoring stronger U.S. military action, even at the risk of a clash with the Soviet Union or China, vs. only 24% opting to wind down the war. Rusk insists that the Administration was right not to capitalize on this sentiment. Says he: "We made a deliberate decision not to whip up war fever in this country. We did not have parades and movie stars selling war bonds, as we did in World War II. We thought that in a nuclear world it is dangerous for a country to become too angry too quickly. That is something people will have to think about in the future."

It certainly is. Viet Nam veterans argue passionately that Americans must never again be sent out to die in a war that "the politicians will not let them win." And by win they clearly mean something like a World War II–style triumph ending with unconditional surrender. One lesson of Viet Nam, observes George Christian, who was L.B.J.'s press secretary, is that "it is very tough for Americans to stick in long situations. We are always looking for the quick fix." But nuclear missiles make the unconditional-surrender kind of war an anachronism. Viet Nam raised, and left unsolved for the next conflict, the question posed by Lincoln Bloomfield, an M.I.T. professor of political science who once served on Jimmy Carter's National Security Council: "How is it that you can 'win' so that when you leave two years later you do not lose the country to those forces who have committed themselves to victory at any cost?"

It is a question that cannot be suppressed much longer. Americans have a deep ambiguity toward military power: they like to feel strong, but often shy away from actually using that strength. There is a growing recognition, however, that shunning all battles less easily winnable than Grenada would mean abandoning America's role as a world power, and that, in turn, is no way to assure the nation's survival as a free society. Americans, observes Secretary of State George Shultz, "will always be reluctant to use force. It is the mark of our decency." But, he adds, "A great power cannot free itself so easily from the burden of choice. It must bear responsibility for the consequences of its inaction as well as for the consequences of its action."

READING REVIEW

1. Why was strong popular support for the war in Vietnam lacking?
2. How do President Johnson's views on the war in Vietnam (Reading 243) compare with those presented in this reading? With which viewpoint do you agree? Why?

245 A Russian Writer's Warning Against Détente

One of the major achievements of American foreign policy under President Nixon was the improvement in United States relations with both Communist China and the Soviet Union. This important effort to end the Cold War and relax world tensions became known as the policy of détente. While détente with both China and the Soviet Union seemed to be widely supported, some important voices spoke out against détente with the Soviet Union. One of them was Aleksandr Solzhenitsyn, a famous Soviet writer.

Solzhenitsyn had spent many years in Russian labor and detention camps for writings that were critical of Stalin and later Soviet leaders. Finally, in 1974, he was compelled to leave the Soviet Union to live in exile in Switzerland. The following selection is from a speech he made on a visit to the United States in 1975.

READING FOCUS

1. Why did Solzhenitsyn oppose détente with the Soviet Union?
2. According to Solzhenitsyn, what was wrong with America's policy of détente?

The Soviet system is so closed that it is almost impossible for you to understand. Everything is done the way the [Communist] Party demands. That's our system. Judge it for yourself.

It's a system where for 40 years there haven't been genuine elections. It's a system which has no legislative bodies. It's a system without a free press or independent judges. The people have no influence either on foreign policy or on internal policy. And thinking which is different from what the government thinks is crushed.

It's a system where leaders who have murdered millions have never been tried in the courts but instead retire with huge pensions and live in the greatest comfort. It's a system where the constitution has never been carried out for a single day. All the decisions are made in secrecy, by a small group responsible to no one, and then are released on us like a bolt of lightning.

And what are the signatures of members of such a group worth? How could anyone trust

Russian writer, Aleksandr Solzhenitsyn

their signatures to documents of détente? Your specialists will tell you that in recent years the Soviet Union has succeeded in creating wonderful chemical weapons and missiles, even better than those used by the United States.

So what are we to conclude from that? Is détente needed or not? Not only is it needed, it's as necessary as air. It's the only way of saving the earth. Instead of a world war, we must have détente—but a true détente.

I would say that there are very few, really only three, main characteristics of such a true détente.

In the first place, there would be disarmament—not only disarmament in terms of war but also in terms of violence. We must stop using the sort of arms [weapons] which are used to destroy one's neighbors, and also the sort of arms which are used to oppress one's fellow citizens. It is not détente if we here with you today can spend our time agreeably while over there people are suffering and dying.

The second sign of détente, I would say, is the following: that it be not one based on

Adapted from "America, We Beg You to Interfere" by Aleksandr I. Solzhenitsyn in the AFL-CIO American Federationist, July 1975. Reprinted by permission of the American Federation of Labor and Congress of Industrial Organizations.

smiles, not on verbal concessions, but only on a firm foundation. There must be a guarantee that it will not be broken overnight. This means that the other party to the agreement must have its actions subject to public opinion, to the press, and to a freely elected parliament. Until such control exists there is absolutely no guarantee.

There is a third simple condition. What sort of détente is it when the Soviet Union uses the kind of inhumane propaganda which is proudly called "ideological warfare"? Let us not have that. If we're going to be friends, let's be friends. If we're going to have détente, then let's have détente and put an end to ideological warfare.

The Soviet Union and the Communist countries can conduct negotiations. They know how to do this. For a long time they don't make any concessions and then they give in a little bit. Then everyone says triumphantly, "Look, they've made a concession. It's time to sign."

But we, from our lives there, have learned that violence can only be withstood by firmness.

You have to understand the nature of communism. The very ideology of communism, all of Lenin's teachings, holds that people who don't take what's lying in front of them are fools. If you can take it, take it. If you can attack, attack. But if there's a wall, then go back. The Communist leaders respect only firmness. They laugh at persons who continually give in to them. Your people are now saying, "Power without any attempt at conciliation will lead to a world conflict." But I would say that power with continual surrender is no power at all.

From our experience I can tell you that only firmness will make it possible to withstand the assaults of Communist totalitarianism. We see many historic examples. Let me give you some of them. Look at tiny Finland in 1939, which by its own forces withstood Russian attack. You, in 1948, defended Berlin only by your firmness of spirit, and there was no world conflict. In Korea in 1950 you stood up against the Communists, only by your firmness, and there was no world conflict. In 1962 you forced the rockets to be removed from Cuba. Again it was only firmness, and there was no world conflict.

We, the dissidents of the USSR [those who openly disagree with Russian policy within the

Soviet Union], don't have any tanks, we don't have any weapons, we have no organization. We don't have anything. Our hands are empty. We have only our hearts and what we have lived through during the past 50 years under the system. And when we have found the firmness within ourselves to stand up for our rights, we have done so. It's only by firmness of spirit that we have withstood. And if I am standing here before you, it's not because of the kindness or the good will of communism, not thanks to détente, but thanks to my own firmness and your firm support. They knew that I would not give in one inch, not one hair. And when they couldn't do more, they themselves fell back.

This is not an easy lesson. In our conditions this was taught to me by the difficulties of my own life. And if you yourselves—any one of you—were in the same difficult situation, you would have learned the same thing.

Today there are two major processes occurring in the world. One is a process of short-sighted concessions. It is a process of giving up, and giving up, and giving up, and hoping that perhaps at some point the wolf will have eaten enough.

The second process is one which I consider the key to everything and which, I will say now, will bring a new future to those under communism. For 20 years in the Soviet Union (and a shorter time in other Communist countries) there has been occurring a liberation of the human spirit. New generations are growing up which are steadfast in their struggle with evil. They are not willing to accept unprincipled compromises. They prefer to lose everything—salary, conditions of existence, life itself—rather than sacrifice conscience or make deals with evil.

This process has now gone so far that in the Soviet Union today, Marxism [the Communist teachings of Karl Marx] has become simply an object of contempt. No serious person in our country today, not even university and high school students, can talk about Marxism without laughing. But this whole process of our liberation, which obviously will involve social changes, is slower than the first one— the process of concessions. Over there, when we see these concessions, we are frightened. Why so quickly? Why give up several countries a year?

You are the allies of our liberation movement in the Communist countries. And I call upon you. Let us think together and try to see how we can adjust the relationship between these two processes. Whenever you help the persons persecuted in the Soviet Union, you're defending not only them but yourselves as well. You're defending your own future. So let us try and see how far we can go to stop this senseless and immoral process of making endless concessions to the aggressor.

On our crowded planet there are no longer any internal affairs. The Communist leaders say, "Don't interfere in our internal affairs. Let us strangle our citizens in peace and quiet." But I tell you: Interfere more and more. Interfere as much as you can. We beg you to come and interfere.

America—in me and among my friends and among people who think the way I do over there, among all ordinary Soviet citizens— brings forth a mixture of admiration and compassion. You're a country of the future; a young country; a country of still unused possibilities; a country of tremendous geographical distances; a country of tremendous spirit; a country of generosity. But these qualities— strength and generosity—usually make a person and even a whole country trusting. This already has done you a disservice several times.

I would like to call upon America to be more careful with its trust and prevent those people who are falsely using the struggle for peace and social justice to lead you down a false road. They are trying to weaken you. They are trying to disarm your strong and magnificent country in the face of this fearful threat—one which has never been seen before in the history of the world. Do not let yourselves be taken in the wrong direction. Let us try to slow down the process of concessions and help the process of liberation!

READING REVIEW

1. What did Solzhenitsyn describe as "a true détente"?
2. According to Solzhenitsyn, what were the weaknesses of the policy of détente being followed by the United States?
3. What role did he think the United States should play in the liberation movement in Communist countries?

246 Kissinger Defends Détente

During the administrations of Richard Nixon and Gerald Ford, from 1969 to 1977, the United States improved its relations with the Communist nations of China and the Soviet Union through détente. A major figure behind this policy was Henry Kissinger, who served as Secretary of State under both Nixon and Ford. Kissinger helped negotiate the treaty ending United States military involvement in Vietnam. He also helped arrange President Nixon's historic visits to China and the Soviet Union in 1972. The following selection is from a 1975 speech that Kissinger made to explain détente.

READING FOCUS

1. According to Kissinger, what principles must guide relations between the Soviet Union and the United States?
2. Why did Kissinger support détente?

Our relationship with the Communist powers has raised difficult questions for Americans ever since the Bolshevik Revolution. [The Russian Revolution took place in 1917–18.] It was understood very early that the Communist system and ideology were in conflict with our own principles. Sixteen years passed before President Franklin Roosevelt extended diplomatic recognition to the Soviet government. He did so in the belief, as he put it, that "through the resumption of normal relations the prospects of peace over all the world are greatly strengthened."

Today again courageous voices remind us of the nature of the Soviet system and of our duty to defend freedom. About this there is no disagreement.

There is, however, a clear conflict between two principles which is at the heart of the problem. Since the beginning of the nuclear age, the world's fears of catastrophe and its hopes for a better future have both depended on the relationship between the two superpowers. In an era of strategic nuclear balance—when both sides have the capacity to destroy

Adapted from Henry Kissinger "The Moral Foundations of Foreign Policy," speech delivered at Minneapolis on July 15, 1975.

civilized life—there is no alternative to co-existence.

In such conditions the necessity of peace is itself a moral principle. As President Kennedy pointed out: "In the final analysis our most basic common link is that we all inhabit this small planet. We all breathe the same air. We all cherish our children's future. And we are all mortal."

It is said, correctly, that the Soviet idea of "peaceful coexistence" is not the same as ours, that Soviet policies aim at the furthering of Soviet objectives. The problem of peace takes on a profound moral and practical difficulty in a world of nuclear weapons capable of destroying humankind; in a century which has seen the use of brutal force; in an age of ideology which turns the domestic policies of nations into issues of international conflict. But the issue, surely, is not whether peace and stability serve Soviet purposes, but whether they also serve our own. Constructive actions in Soviet policy are desirable whatever the Soviet motives.

This government has stated clearly and constantly the principles which we believe must guide relations between the Soviet Union and the United States and international conduct, principles that are consistent with both our values and our interests:

—We will maintain a strong and flexible military position to preserve our security. We will as a matter of principle and national interest oppose attempts by any country to achieve global or regional predominance.

—We will judge the state of U.S.-Soviet relations according to whether concrete problems are successfully resolved.

—All negotiations will be a two-way street, based on mutual benefit and observance of agreements.

—We will insist, as we always have, that progress in U.S.—Soviet economic relations must reflect progress toward stable political relationships.

—We will never abandon our ideals or our friends. We will not negotiate over the heads of, or against the interests of, other nations.

—We will respond firmly to attempts to achieve advantage by one side.

Beyond the necessities of coexistence there is the hope of a more positive relationship. The American people will never be satisfied with simply reducing tension and easing the danger of nuclear disaster. Over the longer term, we hope that firmness in the face of pressure and the creation of motives for cooperative action may bring about a more lasting pattern of stability and responsible conduct.

Today's joint manned mission in space—an area in which 15 years ago we saw ourselves in rivalry—is symbolic of the distance we have traveled. [He is referring to the Apollo-Soyuz space flight in 1975, in which an American and a Russian spacecraft met and docked in space.] Practical progress has been made on many problems. Berlin is no longer a source of conflict between East and West. Crises have been avoided. The frequency of U.S.-Soviet consultation is unprecedented. The cooperation in many fields is in dramatic contrast to the state of affairs ten, even five, years ago. The agreements already achieved to limit strategic armament programs are unparalleled in the history of diplomacy.

Our immediate attention is on the international actions of the Soviet Union not because it is our only moral concern, but because it is the sphere of action that we can most directly and confidently affect. As a result of improved foreign policy relationships, we have successfully used our influence to promote human rights. But we have done so quietly, keeping in mind the delicacy of the problem and stressing results rather than public confrontation.

Therefore critics of détente must answer: What is the alternative that they propose? What precise policies do they want us to change? Are they prepared for a prolonged situation of dramatically increased international danger? Do they wish to return to the constant crises and high arms budgets of the Cold War? Does détente encourage repression? Or is it détente that has brought about the demands for openness that we are now witnessing? Can we ask our people to support confrontation unless they know that every reasonable alternative has been explored?

In our relations with the Soviet Union, the United States will maintain its strength, defend its interests, and support its friends with determination and without illusion. We will speak up for our beliefs with vigor and without self-deception. We consider détente a means to regulate a competitive relationship—not a substitute for our own efforts in building the strength of the free world. We will continue on

Henry Kissinger

this course because it offers hope to our children of a more secure and a more just world.

The considerations raise a more general question: To what extent are we able to affect the internal policies of other governments and to what extent is it desirable?

There are some 150 nations in the world. Barely 20 of them are democracies in any real sense. The rest are nations whose ideology or political practices are inconsistent with our own. Yet we have political relations and often alliances with some of these countries in Asia, Latin America, Africa, and Europe.

We do not and will not overlook repressive practices. We have used, and we will use, our influence against repressive practices. Our traditions and our interests demand it.

But truth also forces a recognition of our limits. The question is whether we promote human rights more effectively by counsel and friendly relations when this serves our interest or by propaganda and discriminatory legislation. And we must also assess how foreign governments act in relation to their history and to the threats they face. We must have some understanding for the problems of countries adjoining powerful, hostile, and totalitarian regimes.

Our alliances and political relationships serve mutual ends. They contribute to regional and world security and thus support the broader welfare. They are not favors to other governments, but reflect a recognition of mutual interests. They should be withdrawn only when our interests change and not as a punishment for some act with which we do not agree.

In many countries, whatever the internal structure, the populations are unified in seeking our protection against outside aggression. In many countries our foreign policy relationships have proved to be no obstacle to the forces of change. And in many countries, especially in Asia, it is the process of American withdrawal that has weakened the sense of security and created a need for greater internal discipline—and at the same time decreased our ability to influence domestic practices.

The attempt to deal with those practices by restrictive American legislation raises a serious problem. This is not because of the moral view it expresses—which we share—but because of the mistaken impression it creates that our security ties are acts of charity. And beyond that, such acts are almost inevitably doomed to fail because they are too public, too inflexible, and too much a stimulus to nationalistic resentment.

There are no simple answers. Painful experience should have taught us that we ought not exaggerate our ability to foresee, let alone to shape, social and political change in other societies. Therefore let me state the principles that will guide our action:

—Human rights are a legitimate international concern and have been so defined in international agreements for more than a generation.

—The United States will speak up for human rights in appropriate international forums and in exchanges with other governments.

—We will be mindful of the limits of our reach. We will be conscious of the difference between public attitudes that satisfy our self-esteem and policies that bring positive results.

—We will not lose sight of either the requirements of global security or what we stand for as a nation.

READING REVIEW

1. Why did Kissinger think that a peaceful relationship between the United States and the Soviet Union was so necessary to the rest of the world?

2. What did Kissinger say to the critics of détente?
3. Do you think his arguments were effective? Explain.

CHAPTER

42 Reaching for Freedom's Promise
(1960 to the Present)

---

247 An Appeal by Martin Luther King, Jr.

One of the greatest of modern American black leaders was Martin Luther King, Jr., a minister and crusader for civil rights. King first became well known during a bus boycott in Montgomery, Alabama, in 1955–56. After several months, black residents succeeded in desegregating local transportation. In the years that followed, King became a powerful leader of the nonviolent protest movement. He and his followers used sit-ins, boycotts, and marches to call attention to inequality and illegality in the treatment of black Americans.

In 1963 some 200,000 Americans, black and white, gathered in Washington, D.C., to publicize the demand for jobs and voting rights for blacks. As one of the leaders of this March on Washington, King made the following speech to the huge crowd assembled before the Lincoln Memorial.

READING FOCUS

1. Why did Martin Luther King, Jr. say the Negro was still not free?
2. What were his dreams for America?

One hundred years ago a great American, in whose symbolic shadow we stand [the demonstration was held at the Lincoln Memorial], signed the Emancipation Proclamation. This

---

Adapted from I Have a Dream *by Martin Luther King, Jr.*

momentous decree came as a great beacon light of hope to millions of Negro slaves who had been seared in the flames of withering injustice. It came as a joyous daybreak to end the long night of captivity.

But one hundred years later we must face the tragic fact that the Negro is still not free. One hundred years later the life of the Negro is still sadly crippled by the chains of segregation and discrimination. One hundred years later the Negro lives on a lonely island of poverty in the midst of a vast ocean of material prosperity. One hundred years later Negroes still find themselves exiles in their own land. So we have come here today to dramatize an appalling condition.

In a sense we have come to our nation's capital to cash a check. When the builders of our republic wrote the magnificent words of the Constitution and the Declaration of Independence, they were signing a promissory note which every American was to inherit. This note was a promise that all people would be guaranteed the unalienable rights of life, liberty, and the pursuit of happiness.

It is obvious today that America has defaulted on this promissory note insofar as its black citizens are concerned. Instead of honoring this sacred obligation, America has given the Negro people a bad check—a check which has come back marked "insufficient funds." But we refuse to believe that the bank of justice is bankrupt. We refuse to believe that there are insufficient funds in the great vaults of opportunity of this nation. So we have come to cash this check—a check that will give us upon demand the riches of freedom and the security of justice. We have also come to this hallowed spot to remind America of the fierce urgency of *now*. This is no time to engage in the luxury of cooling off or gradualism [the idea of proceeding slowly in carrying out change]. *Now* is the time to make real the promises of democracy. *Now* is the time to rise from the dark and desolate valley of segregation to the sunlit path of racial justice. *Now* is the time to open the doors of opportunity to all of God's children. *Now* is the time to lift our nation from the quicksands of racial injustice to the solid rock of brotherhood.

It would be fatal for the nation to overlook the urgency of the moment and to underestimate the determination of the Negro. This sweltering summer of the Negro's legitimate discontent will not pass until there is an invigorating autumn of freedom and equality. The year 1963 is not an end, but a beginning. Those who hope that the Negro needed to blow off steam and will now be content will have a rude awakening if the nation returns to business as usual. There will be neither rest nor tranquility in America until the Negro is granted citizenship rights. The whirlwinds of revolt will continue to shake the foundations of our nation until the bright day of justice emerges.

But there is something that I must say to my people who stand on the warm threshold which leads into the palace of justice. In the process of gaining our rightful place we must not be guilty of wrongful deeds. Let us not seek to satisfy our thirst for freedom by drinking from the cup of bitterness and hatred. We must forever conduct our struggle with dignity and discipline. We must not allow our creative protest to turn into physical violence. Again and again we must rise to the majestic heights of meeting physical force with soul force. The marvelous new militancy which has taken over the Negro community must not lead us to a distrust of all white people. Many of our white brothers, as shown by their presence here today, have come to realize that their destiny is tied up with our destiny. Their freedom is bound to our freedom. We cannot walk alone.

The Civil Rights March in Washington, D.C., 1963

And as we walk, we must make the pledge that we shall march ahead. We cannot turn back. There are those who are asking us, "When will you be satisfied?" We can never be satisfied as long as the Negro is the victim of the unspeakable horrors of police brutality. We can never be satisfied as long as we cannot gain lodging in the motels of the highways and the hotels of the cities. We cannot be satisfied as long as the Negro's basic mobility is from a smaller ghetto to a larger one. We can never be satisfied as long as a Negro in Mississippi cannot vote, and a Negro in New York believes he has nothing for which to vote. No, no, we are not satisfied, and we will not be satisfied until justice rolls down like water and righteousness like a mighty stream.

I know that some of you have come here out of great trouble. Some of you have come fresh from narrow jail cells. Some of you have come from areas where your search for freedom left you battered by the storms of persecution and staggered by the winds of police brutality. You have been the veterans of creative suffering. Continue to work with the faith that unearned suffering is redeeming.

Go back to Mississippi, go back to Alabama, go back to South Carolina, go back to Georgia, go back to Louisiana, go back to the slums and ghettos of our modern cities, knowing that somehow this situation can and will be changed. Let us not wallow in the valley of despair.

I say to you today, my friends, that in spite of the difficulties and frustrations of the moment I still have a dream. It is a dream deeply rooted in the American dream.

I have a dream that one day this nation will rise up and live out the true meaning of its creed: "We hold these truths to be self-evident: that all men are created equal."

I have a dream that one day on the red hills of Georgia the sons of former slaves and the sons of former slaveowners will be able to sit down together at the table of brotherhood.

I have a dream that one day even the state of Mississippi will be transformed into an oasis of freedom and justice.

I have a dream that my four little children will one day live in a nation where they will not be judged by the color of their skin but by the content of their character.

I have a dream today.

I have a dream that one day the state of Alabama will be changed into a situation where little black boys and black girls will be able to join hands with little white boys and white girls and walk together as sisters and brothers.

I have a dream today.

This is our hope. This is the faith with which I return to the South. With this faith we will be able to cut out of the mountain of despair a stone of hope. With this faith we will be able to change the jangling discords of our nation into a beautiful symphony of brotherhood. With this faith we will be able to work together, to pray together, to struggle together, to go to jail together, to stand up for freedom together, knowing that we will be free one day.

This will be the day when all of God's children will be able to sing with new meaning "My country 'tis of thee, sweet land of liberty, of thee I sing. Land where my fathers died, land of the pilgrim's pride, from every mountainside, let freedom ring."

And if America is to be a great nation this must become true. So let freedom ring from the hilltops of New Hampshire. Let freedom ring from the mountains of New York. Let freedom ring from the Alleghenies of Pennsylvania!

Let freedom ring from the snow-capped Rockies of Colorado!

Let freedom ring from the peaks of California!

But not only that; let freedom ring from Stone Mountain of Georgia!

Let freedom ring from Lookout Mountain of Tennessee!

Let freedom ring from every hill and molehill of Mississippi. From every mountainside, let freedom ring.

When we let freedom ring, when we let it ring from every village and every hamlet, from every state and every city, we will be able to speed up that day when all of God's children, black people and white people, Jews, Protestants, and Catholics, will be able to join hands and sing in the words of the old Negro spiritual, "Free at last! free at last, thank God almighty, we are free at last!"

READING REVIEW

1. How, according to King, had America failed to live up to its "sacred obligation"?
2. What did he mean when he spoke of "meeting physical force with soul force"?

3. **(a)** How would you describe King's dreams? **(b)** Do you think his dreams have been realized in today's society? Cite evidence from your textbook to support your conclusion.

Protestors march for civil liberties

248 An Assessment of Black Progress

The historic decision in Brown v. Board of Education of Topeka—*calling for desegregation in public education—was handed down by the Supreme Court in 1954. Twenty-four years later a group of scholars met in Mississippi to debate the question, "Have we overcome?" The words came from the unofficial anthem of the civil rights movement, "We Shall Overcome." Here black writer Lerone Bennett, Jr., offered an answer and an explanation.*

READING FOCUS

1. How did Bennett answer the question, "Have we overcome?"
2. What did the civil rights movement accomplish?

The question is have we overcome?

And my question is how are we to understand that dangerous word *we*?

And what does it mean *to overcome*?

Well, in the context of the song and the struggle, *we* means black people and white people who are committed to and involved in the struggle for equality and racial justice. And *to overcome,* again in the context of the song and the struggle, means the act of destroying all racial barriers and creating a new land of freedom and equality for all men, all women, and all children.

"Oh, deep in my heart I do believe we shall overcome." We shall overpass, triumph over mean sheriffs, robed riders, assassins of the spirit, segregation, discrimination, hunger, poverty, and humiliation.

Have we done it? No, a thousand times no.

We were there, some of us, and we sang the song, some of us, and saw the blood, some of us. And we know—deep in our hearts—that

Adapted from "Have We Overcome?" by Lerone Bennett, Jr. in Have We Overcome? Race Relations Since Brown.

what the singers and dreamers and victims hoped for . . . what they struggled and died for . . . has not happened yet. Because of the passion and the pain of the singers and victims and dreamers, we have, in the past twenty-four years, crossed many barriers . . . but we are nowhere near the end of our journey, and we have miles to go before we sleep.

And so, it is necessary to say here, in the name of the dreamers and victims, that we have not yet started the process of grappling with the depth and the height of the dream. As a matter of fact, we haven't even defined what we must do in order to overcome.

To cite only one point, the admission of a handful of gifted black students and athletes to a white university controlled by whites is not—repeat—*not* integration. It is at best desegregation and a prelude to that great American dream which was written down on pieces of paper, which was promised, and which has never existed anywhere in America, except in the hearts of a handful of men and women. By any reasonable standard, then, we have failed to meet the goal.

How remote, how unimaginably distant and remote that May day [of the *Brown* decision] seems today. The events of the intervening years—Montgomery, the sit-ins, the freedom rides, the marches, and urban rebellions—came so suddenly, so dramatically. Our sense of time has been distorted and incidents and personalities of only a few days ago have been pushed into the distant past.

The internal and external changes flowing from this event have been profound and dramatic. So have the costs. Martin Luther King, Jr., is dead; Malcolm X is dead. Whitney Young, Medgar Evers, Fred Hampton [other figures associated with the civil rights movement] are all dead. And the movement they led and symbolized has ended.

It is true, and important, that blacks are going places today they couldn't go twenty-four years ago. *Everything, in fact, has changed in Mississippi and America, and yet, paradoxically, nothing has changed.*

Despite the court orders and civil rights laws, blacks are still the last hired and the first fired. They are still systematically exploited as consumers and citizens. To come right out with it, the full privileges and immunities of the U.S. Constitution do not apply to blacks tonight, in Mississippi or in Massachusetts, and they never have. You want to know how bad things are? Listen to the facts cited by Robert B. Hill of the National Urban League in a recent booklet, entitled *The Illusion of Black Progress.*

Contrary to popular belief, the economic gap between blacks and whites is widening. Between 1975 and 1976, the black to white family income ratio fell sharply from 62 to 59 percent.

Not only is black unemployment at its highest level today, but the jobless gap between blacks and whites is the widest it has ever been. . . . The proportion of middle-income black families has not significantly increased. The proportion of upper-income black families has steadily declined. White high school dropouts have lower unemployment rates (22.3%) than black youth with college education (27.2%).

These figures are terrible, and the reality is worse. How did this happen? How is it possible for black America to be in so much trouble after all the demonstrations, and marches, and court orders? What is the meaning of this terrible indictment?

The short answer to these questions is that we stopped marching too soon. The long . . . and scholarly . . . answer is embedded in the history of our journey.

It is possible, indeed likely, that the post-*Brown* struggle, despite its limitations, was a necessary stage in the social maturing of black people. And there can be little doubt that it created black America's finest hours and one of the finest hours in the history of the republic.

Because of that struggle, we have made significant gains on the political front and in the middle sectors. The movement changed, destroyed, wiped out the visible and dramatic signs of racism, but it did not and perhaps could not at that time deal with the subtle forms of institutional racism. Nor did it change or even make a dent in the economic inequities of a society that can make work for black men inside prisons after they commit crimes but cannot find work for black men outside prisons before they commit crimes.

And so, as a result of the failure of the movement to make a total breakthrough on the racial front, we find ourselves in the post-revolutionary phase of a revolution that never happened.

Does this mean that the movement was a failure? By no means. As a result of that struggle, one-third of this nation—the South—was changed, perhaps forever, and the rest of the nation made its first tentative steps toward democracy. Beyond all that, the movement created the foundations for future change.

The leaders [of the civil rights movement] didn't start the Montgomery boycott: the people started it. And when the energy of the people ran out, when they had tried everything, or almost everything, the people withdrew to retool and rethink. And what we've got to understand tonight is that this temporary withdrawal was and is natural under the circumstances. The law of history is that people cannot live forever on the heights. The law of history is that a people advance and retreat, advance and retreat, advance and retreat, until they reach a collective decision to go for broke. And this entitles us to say, I think, that if the sun continues to shine and the wind continues to blow, the movement of the sixties will reemerge in America on a higher level of development.

The sixties taught us four great lessons. First, the struggle to overcome is not a hundred-yard dash but a long-distance run. We must prepare, therefore, for the long haul. We must prepare for a struggle of five, ten, fifteen, or even fifty years.

The second lesson, growing out of the first,

is that people change only when they have to change, and that it is the task of the oppressed to do whatever is required to force change.

The third is that we cannot overcome and the gains of the post-*Brown* years cannot be preserved without a total struggle for fundamental change. There have to be real changes in the tax structure and the relations between the private and public sectors, a redefinition of values, and a redistribution of income.

Finally, and most importantly, the white South and white North are going to have to deal with themselves. The great lesson of the sixties, a lesson heeded almost nowhere, is that there is no Negro problem in Mississippi and in America. The problem of race in Mississippi, and in America, is a white problem, and we shall not overcome until we confront that problem.

READING REVIEW

1. **(a)** How did Bennett answer the question "Have we overcome?" **(b)** What evidence did he offer to support his answer to this question?
2. **(a)** What did the civil rights movement accomplish? **(b)** Did Bennett feel that it was successful? Why or why not?
3. As Bennett saw it, what lessons did the 1960's teach?
4. What did Bennett mean when he said, "Everything, in fact, has changed in Mississippi and America, and yet paradoxically, nothing has changed"?

---

249 The Unending Dream

With all its problems, the United States in the 1980's still has a worldwide image as a land of opportunity. Every year thousands of foreigners immigrate in hopes of finding a better life. Thousands more come illegally with the same hope. In the interview that follows, Leonel Castillo, former head of the United States Immigration and Naturalization Service, talked about the American Dream. Himself the grandson of a Mexican immigrant, he was especially concerned with Mexican, and other, illegal (or undocumented) aliens.

READING FOCUS

1. What did Castillo say were the outstanding characteristics of illegal aliens?
2. What was the author's attitude toward illegal aliens?

New immigrants are trying all over again to integrate themselves into the system. They have the same hunger. On any given day, there are about three million throughout the world who are applying to come to the United States and share the American Dream. . . .

The Vietnamese boat people [who fled Southeast Asia after the Communist takeover in 1975] express it as well as anyone. They don't know if they're gonna land, if the boat's gonna sink. They don't know what's gonna happen to 'em, but they've a hunch they might make it to the U.S. as the "freedom place."

There is the plain hard fact of hunger. In order to eat, a person will endure tremendous hardship. Mexican people who come here usually are not the poorest. Someone who's too poor can't afford the trip. . . .

Sometimes the whole family saves up and gives the bright young man or the bright young woman the family savings. It even goes into debt for a year or two. They pin all their hopes on this one kid, put him on a bus, let him go a thousand miles [1600 kilometers]. He doesn't speak a word of English. He's only seventeen, eighteen years old, but he's gonna save that family. A lot rides on that kid who's a busboy in some hotel.

Adapted from American Dreams: Lost and Found *by Studs Terkel.*

Vietnamese boat people

We've had some as young as eleven who have come a thousand miles [1600 kilometers]. You have this young kid, all his family savings, everything is on him. There are a lot of songs and stories about mother and child, the son leaving who may never return. We end up deporting him [sending him back home]. It's heartrending.

He's the bright kid in the family. The slow one might not make it, might get killed. The one who's sickly can't make the trip. He couldn't walk through the desert. He's not gonna be too old, too young, too destitute, or too slow. He's the brightest and the best.

He's gonna be the first hook, the first pioneer coming into an alien society, the United States. . . . He works as a busboy all night long. They pay him minimum or less, and work him hard. He'll never complain. He might even thank his boss. He'll say as little as possible because he doesn't want anyone to know what his status is. He will often live in his apartment, except for the time he goes to work or to church or to a dance. He will stay in and watch TV. If he makes a hundred a week, he will manage to send back twenty-five. All over the country, if you go to a Western Union office on the weekend, you'll find a lot of people there sending money orders to Mexico.

After the kid learns a bit, because he's healthy and young and energetic, he'll probably get another job as a busboy. He'll work at another place as soon as the shift is over. He'll try to work his way up to be a waiter. He'll work incredible hours. He doesn't care about union scale, he doesn't care about conditions, about humiliations. He accepts all this as his fate.

He's burning underneath with this energy and ambition. He outworks the U.S. busboys and eventually becomes the waiter. Where he can maneuver, he tries to become the owner and gives a lot of competition to the locals. Restaurant owners tell me, if they have a choice, they'll always hire foreign nationals first. They're so eager and grateful. There's a little greed here, too. They pay 'em so little. . .

At least a quarter of a million apprehensions were made last year. If we apprehend them at the border, we turn 'em around and ask them to depart voluntarily. They turn around and go back to Mexico. A few hours later, they try again. In El Paso, we deported one fellow six times in one day. There's a restaurant in Hollywood run by a fellow we deported thirty-seven times. We've deported some people more than a hundred times. They always want to come back. There's a job and there's desperation. . . .

Half the people here without papers are not Mexicans. They're from all over the world. They came legally, with papers, as tourists ten years ago. . . . All too often, the public gets the impression that all immigrants are on welfare. It's the exact opposite. Very few go on welfare. We get people coming in from Haiti, the poorest country in the western hemisphere. They come over by boat and land in Florida.

We make three thousand apprehensions at the border every weekend. It's just a little 14-mile [22-kilometer] stretch. Our border patrol knows this little fellow comin' across is hungry. He just wants to work. They know he's no security threat. They say: "It's my job." Many of them come to have a great deal of respect for the people they're deporting. What do you think of a person you deport three, four times, who just keeps coming back? You would never want to get in the same ring with that person.

I'm torn. I saw it in the Peace Corps, when I was in the Philippines. A mother offered you her infant. You're just a twenty-one-year-old kid and she says: "Take my child, take him with you to the States." When you see this multiplied by thousands, it tears you up. . . .

The only thing that helps me is remembering the history of this country. We've always managed . . . to rejuvenate ourselves, to bring in new people. Every new group comes in believing more firmly in the American Dream than the one that came a few years before. Every new group is scared of being in the welfare line or in the unemployment office. They go to night school, they learn about America. We'd be lost without them.

The old dream is still dreamt. The old neighborhood Ma-Pa stores [small stores owned and run by a husband and wife] are still around. They are not Italian or Jewish or Eastern European any more. Ma and Pa are now Korean, Vietnamese, Iraqi, Jordanian, Latin American. They live in the store. They work seven days a week. Their kids are doing well in school. They're making it. Sound familiar?

Near our office in Los Angeles is a little cafe with a sign: KOSHER BURRITOS. A *burrito* is a Mexican tortilla with meat inside. Most of the customers are black. The owner is Korean.

The banker, I imagine, is WASP. This is what's happening in the United States today. It is not a melting pot, but in one way or another, there is a blending of cultures.

I see all kinds of new immigrants starting out all over again, trying to work their way into the system. They're going through new battles, yet they're old battles. They want to share in the American Dream. The stream never ends.

READING REVIEW

1. **(a)** How did Castillo describe the typical undocumented newcomer? **(b)** Do you think this description is valid for all illegal aliens? Why or why not?
2. What were Castillo's feelings about illegal aliens?
3. What does the American Dream mean to you?

250 Four Minority Voices

The United States was settled and built by people of many different racial and national backgrounds. In many cases the newcomers or their descendants discarded their cultural differences and became "Americanized." Indeed, for a long time the ideal America was a "melting pot." In it all the various peoples would blend, losing their individuality and ethnic identity. Instead of being Poles or Filipinos or Haitians, they would become, simply, Americans.

In recent years, however, the trend has been to emphasize ethnic consciousness—the feeling of belonging to a special group. Members of many minority groups have felt a new awareness of their cultures. This selection presents the views of four minority group members: a Mexican American, a Puerto Rican, a Chinese American, and an American Indian.

READING FOCUS

1. How did each of these representatives of minority groups feel about their national background?
2. What did they have in common?

[FORRESTO GARCIA]

I am Forresto Garcia and sixteen years old. I have five brothers and four sisters. I know how it is to work in the fields but I have been lucky and graduated from my grade school. I like to help poor people and I want to be somebody that helps poor people.

American Indians demand greater rights.

We have just come from Texas to California in our car with a trailer attached to it, and we put all our belongings in the trailer. When we arrived here we looked for a rancher, and he said, "Do you want to work picking cotton?" And we said, "Yes, we want to work," and he said, "Well, I'll give you a house if you work for me for the cotton season," and he gives us a house and that's the way we live. And when the cotton is finished we move to another town and look for another crop. When there is no house we set up our trailer near the rest of the families, but mostly we live outside the trailer. But when we are naughty my father quietly tells us to go into the trailer. You obey right away just by hearing the way he speaks. He has a twig from the prune tree and when he hits you with it you know it. Just once or twice.

We get up at five in the morning so we can start work at six. My sisters get up earlier because they have to make breakfast for my dad and my brothers and then make food for the fields. We make an early start so we could earn enough money for the day. We work until about four in the afternoon.

I am trying to get a steady job to help my family so they can have more money. In Texas I have seen many American-Mexicans without shoes, with their feet all dirty, and their faces and hands dirty, and no water to take a bath.

I sometimes just stay home doing nothing but thinking about my family. On Sunday when there is no work we go to the picnic grounds and cook on an open fire and when it gets very hot we swim in the stream that runs by our house.

Forresto Garcia's story adapted from Small Hands, Big Hands *by Sandra Weiner.*

It makes me feel bad to see poor people. My brother, he works for the union and he talks a lot about the union and what the union is doing and I like it. When I meet some guys working in the field I say, "How would you like to join the union?" and they say, "No, I'm O.K. and I don't like to help poor people." I get mad at them.

Now when my older brothers and my father picket against picking grapes I help them. I like to see them win what they are fighting for. Some employers are better than others, but some take advantage of the workers. They are rich and my people are so poor.

[RICKY]

My name is Ricky and I'm Puerto Rican. The best thing about being Puerto Rican is just being Puerto Rican. That's where it's at. I believe Puerto Rican people are the best. They treat me very good—very good. Like they aren't cheap with their stuff. Like you're at a party and it's late. And they say right away, "We got an extra bed. Sleep here." And they feed you and they do everything for you. And they don't have that much. But they've always given to everyone, and they'll give you what they got because they're generous.

Where I live now it looks like a ghetto. But it used to be real pretty. When I was young there were no addicts there and nobody was uptight about drugs. Now everybody is, because there's a lot of junkies [drug users] hanging around all over the neighborhood. Puerto Ricans. Blacks. Dominicans. All the races mix. It doesn't matter.

There's a lot of violence where I live. I watch not because I'm interested, but because you have no choice. After all, if I'm there, what am I going to do—just look the other way? But I like to see people who deserve to get hurt get theirs, you know? The guys that hurt other people. Like the junkies—most people who get hurt in these fights are junkies, because they're the ones who go around hurting people and the others get even. They mug people, kill people, and rob houses, and the people around my way they don't have that much. Maybe they save a year for a television set, and they enjoy watching it. And then here comes somebody, some junkie after money, and he robs these people and takes all they've got and leaves them with nothing.

I know a whole lot of junkies, but they're not my friends—I don't hang out with them. I don't know how people become junkies in the first place. Maybe they're influenced by their friends or they pick it up in school—but something happens to them.

I never smoked marijuana cause I don't need it. I don't need anything. Maybe other people need to feel nice. Maybe it makes them feel like a big man. It's the same with violence, guns, and killings, I guess.

I feel nice when I shoot pool. I'm pretty good, too. I make money from it, in fact. I can make thirty or forty dollars on a weekend. I just go up to a guy and say, "Hey, do you want to shoot pool?" I lose a lot of times, but I've won more money than I lost. And I also like to play poker.

Another thing I've always liked to do is turn on the fire hydrant. It's fun getting wet and running around getting other people wet. One time when I was little I was playing with the fire hydrant and I was covering myself with a box so I didn't see a car coming. And I guess the car didn't see me either and the driver didn't pay any attention to the water and I got hit. That happened twice more. The person that hit me the third time was my lawyer. He was going to my house to talk to my parents about the first two cases and then he hit me. I tried to sue but I don't know what happened. I wasn't badly hurt.

I'd still like to play with the fire hydrant, but the cops picked me up for opening one last summer. The only other time I got into trouble with the police was once when they asked me my name. I gave them a phony name and a phony address. I told them I didn't have a phone number, and they believed me.

When a cop gets shot, I say that's bad. Like, they have to take care of people and they're just people, too. They weren't born cops, they just got in it. In fact, I like Puerto Rican cops. They're together people. Puerto Ricans are proud and that's good. Maybe that's why we fight a lot. We are proud people and we don't take anything off of people. We don't ask nobody for nothing. I wouldn't even borrow money from my friends. That's how proud I am.

Adaptation of "Ricky's Story" from Growing Up Puerto Rican *by Paulette Cooper.*

[CLARENCE CHEN]

For most of my life I have taken for granted the fact that I am racially different from most of the people I have met and known—they are mostly Caucasian and I am not. When it occurred to me to think about who I was I would think of myself first as a boy, a student, a son, and then, somewhere near the end of the list, as a Chinese.

After all, I was like all of my American friends; we spoke the same slang, played the same games, listened to the same music, wore the same type of clothes. When we were boys, we lived and would have died for the same local baseball team—the White Sox. We played cowboys and Indians. As an adolescent, I had the same financial, emotional, and social crises everyone else did. For all practical purposes, I grew up as a typical American boy who happened to be Chinese.

Throughout my years of growing up, I encountered relatively little outward racial prejudice directed against me. The general lack of racial prejudice directed against me was at least partially due to the absence of any other Chinese people. My family were the first Chinese (and nonwhite) to move into that neighborhood on the South Side of Chicago. My brother and I were the first Chinese students at our elementary and high schools.

But while I am an American for all practical purposes, there have been times when I was acutely and uncomfortably aware that I was also different. Though my mannerisms, speech, and dress were American, my physical appearance was quite obviously Oriental. When I was about five, I believed that my Oriental features made me ugly even though I cannot recall having been told that by anyone.

In school, whenever a topic related to China was brought up in a social studies class, I would notice the other kids looking in my direction—expecting me to be knowledgeable on the subject. Since I knew practically nothing of Chinese history, culture, or language, I generally passed such moments by slumping into my seat and becoming suddenly interested in my books.

Clarence Chin's story adapted from "The Security Blanket of Racial Anonymity" by Clarence Chen in Bridge: An Asian American Perspective.

Unfortunately, some of my meetings with other Chinese have been similarly embarrassing. Whenever I have met Chinese people who have been brought up in the Chinese culture, I have been met with two sets of responses. Either I am Chinese and able to speak and act Chinese, or I am not Chinese at all but completely American or perhaps Japanese. In the former case, the other person is usually disappointed and embarassed to learn I cannot speak Chinese. In the latter case, the other person is usually surprised and amused to find I am racially 100 percent Chinese, that my family came to this country just one generation ago, and that I actually know a few phrases in Chinese such as "Thank you" and "See you again."

Several years ago I made a trip to Taiwan. My uncles and aunts, while warmly receiving me as a member of the family, could not help but see me as more American than Chinese. They affectionately called me *wai gwo ren*—a term meaning "foreigner" but also suggesting "Westerner" or "white man." I felt I was viewed as somewhat stupid because of my inability to speak Chinese. There must have been something about my appearance and manner—perhaps my American-style clothes and hair length or my un-Chinese assertiveness—which branded me as an alien; for storekeepers, cab drivers, and waiters quickly knew I was an outsider even before I spoke.

I do not mean to suggest that I have never gotten along with other Chinese. Yes, some of my best friends are Chinese. But they have come from white-collar, middle-class families like mine who have been pretty much assimilated into the mainstream of American culture.

While it may sound as if I have never been genuinely comfortable in the company of either Americans or Chinese, the reality has not been that difficult. Most of the time when I am with other non-Chinese people, the matter of our racial differences never crosses our minds.

While I have occasionally felt uncomfortable being Chinese in a mainly Caucasian country, I am fortunate in belonging to a group of Chinese-Americans in which I can feel very much at home. This group, consisting of eight families scattered around the Chicago area, began as an informal association of Chinese student couples who found themselves stranded in the United States after the Communists came to power in China. The members meet socially once a month at one another's homes.

The people of my generation in this group will, no matter how Americanized they seem to become, always have a unique aspect in their backgrounds—their parents grew up and were brought up in the Chinese culture. Thus, despite our American characteristics, we (the American-born Chinese) have been influenced in certain ways by the traditional culture. All of us have high achievement motivations and have all won superior academic credentials. (Scholarship was, for thousands of years in China, the most honored and respected path to higher status and public recognition.) Furthermore, academic and nonacademic achievements have been felt in our group to reflect shamefully or proudly on the individual and also on the individual's family. It is quite common in our eight-family gatherings to hear one parent praising another parent for his or her offspring's accomplishment. This is a reflection of a traditional Chinese concept: a person's reputation, whether honorable or dishonorable, directly affects the family's reputation. "Good" children in China were those who brought honor to the family name.

Last summer I went to a "Chinese Family Camp" to serve as a counselor. About thirty yards [27 meters] off the shore of Lake Wawasee, Indiana, was an anchored raft that could be used by anyone who swam out to it. One afternoon I was resting on it when I suddenly realized that the five or six of us on the raft were all Chinese-American. In that moment, a deep, warm feeling swept through me. I was just where I belonged—a temporary island on which disguises dissolved and I could be what I am—not really American, not really Chinese, but really Chinese-American.

[BETTY]

I'm like my brother. He says we're *both* going to be different Hopis than our parents were. We would like to leave the reservation. We wouldn't mind seeing how Indians live in cit-

ies. A lot of Hopis say you stop being a Hopi when you go into a city and live in big buildings and forget about our land, and our hills, and the sky over us. Maybe. I don't know. The Indian can't just sit and think of his past. My mother says it's a pity; our people were happy here for so long. Now, a lot of us want to leave. But she admits that we are living better than we used to live. And she says we can still be Hopis, even if we get the white man's knowledge, and spend some of our lives living in his land, not ours.

We're not going to have cities here. We're not going to let the white man come and tear our land up, like he's done elsewhere. But we have to live so that our children don't get sick and die, when they could live if there was a doctor and a hospital near. And we have to live in houses where the children don't freeze in the winter. Our mother said her old mother and old aunt didn't like the house we lived in at first. They said it was a white man's house. They didn't like the electricity when it was first brought in. But now they do. They wouldn't know how to get by without it. That's why I tell my brother: it's all right to be a white man, and you can still be a Hopi.

My aunt is very fond of me. She asks me a lot of the time what I will do when I grow older. Will I stay in school? Have I thought of someone I'd like to marry? Questions like that. I have always confided in her. I told her once that I wouldn't mind going away for a while and living among white people. She wasn't as upset as my mother would be. But I don't think she really believes I'm going to go—and I'm not sure either.

She said it was all right to want to know about the white man and his cities. She said it's because of school; we learn so much. When she was young, she didn't go to school. She is right about schools. They show us pictures and movies and we read books. I read a book about France. I would like to go to Paris. I read another book about England, I would like to go to London. I would also like to see California. I would *not* like to visit Washington, D. C. That is where the BIA [Bureau of Indian Affairs] has its office.

My old aunt always asks me the same question at the end of a talk: would you come back if you traveled far away? I say yes, and she is happy. But I'm not sure. What would happen if I traveled far and liked living where I was?

Betty's story adapted from pp. 504–507 in Eskimos, Chicanos, Indians: Volume IV of Children of Crisis *by Robert Coles.*

Would I come back then? I don't know. The white people live a different life than we do. And my father is right, they kill each other in automobile crashes when they travel, and they are always starting a war or trying to end one. And our people have lost so much to them. Our men still fight in their wars, and a long time ago, they were making war against us, and we lost a lot of people then. But the Hopis never fought the whites the way the Navajos and the Apaches did. The teachers told us that in school, and my father said they are right because we have not been fighters. My father tells us that to fight is to admit that you are weak and without control over yourself—wilder than any animal.

But the white people aren't just fighting all the time. They can be friends of the Indians; some white people are volunteers. They try to help people—and they even work for the same federal government that sends us the BIA people. My father admits that even a few of the BIA people are getting better. I think in the future Hopis and white people will become friendlier, and the Hopi people will travel more.

READING REVIEW

1. What did being Mexican American mean to Forresto Garcia?
2. What were Ricky's feelings about his Puerto Rican identity?
3. How did Clarence Chen describe his experience as a Chinese American?
4. How would you summarize Betty's attitude toward being an American Indian?
5. What common experiences or attitudes did these four young people share?

251 Women's Dissatisfaction

In the 1950's most American women were full-time wives and mothers; only about 30 percent worked outside the home. There were very few women in politics, in the professions, or in executive positions in business and industry. Society praised the role of the housewife—but not all of those who held the job were satisfied with it.

One woman who felt that there must be more to life was a suburban mother of three, named Betty Friedan. She investigated how other women felt about themselves and reported her findings in a best-selling book, *The Feminine Mystique*. Its major point was that millions of American women were becoming aware that the world of home and family did not offer them fulfillment.

In 1964 Friedan helped found the National Organization for Women. It revived the feminist movement and led a renewed struggle for equal rights for women in employment, education, and other areas of American society.

READING FOCUS

1. According to the author, what was the "feminine mystique"?
2. What was "the problem that has no name"?

The problem lay buried, unspoken, for many years in the minds of American women. It was a strange stirring, a sense of dissatisfaction, a yearning that women suffered in the 1950's in the United States. Each suburban wife struggled with it alone. As she made the beds, shopped for groceries, matched slipcover material, ate peanut butter sandwiches with her children, drove around Cub Scouts and Brownies, she was afraid to ask herself the silent question—"Is this all?"

Adapted from The Feminine Mystique *by Betty Friedan.*

Betty Friedan

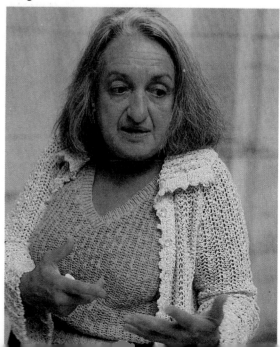

For over fifteen years there was no word of this yearning in the millions of words written about women and for women by experts telling them that their role was to seek fulfillment as wives and mothers. Over and over women heard that they could desire no greater destiny than to glory in their own femininity. Experts told them how to catch a man and keep him, how to handle children; how to buy a dishwasher, bake bread, cook gourmet snails; how to dress, look, and act more feminine and make marriage more exciting. They were taught to pity the neurotic, unfeminine, unhappy women who wanted to be poets or physicists or presidents. They learned that truly feminine women do not want careers, higher education, political rights—the independence and the opportunies that the old-fashioned feminists fought for. A thousand expert voices praised women's new maturity. All they had to do was devote their lives from earliest girlhood to finding a husband and having children.

By the end of the 1950's the average marriage age of women in America had dropped to 20, and was still dropping, into the teens. Fourteen million girls were engaged by 17. The proportion of women attending college in comparison with men dropped from 47 percent in 1920 to 35 percent in 1958. A hundred years earlier, women had fought for higher education; now girls went to college to get a husband. By the mid-1950's, 60 percent dropped out of college to marry, or because they were afraid too much education would hurt their chances for marriage.

By the end of the 1950's the United States birthrate was overtaking India's. Statisticians were especially astounded at the fantastic increase in the number of babies born to college-educated women. Where once they had two children, now they had four, five, six.

Girls were growing up in America without ever having jobs outside the home. Fewer and fewer women were entering professional work. The shortages in the nursing, social work, and teaching professions caused crises in almost every American city. Concerned over the Soviet Union's lead in the space race, scientists noted that America's greatest source of unused brainpower was women. But girls would not study physics: it was "unfeminine."

The suburban housewife—she was the dream image of young American women. She was the envy, it was said, of women all over the world. The American housewife was freed by science and labor-saving appliances from the drudgery, the dangers of childbirth, and the illnesses of her grandmother. She was healthy, beautiful, educated, concerned only about her husband, her children, her home. She had found true feminine fulfillment. As a housewife and mother, she was respected as a full and equal partner to man in his world. She was free to choose automobiles, clothes, appliances, supermarkets. She had everything that women had ever dreamed of.

In the fifteen years after World War II, this mystique of feminine fulfillment became the cherished center of American culture. Millions of women lived their lives in the image of the American suburban housewife, kissing their husbands goodbye in front of the picture window, leaving their stationwagonsful of children at school, and smiling as they ran the new electric waxer over the spotless kitchen floor. They gave no thought to the unfeminine problems of the world outside the home; they wanted the men to make the major decisions. They gloried in their role as women, and wrote proudly on the census blank: "Occupation: housewife."

For over fifteen years, the words written for women, and the words women used when they talked to each other, were about problems with their children, or how to keep their husbands happy, or improve their children's school, or cook chicken or make slipcovers. Nobody argued whether women were inferior or superior to men; they were simply different. Words like "emancipation" and "career" sounded strange and embarrassing; no one had used them for years.

If a women had a problem in the 1950's and 1960's, she knew that something must be wrong with her marriage, or with herself. Other women were satisfied with their lives, she thought. What kind of woman was she if she did not feel this mysterious fulfillment waxing the kitchen floor? She was so ashamed to admit her dissatisfaction that she never knew how many other women shared it. If she tried to tell her husband, he didn't understand what she was talking about.

But on an April morning in 1959, I heard a mother of four, having coffee with four other mothers, say in a tone of quiet desperation, "the problem." And the others knew, without words, that she was not talking about a problem with her husband, or her children, or her home. Suddenly they realized they all shared the same problem, the problem that has no name. They began, hesitantly, to talk about it. Later, after they had picked up their children at nursery school and taken them home to nap, two of the women cried, in sheer relief, just to know they were not alone.

Gradually I came to realize that the problem that has no name was shared by countless women in America. Sometimes I sensed the problem, not as a reporter, but as a suburban housewife, for during this time I was also bringing up my own three children.

Just what was this problem that has no name? What were the words women used when they tried to express it? Sometimes a woman would say, "I feel empty somehow—incomplete." Or she would say, "I feel as if I don't exist." Sometimes she got rid of the feeling with a tranquilizer. Sometimes she thought the problem was with her husband, or her children, or that what she really needed was to redecorate her house, or move to a better neighborhood, or have another baby. Sometimes she went to a doctor with symptoms she could hardly describe: "A tired feeling—I get so angry with the children it scares me—I feel like crying without any reason."

In 1960 the problem that has no name burst through the image of the happy American housewife. In the television commercials the pretty housewives still smiled over their foaming dishpans. But the actual unhappiness of the American housewife was suddenly being reported, although almost everybody who talked about it found some easy reason to explain it away.

The problem was explained away by telling the housewife she didn't realize how lucky she was. What if she wasn't happy—did she think men were happy in this world? Did she really, secretly, still want to be a man? Didn't she know yet how lucky she was to be a woman?

The problem was also explained away by saying that there are no solutions. This is what being a woman means. What is wrong with American women that they can't accept their role gracefully?

By 1962 the plight of the trapped American housewife had become a national game. Whole issues of magazines, newspaper columns, books, educational conferences, and television panels were devoted to the problem.

Even so, most men, and some women, still did not know that this problem was real. But those who had faced it honestly knew that all the easy remedies did not work. They got all kinds of advice on how to adjust to their role as housewives. No other road to fulfillment was offered to American women in the 1950's. Most adjusted to their role and suffered or ignored the problem that has no name.

* * * *

It is no longer possible to ignore, to explain away, the desperation of so many American women. This is not what being a woman means, no matter what the experts say. Perhaps the reason has not been found because the right questions have not been asked, or pressed far enough. The women who suffer from this problem have a hunger that food cannot fill. It may not even be felt by women with desperate problems of hunger, poverty, or illness. And women who think it will be solved by more money, a bigger house, a second car, moving to a better suburb, often discover it gets worse.

It is no longer possible today to blame the problem on loss of femininity, or to say that education and independence and equality with men have made American women unfeminine. I have heard so many women try to deny this dissatisfied voice within themselves because it does not fit the pretty picture of femininity the experts have given them.

If I am right, the problem that has no name stirring in the minds of so many American women today is not a matter of loss of femininity or too much education or the demands of taking care of a house and family. It is far more important than anyone recognizes. It is the key to these other new and old problems which have been torturing women and their husbands and children for years. It may well be the key to our future as a nation and a culture. We can no longer ignore that voice within women that says: "I want something more than my husband and my children and my home."

READING REVIEW

1. Describe the "feminine mystique."
2. What was "the problem" as women saw it in the 1950's?
3. How did many people try to explain the problem?
4. Did Friedan agree with the solutions explaining the problem? Why or why not?

252 The Gains of Feminism

When Linda Gray Sexton graduated from college in the mid-1970's, she and her classmates felt that all options were open to them: career, marriage, and motherhood. Sexton's mother had given her a copy of *The Feminist Mystique* when she was a girl, and she had found Betty Friedan "a friendly girder of support" as she contemplated living in the "two worlds" of career woman and wife-mother.

But reality seemed more complex. Some of Sexton's friends were poorly prepared for vocations. Others, trying to exercise all their options, teetered constantly on the edge of exhaustion. What was wrong? Like Friedan before her, Sexton (about the right age to be Friedan's daughter) embarked on a series of interviews. Here she summarized her findings.

READING FOCUS

1. What was the difference between the femin*ine* mystique and the femin*ist* mystique?
2. According to Sexton, what had the women's movement achieved?

The femin*ine* mystique preached that women didn't need a variety of choices because biology determined that they would be wives and mothers. The femin*ist* mystique said that women didn't need a variety of choices because

---

Adapted from Between Two Worlds *by Linda Gray Sexton.*

Demonstrators support the Equal Rights Amendment.

choice in itself was unnecessary, limiting, and defeatist. In the long run, then, there was only one difference between the two. One gave birth to boredom—for those not suited to house-wifery. The other led to exhaustion—for those not geared to "Superwomanhood." From the women I interviewed, one message stood out clearly: blind acceptance of the femin*ist* mystique is as much an unthinking observance of a new tradition as blind acceptance of the femin*ine* mystique was an unthinking observance of the old. Once again, a problem has arisen because a system of values has been applied to an entire population.

A few months ago, in the midst of my writing, an acquaintance told me a story that seemed to sum up some of the problems faced by our generation. She had recently become a mother, while simultaneously teaching full time at a nearby university. Using a day-care center—which she had applied to months in advance—she clockworked her schedule down to the minute. Racing between home, the university, and the center, she managed to keep it all together. Both she and her husband worked four days a week as a compromise. But now, even looking back on that time makes her feel exhausted. She realizes that her attempt not to shortchange the needs of her baby, her husband, or her career resulted in short-changing the most important needs of all—her own. She had proved she could do it, but at what cost to herself?

The oversimplified teachings of women's liberation have been no cure-all. The movement promised that if women worked they would be happy and fulfilled. But as more and more of us have ventured out into the business world, universal happiness has not descended. Universal confusion has, however. Women are finally beginning to wake up to a basic truth, a truth men have taken for granted and accepted for generations: work is *work*—not play. Work is not always fulfillment. It is 90 percent drudgery and 10 percent illumination—like motherhood. Its satisfactions are not sufficient for everyone.

The Women's Movement has made great strides in winning the equal rights women deserve as a group. But it has failed as a miracle drug—it has not cured the unhappiness of all individual American women. Before we are women, after all, we are people. Many of our discontents can only be solved by us alone, for ourselves alone. Even when a woman adopts feminist teachings wholeheartedly and makes no choice between parenthood and career, even when her husband rearranges his own career, there is still a price to be paid. And, ultimately, it is the woman herself who bears the cost.

With nearly all doors open to us, with increasing legislation in our favor, with more and more of us flowing into the job market at one time or another, are we more content, more fulfilled than our mothers were? I think not. I think it would be accurate to say we are overwhelmingly confused about who we are—just as confused as our mothers were, if not more so. We are trapped between one mystique and the other, and the way to freedom is not at all clear. Even worse, we are often ashamed to voice our feelings of conflict because we live in a time when women are supposed to be free of conflict.

We are the products of two vastly different worlds, forged in the fire of dissent and strife. While it is difficult to generalize about fifteen women so very different as those presented [in the book Sexton has written], one feeling common to them all is frighteningly clear. Wherever they come from, whatever they do, whoever they are, they all feel an increasing need to choose between the two worlds, to simplify their lives, to stop straddling the fence. I see a new and painful light dawning in their eyes, a new acknowledgement of the need to choose. Some realize it with horror, as it increases the immediate pressure. Others realize it with heartfelt relief because facing it releases some of the tension.

Each and every one of us finds the idea of making choices frightening: to make a choice is to take a risk. Studies show that women don't like risk—they see it as a possibility only for loss, while men tend to see it as an equally balanced chance for loss *or gain*. Now, for the first time in history, an entire generation of women is being asked—as men have been for years—to choose their destiny, to take risks. Now, even if a woman elects traditional family-oriented life, it is a *choice*, a gamble—not a passive assumption of the inevitable.

Contrary to what the Women's Movement says, it matters little which kind of choice we make, so long as we take the risk of making that choice for ourselves. The opportunity to choose is that which, in the long run, feminism has really given us. This is what we have

gained—and it is both a blessing and a curse, both liberating and painful, but never, as we were taught, easy or natural.

READING REVIEW

1. What, according to Sexton, was the "feminist mystique"?
2. Why had the women's movement failed to solve all of women's problems?
3. List two achievements of the women's movement during the 1970's.

CHAPTER
43 Into the Future
(1960 to the Present)

---

253 Improving the Quality of Life

As the United States entered the last decades of the 1900's, Americans were deeply concerned about the nation's economy. They were increasingly concerned, too, about the quality of life. There was a feeling that material progress alone was not enough to satisfy society's needs. Here one observer, Angus Campbell, discussed what he called "the public sense of well-being."

READING FOCUS

1. Why were Americans dissatisfied with the quality of their lives?
2. Why were "nonmaterial needs" important?

In his State of the Union Message in 1970, Richard M. Nixon observed: "In the next 10 years we will increase our wealth by 50 percent. The profound question is, Does this mean that we will be 50 percent richer in any real sense, 50 percent better off, 50 percent happier?" Now, 10 years later, it is clear that he overestimated the nation's economic growth.

Now, Psychological Man *by Angus Campbell in* The New York Times, *October 31, 1980.*

Many Americans enjoy a high standard of living.

a growing fear of criminal assault, the development of a widespread drug culture, a spreading distrust of government, and a general dissatisfaction with the state of the nation. National surveys demonstrate that as economic welfare increased during the postwar period, psychological well-being declined, especially among the young, the affluent, and the well-educated.

Many factors contributed to this turn of events. One appears to be the nature of affluence itself. Public aspirations and values can no longer be as readily satisfied by simple increases in economic affluence as they may have been earlier in our history. There appear to be a growing number of people for whom economic circumstances are no longer what determines their sense of well-being. Economic man is being replaced by psychological man. These are people for whom "higher needs" have become important. This conclusion is supported by studies in [Europe], Canada and this country that find income to be losing its relationship to the way people describe the psychological quality of their lives.

This decline in the significance of income occurs primarily among the more advantaged parts of the population. It does not mean that people have lost interest in having the material things and other benefits that income makes possible.

What appears to have happened is that an increasing number of people have achieved a degree of economic security. This has liberated them from an overwhelming concern with income. Thus there is an increase in the importance of nonmaterial needs—the need for a sensitive and responsive marital relationship, for challenging and significant work, for the respect and approval of friends, for identification with community, and for a stimulating and fulfilling life.

Senator Daniel Patrick Moynihan [of New York] once observed that governments seldom do anything about a problem until they have learned to count it. Governments have well-established ways of responding to public needs for a minimum income, adequate housing, and medical care. But they have a more difficult time with such feelings as boredom, job dissatisfaction, fear of crime, loneliness, resentment of discrimination, loss of confidence in authority, and other conditions that diminish the quality of people's lives. They do not have

But his "profound question" still remains: Does increasing affluence mean a greater sense of public well-being?

For the last 100 years, we have had a strong faith in the power of economic prosperity to bring about the good life. It would be hard to argue that over that century of increasing affluence, the life of the average American has not been improved. Small wonder that the Gross National Product [the yearly total value of all the goods and services produced by the nation] and other economic indicators have, as a government publication put it, "become so much a part of our thinking that we tend to equate a rising national income with national well-being."

Sometime during the 30 years following World War II, however, something went wrong with this simple tie between economic welfare and the public sense of well-being. Americans experienced one of the most dazzling rises in economic affluence in the nation's history. Average family income went up by about two-thirds between 1945 and 1973, a remarkable national achievement. But, as we increased the ability of our people to purchase the material things of life, we also experienced a great increase in divorce, illegitimacy, juvenile delinquency, and suicide. In addition, there was a clear sense of how widespread these problems are or a sure feeling of how to deal with them.

At present, inflation and unemployment are creating economic stress for many Americans. Our governmental officials are understandably obsessed with their problems. Eventually, however, the national agenda will have to give greater prominence to the psychological needs of the population than it has in the past.

We must recognize that people may be deprived psychologically as well as economically. As economic needs are met, psychological needs assume priority.

A government that aspires to raise the national quality of life must concern itself with both.

READING REVIEW

1. In the thirty years after World War II, what happened to economic life in America?
2. What trends caused dissatisfaction among Americans?
3. What "nonmaterial needs" did people want to satisfy?
4. (a) According to Campbell, why had government not dealt with these needs? (b) What role do you think government should play in dealing with the nonmaterial needs of society?

254 A Troubled Economy

Beginning in the early 1970's, inflation became a serious problem in the United States. Americans were deeply concerned about its impact on their lives. They asked what could be done to help the troubled economy.

The two selections that follow discuss the nation's economic difficulties. In the first, Lester Thurow, an economist at the Massachusetts Institute of Technology, explains why he thinks the economy is in trouble. In the second, President Reagan puts forward his program for recovery.

READING FOCUS

1. What were the economic condition of America during the early 1970's?
2. How should the government's taxing power be used?

[THUROW]

[By the late 1970's] seemingly unsolvable problems were emerging everywhere—inflation, unemployment, slow growth, environmental decay, conflicting group demands, and complex, cumbersome regulations. Were the problems unsolvable or were our leaders incompetent? Had Americans lost the work ethic? Had we stopped inventing new processes and products? Should we invest more and consume less? Do we need to junk our social welfare, health, safety, and environmental protection systems in order to compete? Why were others doing better?

The hard-core conservative solution [to our economic problems] is to "liberate free enterprise," reduce social expenditures, restructure taxes to encourage saving and investment (shift the tax burden from those who save, the rich, to those who consume, the poor), and eliminate government rules and regulations that do not help business. Only by returning to the virtues of hard work and free enterprise can the economy be saved.

In thinking about this solution, it is well to remember that none of our competitors became successful by following this route. Government absorbs slightly over 30 percent of the GNP [Gross National Product] in the United States, but over 50 percent of the GNP in West Germany. Fifteen other countries collect a larger fraction of their GNP in taxes.

Ours is not the economy with the most rules and regulations. On the contrary, it is the one with the fewest rules and regulations. As many American firms have discovered to their horror, it simply isn't possible to fire workers abroad as it is here. It is a dubious achievement, but nowhere in the world is it easier to lay off workers.

Nor have our competitors unleashed work effort and savings by increasing some differentials [that is, allowing bigger gaps between rich and poor]. Indeed, they have done exactly the opposite. If you look at the earnings gap between the top and bottom 10 percent of the population, the West Germans work hard with 36 percent less inequality than we, and the Japanese work even harder with 50 percent less inequality. If income differentials encourage individual initiative, we should be full of initiative, since among industrialized countries, only the French surpass us in terms of inequality.

From The Zero-Sum Society *by Lester C. Thurow.*

Moreover, our own history shows that our economic performance since the New Deal and the onset of governmental "interference" has been better than it was prior to the New Deal. As both our experience and foreign experience demonstrate, there is no conflict between social spending or government intervention and economic success. As we, and others, have shown, social reforms can be productive, as well as just, if done in the right way. If done in the wrong way, they can, of course, be both disastrous and unjust. There may also be some merit in "liberating free enterprise" if it is done in the right way. There are certainly unnecessary rules and regulations that are now strangling our economy. The trick is not rules versus no rules, but finding the right rules.

The American problem is not returning to some golden age of economic growth (there was no such golden age) but in recognizing that we have an economic structure that has never in its entire history performed as well as Japan and West Germany have performed since World War II. We are now the ones who must copy and adapt the policies and innovations that have been successful elsewhere. To retreat into our mythical past is to guarantee that our days of economic glory are over.

But our problems are not limited to slow growth. Throughout our society there are painful, persistent problems that are not being solved. Energy, inflation, unemployment, environmental decay, ever-spreading waves of regulations, sharp income gaps between minorities and majorities—the list is almost endless. Because of our inability to solve these problems, the lament is often heard that the U.S. economy and political system have lost their ability to get things done.

The problem is real, but it has not been properly diagnosed. One cannot lose an ability that one never had. What is perceived as a lost ability to act is in fact (1) a shift from international cold war problems to domestic problems. It is also (2) an inability to impose large economic losses explicitly [that is, openly and frankly].

As domestic problems rise in importance relative to international problems, action becomes increasingly difficult. International conflicts can be, and to some extent are, portrayed as situations where everyone is fairly sharing sacrifices to hold the foreign enemy in check.

Since every member of society is facing a common threat, an overwhelming consensus can be achieved. Domestic problems are much more difficult. When policies are adopted to solve domestic problems, there are American winners and American losers. Some incomes go up as a result of the solution, but others go down. Individuals do not sacrifice equally. Some gain; some lose. A program to raise the occupational position of women and minorities automatically lowers the occupational position of white men. Every black or female appointed to a President's cabinet is one less white male who can be appointed.

Secondly, the solutions to our problems have a common characteristic. Each requires that some large group—sometimes a minority and sometimes the majority—be willing to tolerate a large reduction in their real standard of living. When the economic pluses and minuses are added up, the pluses usually exceed the minuses. But there are large economic losses. These have to be allocated to someone, and no group wants to be the group that must suffer economic losses for the general good.

This is the heart of our fundamental problem. Our political and economic structure simply isn't able to cope with an economy that has a substantial zero-sum element. A zero-sum game is any game where the losses exactly equal the winnings. All sporting events are zero-sum games. For every winner there is a loser. Winners can only exist if losers exist. What the winning gambler wins, the losing gambler must lose.

When there are large losses to be allocated, any economic decision has a large zero-sum element. The economic gains may exceed the economic losses, but the losses are so large as to [cancel out much of the gain]. What is more important, the gains and losses are not allocated to the same individuals or groups. On average, society may be better off, but this average hides a large number of people who are much better off and large numbers of people who are much worse off.

The problem with zero-sum games is that the essence of problem solving is loss allocation [deciding who will suffer losses]. But this is precisely what our political process is least capable of doing. When there are economic gains to be allocated, our political process can allocate them. When there are large economic losses to be allocated, our political process is paralyzed. And with political paralysis comes economic paralysis.

Lacking a consensus on whose income ought to go down, or even the recognition that this is at the heart of the problem, we are paralyzed. We dislike the current situation, we wish to do something about our problems, but we endure them because we have not learned to play an economic game with a substantial zero-sum element.

[REAGAN]

I'm here tonight to ask that we share in restoring the promise that is offered to every citizen by this, the last, best hope of man on earth.

All of us are aware of the punishing inflation which has, for the first time in 60 years, held to double-digit figures for two years in a row [that is, figures over 9 percent]. Interest rates have reached absurd levels of more than 20 percent and over 15 percent for those who would borrow to buy a home. All across this land one can see newly built homes standing vacant, unsold because of mortgage interest rates.

Almost eight million Americans are out of work. These are people who want to be productive. But as the months go by, despair dominates their lives. The threats of layoff and unemployment hang over other millions, and all who work are frustrated by their inability to keep up with inflation.

One worker in a Midwest city put it to me this way. He said: "I'm bringing home more dollars than I ever believed I could possibly earn but I seem to be getting worse off." And he is. Not only have hourly earnings of the American worker, after adjusting for inflation, declined 5 percent over the past five years, but in these five years, Federal personal taxes for the average family have increased 67 percent.

We can no longer procrastinate and hope that things will get better. They will not. Unless we act forcefully, and now, the economy will get worse.

Can we who man the ship of state deny it is somewhat out of control? Our national debt is approaching $1 trillion. The interest on the public debt this year will be over $90 billion.

"A Troubled Economy" from "State of the Union Message on Economic Recovery" by Ronald Reagan in The New York Times, February 19, 1981.

President Reagan explains his economic program.

Adding to our troubles is a mass of regulations imposed on the shopkeeper, the farmer, the craftsman, professionals and major industry that is estimated to add $100 billion to the price of the things we buy. And it reduces our ability to produce. The rate of increase in American productivity, once one of the highest in the world, is among the lowest of all major industrial nations. Indeed, it has actually declined in the last three years.

Now I've painted a pretty grim picture, but I think I've painted it accurately. It is within our power to change this picture and we can act with hope. There's nothing wrong with our internal strengths. There has been no breakdown in the human, technological and natural resources upon which the economy is built.

Based on this confidence in a system which has never failed us—but which we have failed through a lack of confidence, and sometimes through a belief that we could fine-tune the economy and get a tune to our liking—I am proposing a comprehensive four-point program.

This plan is aimed at reducing the growth in Government spending and taxing, reforming and eliminating regulations which are unnecessary and unproductive, or counterproductive, and encouraging a policy aimed at maintaining the value of the currency.

If enacted in full, this program can help America create 13 million new jobs, nearly three million more than we would without these measures. It will also help us to gain control of inflation.

It's important to note that we're only reducing the rate of increase in taxing and spending. We are not attempting to cut either spending or taxing levels below that which we presently have. This plan will get our economy moving again and thus create the jobs that our people must have.

[Reagan next discusses some details of his four main proposals: (1) reducing federal spending by tightening or eliminating various aid programs; (2) across-the-board tax cuts for individuals and businesses; (3) reducing the number of federal regulations; and (4) slowing the growth of the money supply.]

This, then, is our proposal. "America's New Beginning: A Program for Economic Recovery." I don't want it to be simply the plan of my Administration—I'm here tonight to ask you to join me in making it our plan. Together, we can embark on this road—not to make things easy, but to make things better.

Our social political and cultural, as well as our economic institutions, can no longer absorb the repeated shocks that have been dealt them over the past decades.

Can we do the job? The answer is yes. But we must begin now.

We are in control here. There's nothing wrong with America that together we can't fix.

I'm sure there will be some who will raise the familiar old cry, "Don't touch my program—cut somewhere else."

I hope I've made it plain that our approach has been even-handed; that only the programs for the truly deserving needy remain untouched.

The question is, are we simply going to go down the same path we've gone down before—carving out one special program here, another special program there? I don't think that's what they want. They are ready to return to the source of our strength.

The substance and prosperity of our nation is built by wages brought home from the factories and the mills, the farms and the shops.

They are the services provided in 10,000 corners of America; the interest on the thrift of our people and the returns for their risk-taking. The production of America is the possession of those who build, serve, create and produce.

For too long now, we've removed from our people the decisions on how to dispose of what they created. We've strayed from first principles. We must alter our course.

The taxing power of Government must be used to provide revenues for legitimate Government purposes. It must not be used to regulate the economy or bring about social change. We've tried that and surely we must be able to see it doesn't work.

Spending by Government must be limited to those functions which are the proper province of Government. We can no longer afford things simply because we think of them.

I would direct a question to those who have indicated already an unwillingness to accept such a plan: Have they an alternative which offers a greater chance of balancing the budget, reducing and eliminating inflation, stimulating the creation of jobs and reducing the tax burden? And, if they haven't, are they suggesting we can continue on the present course without coming to a day of reckoning?

If we don't do this, inflation and the growing tax burden will put an end to everything we believe in and our dreams for the future. We don't have an option of living with inflation and its attendant tragedy, millions of productive people willing and able to work but unable to find a buyer for their work in the job market.

We have an alternative and that is a program for economic recovery.

True, it will take time for the favorable effects of our proposal to be felt. So we must begin now.

The people are watching and waiting. They don't demand miracles. They do expect us to act. Let us act together.

READING REVIEW

1. According to Thurow, what was a "zero-sum game"?
2. Why does Thurow feel the nation's economy is unable to handle such a situation?
3. (a) According to Reagan, what should the government's taxing power be used for? (b) What should it *not* be used for?
4. (a) Do you find areas where Thurow and Reagan agree? (b) where they disagree?

255 The Energy Crisis

One of the foundations of American prosperity was cheap energy. At home, coal and oil were abundant. Additional supplies from foreign sources seemed assured. Suddenly, in 1973, the situation changed. At this time Israel was successfully pushing back Egypt and Syria after attacks by these two Arab nations. In response the largely Arab membership of the Organization of Petroleum Exporting Countries (OPEC) cut back oil production and began an embargo of the United States and several other nations friendly to Israel. Although the boycott ended in a few months, the price of oil had soared and continued to rise in following years.

Most Americans agreed that they faced an energy crisis. They disagreed, though, about its nature and how best to cope with it. One set of solutions was offered in a report of the Energy Project of the Harvard Business School. The selection that follows is from the report's introductory chapter.

READING FOCUS

1. As the editors saw it, what was the "key contradiction" of the energy crisis?
2. What solutions did the report offer to alleviate the energy crisis?

In 1970, some 111 years after the birth of the American oil industry, domestic production peaked and began to decline. But the demand for oil continued to surge. That demand could be met only by more and more oil from the Middle East. This meant increasing dependence—and increasing vulnerability. The idea that there was something threatening in the growing dependence was an idea better ignored. Even if one recognized a potential problem, what to do about it was hardly clear. . . .

The first oil shock, in late 1973 and early 1974, definitely marked the end of the era of secure and cheap oil. Arab oil producers embargoed the United States and reduced overall output and shipments to other nations. For the first time, these producers stopped negotiating a price with the oil companies. Instead they set the price on a take-it-or-leave-it basis. The oil buyers had no choice, and they took it, paying the higher price—eight times higher by the end of 1974 than five years earlier. And so

the petroleum exporting countries defined a new era for the rest of the world—one of insecure supplies of expensive oil.

Yet today, as we enter the 1980's, even after the second oil shock that accompanied the fall of the Shah of Iran, the cause and consequences of the new era of oil have yet to be taken seriously in the United States. The key contradiction is this: While the declared aim of American policy is to reduce the use of imported oil, the United States is in fact becoming more and more dependent upon it. Between 1973 and early 1979, U.S. oil imports almost doubled, and had begun to provide half of the nation's oil. By current trends the United States will be even more dependent on imported oil in the 1980's.

Does this matter?

From Energy Future: Report of the Energy Project at the Harvard Business School, *edited by Robert Stobaugh and Daniel Yergin.*

OPEC members discuss oil prices.

We think it does. . . . Imported oil poses too many risks to be calmly accepted. . . . The United States should make a much greater attempt to stop the growth of its oil imports.

But can the United States do this? There are four conventional sources of domestic energy: oil, natural gas, coal, and nuclear power. But all four are likely to deliver less energy than their advocates would lead one to believe.

In the debate about oil, three main domestic oil "solutions" have been put forward as alternatives to imported petroleum. They are to break up the industry, to decontrol oil prices (and lease more land), and to use unconventional technology. The first two are important and controversial political questions because they affect the distribution of income and power in America. But the "solutions" have little to do with increasing production. Whether the industry is or is not broken up, whether prices are or are not deregulated, the physical production of oil from conventional sources will continue to decline. At best, . . . unconventional means can help to keep domestic supplies flowing at current levels. To be sure, outside the United States new oil fields in Mexico and China are important and will add to world supplies. But they are unlikely to make a substantial change in the world oil balance.

Natural gas accounts for over a quarter of America's energy needs. It has also been caught in a great domestic debate. Should it continue to be deregulated, with price based on value? As in the case of oil, the debate is about money and who gets it. But . . . the best that one can expect is that a deregulated price will enable natural gas production to remain at current levels.

A major goal of President Carter's National Energy Plan has been the substitution of domestically produced coal for imported oil. Given America's great coal reserves, this appears possible on paper, but in practice it probably is not. For coal to do what the Carter Administration wants it to do, a traditionally backward industry must be suddenly transformed into a modern, technologically advanced one. Potential users are reluctant to commit themselves to coal, especially because of the uncertainty about meeting environmental requirements. Coal's contribution, . . . therefore, is likely to prove more limited than the Administration plans. However, its impor-

tance is still likely to grow, particularly for utilities.

Nuclear power is the other conventional alternative in which high hopes are placed. Yet, the further development of nuclear power is hindered by controversy. . . . It is too soon to judge the long-term consequences for the nuclear power industry of the nuclear accident at Harrisburg [the 1979 accident at Three Mile Island]. It seems safe to say that it hardly improves the industry's prospects. Even without a Harrisburg, however, the problem of what to do with nuclear waste is so confused, and so far from being settled, that it could result in a decline in the energy produced by nuclear power in the next decade. Moreover, one should remember how limited the potential of atomic power is under the best circumstances. If nuclear power capacity *doubled* in ten years, it would still be providing less than 7 percent of America's total energy.

In short, there is little reason to expect conventional alternatives to make a sizable contribution to reducing our dependence on imported oil. These energy sources . . . as a group can increase their contribution to cover, at most, one third to one half of the nation's additional energy needs over the next decade.

On the other hand, the unconventional alternatives, which tend to be played down, can make a much greater contribution than is normally assumed. The unconventional . . . alternatives should be given a fair chance. To date, they have not received anything like that. According to one estimate, conventional energy sources have received more than $120 billion in incentives and subsidies. At the same time, the unconventional sources have received virtually nothing by comparison. . . .

Among the unconventional sources of energy, conservation offers the most immediate opportunity. It should be regarded as a largely untapped source of energy. Indeed, conservation—not coal or nuclear energy—is the major alternative to imported oil. It could perhaps "supply" up to 40 percent of America's current energy usage, although we do not predict that it will. Moreover, the evidence suggests that . . . a conservation strategy could actually spur economic growth. Conservation does not require technological breakthroughs. But it has been difficult to tap, because a consistent set of signals—price, incentives, and regulations—is not in place. Moreover, . . . decisions to conserve, unlike decisions to produce energy, have to be made by millions and millions of often poorly informed people.

The range of energy possibilities grouped under the heading "solar" could meet one fifth of U.S. energy needs within two decades. Like conservation, solar energy faces a problem of decentralized decision-making. Moreover, the most promising short-term solar energy applications use existing, relatively simple technologies. These are receiving less support than the more uncertain more distant high-technology solar applications. Low-technology solar energy can make a significant contribution. But like conservation, it needs a more consistent framework of price, incentive, and regulation.

Some people may charge that the authors are romantics opposed to economic growth, or that we advocate basic changes in the way the society is organized. We are not and we do not. . . . Genuine alternatives for energy do exist and we want to contribute to the clarification of the choices. We also believe that it is unwise to ask conventional sources to do more than they really can and by so doing to block the move to a more balanced energy system. . . .

No easy remedy will solve the energy crisis. Solutions, however, will emerge from a recognition and comparison of benefits and risks, possibilities and obstacles, across a wide range. Political choices are therefore involved, which is why the energy crisis is a crisis of our political system.

READING REVIEW

1. Why was the United States policy regarding foreign oil contradictory?
2. (a) What future did the authors of the report see for the four conventional sources of domestic energy? (b) What unconventional source did they regard most highly? Why?

256 Concern for the Environment

For a long time Americans exploited the rich resources of their land with little thought of the future. They stripped trees and minerals from the earth, poured wastes into the water, and filled the air with smoke and chemicals. Not until the mid-1900's did they begin to see what was happening to their environment.

A major factor in their new awareness was the warning voice of Rachel Carson. A zoologist, she was particularly concerned about the effects of such insecticides and pesticides as DDT. In 1962 she published a book called *Silent Spring,* which was widely read and enormously influential. Carson's title referred to some future spring season when migratory birds—their numbers greatly reduced by pollution—would fail to arrive. It was a frightening picture of a world slowly dying. In this selection Carson warns that human beings have acquired significant power to change the nature of their world.

READING FOCUS

1. What harmful effects do chemicals have on the environment? On human beings?
2. According to Carson, why is it impossible for life to adjust to the endless stream of manufactured chemicals?

The history of life on earth has been a history of interaction between living things and their surrounding. To a large extent, the physical form and the habits of the earth's vegetation and its animal life have been molded by the environment. Considering the whole span of earthly time, the opposite effect, in which life actually modifies its surroundings, has been relatively slight. Only within the moment of time represented by the present century has one species—man—acquired significant power to alter the nature of his world.

Excerpt from Silent Spring *by Rachel Carson.*

Writer and conservationist, Rachel Carson

During the past quarter century, this power has not only increased to one of disturbing magnitude but it has changed in character. The most alarming of all man's assaults upon the environment is the contamination of air, earth, rivers, and sea with dangerous and even lethal materials. This pollution is for the most part irrecoverable; the chain of evil it initiates not only in the world that must support life but in living tissues is for the most part irreversible. In this now universal contamination of the environment, chemicals are the sinister and little recognized partners of radiation in changing the very nature of the world—the very nature of its life. Strontium 90, released through nuclear explosions into the air, comes to earth in rain or drifts down as fallout, lodges in soil, enters into the grass or corn or wheat grown there, and in time takes up its abode in the bones of a human being, there to remain until his death. Similarly, chemicals sprayed on croplands or forests or gardens lie long in soil, entering into living organisms, passing from one to another in a chain of poisoning and death. Or they pass mysteriously by underground streams until they emerge and through the alchemy of air and sunlight, combine into new forms that kill vegetation, sicken cattle, and work unknown harm on those who drink from once pure wells. As Albert Schweitzer has said, "Man can hardly even recognize the devils of his own creation."

It took hundreds of millions of years to produce the life that now inhabits the earth—eons of time in which that developing and evolving and diversifying life reached a state of adjustment and balance with its surroundings. The environment, rigorously shaping and directing the life it supported, contained elements that were hostile as well as supporting. Certain rocks gave out dangerous radiation; even within the light of the sun, from which all life draws its energy, there were short-wave radiations with power to injure. Given time—time not in years but in millennia—life adjusts, and a balance has been reached. For time is the essential ingredient; but in the modern world there is no time.

The rapidity of change and the speed with which new situations are created follow the impetous and heedless pace of man rather than the deliberate pace of nature. Radiation is no longer merely the background radiation of rocks, the bombardment of cosmic rays, the ultraviolet of the sun that have existed before there was any life on earth; radiation is now the unnatural creation of man's tampering with the atom. The chemicals to which life is asked to make its adjustment are no longer merely the calcium and silica and copper and all the rest of the minerals washed out of the rocks and carried in rivers to the sea; they are the synthetic creations of man's inventive mind, brewed in his laboratories, and having no counterparts in nature.

To adjust to these chemicals would require time on the scale that is nature's; it would require not merely years of a man's life but the life of generations. And even this, were it by some miracle possible, would be futile, for the new chemicals come from our laboratories in an endless stream; almost five hundred annually find their way into actual use in the United States alone. The figure is staggering and its implications are not easily grasped— 500 new chemicals to which the bodies of men and animals are required somehow to adapt each year, chemicals totally outside the limits of biologic experience.

Among them are many that are used in man's war against nature. Since the mid-1940's over 200 basic chemicals have been created for use in killing insects, weeds, rodents, and other organisms described in the modern vernacular as "pests"; and they are sold under several thousand different brand names.

These sprays, dusts, and aerosols are now applied almost universally to farms, gardens, forests, and homes—nonselective chemicals that have the power to kill every insect, the "good" and the "bad," to still the song of birds and the leaping of fish in the streams, to coat the leaves with deadly film, and to linger on in soil—all this though the intended target may be only a few weeds or insects. Can anyone believe it is possible to lay down such a barrage of poisons on the surface of the earth without making it unfit for all life? They should not be called "insecticides," but "biocides."

The whole process of spraying seems caught up in an endless spiral. Since DDT was released for civilian use, a process of escalation has been going on in which ever more toxic materials must be found. This has happened because insects in a triumphant vindication of Darwin's principle of the survival of the fittest, have evolved super races immune to the par-

The disposal of toxic waste is a growing problem in the 1980's.

ticular insecticide used, hence a deadlier one has always to be developed—and then a deadlier one than that. It has happened also because, for reasons to be described later, destructive insects often undergo a "flareback," or resurgence, after spraying, in numbers greater than before. Thus the chemical war is never won, and all life is caught in its violent crossfire.

Along with the possibility of the extinction of mankind by nuclear war, the central problem of our age has therefore become the contamination of man's total environment with such substances of incredible potential for harm—substances that accumulate in the tissues of plants and animals and even penetrate the germ cells to shatter or alter the very material of heredity upon which the shape of the future depends.

Some would-be architects of our future look toward a time when it will be possible to alter the human germ plasm by design. But we may easily be doing so now by inadvertence, for many chemicals, like radiation, bring about gene mutations. It is ironic to think that man might determine his own future by something so seemingly trivial as the choice of an insect spray.

All this has been risked—for what? Future historians may well be amazed by our distorted sense of proportion. How could intelligent beings seek to control a few unwanted species by a method that contaminated the entire environment and brought the threat of disease and death even to their own kind? Yet this is precisely what we have done. We have done it, moreover, for reasons that collapse the mo-

ment we examine them. We are told that the enormous and expanding use of pesticides is necessary to maintain farm production. Yet is our real problem not one of *overproduction?* Our farms, despite measures to remove acreages from production and to pay farmers *not* to produce, have yielded such staggering excess of crops that the American taxpayer in 1962 is paying out more than one billion dollars a year as the total carrying cost of the surplus-food storage program. And is the situation helped when one branch of the Agriculture Department tries to reduce production while another states, as it did in 1958, "It is believed generally that reduction of crop acreages under provisions of the Soil Bank will stimulate interest in use of chemicals to obtain maximum production on the land retained in crops."

All this is not to say there is no insect problem and no need of control. I am saying, rather, that control must be geared to realities, not to mythical situations, and that the methods employed must be such that they do not destroy us along with the insects.

READING REVIEW

1. Why are synthetic chemicals more harmful than contaminates found in nature?
2. How does the use of pesticides create an "endless spiral" of chemical pollution?
3. Why did Carson say that "something as trivial as the choice of an insect spray" might determine man's future?
4. According to Carson, what was the real problem in American agriculture? Cite two pieces of evidence Carson used to support her opinion.

INDEX OF AUTHORS

Author	Reading Title	Page

Author	Reading Title	Page

INDEX OF TITLES

Reading Title	Author	Page

A 5
B 6
C 7
D 8
E 9
F 0
G 1
H 2
I 3
J 4